MW00576006

EDITORIAL BOARD

SAUL LEVMORE
DIRECTING EDITOR
William B. Graham Distinguished Service Professor of Law and
Former Dean of the Law School
University of Chicago

DANIEL A. FARBER
Sho Sato Professor of Law
University of California at Berkeley

HEATHER K. GERKEN
Dean and the Sol & Lillian Goldman Professor of Law
Yale University

SAMUEL ISSACHAROFF
Bonnie and Richard Reiss Professor of Constitutional Law
New York University

HAROLD HONGJU KOH
Sterling Professor of International Law and
Former Dean of the Law School
Yale University

THOMAS W. MERRILL
Charles Evans Hughes Professor of Law
Columbia University

ROBERT L. RABIN
A. Calder Mackay Professor of Law
Stanford University

HILLARY A. SALE
Professor of Law and Affiliated Faculty
McDonough School of Business, Georgetown University

UNIVERSITY CASEBOOK SERIES®

LEGAL METHODS

CASE ANALYSIS AND STATUTORY INTERPRETATION

FIFTH EDITION

JANE C. GINSBURG
Morton L. Janklow Professor of Literary and Artistic Property Law
Columbia University School of Law

DAVID S. LOUK
Academic Fellow
Columbia University School of Law

Illustrations by
Adine Varah, Esq.

FOUNDATION
PRESS

The publisher is not engaged in rendering legal or other professional advice, and this publication is not a substitute for the advice of an attorney. If you require legal or other expert advice, you should seek the services of a competent attorney or other professional.

University Casebook Series is a trademark registered in the U.S. Patent and Trademark Office.

© 1996, 2003, 2004 FOUNDATION PRESS
© 2008 by THOMSON REUTERS/FOUNDATION PRESS
© 2014 LEG, Inc. d/b/a West Academic
© 2020 LEG, Inc. d/b/a West Academic
    444 Cedar Street, Suite 700
    St. Paul, MN 55101
    1-877-888-1330

Nothing in this casebook is based on any non-public information.

Printed in the United States of America

ISBN: 978-1-68328-997-5

I was much troubled in spirit, in my first years upon the bench, to find how trackless was the ocean on which I had embarked. I sought for certainty. I was oppressed and disheartened when I found that the quest for it was futile. I was trying to reach land, the solid land of fixed and settled rules, the paradise of a justice that would declare itself by tokens plainer and more commanding than its pale and glimmering reflections in my own vacillating mind and conscience. I found ". . . that the real heaven was always beyond." As the years have gone by, I have become reconciled to the uncertainty, because I have grown to see that the process in its highest reaches is not discovery, but creation; and that the doubts and misgivings, the hopes and fears, are part of the travail of mind, the pangs of death and the pangs of birth, in which principles that have served their day expire, and new principles are born.

Benjamin Nathan Cardozo, *The Nature of the Judicial Process* 166 (1921)

To George
and Paul and Clara
and Lucrezia

To Linda and AV

PREFACE

This casebook serves a course in introduction to legal reasoning. It is designed to initiate students in the legal methods of case law analysis and statutory interpretation. In a course of this kind, students should acquire or refine the techniques of close reading, analogizing, distinguishing, positing related fact patterns, and criticizing judicial and legislative exposition and logic. All of this is fairly standard to the first year, indeed, the first semester, of law school. We hope that students learn from a course in legal methods not only familiarity with these new techniques, but sufficient mastery of them to avoid losing sight of the practical consequences of their implementation.

Law students' introduction to law can be unsettling: the sink or swim approach favored by many schools casts students adrift in a sea of substantive rules, forms, and methods. By contrast, the Legal Methods casebook seeks to acquaint students with their new rhetorical and logical surroundings before, or together with, the students' first encounters with the substance of contracts, torts, or other first year courses. This approach may not only be user friendly; it should also prompt students to take a critical distance from the wielding of the methods. In this way, one hopes, students may avoid (or at least broaden) the tunnel vision that so often afflicts beginning law students. They should learn that "thinking like a lawyer" does not mean letting oneself be seduced by the artifice of enunciating and manipulating legal categories. Nor does it mean diligently and complacently working one's way through a text without stepping back to inquire whether the resulting interpretation makes any common sense.

Indeed, "common lawyers" have long understood that it is more important to attend to a decision's reasoning than simply to parrot the rule for which a decision is said to stand. Thomas Littleton, an English treatise writer who died in 1481, cautioned his son the aspiring lawyer not to take for granted that things written in treatises (including his own) in fact correctly state the law; rather, they are guideposts to understanding the law that emerges from "the arguments and reasons":

> Notwithstanding that certain things that be noted and specified in the said books be not law, yet [they are] such things that make thee more apt and able to understand, and learn the arguments and the reasons of the law. For by the arguments and the reasons in the law, a man may sooner come to the certainty and to the knowledge of the law.

Littleton's Tenures in English, London 1556.

This edition of the casebook largely retains the comparative law dimension of its predecessor, thanks to Professor Gary Bell's introductory Note on comparative law, now expanded to include a reflection on legal pluralism and the challenges of incorporating distinctive legal cultures and traditions within a single legal jurisdiction, particularly in the West.

The Note continues to provide important coverage of non-Western legal systems, as well as materials on civil law and on the variations among common law jurisdictions. American lawyers should learn, from the outset, that our legal methods are neither the only, nor necessarily the best, ones. This casebook does not purport to provide systematic instruction in foreign law, however. Its aspiration is more modest, yet also more fundamental: by offering an occasional comparative law perspective, to challenge the insularity that too often characterizes American legal thought and practice. An appreciation of other common law approaches as well as of civil law systems is likely to become increasingly important to tomorrow's lawyers; the start of legal studies is as good a place as any to begin to promote that understanding.

The current edition also reorganizes and augments the statutory materials. While students tend to adapt readily to case law analysis, they often find statutory interpretation less congenial. Cases tell stories; statutes enunciate rules. And the enunciation may be extremely opaque. Perhaps because statutory text lacks both the human drama and the expository charm of case law, casebooks on statutory interpretation, including earlier editions of this one, tend to present issues of interpretation through judicial opinions that construe the statutes in question, rather than confronting students directly with the statutes themselves. To remedy that shortcoming, this edition precedes several of the judicial opinions construing statutes with extensive excerpts from the statutes at issue. This edition also invites students to assess prevailing approaches to statutory interpretation from the standpoint of *method*. Courts interpret statutes against the backdrop of legislative supremacy, and legislatures rarely set out determinative rules for the interpretation of their statutes. Thus, in contrast to the judicial exposition of common law rules, judicial statutory interpretation entails the use of interpretive methods whose legitimacy or pertinence are almost always open to debate. This edition regularly prompts students to assess the (often unstated) empirical and jurisprudential assumptions that courts make when employing these methods. The materials in Part III thus encourage students to decipher the text in order to understand the problem to which the statutory text responds and the ways the text addresses the problem, as well as to examine critically how a variety of interpretive methods yield often conflicting answers. This edition also provides further discussion problems consisting exclusively of statutory text. The Review Problems in Part IV have been revised to provide students with the opportunity to work through problems in common law method, statutory method, as well as problems that require the synthesis of both approaches.

Finally, we hope a course, and a casebook, like these will constantly prompt the student to ask whether an analysis leads to outcomes the student would have approved before starting law school. One goal of a Legal Methods course is to push the student to go beyond stating a conclusion, to articulate and evaluate the steps, methods, and arguments leading to that conclusion. But if "thinking like a lawyer" may require students to think differently than before they began law school, because it demands that they spell out their reasoning and justify their responses, it by no means advocates that they believe in different goals or principles than before. On the contrary, by mastering "the arguments and the reasons in the law," students should be all the better equipped to advance the positions to which they subscribe.

———————

The illustrations of Adine Kernberg Varah, Esq. (Columbia Law School JD '95) that enlivened the earlier editions reappear in this edition, along with additional illustrations newly created for this edition. Ms. Varah's unique depictions encapsulate a variety of concepts in legal methods with humor and striking acumen. We trust that readers will agree that her contributions have made this book both more thought-provoking and more fun.

Many thanks to our research assistants: Emily Gerry, Columbia Law School class of 2020, and Robert Koehler, Evan Rocher, and Sankeerth Saradhi, Columbia Law School class of 2021. Thanks also to Columbia colleagues and former Associates in Law for advice and suggestions over the years, as well as to Jessica Copland for administrative support.

JANE C. GINSBURG
DAVID S. LOUK

May 2020

SUMMARY OF CONTENTS

TABLE OF CONTENTS

TABLE OF CASES

The principal cases are in bold type.

UNIVERSITY CASEBOOK SERIES®

LEGAL METHODS

CASE ANALYSIS AND STATUTORY INTERPRETATION

FIFTH EDITION

And know thou my sonne, that I will not that thou beleue, that all that I haue said in the sayd bookȝ is law, foȝ that will I not take vpon me noȝ presume. But of those thynges that be not lawe, enquyȝe and learne of my wyse maysters learned in the law. Not withstandyng though that certain thinges that be noted and specified in the sayd bokes be not law, yet suche thinges shall make the moȝe apte and able to vnderstande and learn the argumentes and the reasons of the lawe. Foȝ by the argumentes and the reasons in the law, a man may moȝe sooner come to the certaynitie and to the knowledge of the law.

Littleton's Tenures,
in English (London 1556)

PART I

GENERAL BACKGROUND[*]

A. CASE LAW

The common law does not work from pre-established truths of universal and inflexible validity to conclusions derived from them deductively. Its method is inductive, and it draws its generalizations from particulars.

Benjamin Nathan Cardozo, The Nature of the Judicial Process 22–23 (Yale Univ. Press 1921).

1. ORIGINS, NATURE AND AUTHORITY

a. HOW CASES MAKE LAW

The decisions of judges, as well as of other officials that the Constitution or the laws of a political entity empower to hear and decide controversies, create case law. As the name "case law" suggests, a particular decision, or a collection of particular decisions, generate law—that is, rules of general application. How is it that a court's determination of the rights and obligations of the particular parties before it can apply to the disputes of persons who were not before the court? From the point of view of the parties to a lawsuit or other contested controversy, what matters is the immediate outcome, the result the tribunal reaches in their case. Suppose that A has sued B for damages for asserted breach of contract, and that the court has reached a decision in their case. For A and B, the decision has immediate, and specific, significance: B either

---

[*] Portions of this casebook, particularly in Part I, are revised and adapted from Harry Jones, Arthur Murphy & John M. Kernochan, Legal Method: Cases and Text Materials (Foundation Press, 1980), used with permission of the authors and Foundation Press.

will or will not have to pay a determined amount of damages to A. In the view of judges, lawyers, and law students, however, the decision takes on broader significance. The decision becomes a possible source of generally applicable case law. In other words, the decision in A v. B becomes authority for determining subsequent controversies. Just as the court in A v. B will have sought guidance from prior similar decisions, so later judges and advocates will look to A v. B for a rule by which to measure later parties' conduct.

The wider authority of prior decisions in individual cases may not seem self-evident at first, but consider the opposite proposition. Suppose a society in which every disputed claim is heard and decided on its own individual merits, and with no regard whatsoever for consistency of the results from case to case. This society offers the means of settling disputes, but the society has no "case law." Each decision presents a result unto itself. Each decision is therefore unpredictable. Unpredictability in adjudication may provoke both instability in social relations, and the fear that little more than personal whim controls the judges' decisions. There is in fact, in most societies, a strong urge to make general law from particular decisions.

How are we to account for this widespread inclination to make general law from particular decisions? Professor Karl N. Llewellyn, the leading spokesman for the generation of mid-century legal philosophers known as the American Legal Realists, offered the following explanation:

> Case law in some form and to some extent is found wherever there is law. A mere series of decisions of individual cases does not of course in itself constitute a system of law. But in any judicial system rules of law arise sooner or later out of such decisions of cases, as rules of action arise out of the solution of practical problems, whether or not such formulations are desired, intended or consciously recognized. These generalizations contained in, or built upon, past decisions, when taken as normative for future disputes, create a legal system of precedent. Precedent, however, is operative before it is recognized. Toward its operation drive all those phases of human make-up which build habit in the individual and institutions in the group: laziness as to the reworking of a problem once solved; the time and energy saved by routine, especially under any pressure of business; the values of routine as a curb on arbitrariness and as a prop of weakness, inexperience and instability; the social values of predictability; the power of whatever exists to produce expectations and the power of expectations to become normative. The force of precedent in the law is heightened by an additional factor: that curious, almost universal, sense of justice which urges that all men are properly to be treated alike in like circumstances. As the social system varies we meet infinite variations as to what

men or treatments or circumstances are to be classed as "like";
but the pressure to accept the views of the time and place
remains.[1]

You will become aware, as your study of law proceeds, that adherence to
precedent has its other side. A court that follows precedents mechanically
or too strictly will at times perpetuate legal rules and concepts that have
outlived their usefulness. In a legal system that recognizes past decisions
as authoritative sources of law for future cases, the continuing problem
is how to maintain an acceptable accommodation of the competing
values: one value is stability in the law, which is served by adherence to
precedent, and the other is responsiveness to social change, which may
call for the abandonment of an outworn legal doctrine. This problem of
stability *versus* change will be a recurring theme in this casebook.

b.   LAW AND EQUITY

Historically in Anglo-American law, law and equity operated as
distinct legal systems with separate procedures, causes, and remedies.[2]
This system originated in the historical distribution of powers found in
the King's Council after the Norman Conquest of England in 1066.[3] As
one commentator summarized the history:

> In the first hundred years after the conquest, central
> government in England was essentially the King in Council, and
> the Council embodied all of the functions of government:
> executive, legislative, and judicial. . . . The King's Chancellor
> was probably the most important member of the Council, with a
> multitude of functions. . . . The common law courts gradually
> emerged out of the Council and became fixed institutions sitting
> at Westminster. However, in those more fluid times, the Council
> and the King himself continued to receive petitions seeking
> justice. The Chancery Court [responsible for equity] had its
> beginnings in the practice of royal disposition of humble
> petitions for justice.[4]

The common law system was writ-based: Writs were issued and
sealed by the Court of Chancery and directed the local sheriff to empanel
a jury to find facts and deliver a verdict when the royal justices took the
case.[5] Eventually, writs became limited in number and formulaic.[6] If the
subject of the litigation did not fit an existing writ, it could not be brought
before the royal courts. In such cases, litigants could petition the King

---

[1]   "Case Law," 3 Encyclopedia of the Social Sciences 249 (1930).

[2]   George L. Clark, Equity § 1 (New York ed. 1921).

[3]   1 John Norton Pomeroy, A Treatise on Equity Jurisprudence §§ 31–36 (5th ed. 1941);
see also, William F. Walsh, A Treatise on Equity § 2 (1930).

[4]   Morton Gitelman, *The Separation of Law and Equity and the Arkansas Chancery
Courts: Historical Anomalies and Political Realities*, 17 U. Ark. Little Rock L.J. 215, 216 (1995).

[5]   *See, e.g.*, Walsh, *supra* note 3, at § 2; Gitelman, *supra* note 4, at 220.

[6]   Henry L. McClintock, Handbook of the Principles of Equity § 1 (2d ed. 1948); Walsh,
supra note 3, at § 2.

and Council to intervene on behalf of justice.[7] The Chancellor acted as part of the Council in this process and eventually became sole recipient of such petitions.[8] The Chancellor assumed judicial powers during the fourteenth century[9] and acted under the direction of the Council until approximately the late fifteenth century, at which point equity jurisdiction became exclusively his.[10]

The Chancellor was originally an ecclesiastic figure who applied the law in accordance with good conscience, leading to the concept of equity as a discretionary tailoring of the law to reach equitable or just results.[11] "Equity," however, has come to be a term of art in law which has a meaning distinct from its colloquial meaning of fairness or fair share:[12]

> The term "equity" is an illustration of [the] proposition that some words have a legal meaning very unlike their ordinary one. In ordinary language "equity" means natural justice; but the beginner must get that idea out of his head when dealing with the system that the lawyers call equity. Originally, indeed, this system was inspired by ideas of natural justice, and that is why it acquired its name; but nowadays equity is no more (and no less) natural justice than the common law, and it is in fact nothing else than a particular branch of the law of England. Equity, therefore, is law. The student should not allow himself to be confused by the lawyer's habit of contrasting "law" and "equity," for in this context "law" is simply an abbreviation for the common law. Equity is law in the sense that it is part of the law of England; it is not law only in the sense that it is not part of the common law.[13]

Even given this meaning, equity is distinguished by its flexibility and is often referred to as discretionary.[14] As discussed above, however, a judge sitting in equity does not have unfettered power but applies equitable concepts within a well-defined system of such remedies.[15] According to one commentator:

> In Anglo-American law equity means the system of distinctive concepts, doctrines, rules, and remedies developed and applied by the court of Chancery in England and by American courts sitting in equity. In short, "equity" and "equitable" refer to the

---

[7]   McClintock, *supra* note 6, at § 1; Pomeroy, *supra* note 3, at §§ 11–12a.

[8]   Walsh, *supra* note 3, at §§ 2–3.

[9]   *Id.* at § 2.

[10]   McClintock, *supra* note 6, at § 2; Gitelman, *supra* note 4, at 221.

[11]   See Clark, *supra* note 2, at § 1; Walsh, *supra* note 3, at § 3.

[12]   See McClintock, *supra* note 6, at § 25; 1 Joseph Story, Commentaries on Equity Jurisprudence § 3 (14th ed. 1918).

[13]   Glanville Williams, Learning the Law 25–26 (11th ed. 1982), reproduced in Black's Law Dictionary (Bryan A. Garner ed., 9th ed. 2009).

[14]   See Story, *supra* note 12, at § 28.

[15]   See C. C. Langdell, A Brief Survey of Equity Jurisdiction 1 (1908) ("Equity jurisdiction is a branch of the law of remedies . . . .").

whole body of equitable precedent and practice. . . . [E]quitable relief was, and is, considered a matter of judicial discretion, not a matter of right. Thus, a party who sought equitable relief could not demand it as a matter of right simply upon a showing of specific facts that would fit the case into one for equitable relief. This is what commentators mean when they say that granting or denying equitable relief is within the discretion of the court. They do not mean that the court has the power to grant equitable relief in every type of case presented as the spirit moves the judge; rather, what they mean is that parties who have placed their case within the category of cases traditionally qualifying for equitable relief were not automatically entitled to it. . . . [P]arties who successfully made a case for equitable relief—showed that theirs was the type of case where equitable relief had been granted in past cases—still had to invoke the discretion of the court to grant such relief.[16]

Today, law and equity are merged in all but three jurisdictions (Delaware, Mississippi, and Tennessee) in the United States. As a result, judges can apply both legal and equitable remedies to controversies given the controlling case and statutory law. Legal remedies involve damages for past wrongs.[17] Equitable remedies include preventive injunctive relief (a court order compelling a party to do or refrain from doing certain actions), as well as other non-compensatory forms of relief such as specific performance (where the defendant is ordered to perform her obligations under a contract rather than pay monetary damages for her default).[18] Restitutional remedies form a second category of equitable remedies. Courts order restitution to prevent unjust enrichment by causing the defendant to return to the plaintiff items or amounts unjustly taken.

Furthermore, "legal" claims (formerly called "actions at law") carry with them the right to a jury trial whereas "equitable" claims (formerly called "bills in equity") do not. As one judge has written: "In civil matters before the district court . . . the distinction between law and equity is now limited to the type of remedy imposed and the parties' right to a jury trial."[19]

As you read cases that refer to "equity," keep in mind the historical basis for the distinction between law and equity, the types of remedies that law and equity afford, and the constraints on judicial discretion that apply.

---

[16] Kevin C. Kennedy, *Equitable Remedies and Principled Discretion: The Michigan Experience*, 74 U. Det. Mercy L. Rev. 609, 610, 613–14 (1997).

[17] Story, *supra* note 12, at § 30.

[18] Id.

[19] Leandra Lederman, *Equity and the Article I Court: Is the Tax Court's Exercise of Equitable Powers Constitutional?*, 5 Fla. Tax Rev. 357, 373 (2001) (quoting The Honorable Marcia S. Krieger, *"The Bankruptcy Court is a Court of Equity": What Does That Mean?*, 50 S.C. L. Rev. 275, 281 (1999)).

c.   THE COMMON LAW DOCTRINE OF PRECEDENT

Professor Llewellyn was undoubtedly right in his contention that
case law can be found "in some form and to some extent" in every legal
system. But case law is uniquely authoritative and influential in a
"common law country," which the United States is by inheritance from
England. The Anglo-American legal system, unlike the "civil law" system
which prevails with variations in most of the other non-Commonwealth
countries of the world, explicitly recognizes the doctrine of precedent,
known also as the principle of *stare decisis*. It is the distinctive policy of
a "common law" legal system that past judicial decisions are formally and
"generally binding"[20] for the disposition of factually similar present
controversies. This basic principle, firmly established centuries ago in the
royal courts of England, was naturalized as American by the "reception"
of the common law in the United States.

When, and for what future cases, will a judicial decision or group of
decisions operate as precedent? The term "precedent" is a crucially
important term of art in the vocabulary of our law. Let us note, first, a
kind of territorial limitation: a judicial decision is a precedent in the full
sense of the word only within the same judicial system or "jurisdiction."
Thus, a decision of the Supreme Court of California is a precedent and so
generally binding in future "like" cases in that court and in "lower"
California courts, but it is not a full-fledged precedent for future cases
arising in the courts of Ohio or Vermont or some other state. Even a
decision of the Supreme Court of the United States is not a binding
precedent in a state court, say the Court of Appeals of New York, unless
the legal issue decided by the Supreme Court decision was a federal
question, that is, one involving the interpretation or effect of a federal
statute or regulation or of the Constitution of the United States. The
possible influence of a judicial decision on future cases arising in other
jurisdictions will be considered in Part II; it is sufficient to note now that
a decision has the full status and effect of precedent only on the deciding
court's home grounds.

A second restriction on what is and is not "precedent" in the full and
technical sense has already been suggested, perhaps, by our discussion
so far. Even within the same jurisdiction, a decision is precedent only for
"like," that is, factually similar, future cases. To put the matter more
precisely, a judicial decision is a precedent, and so generally binding, only
in future cases involving the *same material facts*. As the first-year law
student will soon discover, this limitation is far easier to state in general
terms than to apply in concrete situations. No two disputes will ever be
identical in every factual particular. How is one to determine, or argue,

---

[20] "Generally" binding is an imprecise but unavoidable way of saying that a court will
follow precedent almost all the time, and except when it is persuaded, in unusual and quite
undefinable circumstances, that the precedent is too unsound or socially unjust to be adhered
to. For a long time in England, precedents were taken to be absolutely binding, but that rigid
notion never caught on in American courts and, since 1966, has been on the way out in England.
See subsection II.B.2 "Overruling," *infra*.

that a factual difference between a past decided case and a case now presented for decision is, or is not, a difference in *material* facts? Case law processes require careful analysis, matching and distinguishing the facts of cases. This is one of the distinctive arts of the common or case lawyer and will be explored in depth in Part II of this casebook. By the end of the first semester, the beginning law student should find that case matching and comparison has become a matter of second nature.

Even when the jurisdiction is the same and the pending new case is found to possess the same material facts, some judicial decisions will have greater weight as precedent than others. Thus, for example, the weight or influence of a precedent is greatly affected by the place of the court that decided it in the judicial hierarchy of its jurisdiction, that is, by whether it was a "higher court" decision or a "lower court" decision. Three tiers of courts exist in the federal judicial structure and in most states: (1) trial courts, (2) intermediate appellate courts, and (3) a highest appellate court or "court of last resort," called the Supreme Court in most jurisdictions. The American state court systems and federal court system are described in some detail at pages 10–21 of this casebook. One should not assign the same force as precedent to the decision of a state intermediate appellate court as to a decision of that state's court of last resort, and should not expect a decision of a United States Court of Appeals to have the same precedent force as a decision of the Supreme Court of the United States. As to the decisions of the trial courts, particularly state trial courts, where most of law's day-to-day business is done, these are rarely published and, even when published, are not likely to have much force as precedent except in future cases in the same trial court. As a result, the overwhelming majority of the cases included in this and most other law school casebooks are decisions of the nation's highest appellate courts.

d. *"RES JUDICATA"* AND *"STARE DECISIS"*; "REVERSAL" AND "OVERRULING"

Every final decision of an appellate court has a dual impact or effect: (1) as an authoritative settlement of the particular controversy then before the court; and (2) as a precedent, or potential precedent, for future cases. A Latin expression denominates each of these effects: *stare decisis,* as we have seen, for the impact of the decision as precedent; *res judicata* for its effect as a resolution of the immediate controversy. Do not confuse these two Latin terms or the concepts they symbolize. The latter addresses a decision's impact in the individual case; the former, its impact on the legal norm of conduct.

The following example should illuminate the difference. Suppose that P (plaintiff) sues D (defendant) advertiser in State X, for using P's photograph without his permission in an advertisement for breakfast cereal. The trial court decides in D's favor, on the ground that in State X, there is no claim against the non-consensual use of private citizens' photographs for purposes of trade, nor have the courts there recognized a "right of privacy." The Supreme Court of X, the court of last resort in that state, affirms the judgment. This decision is a final and conclusive settlement of the controversy between P and D: The case is now *res judicata,* and the losing party, P, cannot bring this claim again.

Now, to make plain the difference between *res judicata* and *stare decisis*, suppose further that the Supreme Court of X, ten years later, and in another case involving the non-consensual use of a private citizen's photograph for purposes of trade, is persuaded that its refusal to recognize a right of privacy in this context is not a sound legal doctrine for present-day conditions, and so "overrules" P v. D, thus finding against the advertiser in the new case. Although this overruling decision is a deviation from the norm of *stare decisis,* U.S. courts of last resort have never regarded precedents as absolutely binding—only as "generally" binding—and have reserved to themselves a largely undefined authority to overrule even clear precedents when considerations of public policy require a change in the case law. (The problem of overruling is the subject of a subsequent section of this casebook, see subsection II.B.2, *infra.*)

What, however, of the particular claim of P v. D? Now that the Supreme Court of X has changed the law, and "overruled" the decision reached in P's case ten years earlier, should not P be able to bring his suit again, and prevail in his claim? The answer is clear, and adverse to P. His particular claim has been finally and conclusively settled against him; the doctrine of *res judicata* bars P from ever suing on that claim again.[21] As a result, the final decision of a court of last resort can be more conclusive and permanent in its aspect as a settlement of a particular case (*res judicata*) than it may be in its aspect as general law for the future (*stare decisis*).

It is important here to underscore one other distinction in legal terminology: between "overruling" and "reversal." In the later privacy case, the Supreme Court of X "overruled" its decision in P v. D. The Supreme Court of X did *not* "reverse" P v. D. The two notions are distinct, and carry different consequences. The highest court of the jurisdiction "overrules" its own precedent. The prior decision continues to bind the parties to it, but the overruled precedent is no longer authoritative as to subsequent controversies. By contrast, a higher court "reverses" the decision of a lower court concerning that same case. When a higher court "reverses" a decision, it reviews the lower court's judgment, and concludes that the lower court has reached an erroneous result (on the facts or on the law) in that case. As a result, the lower court's judgment is set aside and is no longer effective as to the parties to that controversy nor as persuasive authority for future controversies.

---

[21] By "that claim," it is important to understand, "on those facts, when they occurred." The Supreme Court of X's overruling of P v. D would entitle P to bring a new claim against D in the event that, *after* the Supreme Court's decision, D were again to use P's photograph in an advertisement without P's permission.

e.   A NOTE ON RESTATEMENTS

As the common law of the various U.S. states became increasingly complex, its "rules" were becoming more uncertain and thus harder to discern. Many believed that orderly "restatements" of the law were necessary to improve and clarify the work of legislators, judges, lawyers and academics. One effort to systematize or organize the law in a variety of common law subjects—such as Agency, Children and the Law, Conflict of Laws, Contracts, Employment, Foreign Relations, Property, Restitution, Security, Torts, and Trusts—has taken the form of Restatements of the Law published by the American Law Institute (ALI). ALI was organized in 1923 following a study by a group of prominent law professors, practicing attorneys and judges known as "The Committee on the Establishment of a Permanent Organization for the Improvement of the Law." The Committee had reported that the two chief defects in American law, its uncertainty and its complexity, had produced a "general dissatisfaction with the administration of justice."[22] William Draper Lewis outlined the Restatement's original objectives in 1937:

> The object of the [American Law] Institute in preparing the Restatement is to present an orderly statement of the general common law of the United States. . . . The object of the Institute is accomplished insofar as the legal profession accepts the restatement as *prima facie* a correct statement of the general law of the United States.

Introduction to *Restatement of Restitution* at ix. (1937).

The founders of ALI included Chief Justice and former President William Howard Taft, future Chief Justice Charles Evans Hughes, and former Secretary of State Elihu Root. Judges Benjamin N. Cardozo and Learned Hand were among its early leaders.[23] While not intended to be enacted as a statute by legislatures, Restatements do assist state and federal courts in determining patterns of prior judicial decisions in the common law. In this way, they have been largely successful in addressing the uncertainty and complexity of the common law. As one judge noted, "[ALI's] monumental first Restatements, pronouncing on the fundamental principles of the common law, have greatly influenced the advancement and unification of legal principles in this country. Revisions of the initial Restatements have permitted the Institute to reassess stated principles and to recognize developing concepts."[24] It is important to note, however, that a particular Restatement provision does not have the force of law in any given state until it is adopted as an authoritative statement by the appellate courts deciding cases in that state.

---

[22]   Am. Law Inst., About ALI, *available at* https://www.ali.org/about-ali/.

[23]   *Id.*

[24]   Herbert P. Wilkins, *Foreword, Symposium on the American Law Institute: Process, Partisanship, and the Restatements of Law*, 26 Hofstra L. Rev. 567 (1998).

E. Allen Farnsworth et al., Selections For Contracts 1–2 (2010) (excerpt from Compilers' Note).

As originally conceived, the first Restatement was to be accompanied by treatises citing and discussing case authority, but experience proved that group production of such volumes was not feasible. As they stand, the Restatements consist of sections stating rules or principles (the so-called black letter), each followed by one or more comments with illustrations, and in the Restatement, Second, also by Reporters' Notes in which supporting authorities are collected. . . .

. . . An eminent critic of the Restatement of Contracts immediately objected that the American Law Institute "seems constantly to be seeking the force of a statute without statutory enactment." Clark, The Restatement of the Law of Contracts, 42 Yale L.J. 643, 654 (1933).[1] To what measure of authority is the Restatement entitled, then, in the courts?

This general question can have only a general answer. The Supreme Court of Oregon has emphasized the difference between statutory and Restatement texts:

Although this court frequently quotes sections of the Restatements of the American Law Institute, it does not literally "adopt" them in the manner of a legislature enacting, for instance, a draft prepared by the Commissioners on Uniform State laws, such as the Residential Landlord and Tenant Act. In the nature of common law, such quotations in opinions are no more than shorthand expressions of the court's view that the analysis summarized in the Restatement corresponds to Oregon law applicable to the facts of the case before the court. They do not enact the exact phrasing of the Restatement rule, complete with comments, illustrations, and caveats. Such quotations should not be relied on in briefs as if they committed this court or lower courts to track every detail of the Restatement analysis in other cases. The Restatements themselves purport to be just that, "restatements" of law found in other sources, although at times they candidly report that the law is in flux and offer a formula preferred on policy grounds.

[Brewer v. Erwin, 600 P.2d 398, 410 n. 12 (Or.1979).]

2. THE JUDICIAL HIERARCHY

As discussed above, precedent operates to bind subordinate courts within the superior court's jurisdiction. Thus, a decision by the court of

---

[1] On occasion a legislature has given statutory backing to the Restatement. The Virgin Islands Code (Title 1, § 4) provides: "The rules of the common law, as expressed in the restatements of the law approved by the American Law Institute . . ., shall be the rules of decision . . . in cases to which they apply, in the absence of local laws to the contrary."

last resort in one state is binding on all courts within that state but not binding on any court in any other state. (The reasoning of a court regarding a new issue, however, may be useful for courts in other jurisdictions when they are considering the same issue for the first time, and this is called "persuasive authority.") A decision by the Supreme Court of the United States is binding on all other courts as to constitutional and other federal questions. A State's highest court (and not the U.S. Supreme Court) has the last word on issues of that state's law.

Because of the important influence of out-of-state decisions as persuasive authority in American common law, law school casebooks covering first-year common-law subjects like Torts and Property usually include cases drawn from many jurisdictions. You will find that the states' appellate courts exhibit a marked degree of mutual respect for each other's decisions. Some decisions will have greater influence than others on the thinking of judges in other states. The prestige of the court that rendered the decision, or the prestige of the particular judge who wrote the opinion of the court, may also affect the persuasiveness of the decision to the courts of other jurisdictions. (For instance, the judicial decisions and academic writings of Benjamin Cardozo, who served first as the Chief Judge of the New York Court of Appeals and later as an Associate Justice of the Supreme Court of the United States, continue to carry outsized influence—note the epigraphs that begin this Part, and conclude Part II!)

Thus, the hierarchical structure of the U.S. court system, set out below, has fundamental implications for the degree of authority that precedent commands. To appreciate the scope of a prior decision's authority, it is therefore very important to understand the placement of a court within the judicial hierarchy. The interaction between Federal and State courts will be discussed in greater detail in other courses you take. For the purposes of this discussion, it suffices to note briefly that principles of federalism (which you will study in your Constitutional Law, Civil Procedure, and other courses) determine the domains of these interacting legal systems.

a.   THE FEDERAL COURTS

There was no regular federal judiciary under the Articles of Confederation. In *The Federalist* No. 22, Alexander Hamilton described this "want of a judiciary power" as "a circumstance which crowns the defects of the confederation," for, he continued, "Laws are a dead letter without courts to expound them and define their true meaning and operation."

Hamilton's views on this issue are an accurate report of the consensus arrived at, with surprisingly little debate or discussion, when the delegates to the Constitutional Convention had assembled in Philadelphia in May 1785. Max Farrand, author of the classic study of the Convention, concluded simply: "That there should be a national judiciary was readily accepted by all."[25] As the Convention proceeded, there were lively disagreements over methods for the selection of federal judges and over the categories of cases to which the federal judicial power was to extend, but the necessity of a federal judiciary—at least of a national Supreme Court as ultimate arbiter of foreseen disputes between states or between a state and the new national government—was universally recognized.

Article III, Section 1 of the Constitution reflects this consensus:

> The judicial Power of the United States, shall be vested in one supreme Court, and in such inferior Courts as the Congress may from time to time ordain and establish.

The Supreme Court is the only federal court directly created by the Constitution itself. The other courts in the federal judicial system are created by Acts of Congress enacted pursuant to Article III. The landmark statute in the evolution of the federal judicial system was passed by the first Congress as one of its early orders of business and became law on September 24, 1789. This statute, entitled "An Act to establish the Judicial Courts of the United States," embodied the first Congress's decision on the issue that the Constitution itself had not resolved: whether there should be federal *trial* courts as well as a Supreme Court or whether the interpretation and enforcement of federal law should be left entirely to the existing state trial and appellate courts, subject to review by the Supreme Court of the United States. The organization of the federal judiciary has greatly changed over the years since 1789, but the decision of the first Congress to establish a federal judicial system, of trial as well as appellate courts (although Congress did not in fact create federal appellate courts until the Judiciary Act of 1891), set the course for the national judicial future.

The basic federal court system as it now exists is a three-tier hierarchy: (1) trial courts of general jurisdiction, known as the *District Courts;* (2) intermediate appellate courts, called the *Courts of Appeals;* and (3) the *Supreme Court,* specifically provided for by Article III of the Constitution and operating as the court of last resort for the federal judicial system and, in matters of federal law, for the state judicial systems as well. There are also a few specialized federal courts (*e.g.,* the Claims Court, the Bankruptcy Court, or the Tax Court), which operate more or less like District Courts in their specialized jurisdiction, as well as the Court of Appeals for the Federal Circuit, whose jurisdiction includes exclusive authority over patent appeals.

---

[25] Max Farrand, The Framing of the Constitution of the United States 79 (1963).

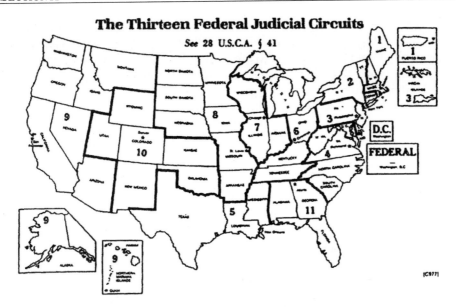

The Thirteen Federal Judicial Circuits
See 28 U.S.C.A. § 41

i.   *The District Courts of the United States*

By existing Congressional legislation, the United States is divided into 94 federal judicial districts,[26] each with its District Court. Every state has at least one District Court; about half the states have only one, *e.g.*, the United States District Court for Nevada. There is one District Court for the District of Columbia and one for Puerto Rico.

The more populous states have been divided into two, three or four districts. In New York, for example, there are four United States District Courts, one each for the Southern, the Northern, the Eastern and the Western District. There are now about 677 federal district judgeships,[27] distributed more or less according to the differing volume of judicial business in the 94 districts. There are also 576 authorized positions for federal magistrate judges.[28] Thus, there are now 44 judges (active and senior) for the Southern District of New York (as well as 15 magistrate

---

[26]   This includes the District of Columbia and Puerto Rico, but does not include the District Courts of the Virgin Islands, Guam, and the Northern Mariana Islands, which for some purposes are treated as District Courts of the United States.

[27]   See Federal Judgeships, U.S. Courts, http://www.uscourts.gov/JudgesAndJudgeships/FederalJudgeships.aspx. There may be fewer active judges than judgeships due to judicial vacancies; furthermore, long-serving judges can elect to take senior status, creating a judicial vacancy while still handling a (reduced) caseload. In 2018, there were 562 active judges and 412 senior judges with staff. See Judicial Facts and Figures 2018, U.S. Courts, https://www.uscourts.gov/statistics/table/11/judicial-facts-and-figures/2018/09/30.

[28]   See Judicial Facts and Figures 2018, *supra*. According to the website for the Federal Magistrate Judges Association: "A United States Magistrate Judge is a federal trial judge appointed to serve in a United States district court for a term of eight years. He or she is appointed by the life-tenured federal judges of a district court, District Judges, who supervise the activities of the Magistrate Judges by assigning civil cases for jury or non-jury trial upon consent of the parties and for pre-trial matters. Similarly criminal cases are assigned to Magistrate Judges on the consent of the parties, except for the trial of felony cases." About, Federal Magistrate Judges Association, https://fmja.org/about/.

judges)[29] and 29 for the Central District of California (with 25 magistrate judges),[30] as against 3 for the Western District of Wisconsin (with 1 full-time and 1 part-time magistrate judge)[31] and 3 for the District of Wyoming (with 2 full-time and 2 part-time magistrate judges).[32] Trials in a District Court are normally presided over by a single judge, although there are a few situations—such as cases challenging the constitutionality of the apportionment of congressional districts or statewide legislative bodies or when injunctions are sought on federal constitutional grounds against the enforcement of state or federal statutes—in which a three-judge panel must be convened.[33]

Although they correspond in essential function to the state trial courts of general jurisdiction, there is a sense in which the jurisdiction of the District Courts of the United States is a limited one: They, like other federal courts, cannot entertain cases that fall outside the "judicial power of the United States" as defined in the Constitution. Article III, Section 2 of the Constitution is the controlling text and sets the outer bounds beyond which the federal courts cannot exercise, or be vested by Congress with, jurisdiction. Article III, Section 2 provides, in pertinent part, as follows:

> The judicial power [of the United States] shall extend to all cases, in Law and Equity, arising under this Constitution, the Laws of the United States, and Treaties made, or which shall be made, under their Authority;—to all Cases affecting Ambassadors, other public Ministers and Consuls;—to all Cases of admiralty and maritime Jurisdiction;—to Controversies to which the United States shall be a Party;—to Controversies between two or more States;—[between a State and Citizens of another State;—]*between Citizens of different States,— between Citizens of the same State claiming Lands under Grants of different States, and between a State, or the Citizens thereof, and foreign States, Citizens or Subjects.

As a result, the jurisdiction of a District Court of the United States must be based either on the *character of the controversy* (for example, that it is a case "arising under this Constitution [or] the laws of the United States") or on the *character of the parties to the controversy* (for example, that it is a controversy "to which the United States shall be a party" or one "between citizens of different States").

---

[29] Judges of the Southern District of New York, U.S. District Court for the Southern District of New York, https://nysd.uscourts.gov/judges.

[30] Judges' Procedures and Schedules, U.S. District Court for the Central District of California, https://www.cacd.uscourts.gov/judges-schedules-procedures.

[31] About the Court, U.S. District Court for the Western District of Wisconsin, https://www.wiwd.uscourts.gov/judges.

[32] Judges' Info, U.S. District Court for the District of Wyoming, https://www.wyd.uscourts.gov/judges-info.

[33] See 28 U.S.C. 2284.

* This provision was repealed by the Eleventh Amendment.

Most of the cases which make up the workload of the District Courts fall within one or another of three categories: (1) cases to which the United States is a party, which includes both civil cases in which the United States is plaintiff or defendant and all prosecutions for violation of federal criminal statutes; (2) cases involving a "federal question," which means a question involving the interpretation or effect of a provision of the Constitution or of a federal statute or regulation; and (3) cases involving "diversity of citizenship," that is, suits between citizens of different states of the United States. For the purposes of this "diversity" jurisdiction, a corporation is deemed to be a "citizen" both of the state in which it is incorporated and of the state in which it has its principal place of business.

Existing federal legislation imposes a further limitation on District Court jurisdiction in some "federal question" and all "diversity of citizenship" cases: The "matter in controversy must exceed $75,000." A case within federal jurisdiction—for example, a controversy between citizens of different states and involving more than $75,000—may, as a matter of "venue," be brought in a district in which either the plaintiff or the defendant resides. If the plaintiff in such a case chooses, as he may, to file his suit not in a federal District Court but in a state trial court, the defendant may in certain circumstances have the case "removed" to the federal court for the same district, where it will then be heard and decided. Note, however, that a "diversity of citizenship" case cannot be removed by the defendant if brought in a state court of the state in which the defendant himself resides, but a "federal question" claim can be removed regardless of the parties' citizenship. The historical origins of "diversity of citizenship" jurisdiction derive from a concern of former times that a citizen of one state might not be fairly treated in the courts of the state of his adversary's residence, and even this old concern is inapplicable when the defendant is, so to speak, sued on his own home grounds.

Whenever you encounter a civil federal court decision in this Legal Methods casebook, or for that matter in any casebook or case reporter, ask yourself why this case is within federal court jurisdiction; *i.e.*, is it based on the nature of the parties, a "diversity of citizenship" case, or does it "arise under" federal law? (In addition to the civil law controversies that predominate in this casebook, Part III also includes a number of cases involving the interpretation federal criminal statutes; questions about federal criminal jurisdiction are central to the advanced course in Federal Criminal Law.)

The federal rules of procedure in the District Courts are formally uniform throughout the United States and takes no account of the differences in court procedures that exist from state to state. In 1934, Congress empowered the Supreme Court to prescribe uniform Rules of Civil Procedure applicable both to "actions at law" and "cases in equity" in District Courts throughout the country. The uniform rules, commonly referred to as the "Federal Rules," were promulgated by the Supreme Court and have been in effect, with occasional amendments, since 1938. The most recent amendments to the rules were effective as of Dec. 1, 2018. Separate Federal Rules of Criminal Procedure govern the prosecution of crimes in the federal courts. The Federal Rules of Evidence, also adopted by the Supreme Court, govern the admission and use of evidence in both civil and criminal federal proceedings.

ii.   Courts of Appeals of the United States

Existing federal legislation also divides the United States into judicial circuits, each with its own Court of Appeals.[34] Appeals lie as a matter of right to each Court of Appeals from the District Courts located within the geographical area comprised by its circuit. There are now thirteen judicial circuits. One of the additions—the Eleventh Circuit—was created by splitting off Alabama, Florida and Georgia from the old fifth circuit. The other later-created circuit, the Federal Circuit, differs from the others in that its jurisdiction is defined in terms of subject matter rather than geography. It was created in 1982 and inherited the appellate jurisdiction of the old Court of Claims and the Court of Customs and Patent Appeals. The number of circuit judges for each Court of Appeals varies similarly—and, in fact, corresponds considerably more closely than existing circuit boundaries do—to contemporary Court of Appeals workloads. Thus, there are presently 29 Circuit Judges for the vast Ninth Circuit, and only 6 for the First Circuit. See 28 U.S.C. § 44(a).

Federal appeals in both civil and criminal cases are heard by panels of three judges, although, on very rare occasions, the full complement of circuit judges may sit "en banc" to hear and decide a case of particular difficulty or importance. Normally the three judges who participate in a federal appeal are all circuit judges, but Congressional legislation authorizes the summoning of district judges to sit temporarily "by designation" in the Courts of Appeals when pressure of appellate business requires. In recent years, as the volume of federal appellate litigation continues to mount, it has become quite common to have federal appeals heard and decided by a Court of Appeals consisting of two circuit judges and one district judge.

iii.   The Supreme Court of the United States

The most important point to grasp and remember about the Supreme Court's function as the court of last resort in the federal system is that only a small fraction of the controversies in which Supreme Court review is sought is ever accepted by the Court for hearing and decision "on the merits." In recent Terms, the Supreme Court has heard around eighty cases a year. By contrast, in 2019 the U.S. Court of Appeals for

---

[34] In older case reports, the student will find the federal intermediate appellate courts referred to as the "Circuit Courts of Appeals." The accurate usage now is simply "Courts of Appeals"; e.g., United States Court of Appeals, Second Circuit.

the Second Circuit decided more than 3,800 appeals. A disappointed litigant cannot secure Supreme Court review merely by contending, however persuasively, that the decision handed down against her was wrong; she must first persuade the Supreme Court that the issues presented by her case are important enough, as issues of general federal law, to justify Supreme Court consideration, for example, because different circuits have decided the same issues differently. In almost all cases, review by the Supreme Court of federal and state appellate court judgments can be obtained only by a "petition for a writ of certiorari," which the Supreme Court may grant or deny in the exercise of the broad discretion conferred upon it by Acts of Congress. As a matter of Supreme Court practice, if four or more of the nine justices vote to take the case, that is, to hear and decide it on its merits, the Court will "grant certiorari." If the petition for certiorari is denied, as the overwhelming majority of them are, the judgment of the Court of Appeals or the state's highest appellate court stands as the authoritative last word in the particular controversy.

It is important to understand that Supreme Court denial of a petition for certiorari does not necessarily imply Supreme Court approval of the theory or result reached by the Court of Appeals or other court from which the review was sought. Denial of certiorari may mean no more than that the justices do not believe the issues involved in the case important enough, in terms of the sound development of *federal law,* for full-dress Supreme Court attention. A sound policy basis underlies the discretionary nature of Supreme Court appellate jurisdiction: if appeal to the Supreme Court were available in all cases, the Court would be overwhelmed with ordinary appeals and unable to give full and deliberate consideration to the novel and socially important cases it must decide with finality as umpire of the federal system, authoritative guardian of constitutional liberties, and final overseer of the consistency and substantial justice of the general law administered in the courts of the United States. Thus, the Court is most likely to take a case if the federal courts of appeals have come out differently on the same question of interpretation of federal law. (This is known as a "Circuit split.") The records for a recent year demonstrate the extent to which the Supreme Court exercises its discretion under the certiorari procedure to keep its adjudicative workload within manageable bounds: during the October 2018 Term, 6,442 cases were filed in the Supreme Court; 73 cases were argued and 69 were disposed of in 66 signed opinions.[35]

b.   THE STATE COURTS

Each of the fifty states of the United States has its own system of courts. Court structures and court nomenclature differ greatly from state

---

[35]   See Supreme Court of the United States, 2019 Year-End Report on the Federal Judiciary 5 (December 31, 2019), https://www.supremecourt.gov/publicinfo/year-end/2019year-endreport.pdf.

to state, but all the state court systems exhibit what may be called a hierarchical structure, that is, a pattern of organization in which the decisions of "lower" courts may be taken for review to a higher-ranking tribunal. Ninety percent or more of the state "cases" a law student reads in casebooks are appellate decisions, but all these appellate cases will have passed through a "trial" stage and perhaps an intermediate appellate stage before reaching the state's "court of last resort."

The following sketch of the tiers in a typical state court hierarchy is unavoidably very much generalized—for example, some states do not have an intermediate appellate court, while others, such as Texas, have separate tribunals for civil and criminal appeals—but should be sufficient for present purposes. A first-year law student will find it interesting and worthwhile to become familiar with the pattern of court organization that exists in the state in which she expects to practice and with the names by which the various courts in her state are known.

i.   Trial Courts of "Inferior" Jurisdiction

Every state has its "inferior" or "petty" trial courts with jurisdiction limited to civil suits involving relatively small amounts of money and to minor violations of the criminal law. In many rural areas, these courts still go by the ancient name, Justice of the Peace (or "J.P.") Courts; in the cities, they are more often called Municipal Courts or City Courts. The civil jurisdiction of an "inferior" or "petty" trial court is usually defined in terms of the amount of money in dispute; thus the jurisdiction of the Justice of the Peace Court may be limited to claims not exceeding $100, while a metropolitan Municipal Court may be empowered to decide claims up to $1,000. Similarly, the jurisdiction of an "inferior" criminal court is likely to be defined in terms of the maximum jail sentence, commonly six months, or maximum fine that may be imposed if the defendant is found guilty of the particular offense charged.

ii. Trial Courts of General Jurisdiction

If a civil claim or criminal prosecution involves an amount of money, or a potential criminal sentence, beyond the jurisdiction of an "inferior" trial court, it must be filed and heard in a "trial court of general jurisdiction," that is, a court empowered to try all kinds of cases, without monetary or subject matter limitation. Practically all the appellate cases in law school casebooks will have been tried originally (or re-tried, on appeal by the losing party, after earlier judgment in an "inferior" court) in a trial court of general jurisdiction.

Every state has a set of trial courts of general jurisdiction, but there are differences in nomenclature from state to state. In some states, the trial court of general jurisdiction is known as the Superior Court ("superior," presumably, to the "petty" courts described above), in other states as the District Court or Circuit Court, names reflecting the typical division of the states into judicial districts or circuits. A few states retain old common law names, *e.g.*, Court of Common Pleas. New York, to the great confusion of out-of-state lawyers and frequent bewilderment of its own electorate, calls its trial court of general jurisdiction the Supreme Court, with the incidental consequence that New York trial judges of general jurisdiction are "justices," whereas the members of the State's distinguished court of last resort—the Court of Appeals—are mere "judges."

In every state, trial courts of general jurisdiction are distributed geographically throughout the state, so that litigants can have access to them without journeying to the state capital. Thus each state is divided into a number of judicial districts or circuits and a court established for each district or circuit, with at least one district or circuit judge for each of these geographical units. In metropolitan districts and other areas of large population, there will be many judges for each district; the Superior Court of Los Angeles, for example, in 2019 had 497 judges.[36] Although their principal function is the trial and initial (and final, if unappealed) determination of important civil and criminal controversies, state trial courts of general jurisdiction typically act also as appellate tribunals to decide appeals from the judgments of "inferior" trial courts and to review the actions of certain state administrative agencies, such as workers' compensation boards, licensing authorities, and public utility commissions.

A complete inventory of any state's trial courts will have to take account, also, of the specialized trial courts that are found in almost every state: Family Courts, Probate Courts, and the like. Some states have separate courts, with specially appointed or elected judges, for probate, divorce or criminal matters. In other states, only the one multi-judge trial court of general jurisdiction exists in each district but specialization is achieved by assigning one or more judges of that court to a particular task (*e.g.*, the Family Court) at the beginning of each judicial term. During the first half of the 20th-century, a number of states still had a set of courts for "common law" actions and another set for "equity" cases, but procedural reforms, specifically the so-called "merger of law and equity," have brought about a virtual disappearance of this terminological survival of days past.

iii. Appellate Courts

Every state has its "court of last resort," the appellate court at the top of the judicial hierarchy and the one which determines with finality (subject to occasional review on "federal questions" by the Supreme Court of the United States) what the particular state's law is and should be. In most states, this highest court in the hierarchy is called the Supreme Court of the state, but other names are in use here and there: Supreme Judicial Court, Supreme Court of Appeals and, as in New York, Court of

---

[36] Judges Roster, California Courts, http://www.courts.ca.gov/2948.htm.

Appeals. "Whatever the name, its function is the same: to review the action of the lower judicial tribunals of the state. This is the exercise of appellate jurisdiction. The scope of judicial review which the court exercises in such cases is relatively narrow; it does not retry the case on the merits, and it does not substitute its idea of justice for those of the trial court; what it does is to review the record of the proceedings to determine whether or not the lower court committed error in its procedure or in applying the substantive law to the facts of the case." Green, "The Business of the Trial Courts," in Jones (ed.), The Courts, the Public and the Law Explosion 7, 16 (1965).

The contemporary idea that one's "day in court" includes the right to appellate review of every adverse trial court judgment is a quite recent development. Appeal was a "matter of grace," not a "matter of right," at English common law and even during the first century or so of American legal history. Under existing statutes in every state, the party who loses at the trial court stage of a litigated controversy has a right to have the trial court judgment reviewed at least once by a court other than the one that originally entered it. One inevitable result of this recognition of appeal as a matter of right was, of course, a vast increase in appellate litigation which, particularly in the more populous states, soon led to hopeless congestion of the dockets of the state courts of last resort.

In response, most States have created intermediate appellate courts, empowered to strain out and finally dispose of the bulk of appellate litigation—cases, for example, that raise no new or difficult issue of law— so that the court of last resort can give its full attention to novel and socially important controversies. The prevailing contemporary policy is to give the court of last resort very wide discretion over the granting or denial of applications for its appellate review. If appeals from a state's intermediate appellate court to its court of last resort were granted too freely, the intermediate appellate court would not be performing the vital "screening out" function for which it was created. As the volume of litigation continues to grow in almost every state, the intermediate appellate courts become increasingly the final tribunal for authoritative disposition of far more cases than will ever reach the state's court of last resort.

The following chart illustrates the variety, and complexity, of the court system of one state—New York.

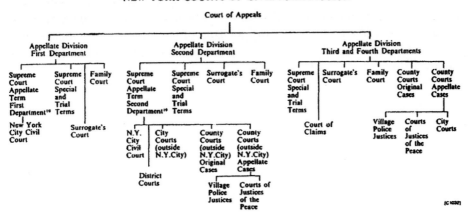

THE COURT SYSTEM IN PRACTICE: THE STRUCTURE OF A CIVIL ACTION

3. THE COURT SYSTEM IN PRACTICE: THE STRUCTURE OF A CIVIL ACTION

Professor Karl Llewellyn once described substantive law as follows:

> [C]ertain bodies of law, which we call substantive—the substance of the law—deal with what ought to be, with whether contracts ought to be enforced at law, and when; with what formalities are necessary to make a last will stick; with how to form a corporation and how to issue its stock, and how to keep investors from having any say in it; and what words are necessary to make an effective lease or deed of land; and so on.[37]

Civil Procedure, by contrast, constitutes the mechanism through which rules of substantive law have effect. Rules of Civil Procedure control all aspects of the manner through which rules of substantive law are applied; whether a particular person has standing to bring a particular suit; the forum in which the suit may be brought; the manner in which her claim must be asserted; the ground rules of proof of his claim; the remedy which is afforded; the manner in which the judgment is enforced. In the words of one scholar, "the road to court-made justice is paved with good procedures."[38]

You will learn about various aspects of civil procedure in other courses, such as Civil Procedure, Evidence, Administrative Law, Federal Courts and Conflicts of Law. But even at this stage you need to know something about procedure. The first portion of the Legal Methods course

---

[37] Karl Llewellyn, The Bramble Bush 16 (1930).

[38] Maurice Rosenberg, *Devising Procedures That Are Civil to Promote Justice That Is Civilized*, 69 Mich. L. Rev. 797 (1971). Professor Rosenberg also observed:

> In a democracy, process is king to a very large extent, and this is especially so in the judicial branch. Even though substantive laws command attention, procedural rules ensure respect. Why is this true? One powerful reason is that when people end up in court, their case typically is not a matter of right against wrong, but of right against right. Decent process makes the painful task of deciding which party will prevail bearable and helps make the decision itself acceptable.

Id. at 797.

is devoted to a study of case law. In reading cases we are seeking to
determine what the case decides as to the substantive law, or, to phrase
it somewhat differently, what proposition of substantive law a case may
be said to stand for. This depends upon the exact question the court had
before it for decision, which in turn depends on the procedure to date in
the case.

At first, the profusion of procedural steps encountered in a civil
lawsuit may prove bewildering. To clarify the subject and put it in
perspective, consider the following outline of a civil action.

a.   THE PLEADING STAGE

The "client," when he first comes to the lawyer, does not have a case;
he has a problem. The lawyer's first task is to ascertain "the facts." This
task is crucial, and it is not as easy as it sounds, even in uncomplicated
situations. Clients are no less—sometimes they are more—prone to
misunderstanding, misimpression, and faulty recollection as the next
person. Sometimes clients lie, and even when they aim at the truth, they
often miss—for all of the reasons encountered in non-legal contexts. In
today's increasingly global legal practice, the "client" may also be a large
multi-national corporate entity comprising of thousands of employees,
any number of whom may have relevant information related to the legal
matter at issue.

To start with a simpler matter, assume that you are a lawyer whose
client (X) tells you the following: X received a series of increasingly
taunting postcards sent by F, his former fiancée, during the course of her
honeymoon with her new husband. As a result, X claims to have suffered
severe emotional distress, resulting in neurological disturbances
(personal injury). Moreover, overcome by a bout of depression while
driving, he drove his car into a tree, destroying the front end (property
damage).[39]

For the purposes of this discussion (but not in real practice), assume
further that you are satisfied that the facts correspond to your client's
assertions, and that they can be proved in court.[40] Next, you will need to
determine if these facts state a claim under the applicable law. In many
instances, the existence of a legal violation (if the facts alleged are
proved) will be clear. For example, if your client alleged that the other
party reneged on a written agreement to sell him her house, your client
would have stated a claim for breach of contract. In other cases, however,
it may be less clear that the defendant has violated a legal norm. For
example, if your client claims to suffer humiliation because a newspaper
published a true account of his divorce or of his filing for personal
bankruptcy, but neither the common law in your jurisdiction, nor local

---

[39] This hypothetical is inspired by a real case, Halio v. Lurie, 222 N.Y.S.2d 759 (N.Y. App.
Div. 1961), discussed in *Flamm v. Van Nierop, infra*, subsection II.B.1.d.

[40] The rules governing what can be proved in court and how to prove it are covered in the
course in Evidence.

legislative authorities have recognized a claim for this kind of invasion of privacy, then the newspaper will have committed no legal violation. Even if you determine that your client does have a legal claim, you should expect the defendant to dispute your client's case both on the facts and on the law, as we shall see.

If you are satisfied that the facts your client alleges can be proved, and that they make out a legal violation, you will now have to determine in what court you will "bring your action." This will depend on what courts have "jurisdiction" of the type of action, which may turn on such factors as the amount of money involved and the states of residence of the parties. Assuming that the court has "subject matter jurisdiction," the person sued (the "defendant") must be subject to the jurisdiction of the court. Without "personal jurisdiction," a court can render no valid judgment against the defendant. A defendant who lives in the state where the court is located (the "forum"), or who has committed the wrongful act there, will usually be answerable to suit in that forum.

Ordinarily, personal jurisdiction is established by the service of process on the defendant. The forms vary in different jurisdictions but in most you will initiate the lawsuit by "serving" a "summons" and "complaint" on the defendant. Service of process is a story in itself which is best left to the course in Civil Procedure.

The complaint is a "pleading" in which the person suing (the "plaintiff") states the facts that in his view entitle him to a judgment against the defendant, F in our case. The complaint must set forth a statement of the allegations clear enough to enable the defendant to prepare her defense. The complaint also must allege facts sufficient to "constitute a cause of action," that is, facts which under the controlling law entitle him to judgment.

Once the complaint has been served, the next move is up to the defendant and her lawyer. Stepping into the role of defense counsel, four courses of action are open to you:

1. *Do nothing,* in which event, the court, after a proper interval, will enter a *"default"* judgment against your client, through which the plaintiff will be able to collect against your client's property. For obvious reasons this is rarely the recommended response.

2. *Serve (and/or file in court) a motion to dismiss for failure to state a claim.* (Older cases and some state rules of procedure refer to this motion as a "demurrer.") By this pleading you would say, in effect, "even if the alleged facts are true, there is no rule of law that permits X to recover against F on those facts." The demurrer is the pleading involved in the *Roberson* and *Garrison* cases, *infra* subsections II.A.1.b and II.B.1.c. Since the motion to dismiss, or demurrer, admits, temporarily, the truth of the

facts alleged by the plaintiff, it raises a pure issue of substantive law.

3. *Serve (and/or file) an answer.* An *answer* denies all (or some) of the facts alleged in the complaint. It thus raises an issue of *fact* between the parties, not an issue of *law*. (Usually, in U.S. pleading, all facts stated in the complaint and not denied by the defendant are taken as true.)

4. *Serve (and/or file) an affirmative defense.* By this pleading, you admit (again temporarily, as in the case of the motion to dismiss) the truth of the facts alleged and also (unlike the motion to dismiss) that those facts standing alone would win for plaintiff, but allege new facts which require a different result. In our supposed case, the pleading might be in effect, "Yes, your statement of facts is true, but the acts you complain of happened more than three years ago and your claim is barred by the statute of limitations."

As noted above, the motion to dismiss for failure to state a claim raises a pure question of substantive law. It is as though the defendant said: I concede (for the sake of argument) that the facts alleged are true, but the law does not provide for a recovery against me on the basis of those facts. For example, suppose that in our case, F said "I admit (for purposes of this motion) that I sent you the postcards intending to hurt your feelings and to cause you emotional harm, but the law in this jurisdiction does not recognize the tort of intentional infliction of emotional distress."

Assuming that the defendant moves to dismiss for failure to state a claim, the motion will be argued before the court and either granted or denied. If it is granted, usually the plaintiff will be given an opportunity to "replead," *i.e.*, to allege additional facts, if they exist, sufficient to state a claim. If he is unable to do so, he may appeal. If the motion to dismiss is denied, and the defendant has, in addition to moving to dismiss, controverted the plaintiffs' allegations of fact, the case will go to trial (or in some jurisdictions the defendant may appeal immediately).[41] If she does not dispute the facts, there is no need for a trial. The case proceeds directly to judgment, on the law, which may be reviewed on appeal.

Up to now, we have been talking about the defendant's motion to dismiss. Precisely the same kind of issue (*i.e.*, an issue of substantive law) may arise when defendant raises an affirmative defense that plaintiff controverts. For example, suppose that F admitted the allegations of the complaint, but asserted that X was negligent in driving a car when he was emotionally unfit to drive. X could challenge the legal sufficiency of F's affirmative defense. X could admit that he drove while suffering from emotional distress, but could deny that driving under those conditions

---

[41] In those jurisdictions where an appeal does not "lie" immediately, the denial may be appealed at the end of the trial.

was negligent. Alternatively, X could challenge the facts F alleged. X could contend that he did not know, and should not have known, that his emotional distress would impair his ability to drive.

b.   THE TRIAL STAGE

Although it may not appear so from casebooks, the overwhelming majority of cases do not raise issues of substantive law. In most cases, the parties do not dispute the law, but only the facts.

Let us assume that an issue of fact has been raised by the pleadings, that is, that your client (now you are representing the defendant), at the pleading stage, filed an answer denying some or all of the facts stated in the plaintiff's complaint. Thus an issue of fact is raised between the parties, which will require trial,[42] before a jury or (if a jury is waived by the parties) trial before a judge sitting as a jury—a "bench trial."

What are the principal procedural events that occur, or can occur, at the trial stage?[43] We begin with the presentation of the plaintiff's case:

1.   Plaintiff's opening statement to the jury, "I expect to prove . . . ." In some states (e.g., New York) this may be followed immediately by defendant's opening statement (if defendant chooses to make one) as to what defendant expects to prove. In other states, defendant's opening statement comes later, at the start of defendant's case.

2.   Next come the direct and cross-examinations of plaintiff's witnesses—the witnesses called by plaintiff's counsel testify and are cross-examined by defendant's counsel. Here you may have "objections" to the introduction of evidence, for example, on the ground that the evidence is inadmissible as hearsay. If the court, after defendant's objection, lets the evidence in, defendant will "except" to the ruling and so preserve her right to challenge the ruling on appeal if the jury verdict goes against her.

3.   At the end of plaintiff's evidence, defendant may ask the trial court for a "directed verdict" or, in the federal courts, for a "judgment as a matter of law."[44] By making one of these motions, defendant is saying, in effect, that plaintiff has not proved enough—i.e., has not offered adequate evidence in support of his allegations of fact—to enable any reasonable jury to bring in a verdict for him. You will note that these motions

---

[42] It is, of course, possible that although the pleadings may raise an issue, there may be "no *genuine* issue of fact" between the parties, i.e., that there is no evidence to support the claim or demand in the pleadings. Such cases may be disposed of without trial by "summary judgment."

[43] This outline omits the very important procedural devices by which the parties obtain information in advance of trial, such as examinations before trial, requests for admission, document discovery and interrogatories. Nor does it discuss the important and interesting process of jury selection. These issues form part of the course in Civil Procedure.

[44] See Fed. R. Civ. P. 50.

attack the sufficiency of plaintiff's proof of facts and, ordinarily, do not raise a question of substantive law.

4.   Assuming that defendant's motions have been made but denied by the court, defendant presents her evidence, *i.e.*, calls witnesses to prove her version of the facts. Thus again, we will have the direct testimony and cross-examination of witnesses and may have objections to evidence (this time from counsel for plaintiff) and exceptions to the court's rulings thereon.

5.   At the end of defendant's evidence, plaintiff may move for a directed verdict (rarely granted, however, to the party with the "burden of proof") or the defendant may again move for a directed verdict on the ground that she has now shown so clearly that plaintiff's asserted version of the facts is not true that no reasonable jury could do otherwise than find for defendant.

6.   If all these motions are denied, plaintiff and defendant sum up before the jury, plaintiff having the right, usually, to make the closing argument.

7.   The next, and crucial, stage of the trial is the "charge to the jury." The judge gives her instructions to the jury as to the applicable law of the case. Thus, for example, in our hypothetical case, the judge might advise the jury about as follows: "If you the jury find that the defendant sent the postcards, with the intention of causing the plaintiff emotional distress, and that the cards did cause the plaintiff to suffer emotional distress, you will bring in a verdict in the amount of his medical expenses and personal suffering. If you find that a reasonable person in plaintiff's position would not or should not have been aware that his emotional distress would impair his ability to drive, then you will also bring in a verdict for the amount of his property damage." The instruction stage is one of the most important for our immediate purposes, and you should know something about its realities:

   a.   In actual practice, few instructions are ever drawn up by the trial judge as a matter of her own literary initiative. What usually happens is that each side draws up draft instructions and submits them to the judge. The judge then looks at the draft instructions submitted by both sides and decides which ones to give to the jury (she will probably revise the words). Either side in the litigation may:

      (i)   except, *i.e.*, record objections, to any instruction or part thereof, which he believes is an erroneous statement of the law; or

      (ii) except to the refusal of the judge to give the instruction proposed by the party.

b.   Since the instruction is, in substance, a statement to the jury of the substantive law applicable to the facts of the case, it is at the instruction stage that you are quite likely to have a sharp issue of law between the parties, decided by the trial judge and specified by the losing party as the ground for his appeal. This is particularly true in tort actions, where a very large percentage of appeals in modern cases come up on, or involve, an appeal from the instructions given to the jury.

8.   After the judge delivers her instructions, the jury retires for deliberation and, ultimately, brings in its "verdict." Most jury verdicts are general, a statement of result in some such form as "We, the jury, find for the plaintiff in the sum of $50,000." So-called "special" verdicts, by which the jury answers specific questions of fact submitted to it by the judge, are becoming more frequent. However, a general verdict with interrogatories (by which the court instructs the jury to reach a general verdict, but requests answers to one or more questions so that the basis for the verdict is disclosed) is less controversial and often preferred by judges over the special verdict.[45]

c.   MOTIONS IN THE TRIAL COURT AFTER VERDICT

After the jury has returned its verdict, but before the trial court has entered "judgment"[46] in the action, the party who lost before the jury can make one or more of several motions. Many appeals come up to the appellate courts from the action of trial courts granting or denying one of these motions, so you should get a general idea now as to the kind of question each motion raises. Terminology and practice will differ considerably from state to state, but it should be possible to get a general understanding without too much difficulty.

Most sweeping of the motions after verdict is the motion for judgment notwithstanding the verdict, which is also referred to by the Latin name "judgment *non obstante veredicto*" (or, familiarly, judgment n.o.v. or j.n.o.v.), in which the party against whom the verdict is pronounced goes so far as to ask that judgment be given for him or her in spite of the jury findings. In the federal courts, this motion is a "renewed motion for a judgment as a matter of law."[47]

More common is the motion to set aside the verdict as against the weight of the evidence and grant a new trial. Both this motion and the

---

[45]   Jack H. Friedenthal et al., Civil Procedure 569–70 (4th ed. 2005).

[46]   Note and remember the difference between "verdict" and "judgment."

[47]   "The standards for granting a motion for a directed verdict and for granting a motion for judgment notwithstanding the verdict are identical. . . . We will take the issue from the jury 'only if all the evidence favors the movant and is susceptible of no reasonable inferences sustaining the position of the non-moving party.'" Ruwitch v. William Penn Life Assur. Co., 966 F.2d 1234 (8th Cir. 1992) (citations omitted).

modern motion for judgment n.o.v. are attacks on the sufficiency of the evidence to support the verdict. You may well ask at this point what gives the judge (to whom all motions are addressed) the right to disregard a verdict of a jury, which in our system is the cherished and time-honored instrument for finding the facts. The answer is that we require *as a matter of law* a minimum amount of evidence to support the jury verdict.[48] This amount, variously phrased as "more than a scintilla," or such that "reasonable persons may not differ," is obviously an imprecise standard and susceptible to abuse. In practice, however, most judges will only rarely displace a jury verdict, and when they do, will ordinarily not grant judgment n.o.v., but instead set aside the verdict and grant a new trial.

The losing party may also move for a new trial on a number of other grounds such as an error by the judge in ruling on evidence, an error in the instructions, misconduct by the jurors, or excessive damages. The usual rule is that a losing party cannot appeal any errors of the trial court which he did not call to the trial court's attention by filing a motion for a new trial.

If all motions after verdict are denied, the trial court formally enters judgment for the party to whom the jury awarded the verdict. This judgment is *res judicata* of the controversy between the parties unless notice of appeal is given by the losing party within a required number of days.

---

[48] The following definition of the test for the correctness of the grant of a motion for a directed verdict is from Combs v. Meadowcraft, Inc., 106 F.3d 1519, 1526 (11th Cir. 1997):

> In conducting our review: "[W]e consider all the evidence, and the inferences drawn therefrom, in the light most favorable to the nonmoving party. If the facts and inferences point overwhelmingly in favor of one party, such that reasonable people could not arrive at a contrary verdict, then the motion was properly granted. Conversely, if there is substantial evidence opposed to the motion such that reasonable people, in the exercise of impartial judgment, might reach differing conclusions, then such a motion was due to be denied and the case was properly submitted to the jury". Carter v. City of Miami, 870 F.2d 578, 581 (11th Cir. 1989).

> Under the foregoing standard, the nonmoving party must provide more than a mere scintilla of evidence to survive a motion for judgment as a matter of law: "[T]here must be a substantial conflict in evidence to support a jury question." *Id.* To summarize, we must consider all the evidence in the light most favorable to [the plaintiff] and determine "whether or not reasonable jurors could have concluded as this jury did based on the evidence presented." Quick v. Peoples Bank, 993 F.2d 793, 797 (11th Cir. 1993) (citation and internal quotation marks omitted).

The test for the granting of a judgment notwithstanding the verdict is substantially the same:

> A district court may enter a judgment notwithstanding the verdict when, viewing the evidence in the light most favorable to the non-moving party, "(1) there is such a complete absence of evidence supporting the verdict that the jury's findings could only have been the result of sheer surmise and conjecture, or (2) there is such an overwhelming amount of evidence in favor of the movant that reasonable and fair minded men could not arrive at a verdict against him."

Haskell v. Kaman Corp., 743 F.2d 113, 120 (2d Cir. 1984) (quoting Mattivi v. South African Marine Corp., 618 F.2d 163, 168 (2d Cir. 1980)).

d. EXECUTION OF THE JUDGMENT

If the plaintiff has obtained a judgment against the defendant and the defendant does not pay or otherwise satisfy the judgment, the plaintiff is entitled to execution. In the case of a judgment for money, (the usual case in our system) the plaintiff obtains a writ from the court directing the sheriff (or similar official) to seize property of the defendant, sell it, and with the proceeds pay to the plaintiff the amount of his judgment.

Execution, like service of process, is a story by itself. Just as it can be very difficult to serve process on a reluctant defendant, it can be very difficult to collect from a determined, unscrupulous, "judgment-proof" debtor. The securing of a judgment can be only the beginning of a long trail to compensation. Execution is of great importance to the client. Inability to enforce a judgment because of the insolvency or intransigence of the defendant may make meaningless all that has gone before. As a result, before initiating an action it is important to assess whether the defendant has the resources, and the compliance, to satisfy a judgment.

e. THE APPELLATE STAGE

Most cases you will read in law school are appellate cases and you need to have some background on the appellate process if you are fully to understand them.

In the U.S. system, the appellate court does not retry the case on its merits or take additional evidence. The focus of the appellate court's scrutiny is on the correctness of the rulings of the trial court below. The documents at which the appellate court will look in its review include the record—the pleadings, the transcript of the testimony at the trial or an edited portion thereof, the exhibits entered into evidence, the trial court's rulings—and the "briefs" of counsel, *i.e.*, statements (usually printed) of the arguments supporting each side's position in the litigation below. No additional testimony is taken, nor is new evidence submitted. Most law libraries have many copies of briefs and records and you should look at a few. Appellate briefs are also available online, particularly filings before the U.S. Supreme Court.[49]

After the briefs and the record are filed, the case is set up for oral argument and argued before the appellate court. After oral argument and study of the briefs and the trial record, the judges of the appellate court meet in conference, discuss the case, and assign the writing of the opinion of the court to one of its members. The opinions are more than individual essays of the judge. When written by the assigned judge, the draft opinion will be circulated for initialing, and when approved by all the members of the panel, or a majority, the opinion is filed as the opinion of the court. There may also be concurring opinions (the concurring judges agreeing

---

[49] *See, e.g.*, https://www.scotusblog.com/case-files/terms/ (containing petitions and briefs from OT 2007 to present).

with the result but differing in some way from the majority opinion) and dissenting opinions.

One other point bears emphasizing. A lawsuit is a complicated and long drawn out proceeding. Many points of dispute will come up. Few, if any, trial judges can avoid error in every ruling in a complicated case. This is particularly true of rulings from the bench during the course of trial. Unlike appellate judges, who enjoy the leisure of hindsight on the trial court's determinations, and time to research and reflect on their own rulings, the trial court frequently must make snap decisions. Sometimes these are wrong. Should all such errors warrant reversal by the appellate court? Many times, the errors are "cured" by subsequent events, or the questions on which erroneous rulings are made turn out to be unimportant. As a result, an error in the trial court will not provoke a reversal unless it is "prejudicial," *i.e.*, unless it did—or might have—prejudicially influenced the outcome of the case.

B. LEGISLATION

1. ATTRIBUTES AND TYPES

a.   THE GENERALITY OF LEGISLATION

In section A, we saw how case law generates rules inferred from prior decisions. Rules of general application derive from an accumulation and synthesis of the results and reasoning in particular controversies. The common lawyer is accustomed to reasoning from the particular to the general. Specific examples play an important role in the common lawyer's approach, as do the facts of individual cases.

But case law is not the only source of law, even in a common law system. Legislation supplies another principal, and increasingly predominant, source of law. The drafting and interpretation of legislation call on skills and analyses different from those honed in the adjudicative process. While case law begins with particular controversies, legislation imposes a general rule. Where case law analysis calls on the lawyer to move upward from specific facts to a general principle to discern how the solution in one case can guide the resolution of another, the interpretation of legislation requires reasoning from the general to the specific, to determine whether and how a rule claiming wide application in fact governs an individual controversy.

Moreover, legislation does not simply declare rules; it expresses them in specific language. With legislation, every word (indeed, every punctuation mark) counts. As the late Edwin W. Patterson wrote in the first Legal Methods casebook, Neal Thomas Dowling, Edwin Wilhite Patterson and Richard R.B. Powell, Materials for Legal Method (1946):

> A proposition of case law may be correctly stated in several
> different ways, each of which is equally "official." A statute

(proposition of legislation) is stated as an exclusive official wording of the rule. Case law is flexible; legislation is (textually) rigid.

Statutory interpretation requires working with the words of the statute. Their meaning may be uncertain, but their presence is not. Interpreting the text should not mean rewriting or paraphrasing it. Courts inevitably have great latitude in determining the meaning and application of statutory language in concrete situations, but only the legislature is authorized to change a statute's wording by the process of amendment. (As you work through the materials in Part III of this casebook, consider to what extent the judicial interpretation of statutes in fact follows these precepts.)

To some extent, the methods of case analysis and statutory interpretation converge. Judges interpret statutes, and their accumulated interpretations become, in effect, the case law of the statutes. Once a court has given a statute a particular interpretation, the principle of *stare decisis* applies to that interpretation: Lower courts in that jurisdiction are as bound by the interpretation as they would be had the rendering court resolved an issue of common law. Of course, the legislator is not bound by the court's interpretation: It is free to amend the statute to impart a different meaning to the text. (On legislative responses to prior judicial interpretations of statutes, see subsection III.G.3 of the casebook, *infra*.)

b. TYPES OF LEGISLATION

Legislative precepts are prescribed general rules expressed in authoritative verbal form. The statutes enacted by Congress and state legislatures are legislation of the classic and most familiar kind. In the present section, however, the term "legislation" will denote not only federal and state statutes but also the other types of general legal rules that are prescribed in administrative regulations, municipal ordinances and the like. Even the Constitution of the United States or a state constitution is "legislation" in this broad sense (although of higher political and legal obligation than "ordinary" legislation), because a constitution, too, is a rule-prescribing instrument, one which expresses in authoritative form the general rules, or principles, that govern the exercise of political power in an organized society and safeguard individual interests from unwarranted governmental intrusion.

Because of the wide dispersion of law-making power in the United States—the constitutional division of legislative authority between the national government and the states and the delegation of subordinate legislative power to administrative agencies and, in the states, to city councils and other municipal bodies—American legislation is an aggregate of precepts from many sources. Conflicting directions are frequently encountered in this mix; a state statute, for example, may be or seem in conflict with existing federal legislation or a state administrative regulation with a municipal ordinance on the same subject. Individuals and corporations, and so the lawyers advising them, are often faced with the problem of what to do when one law-maker has commanded certain behavior and another law-maker has ordered a quite different course of action. In determining which of two competing legislative commands is the one to be obeyed, or to be given controlling force by a court in a litigated case, the manifest first step is to consider the degree of authority with which each of the two law-makers spoke to the subject at hand. The types of legislation briefly sketched in the following paragraphs therefore follow our legal system's hierarchy of legislative norms, from most to least authoritative.

i.   The Constitution of the United States

The Constitution sets out the norms that govern the distribution of political powers in our society and the ways in which—and purposes for which—these powers are to be exercised. In our legal order the Constitution is "law," and law of the highest authoritativeness and obligation. Even a deliberately enacted federal statute can be challenged in the courts as beyond the legislative power delegated to the Congress by the Constitution or as violative of some provision of the Bill of Rights or other constitutional guarantee of individual interests against impairment by government action. Similarly, the Constitution of the United States, as "supreme Law of the Land," is the ultimate authority to which reference must be made to determine the validity of state and municipal legislation. The Constitution, in its inception, related almost entirely to the structure and operations of the national (or "federal") government, but since the adoption of the Reconstruction Amendments (the Thirteenth, Fourteenth and Fifteenth Amendments) in the years following the Civil War, the prohibitions of the Constitution have been of equal importance in relation to state legislation and to action taken by state and local officials.

ii.   Federal Statutes

Article I, Section 1 of the Constitution of the United States provides that "all legislative Powers herein granted shall be vested in a Congress of the United States." The powers so granted to Congress are enumerated in considerable detail in Article I, Section 8, which concludes with a broadly worded grant of authority to "make all Laws which shall be necessary and proper for carrying into Execution the foregoing Powers." What are the constitutional and legal consequences when Congress, as it has done quite often in recent years, enacts a statute which, although clearly within the scope of its law-making authority under Article I, Section 8, conflicts directly with existing state legislation or state constitutional provisions? The "supremacy clause" (Article VI, paragraph 2) of the Constitution supplies the answer.

The supremacy clause, one of the key provisions of the Constitution, provides in full as follows:

> This Constitution, and the Laws of the United States which shall be made in Pursuance thereof; and all Treaties made, or which shall be made, under the Authority of the United States, shall be the supreme Law of the Land; and the Judges in every State shall be bound thereby, any Thing in the Constitution or Laws of any State to the Contrary notwithstanding.

The words are carefully chosen and their meaning and effect clear. A federal statute "made in pursuance" of the Constitution is a part of "the supreme Law of the Land" and so of superior authoritativeness to any state constitutional provision, state statute or other type of state legislation.

iii. Treaties

> Article II, Section 2 of the Constitution provides that the President shall have power, by and with the Advice and Consent of the Senate, to make Treaties, provided two-thirds of the Senators present concur.

A treaty in its essence is a diplomatic instrument, a compact between nations, and it may seem strange to see treaties included in an inventory of the types of legislation. Nonetheless, there are a few circumstances in which a treaty made by the President with the advice and consent of the Senate has much the same legal effect as a federal statute. Suppose, for example, that a treaty between the United States and some other nation provides that the citizens of each country shall be fully entitled to inherit property or to engage in all kinds of business in the other country. By the explicit terms of the supremacy clause of the Constitution of the United States, just considered in its relation to federal statutes, this treaty is a part of the "supreme law of the land" and so is superior in legal authoritativeness to any type of state legislation. The citizens of the nation with whom the supposed treaty was made are thus entitled to inherit property or to engage in any kind of business in State X, even if State X has a statute or state constitutional provision restricting the inheritance of property or the carrying on of designated kinds of business to American citizens. The place of treaties and the treaty power in our constitutional system raises many complex questions, some of them of lively contemporary importance, but these questions must be left to later courses in International Law and Constitutional Law. It is sufficient now to note the possibility that a treaty may have an incidental side-effect as federal legislation.

iv. State Constitutions

State constitutions existed before the drafting of the Constitution of the United States. Almost all of the thirteen original states adopted constitutions in 1776 or 1777. These first state constitutions and those adopted early in the 19th century were much like the Constitution of the United States in content and style, that is, they were largely confined to essential matters like basic governmental structure and the definition and distribution of political powers and, except in their bills of individual rights, expressed in terms of broad principles or standards as distinguished from narrowly stated rules.

Every state has its constitution, and the typical state constitution of today is a far bulkier document and is likely to deal at length and in very specific terms with subjects like school and police administration, lotteries, state and municipal budgeting, the tenure of civil service employees, and the powers to be exercised by irrigation and sewer districts. Such explicit and detailed provisions are written into a state constitution for the manifest purpose of making it impossible for a subsequent state legislature to change the law on the subject by simple statutory enactment. It is far harder politically to amend a state constitution than to repeal or amend a statute; a two-thirds majority in each house of the state legislature is commonly required to propose a state constitutional amendment, and an amendment so proposed must typically be approved by popular referendum which may, in its turn, require more than a simple-majority vote of the electorate.

State statutes are, of course, subject to challenge in the courts on federal constitutional grounds, but, because of the great specificity of most state constitutions, the state constitutional barrier may be the more difficult one to overcome. A state statute that would unquestionably pass Supreme Court scrutiny as consistent with the Constitution of the United States can nonetheless be held invalid by a state court of last resort as a violation of some provision of the local state constitution. And that will be a final and conclusive determination because the Supreme Court of the United States is not superior in authority to state courts on questions of state law.

v.   State Statutes

It is sometimes said that state statutes are less important in the day-to-day work of lawyers than they once were, because federal regulatory activity has vastly expanded. To say this is to overlook two other developments during approximately the same time: (1) the extension and intensification of state controls, imposed by or based on statutes, in such areas as consumer protection, environmental management, and equal employment opportunity; and (2) the increasing tendency of state legislatures to intervene in traditional private law fields by replacing old case law rules with new and presumably more up-to-date legislative norms.

The effectiveness of a state statutory provision as an authoritative rule may be challenged in court on one or more of several grounds: that it violates some more or less explicit prohibition in the Constitution of the United States, that it contravenes some provision of the state constitution, or that it conflicts with some more authoritative federal statute, treaty or administrative regulation. But it is misleading to concentrate too much on the possible vulnerability of state statutes to constitutional challenge. Ninety percent or more of the statutes enacted by a busy state legislature at one of its sessions will raise no serious question of federal or state constitutional law. The lawyer's work in dealing with state statutes is chiefly a work of interpretation, of determining the meaning and effect of enacted statutory language for specific cases and counseling situations.

vi. *Municipal Ordinances*

The rules enacted by the legislative branch of a local or "municipal" unit of government are authoritative precepts of legislation within the unit's territorial limits. These prescribed rules of local legislative origin are commonly called "ordinances" (to distinguish them from the "statutes" enacted by Congress and the state legislatures), and that is what we shall call them here, even though they sometimes bear another name (*e.g.*, "by-law"). A municipal ordinance is, of course, legally ineffective if inconsistent with a higher norm of federal law or with a provision of the state constitution and is usually, but not always, inferior in authoritativeness to a conflicting state statute—"not always" because many state constitutions contain so-called "home rule" provisions which, to one or another extent, may empower cities and other municipal units to enact ordinances, on a few designated subjects, that are not vulnerable to disapproval or modification by the state legislature. Insofar as the law-making power of the municipal unit comes to it by statutory delegation from the state legislature, however, the rule prescribed by a municipal ordinance must yield to the conflicting direction of a state statute and may, like an administrative regulation, be repealed or modified by subsequent action of the legislature.

c.   NOTE ON UNIFORM CODES

One way to systematize the law and make it uniform across state jurisdictions is to reduce the common law to statutory form and seek adoption by state legislators. The Uniform Commercial Code (UCC), developed and monitored by the American Law Institute (ALI) in collaboration with the National Conference of Commissioners on Uniform State Laws (NCCUSL), represents the most successful of such efforts.[50] The UCC is a comprehensive code aimed at simplifying and

---

[50] Other ALI proposals for law reform include model statutory formulations such as the Model Code of Evidence, the Model Penal Code, a Model Code of Pre-Arraignment Procedure, a Model Land Development Code, and a proposed Federal Securities Code. In 2012, the Council approved several new projects including Restatements of consumer contracts law, American Indian law, and intentional torts to persons. The ALI also plans on updating the Restatement of the Foreign Relations Law of the United States and the Model Penal Code's provisions on sexual assault and related offenses. See https://www.ali.org/media/filer_public/be/2d/be2d7c2d-58c6-427d-b5ce-a2176cc072a0/annual-report-2019-web.pdf.

standardizing (rather than restating) most aspects of commercial law. You are likely to study sections of the UCC closely in your contracts class. Helping to promote commerce between states by making it simpler to pursue transactions in various jurisdictions, the Code covers the sales of goods, commercial paper, bank deposits and collections, letters of credit, investment securities, and secured transactions. The UCC which took ten years to complete and another 14 years before it was enacted across the country[51] is generally viewed as one of the most important developments in American law. It has been enacted (with some local variations) in 49 states and in the District of Columbia and the Virgin Islands, as well as partially in Louisiana.[52]

In addition to collaborating with the ALI on the UCC, the NCCUSL has drafted more than 200 uniform laws on numerous subjects and in various fields of law since its organization in 1892. The conference comprises more than 300 lawyers, judges and law professors, appointed by the states as well as the District of Columbia, Puerto Rico and the U.S. Virgin Islands, to "draft proposals for uniform and model laws on subjects where uniformity is desirable and practicable, and work toward their enactment in legislatures."[53] Uniform acts include the Uniform Probate Code, the Uniform Child Custody Jurisdiction Act, the Uniform Partnership Act, the Uniform Anatomical Gift Act, the Uniform Limited Partnership Act, and the Uniform Interstate Family Support Act.[54] Recently promulgated uniform acts include the Uniform Foreign-Country Money Judgments Recognition Act, the Uniform Representation of Children in Abuse, Neglect, and Custody Proceedings Act, and the Uniform Rules Relating to Discovery of Electronically Stored Information.[55] As with the Restatements (discussed *supra* at pp. 9–10), the Conference can only propose laws, and no uniform law is effective until adopted by a state legislature. For example, as of April 2019, New York has enacted more than 78 Uniform Acts since 1897.[56]

More recently, conservative and progressive organizations have also been involved in preparing model laws, first on the right (the American Legislative Exchange Council, or "ALEC"), and, more recently and in response, on the left (originally the American Legislative and Issue Campaign Exchange, or "ALICE," now known as the State Innovation Exchange, or "SIX"). In contrast to the ALI and the UCC, these organizations prepare model legislation to achieve specifically

---

[51] See http://www.uniformlaws.org.

[52] See Uniform Commercial Code, Uniform Law Commission, https://www.uniformlaws.org/acts/ucc.

[53] http://www.uniformlaws.org.

[54] The texts of all acts and drafts can be found at the Uniform Law Commission's website: http://www.uniformlaws.org/acts/overview.

[55] See http://www.uniformlaws.org.

[56] See Richard B. Long, Uniform State Laws: Where Do They Come From and Why Do They Matter, NYSBA J., Apr. 2019, 32–35, https://nysba.org/NYSBA/Publications/Bar%20Journal/PastIssues2000present/2019/NYSBA%20Journal%20April%202019_WEB.pdf.

conservative or progressive policy objectives. Because many state legislatures operate on a part-time basis and sit for only a few months in any two-year legislative term, model legislation has proven to be an extremely effective way to implement state-level legal change at a rapid pace by providing state legislators with ready-made draft bills, though not without some controversy.[57]

2. THE LEGISLATIVE PROCESS

At the beginning of this introductory section, we devoted substantial attention to the organization and operation of courts in order to provide a basis for a better understanding of the case law the courts produce. In the same way, we now consider legislative institutions and processes to assist in the understanding of legislative law. After reviewing the legislative process, we will take up the interpretation of statutes in Part III of this casebook.

a. INTRODUCTION

Of all the professional tasks a lawyer is asked to perform, one of the most frequent is that of interpreting legislation. She may be called on for interpretation, for example, as counsel advising clients of their rights under statutes, or as advocate urging, or defending against, a statutory claim, or as a judge or administrator ruling on the application of legislative language, or as a scholar explaining or appraising its significance. Many of the cases in Part III offer notable examples of judicial inquiry into legislative history in aid of interpretation.[58]

As you read the following discussion of the stages of the federal legislative process, it may be helpful to keep in view some general and specific questions. As a general question, a reader might well ask himself at each stage—what does this aspect of the legislature or its procedures disclose about the nature of the legislative institution, about the special advantages and disadvantages of legislative lawmaking and its part in the American legal system? More specifically, and with an eye to the practical use of the process, he should also ask himself the legislative advocate's (lobbyist's) question—what can be done at this stage to speed a bill on its way or obstruct its advance? The effort to answer this last question will surely shed light on the more general question first suggested. Finally, with an eye to interpretive considerations, it is instructive to ask—what does this phase of the process yield in the way of records of legislative deliberations and where are they to be found? What is or should be the weight of these particular records in the search

---

[57] See Molly Jackman, ALEC's Influence over Lawmaking in State Legislatures, Brookings Institute, Dec. 6, 2013, https://www.brookings.edu/articles/alecs-influence-over-law making-in-state-legislatures/.

[58] Some of the decisions debate the relevance of legislative history in the interpretation of statutes. An understanding of the legislative process should also help you appreciate why this debate is occurring.

for "legislative intent"? (As you will see, some jurists resist seeking legislative intent beyond the enacted text of the statute itself.)

b. STRUCTURE, POWERS, FUNCTIONS OF CONGRESS

The primary function of Congress is to make laws. All the legislative power entrusted by the Constitution to the national government is conferred upon the Congress in Article I, Section 1. The enumeration of Congress's legislative powers in Article I, Section 8 of the Constitution— including familiar powers to tax, borrow, and spend, to regulate commerce, to provide for defense and for the general welfare, etc.— merely sketches the underpinning of the vast power Congress today wields. On this constitutional foundation of granted powers, generously construed by the courts, Congress legislates today for the ongoing needs of a huge government establishment and for substantive concerns as diverse as tariffs, public lands, currency, sale of securities, transportation, highways, aviation, healthcare, nuclear energy, space exploration, urban renewal, communications, environmental protection, social security, welfare, housing, education, anti-discrimination, industrial safety, wages and hours, labor-management relations, agriculture, intellectual property, foreign aid, defense, national security, armed services, and so forth. Its responsibilities for public finance, for taxes and other revenue, for borrowing and for appropriations inevitably require it to scrutinize and deal with an enormous range of activities embracing all those just mentioned by way of illustration and others too numerous to itemize. Lawyers, in particular, should be mindful too that Congressional responsibilities include the revision and updating of the substantial body of federal statute law, to say nothing of "back-up" work in dealing with unsatisfactory lawmaking or interpretation by judicial and administrative agencies. Beyond all these aspects of general legislation, there is a continuing and not negligible concern with private legislation in settlement, for example, of individual claims against the government or individual immigration or naturalization cases.

Lawmaking is not the only function of Congress or Congressmen. There is too, for example, the conduct of investigations—commonly in aid of lawmaking and often in pursuit of another major Congressional concern, that of checking on the administration of the laws. The Legislative Reorganization Act of 1946 focused a spotlight on this last concern and called for "continuous oversight" by Congressional committees of the administrative arms of government. Such checking seemed to the sponsors and has seemed to many since to be particularly necessary at a time when the speed and complexity of modern industrial society have required Congress to delegate much power to administrators. "Oversight" permits Congress to appraise administrative performance and to revise the machinery and rules and to provide funds for administrative activity as appropriate.

c.   SOURCE AND DEVELOPMENT OF LEGISLATIVE PROPOSALS

John V. Sullivan, "How Our Laws Are Made," H. Doc. 110–49 (2007) (excerpt):

Sources of ideas for legislation are unlimited and proposed drafts of bills originate in many diverse quarters. Primary among these is the idea and draft conceived by a Member. This may emanate from the election campaign during which the Member had promised, if elected, to introduce legislation on a particular subject. The Member may have also become aware after taking office of the need for amendment to or repeal of an existing law or the enactment of a statute in an entirely new field.

In addition, the Member's constituents, either as individuals or through citizen groups, may avail themselves of the right to petition and transmit their proposals to the Member. The right to petition is guaranteed by the First Amendment to the Constitution. Similarly, state legislatures may "memorialize" Congress to enact specified federal laws by passing resolutions to be transmitted to the House and Senate as memorials. If favorably impressed by the idea, a Member may introduce the proposal in the form in which it has been submitted or may redraft it. In any event, a Member may consult with the Legislative Counsel of the House or the Senate to frame the ideas in suitable legislative language and form.

In modern times, the "executive communication" has become a prolific source of legislative proposals. The communication is usually in the form of a message or letter from a member of the President's Cabinet, the head of an independent agency, or the President himself, transmitting a draft of a proposed bill to the Speaker of the House of Representatives and the President of the Senate. Despite the structure of separation of powers, Article II, Section 3, of the Constitution imposes an obligation on the President to report to Congress from time to time on the "State of the Union" and to recommend for consideration such measures as the President considers necessary and expedient. Many of these executive communications follow on the President's message to Congress on the state of the Union. The communication is then referred to the standing committee or committees having jurisdiction of the subject matter of the proposal. The chairman or the ranking minority member of the relevant committee often introduces the bill, either in the form in which it was received or with desired changes. This practice is usually followed even when the majority of the House and the President are not of the same political party, although there is no constitutional or statutory requirement that a bill be introduced to effectuate the recommendations.

The most important of the regular executive communications is the annual message from the President transmitting the proposed budget to Congress. The President's budget proposal, together with testimony by officials of the various branches of the government before the Appropriations Committees of the House and Senate, is the basis of the several appropriation bills that are drafted by the Committees on Appropriations of the House and Senate.

The drafting of statutes is an art that requires great skill, knowledge, and experience. In some instances, a draft is the result of a study covering a period of a year or more by a commission or committee designated by the President or a member of the Cabinet. The Administrative Procedure Act and the Uniform Code of Military Justice are two examples of enactments resulting from such studies. In addition, congressional committees sometimes draft bills after studies and hearings covering periods of a year or more.

d. INTRODUCTION AND REFERENCE

Once the drafting of the legislative proposal has been completed and the bill is ready for Congressional consideration, it is necessary to take the appropriate formal steps to lay it before the Congress—*i.e.*, to introduce the bill in one or both chambers. In contrast to the British Parliament where cabinet members may introduce bills, only a Representative can introduce legislation in the House of Representatives, only a Senator in the Senate. Thus the supporters of a proposal must find one or more sponsors in one or both chambers to assume responsibility for the bill and accomplish its introduction.

The choice of a sponsor or sponsors can be important. Sponsorship may represent a burdensome commitment and sponsors not infrequently have a degree of power over the fate of a measure. The sponsor identified with a bill is assumed to have taken a position in its favor (to avoid this, members sometimes insist on adding the phrase "by request" to the notice of their sponsorship) and frequently must defend this position in correspondence, in the Congress and in public discussion and in meeting proposals for amendment. From the proponents' point of view it is vital to know whether a potential sponsor or sponsors is truly in favor of the proposal. Will he take his commitment seriously? Is he strategically placed—say as a member of the Congressional leadership or as chair of a standing committee (or, at least, as an influential member of it) and as a member of the majority party—so as to make his support most telling? Is he a tenacious and effective fighter if there are storms in the offing, as, for example, New York's Senator Wagner was in sponsoring the National Labor Relations Act and the Social Security Act? Significant Administration bills, which account for much of Congressional time and effort, are commonly introduced by the chairs of the committees or subcommittees concerned with the subject-matter or, especially if the committee's support is in question, by a leader of the President's party in Congress. Multiple sponsorship of bills is possible in both houses. Whether co-sponsorship is desirable or not in a given case may depend on the circumstances. Dilution of responsibility and prestige must be weighed against a possible broadening of the base of support.

Once the issue of sponsorship has been settled, the sponsor or one of them introduces the legislative proposal. Assume that the proposal is to begin its legislative career in the House. In this case introduction involves nothing more than dropping the proposed bill, with the sponsor's name endorsed upon it, into the hopper at the clerk's desk in the chamber of the House of Representatives. Although there is no opportunity for sponsors to make statements as they introduce legislation in the House, most sponsors will insert an explanatory statement about their bills in the Congressional Record at some time on the day of introduction. In the Senate, the sponsor may make a statement about the bill, if she is present on the floor of the Senate and is recognized. If the bill is ultimately enacted, the statement made about it by the Senate sponsor at the time of Senate introduction, and the explanatory remarks of the House sponsor sometime after House introduction, will be components of the bill's legislative history that the courts will weigh in ascertaining legislative intent. Lawyers need to be aware that such materials will generally be found in the Congressional Record.

The first action on our bill after introduction is an important one: the referring of the bill to the appropriate House standing committee for consideration. The committees and their operation will be discussed in some detail in section e, below. For the moment it is enough to point out that bills are normally referred to whichever of the numerous House standing committees has jurisdiction, under House rules, of the bill's subject-matter. See the Table, *infra* p. 47. A sponsor may request a desired reference. The decision on reference, usually a routine one, is made by the Speaker with the assistance of the Parliamentarian and is recorded in the Congressional Record. From time to time difficult problems of choice arise where bills arguably fall within the jurisdiction of more than one committee. Occasionally, a disputed reference, when the Speaker's ruling is not accepted, has led to a floor fight and a decision by the House itself.

110TH CONGRESS
1ST SESSION

H. R. 1524

To amend the Internal Revenue Code of 1986 to provide that a deduction equal to fair market value shall be allowed for charitable contributions of literary, musical, artistic, or scholarly compositions created by the donor.

IN THE HOUSE OF REPRESENTATIVES

MARCH 14, 2007

Mr. LEWIS of Georgia (for himself, Mr. RAMSTAD, and Mr. DOGGETT) introduced the following bill; which was referred to the Committee on Ways and Means

---

A BILL

To amend the Internal Revenue Code of 1986 to provide that a deduction equal to fair market value shall be allowed for charitable contributions of literary, musical, artistic, or scholarly compositions created by the donor.

1   *Be it enacted by the Senate and House of Representa-*

2 *tives of the United States of America in Congress assembled,*

3 **SECTION 1. SHORT TITLE.**

4   This Act may be cited as the "Artist-Museum Part-

5 nership Act".

A House rule calls on the Speaker to refer bills in such a way that, as far as may be, each committee that has jurisdiction over any provision of a bill will have responsibility for considering and reporting on that provision. This may be accomplished by having committees consider legislation concurrently or successively, or by dividing up the bill, or by creating a special ad hoc committee with members drawn from the various standing committees interested in the measure.

In the Senate, the reference process is much the same as in the House, with the decision on reference being made by the presiding officer at the time. Under the Senate rules any controversy as to jurisdiction is to be decided by the presiding officer (subject to an appeal) in favor of that committee which has jurisdiction over the subject matter which predominates in the bill. Upon motion by both the Majority and Minority Leaders or their designees, the bill may be referred to two or more committees jointly or sequentially and may be divided up between the committees.

After introduction and reference, the proposed bill is given a number and sent to the Government Printing Office. The next morning printed copies are available in the Senate and House document rooms. The print of the bill following introduction appears as indicated by the example above. The designation—H.R.1524 (note that H.R. means House of Representatives)—will often be used to refer to the bill thereafter. Had it been a Senate bill the designation would have been the letter "S" followed by the bill number.

As you become accustomed to seeing or reading bills or statutes, you will note that their structure commonly contains such elements as these (items 1, 2, 4, and 8 always being present):

1.   *Identifying Designation*—"H.R." or "S." and a number for federal bills, "Chapter" or "Public Law" and a number for federal statutes. State bills have comparable designations.

2.   *Title*—This succinctly states the subject or aim of the legislation.

3.   *Preamble*—This is found mainly in older legislation. Utilizing one or more "whereas" clauses, a preamble typically has purposes similar to those of the now more widely used Legislative Findings, Purpose or Policy (see below).

4.   *Enacting Clause*—This states that the legislature adopts as law what follows.

5.   *Short Title*—This gives an easy "handle" or name to the legislation.

6.   *Legislative Findings, Purpose or Policy*—This embraces some or all of the following: The reasons or the occasion for the legislation, or the facts found as a basis for it, or arguments for its adoption or constitutionality. Unlike a preamble, it is a part of the Act, since it follows the enacting clause, and, unlike a preamble, it is frequently carried into codifications.

7.   *Definitions*—These save repetition and attempt to clarify meaning. Sometimes they are found at the end of a bill or statute.

8.   *Purview*—This is the main body of the law containing the administrative, substantive and remedial provisions, etc.

9. *Standard Clauses*—These may comprehend all or some of the following commonly encountered types of clauses:

a.   Severability Clause—This is a clause that keeps the remaining provisions of the bill or statute in force if any portion of it is judicially declared void or unconstitutional.

b.   Saving Clause—This is a clause exempting from coverage something that would otherwise be included. Colloquially, this kind of clause is also referred to as a "grandfathering" clause. It is generally used in a repealing act to preserve rights and claims that would otherwise be lost.

c.   Repealer Clause—This may be (1) a general repealer repealing in general terms all laws inconsistent with the legislation in question, or (2) a specific schedule explicitly listing laws repealed or (3) both.

d.   Effective Date Clause—This designates the time when the legislation takes effect.

We have spoken only of bills but it is well to note that legislative action by the Congress or its chambers can take other legislative forms. These include joint resolutions, designated as "H.J.Res." or "S.J.Res.," which go through the same legislative process as bills, including signature by the President, and have the same effect, except in the case of joint resolutions proposing constitutional amendments which must be approved by two-thirds of each house and are not signed by the President. There is little, if any, practical difference between bills and those joint resolutions that do not propose constitutional amendments and these forms are sometimes used interchangeably. The bill form tends to be used routinely for general legislation. The Joint Resolution tends to be used for miscellaneous special cases such as authorizing invitations to foreign governments, or extending statutes due to expire.

There are, in addition, concurrent resolutions, designated as "H.Con.Res." or "S.Con.Res.," which are not submitted to the President and so are not equal in status or legal effect to bills or joint resolutions. They are not used for general legislation but normally deal with matters affecting only the Congress and express principles, opinions and purposes of the two Houses. And there are, finally, simple resolutions, designated "H.Res." and "S.Res.," which are promulgated by one House only and deal with concerns of the enacting House such as the establishment of a committee or the expression of the sense of one House on some public or intra-mural issue.

Joint and Concurrent Resolutions, like enacted bills, are printed in the Statutes at Large after adoption; simple resolutions are not but may be found in the Congressional Record. The Library of Congress's congress.gov website has the text of bills and resolutions going back to the 101st Congress.[59]

---

[59] See http://congress.gov.

e.   THE COMMITTEE STAGE

John V. Sullivan, "How Our Laws Are Made," H.Doc. 110–49 (2007) (excerpt):

Perhaps the most important phase of the legislative process is the action by committees. The committees provide the most intensive consideration to a proposed measure as well as the forum where the public is given their opportunity to be heard. A tremendous volume of work, often overlooked by the public, is done by the Members in this phase. There are, at present, 20 standing committees in the House and 16 in the Senate as well as several select committees. In addition, there are four standing joint committees of the two Houses, with oversight responsibilities but no legislative jurisdiction. The House may also create select committees or task forces to study specific issues and report on them to the House. A task force may be established formally through a resolution passed by the House or informally through organization of interested Members by the House leadership.

Each committee's jurisdiction is defined by certain subject matter under the rules of each House and all measures are referred accordingly. For example, the Committee on the Judiciary in the House has jurisdiction over measures relating to judicial proceedings and 18 other categories, including constitutional amendments, immigration policy, bankruptcy, patents, copyrights, and trademarks. In total, the rules of the House and of the Senate each provide for over 200 different classifications of measures to be referred to committees. Until 1975, the Speaker of the House could refer a bill to only one committee. In modern practice, the Speaker may refer an introduced bill to multiple committees for consideration of those provisions of the bill within the jurisdiction of each committee concerned. Except in extraordinary circumstances, the Speaker must designate a primary committee of jurisdiction on bills referred to multiple committees. The Speaker may place time limits on the consideration of bills by all committees, but usually time limits are placed only on additional committees to which a bill has been referred following the report of the primary committee.

In the Senate, introduced measures and House-passed measures are referred to the one committee of preponderant jurisdiction by the Parliamentarian on behalf of the Presiding Officer. By special or standing order, a measure may be referred to more than one committee in the Senate.

Membership on the various committees is divided between the two major political parties. The proportion of the Members of the minority party to the Members of the majority party is determined by the majority party, except that half of the members on the Committee on Standards of Official Conduct are from the majority party and half from the minority party. The respective party caucuses nominate Members of the caucus to be elected to each standing committee at the beginning of each Congress. Membership on a standing committee during the course of a Congress is contingent on continuing membership in the party caucus that nominated a Member for election to the committee. If a Member ceases to be a Member of the party caucus, a Member automatically ceases to be a member of the standing committee.

Members of the House may serve on only two committees and four subcommittees with certain exceptions. However, the rules of the caucus of the majority party in the House provide that a Member may be chairman of only one subcommittee of a committee or select committee with legislative jurisdiction, except for certain committees performing housekeeping functions and joint committees.

A Member usually seeks election to the committee that has jurisdiction over a field in which the Member is most qualified and interested. For example, the Committee on the Judiciary traditionally is populated with numerous lawyers.

Members rank in seniority in accordance with the order of their appointment to the full committee and the ranking majority member with the most continuous service is often elected chairman. The rules of the House require that committee chairmen be elected from nominations submitted by the majority party caucus at the commencement of each Congress. No Member of the House may serve as chairman of the same standing committee or of the same subcommittee thereof for more than three consecutive Congresses, except in the case of the Committee on Rules.

The rules of the House provide that a committee may maintain no more than five committees, but may have an oversight committee as a sixth. The standing rules allow a greater number of subcommittees for the Committees on Appropriations and Oversight and Government Reform. In addition, the House may grant leave to certain committeess [sic] to establish additional subcommittees during a given Congress.

Each committee is provided with a professional staff to assist it in the innumerable administrative details involved in the consideration of bills and its oversight responsibilities. For standing committees, the professional staff is limited to 30 persons appointed by a vote of the committee. Two-thirds of the committee staff are selected by a majority vote of the majority committee members and one-third of the committee staff are selected by a majority vote of minority committee members. All staff appointments are made without regard to race, creed, sex, or age. Minority staff requirements do not apply to the Committee on Standards of Official Conduct because of its bipartisan nature. The Committee on Appropriations has special authority under the rules of the House for appointment of staff for the minority.

Standing House Committees, 116th Congress (2019–2021)

Committee	Total Members	D	R	No. of Subcom.
Agriculture	47	26	21	6
Appropriations	53	30	23	12
Armed Services	58	32	26	6
Budget	36	22	14	0
Education and Labor	52	30	22	5
Energy and Commerce	54	30	24	6
Ethics	10	5	5	0
Financial Services	60	34	26	6
Foreign Relations	47	26	21	6
Homeland Security	31	18	13	6
House Administration	9	6	3	1
Judiciary	41	24	17	5
Natural Resources	44	25	19	5
Oversight and Government Reform	42	24	18	5
Rules	13	9	4	3
Science, Space and, Technology	39	227	17	5
Small Business	24	14	10	5
Transportation and Infrastructure	67	37	30	6
Veterans' Affairs	28	16	12	5
Ways and Means	42	25	17	6

Select Committees of the House

Permanent Select Committee on Intelligence
Select Committee on the Climate Crisis
Select Committee on the Modernization of Congress

Standing Senate Committees, 116th Congress (2019–2021)

Committee	Total Members	R	D	No. of Subcom.
Agriculture	20	11	9	5
Appropriations	31	16	15	12
Armed Services	27	14	13	7
Banking, Housing, and Urban Affairs	25	13	12	5
Budget	21	11	10	0
Commerce, Science, and Transportation	26	14	12	6
Energy and Natural Resources	20	11	9	4
Environment and Public Works	21	11	10	4
Finance	28	15	13	6
Foreign Relations	22	12	10	7
Health, Education, Labor, and Pensions	23	12	11	3
Homeland Security and Governmental Affairs	14	8	6	3
Judiciary	22	12	10	6
Rules and Administration	19	10	9	0
Small Business and Entrepreneurship	19	10	8	0
Veterans' Affairs	17	9	8	0

Select Committees of the Senate

Select Committee on Ethics

Select Committee on Intelligence

Special Committee on Aging

Committee on Indian Affairs

Joint Committees

Joint Economic Committee

Joint Committee on the Library

Joint Committee on Printing

Joint Committee on Taxation

What happens when a bill has been referred to a standing committee? In most cases, the standing committee chairman will refer the bill to a subcommittee for consideration, if the committee has subcommittees, as most do. Also, copies will often be transmitted to the executive departments or agencies with a request for their views. One must remark at this point, on the power of the committee as a whole and the power of the standing committee chair in particular. Only a small percentage of bills referred to committees is reported out. The power the committee possesses to block or to report legislation, with or without amendment—and we shall later see further reasons for its life and death powers—helps to make the committee a crucial factor in almost any bill's history.

The Committee chair has other practical powers stemming from her other functions—such as calling and presiding over meetings and hearings, setting the agenda, developing and controlling staff, negotiating for floor consideration, designating the floor manager for the bill and participating in conference proceedings. In turn, the subcommittee chair will have major power over the fate of the bill and much to say, subject to the power of the full committee and its chair, over whether the measure is to languish or be pursued with more or less vigor. The subcommittee's decision to table or to endorse or to reshape is often accepted by the full committee and ultimately by the Congress. The Appropriations Committees, for example, regularly endorse the work of their subcommittees. Thus, the work of a very few Senators or Representatives and of the chair may be decisive. The extraordinary fragmentation of Congressional power becomes evident.

Whether the bill is considered by the full committee or a subcommittee, and especially if it is a significant bill and in some degree controversial, the chair or subcommittee chair as the case may be will probably decide to hold public hearings on it; he or she has much discretion over whether and how such hearings will be conducted. With the staff, who are subject to his or her control, the chair concerned will schedule the hearings, give notice, plan the pattern of witnesses, and issue requests to testify or, perhaps, subpoenas. On the appointed hearing day, an official reporter will be present to record testimony. After introductory statements by committee or subcommittee members, the Senators and Representatives who seek to be heard will receive preference as witnesses; officials of the executive departments or agencies may also then be heard, as well as the representatives of interest groups and other private persons. Prepared statements will often be submitted and witnesses will be questioned. Owing to the multiple burdens of committee work that affect legislators, the hearing may only be sparsely attended by members of the sponsoring committee or subcommittee.

The purposes of hearings may vary widely depending on the measure and the aims of the legislators. If well organized by chairman and staff to that end, they can serve as a valuable means for gathering information and for testing the proposal's impact on segments of the public. In this aspect it is instructive to compare the modest research and data-gathering capability of the courts to the capabilities of Congressional committees, with their staffs, their access to the Congressional Research Service and the Offices of Legislative Counsel, and their access through hearings and otherwise to the expertise of governmental and private sources. But hearings are not always well managed to serve this informational purpose and may be used to serve, instead or in addition, such other purposes as mobilizing public support or opposition, providing publicity for legislators, stalling the legislative progress of a bill, furnishing a "safety valve" for disturbances, and so forth.

After the hearings, the hard work begins on the bill. A transcript of the hearings is made available. With the help of staff, other data, analyses and drafts are assembled. The legislators then meet, with or without preliminary caucusing and with staff personnel and sometimes representatives of governmental departments (and sometimes representatives of private interests) in attendance. They discuss the bill and any amendments and decide whether and on what terms to report it out. If the vote is to table, that will often be the end of a bill unless pressures in the full committee (in the case of a bill first considered by a subcommittee) or in the chamber as a whole can force a different result. If the bill is not tabled, the next step is to "mark up" the bill and it will often receive its definitive shape in the course of compromises and negotiations on this level at the hands of members and staff and drafters. Note must be taken here of the ease with which a proposal can be blocked by a strategically placed minority at this stage—unless the pressures against it can be overcome by intense pressures in its behalf.

When a bill is reported out, with or without amendment, by a subcommittee, it must run the gauntlet of the full committee, which typically has regular meeting days on which subcommittee reports are taken up. Sometimes the subcommittee's work will be accepted; at other times, the whole process of hearings and "marking up" or revision will be repeated in the full committee, which in any event must ultimately vote on its own to table the bill or to report it in some form. Again, there is opportunity for delay and defeat and much may depend on the attitude and practice of the full committee chair toward the proposal. From the standpoint of the lobbyist, of course, the subcommittee and committee phases of action are key points for the application of favorable or adverse pressures and the same is apt to be true at other points of the process where a small number of persons exercise great power over a measure's progress.

Notice at the committee stage that three kinds of documents emerge that may be vital elements in the legislative history of the bill when its meaning is later sought by lawyers, administrators, judges or by the public. The first of these is the hearings, if they are printed and made generally available to the Congress and the public.[60] These may contain important clues to the impact or sense of legislative provisions, especially, for example, when amendments are made in response to points made at the hearings. The second is the different versions of the bill considered by the committee. Changes in language between the bill as referred to the committee and the bill as reported out may shed significant light on the bill's final meaning. The third and perhaps most important document at this stage is the full committee's formal report accompanying the bill when it is transmitted by the committee to the chamber as a whole. This formal report normally discusses the purposes of and reasons for the bill and analyzes its provisions. Committee amendments are indicated and communications from the executive regarding the bill are commonly incorporated in the report. There may be a minority report—*i.e.*, dissenting views—on the same bill. Both the committee report (which will be given a number) and the bill as reported will be printed up and made available promptly after filing. The report has special significance for interpretive purposes, representing, as it does, an expression of views about the bill by the Congressional group charged with detailed knowledge and responsibility. It constitutes a prime source of information about the bill for the members of Congress as well, a source to which they can refer as a basis for their vote. So important is it for this purpose that House and Senate normally require that committee reports be available to the membership for several days before consideration of the measures to which they are addressed.

We have been considering the committee stage in relation to a bill. But if it is to become law, the bill must somehow be laid before the chambers themselves to be voted on and approved by the membership as a whole. In the House, serious risks of delay and obstruction attend the process of getting to the floor but rigid, expeditious procedures speed it to its fate thereafter; on the other hand, in the Senate, getting to the floor is notably less difficult, but serious risks of delay and obstruction arise in connection with floor consideration.

f.   FLOOR ACTION ON THE BILL

i.   *On the House Floor*

Let us look first at the patterns of floor action in the House. Assuming the bill is important and controversial, it will in all probability, as we saw, be the subject of a special rule from the Rules Committee. Even bills privileged in their own right, such as revenue bills, not infrequently are brought before the House by preference under a special rule from the Rules Committee limiting the terms of debate. The initial step then in the floor proceedings on our bill—unlike privileged bills or

---

[60] A printed version of the hearings may not be available until many months after the hearings have taken place. Each committee, however, posts the hearing transcripts on its website shortly after the hearing.

bills coming up on the Private or Consent or Discharge Calendar or Suspension of the Rules or as District of Columbia business—will be the Speaker's recognition of a member of the Rules Committee to call up the rule relating to our bill. Special rules of this kind may be debated for an hour but the debate does not normally consume the allotted time and such rules are often adopted without difficulty by voice vote. Following is an example of a typical special rule, of the "open" kind, for a bill on the Union Calendar:

> *Resolved,* That upon the adoption of this resolution it shall be in order to move that the House resolve itself into the Committee of the Whole House on the State of the Union for the consideration of the bill (H.R. ___) to (here insert the purpose of the bill). After general debate, which shall be confined to the bill and shall continue not to exceed two hours, to be equally divided and controlled by the chairman and ranking minority member of the Committee on ___, the bill shall be read for amendment under the five-minute rule. At the conclusion of the consideration of the bill for amendment, the Committee shall rise and report the bill to the House with such amendments as may have been adopted, and the previous question shall be considered as ordered on the bill and amendments thereto to final passage without intervening motion except one motion to recommit.

The text of the resolution is of great importance as it sets the pattern for what follows.

Upon adoption of the special rule the House resolves itself into the Committee of the Whole House on the State of the Union. This step, applicable to most significant pieces of legislation, has a number of consequences. In essence it makes less formal, and speeds, the action of the House. In the Committee of the Whole, the House can operate with a quorum of 100 members (as against 218 for the House itself). Time-consuming yea and nay votes are avoided. For the deliberations of the Committee of the Whole, the Speaker steps down from the chair, appointing another chairman in his place.

As the above special rule indicates, the next step in relation to our bill is general debate. The time the rule allows is equally divided between (a) the bill's floor manager, who is normally the chair of the responsible standing committee or subcommittee, and, (b) his or her principal opponent, who is usually a ranking minority member of the same committee or subcommittee. The floor manager speaks first, followed by his or her opposite number. Both yield time to others for further speeches regarding the bill. Note once again the pervasive role of the standing committee and its leaders in the legislative process.

Following the general debate, the bill is open to amendment, committee amendments having priority. The sponsor of an amendment has five minutes to explain and support his or her amendment; additional time requires unanimous consent. The floor manager has five minutes to respond. If other members want time to discuss an amendment, they offer fictional or pro forma amendments (motions to "strike the last word") as a basis for receiving five minutes of speaking time. Members of the standing committee are also entitled to preference in recognition. Debate on an amendment can continue for some little time under this system and may be closed by unanimous consent or by motion requiring a majority vote. While there are possibilities for delay in House procedure, there is no real opportunity to stop a bill or amendment from being voted on.

Votes on amendments in the Committee of the Whole may be voice votes. If the vote is close or doubtful, a vote by division (proponents and opponents stand in turn to be counted) may be demanded. A roll call vote may be had if the division reveals the lack of a quorum.

The amending stage is crucial in the progress of a bill. The amendments offered may be and often are of such character as to change the bill substantially or weaken it drastically. Their adoption might undermine such support for the bill as already exists. In any case, the skill, dedication and prestige of the floor manager may make the difference between success and failure in warding off crippling revisions. Once again it is appropriate to point to the life and death role of the committee personnel who, having addressed the bill in the committee itself and championed it before the Rules Committee, are now proponents for the bill on the floor. The support or opposition of the bill's standing committee proponents with respect to a particular amendment may influence a member of Congress' vote on the amendment. In theory, doubts should be resolved in favor of the committee that has done the detailed work on the bill. If the committee represents a cross-section of the House, it may have foreseen and met the need to compromise adequately the divergent interests represented in the full House. Weight may attach, too, to the position of the leadership; and in the case of amendments proposed by minority party spokespersons, party loyalty may play a role. Incidentally, one of the most difficult tasks of those managing bills is to see that needed supporters are available on the floor when critical votes are taken.

Note, for purposes of later comparison with the Senate, that amendments put forward in the Committee of the Whole must be germane to the bill and to that portion of the bill they purport to revise. It may be possible to tack a non-germane amendment to a bill when the Rules Committee's special rule waives points of order against the bill or when the amendment concerned has specifically been made in order.

Not only is the bill open to amendment under the procedures we have been discussing, but it is also possible—though rare—to kill the bill in its entirety if a motion to strike the enacting clause is offered and sustained. If this preferential motion—which must be considered at once and allows ten minutes of debate—is upheld in the Committee of the Whole, the

Committee rises and reports back to the full House which then has an opportunity to vote on the same question. If the full House sustains the defeat, the bill is killed; if not, the House resolves itself back into Committee of the Whole and resumes debate.

The process of amending the bill in Committee of the Whole, if not limited by the provisions of the special rule, will normally continue until there are no amendments left to consider, but it may be brought to an end by a unanimous consent agreement or by a motion disposed of by majority vote. Here, too, the inexorable march and expedition of House procedures deserve comparison with the Senate.

When the process of reading the bill for amendment has concluded, the Committee of the Whole rises, its action is reported to the House itself, the Speaker resumes the chair, the quorum requirement is once again 218 members, and the House itself takes over consideration at this point. Note again the terms of the special rule, *supra*, governing the remaining steps, and these steps will generally be quite similar as a practical matter even when a privileged measure—such as an appropriation bill—is being considered without a special rule. Under the rule the "previous question" is deemed ordered, a highly privileged procedure which calls for final vote forthwith on the merits.

The House itself now takes up without debate the amendments, if any, reported by the Committee of the Whole and usually, though not necessarily, votes on them en bloc. Amendments rejected in Committee of the Whole are not reported and, in practice, they are lost and may not be voted on again. Once the amendments approved in Committee of the Whole have been voted on by the House—and the House commonly approves the work of the Committee of the Whole—the question before the House is the adoption of the amended bill itself. After vote on engrossment and third reading of the bill a member of the opposition may make a motion to recommit the bill to the original standing committee with or without instructions. If such a motion without instructions carries, the bill is stopped *pro tem* and goes back to the committee which may however report it back again at some later date for another attempt at passage. If the motion is made and approved with instructions to amend the bill in specified ways—often ways that were defeated in the Committee of the Whole—and to report forthwith, the bill as revised by the standing committee in accordance with the instructions is reported back to the House and put to a vote. When the motion to recommit is defeated, as it normally is, the question before the House becomes the final passage of the bill. The final vote will be a roll-call vote if one fifth of the members so demand.

House floor procedure, taken as a whole, is notable then for the power it gives the majority, the continuing power exercised by the committee, the short shrift (*e.g.*, the 5-minute rule, the "previous question") given to dilatory tactics and to efforts to block a final vote. While the amending process can be used to delay and perhaps destroy, such action is subject to majority approval and is part and parcel of the ongoing Congressional task of reconciling divergent interests as a basis for social action.

ii. *On the Senate Floor*

Compare the operation of the Senate when it takes up a bill on the floor, especially its handling of amendments and the limitation of debate. Commonly a bill will come before the Senate pursuant to a unanimous consent arrangement worked out by the majority leader in consultation with the minority leader and other interested Senators. Failing that, a motion may be made to take up the bill. Such a motion is vulnerable to the filibuster tactic (see below). Pursuant to such a motion, if adopted, or to a unanimous consent agreement, floor consideration of the bill begins—usually with an opening statement by the floor manager who will probably be either the responsible subcommittee chair or, especially on major bills, the chair of the standing committee itself. Members of the committee will most likely be on hand on the floor at this point and the opposition will be led by the appropriate ranking minority committee member. There is no reserved time for general debate as in the House and the amendment of the bill is in order at once. Committee amendments are taken up first, then non-committee amendments. This amendment stage is no less critical, no less dependent on the skill and prestige of the floor managers, than it is in the House. Note, however, that in contrast to the House, where the requirement of germaneness regulates the amending process, in the Senate an amendment to a bill need not be germane to a bill, unless it is a general appropriation bill.

The central characteristic of Senate floor procedure that differentiates it from that of the House and, indeed, from that of most other legislative bodies, is the difficulty of limiting debate. At this time, there are only three ways in which debate may close. First, when all Senators have said all they wish to say on a proposal the debate will come to a halt. Second, there is the possibility of a unanimous consent agreement to limit debate on a particular measure. Even on many relatively controversial bills, the discussion is ended pursuant to such agreements. But such a device is not available to close debate against the wishes of even a single Senator. Absent unanimous consent, or the exhaustion of all desires to speak, the only recourse is the so-called cloture rule.

John V. Sullivan, "How Our Laws Are Made," H. Doc. 110–49 (2007) (excerpt):

> On occasion, Senators opposed to a measure may extend debate by making lengthy speeches or a number of speeches at various stages of consideration intended to prevent or defeat action on the measure. This is the tactic known as "filibustering." Debate may be closed, however, if 16 Senators sign a motion to that effect and the motion is carried by three-fifths of the Senators

duly chosen and sworn. Such a motion is voted on one hour after the Senate convenes, following a quorum call on the next day after a day of session has intervened. This procedure is called "invoking cloture." In 1986, the Senate amended its rules to limit "post-cloture" consideration to 30 hours. "Post-cloture," a Senator may speak for not more than one hour and may yield all or a part of that time to the majority or minority floor managers of the bill under consideration or to the Majority or Minority leader. The Senate may increase the time for "post-cloture" debate by a vote of three-fifths of the Senators duly chosen and sworn. After the time for debate has expired, the Senate may consider only amendments actually pending before voting on the bill.

There has been much argument over the merits of unlimited debate, or filibustering, and the weak cloture rule. On the one hand, the arguments made have cited the importance of unfettered debate in at least one chamber and have stressed the desirability of assuring that legislation with drastic consequences cannot be adopted by ruthless majorities over the intense opposition of a numerous minority. On the other hand there have been arguments based on the desirability of a majority's being ultimately able to prevail in a democratic society. The upshot of the present rule certainly is, in any case, to allow an intense minority to prevail, to block action, unless an extraordinary majority can be mobilized on the other side. And this state of affairs has pervasive implications for Senate procedure and decision-making. A majority cannot act if a large and determined minority opposes. The filibuster and threat of filibuster—even by individuals—offer a tremendous weapon for extracting concessions and compromises in legislative bargaining, especially in the crowded hours before sessions draw to a close. The difficulty of building winning coalitions is greatly increased. The further dispersion of already dispersed Congressional power should be plain enough to any observer.

The Senate conducts a great deal of business, nonetheless, without encountering the occasional barrier of an actual filibuster. Assuming the bill is a part of such normal business, it will come in due course to a vote. Unlike the House, the Senate does not deliberate in a Committee of the Whole, but it conducts its voting as the House does—by voice, by division and, on the request of one-fifth of a quorum, by roll-call (the yeas and nays). Roll-call votes, due to the chamber's smaller size, are easier and more frequent in the Senate.

When the vote has been taken, any Senator on the prevailing side may move to reconsider it within two days. In order to make the result definite and final, this motion to reconsider is generally made promptly after the final vote and another Senator moves to table the motion while the supporters of the final vote are still on hand. Tabling the motion has the effect of making the final vote conclusive; it usually is approved by voice vote. Once in a while, after a close vote, a change of heart or the arrival of new troops can dramatically upset the result. In the House, as we saw, it is common for the opponents of a bill to move to recommit; the same motion is possible in the Senate, but infrequent. Generally, when the motion to reconsider is tabled, the Senate's deliberations—short of conference—on a bill are finished. Such deliberations, it should now be apparent, are far more flexible and leisurely than the House's, more prone to delay and liable as well to serious minority obstruction.

The student of votes in the Congressional Record will note references to "pairs." The practice of pairing is followed in both chambers. Pairing permits absent, or otherwise nonvoting, Senators to record their position. Thus, two absent Senators on opposite sides may "pair" with each other and their positions will be noted but will not be counted in the voting tallies.

iii.   The Congressional Record

Lawyers investigating the history of bills, and other students of the legislative process will inevitably make extensive use of the Congressional Record, which reports the floor proceedings of Congress and contains other information as well. The Record has been published since 1873. Before that time the proceedings of Congress were published in the Annals of Congress (1789–1824), the Register of Debates (1824–1837) and the Congressional Globe (1833–1873). The modern Record is published daily while Congress is in session. Bound volumes appear later. The bound volumes do not necessarily match the daily edition exactly and, as to both, it must be noted that the Record purports only to be "substantially a verbatim report of proceedings." Unfortunately, the practice of Representatives and Senators in revising or extending their remarks or inserting undelivered speeches has marred the accuracy of the Record as a transcript of what occurred on the floor. A modest step was taken on March 1, 1978 in both House and Senate toward identifying in the Record materials not actually uttered on the floor. Now, in the House section of the Congressional Record, undelivered speeches and other extraneous material are printed in a different type style to distinguish them from speeches actually given on the Floor; in the Senate section, statements or insertions that are not spoken by a Senator from the Floor are preceded by a "bullet." However, because in the Senate, with unanimous consent, remarks are printed as if spoken, the system adopted falls far short of enabling the reader reliably to know how much of what is printed was in fact said in debate. Although only substantially verbatim, the Record is the best source available and lawyers must learn to make effective use of it. It is necessary to remember that the Record fulfills many purposes for the legislator besides that of providing an accurate record for judicial use. A glance at its pages seasoned with articles, occasional speeches, editorials, etc. and at its swollen Appendix will give some idea of the problem. But it does provide a record of some kind of the floor proceedings, the texts of amendments (which may also be available separately and may be crucial for interpretive purposes), and conference reports, and it contains indices invaluable to the researcher such as the Daily Digest, and, in the permanent edition, the History of Bills and Resolutions. In the Congressional Record and in the headings of bills, one peculiarity appears (particularly in the Senate proceedings) which should be mentioned. That is the phenomenon of the "legislative day." Because the Senate is apt to recess, rather than adjourn, from day to day and because recessing overnight does not trigger a new legislative day when the Senate reconvenes in the morning, the Senate may be still operating on a legislative day, begun much earlier, which does not coincide with the calendar day. In the study of the rules this can be important as they may provide for lapses of time in terms of legislative days or calendar days and the difference must be noted.

g.   INTER-HOUSE COORDINATION

The House and Senate, acting successively or concurrently in accordance with the procedures already described, may adopt identical measures. When they do, there is nothing to prevent or delay presentation of the legislation to the President for his signature. The same is true, even when the chambers pass different versions of a bill, if one chamber is willing, without more, to accept the other's version.

When the differences between the chambers regarding a bill are controversial in character, however, and neither chamber is, or seems, likely to yield its position, special action to compose differences may be needed. Normally a conference will be requested. Conferees or managers from each chamber are appointed by, respectively, the Speaker of the House and the presiding officer of the Senate. At least three conferees— but there may be more—are designated in each chamber. In selecting them, the presiding officer generally follows the recommendations of the appropriate standing committee chair. Each chamber's team of conferees or managers is very likely to include senior members of the standing committee. Such persons as the standing committee chair, the ranking majority and minority members, the appropriate subcommittee chair and the ranking minority subcommittee member will probably be selected. A House rule provides that in appointing conference committee members the Speaker "shall appoint no less than a majority of members who generally supported the House position as determined by the Speaker." Another rule requires the Speaker, to the extent feasible, to name as conferees the authors of the principal amendments to the proposed bill. Both political parties are commonly represented on the committee, with the majority party having the larger representation. Because the Senate and House delegations vote separately on all questions arising in the conference committee and because a majority of each delegation must approve every action, it is not essential that the two delegations be of the same size and they frequently are not. Note here, as elsewhere in the federal legislative process the pervasive influence of the standing committee and its chair.

The designated conferees meet to discuss the bill, typically under great pressure to reach an accommodation and often under great pressure of time. On rare occasions, conference delegations operate under direction from the parent chamber, but generally there are no instructions. The conferees are generally free to negotiate and resolve all matters in dispute between the chambers, although House rules restrict the power of House conferees to agree to non-germane Senate amendments. The conferees may trade off Senate provisions against House provisions and vice versa; they may seek a middle ground between the Senate and House provisions. They may not add new provisions or change provisions already agreed on by both chambers. Nonetheless they have, in practice, substantial leeway to compose differences; moreover it is difficult to enforce strict limitations. Sometimes, one chamber will have amended a bill originating in the other by striking out all that follows the enacting clause and inserting its own provisions. When such an amendment "in the nature of a substitute" comes before the conference, the conferees have the entire subject matter before them and are much more free to make changes, even to draw a new bill. In such cases, the conferees may not include in their report matter not committed to them by either house; but they may include matter which is a germane modification of subjects in disagreement.

The deliberations of a small group with a large measure of power over the shape and fate of a controversial bill are a natural target for pressure from special interests for this or that modification of the bill's provisions. By any yardstick, the conference is crucial for a bill, and any experienced lobbyist cannot fail to be aware of this. Once more there is a major opportunity for blocking action.

As the figures quoted earlier suggest, conference committees are usually able to arrive at some sort of accommodation of Senate-House differences and to agree on provisions to be recommended to the chambers. If the chambers cannot be thus brought to agreement, the bill is lost. Assuming, however, that the conferees do concur in recommendations for adjusting the differences, they incorporate these recommendations in a report which must be signed by a majority of each delegation of the conferees and filed with their respective houses. The dissenting managers have no authority to file statements of minority views. The recommendations are accompanied by a statement on the part of the managers explaining the effect of actions recommended. The conference report containing the recommendations and statement is made available in print separately and in the Congressional Record. As a document representing the late and detailed views of representatives of both chambers it is a very important aid to judicial interpretation of the enacted bill.

The engrossed bill and amendments, together with a copy of the report of the conference committee, are transmitted to the chamber which is to act first on the conference report (normally to the house other than the one requesting the conference). Whichever chamber takes up the conference report, it represents a matter of high privilege. In the House of Representatives, for example, the report and bill do not need help from the Rules Committee to reach the floor quickly.

The chamber first approving the conference report sends the documents to the other house for final action. When both chambers have approved the conference bill it is sent to the enrolling clerk of the chamber in which the bill had its origin. It is then ready for the last stage of its journey to enactment.

h.   EXECUTIVE ACTION

When the bill has weathered the stages of committee review, of getting to the floor, of floor consideration, of inter-house coordination, it faces at least one more critical test—that of Presidential review. In fact, the President's concern with an important bill is not something that merely springs into being at the end of the long process just described. When discussing the sources of legislation, we noted the President's major role as an initiator of enactments. Through public statements and personal communications, through Cabinet members, staff aides, administrative agency officials and otherwise, the President maintains active contact with the Congress in regard to bills important to him as they make their way forward from stage to stage of the process. His participation in that process comes to a climax or focus, however, when the moment arrives for exercise of the power to approve or veto conferred on him by the Constitution.

Once the bill is approved in identical form by both House and Senate, it is transmitted to the enrolling clerk of the chamber in which it originated, who undertakes the often complex and difficult task of preparing the so-called enrolled bill, incorporating as accurately as may be all amendments adopted along the way. The enrolled bill is printed and when the proper committee approves the bill as truly enrolled, it is transmitted for signature first to the Speaker of the House, then to the President of the Senate. When both have affixed their signatures to the enrolled bill, it is delivered to the White House and a receipt is secured for it. This delivery is normally regarded as presentation to the President and as triggering the start of the ten day period allowed for Presidential action by the Constitution. Occasionally, in the past, when a President has had to be absent for an extended period—as Wilson was in 1919 and as Franklin D. Roosevelt was some decades later—the step of delivery to the White House has been deferred for a time so as not to trigger the ten day period at an inconvenient moment.

The President has several choices in dealing with a bill presented to him. If he decides to approve the measure, he may do so affirmatively by signing it, or passively, if Congress is still in session at the end of ten days following presentation, by leaving it unsigned. In either case the bill becomes a law. In neither of these cases does the Constitution require any statement by the President. By the mid-twentieth century, special occasions arose—for example, President Truman's approval of the Hobbs Anti-Racketeering Act of 1946 and the Portal-to-Portal Act of 1947— when the chief executive upon approving a bill sent a formal message to Congress explaining his approval and discussing the provisions of the legislation concerned. Whether or not there is a formal communication to Congress, the President may in any case issue a more or less detailed public statement on signing the bill, a practice that has become more regular in recent decades. President George W. Bush frequently filed "signing statements" with signed bills, in which he asserted that the Constitution gives him the right to ignore certain sections of the bills. Although President Bush was not the first president to use signing statements, his use of signing statements functioned to assert his authority as President to "supervise the unitary executive branch" and to undertake an independent determination as to the constitutionality of legislative enactments, a practice that his predecessors Ronald Reagan, George H.W. Bush, and Bill Clinton also engaged in. President Obama also occasionally issued signing statements, albeit with less frequency.

If the President objects to a bill, the Constitution provides that within ten days after presentation "he shall return it, with his objections to the House in which it shall have originated, who shall enter the objections at large on their Journal and proceed to reconsider it." The President's veto may be overridden by a two-thirds vote of both Senate and House. In that event the bill becomes a law; without such overriding it does not. There is also the possibility of a "pocket veto." This occurs when the President fails to sign a measure and Congress adjourns before the end of the ten-day period allowed for Presidential action. In this case the bill is lost; Congress has no opportunity to override the veto. When the President vetoes by returning a bill to Congress, there is an obligatory Presidential message that goes with it. Although such a message is not required with a "pocket veto," it has been a Presidential practice to give the press and the public a full statement of reasons for each "pocket veto."

How is the decision made to veto or approve a bill? At the point where an enrolled bill is presented to the President, the Legislative Reference Division of the President's Office of Management and Budget undertakes a searching review process. Copies of the bill are sent to the executive departments and agencies concerned with its provisions and their recommendations are sought within forty-eight hours as to whether the President should veto or approve. While this may sound like a short period for response, it must be remembered that the departments and agencies in question will generally have been active in the legislative process on the bill—*e.g.*, providing expert views and aid to the

Congressional committees in hearings and otherwise—and so will commonly be very familiar with the measure. When agency responses are received, the Legislative Reference Division has several days to prepare its own "enrolled bill memorandum" for the chief executive. In that memorandum will be the arguments advanced by the agencies for and against the bill, together with the Division's own analysis and recommendations. In the end the President must weigh all this argumentation in relation to his perception of the national interest, his programs and promises, his obligations, his party position, the counsels of staff and other close advisers, and so forth. Note that the lobbying pressures on the President and his advisers may be as intense at this point as they are at earlier critical points in the legislative process. Note also that the President with his national constituency and his own objectives and resources, brings to the decisional process still another perspective from that applied by the Senators and Representatives who have previously passed on it.

One way or another, the President must decide. Much of the time, the decision is to approve. The number of Presidential vetoes is not in fact very large in comparison to the total number of bills which are presented for signature and become law without exercise of the veto power. But the number of vetoes should not be taken as an index of the veto power's importance. The existence of the veto power and the threat of its possible use extend the President's influence throughout the legislative process. His position must be reckoned with by proponents and opponents at every stage. Here is one more center of power in the panorama of dispersed and divided powers that the Federal legislative processes offer to view. Here is one more opportunity to block action.

If the decision is to approve, and unless the President allows the bill to become law without his signature, there may be more or less elaborate signing ceremonies. Notice of the signing is generally sent by message to the chamber where the bill originated and that chamber informs the other. The action is noted in the Congressional Record.

If the President vetoes a bill, other than by "pocket veto," the bill and his veto message are, as we saw, returned to the chamber of origin. A vetoed bill returned to the Congress in this way is accorded high privilege (there is no need for recourse to the Rules Committee in the House) and will generally be disposed of quickly. Amendments are not in order; in the House, only a limited time is allowed for debate. If there is no real possibility the veto may be overridden, the bill may be tabled or sent back to committee. Otherwise the question is put, "Shall the bill pass, the objections of the President to the contrary notwithstanding?" To override the veto, each chamber must separately vote to do so by a vote of at least two-thirds of those present, a quorum being required to be on hand. A negative vote kills the bill and if it occurs in the first chamber a message is normally sent to the other advising of the decision that the bill is not to pass.

If the President signs the bill or allows it to become law without signature, or if the chambers vote to override a veto, then, as the case may be, the President or the chamber last voting to override will transmit the bill to the General Services Administration for publication. There, a public law number will be given to the bill (the public law number contains the number of the enacting Congress and a number indicating the order in which the bill was adopted as compared with other enactments by the same Congress). The bill is forthwith made available in published form. First, it is made available as a slip law in unbound pamphlet form printed by offset process from the enrolled bill. Later, this and other new laws will be published in bound volumes of the Statutes at Large, an official authoritative compilation containing the laws of each Congress in the chronological order of their enactment.

Later also, the bill will be incorporated in the United States Code, a compilation consolidating and codifying the general and permanent laws of the United States and arranging them by subject-matter under 50 titles. Congress's Office of the Law Revision Counsel transmutes the enacted statute at large into specific and segmented provisions of the U.S. Code; often left out altogether are important portions of the bill, such as the legislative findings and purposes—which may help to clarify the legislative purpose and intent of the statute.[61] Notwithstanding the possibility that portions of the statute may be lost in transmutation, for most lawyers, the Code is a much more readily usable research tool than the chronologically arranged Statutes at Large. Certain titles of the Code have been enacted into positive law in an ongoing codification effort; as to these titles the Code is the official and authoritative source of the statute law. The Statutes at Large and the Revised Statutes (an early compilation of the laws in force as of Dec. 1, 1873) remain the official and authoritative source, however, for laws not included in these titles. These versions of the bill—the slip law, the text in the Statutes at Large, the version in the U.S. Code—are primary sources for lawyers working with legislation. Other materials, such as veto or approval messages, may be of high importance as aids to understanding the bill, now a statute, when it comes before lawyers, courts or administrators for interpretation. Many of these materials are located on the Library of Congress's congress.gov website. This collection includes bills, resolutions, public laws, Senate and House Roll Call Votes, the Congressional Record, committee reports, and treaties.[62]

C. ADMINISTRATIVE LAW

While case and statutory law will occupy almost all of your studies during your first year, administrative law is an important and increasingly pervasive source of law in practice. Administrative agencies

---

[61] See Jarrod Shobe, *Enacted Legislative Findings and Purposes*, 86 U. Chi. L. Rev. 669, 673 (2019).

[62] See http://congress.gov.

run adjudicatory proceedings which, for the parties involved, are essentially indistinguishable from court proceedings. And administrative agencies also promulgate rules, which for all intents and purposes, function as statutes. The following provides an overview of these administrative functions in the U.S. legal system.

1. BACKGROUND AND HISTORY

Ronald M. Levin and Jeffrey S. Lubbers, Administrative Law and Process in a Nutshell 1–3 (6th ed. 2017), offer the following observations on the reasons for establishing administrative agencies (instead of relying on the courts and the legislature):

> Administrative agencies usually are created to deal with current crises or to redress serious social problems. Throughout the modern era of administrative regulation, which began in the late nineteenth century, the government's response to a public demand for action has often been to establish a new agency, or to grant new powers to an existing bureaucracy. Near the turn of the century, agencies like the Interstate Commerce Commission and the Federal Trade Commission were created in an attempt to control the anticompetitive conduct of monopolies and powerful corporations. . . . In the 1960's when the injustices of poverty and racial discrimination became an urgent national concern, the development of programs designed to redress these grievances expanded the scope of government administration. More recently, increased public concern about risks to human health and safety and threats to the natural environment, as well as national security concerns, have resulted in new agencies and new regulatory programs.

> The primary reason why administrative agencies have so frequently been called upon to deal with such diverse social problems is the great flexibility of the regulatory process. In comparison to courts or legislatures or elected executive officials, administrative agencies have several institutional strengths that equip them to deal with complex problems. Perhaps the most important of these strengths is specialized staffing: an agency is authorized to hire people with whatever mix of talents, skills and experience it needs to get the job done. Moreover, because the agency has responsibility for a limited area of public policy, it can develop the expertise that comes from continued exposure to a problem area. . . .

> However, these potential strengths of the administrative process can also be viewed as a threat to other important values. Administrative "flexibility" may simply be a mask for unchecked power, and in our society unrestrained government power has traditionally been viewed with great and justifiable suspicion. Thus, the fundamental policy problem of the administrative

process is how to design a system of checks which will minimize the risks of bureaucratic arbitrariness and overreaching, while preserving for the agencies the flexibility they need to act effectively.

For the historical context of the shift in lawmaking from legislatures to administrative agencies, consider the following developments traced in 1 Richard J. Pierce, Jr., Administrative Law Treatise § 1.4 (5th ed. 2010):

> [T]he powers and roles of agencies increased and expanded significantly in the twentieth century. Peter Strauss has illustrated the increases in the roles of agencies by comparing the Federal Railway Safety Appliances Act of 1893 with the National Traffic and Motor Vehicle Safety Act of 1966. Strauss, Legislative Theory and the Rule of Law: Some Comments on Rubin, 89 Colum. L. Rev. 427, 428–30 (1989). In both cases Congress responded to the widespread perception that the then-dominant form of transportation was unsafe. Its 1966 response differed significantly from its 1893 response. In the process of enacting the Rail Safety Act, Congress debated and resolved the major policy issues concerning rail safety; it specified detailed safety rules by statute. Seventy years later when Congress passed the Motor Vehicle Safety Act, it debated and resolved none of the major policy issues; rather, Congress instructed an agency to further motor vehicle safety subject only to loosely worded general guidance in the statute delegating power to the agency. . . .

> For a broad perspective about the early development of American administrative law, one must seek help from a leading legal and social historian, such as James Willard Hurst. In his book, Law and Social Order in the United States 35–41 (1977), Hurst declared:

> > One can plot a curve of statute law that begins at a modest and yet substantial level, rises considerably from the 1830's to the 1880's, then shows a marked increase of pitch and takes off into an ascending line, which in the 1970's shows no sign of turning down. . . . From the 1880's, but most markedly from the take-off decade of 1905–1915, the regulatory component of statute law became much more prominent and added considerably to the volume of legislation, a shift of emphasis that brought a new type of statute law concerning organized relationships. The focus changed from enabling organized action to injecting more public management or supervision of affairs and providing more sustained, specialized means of defining and enforcing public policy. Symbolic of this turn of affairs were the statutes creating the modern federal and state administrative apparatus; typical was the shift from factory

safety laws that simply commanded employers to provide safe work places to law implemented by provision for administrative rulemaking and inspection. . . . United States legal history began with distrust of and hence deliberate restriction of executive power and with only rudimentary administrative machinery. . . . Well into the last quarter of the nineteenth century legislative processes—especially in the states—were crude. Legislators worked with little experience and little precedent to guide their jobs; sessions were short; legislators were part-time amateurs at public policy making; only slowly did a standing committee system develop. . . . Our chart will show [no] great contribution to the body of law from executive offices or administrative agencies until the 1890's. . . . We can plot major executive administrative contributions from the decade 1905–1915, which first saw the grant of substantial rule-making, rule-enforcement, and adjudicative powers to executive offices and independent administrative agencies. . . . Indeed, by the mid-twentieth century the curve for administrative legislation perhaps topped that for statute law: by the 1950's lawyers with business clients and individuals with demands on the increasing service functions of government had to turn more to administrative rule books than to statute books to locate the legal frame of reference for their affairs. . . .

Elihu Root, in a 1916 address as President of the American Bar Association, made a statement that could hardly be improved upon with the hindsight of nearly a century later:

There is one special field of law development which has manifestly become inevitable. We are entering upon the creation of a body of administrative law quite different in its machinery, its remedies, and its necessary safeguards from the old methods of regulation by specific statutes enforced by the courts. As any community passes from simple to complex conditions, the only way in which government can deal with the increased burdens thrown upon it is by the delegation of power to be exercised in detail by subordinate agents, subject to the control of general directions prescribed by superior authority. The necessities of our situation have already led to an extensive employment of that method. . . . Before these agencies the old doctrine prohibiting the delegation of legislative power has virtually retired from the field and given up the fight. There will be no withdrawal from these experiments. We shall go on; we shall expand them, whether we approve theoretically or not, because such agencies furnish protection to rights and obstacles to wrongdoing which under our new social and industrial conditions cannot be practically accomplished by the old and simple procedure of legislatures and courts as in the last generation.

Elihu Root, Public Service by the Bar: Address by Elihu Root as President of the American Bar Association at the Annual Meeting in Chicago 14–15, reprinted in 41 A.B.A.R. 355, 368–69 (1916).

In his clarity of perception, Elihu Root may have been a generation or more ahead of other leaders of the bar. At the same time, he uttered important words of caution:

> If we are to continue a government of limited powers, these agencies of regulation must themselves be regulated. The limits of their power over the citizen must be fixed and determined. The rights of the citizen against them must be made plain. A system of administrative law must be developed, and that with us is still in its infancy, crude and imperfect.

Id. at 15

2. ADMINISTRATIVE ADJUDICATION

The courts are our society's traditional instrumentalities for the authoritative disposition of controversies and, at the start of the 20th century, seemed to have a virtual monopoly of the public business of dispute-settlement. But just as legislation has made great inroads into what were once the largely exclusive preserves of the case law, administrative agencies like the National Labor Relations Board and the Federal Trade Commission have come to exercise powers of adjudication in many areas of American social and economic life.

The following are examples of disputes remitted to administrative adjudication. If a person has a disputed claim for federal retirement benefits, he or she does not begin by going to court to sue on it; the claim will be judged and authoritatively determined, at least as a matter of first instance, by an adjudicatory official in the Social Security Administration. A power company that wishes to construct a nuclear reactor applies for the required license not to a court but to the Nuclear Regulatory Commission, which, after proper hearing and deliberation by its atomic safety and licensing board, will grant or deny the application. Administrative agencies entrusted with power to hear and pass upon claims, applications and charges of law violation are found everywhere in the federal governmental structure, sometimes as divisions within cabinet departments, sometimes as independent regulatory establishments. Quantitatively, far more controversies are decided by federal administrative agencies than by all the federal courts.

Administrative adjudication has similarly been a growth industry in the state and local governments. Administrative bodies are empowered to issue or refuse, and to revoke or suspend, the licenses required to engage in a wide variety of professions and businesses. Workers' compensation commissions hear and decide claims arising from industrial accidents, and public utility commissions pass on applications for rate increases submitted by gas, light and water companies. Every municipal government has its administrative complex of local tax boards, licensing officials, zoning appeals boards and the like, all performing in one way or another the essentially judicial function—or quasi-judicial function—of hearing and deciding particular claims, charges and disputes. The decisions reached by federal, state and local administrative agencies are, to one or another extent, subject to judicial review in the (regular) courts, but the scope of this review is usually limited and constitutes not a retrial of the case or claim but an inquiry into whether the administrative adjudicative agency has acted illegally, arbitrarily or without sufficient evidence to support its findings.

In the early part of the twentieth century, many lawyers looked with distrust and hostility on the proliferation of administrative agencies and the extension of their decision-making powers. Despite this, the growing consensus seemed to be that administrative adjudication was inevitable, given the vastly increased range of government's regulatory and public welfare programs, and, being here to stay, should be ordered and regularized. The great step in this direction, insofar as the federal agencies are concerned, was the enactment in 1946 of the Administrative Procedure Act. By this Act, which was passed by the unanimous vote of both houses of Congress, the adjudicative processes of the federal agencies were largely "judicialized," that is, subjected to uniform procedural standards designed to secure fairness in the hearing, determination and review of particular cases. Many states have enacted similar legislation to regularize the processes of administrative adjudication in the state and local governments. More recently, a new generation of scholars and jurists have raised renewed questions about the legitimacy and legality of such practices.[63]

3.   RULE PROMULGATION

a.   FEDERAL ADMINISTRATIVE REGULATIONS

Administrative adjudication is an important element in the contemporary American pattern of controversy-settlement. But administrative agencies do not only apply law in particular cases; they also make law, and the general rules formulated and prescribed by the agencies constitute a major ingredient of American legislation. Dozens of federal agencies, some of them established as independent commissions and others as more or less separate branches within cabinet

---

[63]   See Philip Hamburger, Is Administrative Law Unlawful? (2014).

departments, are now involved in the regulation of business and other private activities. Most have been entrusted by Acts of Congress with subordinate legislative power, subordinate in the sense that the regulations made and issued by an administrative agency must be within the scope of the authority delegated to the agency by Congress.

Regulations prescribed by a federal agency within the scope of its delegated rule-making power are authoritative norms of the legal order and, assuming the constitutional validity of the underlying federal statute, superior in authoritativeness to state law. Thus a properly issued regulation of the Securities and Exchange Commission, the National Labor Relations Board, or the Food and Drug Administration has legal effect everywhere in the United States, and any conflicting rule on the same subject in a state's case law or statutes, or even in its constitution, must yield to the superior authority of the federal regulation. The rule-making processes of the federal administrative agencies, like their adjudicatory processes, are governed by the Administrative Procedure Act. Acts of Congress require publication of administrative regulations in a daily and official gazette called the Federal Register, and further require that regulations be systematically arranged and codified, by a continuing process, in the Code of Federal Regulations. The rule-making functions of administrative agencies, as well as their adjudicatory and executive (largely enforcement) functions, are examined intensively in law school courses on Administrative Law.

b.   STATE ADMINISTRATIVE REGULATIONS

State governments have vested administrative agencies with the provision of public services and the supervision of private activity. The list of regulated activities differs from state to state, reflecting differences in economic conditions and in prevailing political attitudes, but it is everywhere a long list. Regulations are prescribed by state and local agencies and officials on an enormous variety of subjects: agriculture, civil service, fishing, horse racing, water resources and zoning, to mention just a few. State administrative regulations, in their vast aggregate, loom large in the picture of American legislation.

D. COMPARATIVE LAW

The U.S. Legal Tradition Among the Legal Traditions of the World
— Gary F. Bell*

Because the United States are a federation, Americans are usually well aware that the law does vary from jurisdiction to jurisdiction. One should note however that all States except Louisiana belong to the

---

*   Thanks to Associate Professor Gary F. Bell of the National University of Singapore for contributing this Note.

common law tradition and therefore their laws are very similar. Even if politically each State is independent and has its own legal system, all States except Louisiana share the same legal tradition and method.

At the international level however, there is much more diversity in legal traditions and methods. Most of the world's national legal systems have been influenced by at least one of a few major legal traditions. In the Western world, there are two main legal traditions—the civil law and the common law. The laws of France and Italy are in some respects different but they both belong to the civil law tradition and share similar assumptions, in the same way California law is in the end not that different from New York law. Mortgage rules may be different in California, New York and England but all have mortgages as opposed to hypothecs as would be the case in France and Italy. And if you want to set up a mortgage you would go to an attorney in both California and New York, and a solicitor in England, but definitely not a notary as you would in France and Italy for a hypothec. Belonging to the same legal tradition means you share the same legal concepts and institutions. And in the case of the common law tradition, you share a common language, English, something the civil law sorely misses since Latin was abandoned as its common language a few centuries ago.

Mainly through colonization, either the civil law or the common law has influenced, at least in part, the laws of almost all countries in the world. Outside of the Western world however, the civil law or the common law often co-exists with other legal traditions, such as the Islamic legal tradition, the Jewish legal tradition, the Hindu legal tradition, as well as many other legal traditions including many indigenous traditions.[64]

For commerce and trade, most national legal systems rely mainly on either the civil law or the common law. This note will therefore introduce you to the origins and development of the common law and the civil law and to the main distinctions between these two systems, especially in terms of legal methods. I will then briefly mention at a few examples of non-Western traditions which do not share the same legal methods as Western legal traditions. I will finally mention how legal pluralism is generally rejected in the West but accepted in many other legal traditions.

1. ORIGINS OF THE TWO MAIN WESTERN LEGAL TRADITIONS AND THEIR DIFFUSION AROUND THE WORLD

a. THE COMMON LAW

The common law tradition originated in England. A new legal order was established as early as 1066 by the Norman Conquest, but the

---

[64] For a fascinating and detailed description of the different legal traditions read H. Patrick Glenn, Legal Traditions of the World (2014).

common law did not exist in 1066. William the Conqueror did not abolish the local customs and the local courts.[65] Local courts continued to apply local customs. There was no law common to the whole kingdom. The King did however establish some royal courts at Westminster. Their jurisdiction was at first very limited but eventually expanded to the point where the local courts fell into disuse. The decisions of the royal courts became the law common to the whole kingdom, the common law.

The common law has its source in previous court decisions. The main traditional source of the common law is therefore not legislation but cases. This is so true that when the common law evolved into an unfair set of rigid and formal procedural rules the King, rather than legislate to amend the law, created a new court. When a subject thought that a common law decision led to an unfair result he would petition the King. There were so many petitions that the King created the court of Chancery which could grant a discretionary relief "in equity" to correct the common law. The decisions of this court gave birth to a body of law called equity which is also based on previous judicial decisions.[66] Both law and equity are now part of what is called the common law tradition.

The British Empire brought the common law to all continents. The common law was "received"[67] in many countries but its reception has been most successful in countries where the European settlers became a majority and imposed (usually unfairly through force) their law over indigenous populations. This was the case in Australia, English Canada, New Zealand and the United States (except Louisiana where the civil law was in place before the United States gained jurisdiction). The common law was also imposed on many other colonies but usually with some adaptation to take into account the local laws and customs. For example, Singapore and Malaysia which are now independent common law countries continue to apply Islamic law to Muslims in family matters. In fact family law and inheritance law, or more generally what is referred to as personal laws, often continue to be governed by indigenous laws rather than the common law. Nevertheless, still today in Africa and Asia, former British colonies for the most part continue to apply the common law. Today, India is the most populous common law country.

In some instances, the new colonial power imposed parts of the common law on newly entrusted territories that used to be civil law jurisdictions under the previous colonial masters (*e.g.*, the USA in the Philippines after centuries of Spanish colonialism, England in South Africa and Quebec after decades of Dutch and centuries of French colonialism). This led to mixed legal systems.

Following the Second World War, the economic hegemony of the United States also contributed to the expansion of the common law.

---

[65] William wanted to be seen as the successor of the previous king and not as a conqueror.

[66] Today, in almost all common law jurisdictions, the same court exercises both the common law and the equity jurisdictions.

[67] "Reception" refers to the process by which one political entity adopts the law of another.

International contracts were often drafted in a common law style with the use of common law terms and international arbitrators often applied common law principles.

A note about the common law in the United States.

Because of the early independence of the United States, the US common law has evolved separately from the common law of England and of other Commonwealth countries. Commonwealth nations became independent only fairly recently, and even long after they were independent, some nations continued to allow appeals to the Judicial Committee of the Privy Council in London (some countries still allow such appeals). This has had a unifying effect on the law of these countries and still today the courts of one country will consider the decisions of the courts of another Commonwealth country as very persuasive. By contrast, only rarely, if ever, does a United States court determining a matter of domestic law invoke a decision of a foreign country's courts.[68] It is therefore even more striking that notwithstanding years of "legal separation" the law of this country still has so much in common with the law of other common law countries.

b.   THE CIVIL LAW

The origins of the civil law go further back. They can be traced to the Twelve Tables of the Republic of Rome (probably in the fifth century B.C.). In its origins, it is the law of the city of Rome, the law applied to a citizen (in Latin, *civis*) of Rome as opposed to the law applied to a non-citizen.[69] The expression "civil law", in Latin *ius civilis,* literally means the law of the citizens of Rome.

After the fall of the Western Roman Empire (476 A.D.), the so-called "barbarians" brought their law to Rome, and although Roman law continued to apply to the Romans, the Germanic influence grew quickly and the law became more and more a mixture of Germanic and Roman law. This would later be known as the vulgarized Roman law. This law was in many ways different from the classical Roman law. In what used to be the Western Roman Empire, Canon law, the law of the Catholic Church, also kept relatively intact many elements of the Roman law. In 529–34, the Eastern Roman Emperor Justinian published the *Corpus Iuris Civilis,* an articulation and reformulation of Roman law mainly in the form of a long compendium of selected and reorganized abstracts of original documents. The *Corpus Iuris Civilis* remained in force in

---

[68]   One of these rare exceptions would be Lawrence v. Texas, 539 U.S. 558 (2003), in which Justice Kennedy used foreign precedents in a constitutional case causing the usual ire of Justice Scalia. See *infra* Section II.B.

[69]   Those of you familiar with the New Testament will remember that St. Paul, because he was a citizen of Rome, was entitled to be tried according to Roman law (Acts 23:27). In fact, according to the New Testament, Paul was even entitled to be tried in Rome in front of an imperial court (Acts 25:11–12).

Byzantium in one form or another until and even after the fifteenth-century conquest by the Ottoman Turks.

At the end of the eleventh century, the University of Bologna started teaching Roman law, more specifically the *Corpus Iuris Civilis*. This was at first a purely intellectual endeavor since this version of Roman law was no longer the law anywhere in Western Europe. This marked the beginning of what would later be known as the resurgence of Roman law. Soon other Western European universities followed Bologna's lead and after a few centuries and for reasons too complex to be considered here, the Roman law was received almost everywhere in continental Europe. It became the *ius commune* (the "common law") of continental Europe.

The Roman law actually "received" was in fact limited to what we call "private law" (persons, property, torts, contracts etc.). That is why civilian jurists refer to what we call private law simply as "the civil law" (persons, property and obligations).

Although most civil law countries now have a civil code,[70] codification is in fact a fairly recent phenomenon. The first modern code, the French Civil Code, dates back only to 1804 and the German Civil Code, to 1896 (in force in 1900).

The French and German Codes are the two main civil law models. Napoleon brought his Code wherever he and his armies traveled. The French model has been influential in Latin countries both in Europe and in America (Central and South America, Louisiana and Quebec). It has also influenced former French, Portuguese, Spanish and Dutch colonies in Africa, the Middle East and Asia, in countries as diverse as Indonesia and the Ivory Coast, Vietnam and Peru.

The German model has influenced the Austrian and Swiss codes as well as the law of many Eastern European countries before the Soviet occupation. German Law has also been received in Japan, Korea and Taiwan and to some extent in pre-Maoist China.

In imposing the civil law on their colonies in Africa and Asia, the colonial powers often left in place local personal laws (customary and religious) to govern family matters and sometimes land law for local populations. In those continents, the civil law, like the common law, often coexisted with indigenous traditions in a form of legal pluralism.

---

[70] Scotland and South Africa—in many respects civil law jurisdictions—do not have a civil code.

2. LEGAL METHODS—A COMPARISON

You must understand that a civil-law legal methods course (if there were such a thing) would be completely different from the course you are now taking. It is important at the beginning of your legal career that you realize that law can take different forms and play different roles in different societies and cultures. What you will be studying is not the law as it necessarily has to be but the law as it is in the United States. Here are a few methodological differences between the civil law and the common law.

Case law v. "jurisprudence"

First and foremost, in common law countries, cases are usually considered to be the primary source of law. Your legal methods class starts with the study of cases. In civil law countries, cases are simply not a source of law—at least not in theory. The reality might well be that legislation has become extremely relevant in common law countries and that cases are becoming more and more relevant in civil law countries, but the attitudes of civilians and common lawyers toward legislation and cases differ greatly.

You will soon get to read a typical French case. When you read the reasons of the court, you will not find a long and detailed exposition of the facts of the case. Instead the court states a few general principles, usually stemming from articles of the civil code or of the law and then

---

*   Cartoon from PASCAL ÉLIE, HUMOUR: FORMAT LEGAL (1987). Reproduced with the permission of the author and of the publisher (Les Éditions Yvon Blais).

concludes "therefore . . . " Typically, French cases have one sentence: "whereas article 100 of the civil code states . . . , whereas it is a general principle of law that . . . , therefore the court decides . . . ." Even if the civil law had a principle of *stare decisis* (which it does not) it would be hard to apply the decision in one case to other cases with similar facts since the facts of the original case are not stated in full. This is not to say that French jurists do not look at cases, or as they call them collectively, at the *"jurisprudence."* Quite to the contrary, they very often look at cases, and the civil code is typically published with copious annotations and summaries of court decisions. French jurists however look at jurisprudence not for binding precedents with similar facts but rather for general principles of law and for specific interpretations of particular provisions of law. Typically, the case law annotations of the civil code state in one sentence a principle of law rather than a set of facts. Understandably therefore the common law technique of distinguishing cases based on facts is not part of the method taught in French law school.

The practice with regards to cases may vary to a certain extent in civil law countries other than France—for example German cases tend to be longer and give a more detailed account of the facts. It remains however that the cases never have in civil law countries the importance they have in common law countries. The law is perceived as enunciated in codes and statutes and the main function of the jurist is to interpret the codes directly, rather than to distinguish or apply previous cases *in concreto.*

Legislative interpretation and drafting

Civil law jurists tend to see the civil code as an all-encompassing document. They will interpret it generously in order to allow it to reach its goal of regulating the whole private law. The code lends itself to this kind of interpretation since its articles are usually drafted in very general and abstract terms. The degree of generality and of abstraction can be stunning. For example, the whole French law of tort (called "delictual obligations") finds its source in this very abstract provision of new law of obligations in the French civil code:

"Art. 1240. Any human action whatsoever which causes harm to another creates an obligation in the person by whose fault it occurred to make reparation for it."[71]

The judges would readily give to the law a teleological interpretation—a purposive interpretation that is not going to be limited to the actual purpose of the legislator in enacting a particular provision, but which will extend to the purpose of the law and of the code in general

---

[71] The Law of Contract, The General Regime of Obligations, and Proof of Obligations, The New Provisions of the Code civil Created by Ordonnance n° 2016–131 of 10 February 2016 translated into English by John Cartwright, Bénédicte Fauvarque-Cosson, and Simon Whittaker. Available at http://www.textes.justice.gouv.fr/art_pix/THE-LAW-OF-CONTRACT-2-5-16.pdf.

in regulating private law. The judges will look at the spirit of the law beyond its letter. As the Swiss Civil Code puts it, in the most radical way:

"(1) The Law must be applied in all cases which come within the letter or the spirit of any of its provisions.

"(2) Where no provision is applicable, the judge shall decide according to the existing Customary Law and, in default thereof, according to the rule which he would lay down if he had himself to act as legislator."[72]

It is unlikely that the judge will narrowly interpret a provision. Even though in the past there have been some civil law judges who were narrow black letter jurists, it is fair to says that generally the civil law judge will look beyond the letter of the law and will often apply some principles by analogy, even though the letter of the law does not apply. He will however nonetheless be rather reluctant to extend a particular provision of the code in a certain direction unless he or she can be convinced that this does not go against the systematic edifice of the code. The code is perceived as a whole and one must try to foresee in advance the effect of a decision on the whole organization or economy of the code. Therefore, in seminal cases, the court will not decide simply to extend a practice to a new set of facts but will decide whether this matter should be regulated by this part or that part of the code or, to put it differently, whether a particular development is consistent with the very structure of the code. The civil law jurist wants a systematic and consistent approach to the law, but is willing to interpret the code generously to achieve such a systematic and all-encompassing approach.

In common law jurisdictions one often has the impression that legislation tends to be considered as an exception to the case law. Of course, in theory, legislation is a higher source of law than cases and courts are now bound by what Congress has decided. In fact, however, the courts often have a tendency to interpret legislation rather restrictively. We often hear judges say that had the legislator intended to cover a certain situation he could have said so more clearly in the statute. In consequence the legislator tends to enunciate legal rules in very specific terms so as to be "clear." This makes for a legislative style that tends to enunciate a list of possible situations, or facts, as in this provision for an extreme example:

"Every person who marks or brands, alters, conceals, disfigures, obliterates, or defaces the mark or brand of any horse, mare, colt, jack, jennet, mule, bull, ox, steer, cow, calf, sheep, goat, hog, shoat or pig belonging to another, with intent thereby to steal the same or to prevent identification thereof by the true owner, shall be guilty of a felony."[73]

Such long lists are almost never heard of in civil law drafting style. Since the judge will not interpret the statute narrowly, there is no need

---

[72] Swiss Civil Code, art. 1 (1907) (translation).

[73] Idaho Code § 25–1901.

for a detailed list—a general statement will suffice. It is true that common law also has recourse to the purposive interpretation of statutes, but one should recognize that it does so in a narrower way than the civil law.

One should not conclude that one drafting style is better than the other. I do not draft a letter to a lover in the same way I draft a letter to an employer. Different drafting style must be adopted to take into account the interpretative style of the reader. The detailed drafting style of the common law is justified by the way statute, and even contracts, are interpreted by common law judges generally. In the same way the drafting style of the civil law, which sticks to general principles in both statutes and contracts, is also justified by the fact that civil law judges will interpret the provisions generously. Each drafting style is justified by the legal method of each legal tradition.

Other differences

Civil law students will read "la doctrine" more than cases. The "doctrine" is the cumulated writings of law professors on what the law is or should be. In civil law the "doctrine" is highly respected. You have to remember that the University, not the courts, reintroduced the civil law in Continental Europe. It is therefore not surprising that law professors still have an important role in defining the law. Common law professors generally do not enjoy a similar prestige within their own jurisdiction. Here the judges get most of the prestige.

Legal education differs a lot from country to country but it is fair to say that American legal education is very original and, in many respects, unique. The "case method" or "Socratic method" is peculiar to this country. It must be clear to you by now that the "case" method could not have been devised in a civil law country. One should also note that in those countries (as is the case in England, and in fact almost everywhere except in the USA, Canada, the Philippines and more recently Japan and South Korea) law is an undergraduate degree.[74] Civil law legal education tends to last longer than the three years typically required in the United States (though generally not as long as the combined seven years of U.S. undergraduate and law school training). The main teaching style is magisterial—the professor exposes the law to his or her students, who take notes and do not intervene in class.

3. A FEW EXAMPLES OF NON-WESTERN LEGAL TRADITIONS

Because colonialism and economic hegemonism has brought the civil law and the common law throughout the world, and because these two

---

[74] It should be noted however that increasingly, some other jurisdictions are adopting the American approach of law as a graduate degree. A graduate JD-like law degree will now be required for practice in Japan and the University of Melbourne now offers law exclusively as a graduate degree (JD).

traditions govern most aspects of trade and commerce around the world, many comparative law books go no further. There are however many other legal traditions, in fact too many for us to cover them all. Even in the West, other legal traditions are known such as Talmudic or Jewish law and Canon law for example. My area of expertise is Indonesian law. Indonesia, which is the largest Muslim-majority country in the world by population, has very many different legal traditions: Civil law (from the Dutch colonizers), but also Islamic law and many different adat laws—the many indigenous laws of the many different ethnic groups. Some of these groups are Hindu (the Balinese for example) and therefore their adat law is influenced by Hindu legal traditions.

In fact in a large number of countries in Asia and Africa, many different laws co-exist within the same jurisdiction in a form or another of legal pluralism: in addition to the former colonial law (civil or common law), indigenous, customary or religious laws, apply to different persons depending of the ethnic group, tribe, or religion to which they belong. In Indonesia for example, aspects of Islamic law (family law, including divorce, inheritance etc.) will apply to Muslims whereas non-Muslim will have the civil law or the adat law of their ethnic community govern the same matters. Even in very "modern" Singapore, we have legal pluralism: Islamic family law for Muslims, secular family law for others. The same is true in Israel where each religious community has its own family law.

I will give you below only a few examples of some of the many legal traditions found in East, South and Southeast Asia. It goes without saying that the legal methods of these other legal traditions would be very different from the legal methods of the civil or common law.[75]

a.   PRE-COLONIAL INDIGENOUS LAWS: THE EXAMPLE OF THE ADAT LAWS

Indigenous laws and aboriginal land titles were often disregarded by the colonial powers but many jurisdictions around the world today recognize indigenous customary laws and aboriginal titles (often called "original Indian titles" in the United States). This is so whether the aboriginals are only a small portion of the citizens of a country (Canada, USA, New Zealand, etc.) or a majority (Indonesia, most countries in Africa etc.).

In Asian and African countries, that is in countries where the local population was not overtaken by European settlers, the colonial powers, after imposing the civil or common law for trade and commerce, often did not abolish the other local or religious legal traditions and they let family matters, and in some cases some land matters, be governed by local laws rather than colonial laws. Therefore, in India to this day both Hindu and

---

[75] Most of what follows is taken and adapted from my earlier contribution to the following book: Michael Hor & Tang Hang Wu, Reading Law in Singapore (2009) at chapter 7.

Islamic laws apply in family matters depending on the religion of the parties.

Many of the indigenous laws found around the world are customary, rather than religious laws. In Indonesia, adat laws are customary: in fact the word adat is an Arabic word (عادة ʿādah) meaning custom or habit and "adat law" (in Dutch "adatrecht") is the name given by the Dutch and British to that part of the adat traditions that they considered to be law, as law is understood in the West (as opposed to the part of adat traditions that related to religion, morals and habits, a distinction the indigenous population did not make). Adat laws are found all over Indonesia and Malaysia and there is great diversity—there is not one adat law but numerous different adat laws, each ethnic group having its own adat. Adat law is still very important in "personal laws," *i.e.*, in family and inheritance law.

b. HINDU LAW

The Hindu legal tradition is one of the oldest ones in the world. The Vedas, the sacred and revealed foundational texts of Hinduism probably date back to 1500–2000 B.C.E. As is the case for almost all non-Western legal traditions, Hinduism does not make a clear distinction between law and religion, law and morals, law and customs or practices. In fact, in Sanskrit there is no word for law as the concept is understood in the West.

Later books, the Dharmasastras, elaborate on personal and royal duties (again making no clear distinction between religious, ritual and social duties on the one hand, and what the West would understand as legal duties on the other). The most famous of them is the Manusmṛti, known in English as the Laws of Manu, written sometime between 200 B.C.E. and 200 C.E. This book and others describe one's duties or dharma and how one must perform one's dharma through good deeds (karma) which (along with bad deeds) will have effects in the future (in reincarnation for example). "Legal" obligations therefore have religious consequences. A king's dharma is to follow the law (an early version of the Rule of Law) and make sure others follow it too—he can use "danda" or punishment to insure this. There is a lot of diversity in Hindu law which tolerates all sorts of local variations. This is consistent with the great tolerance of others found in the Hindu tradition (though not in the recent Hindu nationalist movement in India which shows a very non-traditional intolerance).

Under the British, Hindu law in India was reduced to personal laws and as the British courts did not fully understand that law, they ended up creating through case law what is often referred to as the "Anglo-Hindu law"—Hindu law as applied by English courts (which is very different from classical Hindu law). Not long after Independence, India "codified" Anglo-Hindu law in four statutes: Hindu Marriage Act (1955), Hindu Succession Act (1956), Hindu Minority and Guardianship Act

(1956), and Hindu Adoptions and Maintenance Act (1956) which formed the basis of the so called "modern Hindu law."

c. ISLAMIC LAW

No other legal tradition is as seriously misunderstood in the West as Islamic law is. Islamic law is the frequent topic of news reports; mainly reports about how extremist regimes apply their version of Islamic law to cut hands and stone adulterers. There is indeed a resurgence of Islamic law, which unfortunately too many non-Muslims associate only with radicalism, but which can also be seen as a call for a renewed approach to law, one that better takes into account moral and religious obligations than Western secular law does. Islamic banking and finance (which are growing very fast and in which many large US banks are involved) try to bring morality into the financial system, something many in the West think is a very good idea. Of course, one should not expect non-Muslims to agree with every aspect of Islamic law—I, for one, am very uncomfortable with some aspects of Islamic law, the same way I am uncomfortable, for moral and religious reasons, with capital punishment as practiced in many states of the United States. I do not however condemn the whole US legal system as unfair and unjust simply because I find one part of it to be abhorrent and contrary to my religious and moral beliefs. In fact I have the greatest admiration for the US legal system notwithstanding the fact that I consider the death penalty repulsive, and I do have great respect for those who disagree with me on the death penalty—they are not evil, backward people following an evil legal system: almost all of them are very nice, rational people who have come to a different conclusion on this issue and they adhere to a legal system for which I have great admiration. As lawyers to be, before passing judgment on a whole legal tradition, you should first get a fair overview of it. Given the growing importance of Islam and Islamic law in world affairs, I strongly recommend you read a good book on Islamic law.[76]

Islamic law is a rich and diverse legal tradition. Contrary to what we too often hear, it can be a tolerant law—within Islam there are different schools of law ("Madhhab," Arabic: مذهب) which disagree on the content of Islamic law but which respect one another—a Sunni Muslim for example can decide to belong to one or the other of the four main schools of Sunni Islamic law. It is also tolerant in that most parts of Islamic law do not apply to non-Muslims who are allowed to follow their own law.

The sources of Islamic law are many. Of course, the Koran, being for Muslims the very words of God, is the first and the highest source of law, but most of the Koran is not about law and much more law was needed

---

[76] I recommend one of these two short excellent books as introductions to Islamic law: Wael B. Hallaq, An Introduction to Islamic Law (2009) and Bernard G. Weiss, The Spirit of Islamic Law (1998).

by the Muslim community (the "ummah") than what law is in the Koran. In the Sunni tradition (I do not have time here to also discuss the Shia tradition) other sources were recognized. The second source is the Sunnah which is the sayings, actions and practices of the Prophet Muhammad and his companions. What the Prophet allowed is allowed and what he prohibited is prohibited. There are different collections of "hadith" or sayings or deeds of the Prophet, some more authentic than others, and some not to be relied on (the validity and authenticity of particular "hadiths" is openly debated among Islamic scholars). Each school of law relies on slightly different hadith collections which at times explain in part their disagreement on many legal issues. The third source is "ijma" or consensus and there is consensus among Sunni schools that consensus is a source of law but disagreement as to how one is to reach a consensus (who should be included in the consensus for example: scholars only or the whole ummah). The fourth source is "Qiyas" or analogical deduction or reason. Finally, a more controversial source of law is "ijtihad", or the independent interpretation through reason as opposed to "taqlid" which reduces the role of the interpreter to one of imitation. Sunni Islam did hold that ijtihad was one of the sources of Islamic law but now most Sunni Islamic scholars seem to adhere to the view that the "Door of Ijtihad" was closed a few centuries ago and that "ijtihad" is no longer a source of law. Many Sunni scholars however strongly contest this. This debate over whether the door of ijtihad is open or closed is one of the most important and vigorous debates in Islamic law today and how it is solved will shape the future of Islamic law.

What should come out clearly from the above discussion of the sources of Islamic law is that Islamic law was in fact developed by scholars. Most of the law is found in scholars' books detailing what they thought was the will of God for the Ummah based on their reading of the main sources of Islamic law. There has always been scholarly debate and diversity in Islamic law—even though there are points on which all schools agree, when one asks "what does Islamic law say on this" the answer should most of the time start with "Sunni or Shia Islam?" And, for example if Sunni, "Which school of Islamic law? The Hanafi, Maliki, Shafi'i or Hanbali School of Law?"

Islamic law, before colonization reduced it to a subservient role (reduced to family law), was a very developed and sophisticated law. Trade was an important part of the Muslim caliphates and empires, and therefore their commercial law was sophisticated and flexible.

d.   BUDDHIST LEGAL TRADITIONS AND CHINESE LEGAL TRADITIONS

There has been a long tradition of Buddhist law in Asia, in particular in Southeast Asia—in Thailand, Laos and Myanmar for example. Comparative lawyers are only starting to recognize the important role that Buddhist law has played in Asia in the past.

There are also Chinese traditions relating to law. Obviously, China is an increasingly important partner in international trade and there are therefore good reasons to study its legal history and its law. But the main reason for my interest in Chinese legal history is that it is nothing short of fascinating. The early debates (although sometime overemphasized) between the Legalists (who believed in or put the emphasis on law to reform people and maintain order) and the followers of Confucius (who believed in education and good administration more than law) are fascinating philosophical debates about what role law should play in society. Confucianism became the state philosophy during the Han Dynasty (in particular under Emperor Wu, 156–87 B.C.E.). Nevertheless, there was still some influence form the Legalist tradition. This blend of Confucian values and sometimes strict laws is very interesting.

Modern China, before the communist revolution, adopted Western law in the form of codes from the civil law tradition, more specifically, German models of laws were adopted. After the revolution, another Western model was followed—Socialist law from the USSR. Later during the Cultural Revolution not much law was tolerated. Now China is reforming again and adopting law in the civil law tradition. What role will law play in China? No one knows precisely, but knowing the different legal traditions and their history in China might provide a better understanding of present Chinese attitudes toward the law.

4. LEGAL PLURALISM TODAY

One of the main differences between the West on the one hand, and most (though not all) countries in Asia (including the Middle East) and in Africa, on the other, is their respective rejection and acceptance of legal pluralism. As mentioned above, there is legal pluralism where, within one country, different laws are applied to different people according to their religion, ethnicity or choice—there is not one national law applicable equally to all but a plurality of laws.[77] For example, as mentioned above, in Israel, the law of marriage is different for Jews, Muslims and Christians.

In the West, since the adoption of the Westphalian concept of State, law has become increasingly synonymous with one (non-plural) State law, but it was not always the case. As mentioned above, for the longest time, Western Europe applied as its main law the civil law inherited from the *Corpus Iuris Civilis* of Justinian. This was the *ius commune* or "common law" of Europe even though Justinian's Empire had long disappeared (in fact, it had never even extended to Western Europe) and

---

[77] Federal States in the West do not have legal pluralism simply because they have different federated States. In any given State, only one state law applies to all. In New York State, in certain matters, New York State law will apply and in other matters, Federal "State" law (the law of the Federal State i.e. federal law) will apply but there will not be a plurality of laws applicable within the State of New York to the same matter. Only one law of a state (federal or State) applies to all. Any conflict between the powers of a State and those of the federal State will be resolved though a constitutional review of the matter, but in the end, one law will apply.

Europe was made up of many different separate countries. The *Corpus Iuris Civilis* and its interpretation by scholars was in fact what we would call today a supra-national scholarly law. It was followed because it was convincing i.e. it was perceived as a good law—no State statute decreed that it should be applied. In addition, many customary and religious laws completed that *ius commune.* Canon law applied by church courts governed the clergy and church matters, Jewish law was applied within Jewish communities. There was therefore legal pluralism in Europe until relatively recently. When the Code Napoléon was adopted in France in 1804, it replaced a plurality of customary and religious laws as well as the *Corpus Iuris Civilis* with a State legislation—it established one state law applicable to all in the territory of France to the exclusion of any other law. This is now the main view of law in the West—one state law fits all.

This is not the prevailing view in many other legal traditions outside the West. The Hindu legal tradition celebrates local customs and practices. Jewish and Islamic law were generally not imposed on non-Jews or on non-Muslims who could keep their own laws. In fact, in Islam itself there is legal pluralism. Shia Islam and Sunni Islam have different interpretations and traditions of Islamic law and even within these two main branches of Islam, there are many different schools of law to which Muslims can adhere. As mentioned above, within Sunni Islam, there are four main schools of law (a مذهب *madhab* in Arabic): the Hanafi, Maliki, Shafi'i and Hanbali Schools of Law. For example, in Singapore where Islamic law applies to Muslims in family matters and a few other matters, the question arises as to which version of Islamic law should be applied. The vast majority of Singaporean Muslims are Sunni and follow the Shafi'i school, but there are also minority Shia Muslims who follow the Jafari School. So when a Muslim from that minority school asks for a legal opinion (a fatwa) from the Mufti, the *Application of Muslim Law Act*[78] provides that the Legal Committee must give an answer according the school of law of that minority—legal pluralism within Islam requires that the members of the legal committee, who all follow the Shafi'i school, must provide an answer according to a school they do not adhere to.

This respect for legal diversity and legal pluralism outside the West clashes with the "one state law fits all" that now prevails in the West. This may not last forever however as, even in the West, it is increasingly accepted that the applicable law is more often than not a matter of choice. It is recognized that in commercial matters for example, one may choose to apply the law of country X to the contract and choose to bring disputes to arbitration in country Y. Different laws will apply to different aspects of the dispute according to the choices of the parties—a form of legal pluralism dealt with by rules of conflicts of laws. The best argument for legal pluralism, one that the West could more easily accept, is one in favor of granting more choices when it comes to which law should apply.

---

[78] S. 33(3) of the *Application of Muslim Law Act* Cap. 3, 1999 Rev. Ed. Sing.

It is my hope that the West will come to accept more readily that in some matters it might be better to let people chose the law that should apply, thus respecting their faiths and cultures.

The problem for the liberal West is when legal pluralism does not allow for some individual choices or allows only for very hard choices, as is unfortunately often the case. In Israel, only religious marriages are recognized—there is no civil marriage. And when it comes to Jewish religious marriages, only marriages celebrated by orthodox rabbis are recognized. It leaves no choice to those who do not adhere to the recognized religions or are of different religions—no choice other than to get married abroad which costs money and cannot be afforded by all.[79] In many jurisdictions where Islamic law is recognized as the personal law of Muslims, one born and raised within Islam cannot leave the religion without being accused of apostasy, often considered a serious crime, and therefore one has effectively no choice—even if one has converted to another faith or has become an atheist, that conversion may not be recognized and Muslim law will still apply.[80] To be consistent with Western liberalism, pluralist personal laws should allow a choice by all citizens of a secular law. It remains however that in most countries that practice legal pluralism, the majority of citizens find it normal that the state applies to them their own religious or customary law—for example, Christians in Pakistan appreciate that their marriages are governed by a statute reflecting their own law rather than by the Islamic law of the majority.[81] Legal pluralism is often a shining example of a legal system's tolerance and respect for the main minorities of a country (if not all minorities—gays, converts and atheists are rarely enjoying such tolerance under most regimes of legal pluralism).

Conclusion

In this era of globalization, one might expect that the differences among legal systems would markedly diminish as the world moves toward greater harmonization and uniformization of law. Though there may be many areas in which uniformity of law may be useful and desirable (trade and commerce for example), in my view, the diversity of legal traditions will and should remain. Moreover, in some respects those differences will become even more apparent. As people travel and migrate around the world, it is increasingly likely that different traditions will meet and sometimes unfortunately clash. Legal traditions are part of a person's identity, maybe not as much as her religious or

---

[79] Surprisingly, Israel recognizes marriages celebrated abroad, even gay marriages, notwithstanding the fact that for marriages celebrated within Israel, it recognizes only religious marriages between persons of the same religion.

[80] See the case of *Lina Joy v Majlis Agama Islam Wilayah Persekutuan* [2007] 4 MLJ 585 in which the Federal Court of Malaysia (the highest court in Malaysia) refused to recognize the conversion of a Muslim to Christianity, thus preventing her from marrying her Christian fiancé since according to Muslim law as applied in Malaysia, a female Muslim cannot marry a Christian man.

[81] Indian Christian Marriage Act, 1872 (Act 15 of 1872) still applicable in Pakistan.

cultural traditions, but nonetheless part of that identity. For example, one's Jewishness is in part defined by Jewish law, one's Catholicism, in part by canon law, one's indigenous status, in part by indigenous law and in particular by claims of legal title over land. Recognizing other legal traditions means recognizing an important component of other people's cultures and identities. An understanding and appreciation of other legal traditions is likely to be more and more relevant to the practice of law in the future. Learning more about the civil law tradition and other legal traditions is like learning another language: to do it well, you don't just learn the words, you try to appreciate the culture behind the words. That in turn, should not only enliven your legal education but enrich your experience in practice as well.

PART II

CASE LAW: THE ANALYSIS AND SYNTHESIS OF JUDICIAL DECISIONS

A. COMMON LAW DECISION-MAKING

1. SELECTED CONTROVERSIES

a. OWNERSHIP OF WRITTEN AND SPOKEN WORDS

Baker v. Libbie

Supreme Judicial Court of Massachusetts, 1912.
210 Mass. 599, 97 N.E. 109.

Bill in Equity, filed in the Superior Court on February 17, 1911, by the executor of the will of Mary Baker G. Eddy, late of Concord in the State of New Hampshire, against the members of a firm engaged in business in Boston as auctioneers of books and manuscripts, alleging that a number of private unpublished letters written by the plaintiff's testatrix had come into the possession of the defendants in the course of their business, that the defendants had advertised such letters for public sale in their auction rooms in Boston and already had printed and published material and substantial parts of the letters in their sale catalogue, that the catalogue was being distributed by the defendants, and would be further distributed to the persons in attendance at such auction and that portions of the letters also had been published in the newspapers of Boston, New York and other cities of the country; and praying that the defendants might be enjoined and restrained "from further printing, publishing, selling, circulating, or in any manner making public or showing said letters, or any of them, or any copy or copies, extract or extracts therefrom, or any of them, to any person or persons," and "from further circulating or distributing or making public in any manner copies of said catalogue containing extracts from any of said letters."

The case came on to be heard before Richardson, J., who by agreement of the parties reserved and reported it, upon the bill and answer, and all questions of law therein, for determination by this court.

■ RUGG, C.J. The plaintiff as executor of the will of Mary Baker G. Eddy, the founder of "Christian Science" so called, seeks to restrain an auctioneer of manuscripts from publishing for advertising purposes and from selling certain autographed letters of his testatrix. These letters were written in her own hand by Mrs. Eddy, as is said, "during one of the most interesting periods of her career, that is, just after the first publication of her 'Science and Health with Key to the Scriptures,'" in 1875. It is averred in the answer that the letters have no attribute of literature, but are merely friendly letters written to a cousin about domestic and business affairs. Extracts from the letters show that they refer to household matters, to health and to the work she was doing. The questions raised relate to the existence, extent and character of the proprietary right of the writer of private letters upon indifferent subjects not possessing the qualities of literature and to the degree of protection to be given in equity to such rights as are found to exist. These points have never been presented before for decision in this Commonwealth. The nearest approach was in Tompkins v. Halleck, 133 Mass. 32, 43 Am.Rep. 480, where the rights of an author of a dramatic composition put upon the stage but not printed were protected against a rival presentation made possible by human memory (overruling upon this point the earlier case of Keene v. Kimball, 16 Gray, 545, 77 Am.Dec. 426) and Dodge Co. v. Construction Information Co., 183 Mass. 62, 66 N.E. 204, 60 L.R.A. 810, 97 Am.St.Rep. 412, where property rights in valuable commercial information distributed to subscribers in writing, in print, by telegraph or orally, were recognized and protected against use by a rival concern. Neither of these decisions touches at all closely the points involved in the case at bar.

The rights of the authors of letters of a private or business nature have been the subject of judicial determination in courts in England and this country for a period of at least one hundred and seventy years. The first English case was Pope v. Curl, 2 Atk. 341, which was in 1741. It was a suit by Alexander Pope to restrain the publication of letters written by him to Swift and others. In continuing an injunction Lord Chancellor Hardwicke, after remarking that no distinction could be drawn between letters and books or other learned works, said, "Another objection has been made . . . that where a man writes a letter, it is in the nature of a gift to the receiver. But I am of opinion that it is only a special property in the receiver, possibly the property of the paper may belong to him; but this does not give a license to any person whatsoever to publish them to the world, for at most the receiver has only a joint property with the writer. . . . It has been insisted . . . that this is a sort of work which does not come within the meaning of the act of Parliament [as to copyright], because it contains only letters on familiar subjects, and inquiries after the health of friends, and cannot properly be called a learned work. It is certain that no works have done more service to mankind, than those which have appeared in this shape, upon familiar subjects, and which perhaps were never intended to be published; and it is this [that] makes them so valuable."

Thompson v. Stanhope, 2 Ambl. 737 (1774) was a suit by the executors of Lord Chesterfield to restrain the publication of his now famous letters to his son, which the widow of the latter proposed to print and sell. Some of these possessed literary merit of a high order. Lord Chancellor Apsley was "very clear" that an injunction should be granted, upon the authority of the foregoing decision and the somewhat kindred cases of Forrester v. Waller, cited 4 Burr. 2331, and Webb v. Rose, cited 4 Burr. 2330, where notes and conveyancer's draughts were held to be the literary property of the writer or his representatives, and Duke of Queensbury v. Shebbeare, 2 Eden, 329, where the publication of a part of Lord Clarendon's History by a possessor of the manuscript was restrained.

Gee v. Pritchard, 2 Swanst. 402, 426, was decided by Lord Eldon in 1818. Letters apparently without literary or other special interest by the plaintiff to the son of her husband were the subject of the suit, and publication was restrained on the ground of the property right of the writer. In Lytton v. Devey, 54 L.J. (N.S.) Ch. 293, 295, it was said: "The property in the letters remains in the person to whom they are sent. The right to retain them remains in the person to whom the letters are sent; but the sender of the letters has still that kind of interest, if not property, in the letters that he has a right to restrain any use being made of the communication which he has made in the letters so sent by him." See also Prince Albert v. Strange, 2 DeG. & Sm. 652; S.C. 1 MacN. & G. 25, 43. This same principle was followed expressly in the Irish case of Earl of Granard v. Dunkin, 1 Ball & Beatty, 207, and in Labouchere v. Hess, 77

L.T. (N.S.) Ch. 559. There are several dicta to the same effect by great English judges. For example, Lord Campbell said in Boosey v. Jefferys, 6 Exch. 580, at 583, "A court of equity will grant an injunction to prevent the publication of a letter by a correspondent against the will of the writer. That is a recognition of property in the writer, although he has parted with the manuscript; since he wrote to enable his correspondent to know his sentiments, not to give them to the world." Lord Cairns said, respecting correspondence in Hopkinson v. Burghley, L.R. 2 Ch. 447, at 448: "The writer is supposed to intend that the receiver may use it for any lawful purpose, and it has been held that publication is not such a lawful purpose." See also Jefferys v. Boosey, 4 H.L.Cas. 815, 867, 962. The latest English case on the subject recognizes this as the well settled rule. Philip v. Pennell, [1907] 2 Ch. 577. In 1804 the Scottish court on the suit of his children interdicted the publication of manuscript letters of Robert Burns. Cadell & Davies v. Stewart, 1 Bell's Com. 116 n.

The earliest case in this country, Denis v. Leclerc, 1 Martin O.S., La., 297, arose in 1811. A single letter of no literary pretension was there in question and its publication was enjoined, and the writer's property interest in the letter was distinctly upheld.

The question was elaborately discussed by Mr. Justice Story in Folsom v. Marsh, Fed.Cas.No. 4901, 2 Story 100, 110 [D.Mass.1841], who held that "The author of any letter or letters, (and his representatives), whether they are literary compositions, or familiar letters, or letters of business, possess the sole and exclusive copyright therein; and that no persons, neither those to whom they are addressed, nor other persons, have any right or authority, to publish the same upon their own account, or for their own benefit."

In Bartlett v. Crittenden, Fed.Cas.No. 1076, 5 McLean, 32, at 42 [D.Ohio 1849], Mr. Justice McLean said: "Even the publication of private letters by the person to whom they were addressed, may be enjoined. This is done upon the ground that the writer has a right of property . . . in the purpose for which they were written."

In Woolsey v. Judd, 11 How.Prac. 49, 4 Duer, 379 [N.Y.1855], the question was considered exhaustively, and all the earlier cases were reviewed. The conclusion was reached that the writer of even private letters of no literary value has such a proprietary interest as required a court of equity at his instance to prohibit their publication by the receiver.

Grigsby v. Breckinridge, 2 Bush, Ky., 480 [65 Ky. 481 (1867)], decided that "the recipient of a private letter, sent without any reservation, express or implied, 'held' the general property, qualified only by the incidental right in the author to publish and prevent publication by the recipient, or any other person." . . .

In Barrett v. Fish, 72 Vt. 18, at 20, 47 A. 174, 51 L.R.A. 754, 82 Am.St.Rep. 914 [1899], it was said "that a court of equity will protect the right of property in such [private] letters, by enjoining their unauthorized publication." The same doctrine has been held, either expressly or by way of dictum, in Dock v. Dock, 180 Pa. 14, 22, 36 A. 411, 57 Am.St.Rep. 617 [1897]; Rice v. Williams, 32 F. 437 [E.D.Wisc.1887]; Eyre v. Higbee, 22 How.Pr. 198, 35 Barb. 502 [N.Y.1861]; Palmer v. DeWitt, 47 N.Y. 532, 536, 7 Am.Rep. 480 [1872].

Against these opinions are Wetmore v. Scovell, 3 Edw.Ch. 515 [N.Y.1842], and Hoyt v. Mackenzie, 3 Barb.Ch. 320, 49 Am.Dec. 178 [N.Y.1848]; decided respectively by Vice-Chancellor McCoun and Chancellor Walworth while sitting alone. They were criticised and overruled in Woolsey v. Judd, 11 How.Prac. 49, 4 Duer, 379, by a court of six judges. There are also certain doubtful dicta by a vice-chancellor in Percival v. Phipps, 2 V. & B. 19, 28 [35 Eng.Rep. 225 (1813)], which are relied upon as asserting a somewhat similar view. But it is not necessary to discuss them in detail, for this review of cases demonstrates that the weight of decisions by courts of great authority, speaking often through judges of high distinction for learning and ability, supports the conclusion that equity will afford injunctive relief to the author against the publication of his private letters upon commonplace subjects without regard to their literary merit or the popular attention or special curiosity aroused by them.

The same conclusion is reached on principle and apart from authority. It is generally recognized that one has a right to the fruits of his labor. This is equally true, whether the work be muscular or mental or both combined. Property in literary productions, before publication and while they rest in manuscript, is as plain as property in the game of the hunter or in the grain of the husbandman. The labor of composing letters for private and familiar correspondence may be trifling, or it may be severe, but it is nonetheless the result of an expenditure of thought and time. The market value of such an effort may be measured by the opinions of others, but the fact of property is not created thereby. A canvas upon which an obscure or unskillful painter has toiled does not cease to be property merely because by conventional standards it is valueless as a work of art. Few products of the intellect reveal individual characteristics more surely than familiar correspondence, entries in diaries or other unambitious writings. No sound distinction in this regard can be made between that which has literary merit and that which is without it. Such a distinction could not be drawn with any certainty. While extremes might be discovered, compositions near the dividing line would be subject to no fixed criterion at any given moment, and scarcely anything is more fluctuating than the literary taste of the general public. Even those counted as experts in literature differ widely in opinion both in the same and in successive generations as to the relative merits of different authors. The basic principle on which the right of the author is sustained even as to writings confessedly literature is not their literary quality, but the fact that they are the product of labor.

The existence of a right in the author over his letters, even though private and without worth as literature, is established on principle and authority. The right is property in its essential features. It is, therefore, entitled to all the protection which the Constitution and laws give to property. . . .

The extent of this proprietary right, as between the writer and the recipient of letters, requires a closer analysis. It depends upon implications raised by law from the circumstances. This test is a general one, and has been applied to the public delivery of lectures, the presentation of dramas, and other analogous cases. Abernethy v. Hutchinson, 3 L.J.Ch. 209; S.C. 1 Hall & Tw. 28. Tompkins v. Halleck, 133 Mass. 32, 43 Am.Rep. 480. Nicols v. Pitman, 26 Ch.D. 374, 380. The relative rights of the writer and receiver may vary with different conditions. If there be a request for return or if the correspondence is marked in definite terms, as personal or confidential, such special considerations would need to be regarded. The case at bar presents the ordinary example of friendly correspondence between kinswomen upon topics of mutual private interest. Under such circumstances, what does the writer retain and what does he give to the person to whom the letter is sent? The property right of the author has been described as "an incorporeal right to print [and it should be added to prevent the printing of, if he desires] a set of intellectual ideas or modes of thinking, communicated in a set of words and sentences or modes of expression. It is equally detached from the manuscript, or any other physical existence whatsoever." Millar v. Taylor, 4 Burr. 2303, at 2396. It has been called also "the order of words in the * * * composition." Jefferys v. Boosey, 4 H.L.Cas. 815, 867. Holmes v. Hurst, 174 U.S. 82, 86, 19 S.Ct. 606, 43 L.Ed. 904. Kalem Co. v. Harper Bros., 222 U.S. 55, 63, 32 S.Ct. 20, 56 L.Ed. 92, Ann.Cas. 1913A, 1285. The right of the author to publish or suppress publication of his correspondence is absolute in the absence of special considerations, and is independent of any desire or intent at the time of writing. It is an interest in the intangible and impalpable thought and the particular verbal garments in which it has been clothed. Although independent of the manuscript, this right involves a right to copy or secure copies. Otherwise, the author's right of publication might be lost. The author parts with the physical and material elements which are conveyed by and in the envelope. These are given to the receiver. The paper upon which the letter is written belongs to the receiver. Oliver v. Oliver, 11 C.B. (N.S.) 139. Grigsby v. Breckinridge, 2 Bush, Ky., 480, 486, 92 Am.Dec. 509. Pope v. Curl, 2 Atk. 341. Werckmeister v. American Lithographic Co., 142 F. 827, 830. A duty of preservation would impose an unreasonable burden in most instances. It is obvious that no such obligation rests upon the receiver, and he may destroy or keep at pleasure. Commonly there must be inferred a right of reading or showing to a more or less limited circle of friends and relatives. But in other instances the very nature of the correspondence may be such as to set the seal of secrecy upon its contents. See Kenrick v. Danube Collieries &

Intention matters

Minerals Co., 39 W.R. 473. Letters of extreme affection and other fiduciary communications may come within this class. There may be also a confidential relation existing between the parties, out of which would arise an implied prohibition against any use of the letters, and a breach of such trust might be restrained in equity. On the other hand, the conventional autograph letters by famous persons signify on their face a license to transfer. Equitable rights may exist in the author against one who by fraud, theft or other illegality obtains possession of letters. The precise inquiry is whether indifferent letters written by one at the time perhaps little known or quite unknown which subsequently acquire value as holographic manuscripts, may be marketed as such. This case does not involve personal feelings or what has been termed the right to privacy. 4 Harvard Law Review, 193. The author has deceased. Moreover, there appears to be nothing about these letters, knowledge of which by strangers would violate even delicate feelings. Although the particular form of the expression of the thought remains the property of the writer, the substance and material on which this thought has been expressed have passed to the recipient of the letter. The paper has received the impression of the pen, and the two in combination have been given away. The thing which has value as an autograph is not the intactable thought, but the material substance upon which a particular human hand has been placed, and has traced the intelligible symbols. Perhaps the autographic value of letters may fluctuate in accordance with their length or the nature of their subject matter. But whatever such value may be, in its essence it does not attach to the intellectual but material part of the letter.

This exact question has never been presented for adjudication, so far as we are aware. There are some expressions in opinions, which dissociated from their connection may be laid hold of to support the plaintiff's contention. See Dock v. Dock, 180 Pa. 14, 22, 36 A. 411, 57 Am.St.Rep. 617; Eyre v. Higbee, 22 How.Pr. 198, 35 Barb. 502; Palin v. Gathercole, 1 Collyer, 565. But on principle it seems to flow from the nature of the right transferred by the author to the receiver and of that retained by the writer in ordinary correspondence, that the extent of the latter's proprietary power is to make or to restrain a publication, but not to prevent a transfer. The rule applicable to the facts of this case, as we conceive it to be, is that in the absence of some special limitation imposed either by the subject matter of the letter or the circumstances under which it is sent, the right in the receiver of an ordinary letter is one of unqualified title in the material on which it is written. He can deal with it as absolute owner subject only to the proprietary right retained by the author for himself and his representatives to the publication or non-publication of idea in its particular verbal expression. In this opinion publication has been used in the sense of making public through printing or multiplication of copies.

The result is that an injunction may issue against publication or multiplication in any way, in whole or in part, for advertising or other purposes, of any of the letters described in the bill, and allowing the plaintiff, if he desires, to make copies thereof within a reasonable time, but going no further.

QUESTIONS

1. What new questions does this case present? Why does it matter?

2. Why does the court seek support from "authority" before inquiring whether the writer's claims are justified in "principle"?

3. What kind of authority does the court invoke? How does the court deal with contrary pronouncements?

4. Why do the two prior Massachusetts decisions cited by the court not "touch at all closely the points involved in the case at bar"?

5. How does the court identify the respective rights of the letter writer and the recipient? To the extent that the rights overlap, how does the court resolve the conflict?

6. Why does the court decline to make literary merit a requirement for protection? What does this tell you about the role of judges deciding the common law?

Estate of Hemingway v. Random House, Inc.

Court of Appeals of New York, 1968.
23 N.Y.2d 341, 296 N.Y.S.2d 771, 244 N.E.2d 250.

■ FULD, C.J. On this appeal—involving an action brought by the estate of the late Ernest Hemingway and his widow against the publisher and author of a book, entitled "Papa Hemingway"—we are called upon to decide, primarily, whether conversations of a gifted and highly regarded writer may become the subject of common-law copyright, even though the speaker himself has not reduced his words to writing.

Hemingway died in 1961. During the last 13 years of his life, a close friendship existed between him and A.E. Hotchner, a younger and far less well-known writer. Hotchner, who met Hemingway in the course of writing articles about him became a favored drinking and traveling companion of the famous author, a frequent visitor to his home and the adapter of some of his works for motion pictures and television. During these years, Hemingway's conversation with Hotchner, in which others sometimes took part, was filled with anecdote, reminiscence, literary opinion and revealing comment about actual persons on whom some of Hemingway's fictional characters were based. Hotchner made careful notes of these conversations soon after they occurred, occasionally recording them on a portable tape recorder.

During Hemingway's lifetime, Hotchner wrote and published several articles about his friend in which he quoted some of this talk at length.

Hemingway, far from objecting to this practice, approved of it. Indeed, the record reveals that other writers also quoted Hemingway's conversation without any objection from him, even when he was displeased with the articles themselves.

After Hemingway's death, Hotchner wrote "Papa Hemingway," drawing upon his notes and his recollections, and in 1966 it was published by the defendant Random House. Subtitled "a personal memoir," it is a serious and revealing biographical portrait of the world-renowned writer. Woven through the narrative, and giving the book much of its interest and character, are lengthy quotations from Hemingway's talks as noted or remembered by Hotchner. Included also are two chapters on Hemingway's final illness and suicide in which Hotchner writing of his friend with obvious feeling and sympathy, refers to events, and even to medical information, to which he was privy as an intimate of the family. . . .

The complaint, which seeks an injunction and damages, alleges . . . that "Papa Hemingway" consists, in the main, of literary matter composed by Hemingway in which he had a common-law copyright. . . .

The plaintiffs moved for a preliminary injunction. The motion was denied (49 Misc.2d 726, affd. 25 A.D.2d 719), and the book was thereafter published. After its publication, the defendants sought and were granted summary judgment. The Appellate Division unanimously affirmed the resulting orders and granted the plaintiffs leave to appeal to this court.

[W]e agree with the disposition made below but on a ground more narrow than that articulated by the court at Special Term. It is the position of the plaintiffs . . . that Hemingway was entitled to a common-law copyright on the theory that his directly quoted comment, anecdote and opinion were his "literary creations," his "literary property," and that the defendant Hotchner's note-taking only performed the mechanics of recordation. And, in a somewhat different vein, the plaintiffs argue that "[w]hat for Hemingway was oral one day would be or could become his written manuscript the next day," that his speech, constituting not just a statement of his ideas but the very form in which he conceived and expressed them, was as much the subject of common-law copyright as what he might himself have committed to paper.

Common-law copyright is the term applied to an author's proprietary interest in his literary or artistic creations before they have been made generally available to the public. It enables the author to exercise control over the first publication of his work or to prevent publication entirely—hence, its other name, the "right of first publication." (Chamberlain v. Feldman, 300 N.Y. 135, 139).[1] No cases

---

[1] Although common-law copyright in an unpublished work lasts indefinitely, it is extinguished immediately upon publication of the work by the author. He must then rely, for his protection, upon Federal statutory copyright. (See Nimmer, Copyright, § 11, pp. 38, 42 and ch. 4, p. 183 et seq.) Section 2 of the Copyright Act (U.S.Code, tit. 17) expressly preserves common-law rights in *unpublished* works against any implication that the field is pre-empted

deal directly with the question whether it extends to conversational speech and we begin, therefore, with a brief review of some relevant concepts in this area of law.

It must be acknowledged—as the defendants point out—that nearly a century ago our court stated that common-law copyright extended to " '[e]very new and innocent product of mental labor which has been *embodied in writing, or some other material form* '". (Palmer v. De Witt, 47 N.Y. 532, 537; emphasis supplied.) And, more recently, it has been said that "an author has no property right in his ideas unless * * * given embodiment in a tangible form." (O'Brien v. RKO Radio Pictures, 68 F.Supp. 13, 14.) However, as a *noted scholar* in the field has observed, "the underlying rationale for common law copyright (*i.e.*, the recognition that a property status should attach to the fruits of intellectual labor) is applicable regardless of whether such labor assumes tangible form" (Nimmer, Copyright, § 11.1, p. 40). The principle that it is not the tangible embodiment of the author's work but the creation of the work itself which is protected finds recognition in a number of ways in copyright law.

One example, with some relevance to the problem before us, is the treatment which the law has accorded to personal letters—a kind of half-conversation in written form. Although the paper upon which the letter is written belongs to the recipient, it is the author who has the right to publish them or to prevent their publication. (See Baker v. Libbie, 210 Mass. 599, 605, 606.) In the words of the Massachusetts court in the *Baker* case (210 Mass., at pp. 605–606), the author's right "is an interest in the intangible and impalpable thought and the particular verbal garments in which it has been clothed." Nor has speech itself been entirely without protection against reproduction for publication. The public delivery of an address or a lecture or the performance of a play is not deemed a "publication," and, accordingly, it does not deprive the author of his common-law copyright in its contents. (See Ferris v. Frohman, 223 U.S. 424; King v. Mister Maestro, Inc., 224 F.Supp. 101, 106; Palmer v. De Witt, 47 N.Y. 532, 543, supra; see, also, Nimmer, Copyright, § 53, p. 208.)

Letters, however—like plays and public addresses, written or not—have distinct, identifiable boundaries and they are, in most cases, only occasional products. Whatever difficulties attend the formulation of suitable rules for the enforcement of rights in such works (see, e.g., Note, Personal Letters: In Need of a Law of Their Own, 44 Iowa L.Rev. 705), they are relatively manageable. However, conversational speech, the distinctive behavior of man, is quite another matter, and subjecting any

---

by the Federal statute. [While the court's statements with respect to common law copyright in unpublished works were accurate when this opinion was written, the Copyright Act of 1976 made unpublished, as well as published, works of authorship exclusively subject to Federal statutory protection. See Act of Oct. 19, 1976, Pub.L. No. 94–553, 90 Stat. 2541.—Ed.].

part of it to the restraints of common-law copyright presents unique problems.

One such problem—and it was stressed by the court at Special Term (SCHWEITZER, J.)[2]—is that of avoiding undue restraints on the freedoms of speech and press and, in particular, on the writers of history and of biographical works of the genre of Boswell's "Life of Johnson". The safeguarding of essential freedoms in this area is, though, not without its complications. The indispensable right of the press to report on what people have *done,* or on what has *happened* to them or on what they have *said in public* (see Time, Inc. v. Hill, 385 U.S. 374; Curtis Pub. Co. v. Butts, 388 U.S. 130; Associated Press v. Walker, 388 U.S. 130) does not necessarily imply an unbounded freedom to publish whatever they may have *said in private conversation,* any more than it implies a freedom to copy and publish what people may have put down in *private writings.*

Copyright, both common-law and statutory, rests on the assumption that there are forms of expression, limited in kind, to be sure, which should not be divulged to the public without the consent of their author. The purpose, far from being restrictive, is to encourage and protect intellectual labor. (See Note, Copyright: Right to Common Law Copyright in Conversation of a Decedent, 67 Col.L.Rev. 366, 367, commenting on the decision denying the plaintiffs before us a preliminary injunction, 49 Misc.2d 726.) The essential thrust of the First Amendment is to prohibit improper restraints on the *voluntary* public expression of ideas; it shields the man who wants to speak or publish when others wish him to be quiet. There is necessarily, and within suitably defined areas, a concomitant freedom *not* to speak publicly, one which serves the same ultimate end as freedom of speech in its affirmative aspect.

The rules of common-law copyright assure this freedom in the case of written material. However, speech is now easily captured by electronic devices and, consequently, we should be wary about excluding all possibility of protecting a speaker's right to decide when his words, uttered in private dialogue, may or may not be published at large. Conceivably, there may be limited and special situations in which an interlocutor brings forth oral statements from another party which both understand to be the unique intellectual product of the principal speaker, a product which would qualify for common-law copyright if such statements were in writing. Concerning such problems, we express no opinion; we do no more than raise the questions, leaving them open for future consideration in cases which may present them more sharply than this one does.

---

[2] Another problem—also remarked by the court—is the difficulty of measuring the relative self-sufficiency of any one party's contributions to a conversation, although it may be, in the case of some kinds of dialogue or interview, that the difficulty would not be greater than in deciding other questions of degree, such as plagiarism. (See, e.g., Nichols v. Universal Pictures Corp., 45 F.2d 119.)

On the appeal before us, the plaintiffs' claim to common-law copyright may be disposed of more simply and on a more narrow ground.

The defendant Hotchner asserts—without contradiction in the papers before us—that Hemingway never suggested to him or to anyone else that he regarded his conversational remarks to be "literary creations" or that he was of a mind to restrict Hotchner's use of the notes and recordings which Hemingway knew him to be accumulating. On the contrary, as we have already observed, it had become a continuing practice, during Hemingway's lifetime, for Hotchner to write articles about Hemingway, consisting largely of quotations from the latter's conversation—and of all of this Hemingway approved. In these circumstances, authority to publish must be implied, thus negativing the reservation of any common-law copyright.

Assuming, without deciding, that in a proper case a common-law copyright in certain limited kinds of spoken dialogue might be recognized, it would, at the very least, be required that the speaker indicate that he intended to mark off the utterance in question from the ordinary stream of speech, that he meant to adopt it as a unique statement and that he wished to exercise control over its publication. In the conventional common-law copyright situation, this indication is afforded by the creation of the manuscript itself. It would have to be evidenced in some other way if protection were ever to be accorded to some forms of conversational dialogue.

Such an indication is, of course, possible in the case of speech. It might, for example, be found in prefatory words or inferred from the circumstances in which the dialogue takes place.[3] Another way of formulating such a rule might be to say that, although, in the case of most intellectual products, the courts are reluctant to find that an author has "published," so as to lose his common-law copyright (see Nimmer, Copyright, § 58.2, pp. 226–228), in the case of conversational speech,— because of its unique nature—there should be a presumption that the speaker has not reserved any common-law rights unless the contrary strongly appears. However, we need not carry such speculation further in the present case since the requisite conditions are plainly absent here.

For present purposes, it is enough to observe that Hemingway's words and conduct, far from making any such reservation, left no doubt of his willingness to permit Hotchner to draw freely on their conversation in writing about him and to publish such material. . . . It follows, therefore, that the courts below were eminently correct in dismissing the . . . cause of action.

---

[3]   This was the situation in Jenkins v. News Syndicate Co. (128 Misc. 284). The plaintiff alleged that she had had a conference with a newspaper editor in which she described in detail the proposed content of some articles she was requested to write. Later, she decided not to write them and the newspaper thereupon published an "interview" with her, precisely quoting much of her conversation with the editor. The court held that she had stated a cause of action for damages on the theory of common-law copyright.

In brief, then, it is our conclusion that, since no triable issues have been raised, the courts below very properly dismissed the complaint.

The orders appealed from should be affirmed, with costs.

■ JUDGES BURKE, SCILEPPI, BERGAN, KEATING, BREITEL and JASEN concur.

Orders affirmed.

QUESTIONS

1. What new questions does this case present? Are they any newer than those presented in *Baker v. Libbie*?

2. What use does the New York Court of Appeals make of *Baker v. Libbie*?

3. Why does the Court of Appeals in *Hemingway* resolve the case on a narrower ground than that invoked by the lower court?

4. What *is* the court's disposition of the case?

b. THE RIGHT OF PRIVACY

Roberson v. Rochester Folding Box Co.

Court of Appeals of New York, 1902.
171 N.Y. 538, 64 N.E. 442.

■ PARKER, C.J. The Appellate Division has certified that the following questions of law have arisen in this case, and ought to be reviewed by this court: 1. Does the complaint herein state a cause of action at law against the defendants or either of them? 2. Does the complaint herein state a cause of action in equity against the defendants or either of them? These questions are presented by a demurrer to the complaint, which is put upon the ground that the complaint does not state facts sufficient to constitute a cause of action. . . .

The complaint alleges that the Franklin Mills Co., one of the defendants, was engaged in a general milling business and in the manufacture and sale of flour; that before the commencement of the action, without the knowledge or consent of plaintiff, defendants, knowing that they had no right or authority so to do, had obtained, made, printed, sold and circulated about 25,000 lithographic prints, photographs and likenesses of plaintiff, made in a manner particularly set up in the complaint; that upon the paper upon which the likenesses were printed and above the portrait there were printed, in large, plain letters, the words, "Flour of the Family," and below the portrait in large capital letters, "Franklin Mills Flour," and in the lower right-hand corner in smaller capital letters, "Rochester Folding Box Co., Rochester, N.Y.;" that upon the same sheet were other advertisements of the flour of the Franklin Mills Co.; that those 25,000 likenesses of the plaintiff thus ornamented have been conspicuously posted and displayed in stores, warehouses, saloons and other public places; that they have been recognized by friends of the plaintiff and other people with the result that plaintiff has been greatly humiliated by the scoffs and jeers of persons who have recognized her face and picture on this advertisement and her good name has been attacked, causing her great distress and suffering both in body and mind; that she was made sick and suffered a severe nervous shock, was confined to her bed and compelled to employ a physician, because of these facts; that defendants had continued to print, make, use, sell and circulate the said lithographs, and that by reason of the foregoing facts plaintiff had suffered damages in the sum of $15,000. The complaint prays that defendants be enjoined from making, printing, publishing, circulating or using in any manner any likenesses of plaintiff in any form whatever, for further relief (which it is not necessary to consider here) and for damages.

It will be observed that there is no complaint made that plaintiff was libeled by this publication of her portrait. The likeness is said to be a very good one, and one that her friends and acquaintances were able to recognize; indeed, her grievance is that a good portrait of her, and, therefore, one easily recognized has been used to attract attention toward the paper upon which defendant mill company's advertisements appear. Such publicity, which some find agreeable, is to plaintiff very distasteful, and thus, because of defendants' impertinence in using her picture without her consent for their own business purposes, she has been caused to suffer mental distress where others would have appreciated the compliment to their beauty implied in the selection of the picture for such purposes; but as it is distasteful to her, she seeks the aid of the courts to enjoin a further circulation of the lithographic prints containing her portrait made as alleged in the complaint, and as an incident thereto, to reimburse her for the damages to her feelings, which the complaint fixes at the sum of $15,000.

There is no precedent for such an action to be found in the decisions of this court; indeed the learned judge who wrote the very able and interesting opinion in the Appellate Division said, while upon the threshold of the discussion of the question: "It may be said in the first place that the theory upon which this action is predicated is new, at least in instance if not in principle, and that few precedents can be found to sustain the claim made by the plaintiff, if indeed it can be said that there are any authoritative cases establishing her right to recover in this action." Nevertheless, that court reached the conclusion that plaintiff had a good cause of action against defendants, in that defendants had invaded what is called a "right of privacy"—in other words, the right to be let alone. Mention of such a right is not to be found in Blackstone, Kent or any other of the great commentators upon the law, nor so far as the learning of counsel or the courts in this case have been able to discover, does its existence seem to have been asserted prior to the year 1890, when it was presented with attractiveness and no inconsiderable ability in the Harvard Law Review (Vol. IV., page 193) in an article entitled, "The Right of Privacy."

The so-called right of privacy is, as the phrase suggests, founded upon the claim that a man has the right to pass through this world, if he wills, without having his picture published, his business enterprises discussed, his successful experiments written up for the benefit of others, or his eccentricities commented upon either in handbills, circulars, catalogues, periodicals or newspapers, and, necessarily, that the things which may not be written and published of him must not be spoken of him by his neighbors, whether the comment be favorable or otherwise. While most persons would much prefer to have a good likeness of themselves appear in a responsible periodical or leading newspaper rather than upon an advertising card or sheet, the doctrine which the courts are asked to create for this case would apply as well to the one publication as to the other, for the principle which a court of equity is asked to assert in support of a recovery in this action is that the right of privacy exists and is enforceable in equity, and that the publication of that which purports to be a portrait of another person, even if obtained upon the street by an impertinent individual with a camera, will be restrained in equity on the ground that an individual has the right to prevent his features from becoming known to those outside of his circle of friends and acquaintances.

If such a principle be incorporated into the body of the law through the instrumentality of a court of equity, the attempts to logically apply the principle will necessarily result, not only in a vast amount of litigation, but in litigation bordering upon the absurd, for the right of privacy, once established as a legal doctrine, cannot be confined to the restraint of the publication of a likeness but must necessarily embrace as well the publication of a word-picture, a comment upon one's looks, conduct, domestic relations or habits. And were the right of privacy once legally asserted, it would necessarily be held to include the same things if spoken instead of printed, for one, as well as the other, invades the right to be absolutely let alone. An insult would certainly be in violation of such a right and with many persons would more seriously wound the feelings than would the publication of their picture. And so we might add to the list of things that are spoken and done day by day which seriously offend the sensibilities of good people to which the principle which the plaintiff seeks to have imbedded in the doctrine of the law would seem to apply. I have gone only far enough to barely suggest the vast field of litigation which would necessarily be opened up should this court hold that privacy exists as a legal right enforceable in equity by injunction, and by damages where they seem necessary to give complete relief.

The legislative body could very well interfere and arbitrarily provide that no one should be permitted for his own selfish purpose to use the picture or the name of another for advertising purposes without his consent. In such event, no embarrassment would result to the general body of the law, for the rule would be applicable only to cases provided for by the statute. The courts, however, being without authority to legislate, are required to decide cases upon principle, and so are necessarily embarrassed by precedents created by an extreme, and, therefore, unjustifiable application of an old principle.

The court below properly said that "while it may be true that the fact that no precedent can be found to sustain an action in any given case, is cogent evidence that a principle does not exist upon which the right may be based, it is not the rule that the want of a precedent is a sufficient reason for turning the plaintiff out of court," provided—I think should be added—there can be found a clear and unequivocal principle of the common law which either directly or mediately governs it or which by analogy or parity of reasoning ought to govern it.

The case that seems to have been more relied upon than any other by the learned Appellate Division in reaching the conclusion that the complaint in this case states a cause of action is Schuyler v. Curtis, 147 N.Y. 434, 31 L.R.A. 286, 49 Am.St. 671. In that case certain persons attempted to erect a statue or bust of a woman no longer living, and one of her relatives commenced an action in equity to restrain such erection, alleging that his feelings and the feelings of other relatives of deceased would be injured thereby. At Special Term an injunction was granted on that ground. 19 N.Y.Supp. 264. The General Term affirmed the decision. 64 Hun, 594. This court reversed the judgment, Judge Peckham writing, and so far as the decision is concerned, therefore, it is not authority for the existence of a right of privacy which entitles a party to restrain another from doing an act which, though not actionable at common law, occasions plaintiff mental distress. In the course of the argument, however, expressions were used which it is now claimed indicate that the court recognized the existence of such a right. A sufficient answer to that contention is to be found in the opinion written on the motion for reargument in Colonial City Tr. Co. v. Kingston City R. Co., 154 N.Y. 493, in which it was said: "It was not our intention to decide any case but the one before us. . . . If, as sometimes happens, broader statements were made by way of argument or otherwise than were essential to the decision of the questions presented, they are the dicta of the writer of the opinion and not the decision of the court. A judicial opinion, like evidence, is only binding so far as it is relevant, and when it wanders from the point at issue it no longer has force as an official utterance." The question up for decision in the Schuyler case was whether the relatives could restrain the threatened action of defendants, and not whether Mrs. Schuyler could have restrained it had she been living. The latter question not being before the court it was not called upon to decide it, and, as we read the opinion, there is no expression in it which indicates an intention either to decide it or to seriously consider it, but rather, it proceeds upon the assumption that if such a right did exist in Mrs. Schuyler, her relatives did not succeed to it upon her death; all of which will sufficiently appear from the following extracts from the opinion:

"This action is of a nature somewhat unusual and dependent for its support upon the application of certain principles which are themselves not very clearly defined or their boundaries very well recognized or plainly laid down. Briefly described, the action is founded upon the alleged violation of what is termed the right of privacy."

"It is not necessary, however, to the view which we take of this case, to lay down precise and accurate rules which shall apply to all cases touching upon this alleged right."

"For the purposes we have in view, it is unnecessary to wholly deny the existence of the right of privacy to which the plaintiff appeals as the foundation of his cause of action."

"While not assuming to decide what this right of privacy is in all cases, we are quite clear that such a right would not be violated by the proposed action of the defendants."

There are two other cases in this state bearing upon this question: Marks v. Jaffa, 26 N.Y.Supp. 908, decided at Special Term, and Murray v. Gast Lithographic & Engraving Co., 8 Misc.Rep. 36, 28 N.Y.Supp. 271, decided at an Equity Term of the Court of Common Pleas at New York. In the first case the relief prayed for was granted upon the authority of the decision of the General Term in the *Schuyler* case, which was subsequently reversed in this court. In the *Murray* case, in a well-reasoned opinion by Judge Bischoff, it is held that a parent cannot maintain an action to enjoin an unauthorized publication of the portrait of an infant child, and for damages for injuries to his sensibilities caused by the invasion of his child's privacy, because "the law takes no cognizance of a sentimental injury, independent of a wrong to person or property." In the course of his opinion he quotes from the opinion of Lumpkin, J., in Chapman v. West. U.T. Co., 88 Ga. 763, 30 Am.St. 183, 17 L.R.A. 430, as follows: "The law protects the person and the purse. The person includes the reputation. The body, reputation and property of the citizen are not to be invaded without responsibility in damages to the sufferer. But, outside these protected spheres, the law does not yet attempt to guard the peace of mind, the feelings or the happiness of everyone by giving recovery of damages for mental anguish produced by mere negligence. There is no right, capable of enforcement by process of law, to possess or maintain, without disturbance, any particular condition of feeling. The law leaves feeling to be helped and vindicated by the tremendous force of sympathy. The temperaments of individuals are various and variable, and the imagination exerts a powerful and incalculable influence in injuries of this kind. There are many moral obligations too delicate and subtle to be enforced in the rude way of giving money compensation for their violation. Perhaps the feelings find as full protection as it is possible to give in moral law and a responsive public opinion. The civil law is a practical business system, dealing with what is tangible, and does not undertake to redress psychological injuries."

Outside of this jurisdiction the question seems to have been presented in two other cases in this country: Corliss v. E.W. Walker Co., 57 Fed. 434; 64 Fed. 280, 31 L.R.A. 283, and Atkinson v. Doherty, 121 Mich. 372, 80 Am.St.Rep. 507, 46 L.R.A. 219. The *Corliss* case was an action in equity to restrain the publication of the biography and picture of Mr. Corliss. It was based upon an alleged invasion of the right of privacy. The court denied the injunction as to the publication of the biography but granted it as to the use of certain plates from which the defendant was to make a picture of Mr. Corliss, upon the ground that they had been obtained upon conditions which defendant had not complied with. In the course of the opinion the court said: "Under our laws one can speak and publish what he desires, provided he commit no offense against public morals or private reputation. . . . There is another objection which meets us at the threshold of this case. The subject-matter of the jurisdiction of a court of equity is civil property, and injury to property, whether actual or prospective is the foundation on which its jurisdiction rests. In re Sawyer, 124 U.S. 200, 210, 31 L.Ed. 402; Kerr, Inj. (2d ed.) p. 1. It follows from this principle that a court of equity has no power to restrain a libelous publication." Both the opinion and the decision necessarily negative the existence of an actionable right of privacy; but subsequently upon a motion to dissolve the injunction, which was granted upon the ground that Mr. Corliss was a public character, and hence the publishers were entitled to use his picture, the learned court expressed the opinion that a private individual has the right to be protected from the publication of his portrait in any form. Now, while this suggestion was obiter, it merits discussion, and an examination of that which it promulgates as doctrine discloses what we deem a fatal objection to the establishment of a rule of privacy. The learned judge says: "I believe the law to be that a private individual has a right to be protected in the representation of his portrait in any form; that this is a property as well as a personal right, and that it belongs to the same class of rights which forbids the reproduction of a private manuscript or painting, or the publication of private letters, or of oral lectures delivered by a teacher to his class, or the revelation of the contents of a merchant's book by a clerk. . . . But, while the right of a private individual to prohibit the reproduction of his picture or photograph should be recognized and enforced, this right may be surrendered or dedicated to the public by the act of the individual, just the same as a private manuscript, book or painting becomes (when not protected by copyright) public property by the act of publication. The distinction in the case of a picture or photograph lies, it seems to me, between public and private characters. A private individual should be protected against the publication of any portrait of himself, but where an individual becomes a public character the case is different. A statesman, author, artist or inventor, who asks for and desires public recognition, may be said to have surrendered his right to the public." This distinction between public and private characters cannot possibly be drawn. On what principle does an author or artist forfeit his right of privacy and a great orator, a great preacher, or a great advocate retain his? Who can draw a line of demarcation between public characters and private characters, let that line be as wavering and irregular as you please? In the very case then before the judge, what had Mr. Corliss done by which he surrendered his right of privacy? In what respect did he by his inventions "ask for and desire public recognition" any more than a banker or merchant who prosecutes his calling? Or is the right of privacy the possession of mediocrity alone, which a person forfeits by giving rein to his ability, spurs to his industry or grandeur to his character? A lady may pass her life in domestic privacy when, by some act of heroism or self-sacrifice, her name and fame fill the public ear. Is she to forfeit by her good deed the right of privacy she previously possessed? These considerations suggest the answer we would make to the position of the learned judge and at the same time serve to make more clear what we have elsewhere attempted to point out, namely, the absolute impossibility of dealing with this subject save by legislative enactment, by which may be drawn arbitrary distinctions which no court should promulgate as a part of general jurisprudence.

Atkinson v. Doherty was a suit in equity brought by the widow of Colonel John Atkinson, a well-known lawyer in Detroit, to enjoin the defendant, a cigar manufacturer, from using the name and portrait of Colonel Atkinson upon boxes of cigars manufactured by defendant. The suit was dismissed by the Circuit Court, and its decree was unanimously affirmed by the Supreme Court. The case quite closely resembles the *Schuyler* case, which was brought to the attention of that court, and in the course of the opinion the contention that the *Schuyler* case intimated the existence of a right of privacy was met as follows: "We think it should not be considered as containing a dictum even in support of the doctrine contended for." The method adopted by the court in the *Atkinson* case in treating the question was different from that employed by this court in the *Schuyler* case, however, for the opinion proceeds to a review of the authorities upon which the right of privacy is said to rest, reaching the conclusion that all of the authorities which are entitled to respect are based upon property or contract rights, and hence "that Colonel Atkinson would himself be remediless were he alive, and the same is true of his friends who survive." The opinion concludes as follows: "This law of privacy seems to have gained a foothold at one time in the history of our jurisprudence—not by that name, it is true—but in effect. It is evidenced by the old maxim, 'the greater the truth the greater the libel,' and the result has been the emphatic expression of public disapproval, by the emancipation of the press and the establishment of freedom of speech, and the abolition in most of the states of the maxim quoted by constitutional provisions. The limitations upon the exercise of these rights being the law of slander and libel, whereby the publication of an untruth that can be presumed or shown to the satisfaction, not of the plaintiff, but of others (*i.e.*, an impartial jury), to be injurious, not alone to the feelings, but to the reputation, is actionable. Should it be thought that it is a hard rule that is applied in this case, it is only necessary to call attention to the fact that a ready remedy is to be found in legislation. We are not satisfied, however, that the rule is a hard one, and think that the consensus of opinion must be that the complainants contend for a much harder one. The law does not remedy all evils. It cannot, in the nature of things; and deliberation may well be used in considering the propriety of an innovation such as this case suggests. We do not wish to be understood as belittling the complaint. We have no reason to doubt the feeling of annoyance alleged. Indeed, we sympathize with it, and marvel at the impertinence which does not respect it. We can only say that it is one of the ills that under the law cannot be redressed."

An examination of the authorities leads us to the conclusion that the so-called "right of privacy" has not as yet found an abiding place in our jurisprudence, and, as we view it, the doctrine cannot now be incorporated without doing violence to settled principles of law by which the profession and the public have long been guided.

The judgment of the Appellate Division and of the Special Term should be reversed and questions certified answered in the negative, without costs, and with leave to the plaintiff to serve an amended complaint within twenty days, also without costs.

■ GRAY, J., dissenting.

These defendants stand before the court, admitting that they have made, published and circulated, without the knowledge or the authority of the plaintiff, 25,000 lithographic portraits of her, for the purpose of profit and gain to themselves; that these portraits have been conspicuously posted in stores, warehouses and saloons, in the vicinity of the plaintiff's residence and throughout the United States, as advertisements of their goods; that the effect has been to humiliate her and to render her ill and, yet, claiming that she makes out no cause of action. They say that no law on the statute books gives her a right of action and that her right to privacy is not an actionable right, at law or in equity.

Our consideration of the question thus presented has not been foreclosed by the decision in Schuyler v. Curtis, 147 N.Y. 434, 49 Am.St.Rep. 671, 31 L.R.A. 286. In that case, it appeared that the defendants were intending to make, and to exhibit, at the Columbian Exposition of 1893, a statue of Mrs. Schuyler, formerly Miss Mary M. Hamilton and conspicuous in her lifetime for her philanthropic work, to typify "Woman as the Philanthropist" and, as a companion piece, a statute of Miss Susan B. Anthony, to typify the "Representative Reformer." The plaintiff, in behalf of himself, as the nephew of Mrs. Schuyler, and of other immediate relatives, sought by the action to restrain them from carrying out their intentions as to the statue of Mrs. Schuyler; upon the grounds, in substance, that they were proceeding without his consent, (whose relationship was conceded to be such as to warrant such an action, if it were maintainable at all), or that of the other immediate members of the family; that their proceeding was disagreeable to him, because it would have been disagreeable and obnoxious to his aunt, if living, and that it was annoying to have Mrs. Schuyler's memory associated with principles, which Miss Susan B. Anthony typified and of which Mrs. Schuyler did not approve. His right to maintain the action was denied and the denial was expressly placed upon the ground that he, as a relative, did not represent any right of privacy which Mrs. Schuyler possessed in her lifetime and that, whatever her right had been, in that respect, it died with her. The existence of the individual's right to be protected against the invasion of his privacy, if not actually affirmed in the opinion, was, very certainly, far from being denied. "It may be admitted," Judge Peckham observed, when delivering the opinion of the court, "that courts have power, in some cases, to enjoin the doing of an act, where the nature, or character, of the act itself is well calculated to wound the sensibilities of an individual, and where the doing of the act is wholly unjustifiable, and is, in legal contemplation, a wrong, even though the existence of no property, as that term is usually used, is involved in the subject."

That the individual has a right to privacy, which he can enforce and which equity will protect against the invasion of, is a proposition which is not opposed by any decision in this court and which, in my opinion, is within the field of accepted legal principles. It is within the very case supposed by Judge Peckham in Schuyler v. Curtis. In the present case, we may not say that the plaintiff's complaint is fanciful, or that her alleged injury is, purely, a sentimental one. Her objection to the defendants' acts is not one born of caprice; nor is it based upon the defendants' act being merely "distasteful" to her. We are bound to assume, and I find no difficulty in doing so, that the conspicuous display of her likeness, in various public places, has so humiliated her by the notoriety and by the public comments it has provoked, as to cause her distress and suffering, in body and in mind, and to confine her to her bed with illness.

If it were necessary, to be entitled to equitable relief, that the plaintiff's sufferings, by reason of the defendants' acts, should be serious, and appreciable by a pecuniary standard, clearly, we might well say, under the allegations of the complaint, that they were of such degree of gravity. However, I am not of the opinion that the gravity of the injury need be such as to be capable of being estimated by such a standard. If the right of privacy exists and this complaint makes out a case of its substantial violation, I think that the award of equitable relief, by way of an injunction, preventing the continuance of its invasion by the defendants, will not depend upon the complainant's ability to prove substantial pecuniary damages and, if the court finds the defendants' act to be without justification and for selfish gain and purposes, and to be of such a character, as is reasonably calculated to wound the feelings and to subject the plaintiff to the ridicule, or to the contempt of others, that her right to the preventive relief of equity will follow; without considering how far her sufferings may be measurable by a pecuniary standard.

The right of privacy, or the right of the individual to be let alone, is a personal right, which is not without judicial recognition. It is the complement of the right to the immunity of one's person. The individual has always been entitled to be protected in the exclusive use and enjoyment of that which is his own. The common law regarded his person and property as inviolate, and he has the absolute right to be let alone. Cooley, Torts, p. 29. The principle is fundamental and essential in organized society that every one, in exercising a personal right and in the use of his property, shall respect the rights and properties of others. He must so conduct himself, in the enjoyment of the rights and privileges which belong to him as a member of society, as that he shall prejudice no one in the possession and enjoyment of those which are exclusively his. When, as here, there is an alleged invasion of some personal right, or privilege, the absence of exact precedent and the fact that early commentators upon the common law have no discussion upon the subject are of no material importance in awarding equitable relief. That the exercise of the preventive power of a court of equity is demanded in a novel case, is not a fatal objection. Niagara Falls Int. Bridge Co. v. Great Western Ry. Co., 39 Barb. 212; Sherman v. Skuse, 166 N.Y. 352; Hamilton v. Whitridge, 11 Md. 145, 69 Am.Dec. 184. In the social evolution, with the march of the arts and sciences and in the resultant effects upon organized society, it is quite intelligible that new conditions must arise in personal relations, which the rules of the common law, cast in the rigid mould of an earlier social status, were not designed to meet. It would be a reproach to equitable jurisprudence, if equity were powerless to extend the application of the principles of common law, or of natural justice, in remedying a wrong, which, in the progress of civilization, has been made possible as the result of new social, or commercial conditions.

Instantaneous photography is a modern invention and affords the means of securing a portraiture of an individual's face and form, in invitum their owner. While, so far forth as it merely does that, although a species of aggression, I concede it to be an irremediable and irrepressible feature of the social evolution. But, if it is to be permitted that the portraiture may be put to commercial, or other, uses for gain, by the publication of prints therefrom, then an act of invasion of the individual's privacy results, possibly more formidable and more painful in its consequences, than an actual bodily assault might be. Security of person is as necessary as the security of property; and for that complete personal security, which will result in the peaceful and wholesome enjoyment of one's privileges as a member of society, there should be afforded protection, not only against the scandalous portraiture and display of one's features and person, but against the display and use thereof for another's commercial purposes or gain. The proposition is, to me, an inconceivable one that these defendants may, unauthorizedly, use the likeness of this young woman upon their advertisement, as a method of attracting widespread public attention to their wares, and that she must submit to the mortifying notoriety, without right to invoke the exercise of the preventive power of a court of equity.

Such a view, as it seems to me, must have been unduly influenced by a failure to find precedents in analogous cases, or some declaration by the great commentators upon the law of a common-law principle which would, precisely, apply to and govern the action; without taking into consideration that, in the existing state of society, new conditions affecting the relations of persons demand the broader extension of those legal principles, which underlie the immunity of one's person from attack. I think that such a view is unduly restricted, too, by a search for some property, which has been invaded by the defendants' acts. Property is not, necessarily, the thing itself, which is owned; it is the right of the owner in relation to it. The right to be protected in one's possession of a thing, or in one's privileges, belonging to him as an individual, or secured to him as a member of the commonwealth, is property, and as such entitled to the protection of the law. The protective power of equity is not exercised upon the tangible thing, but upon the right to enjoy it; and, so, it is called forth for the protection of the right to that which is one's exclusive possession, as a property right. It seems to me that the principle, which is applicable, is analogous to that upon which courts of equity have interfered to protect the right of privacy, in cases of private writings, or of other unpublished products of the mind. The writer, or the lecturer, has been protected in his right to a literary property in a letter, or a lecture, against its unauthorized publication; because it is property, to which the right of privacy attaches. Woolsey v. Judd, 4 Duer, 399; Gee v. Pritchard, 2 Swanst. 402; Abernathy v. Hutchinson, 3 L.J.Ch. 209; Folsom v. Marsh, 2 Story, 100. I think that this plaintiff has the same property in the right to be protected against the use of her face for defendants' commercial purposes, as she would have, if they were publishing her literary compositions. The right would be conceded, if she had sat for her photograph; but if her face, or her portraiture, has a value, the value is hers exclusively; until the use be granted away to the public. Any other principle of decision, in my opinion, is as repugnant to equity, as it is shocking to reason.

The right to grant the injunction does not depend upon the existence of property, which one has in some contractual form. It depends upon the existence of property in any right which belongs to a person. In Pollard v. Photographic Co., 40 Ch.Div. 345, it was held that the right to grant an injunction against selling copies of plaintiff's photographs did not depend upon the existence of property and that "it is quite clear that independently of any question as to the right at law, the Court of Chancery always had an original and independent jurisdiction to prevent what that court considered and treated as a wrong, whether arising from a violation of an unquestionable right, or from breach of confidence, or contract, as was pointed out by Lord Cottenham in Prince Albert v. Strange, 1 Macn. & G. 25." In Prince Albert v. Strange, Lord Chancellor Cottenham sustained the issuance of an injunction, upon the ground that the right of privacy had been invaded by the publication and sale of etchings, made by Prince Albert and Queen Victoria. Upon the original hearing, Vice-Chancellor Knight-Bruce, in granting the injunction, observed that, "upon the principle of protecting property, it is that the common law, in cases not aided or prejudiced by statute, shelters the privacy and seclusion of thoughts and sentiments committed to writing, and desired by the author to remain not generally known."

It would be, in my opinion, an extraordinary view which, while conceding the right of a person to be protected against the unauthorized circulation of an unpublished lecture, letter, drawing, or other ideal property, yet, would deny the same protection to a person, whose portrait was unauthorizedly obtained, and made use of, for commercial purposes. The injury to the plaintiff is irreparable; because she cannot be wholly compensated in damages for the various consequences entailed by defendants' acts. The only complete relief is an injunction restraining their continuance. Whether, as incidental to that equitable relief, she should be able to recover only nominal damages is not material; for the issuance of the injunction does not, in such a case, depend upon the amount of the damages in dollars and cents.

A careful consideration of the question presented upon this appeal leads me to the conclusion that the judgment appealed from should be affirmed.

■ O'BRIEN, CULLEN and WERNER, JJ., concur with PARKER, CH.J.; BARTLETT and HAIGHT, JJ., concur with GRAY, J.

Judgment reversed, etc.

Pavesich v. New England Life Insurance Co.

Supreme Court of Georgia, 1905.
122 Ga. 190, 50 S.E. 68.

Paolo Pavesich brought an action against the New England Mutual Life Insurance Company, a non-resident corporation, Thomas B. Lumpkin, its general agent, and J.Q. Adams, a photographer, both residing in the city of Atlanta. The allegations of the petition were, in substance, as follows: In an issue of the Atlanta Constitution, a newspaper published in the city of Atlanta, there appeared a likeness of the plaintiff, which would be easily recognized by his friends and acquaintances, placed by the side of the likeness of an ill-dressed and sickly looking person. Above the likeness of the plaintiff were the words, "Do it now. The man who did." Above the likeness of the other person were the words, "Do it while you can. The man who didn't." Below the two pictures were the words, "These two pictures tell their own story." Under the plaintiff's picture the following appeared: "In my healthy and productive period of life I bought insurance in the New England Mutual Life Insurance Co., of Boston, Mass., and to-day my family is protected and I am drawing an annual dividend on my paid-up policies." Under the other person's picture was a statement to the effect that he had not taken insurance, and now realized his mistake. The statements were signed, "Thomas B. Lumpkin, General Agent." The picture of the plaintiff was taken from a negative obtained by the defendant Lumpkin, or someone by him authorized, from the defendant Adams, which was used with his consent and with knowledge of the purpose for which it was to be used. The picture was made from the negative without the plaintiff's consent, at the instance of the defendant insurance company, through its agent Lumpkin. Plaintiff is an artist by profession, and the publication is peculiarly offensive to him. The statement attributed to plaintiff in the publication is false and malicious. He never made any such statement, and has not and never has had a policy of life-insurance with the defendant company. The publication is malicious and tends to bring plaintiff into ridicule before the world, and especially with his friends and acquaintances who know that he has no policy in the defendant company. The publication is "a trespass upon plaintiff's right of privacy, and was caused by breach of confidence and trust reposed" in the defendant Adams. The prayer was for damages in the sum of $25,000. The petition was demurred to generally .... The court sustained the general demurrer, and the plaintiff excepted.

■ COBB, J. .... The question to be determined is whether an individual has a right of privacy which he can enforce and which the courts will protect against invasion. It is to be conceded that prior to 1890 every

[margin note: Right to privacy not recognized, but absence of precedent isn't enough to disqualify]

adjudicated case, both in this country and in England, which might be said to have involved a right of privacy, was not based upon the existence of such right, but was founded upon a supposed right of property, or a breach of trust or confidence, or the like; and that therefore a claim to a right of privacy, independent of a property or contractual right or some right of a similar nature, had, up to that time, never been recognized in terms in any decision. The entire absence for a long period of time, even for centuries, of a precedent for an asserted right should have the effect to cause the courts to proceed with caution before recognizing the right, for fear that they may thereby invade the province of the lawmaking power; but such absence, even for all time, is not conclusive of the question as to the existence of the right. The novelty of the complaint is no objection when an injury cognizable by law is shown to have been inflicted on the plaintiff. In such a case "although there be no precedent, the common law will judge according to the law of nature and the public good." Where the case is new in principle, the courts have no authority to give a remedy, no matter how great the grievance; but where the case is only new in instance, and the sole question is upon the application of a recognized principle to a new case, "it will be just as competent to courts of justice to apply the principle to any case that may arise two centuries hence as it was two centuries ago." Broom's Legal Maxims (8th ed.), 193. . . .

[margin note: naturally, people want to be left alone sometimes]

The individual surrenders to society many rights and privileges which he would be free to exercise in a state of nature, in exchange for the benefits which he receives as a member of society. But he is not presumed to surrender all those rights, and the public has no more right, without his consent, to invade the domain of those rights which it is necessarily to be presumed he has reserved than he has to violate the valid regulations of the organized government under which he lives. The right of privacy has its foundation in the instincts of nature. It is recognized intuitively, consciousness being the witness that can be called to establish its existence. Any person whose intellect is in a normal condition recognizes at once that as to each individual member of society there are matters private and there are matters public so far as the individual is concerned. Each individual as instinctively resents any encroachment by the public upon his rights which are of a private nature as he does the withdrawal of those of his rights which are of a public nature. A right of privacy in matters purely private is therefore derived from natural law. . . .

It is one of those rights referred to by some law-writers as absolute; "such as would belong to their persons merely in a state of nature, and which every man is entitled to enjoy, whether out of society or in it." [Citation.]

Among the absolute rights referred to by the commentator just cited is the right of personal security and the right of personal liberty. In the first is embraced a person's right to a "legal and uninterrupted enjoyment of his life, his limbs, his body, his health, and his reputation;" and in the second is embraced "the power of locomotion, of changing situation, or moving one's person to whatsoever place one's own inclination may direct, without imprisonment or restraint, unless by due course of law." 1 Bl. 129, 134. While neither Sir William Blackstone nor any of the other writers on the principles of the common law have referred in terms to the right of privacy, the illustrations given by them as to what would be a violation of the absolute rights of individuals are not to be taken as exhaustive, but the language should be allowed to include any instance of a violation of such rights which is clearly within the true meaning and intent of the words used to declare the principle. When the law guarantees to one the right to the enjoyment of his life, it gives to him something more than the mere right to breathe and exist. While of course the most flagrant violation of this right would be deprivation of life, yet life itself may be spared and the enjoyment of life entirely destroyed. An individual has a right to enjoy life in any way that may be most agreeable and pleasant to him, according to his temperament and nature, provided that in such enjoyment he does not invade the rights of his neighbor or violate public law or policy. . . .

All will admit that the individual who desires to live a life of seclusion can not be compelled, against his consent, to exhibit his person in any public place, unless such exhibition is demanded by the law of the land. He may be required to come from his place of seclusion to perform public duties,—to serve as a juror and to testify as a witness, and the like; but when the public duty is once performed, if he exercises his liberty to go again into seclusion, no one can deny him the right. One who desires to live a life of partial seclusion has a right to choose the times, places, and manner in which and at which he will submit himself to the public gaze. Subject to the limitation above referred to, the body of a person can not be put on exhibition at any time or at any place without his consent. The right of one to exhibit himself to the public at all proper times, in all proper places, and in a proper manner is embraced within the right of personal liberty. The right to withdraw from the public gaze at such times as a person may see fit, when his presence in public is not demanded by any rule of law is also embraced within the right of personal liberty. Publicity in one instance and privacy in the other is each guaranteed. If personal liberty embraces the right of publicity, it no less embraces the correlative right of privacy; and this is no new idea in Georgia law. In Wallace v. Railway Company, 94 Ga. 732, it was said: "Liberty of speech and of writing is secured by the constitution, and incident thereto is the correlative liberty of silence, not less important nor less sacred." . . .

Instances might be multiplied where the common law has both tacitly and expressly recognized the right of an individual to repose and privacy. The right of the people to be secure in their persons, houses, papers, and effects against unreasonable searches and seizures, which is so fully protected in the constitutions of the United States and of this State (Civil Code, §§ 6017, 5713), is not a right created by these instruments, but is an ancient right which, on account of its gross violation at different times, was preserved from such attacks in the future by being made the subject of constitutional provisions. . . .

It may be said that to establish a liberty of privacy would involve in numerous cases the perplexing question to determine where this liberty ended and the rights of others and of the public began. This affords no reason for not recognizing the liberty of privacy and giving to the person aggrieved legal redress against the wrong-doer in a case where it is clearly shown that a legal wrong has been done. It may be that there will arise many cases which lie near the border line which marks the right of privacy on the one hand and the right of another individual or of the public on the other. But this is true in regard to numerous other rights which the law recognizes as resting in the individual. In regard to cases that may arise under the right of privacy, as in cases that arise under other rights where the line of demarkation is to be determined, the safeguard of the individual on the one hand and of the public on the other is the wisdom and integrity of the judiciary. Each person has a liberty of privacy, and every other person has as against him liberty in reference to other matters, and the line where these liberties impinge on each other may in a given case be hard to define; but that such a case may arise can afford no more reason for denying to one his liberty of privacy than it would to deny to another his liberty, whatever it may be. In every action for a tort it is necessary for the court to determine whether the right claimed has a legal existence, and for the jury to determine whether such right has been invaded, and to assess the damage if their finding is in favor of the plaintiff. This burden which rests upon the court in every case of the character referred to is all that will be imposed upon it in actions brought for a violation of the right of privacy. No greater difficulties will be encountered in such cases in determining the existence of the right than often will be encountered in determining the existence of other rights sought to be enforced by action. The courts may proceed in cases involving the violation of a right of privacy as in other cases of a similar nature, and the juries may in the same manner proceed to a determination of those questions which the law requires to be submitted for their consideration. With honest and fearless trial judges to pass in the first instance upon the question of law as to the existence of the right in each case, whose decisions are subject to review by the court of last resort, and with fair and impartial juries to pass upon the questions of fact involved and assess the damages in the event of a recovery, whose verdict is, under our law, in all cases subject to supervision and scrutiny by the trial judge, [who may,] within the limits of a legal discretion[, control their findings], there need be no more fear that the right of privacy will be the occasion of unjustifiable litigation, oppression, or wrong than that the existence of many other rights in the law would bring about such results.

[The Court reviewed prior decisions, concluding with *Roberson v. Rochester Folding Box Co.*]

We have no fault to find with what is said by the distinguished and learned judge who voiced the views of the majority, as to the existence of decided cases, and agree with him in his analysis of the various cases which he reviews, that the judgment in each was based upon other grounds than the existence of a right of privacy. We also agree with him so far as he asserts that the writers upon the common law and the principles of equity do not in express terms refer to this right. But we are utterly at variance with him in his conclusion that the existence of this right can not be legitimately inferred from what has been said by commentators upon the legal rights of individuals, and from expressions which have fallen from judges in their reasoning in cases where the exercise of the right was not directly involved. So far as the judgment in the case is based upon the argument ab inconvenienti, all that is necessary to be said is that this argument has no place in the case if the right invoked has an existence in the law. But if it were proper to use this argument at all, it could be said with great force that as to certain matters the individual feels and knows that he has a right to exercise the liberty of privacy, and that he has a right to resent any invasion of this liberty; and if the law will not protect him against invasion, the individual will, to protect himself and those to whom he owes protection, use those weapons with which nature has provided him as well as those which the ingenuity of man has placed within his reach. Thus the peace and good order of society would be disturbed by each individual becoming a law unto himself to determine when and under what circumstances he should avenge the outrage which has been perpetrated upon him or a member of his family. The true lawyer, when called to the discharge of judicial functions, has in all times, as a general rule, displayed remarkable conservatism; and wherever it was legally possible to base a judgment upon principles which had been recognized by a long course of judicial decision, this has been done, in preference to applying a principle which might be considered novel. It was for this reason that the numerous cases, both in England and in this country, which really protected the right of privacy were not placed upon the existence of this right, but were allowed to rest upon principles derived from the law of property, trust, and contract. Any candid mind will, however, be compelled to concede that in order to give relief in many of those cases it required a severe strain to bring them within the recognized rules which were sought to be applied. The desire to avoid the novelty of recognizing a principle which had not been theretofore recognized was avoided in such cases by the novelty of straining a well-recognized principle to cover a state of facts to which it had never before been applied. This conservatism of the judiciary has sometimes unconsciously led judges to the conclusion that because the case was novel the right claimed did not exist. With all due respect to Chief Judge Parker and his associates who concurred with him, we think the conclusion reached by them was the result of an unconscious yielding to the feeling of conservatism which naturally arises in the mind of a judge who faces a proposition which is novel. The valuable influence upon society and upon the welfare of the public of the conservatism of the lawyer, whether at the bar or upon the bench, can not be overestimated; but this conservatism should not go to the extent of refusing to recognize a right which the instincts of nature prove to exist, and which nothing in judicial decision, legal history, or writings upon the law can be called to demonstrate its non-existence as a legal right.

We think that what should have been a proper judgment in the *Roberson* case was that contended for by Judge Gray in his dissenting opinion, . . .[quotations from Judge Gray's opinion have been omitted].

The effect of the reasoning of the learned judge . . . is to establish conclusively the correctness of the conclusion which we have reached, and we prefer to adopt as our own his reasoning in his own words rather than to paraphrase them into our own. The decision of the Court of Appeals of New York in the *Roberson* case gave rise to numerous articles in the different law magazines of high standing in the country, some by the editors and others by contributors. In some the conclusion of the majority of the court was approved; in others the views of the dissenting judges were commended; and in still others the case and similar cases were referred to as apparently establishing that the claim of the majority was correct, but regret was expressed that the necessity was such that the courts could not recognize the right asserted. An editorial in the American Law Review (vol. 36, p. 636) said: "The decision under review shocks and wounds the ordinary sense of justice of mankind. We have heard it alluded to only in terms of regret." . . .

So thoroughly satisfied are we that the law recognizes within proper limits, as a legal right, the right of privacy, and that the publication of one's picture without his consent by another as an advertisement, for the mere purpose of increasing the profits and gains of the advertiser, is an invasion of this right, that we venture to predict that the day will come that the American bar will marvel that a contrary view was ever entertained by judges of eminence and ability; just as in the present day we stand amazed that . . . Lord Hale, with perfect composure of manner and complete satisfaction of soul, imposed the death penalty for witchcraft upon ignorant and harmless women.

Judgment reversed. All the Justices concur.

NOTES AND QUESTIONS

1.   Articulate the differences in the starting points of the *Roberson* majority's and the *Pavesich* court's analyses.

2.   How do the two decisions treat prior authority? Whose treatment do you think is more persuasive? Why?

3. If, after *Pavesich,* the New York Court of Appeals had to rule on another claim involving the unauthorized publication of personal photographs for purposes of trade, would the New York court adopt the Georgia court's approach? Why or why not?

c.   THE DUTY OF CARE

Hynes v. New York Cent. R.R. Co.

Court of Appeals of New York, 1921.
231 N.Y. 229, 131 N.E. 898.

Appeal from a judgment of the Appellate Division of the Supreme Court in the second judicial department, entered January 12, 1920, affirming a judgment in favor of defendant entered upon a dismissal of the complaint by the court at a Trial Term.

■ CARDOZO, J. On July 8, 1916, Harvey Hynes, a lad of sixteen, swam with two companions from the Manhattan to the Bronx side of the Harlem river or United States Ship Canal, a navigable stream. Along the Bronx side of the river was the right of way of the defendant, the New York Central Railroad, which operated its trains at that point by high tension wires, strung on poles and crossarms. Projecting from the defendant's bulkhead above the waters of the river was a plank or springboard from which boys of the neighborhood used to dive. One end of the board had been placed under a rock on the defendant's land, and nails had been driven at its point of contact with the bulkhead. Measured from this point of contact the length behind was five feet; the length in front eleven. The bulkhead itself was about three and a half feet back of the pier line as located by the government. From this it follows that for seven and a half feet the springboard was beyond the line of the defendant's property, and above the public waterway. Its height measured from the stream was three feet at the bulkhead, and five feet at its outermost extremity. For more than five years swimmers had used it as a diving board without protest or obstruction.

On this day Hynes and his companions climbed on top of the bulkhead intending to leap into the water. One of them made the plunge in safety. Hynes followed to the front of the springboard, and stood poised for his dive. At that moment a cross-arm with electric wires fell from the defendant's pole. The wires struck the diver, flung him from the shattered board, and plunged him to his death below. His mother, suing as administratrix, brings this action for her damages. Thus far the courts have held that Hynes at the end of the springboard above the public waters was a trespasser on the defendant's land. They have thought it immaterial that the board itself was a trespass, an encroachment on the public ways. They have thought it of no significance that Hynes would have met the same fate if he had been below the board and not above it. The board, they have said, was annexed to the defendant's bulkhead. By force of such annexation, it was to be reckoned as a fixture, and thus constructively, if not actually, an extension of the land. The defendant was under a duty to use reasonable care that bathers swimming or standing in the water should not be electrocuted by wires falling from its right of way. But to bathers diving from the springboard, there was no duty, we are told, unless the injury was the product of mere willfulness or wantonness, no duty of active vigilance to safeguard the impending structure. Without wrong to them, cross-arms might be left to rot; wires highly charged with electricity might sweep them from their stand, and bury them in the subjacent waters. In climbing on the board, they became trespassers and outlaws. The conclusion is defended with much subtlety of reasoning, with much insistence upon its inevitableness as a merely logical deduction. A majority of the court are unable to accept it as the conclusion of the law.

We assume, without deciding, that the springboard was a fixture, a permanent improvement of the defendant's right of way. Much might be said in favor of another view. We do not press the inquiry, for we are persuaded that the rights of bathers do not depend upon these nice distinctions. Liability would not be doubtful, we are told, had the boy been diving from a pole, if the pole had been vertical. The diver in such a situation would have been separated from the defendant's freehold. Liability, it is said, has been escaped because the pole was horizontal. The plank when projected lengthwise was an extension of the soil. We are to concentrate our gaze on the private ownership of the board. We are to ignore the public ownership of the circumambient spaces of water and of air. Jumping from a boat or a barrel, the boy would have been a bather in the river. Jumping from the end of a springboard, he was no longer, it is said, a bather, but a trespasser on a right of way.

Rights and duties in systems of living law are not built upon such quicksands.

Bathers in the Harlem river on the day of this disaster were in the enjoyment of a public highway, entitled to reasonable protection against destruction by the defendant's wires. They did not cease to be bathers entitled to the same protection while they were diving from encroaching objects or engaging in the sports that are common among swimmers. Such acts were not equivalent to an abandonment of the highway, a departure from its proper uses, a withdrawal from the waters, and an entry upon land. A plane of private right had been interposed between the river and the air, but public ownership was unchanged in the space below it and above. The defendant does not deny that it would have owed a duty to this boy if he had been leaning against the springboard with his feet upon the ground. He is said to have forfeited protection as he put his feet upon the plank. Presumably the same result would follow if the plank had been a few inches above the surface of the water instead of a few feet. Duties are thus supposed to arise and to be extinguished in alternate zones or strata. Two boys walking in the country or swimming in a river stop to rest for a moment along the side of the road or the margin of the stream. One of them throws himself beneath the overhanging branches of a tree. The other perches himself on a bough a foot or so above the ground. Hoffman v. Armstrong, 48 N.Y. 201, 8 Am.Rep. 537. Both are killed by falling wires. The defendant would have us say that there is a remedy for the representatives of one, and none for the representatives of the other. We may be permitted to distrust the logic that leads to such conclusions.

[handwritten margin note: If we accept this logic leads to absurd conclusions]

The truth is that every act of Hynes, from his first plunge into the river until the moment of his death, was in the enjoyment of the public waters, and under cover of the protection which his presence in those waters gave him. The use of the springboard was not an abandonment of his rights as bather. It was a mere by-play, an incident, subordinate and ancillary to the execution of his primary purpose, the enjoyment of the highway. The by-play, the incident, was not the cause of the disaster. Hynes would have gone to his death if he had been below the springboard or beside it. Laidlaw v. Sage, 158 N.Y. 73, 97, 52 N.E. 679, 44 L.R.A. 216. The wires were not stayed by the presence of the plank. They followed the boy in his fall, and overwhelmed him in the waters. The defendant assumes that the identification of ownership of a fixture with ownership of land is complete in every incident. But there are important elements of difference. Title to the fixture, unlike title to the land, does not carry with it rights of ownership usque ad coelum. There will hardly be denial that a cause of action would have arisen if the wires had fallen on an aeroplane proceeding above the river, though the location of the impact could be identified as the space above the springboard. The most that the defendant can fairly ask is exemption from liability where the use of the fixture is itself the efficient peril. That would be the situation, for example, if the weight of the boy upon the board had caused it to break and thereby throw him into the river. There is no such causal connection here between his position and his injuries. We think there was no moment when he was beyond the pale of the defendant's duty—the duty of care and vigilance in the storage of destructive forces.

[handwritten margin note: Plank was not the cause of death]

[handwritten margin note: below + above]

This case is a striking instance of the dangers of "a jurisprudence of conceptions" (Pound, Mechanical Jurisprudence, 8 Columbia Law Review, 605, 608, 610), the extension of a maxim or a definition with relentless disregard of consequences to a "dryly logical extreme." The approximate and relative become the definite and absolute. Landowners are not bound to regulate their conduct in contemplation of the presence of trespassers intruding upon private structures. Landowners are bound to regulate their conduct in contemplation of the presence of travelers upon the adjacent public ways. There are times when there is little trouble in marking off the field of exemption and immunity from that of liability and duty. Here structures and ways are so united and commingled, super-imposed upon each other, that the fields are brought together. In such circumstances, there is little help in pursuing general maxims to ultimate conclusions. They have been framed alio intuitu.

They must be reformulated and readapted to meet exceptional conditions. Rules appropriate to spheres which are conceived of as separate and distinct cannot, both, be enforced when the spheres become concentric. There must then be readjustment or collision. In one sense, and that a highly technical and artificial one, the diver at the end of the springboard is an intruder on the adjoining lands. In another sense, and one that realists will accept more readily, he is still on public waters in the exercise of public rights. The law must say whether it will subject him to the rule of the one field or of the other, of this sphere or of that. We think that considerations of analogy, of convenience, of policy, and of justice, exclude him from the field of the defendant's immunity and exemption, and place him in the field of liability and duty. Beck v. Carter, 68 N.Y. 283, 23 Am.Rep. 175; Jewhurst v. City of Syracuse, 108 N.Y. 303, 15 N.E. 409; McCloskey v. Buckley, 223 N.Y. 187, 192, 119 N.E. 395.

The judgment of the Appellate Division and that of the Trial Term should be reversed, and a new trial granted, with costs to abide the event.

■ HOGAN, POUND and CRANE, JJ., concur; HISCOCK, CH.J., CHASE and McLAUGHLIN, JJ., dissent.

NOTES AND QUESTIONS

1.   Judge Cardozo in THE GROWTH OF THE LAW 99–103 (1924) thus commented on the above decision:

> We had in my court a year or more ago a case that points my meaning. A boy was bathing in a river. He climbed upon a springboard which projected from a bank. As he stood there, at the end of the board, poised for his dive into the stream, electric wires fell upon him, and swept him to his death below. In the suit for damages that followed, competitive analogies were invoked by counsel for the administratrix and counsel for the railroad company, the owner of the upland. The administratrix found the analogy that suited her in the position of travelers on a highway. The boy was a bather in navigable waters; his rights were not lessened because his feet were on the board. The owner found the analogy to its liking in the position of a trespasser on land. The springboard, though it projected into the water, was, nonetheless, a fixture, and as a fixture it was constructively a part of the land to which it was annexed. The boy was thus a trespasser upon land in private ownership; the only duty of the owner was to refrain from wanton and malicious injury; if these elements were lacking, the death must go without requital. Now, the truth is that, as a mere bit of dialectics, these analogies would bring a judge to an impasse. No process of merely logical deduction could determine the choice between them. Neither analogy is precise, though each is apposite. There had arisen a new situation which could not force itself without mutilation into any of the existing moulds. When we find a situation of this kind, the choice that will approve itself to this judge or to that, will be determined largely by his conception of the

end of the law, the function of legal liability; and this question of ends and functions is a question of philosophy.

In the case that I have instanced, a majority of the court believed that liability should be adjudged. The deductions that might have been made from preestablished definitions were subordinated and adapted to the fundamental principles that determine, or ought to determine, liability for conduct in a system of law wherein liability is adjusted to the ends which law should serve. Hynes v. The New York Central Railroad Co., was decided in May, 1921. Dean Pound's Introduction to the Philosophy of Law had not yet been published. It appeared in 1922. In these lectures, he advances a theory of liability which it may be interesting to compare with the theory of liability reflected in our decision. "The law," he says, "enforces the reasonable expectations arising out of conduct, relations and situations." I shall leave it to others to say whether the cause of the boy diving from the springboard would be helped or hindered by resort to such a test. This much I cannot doubt. Some theory of liability, some philosophy of the end to be served by tightening or enlarging the circle of rights and remedies, is at the root of any decision in novel situations when analogies are equivocal and precedents are silent. As it stands today, the judge is often left to improvise such a theory, such a philosophy, when confronted overnight by the exigencies of the case before him. Often he fumbles about, feeling in a vague way that some such problem is involved, but missing the universal element which would have quickened his decision with the inspiration of a principle. If he lacks an adequate philosophy, he either goes astray altogether, or at least does not rise above the empiricism that pronounces judgment upon particulars. We must learn that all methods are to be viewed not as idols but as tools. We must test one of them by the others, supplementing and reenforcing where there is weakness, so that what is strong and best in each will be at our service in the hour of need. Thus viewing them we shall often find that they are not antagonists but allies.

What *was* the "theory of liability" of the majority of the Court of Appeals in Hynes?

2. Suppose that, following the *Hynes* decision, one of Harvey's friends swam across the Harlem River to the Bronx side and clambered up on the New York Central Rail Road's bulkhead. Poised for his dive from the edge of the bulkhead, the young man was struck by yet another falling wire, and was swept to his death. Had he already been in the water, he would have suffered the same fate. How should the court rule on the boy's parents' wrongful death claim against the NYCRR?

3. Suppose that, following the *Hynes* decision, another of Harvey's friends swam across the Harlem River to the Bronx side, clambered onto the NYCRR's land, and was making his way to the diving board along a path on the NYCRR's land, when yet another wire broke loose, sweeping the boy out past the path and the bulkhead, into the river, where he drowned. Had he

already been in the water, he would have suffered the same fate. How should the court rule on the boy's parents' wrongful death claim against the NYCRR?

4. Suppose that, following the *Hynes* decision, yet another of Harvey's friends swam across the Harlem River to the Bronx side, clambered onto the NYCRR's land, where he decided to have a picnic, before returning to enjoy the waters. As he was spreading out his lunch, still another wire snapped, sweeping the boy, and his lunch, out past the path and the bulkhead, into the river, where he drowned. Had he already been in the water, he would have suffered the same fate. How should the court rule on the boy's parents' wrongful death claim against the NYCRR?

Murphy v. Steeplechase Amusement Co.

Court of Appeals of New York, 1929.
250 N.Y. 479, 166 N.E. 173.

■ CARDOZO, C.J. The defendant, Steeplechase Amusement Company, maintains an amusement park at Coney Island, New York.

One of the supposed attractions is known as The Flopper." It is a moving belt, running upward on an inclined plane, on which passengers sit or stand. Many of them are unable to keep their feet because of the movement of the belt, and are thrown backward or aside. The belt runs in a groove, with padded walls on either side to a height of four feet, and with padded flooring beyond the walls at the same angle as the belt. An electric motor, driven by current furnished by the Brooklyn Edison Company, supplies the needed power.

Plaintiff, a vigorous young man, visited the park with friends. One of them, a young woman, now his wife, stepped upon the moving belt. Plaintiff followed and stepped behind her. As he did so, he felt what he describes as a sudden jerk, and was thrown to the floor. His wife in front and also friends behind him were thrown at the same time. Something more was here, as every one understood, than the slowly-moving escalator that is common in shops and public places. A fall was foreseen as one of the risks of the adventure. There would have been no point to the whole thing, no adventure about it, if the risk had not been there. The very name above the gate, the Flopper, was warning to the timid. If the name was not enough, there was warning more distinct in the experience of others. We are told by the plaintiff's wife that the members of her party stood looking at the sport before joining in it themselves. Some aboard the belt were able, as she viewed them, to sit down with decorum or even to stand and keep their footing; others jumped or fell. The tumbling bodies and the screams and laughter supplied the merriment and fun. I took a chance," she said when asked whether she thought that a fall might be expected.

Plaintiff took the chance with her, but, less lucky than his companions, suffered a fracture of a knee cap. He states in his complaint that the belt was dangerous to life and limb in that it stopped and started violently and suddenly and was not properly equipped to prevent injuries to persons who were using it without knowledge of its dangers, and in a bill of particulars he adds that it was operated at a fast and dangerous rate of speed *and was not supplied with a proper railing, guard or other device to prevent a fall therefrom. No other negligence is charged.*

We see no adequate basis for a finding that the belt was out of order. It was already in motion when the plaintiff put his foot on it. He cannot help himself to a verdict in such circumstances by the addition of the facile comment that it threw him with a jerk. One who steps upon a moving belt and finds his heels above his head is in no position to discriminate with nicety between the successive stages of the shock, between the jerk which is a cause and the jerk, accompanying the fall, as an instantaneous effect. There is evidence for the defendant that power was transmitted smoothly, and could not be transmitted otherwise. If the movement was spasmodic, it was an unexplained and, it seems, an inexplicable departure from the normal workings of the mechanism. An aberration so extraordinary, if it is to lay the basis for a verdict, should rest on something firmer than a mere descriptive epithet, a summary of the sensations of a tense and crowded moment (Matter of Case, 214 N. Y. 199; Dochtermann v. Brooklyn Heights R. R. Co., 32 App. Div. 13, 15; 164 N. Y. 586; Foley v. Boston & Maine R. R. Co., 193 Mass. 332, 335; Work v. Boston El. Ry. Co., 207 Mass. 447, 448; N. & W. Ry. Co. v. Birchett, 252 Fed. Rep. 512, 515). But the jerk, if it were established, would add little to the case. Whether the movement of the belt was uniform or irregular, the risk at greatest was a fall. This was the very hazard that was invited and foreseen (Lumsden v. Thompson Scenic Ry. Co., 130 App. Div. 209, 212, 213).

Volenti non fit injuria. One who takes part in such a sport accepts the dangers that inhere in it so far as they are obvious and necessary, just as a fencer accepts the risk of a thrust by his antagonist or a spectator at a ball game the chance of contact with the ball (Pollock, Torts [11th ed.], p. 171; Lumsden v. Thompson Scenic Ry. Co., supra; Godfrey v. Conn. Co., 98 Conn. 63; Johnson v. City of N. Y., 186 N. Y. 139, 148; McFarlane v. City of Niagara Falls, 247 N. Y. 340, 349; cf. 1 Beven, Negligence, 787; Bohlen, Studies in the Law of Torts, p. 443). The antics of the clown are not the paces of the cloistered cleric. The rough and boisterous joke, the horseplay of the crowd, evokes its own guffaws, but they are not the pleasures of tranquillity. The plaintiff was not seeking a retreat for meditation. Visitors were tumbling about the belt to the merriment of onlookers when he made his choice to join them. He took the chance of a like fate, with whatever damage to his body might ensue from such a fall. The timorous may stay at home.

A different case would be here if the dangers inherent in the sport were obscure or unobserved (Godfrey v. Conn. Co., supra; Tantillo v.

Goldstein Bros. Amusement Co., 248 N. Y. 286), or so serious as to justify the belief that precautions of some kind must have been taken to avert them (cf. O'Callaghan v. Dellwood Park Co, 242 Ill. 336). Nothing happened to the plaintiff except what common experience tells us may happen at any time as the consequence of a sudden fall. Many a skater or a horseman can rehearse a tale of equal woe. A different case there would also be if the accidents had been so many as to show that the game in its inherent nature was too dangerous to be continued without change. The president of the amusement company says that there had never been such an accident before. A nurse employed at an emergency hospital maintained in connection with the park contradicts him to some extent. She says that on other occasions she had attended patrons of the park who had been injured at the Flopper, how many she could not say. None, however, had been badly injured or had suffered broken bones. Such testimony is not enough to show that the game was a trap for the unwary, too perilous to be endured. According to the defendant's estimate, two hundred and fifty thousand visitors were at the Flopper in a year. Some quota of accidents was to be looked for in so great a mass. One might as well say that a skating rink should be abandoned because skaters sometimes fall.

There is testimony by the plaintiff that he fell upon wood, and not upon a canvas padding. He is strongly contradicted by the photographs and by the witnesses for the defendant, and is without corroboration in the testimony of his companions who were witnesses in his behalf. If his observation was correct, there was a defect in the equipment, and one not obvious or known. The padding should have been kept in repair to break the force of any fall. The case did not go to the jury, however, upon any such theory of the defendant's liability, nor is the defect fairly suggested by the plaintiff's bill of particulars, which limits his complaint. The case went to the jury upon the theory that negligence was dependent upon a sharp and sudden jerk.

The judgment of the Appellate Division and that of the Trial Term should be reversed, and a new trial granted, with costs to abide the event.

[The dissent of O'BRIEN, J., has been omitted.]

QUESTIONS

1.   Is *Murphy* consistent with *Hynes*? How would you reconcile their different outcomes?

2.   Why did Chief Judge Cardozo reject the plaintiff's contention that he fell upon wood rather than canvas padding?

3.   Note how Chief Judge Cardozo's characterizations of Murphy as "a robust young man" and of Harvey Hynes as "a lad of sixteen" foretell the court's result. What if plaintiff in *Murphy* had been "a tot of three"?

France: Court of Cassation (all chambers assembled), Judgment of February 13, 1930

(Jand'heur v. Aux Galeries Belfortaises)

Cass ch. Réuns., Feb. 13, 1930, D.P. I, 57

THE COURT:– Having seen article 1384 [of the Civil Code] clause 1 [which states: "One is liable not only for the harm that one causes by one's own fault, but also for that which is caused by the acts of persons for whom one is responsible, or by the things one has under one's care."]

– Whereas the presumption of liability established by this article against the person who has under his care the inanimate thing which has caused harm to another may not be rebutted except by proof of an unforeseeable and unavoidable event ("*cas fortuit*") or of an Act of God ("*force majeure*"), or of a foreign cause not imputable to him; that it does not suffice to prove that such person has committed no wrongful act ("*faute*"), or that the cause of the harmful act remains unknown;

– Whereas, on April 22, 1925, a truck belonging to the *Société Aux Galeries Belfortaises* overturned and wounded the minor child Lise Jand'heur; that the decision appealed from refused to apply the above text on the ground that the accident caused by a moving car, under the impulse and direction of a man, did not constitute, when no proof existed that it was due to an inherent defect in the car, the act of a thing which one has under one's care in the terms of art. 1384 clause 1, and that, as a result, the victim was obliged, in order to recover for her harm, to establish with regard to the driver a wrongful act imputable to him;

– But whereas the law, by application of the presumption which it edicts, does not distinguish according to whether the thing was or was not activated by man's hand; that it is not necessary that there have been an inherent defect in the nature of the thing which was susceptible to cause harm, art. 1384 attaching liability to having the care of the thing, not to the thing itself;

– Therefore it follows that, in ruling as it did, the decision appealed from has reversed the legal text's order of proof and violated the text of the above-referenced law.

– By these reasons, the decision below is broken and the decision is remanded to the Court of Appeals of Dijon.

NOTES AND QUESTIONS

(English translation by Jane C. Ginsburg; the translation endeavors to capture the original's stilted style.)

1.   This is a decision of France's highest private law court, the Court of Cassation—literally "breaking": when the court reverses the intermediate appellate court's decision, it "breaks" it and remands to another appellate court to apply the law as articulated by the high court.

2. How does the court present the facts and the applicable law? In what order?

3. What can you infer about the state of the law before this case? How does the court address the prior caselaw? Who wrote the decision?

4. *Jand'heur* was in fact a landmark decision, though its presentation typically discloses neither its departures from prior judicial exposition, nor the heated doctrinal debate surrounding the bases of tort liability. France's High Court was at this time expansively reading art. 1384 of the Civil code, beginning a shift in tort law from fault-based liability toward risk allocation based on dominion and control over the harm-causing object. Thus, the court's formulation of the basis for liability under art. 1384 foregoes mention of "fault." Commentators disputed whether liability henceforth would be founded simply on ownership of the harm-causing object, or instead on a legal obligation to maintain and control it. *Compare* L. Josserand, La responsabilité du fait des automobiles devant les chambres réunies de la Cour de cassation, 1930 D.H. Chr. 25, 28 *with* Cass. ch. Réuns., Feb. 13, 1930, D.P. I, 57, note Ripert. Under one interpretation, the court would have adopted a strict liability risk allocation approach, while under the other, fault would in effect have been presumed: if the object caused harm, its owner must have failed to fulfill his or her legal obligation to "care" for the object. Under neither approach, however, would the victim have had to prove acts by the defendant demonstrating breach of its duty of care.

5. How might the French court have decided a case presenting the *Hynes* facts? How might the *Hynes* majority have analyzed *Jand'heur*?

2. THE EFFECT OF PRECEDENT ON A SUBSEQUENT CASE

In this and other courses during your first year in law school, you will begin to develop a "feel" for certain of the basic skills and arts of the case lawyer: for example, distinguishing cases on their facts, narrowing an asserted precedent in terms of its procedural issue, and following the distinguishable case. But the role of precedents in the common law judicial process cannot be grasped unless you know what a judge or a lawyer means when he speaks of the "holding" or *ratio decidendi* of a case and what he means when he says that a statement in a judicial opinion is "dictum" or *obiter dictum*. The distinction between "holding" and "dictum" runs through Anglo-American legal literature and is a recurring theme in case method law classes.

If you have ever heard an oral argument in an appellate court, you undoubtedly have heard counsel for one side or the other quote a statement from some past judicial opinion in support of his legal argument in the case then before the court. And, it is almost equally certain, you have heard some member of the court interrupt the quoting counsel and ask: "Yes, but what were the *facts* of that case?" Why do judges—and law professors, for that matter—insist on asking that question? If the quoted statement was, in truth, made in the earlier judicial opinion, what difference does it make what the *facts* of that case were? After you have read and thought through the cases and other materials in this Section, you should be able to see that the question, "What were the facts of that [earlier] case?" is, essentially, another way of asking, "Was the statement in the past judicial opinion 'holding' or 'dictum' in that case?"

By then, too, you will have realized that the question is deceptively simple. Central as it is to our system of precedent, the concept of holding and dictum is elusive.

Let us start our analysis by accepting at face value the importance of the distinction. The holding of a case, under our system, must be followed in similar cases, until overruled. Dicta are pronouncements which may be persuasive, but are not binding. You will soon realize that this is a somewhat oversimplified view of case law but let us start there.

How does one tell the difference? The conventional definition is that dictum is any statement in a judicial opinion not necessary to the decision of the case actually before the court. The following is a typical statement of the matter:

> if it [the point of law commented on in the opinion] might have been decided either way without affecting any right brought into question, then, according to the principles of the common law, an opinion on such a question is not a decision. To make it so, there must have been an application of the judicial mind to the precise question necessary to be determined, to fix the rights of the parties, and to decide to whom the property in contestation belongs. And, therefore, this court, and other courts organized under the common law, has never held itself bound by any part

of an opinion, in any case, which was not needful to the ascertainment of the right or title in question between the parties.

Carroll v. Carroll's Lessee, 57 U.S. (16 How.) 275, 286–287, 14 L.Ed. 936 (1853). Statements such as "it would be otherwise if . . ." or "Assuming, without deciding" (see *Estate of Hemingway v. Random House, infra*) signal that the court is speculating, rather than deciding the precise controversy before it.

You may well ask why any distinction should be made between holding and dictum. We have designated certain officials judges and made them, subject to legislative overruling, the final law makers in certain spheres. Why should we not give binding effect to all their official pronouncements? Is the following a sufficient answer?

> No *dictum* is authority of the highest sort. To give it such weight would be to give judges power to decide in advance a case not before them for adjudication, a merely hypothetical case, and to bind by their opinion the court before which that hypothetical case may eventually become a practical problem. This would be a legislative power, and, still worse, a power exercised in the absence of full argument of the hypothetical case.

Wambaugh, The Study of Cases 19 (2d ed.1894).

The last clause deserves reemphasis. It is a cardinal tenet of the Anglo-American judicial system that the best result will be produced through "the fire of controversy." At least in theory, given adequate legal representation on both sides, the court will have presented to it the best possible arguments for alternative decisions on a disputed point; the defects of either position will be shown up and the best course to pursue be made apparent. The critical word is "disputed" and therein lies the reason for the distinction between holding and dictum: Dicta are pronouncements on points which need not be considered in order to reach a decision and are, therefore, in most cases, pronouncements on points on which the court has not had the benefit of argument.

Humphrey's Executor v. United States

Supreme Court of the United States, 1935.
295 U.S. 602, 55 S.Ct. 869, 79 L.Ed. 1611.

[Plaintiff brought suit in the Court of Claims to recover a sum of money alleged to be due to the deceased, William E. Humphrey, for salary as a Federal Trade Commissioner from October 8, 1933, when President Roosevelt undertook to remove him from office, to the time of his death, on February 14, 1934. At the time of the attempted removal, Humphrey had almost five years left to serve of the seven-year term to which he had been appointed by President Hoover in 1931. The Court of Claims certified the following two questions to the Supreme Court:

"1. Do the provisions of Section 1 of the Federal Trade Commission Act, stating that 'any commissioner may be removed by the President for inefficiency, neglect of duty, or malfeasance in office' restrict or limit the power of the President to remove a commissioner except upon one or more of the causes named?

"If the foregoing question is answered in the affirmative, then—

"2. If the power of the President to remove a commissioner is restricted or limited as shown by the foregoing interrogatory and the answer made thereto, is such a restriction or limitation valid under the Constitution of the United States?"]

■ MR. JUSTICE SUTHERLAND delivered the [unanimous] opinion of the Court. . . .

[T]he language of the act, the legislative reports, and the general purposes of the legislation as reflected by the debates, all combine to demonstrate the Congressional intent to create a body of experts who shall gain experience by length of service—a body which shall be independent of executive authority, except in its selection, and free to exercise its judgment without the leave or hindrance of any other official or any department of the government. To the accomplishment of these purposes, it is clear that Congress was of opinion that length and certainty of tenure would vitally contribute. And to hold that, nevertheless, the members of the commission continue in office at the mere will of the President, might be to thwart, in large measure, the very ends which Congress sought to realize by definitely fixing the term of office.

We conclude that the intent of the act is to limit the executive power of removal to the causes enumerated, the existence of none of which is claimed here; and we pass to the second question.

Second. To support its contention that the removal provision of section 1, as we have just construed it, is an unconstitutional interference with the executive power of the President, the government's chief reliance is Myers v. United States, 272 U.S. 52, 47 S.Ct. 21, 71 L.Ed. 160. That case has been so recently decided, and the prevailing and dissenting opinions so fully review the general subject of the power of executive removal, that further discussion would add little of value to the wealth of material there collected. These opinions examine at length the historical, legislative, and judicial data bearing upon the question, beginning with what is called "the decision of 1789" in the first Congress and coming down almost to the day when the opinions were delivered. They occupy 243 pages of the volume in which they are printed. Nevertheless, the narrow point actually decided was only that the President had power to remove a postmaster of the first class, without the advice and consent of the Senate as required by act of Congress. In the course of the opinion of the court, expressions occur which tend to sustain the government's contention, but these are beyond the point involved and, therefore, do not come within the rule of *stare decisis*. Insofar as they are out of harmony with the views here set forth, these expressions are disapproved. A like situation was presented in the case of Cohens v. Virginia, 6 Wheat. 264, 399, 5 L.Ed. 257, in respect of certain general expressions in the opinion in Marbury v. Madison, 1 Cranch, 137, 2 L.Ed. 60. Chief Justice Marshall, who delivered the opinion in the *Marbury* Case, speaking again for the court in the Cohens Case, said: "It is a maxim, not to be disregarded, that general expressions, in every opinion, are to be taken in connection with the case in which those expressions are used. If they go beyond the case, they may be respected, but ought not to control the judgment in a subsequent suit, when the very point is presented for decision. The reason of this maxim is obvious. The question actually before the court is investigated with care, and considered in its full extent. Other principles which may serve to illustrate it, are considered in their relation to the case decided, but their possible bearing on all other cases is seldom completely investigated."

And he added that these general expressions in the case of *Marbury v. Madison* were to be understood with the limitations put upon them by the opinion in the *Cohens* Case. See, also, Carroll v. Lessee of Carroll et al., 16 How. 275, 286–287, 14 L.Ed. 936; O'Donoghue v. United States, 289 U.S. 516, 550, 53 S.Ct. 740, 77 L.Ed. 1356.

The office of a postmaster is so essentially unlike the office now involved that the decision in the *Myers* Case cannot be accepted as controlling our decision here. A postmaster is an executive officer restricted to the performance of executive functions. He is charged with no duty at all related to either the legislative or judicial power. The actual decision in the *Myers* Case finds support in the theory that such an officer is merely one of the units in the executive department and, hence, inherently subject to the exclusive and illimitable power of removal by the Chief Executive, whose subordinate and aid he is. Putting aside dicta, which may be followed if sufficiently persuasive but which are not controlling, the necessary reach of the decision goes far enough to include all purely executive officers. It goes no farther; much less does it include an officer who occupies no place in the executive department and who exercises no part of the executive power vested by the Constitution in the President. . . .

The result of what we now have said is this: Whether the power of the President to remove an officer shall prevail over the authority of Congress to condition the power by fixing a definite term and precluding a removal except for cause will depend upon the character of the office; the *Myers* decision affirming the power of the President alone to make the removal, is confined to purely executive officers; and as to officers of the kind here under consideration, we hold that no removal can be made during the prescribed term for which the officer is appointed, except for one or more of the causes named in the applicable statute.

To the extent, that between the decision in the *Myers* Case, which sustains the unrestrictable power of the President to remove purely executive officers, and our present decision that such power does not extend to an office such as that here involved, there shall remain a field of doubt, we leave such cases as may fall within it for future consideration and determination as they may arise.

In accordance with the foregoing, the questions submitted are answered:

Question No. 1, Yes.

Question No. 2, Yes.

Mr. Justice McReynolds agrees that both questions should be answered in the affirmative. [The separate opinion of Justice McReynolds has been omitted.]

NOTES AND QUESTIONS

1.   The opinion in the *Myers* case occupies about 70 pages of Volume 272 of the United States Reports. To what language in that case does the court in *Humphrey's Executor* point as embodying the "holding"?

Would it have changed the situation if the Court in *Myers* had said, on one of those 70 pages: "We hold that the President may at his discretion, remove from office any person appointed by him or a predecessor"?

The point of these questions is to emphasize that when we speak of the holding of a case we refer not to anything which was *said,* but to what was decided. It is true that we may conclude that a particular formulation of words in a decision is an accurate statement of the holding of the case but, as we shall see, a court's statement that it is "holding" in a particular way does not necessarily control in subsequent cases.

2.   Is the following statement on page 130, *supra*, holding or dictum? "Insofar as they are out of harmony with the views here set forth, these expressions are disapproved."

3.   Suppose that after the decision in the *Myers* case, but before the *Humphrey's Executor* case, you had been writing a law review article and had stated that in *Myers* the Supreme Court held that Congress may not constitutionally limit the President's power to remove a presidential appointee from office. Would you have been wrong?

Suppose that during that same period you were working in the Justice Department and the President had asked you whether he could fire Humphrey. If you had told him that *Myers* held he could, would you have been wrong?

Suppose, instead, you had been Humphrey's lawyer, and he asked you if he should take another job. If you had said, "Yes, under *Myers* you don't have a claim for your salary," would you have been wrong?

Morrison v. Olson

Supreme Court of the United States, 1988.
487 U.S. 654, 108 S.Ct. 2597, 101 L.Ed.2d 569.

[The Ethics in Government Act of 1978 allowed the Attorney General to ask a special federal court to appoint an independent counsel to investigate allegations against high level members of the Executive Branch (*e.g.*, an official in the Attorney General's office). Under the statute, only the Attorney General had the power to remove the independent counsel; this power was further limited to discharge on the basis of "good cause, physical disability, mental incapacity, or any other condition that substantially impairs the performance of [her] duties."

In Morrison, appellee Olson, an official of the Attorney General's Office, allegedly gave false testimony during an Environmental Protection Agency investigation. As a result of the Attorney General's request, the special court appointed a special prosecutor, appellant Morrison. A dispute subsequently arose between the Attorney General and the special prosecutor. Olson moved in Federal District Court to declare the independent counsel provision unconstitutional, on the ground that the provision limited the removal power of the Executive Branch. The district court upheld the provision. The Court of Appeals reversed. The Supreme Court reversed the Court of Appeals' disposition.]

■ CHIEF JUSTICE REHNQUIST delivered the opinion of the Court[, in which JUSTICE BRENNAN, JUSTICE WHITE, JUSTICE MARSHALL, JUSTICE BLACKMUN, JUSTICE STEVENS, and JUSTICE O'CONNOR joined.] . . .

V

We now turn to consider whether the Act is invalid under the constitutional principle of separation of powers. Two related issues must be addressed: The first is whether the provision of the Act restricting the Attorney General's power to remove the independent counsel to only those instances in which he can show "good cause," taken by itself, impermissibly interferes with the President's exercise of his constitutionally appointed functions. . . .

A

Two Terms ago we had occasion to consider whether it was consistent with the separation of powers for Congress to pass a statute that authorized a Government official who is removable only by Congress to participate in what we found to be "executive powers." *Bowsher v. Synar*, 478 U.S. 714, 730 (1986). We held in *Bowsher* that "Congress cannot reserve for itself the power of removal of an officer charged with the execution of the laws except by impeachment." Id., at 726. A primary antecedent for this ruling was our 1926 decision in *Myers v. United States*, 272 U.S. 52. *Myers* had considered the propriety of a federal statute by which certain postmasters of the United States could be removed by the President only "by and with the advice and consent of the Senate." There too, Congress' attempt to involve itself in the removal of an executive official was found to be sufficient grounds to render the statute invalid. As we observed in *Bowsher*, the essence of the decision in *Myers* was the judgment that the Constitution prevents Congress from "draw[ing] to itself . . . the power to remove or the right to participate in the exercise of that power. To do this would be to go beyond the words and implications of the [Appointments Clause] and to infringe the constitutional principle of the separation of governmental powers." *Myers*, supra, at 161.

Unlike both *Bowsher* and *Myers*, this case does not involve an attempt by Congress itself to gain a role in the removal of executive officials other than its established powers of impeachment and conviction. The Act instead puts the removal power squarely in the hands of the Executive Branch; an independent counsel may be removed from office, "only by the personal action of the Attorney General, and only for good cause." § 596(a)(1). There is no requirement of congressional approval of the Attorney General's removal decision, though the decision is subject to judicial review. § 596(a)(3). In our view, the removal provisions of the Act make this case more analogous to *Humphrey's Executor v. United States*, 295 U.S. 602 (1935), than to *Myers* or *Bowsher*.

In *Humphrey's Executor*, the issue was whether a statute restricting the President's power to remove the Commissioners of the Federal Trade Commission (FTC) only for "inefficiency, neglect of duty, or malfeasance in office" was consistent with the Constitution. 295 U.S., at 619. We stated that whether Congress can "condition the [President's power of removal] by fixing a definite term and precluding a removal except for cause, will depend upon the character of the office." *Id.*, at 631. Contrary to the implication of some dicta in *Myers*, the President's power to remove Government officials simply was not "all-inclusive in respect of civil officers with the exception of the judiciary provided for by the Constitution." 295 U.S., at 629. At least in regard to "quasi-legislative" and "quasi-judicial" agencies such as the FTC, "[t]he authority of Congress, in creating [such] agencies, to require them to act in discharge of their duties independently of executive control . . . includes, as an appropriate incident, power to fix the period during which they shall continue in office, and to forbid their removal except for cause in the meantime." *Ibid.* In *Humphrey's Executor*, we found it "plain" that the Constitution did not give the President "illimitable power of removal" over the officers of independent agencies. *Ibid.* Were the President to have the power to remove FTC Commissioners at will, the "coercive influence" of the removal power would "threate[n] the independence of [the] commission." *Id.*, at 630. . . .

Appellees contend that *Humphrey's Executor* [is] distinguishable from this case because they did not involve officials who performed a "core executive function." They argue that our decision in *Humphrey's Executor* rests on a distinction between "purely executive" officials and officials who exercise "quasi-legislative" and "quasi-judicial" powers. In their view, when a "purely executive" official is involved, the governing precedent is *Myers*, not *Humphrey's Executor*. See *Humphrey's Executor*, supra, at 628. And, under *Myers*, the President must have absolute discretion to discharge "purely" executive officials at will. See *Myers*, 272 U.S., at 132–134.

We undoubtedly did rely on the terms "quasi-legislative" and "quasi-judicial" to distinguish the officials involved in *Humphrey's Executor* . . . from those in *Myers*, but our present considered view is that the determination of whether the Constitution allows Congress to impose a "good cause"-type restriction on the President's power to remove an official cannot be made to turn on whether or not that official is classified as "purely executive." The analysis contained in our removal cases is designed not to define rigid categories of those officials who may or may not be removed at will by the President, but to ensure that Congress does not interfere with the President's exercise of the "executive power" and his constitutionally appointed duty to "take care that the laws be faithfully executed" under Article II. Myers was undoubtedly correct in its holding, and in its broader suggestion that there are some "purely executive" officials who must be removable by the President at will if he is to be able to accomplish his constitutional role. See 272 U.S., at 132–134. But as the Court noted in *Wiener v. United States*, 357 U.S. 349 (1958):

> "The assumption was short-lived that the *Myers* case recognized the President's inherent constitutional power to remove officials no matter what the relation of the executive to the discharge of their duties and no matter what restrictions Congress may have imposed regarding the nature of their tenure." 357 U.S., at 352.

At the other end of the spectrum from *Myers*, the characterization of the agencies in *Humphrey's Executor* as "quasi-legislative" or "quasi-judicial" in large part reflected our judgment that it was not essential to the President's proper execution of his Article II powers that these agencies be headed up by individuals who were removable at will. We do not mean to suggest that an analysis of the functions served by the officials at issue is irrelevant. But the real question is whether the removal restrictions are of such a nature that they impede the President's ability to perform his constitutional duty, and the functions of the officials in question must be analyzed in that light.

Considering for the moment the "good cause" removal provision in isolation from the other parts of the Act at issue in this case, we cannot say that the imposition of a "good cause" standard for removal by itself unduly trammels on executive authority. There is no real dispute that the functions performed by the independent counsel are "executive" in the sense that they are law enforcement functions that typically have been undertaken by officials within the Executive Branch. As we noted above, however, the independent counsel is an inferior officer under the Appointments Clause, with limited jurisdiction and tenure and lacking policymaking or significant administrative authority. Although the counsel exercises no small amount of discretion and judgment in deciding how to carry out his or her duties under the Act, we simply do not see how the President's need to control the exercise of that discretion is so central to the functioning of the Executive Branch as to require as a matter of constitutional law that the counsel be terminable at will by the President.

Nor do we think that the "good cause" removal provision at issue here impermissibly burdens the President's power to control or supervise the independent counsel, as an executive official, in the execution of his or her duties under the Act. This is not a case in which the power to remove an executive official has been completely stripped from the President, thus providing no means for the President to ensure the "faithful execution" of the laws. Rather, because the independent counsel may be terminated for "good cause," the Executive, through the Attorney General, retains ample authority to assure that the counsel is competently performing his or her statutory responsibilities in a manner that comports with the provisions of the Act. Although we need not decide in the case exactly what is encompassed within the term "good cause" under the Act, the legislative history of the removal provision also makes clear that the Attorney General may remove an independent counsel for "misconduct." See H.R.Conf.Rep. No. 100–452, p. 37 (1987). Here, as with the provision of the Act conferring the appointment authority of the independent counsel on the special court, the congressional determination to limit the removal power of the Attorney General was essential, in the view of Congress, to establish the necessary independence of the office. We do not think that this limitation as it presently stands sufficiently deprives the President of control over the independent counsel to interfere impermissibly with his constitutional obligation to ensure the faithful execution of the laws. . . .

■ JUSTICE KENNEDY took no part in the consideration or decision of this case.

[The dissenting opinion of JUSTICE SCALIA has been omitted.]

QUESTIONS

1. In light of the following statement, do the categories of "purely executive," "quasi-legislative," and "quasi-judicial" officials still have relevance?

> We do not mean to suggest that an analysis of the functions served by the officials at issue is irrelevant. But the real question is whether the removal restrictions are of such a nature that they impede the President's ability to perform his . . . duty.

487 U.S. at 691. What, in light of *Morrison* did *Humphrey's Executor* hold? What did *Myers* hold?

2. Suppose Congress passed a law restricting to good cause the ability of the President to remove the Secretary of State or the Secretary of Defense. Would this be held valid under *Morrison*? Under *Humphrey's Executor*? Under *Myers*?

3. After *Morrison*, suppose that Congress imposed a good cause limitation on the removal of a postmaster of the first class (or modern equivalent); would this violate the constitutional principle of separation of powers?

Free Enterprise Fund v. Public Company
Accounting Oversight Board

Supreme Court of the United States, 2010.
561 U.S. 477, 130 S.Ct. 3138, 177 L.Ed.2d 706.

[In the wake of a series of accounting scandals, Congress enacted the Sarbanes-Oxley Act of 2002, which established the five-member Public Company Accounting Oversight Board ("the Board") charged with regulating every accounting firm that participates in auditing public companies under federal securities laws. The Board's responsibilities include promulgating auditing and ethics standards, performing routine inspections of all accounting firms, and initiating formal investigations and disciplinary proceedings. The willful violation of any Board rule is treated as a willful violation of the Securities and Exchange Act of 1934, and hence is a federal crime.

The Sarbanes-Oxley Act places the Board under the oversight of the Securities and Exchange Commission (SEC). The SEC appoints the Board's members for staggered five-year terms, and the Board's rules are subject to the SEC's approval. In addition to this oversight the Sarbanes-Oxley Act created two tiers of restraint on the President's ability to remove Board members' from their positions.

First, the SEC may remove Board members only "for good cause shown," and "in accordance with" certain procedures. 15 U.S.C. § 7211(e)(6). Specifically, in order to remove a Board member for cause, the SEC must make a finding, "on the record" and "after notice and opportunity for a hearing" that the Board member

(A) has willfully violated any provision of th[e] Act, the rules of the Board, or the securities laws;

(B) has willfully abused the authority of that member; or

(C) without reasonable justification or excuse, has failed to enforce compliance with any such provision or rule, or any professional standard by any registered public accounting firm or any associated person thereof.

15 U.S.C. § 7217(d)(3). Removal of a Board member requires a formal judicial order and is subject to judicial review.

Second, the SEC's Commissioners cannot themselves be removed at will. Rather, the President of the United States may remove

Commissioners only on the grounds of "inefficiency, neglect of duty, or malfeasance in office." *Humphrey's Executor v. United States*, 295 U.S. 602 (1935).

The Free Enterprise Fund is a pro-business advocacy group whose members include an accounting firm, Beckstead and Watts, LLP, which was the subject of a critical report and a formal investigation by the Board. The Free Enterprise Fund and Beckstead and Watts sued the Board, seeking a declaratory judgment that the Board is unconstitutional. Among other claims, the Free Enterprise Fund and Beckstead and Watts contended that the two tiers of restraint on Board members' removal violate the separation of powers by insulating the Board from Presidential control. The District Court granted summary judgment to the Board. A divided Court of Appeals affirmed, and the Supreme Court granted certiorari.]

■ CHIEF JUSTICE ROBERTS delivered the opinion of the Court[, in which JUSTICE SCALIA, JUSTICE KENNEDY, JUSTICE THOMAS, and JUSTICE ALITO joined].

Our Constitution divided the "powers of the new Federal Government into three defined categories, Legislative, Executive, and Judicial." *INS* v. *Chadha*, 462 U.S. 919, 951 (1983). Article II vests "[t]he executive Power . . . in a President of the United States of America," who must "take Care that the Laws be faithfully executed." Art. II, § 1, cl. 1; *id.* § 3. In light of "[t]he impossibility that one man should be able to perform all the great business of the State," the Constitution provides for executive officers to "assist the supreme Magistrate in discharging the duties of his trust." 30 Writings of George Washington 334 (J. Fitzpatrick ed. 1939).

Since 1789, the Constitution has been understood to empower the President to keep these officers accountable—by removing them from office, if necessary. See generally *Myers* v. *United States*, 272 U.S. 52 (1926). This Court has determined, however, that this authority is not without limit. In *Humphrey's Executor* v. *United States*, 295 U.S. 602 (1935), we held that Congress can, under certain circumstances, create independent agencies run by principal officers appointed by the President, whom the President may not remove at will but only for good cause. Likewise, in *United States* v. *Perkins*, 116 U.S. 483 (1886), and *Morrison* v. *Olson*, 487 U.S. 654 (1988), the Court sustained similar restrictions on the power of principal executive officers—themselves responsible to the President—to remove their own inferiors. The parties do not ask us to reexamine any of these precedents, and we do not do so.

We are asked, however, to consider a new situation not yet encountered by the Court. The question is whether these separate layers of protection may be combined. May the President be restricted in his ability to remove a principal officer, who is in turn restricted in his ability to remove an inferior officer, even though that inferior officer determines the policy and enforces the laws of the United States?

We hold that such multilevel protection from removal is contrary to Article II's vesting of the executive power in the President. The President cannot "take Care that the Laws be faithfully executed" if he cannot oversee the faithfulness of the officers who execute them. Here the President cannot remove an officer who enjoys more than one level of good-cause protection, even if the President determines that the officer is neglecting his duties or discharging them improperly. That judgment is instead committed to another officer, who may or may not agree with the President's determination, and whom the President cannot remove simply because that officer disagrees with him. This contravenes the President's "constitutional obligation to ensure the faithful execution of the laws." *Id.* at 693. . . .

III

We hold that the dual for-cause limitations on the removal of Board members contravene the Constitution's separation of powers.

A

The Constitution provides that "[t]he executive Power shall be vested in a President of the United States of America." Art. II, § 1, cl. 1. As Madison stated on the floor of the First Congress, "if any power whatsoever is in its nature Executive, it is the power of appointing, overseeing, and controlling those who execute the laws." 1 Annals of Cong. 463 (1789). . . .

The landmark case of *Myers* v. *United States* reaffirmed the principle that Article II confers on the President "the general administrative control of those executing the laws." 272 U.S., at 164. It is *his* responsibility to take care that the laws be faithfully executed. The buck stops with the President, in Harry Truman's famous phrase. As we explained in *Myers*, the President therefore must have some "power of removing those for whom he can not continue to be responsible." *Id.* at 117.

Nearly a decade later in *Humphrey's Executor*, this Court held that *Myers* did not prevent Congress from conferring good-cause tenure on the principal officers of certain independent agencies. That case concerned the members of the Federal Trade Commission, who held 7 year terms and could not be removed by the President except for " 'inefficiency, neglect of duty, or malfeasance in office.' " 295 U.S. at 620 (quoting 15 U.S.C. § 41). The Court distinguished *Myers* on the ground that *Myers* concerned "an officer [who] is merely one of the units in the executive department and, hence, inherently subject to the exclusive and illimitable power of removal by the Chief Executive, whose subordinate and aid he is." 295 U.S. at 627. By contrast, the Court characterized the FTC as "quasi-legislative and quasi-judicial" rather than "purely executive," and held that Congress could require it "to act . . . independently of executive control." *Id,* at 627–29. Because "one who holds his office only during the pleasure of another, cannot be depended upon to maintain an attitude of independence against the latter's will," the Court held that Congress had power to "fix the period during which [the Commissioners] shall continue in office, and to forbid their removal except for cause in the meantime." *Id.* at 629.

Humphrey's Executor did not address the removal of inferior officers, whose appointment Congress may vest in heads of departments. If Congress does so, it is ordinarily the department head, rather than the President, who enjoys the power of removal. See *Myers, supra,* at 119, 127; [*Ex parte*] *Hennen,* [38 U.S. 230,] 259–60. This Court has upheld for-cause limitations on that power as well. . . .

[*Morrison v. Olson*] concerned the Ethics in Government Act, which provided for an independent counsel to investigate allegations of crime by high executive officers. The counsel was appointed by a special court, wielded the full powers of a prosecutor, and was removable by the Attorney General only " 'for good cause.' " 487 U.S. at 663 (quoting 28 U.S.C. § 596(a)(1)). We recognized that the independent counsel was undoubtedly an executive officer, rather than " 'quasi-legislative' " or " 'quasi-judicial,' " but we stated as "our present considered view" that Congress had power to impose good-cause restrictions on her removal. 487 U.S. at 689–91. The Court noted that the statute "g[a]ve the Attorney General," an officer directly responsible to the President and "through [whom]" the President could act, "several means of supervising or controlling" the independent counsel—"[m]ost importantly . . . the power to remove the counsel for good cause." *Id.* at 695–96 (internal quotation marks omitted). Under those circumstances, the Court sustained the statute. *Morrison* did not, however, address the consequences of more than one level of good-cause tenure—leaving the issue, as both the court and dissent below recognized, "a question of first impression" in this Court. 537 F.3d at 679; see *id.* at 698 (dissenting opinion).

B

As explained, we have previously upheld limited restrictions on the President's removal power. In those cases, however, only one level of protected tenure separated the President from an officer exercising executive power. It was the President—or a subordinate he could remove at will—who decided whether the officer's conduct merited removal under the good-cause standard. The Act before us does something quite different. It not only protects Board members from removal except for good cause, but withdraws from the President any decision on whether that good cause exists. That decision is vested instead in other tenured officers—the Commissioners—none of whom is subject to the President's direct control. The result is a Board that is not accountable to the President, and a President who is not responsible for the Board. The added layer of tenure protection makes a difference. Without a layer of insulation between the Commission and the Board, the Commission could remove a Board member at any time, and therefore would be fully responsible for what the Board does. The President could then hold the

Commission to account for its supervision of the Board, to the same extent that he may hold the Commission to account for everything else it does. A second level of tenure protection changes the nature of the President's review. Now the Commission cannot remove a Board member at will. The President therefore cannot hold the Commission fully accountable for the Board's conduct, to the same extent that he may hold the Commission accountable for everything else that it does. The Commissioners are not responsible for the Board's actions. They are only responsible for their own determination of whether the Act's rigorous good-cause standard is met. And even if the President disagrees with their determination, he is powerless to intervene—unless that determination is so unreasonable as to constitute "inefficiency, neglect of duty, or malfeasance in office." *Humphrey's Executor*, 295 U.S. at 620 (internal quotation marks omitted).

This novel structure does not merely add to the Board's independence, but transforms it. Neither the President, nor anyone directly responsible to him, nor even an officer whose conduct he may review only for good cause, has full control over the Board. The President is stripped of the power our precedents have preserved, and his ability to execute the laws—by holding his subordinates accountable for their conduct—is impaired.

That arrangement is contrary to Article II's vesting of the executive power in the President. Without the ability to oversee the Board, or to attribute the Board's failings to those whom he *can* oversee, the President is no longer the judge of the Board's conduct. He is not the one who decides whether Board members are abusing their offices or neglecting their duties. He can neither ensure that the laws are faithfully executed, nor be held responsible for a Board member's breach of faith. This violates the basic principle that the President "cannot delegate ultimate responsibility or the active obligation to supervise that goes with it," because Article II "makes a single President responsible for the actions of the Executive Branch." *Clinton v. Jones*, 520 U.S. 681, 712–13 (1997) (BREYER, J., concurring in judgment).

Indeed, if allowed to stand, this dispersion of responsibility could be multiplied. If Congress can shelter the bureaucracy behind two layers of good-cause tenure, why not a third? At oral argument, the Government was unwilling to concede that even five layers between the President and the Board would be too many. Tr. of Oral Arg. 47–48. The officers of such an agency—safely encased within a Matryoshka doll of tenure protections—would be immune from Presidential oversight, even as they exercised power in the people's name.

Perhaps an individual President might find advantages in tying his own hands. But the separation of powers does not depend on the views of individual Presidents, see *Freytag v. Commissioner*, 501 U.S. 868, 879–80 (1991), nor on whether "the encroached-upon branch approves the encroachment," *New York v. United States*, 505 U.S. 144, 182 (1992). The

President can always choose to restrain himself in his dealings with subordinates. He cannot, however, choose to bind his successors by diminishing their powers, nor can he escape responsibility for his choices by pretending that they are not his own.

The diffusion of power carries with it a diffusion of accountability. The people do not vote for the "Officers of the United States." Art. II, § 2, cl. 2. They instead look to the President to guide the "assistants or deputies . . . subject to his superintendence." The Federalist No. 72, p. 487 (J. Cooke ed. 1961) (A. Hamilton). Without a clear and effective chain of command, the public cannot "determine on whom the blame or the punishment of a pernicious measure, or series of pernicious measures ought really to fall." *Id.* No. 70, at 476 (same). That is why the Framers sought to ensure that "those who are employed in the execution of the law will be in their proper situation, and the chain of dependence be preserved; the lowest officers, the middle grade, and the highest, will depend, as they ought, on the President, and the President on the community." 1 Annals of Cong., at 499 (J. Madison).

By granting the Board executive power without the Executive's oversight, this Act subverts the President's ability to ensure that the laws are faithfully executed—as well as the public's ability to pass judgment on his efforts. The Act's restrictions are incompatible with the Constitution's separation of powers. . . .

The Constitution that makes the President accountable to the people for executing the laws also gives him the power to do so. That power includes, as a general matter, the authority to remove those who assist him in carrying out his duties. Without such power, the President could not be held fully accountable for discharging his own responsibilities; the buck would stop somewhere else. Such diffusion of authority "would greatly diminish the intended and necessary responsibility of the chief magistrate himself." The Federalist No. 70, at 478.

While we have sustained in certain cases limits on the President's removal power, the Act before us imposes a new type of restriction—two levels of protection from removal for those who nonetheless exercise significant executive power. Congress cannot limit the President's authority in this way.

The judgment of the United States Court of Appeals for the District of Columbia Circuit is affirmed in part and reversed in part, and the case is remanded for further proceedings consistent with this opinion. . . .

■ JUSTICE BREYER, with whom JUSTICE STEVENS, JUSTICE GINSBURG, and JUSTICE SOTOMAYOR join, dissenting.

The Court holds unconstitutional a statute providing that the Securities and Exchange Commission . . . can remove members of the Public Company Accounting Oversight Board from office only for cause. It argues that granting the "inferior officer[s]" on the Accounting Board "more than one level of good-cause protection . . . contravenes the

President's 'constitutional obligation to ensure the faithful execution of the laws.'" I agree that the Accounting Board members are inferior officers. But in my view the statute does not significantly interfere with the President's "executive Power." Art. II, § 1. It violates no separation-of-powers principle. And the Court's contrary holding threatens to disrupt severely the fair and efficient administration of the laws. I consequently dissent.

I

A

The legal question before us arises at the intersection of two general constitutional principles. On the one hand, Congress has broad power to enact statutes "necessary and proper" to the exercise of its specifically enumerated constitutional authority. Art. I, § 8, cl. 18. . . . And Congress has drawn on that power over the past century to create numerous federal agencies in response to "various crises of human affairs" as they have arisen. [Citation.]

On the other hand, the opening sections of Articles I, II, and III of the Constitution separately and respectively vest "all legislative Powers" in Congress, the "executive Power" in the President, and the "judicial Power" in the Supreme Court (and such "inferior Courts as Congress may from time to time ordain and establish"). In doing so, these provisions imply a structural separation-of-powers principle. [Citation.] And that principle, along with the instruction in Article II, § 3 that the President "shall take Care that the Laws be faithfully executed," limits Congress' power to structure the Federal Government. [Citation.] Indeed, this Court has held that the separation-of-powers principle guarantees the President the authority to dismiss certain Executive Branch officials at will. *Myers* v. *United States*, 272 U.S. 52 (1926).

But neither of these two principles is absolute in its application to removal cases. The Necessary and Proper Clause does not grant Congress power to free *all* Executive Branch officials from dismissal at the will of the President. *Id.* Nor does the separation-of-powers principle grant the President an absolute authority to remove *any and all* Executive Branch officials at will. Rather, depending on, say, the nature of the office, its function, or its subject matter, Congress sometimes may, consistent with the Constitution, limit the President's authority to remove an officer from his post. See *Humphrey's Executor* v. *United States*, 295 U.S. 602 (1935), overruling in part *Myers, supra; Morrison* v. *Olson*, 487 U.S. 654 (1988). And we must here decide whether the circumstances surrounding the statute at issue justify such a limitation. . . .

[T]his Court's precedent [does not] fully answer the question presented. At least it does not clearly invalidate the provision in dispute. In *Myers, supra,* the Court invalidated—for the first and only time—a congressional statute on the ground that it unduly limited the President's authority to remove an Executive Branch official. But soon thereafter the

Court expressly disapproved most of *Myers'* broad reasoning. See *Humphrey's Executor*, 295 U.S., at 626–27, overruling in part *Myers, supra*; *Wiener v. United States*, 357 U.S. 349, 352 (1958) (stating that *Humphrey's Executor* "explicitly 'disapproved' " of much of the reasoning in *Myers*). Moreover, the Court has since said that "the essence of the decision in *Myers* was the judgment that the Constitution prevents Congress from *'draw[ing] to itself* . . . the power to remove or the right to participate in the exercise of that power.'" *Morrison, supra,* at 686. And that feature of the statute—a feature that would *aggrandize* the power of Congress—is not present here. Congress has not granted itself any role in removing the members of the Accounting Board. [Citation.] Compare *Myers, supra,* (striking down statute where Congress granted *itself* removal authority over Executive Branch official), with *Humphrey's Executor, supra,* (upholding statute where such aggrandizing was absent); [citation;] *Morrison, supra* (same). . . .

In short, the question presented lies at the intersection of two sets of conflicting, broadly framed constitutional principles. And no text, no history, perhaps no precedent provides any clear answer. Cf. *Chicago v. Morales*, 527 U.S. 41, 106 (1999) (THOMAS, J., joined by REHNQUIST, C.J., and SCALIA, J., dissenting) (expressing the view that "this Court" is "most vulnerable" when "it deals with judge-made constitutional law" that lacks "roots in the language" of the Constitution (internal quotation marks omitted)).

B

When previously deciding this kind of nontextual question, the Court has emphasized the importance of examining how a particular provision, taken in context, is likely to function. . . .

The functional approach required by our precedents . . . recognizes the various ways presidential power operates within [the] context [of administrative complexity]—and the various ways in which a removal provision might affect that power. As human beings have known ever since Ulysses tied himself to the mast so as safely to hear the Sirens' song, sometimes it is necessary to disable oneself in order to achieve a broader objective. Thus, legally enforceable commitments—such as contracts, statutes that cannot instantly be changed, and, as in the case before us, the establishment of independent administrative institutions—hold the potential to empower precisely because of their ability to constrain. If the President seeks to regulate through impartial adjudication, then insulation of the adjudicator from removal at will can help him achieve that goal. And to free a technical decisionmaker from the fear of removal without cause can similarly help create legitimacy with respect to that official's regulatory actions by helping to insulate his technical decisions from nontechnical political pressure. . . .

Thus, here, as in similar cases, we should decide the constitutional question in light of the provision's practical functioning in context. And our decision should take account of the Judiciary's comparative lack of institutional expertise.

II

A

To what extent then is the Act's "for cause" provision likely, as a practical matter, to limit the President's exercise of executive authority? In practical terms no "for cause" provision can, in isolation, define the full measure of executive power. This is because a legislative decision to place ultimate administrative authority in, say, the Secretary of Agriculture rather than the President, the way in which the statute defines the scope of the power the relevant administrator can exercise, the decision as to who controls the agency's budget requests and funding, the relationships between one agency or department and another, as well as more purely political factors (including Congress' ability to assert influence) are more likely to affect the President's power to get something done. That is why President Truman complained that " 'the powers of the President amount to' " bringing " 'people in and try[ing] to persuade them to do what they ought to do without persuasion.' " C. Rossiter, The American Presidency 154 (2d rev. ed. 1960). And that is why scholars have written that the President "is neither dominant nor powerless" in his relationships with many Government entities, "whether denominated executive or independent." Strauss, The Place of Agencies in Government: Separation of Powers and the Fourth Branch, 84 Colum. L. Rev. 573, 583 (1984). Those entities "are *all* subject to presidential direction in significant aspects of their functioning, and [are each] able to resist presidential direction in others." *Id.* (emphasis added).

Indeed, notwithstanding the majority's assertion that the removal authority is "*the* key" mechanism by which the President oversees inferior officers in the independent agencies, it appears that no President has ever actually sought to exercise that power by testing the scope of a "for cause" provision. [Citation.]

But even if we put all these other matters to the side, we should still conclude that the "for cause" restriction before us will not restrict presidential power significantly. For one thing, the restriction directly limits, not the President's power, but the power of an already independent agency. The Court seems to have forgotten that fact when it identifies its central constitutional problem: According to the Court, the President "is powerless to intervene" if he has determined that the Board members' "conduct merit[s] removal" because "[t]hat decision is vested instead in other tenured officers—the Commissioners—none of whom is subject to the President's direct control." But so long as the President is *legitimately* foreclosed from removing the *Commissioners* except for cause (as the majority assumes), nullifying the Commission's power to remove Board members only for cause will not resolve the problem the Court has identified: The President will *still* be "powerless to intervene" by removing the Board members if the Commission reasonably decides not to do so.

In other words, the Court fails to show why *two* layers of "for cause" protection—Layer One insulating the Commissioners from the President, and Layer Two insulating the Board from the Commissioners—impose any more serious limitation upon the *President's* powers than *one* layer. Consider the four scenarios that might arise:

1.   The President and the Commission both want to keep a Board member in office. Neither layer is relevant.

2.   The President and the Commission both want to dismiss a Board member. Layer Two stops them both from doing so without cause. The President's ability to remove the Commission (Layer One) is irrelevant, for he and the Commission are in agreement.

3.   The President wants to dismiss a Board member, but the Commission wants to keep the member. Layer One allows the Commission to make that determination notwithstanding the President's contrary view. Layer Two is irrelevant because the Commission does not seek to remove the Board member.

4.   The President wants to keep a Board member, but the Commission wants to dismiss the Board member. Here, Layer Two *helps the President*, for it hinders the Commission's ability to dismiss a Board member whom the President wants to keep in place.

Thus, the majority's decision to eliminate only *Layer Two* accomplishes virtually nothing. And that is because a removal restriction's effect upon presidential power depends not on the presence of a "double-layer" of for-cause removal, as the majority pretends, but rather on the real-world nature of the President's relationship with the Commission. If the President confronts a Commission that seeks to *resist* his policy preferences—a distinct possibility when, as here, a Commission's membership must reflect both political parties, 15 U.S.C. § 78d(a)—the restriction on the *Commission's* ability to remove a Board member is either irrelevant (as in scenario 3) or may actually help the President (as in scenario 4). And if the President faces a Commission that seeks to *implement* his policy preferences, Layer One is irrelevant, for the President and Commission see eye to eye.

In order to avoid this elementary logic, the Court creates two alternative scenarios. In the first, the Commission and the President *both* want to remove a Board member, but have varying judgments as to whether they have good "cause" to do so—*i.e.*, the President and the Commission both conclude that a Board member should be removed, but disagree as to whether that conclusion (which they have both reached) is *reasonable*. In the second, the President wants to remove a Board member and the Commission disagrees; but, notwithstanding its freedom to make reasonable decisions independent of the President (afforded by Layer One), the Commission (while apparently telling the President that it agrees with him and would like to remove the Board member) uses Layer Two as an "excuse" to pursue its actual aims—an excuse which, given Layer One, it does not need.

Both of these circumstances seem unusual. I do not know if they have ever occurred. But I do not deny their logical possibility. I simply doubt their importance. And the fact that, with respect to the President's power, the double layer of for-cause removal sometimes might help, sometimes might hurt, leads me to conclude that its overall effect is at most indeterminate.

But once we leave the realm of hypothetical logic and view the removal provision at issue in the context of the entire Act, its lack of practical effect becomes readily apparent. That is because the statute provides the Commission with full authority and virtually comprehensive control over all of the Board's functions. . . .

[T]he Court is simply wrong when it says that "the Act nowhere gives the Commission effective power to start, stop, or alter" Board investigations. On the contrary, the Commission's control over the Board's investigatory and legal functions is virtually absolute. . . .

Everyone concedes that the President's control over the Commission is constitutionally sufficient. And if the President's control over the Commission is sufficient, and the Commission's control over the Board is virtually absolute, then, as a practical matter, the President's control over the Board should prove sufficient as well. . . .

C

Where a "for cause" provision is so unlikely to restrict presidential power and so likely to further a legitimate institutional need, precedent strongly supports its constitutionality. First, in considering a related issue in *Nixon v. Administrator of General Services*, 433 U.S. 425 (1977), the Court made clear that when "determining whether the Act disrupts the proper balance between the coordinate branches, the proper inquiry focuses on the extent to which it prevents the Executive Branch from accomplishing its constitutionally assigned functions." *Id.* at 443. The Court said the same in *Morrison*, where it upheld a restriction on the President's removal power. 487 U.S. at 691 ("[T]he real question is whether the removal restrictions are of such a nature that they impede the President's ability to perform his constitutional duty, and the functions of the officials in question must be analyzed in that light"). Here, the removal restriction may somewhat diminish the *Commission's* ability to control the Board, but it will have little, if any, negative effect in respect to the President's ability to control the Board, let alone to coordinate the Executive Branch. Indeed, given *Morrison*, where the Court upheld a restriction that significantly interfered with the

President's important historic power to control criminal prosecutions, a " 'purely executive' " function, 487 U.S. at 687–89, the constitutionality of the present restriction would seem to follow *a fortiori*. . . .

In sum, the Court's prior cases impose functional criteria that are readily met here. Once one goes beyond the Court's elementary arithmetical logic (*i.e.,* "one plus one is greater than one") our precedent virtually dictates a holding that the challenged "for cause" provision is constitutional. . . .

QUESTIONS

1. Recall the factors that the *Morrison* Court said were relevant to whether a for-cause removal provision unconstitutionally interferes with the President's executive powers. When deciding whether it violates the separation of powers to grant members of the Public Accounting Oversight Board two levels of for-cause protection, does the majority in *Free Enterprise Fund* consider these factors? Does the dissent?

2. Does the lack of presidential accountability that the *Free Enterprise Fund* majority condemns result from the double layer of for-cause review, or from *Humphrey's Executor*?

3. Prior to *Free Enterprise Fund*, as both the majority and the dissent acknowledge, the Court had never considered whether it is unconstitutional for Congress to grant an executive officer more than one level of tenure protection. But consider the following statements from the *Free Enterprise Fund* opinions:

(a)   (from the majority opinion) "*Morrison* did not . . . address the consequences of more than one level of good-cause tenure—leaving the issue . . . 'a question of first impression' in this Court."

(b)   (from the dissent): "[H]ere, as in similar cases, we should decide the constitutional question in light of the provision's practical functioning in context."

What does the majority mean when it characterizes the question before the Court as one "of first impression"? Does the dissent agree? If a Justice deciding *Free Enterprise Fund* disagrees with the *Morrison* Court's approach to deciding whether a removal provision violates the separation of powers, is the Justice free to reject that approach when evaluating "the consequences of more than one level of good-cause tenure?" Do the statements above suggest that the majority and the dissent hold different views on this question?

These questions are meant to illustrate the difficulties that sometimes arise when determining whether precedent controls the outcome of a particular case. The holding of a case, as we have seen, includes (at the very least) both the result of the case and the analysis that was necessary for the court to reach that result. It follows that, if a court is bound to follow the holding of a case, it is obligated to follow the reasoning necessary to reach the result of that case. The doctrine of precedent, however, requires courts to follow the holding of a prior case only when a similar issue arises in the future. Accordingly, whether the holding of a case is binding in a particular circumstance will depend on how one frames the issue that was decided in the case. A judge who is critical of the court's analysis in a prior case may wish to frame the issue being decided in that case as narrowly as possible, while a judge who wishes to extend that analysis will have an incentive to frame the issue broadly.

4.   Suppose that you had been advisor to the President after *Morrison* had been decided, but before the decision in *Free Enterprise Fund*, and a member of the Public Accounting Oversight Board had committed a well-publicized act of misconduct. The SEC has formally found that there are grounds for removing the Board member for cause, but has declined to do so. The President is infuriated, and asks for your opinion on whether he may fire the SEC Commissioners. The removal provision at issue in *Free Enterprise Fund* states that, after making the appropriate findings, the SEC "may, as necessary or appropriate in the public interest, for the protection of investors, or otherwise in furtherance of the purposes of this Act or the securities laws, remove from office or censure" a Board member. 15 U.S.C. § 7217(d)(3). What is your advice to the President? Suppose the statute simply said that, if it has found that a Board member has committed misconduct, the SEC "must remove from office or censure" a Board member. Would your advice to the President change? Under the Court's holding in *Free Enterprise Fund*, are the answers to these questions relevant to whether the removal provision violates the separation of powers? Are they relevant under the Court's approach in *Morrison*?

PROBLEM CASE

The following is the opinion of the court in the recent case of *Koehler v. Gerry*, decided by the Supreme Court of the [hypothetical] State of New Hazard in January, 2020.

> SARADHI, J. The facts in this case can be simply stated. Early in 2010, the defendant Emily Gerry purchased a new Toyota automobile for the use of herself and the members of her immediate family. On March 6, 2018, the defendant Gerry gave her 16-year-old daughter, Clara, permission to drive the Ford to the lab where she works after school. As is well known, the law of this State forbids the issuance of a driver's license to any person under 18 years of age. While Clara was driving through the streets of Louktown on the way to the lab, she lost control of the car, which ran up on the curb and seriously injured the plaintiff Koehler.

> The facts stated in the foregoing paragraph are alleged in the plaintiff Koehler's complaint in this action. The jury brought in a verdict for $150,000 damages in plaintiff Koehler's favor, and the defendant Gerry moved for a new trial. The motion for a new trial was denied by the trial court, and the defendant appeals to this Court.

> The development of the law on this subject has been attended by a slow process of clarification. When the automobile was new and

regarded as no more dangerous than the horse and buggy, courts were disposed to hold that no strict liability attached to a registered car owner. Today, mounting traffic accident statistics have brought home to us that the modern, 100-mile-an-hour automobile is, indeed, fraught with such possibility for harm that the owner must bear strict responsibility for its use. When a person purchases a high-powered automobile and allows her spouse or child to use it, she is responsible for all injuries to pedestrians which may result from the spouse's or child's negligence in the operation of the automobile. The question of law is, remarkably, one of first impression in this jurisdiction, but we have no doubt at all about it.

Because, as stated in Judge Saradhi's opinion, the decision in *Koehler v. Gerry* is the first decision in New Hazard on the subject of the liability of a car owner for injuries resulting from another's operation of her car, it is important to determine the scope of the principle of law for which *Koehler v. Gerry* can be taken as authority. What *is* the holding of *Koehler v. Gerry*?

Cullings v. Goetz

Court of Appeals of New York, 1931.
256 N.Y. 287, 176 N.E. 397.

[Action by Joseph Cullings against Edward Goetz and others. From a judgment (231 App.Div. 266, 247 N.Y.S. 109), reversing a judgment of the Trial Term in favor of the plaintiff, and dismissing the complaint, the plaintiff appeals.]

■ CARDOZO, C.J. Plaintiff brought his automobile to a garage, intending to drive in. There were two sliding doors at the entrance, one open, the other closed. He tried to push the closed one open, but it did not move upon its track. When he shook it with some force, it fell upon his back, causing injuries for which he sues. His action is against Goetz, lessee of the garage, and the Nickleys, the owners, who were also the lessors. The lease was an oral one, and ran from month to month. The trial judge left the question to the jury whether as one of its provisions the owners had agreed to make the necessary repairs. In the event of that agreement and of failure to repair after notice of the need, owners as well as lessee were to be held for any negligence in the unsafe condition of the doors. The jury found a verdict against all the parties sued. On an appeal by the owners, the Appellate Division reversed, and dismissed the complaint upon the ground that the failure of the owners to keep the promise to repair was unavailing to charge them with liability in tort.

The evidence of the supposed promise is at best confused and uncertain, if there be evidence at all. For the purpose of this appeal we assume without deciding that it permits conflicting inferences. We assume also that there was freedom from contributory negligence, though another entrance was available, and there is evidence of notice that the one chosen was out of use. Giving the plaintiff's case the aid of these assumptions, we concur with the Appellate Division in its ruling that liability in tort must be confined to the lessee, whose possession and dominion were exclusive and complete.

The subject has divided juridical opinion. Generally, however, in this country as in England, a covenant to repair does not impose upon the lessor a liability in tort at the suit of the lessee or of others lawfully on the land in the right of the lessee. [Citations.] There are decisions to the contrary [citation], but they speak the voice of a minority. Liability in tort is an incident to occupation or control. American Law Inst., Restatement of the Law of Torts, § 227. By preponderant opinion, occupation and control are not reserved through an agreement that the landlord will repair. Cavalier v. Pope, [1906] A.C. 428, at page 433; Pollock, Torts (13th Ed.) 532; Salmond, Torts (7th Ed.) 477. The tenant and no one else may keep visitors away till the danger is abated, or adapt the warning to the need. The landlord has at most a privilege to enter for the doing of the work, and at times not even that if the occupant protests. "The power of control necessary to raise the duty * * * implies something more than the right or liability to repair the premises. It implies the power and the right to admit people to the premises and to exclude people from them." Cavalier v. Pope, supra. In saying this we assume the possibility of so phrasing and enlarging the rights of the lessor that occupation and control will be shared with the lessee. There are decisions in Massachusetts that draw a distinction between a covenant merely to repair and one to maintain in safe condition with supervision adequate to the end to be achieved. [Citations.] In the case now at hand, the promise, if there was any, was to act at the request of the lessee. What resulted was not a reservation by an owner of one of the privileges of ownership. It was the assumption of a burden for the benefit of the occupant with consequences the same as if there had been a promise to repair by a plumber or a carpenter. [Citations.]

The rule in this state is settled in accord with the prevailing doctrine. Dicta, supposed to be inconsistent, are summoned to the support of a contrary position. They will be considered later on. Whatever their significance, they cannot overcome decisions directly to the point. As often as the question has been squarely up, the answer has been consistent that there is no liability in tort. Some of the decisions rejecting liability are judgments of this court. [Citations.] Others, too many to be fully numbered, are in courts of intermediate appeal. [Citations.] The doctrine, wise or unwise in its origin, has worked itself by common acquiescence into the tissues of our law. It is too deeply imbedded to be superseded or ignored. Hardly a day goes by in our great centers of population but it is applied by judges and juries in cases great and small. Countless tenants, suing for personal injuries and proving nothing more than the breach of an agreement, have been dismissed without a remedy in adherence to the authority of Schick v. Fleischhauer and Kushes v. Ginsberg. Countless visitors of tenants and members of a tenant's family have encountered a like fate. If there is no remedy for the tenant, there is none for visitors or relatives present in the tenant's right. Miles v. Janvrin, supra, 196 Mass. at page 440, 82 N.E. 708, 13 L.R.A. (N.S.) 378, 124 Am.St.Rep. 575; Elefante v. Pizitz, 182 App.Div. 819, 821, 169 N.Y.S. 910. Liability has been enlarged by statute where an apartment in an tenement house in a city of the first class is the subject of the lease. Altz v. Leiberson, 233 N.Y. 16, 134 N.E. 703. The duty in such instances is independent of the contract. It is one imposed by law, with liability in tort where the duty is ignored. Here the plaintiff was injured in the use of a garage. His remedy is against the tenant at whose invitation he was there.

We have spoken of dicta that are cited to the contrary. They do not touch the liability of the landlord for conditions within the premises affecting only the lessee or those who enter upon the premises in the right of the lessee. They have to do with nuisances threatening danger to the public beyond the land demised. [Citations.] Even when thus confined, they are dicta, and nothing more, at least in this state, though reiteration may have given them an authority not otherwise belonging to them. Be that as it may, the fact remains that the decision in every instance exonerated the lessor. One case, it is true, there is (Kilmer v. White, 254 N.Y. 64, 69, 171 N.E. 908), which had to do with conditions within the premises, and not with those outside, but it cites Jaffe v. Harteau, supra, and does not suggest even remotely a purpose to establish a new rule. There is merely a cautious reservation of the doctrine to be applied in situations different from any before us at the time. . . .

Other grounds of liability suggested in the plaintiff's argument have been considered and are found to be untenable.

We state for greater caution, though the caution should be needless, that nothing said in this opinion has relation to a case where a part only of the building is in the possession of the lessee, and the dangerous condition is in the ways or other parts retained by the lessor. [Citations.]

The judgment should be affirmed with costs.

■ Pound, Crane, Lehman, Kellogg, O'Brien, and Hubbs, JJ., concur.

Judgment affirmed.

Note and Question

1. One can infer from the opinion of the court in *Cullings v. Goetz* that counsel for the plaintiff-appellant Cullings had cited past decisions of the Court of Appeals in which the opinions had contained statements generally supporting the plaintiff-appellant's position in the principal case. What is the theory on which Judge Cardozo, in his opinion for the court in the principal case, characterizes these past judicial utterances as dicta?

2. Note the care with which Judge Cardozo, in the final paragraph of his opinion, attempts to make it certain that *Cullings v. Goetz* will not, in its turn, be cited out of context by counsel for the defendant in some future suit against a lessor in part possession of a building.

STARE DECISIS IN OPERATION: THE SCOPE OF A PRECEDENT

It should be apparent by now that to ask the question, "What is the holding of a case?" is really to ask, "What fact situations can the rule of law of that case be said to govern?" *i.e.*, "As to what future cases does the decision of the case constitute binding authority?" Since the decision as to whether or not a precedent governs a particular case rests, in the last analysis, with the court deciding the later case, the answer to the question "What is the holding?" is a prediction that as to certain future fact situations the court will consider the decision governing. Whether the prediction is accurate will not be known until the question is finally adjudicated.

The principle of *stare decisis*, simply stated, is that the decision in a case should govern the decision in all like cases—but only in like cases. The best guide in the determination of what are "like cases" is a constant awareness of the underlying assumption of the Anglo-American system of case-by-case progress: that the court in every case will have before it all the facts necessary to a decision and that it will make its decision cognizant of all factors that should be considered. Here we have a standard by which to judge what are "like cases"—they are those whose fact situations present to the court the same factors to be considered in reaching a decision.

There are in any case a number of facts which obviously play no part in the determination, *i.e.*, facts whose absence will not change the factors that the court must consider in reaching its decision. In formulating our statement of the rule of law established by that case, we can safely exclude these obviously nonsignificant (immaterial) facts from our consideration. So stated, the rule of law derived from that case will cover only fact situations so similar to that case that no court can distinguish it without resorting to painfully obvious sophistry, a course courts are usually reluctant to pursue. Here we have the minimum of what can be called the holding.

As we continue to abstract from the facts of our case we eventually reach a level of generalization that clearly includes fact situations materially different from that of the case, *i.e.*, fact situations containing facts that present different considerations for the court to take account of in reaching its decision. When we reach this level of generalization we have gone beyond the maximum of what can be called the holding. An example of such a generalization is that of *Baker v. Libbie*—that all creators are entitled to the fruits of their labors.

These limits, however, guide us only in the easy cases. Between these limits lies a large area in which no one can be sure that his statement of the holding is not too general or too specific—that his view of what the material facts were is the right one—until the court has decided the case. This is the area in which most litigated cases fall. The best that can be done in this area is to state a reasonable rule of law abstracted from the precedent case. Your job as a counselor will be to make a reasonable prediction as to the extent to which a precedent will control. Your initial job as an advocate will be to state the holding of the precedent case in sufficiently general terms so that it covers the facts of your case. Your opponent will be stating the holding in much narrower terms—sufficiently narrow so that it does not cover the facts of your case (she will be "distinguishing the case on its facts"). Until the new case is decided, no one can say with certainty that either statement of the holding is right or wrong. Each statement may be eminently reasonable and until the court has been persuaded to adopt one or the other, there can be no flat answer to the question of which statement more nearly approximated the holding of the precedent case. It may (or may not) be some consolation that judges often disagree as to what the prior case held.

The job of stating a reasonable rule of law—of predicting the decision of the court on the new facts—is not easy; it is an art rather than a science and as such is primarily a matter of feel—a feel you will develop as you read and use more cases, know your courts better and know better the circumstances out of which the first decision came and the different circumstances, if any, of your own case.

The key to the determination is policy. What was the policy (or policies) underlying the earlier decision? Are there facts in the new case that raise different policy considerations? Of course, if the court believes the policy of the original decision was wrong, it may overrule it or, as we shall see, "confine it to its special facts," but usually one stands a better chance to win by arguing that the facts are "materially different." How do we know what the policies underlying the first decision were?

An important guide is the language of the court deciding the case; while not absolutely controlling, it often shows you which facts the court thought significant and makes the job of distinguishing a subsequent case much more difficult where that job involves emphasizing facts other than those the court thought significant. It is not, as you will see in the cases on intentional infliction of emotional distress, an insurmountable handicap, but no good lawyer fails to take the language of the court into account.

But useful as the language may be, the most important element of any case is its facts; the first job you must do is to compare the facts of your case with the facts of those cases upon which you intend to rely as precedent; you must be prepared to reconcile factual differences if any exist.

THE USES OF DICTUM

Should a competent advocate cite dicta supporting her position, particularly when there is no past case squarely in point? As you read these cases, is a dictum merely to be discounted—or to be disregarded altogether? Note Justice Sutherland's reference (in *Humphrey's Executor, supra*) to "dicta, which may be followed if sufficiently persuasive, but which are not controlling." And compare Chief Justice Marshall's statement in Cohens v. Virginia, 19 U.S. 264, 399 (1821), that "they [*i.e.*, dicta] may be respected, but ought not to control the judgment in a subsequent suit when the very point is presented for decision." Another frequent formulation is the following:

> Nevertheless some weight is very properly given to a dictum, a weight similar to that assigned to the sayings of learned text-writers; and in this sense a dictum is authority, its weight varying

with the learning of the court and with the amount of thought bestowed by the court upon the point covered by the dictum.

Wambaugh, The Study of Cases 19 (2d ed. 1894).

But these formulations tend to stress the mechanistic aspects. While courts are not required to follow dictum, if one is looking for guidance as to what courts will do, a well-considered recent dictum may be a better guide than an old holding. Consider in this respect the decision of the United States Supreme Court in Banco Nacional de Cuba v. Sabbatino, 376 U.S. 398 (1964). One of the unsettled questions involved in the controversy was whether state or federal law controlled. In *Sabbatino*, it did not matter since New York law (which would have been applicable if state law controlled) and federal law were the same. Nevertheless, the Court said:

> We could perhaps in this diversity action avoid the question whether federal or state law is applicable. . . . However, we are constrained to make it clear that an issue concerned with a basic choice regarding the competence and function of the Judiciary . . . must be treated exclusively as an aspect of federal law.

376 U.S. at 424–25. Who in a subsequent case would be brave enough to tell the Court that its statement should be ignored as mere dictum—or so foolish as to advise a client that the dictum did not represent "the law"?

THE POSITIVE ASPECTS OF THE DOCTRINE

Do you agree with the following statement of Judge Jerome Frank?

> *Stare decisis* has no bite when it means merely that a court adheres to a precedent it considers correct. It is significant only when a court feels constrained to stick to a former ruling although the Court has come to regard it as unwise or unjust.

United States v. Shaughnessy, 234 F.2d 715, 719 (2d Cir. 1955).

Most discussions of holding and dictum focus exclusively on the negative aspects of the concept: the extent to which the holding of a case is "binding" on subsequent cases. But the concept has another, very important aspect. As noted above, it is possible to phrase the holding of a case at many levels of generality. By restricting the prior "holding" to its narrowest formulation, judges can avoid the binding effect; but they also can, by using the broadest formulation, move the law significantly without seeming to do violence to the doctrine of precedent. When you study the cases on intentional infliction of emotional distress, observe how much flexibility there is in the system and how much courts move the law while they purport to be following binding precedent.

B. HOW PRECEDENT WORKS OVER TIME

1. EVOLUTION OF A CLAIM: INTENTIONAL INFLICTION OF EMOTIONAL DISTRESS

It should be clear by now that one case standing by itself does not tell us much about the law in a particular field. To know "what the law is" we need to put together all the related cases to "synthesize" them. The process of synthesis is the most important element in working with case law; one synthesizes decisions for a number of purposes: to write scholarly articles, to write opinion letters, to write briefs, indeed, just about every time one makes a statement about what the law is. In law practice, before you synthesize you will need to find the cases; here, this section of the casebook gives you a ready-made, albeit not complete, group of cases for you to synthesize.

The primary objective of this section is to show you how over time the law relating to liability for intentional infliction of emotional distress changed as new fact situations arose for decision or, more fundamentally, as the social, political and economic environment evolved. It also shows how this change has taken place within our doctrine of precedent, largely without benefit of statute. Your emphasis should be on learning *how* the law has changed, although you should also contemplate *why*.

In order to get the most out of this exercise, you should put yourself in the position of the lawyers who had to deal with the law during its development. It is easy to find others' descriptions of what happened, and why, but resort to such sources will be self-defeating. When you are faced with the task of making your own predictions, it will not be possible to peek ahead; all you will have to go on are the cases decided to date and your own understanding of the process by which law is made and unmade in our system. After each case, then, you should try to synthesize that case and the earlier cases as though they were all the information that was available, and to formulate a "rule of law" that will accommodate these cases. (Moreover, you should do it *before* you discuss the cases in class.) Professor Llewellyn described this process in the context of the required simultaneous existence of "offer" and "acceptance" in the law of contracts:

> The first case involves a man who makes an offer and gets in his revocation before his offer is accepted. The court decides that he cannot be sued upon his promise, and says that no contract can be made unless the minds of both parties are at one at once. The second case involves a man who has made a similar offer and has mailed a revocation, but to whom a letter of acceptance has been sent before his revocation was received. The court holds that he can be sued upon his promise, and says that his offer was being repeated every moment from the time that it arrived until the letter of acceptance was duly mailed. Here are two rules which are a little difficult to put together, and to square with sense, and which are, too, a little hard to square with the two holdings in the cases. We set to work to seek a way out which will do justice to the holdings. We arrive perhaps at this, that it is not necessary for the two minds to be at one at once, if the person who has received an offer thinks, and thinks reasonably, as he takes the last step of acceptance, that the offeror is standing by the offer.

Karl Llewellyn, The Bramble Bush 49–50 (1930).

(1) minds not one → no contract

(2) minds not one → contract

a. CLAIM REJECTED

Terwilliger v. Wands

Court of Appeals of New York, 1858.
17 N.Y. 54.

ACTION for slander. The plaintiff proved by La Fayette Wands that the defendant asked him, Wands, what the plaintiff was running to Mrs. Fuller's so much for he knew he went there for no good purpose. Mrs. Fuller was a bad woman, and plaintiff had a regular beaten path across his land to Fuller's; defendant said plaintiff went there to have intercourse with Mrs. Fuller, and that plaintiff would do all he could to keep Mrs. Fuller's husband in the penitentiary so that he could have free access there.

The plaintiff proved by Neiper that the defendant said about the same words to that witness, and that he, being an intimate friend of the plaintiff's and a brother-in-law of Mrs. Fuller, communicated to the plaintiff what the defendant had told him, and that the story was all over the country. Other witnesses testified to similar imputations by the defendant, but there was no proof that what the defendant said to them was communicated to the plaintiff.

The only damages proved were that the plaintiff was prostrated in health and unable to attend to business after hearing of the reports circulated by the defendant. A motion for a nonsuit was sustained upon the grounds that the damage, if any, was occasioned by the speaking of the words by the defendant. The judgment was affirmed by the General Term. The plaintiff appealed.

■ STRONG, J. The words spoken by the defendant not being actionable of themselves, it was necessary, in order to maintain the action, to prove that they occasioned special damages to the plaintiff. The special damages must have been the natural, immediate and legal consequence of the words. (*Stark. on Sland. by Wend., 2nd ed.,* 203; 2 *id.* 62, 64; Beach v. Ranney, 2 Hill, 309; Crain v. Petrie, 6 *id.* 522; Kendall v. Stone, 5 *N.Y.* 14.)

The special damages relied upon are not of such a nature as will support the action. The action for slander is given by the law as a remedy for "injuries affecting a man's reputation or good name by malicious, scandalous and slanderous words, tending to his damage and derogation." (3 *Bl.Com.* 123; *Stark, on Sland., Prelim. Obs.* 22–29; 1 *id.* 17, 18.) It is injuries affecting the reputation only which are the subject to the action. In the case of slanderous words actionable *per se,* the law, from their natural and immediate tendency to produce injury, adjudges them to be injurious, though no special loss or damage can be proved. "But with regard to words that do not apparently and upon the face of them import such defamation as will of course be injurious, it is necessary that the plaintiff should aver some particular damage to have happened."

(3 *Bl.Com.* 124.) As to what constitutes special damages, Starkie mentions the loss of a marriage, loss of hospitable gratuitous entertainment, preventing a servant or bailiff from getting a place, the loss of customers by a tradesman; and says that in general whenever a person is prevented by the slander from receiving that which would otherwise be conferred upon him, though gratuitously, it is sufficient. (1 *Stark. on Sland.* 195, 202; *Cook's Law of Def.* 22–24.) In Olmstead v. Miller (1 Wend. 506), it was held that the refusal of civil entertainment at a public house was sufficient special damage. So in *Williams v. Hill* (19 Wend. 305), was the fact that the plaintiff was turned away from the house of her uncle and charged not to return until she had cleared up her character. So in Beach v. Ranney, was the circumstance that persons, who had been in the habit of doing so, refused longer to provide fuel, clothing, etc. (2 *Stark, on Ev.* 872, 873.) These instances are sufficient to illustrate the kind of special damage that must result from defamatory words not otherwise actionable to make them so; they are damages produced by, or through, impairing the reputation.

It would be highly impolitic to hold all language, wounding the feelings and affecting unfavorably the health and ability to labor, of another, a ground of action; for that would be to make the right of action depend often upon whether the sensibilities of a person spoken of are easily excited or otherwise; his strength of mind to disregard abusive, insulting remarks concerning him; and his physical strength and ability to bear them. Words which would make hardly an impression on most persons, and would be thought by them, and should be by all, undeserving of notice, might be exceedingly painful to some, occasioning sickness and an interruption of ability to attend to their ordinary avocations. There must be some limit to liability for words not actionable *per se,* both as to the words and the kind of damages; and a clear and wise one has been fixed by the law. The words must be defamatory in their nature; and must in fact disparage the character; and this disparagement must be evidenced by some positive loss arising therefrom directly and legitimately as a fair and natural result. In this view of the law words which do not degrade the character do not injure it, and cannot occasion loss. In *Cook's Law of Def.* (p. 24), it is said: "In order to render the consequence of words spoken special damage, the words must be in themselves disparaging; for if they be innocent the consequence does not follow naturally from the cause." In Kelly v. Partington (5 Barn. & Adol. 645), which was an action for slander, the words in the declaration were "she secreted 1*s.* 6*d.* under the till, stating these are not times to be robbed." It was alleged as special damage that by reason of the speaking of the words a third person refused to take the plaintiff into service. The plaintiff recovered one shilling damages, and the defendant obtained a rule *nisi* for arresting the judgment on the ground that the words, taken in their grammatical sense, were not disparaging to the plaintiff and, therefore, that no special damage could result from them. Denman, Ch. J., said: "The words do not of necessity import, any thing injurious to the plaintiff's character, and we think the judgment must be arrested unless there be something on the face of the declaration from which the court can clearly see that the slanderous matter alleged is injurious to the plaintiff. Where the words are ambiguous, the meaning can be supplied by *innuendo;* but that is not the case here. The rule for arresting the judgment must, therefore be made absolute." Littledale, J., said: "I cannot agree that words laudatory of a party's conduct would be the subject of an action if they were followed by special damage. They must be defamatory or injurious in their nature. *In Comyn's Digest, title 'Action on the case for Defamation'* (D., 730), it is said generally that any words are actionable by which the party has a special damage, but all the examples given in illustration of the rule are of words defamatory in themselves, but not actionable, because they do not subject the party to a temporal punishment. In all the instances put the words are injurious to the reputation of the person of whom they were spoken."

It is true that this element of the action for slander in the case of words not actionable of themselves—that the special damages must flow from impaired reputation—has been overlooked in several modern cases, and loss of health and consequent incapacity to attend to business held sufficient special damage (Bradt v. Towsley, 13 Wend. 253; Fuller v. Fenner, 16 Barb. 333); but these cases are a departure from principle and should not be followed.

Where there is no proof that the character has suffered from the words, if sickness results it must be attributed to apprehension of loss of character, and such fear of harm to character, with resulting sickness and bodily prostration, cannot be such special damage as the law requires for the action. The loss of character must be a substantive loss, one which has actually taken place.

■ ROOSEVELT, J., dissented.

Murray v. Gast Lithographic & Engraving Co.

Common Pleas of New York, 1894.
8 Misc. 36, 28 N.Y.S. 271.

[Re-read the excerpt from this decision included in the majority opinion in *Roberson v. Rochester Folding Box, supra* at p. 103.]

QUESTIONS

1.   What is the difference between "special damage" and the harm the *Terwilliger* plaintiff claimed to suffer?

2.   Why do the *Terwilliger* and *Murray v. Gast* courts reject the plaintiffs' claims? Does their reasoning foreclose all claims for intentional infliction of emotional distress?

b.   CLAIM SUSTAINED IF DEFENDANT OWED A SPECIAL DUTY TO PLAINTIFF

Gillespie v. Brooklyn Heights R. Co.

Court of Appeals of New York, 1904.
178 N.Y. 347, 70 N.E. 857.

APPEAL from a judgment of the Appellate Division of the Supreme Court in the second judicial department, entered March 20, 1903, affirming a judgment in favor of defendant entered upon a verdict directed by the court in favor of plaintiff for nominal damages.

On the twenty-sixth of December, 1900, the plaintiff, who was a practicing physician, boarded one of the defendant's cars at the corner of Nostrand avenue and Fulton street at about 10:20 in the morning. As to what thereafter occurred, the plaintiff testified: "I know who the conductor was on that car, Conductor Wright. He came to collect my fare just a few minutes after I got on the car. I gave him a twenty-five cent piece and said to him, 'A transfer, please, to Reid Avenue.' Just at that moment a lady on the opposite side called to him. He crossed and he went to punch a transfer and I thought it was mine, and I said to him, 'Please don't do that until I speak with you.' He paid no attention. After he gave the lady her transfer I said to him, 'Won't you please come here? I wish to speak to you about the transfer?' So he came across very growly and roughly, and wanted to know, 'What is the matter with yez?' I said, 'Won't you please tell me—I don't know much about those streets away up here—which would be the nearest, Reid Avenue or Sumner Avenue, to Stuyvesant Avenue.' He said, 'We don't have any Reid Avenue transfers; we transfer at Sumner Avenue.' 'Well,' I said then, 'I thank you; please give me a transfer for Sumner Avenue and my change,' and he actually hollered at me, 'What change?' I said, 'The money I gave you, twenty-five cents, and I want my change,' and he put his hands in his pocket and he pulled out a whole handful of pennies or nickels; he said, 'do you see any twenty-five cents there?' He said, 'It is the likes of ye—you are a dead beat; you are a swindler. I know the likes of ye;' he said, 'You didn't give me twenty-five cents.' The lady that sat next to me set the conductor right. She said to him, 'I am sure, sir, she gave you a quarter of a dollar; I saw her give it to you,' and he turned—'Well, perhaps you are a friend of hers.' Then he said that dead beats like me, he knew that every day they were traveling on the cars; he knew the swindlers and the dead beats—'But you can't dead beat me. I know you; you belong to them,' and he said then, 'Why, only here the other day, I had just such a woman as you trying to dead beat me out of money,' and I said, 'I want my change and I don't want such insolence.' Then he walked back and two gentlemen got on the car, and he called the attention of those gentlemen to me and said, pointing to me—I went to the door, and he was telling them how I was trying to swindle him, 'But,' he said, 'I know them; they are all dead beats; she can't beat me.' I said to him, 'Look here, sir, I know President

Rossiter, and I shall make a complaint of you,' and he came over close to me—he said, 'Ah, the likes of you,' he said. 'You couldn't make a complaint to President Rossiter,' he said: 'I have been on this road too long for you to have any authority with him—no, no.' 'Well,' I said, 'I shall tell him,' and I went back and sat down."

The plaintiff further and in substance testified that she noticed that there was a smell of whisky in the conductor's breath; that he did not give her her change at all; that he gave her no transfer; that he said nothing except merely that he had nothing to do with her, and that "I was a dead beat and a swindler." She then testified as to her efforts to see President Rossiter; that when she reached his office she was about four miles from home; that she walked that distance because she had no money with which to pay her fare; that she became sick, was confined to the bed for two days, and as to its effect upon her business. All this evidence was undisputed.

At the close of the plaintiff's case the defendant made a motion for a dismissal of the complaint, and the court said: "The allegation of the complaint is that it was done maliciously by the servant of the corporation, so that takes it out of the action against the corporation anyway, so far as the slander part of it is concerned. The only question now is whether she is entitled to recover the amount that she paid for the fare." The plaintiff claimed she was entitled to recover more. The court thereupon said: "On the testimony as it stands they (the company) did receive it; it is uncontradicted now that they did receive it. I think I will direct a verdict for the twenty cents if you (referring to the defendant's counsel) want to."

The plaintiff excepted to the direction of a verdict and asked to go to the jury "upon the facts in the case, upon the wrong and the wrongful detention of this woman's money, and the suffering occasioned by it," and the court directed a verdict for the plaintiff for twenty cents, and held that that was the extent to which the railroad company was liable and that "the other damages, if any have grown out of it, are not the proximate result of the act of the conductor." The verdict was directed with the consent of the defendant's counsel.

■ MARTIN, J. The principal and practically the only question involved upon this appeal is whether the plaintiff was entitled to recover for the tort or breach of contract proved, an amount in excess of the sum she actually overpaid the defendant's conductor. Confessedly the plaintiff was a passenger on the defendant's car and entitled to be carried over its road. That at the time of this occurrence the relation of carrier and passenger existed between the defendant and the plaintiff is not denied. The latter gave the conductor a quarter of a dollar from which to take her fare, he received it, but did not return her the twenty cents change to which she was entitled. She subsequently asked him for it, when he, in an abusive and impudent manner, not only refused to pay it, but also grossly insulted her by calling her a dead beat and a swindler, and by the use of other insulting and improper language, even after a fellow-passenger had informed him that she had given him the amount she claimed.

In this case there was obviously a breach of the defendant's contract and of its duty to its passenger. It was its duty to receive any coin or bill not in excess of the amount permitted to be tendered for fare on its car under its rules and regulations, and to make the change and return it to the plaintiff or person tendering the money for the fare. That certainly must have been a part of the contract entered into by the defendant, and the refusal of the conductor to return her change was a tortious act upon his part, performed by him while acting in the line of his duty as the defendant's servant. To that extent, at least, the contract between the parties was broken, and as an incident to and accompanying that breach, the language and tortious acts complained of were employed and performed by the defendant's conductor.

This brings us to the precise question whether, in an action to recover damages for the breach of that contract and for the tortious acts of the conductor in relation thereto, the conduct of such employee and his treatment of the plaintiff at the time may be considered upon the question of damages and in aggravation thereof. That the plaintiff suffered insult and indignity at the hands of the conductor, and was treated disrespectfully and indecorously by him under such circumstances as to occasion mental suffering, humiliation, wounded pride and disgrace, there can be little doubt. At least the jury might have so found upon the evidence before them.

This question was treated on the argument as a novel one, and as requiring the establishment of a new principle of law to enable the plaintiff to recover damages in excess of the amount retained by the defendant's conductor which rightfully belonged to her. In that, we think counsel were at fault, and that the right to such a recovery is established beyond question, as will be seen by the authorities which we shall presently consider. The consideration of this general question involves two propositions: The first relates to the duties of carriers to their passengers; and the second to the rule of damages when there has been a breach of such duty.

The relation between a carrier and its passenger is more than a mere contract relation, as it may exist in the absence of any contract whatsoever. Any person rightfully on the cars of a railroad company is entitled to protection by the carrier, and any breach of its duty in that respect is in the nature of a tort and recovery may be had in an action of tort as well as for a breach of the contract. (2 Sedgwick on Damages, 637.) In considering the duties of carriers to their passengers, we find that the elementary writers have often discussed this question, and that it has frequently been the subject of judicial consideration. Thus in Booth on Street Railways (§ 372) it is said: "The contract on the part of the company is to safely carry its passengers and to compensate them for all unlawful and tortious injuries inflicted by its servants. It calls for safe carriage, for safe and respectful treatment from the carrier's servants, and for immunity from assaults by them, or by other persons if it can be prevented by them. No matter what the motive is which incites the servant of the carrier to commit an improper act towards the passenger during the existence of the relation, the master is liable for the act and its natural and legitimate consequences. Hence, it is responsible for the insulting conduct of its servants, which stops short of actual violence." . . .

Having thus considered a portion of the elementary authorities relating to this question, we will now consider a few of the many decided cases relating to the same subject. In Chamberlain v. Chandler (3 Mason, 242, 245), Judge STORY, who delivered the opinion of the court, in discussing the duties, relations and responsibilities which arise between the carrier and passenger, said: "In respect to passengers, the case of the master is one of peculiar responsibility and delicacy. Their contract with him is not for mere ship room, and personal existence, on board, but for reasonable food, comforts, necessaries and kindness. It is a stipulation, not for toleration merely, but for respectful treatment, for that decency of demeanor, which constitutes the charm of social life, for that attention, which mitigates evils without reluctance, and that promptitude, which administers aid to distress. In respect to females, it proceeds yet farther, it includes an implied stipulation against general obscenity, that immodesty of approach which borders on lasciviousness, and against that wanton disregard of the feelings, which aggravates every evil, and endeavors by the excitement of terror, and cool malignancy of conduct, to inflict torture upon susceptible minds. * * * It is intimated that all these acts, though wrong in morals, are yet acts which the law does not punish; that if the person is untouched, if the acts do not amount to an assault and battery, they are not to be redressed. The law looks on them as unworthy of its cognizance. The master is at liberty to inflict the most severe mental sufferings, in the most tyrannical manner, and yet if he withholds a blow, the victim may be crushed by his unkindness. He commits nothing within the reach of civil jurisprudence. My opinion is, that the law involves no such absurdity. It is rational and just. It gives compensation for mental sufferings occasioned by acts of wanton injustice, equally whether they operate by way of direct, or of consequential, injuries. In each case the contract of the passengers for the voyage is in substance violated; and the wrong is to be redressed as a cause of damage." . . .

In Cole v. Atlanta and West Point R.R. Co. (102 Ga. 474, 477) it was held that it was the unquestionable duty of a railroad company to protect a passenger against insult or injury from its conductor, and that the unprovoked use by a conductor to a passenger of opprobrious words and abusive language tending to humiliate the passenger or subject him to mortification, gives to the latter a right of action against the company. In that case it was said: "The carrier's liability is not confined to assaults committed by its servants, but it extends also to insults, threats, and other disrespectful conduct." In Goddard v. Grand Trunk R. Co. (57 Maine, 202, 213) it was held that a common carrier of passengers is responsible for the misconduct of his servant towards a passenger. In that case, WALTON, J., delivering the opinion of the court, said: "The carrier's obligation is to carry his passenger safely and properly, and to treat him respectfully, and if he intrusts the performance of this duty to his servants, the law holds him responsible for the manner in which they execute the trust. The law seems to be now well settled that the carrier is obliged to protect his passenger from violence and insult, from whatever source arising. * * * He must not only protect his passenger against the violence and insults of strangers and co-passengers, but *a fortiori,* against the violence and insults of his own servants. If this duty to the passenger is not performed, if this protection is not furnished, but, on the contrary, the passenger is assaulted and insulted, through the negligence or the willful misconduct of the carrier's servant, the carrier is necessarily responsible," [citation].

The duties arising between a carrier and passenger have been several times discussed in this state, as in Stewart v. Brooklyn and Crosstown R.R. Co. (90 N.Y. 588, 590), where it was said: "By the defendant's contract with the plaintiff, it had undertaken to carry him safely and to treat him respectfully; and while a common carrier does not undertake to insure against injury from every possible danger, he does undertake to protect the passenger against any injury arising from the negligence or willful misconduct of its servants while engaged in performing a duty which the carrier owes to the passenger. * * * 'The carrier's obligation is to carry his passenger safely, and properly, and to treat him respectfully, and if he intrusts this duty to his servants, the law holds him responsible for the manner in which they execute the trust.'" The court then quoted with approval the decision in Nieto v. Clark (1 Cliff. 145, 149) where it was said: "In respect to female passengers, the contract proceeds yet further, and includes an implied stipulation that they shall be protected against obscene conduct, lascivious behavior, and every immodest and libidinous approach. * * * A common carrier undertakes absolutely to protect his passengers against the misconduct of their own servants engaged in executing the contract." Subsequently in Dwinelle v. N.Y.C. & H.R. R.R. Co. (120 N.Y. 117, 125) the same doctrine was held and the foregoing portion of the opinion in the *Stewart* case was quoted and reaffirmed by this court. It was then added: "These and numerous other cases hold that no matter what the motive is which incites the servant of the carrier to commit an unlawful or improper act toward the passenger during the existence of the relation of carrier and passenger, the carrier is liable for the act and its natural and legitimate consequences." Again, in Palmeri v. Manhattan R. Co. (133 N.Y. 261, 266) it was held that the corporation is liable for the acts of injury and insult by an employee, although in departure from the authority conferred or implied, if they occur in the course of the employment. In that case the employee alleged that the plaintiff was a counterfeiter and a common prostitute, placed his hand upon her and detained her for a while, but let her go without having her arrested. The action was to recover damages for unlawful imprisonment accompanied by the words alleged to have been spoken. This court held she was entitled to recover. The judge then said: "Though injury and insult are acts in departure from the authority conferred, or implied, nevertheless, as they occur in the course of the employment, the master becomes responsible for the wrong committed." The foregoing authorities render it manifest that the defendant was not only liable to the plaintiff for the money wrongfully retained by its conductor, but also for any injury she suffered from the insulting and abusive language and treatment received at his hands.

This brings us to the consideration of the elements of damages in such a case, and what may be considered in determining their amount. Among the elements of compensatory damages for such an injury are the humiliation and injury to her feelings which the plaintiff suffered by reason of the insulting and abusive language and treatment she received, not, however, including any injury to her character resulting therefrom. . . .

In Shepard v. Chicago, R.I. & P.R. Co. (77 Iowa, 54) the court charged the jury, "When a passenger is wrongfully compelled to leave a train, and suffer insult and abuse, the law does not exactly measure his damages, but it authorizes the jury to consider the injured feelings of the party, the indignity endured, the humiliation, wounded pride, mental suffering, and the like, and to allow such sum as the jury may say is right," and it was held that his instruction was not subject to the objection that it authorized an allowance of exemplary damages, because damages may properly be allowed for mental suffering caused by indignity and outrage, and such damages are compensatory and not exemplary. . . .

After this somewhat extended review of the authorities bearing upon the subject, we are led irresistibly to the conclusion that the defendant is liable for the insulting and abusive treatment the plaintiff received at the hands of its servant; that she is entitled to recover compensatory damages for the humiliation and injury to her feelings occasioned thereby, and that the trial court erred in directing a verdict for the plaintiff for twenty cents only and in refusing to submit the case to the jury.

The judgments of the Appellate Division and trial court should be reversed and a new trial granted, with costs to abide the event.

■ GRAY, J. (dissenting.) I dissent; because I think it is extending unduly the doctrine of a common carrier's liability in making it answerable in damages for the slanderous words spoken by one of its agents.

■ BARTLETT, HAIGHT and CULLEN, JJ., concur with MARTIN, J.; PARKER, CH. J., and O'BRIEN, J., concur with GRAY, J.

Judgments reversed, etc.

De Wolf v. Ford

Court of Appeals of New York, 1908.
193 N.Y. 397, 86 N.E. 527.

■ WERNER, J. . . . As no evidence was taken at the trial, the dismissal of the complaint compels us to assume the truth of all the allegations of fact contained in that pleading. Sheridan v. Jackson, 72 N.Y. 170; Baylies Trial Pr. (2d ed.) 247. The facts which must, therefore, be regarded as established for the purposes of this review are that the relation of innkeeper and guest existed between the defendants and the plaintiff at the time when the servant of the former forced his way into the room of the latter; that this forcible entry was made without invitation from the guest and against her protest; that she was there subjected to the mortification of exposing her person in scant attire, and to the ignominy of being accused of immoral conduct; that she and her visitor were ordered to depart from the hotel, and that all this was done by the defendants' servant without justification and in the course of his regular employment. If the defendants, in these circumstances, are not to be held responsible, it must be upon the theory that they owed no duty to the plaintiff in respect of her convenience, privacy, safety and comfort while she was their guest, and that an innkeeper is immune from liability for any maltreatment which he or his servants may inflict upon a guest be it ever so wilful or flagrant. We think it may safely be asserted that this has never been the law, and that no [principle] so repugnant to common decency and justice can ever find lodgment in any enlightened system of jurisprudence. . . .

The innkeeper holds himself out as able and willing to entertain guests for hire, and, in the absence of a specific contract, the law implies that he will furnish such entertainment as the character of his inn and reasonable attention to the convenience and comfort of his guests will afford. If the guest is assigned to a room upon the express or implied understanding that he is to be the sole occupant thereof during the time that it is set apart for his use, the innkeeper retains a right of access thereto only at such proper times and for such reasonable purposes as may be necessary in the general conduct of the inn or in attending to the needs of the particular guest. When a guest is assigned to a room for his exclusive use, it is his for all proper purposes and at all times until he gives it up. This exclusive right of use and possession is subject to such emergent and occasional entries as the innkeeper and his servants may find it necessary to make in the reasonable discharge of their duties; but these entries must be made with due regard to the occasion and at such times and in such manner as are consistent with the rights of the guest. One of the things which a guest for hire at a public inn has the right to insist upon is respectful and decent treatment at the hands of the innkeeper and his servants. That is an essential part of the contract whether it is express or implied. This right of the guest necessarily implies an obligation on the part of the innkeeper that neither he nor his servants will abuse or insult the guest, or indulge in any conduct or speech that may unnecessarily bring upon him physical discomfort or distress of mind. . . .

Upon the facts of record, considered in the light of this very general statement of the rules which govern the relation of innkeeper and guest, it is clear that the defendants were guilty of a most flagrant breach of duty towards the plaintiff. As a guest for hire in the inn of the defendants the plaintiff was entitled to the exclusive and peaceable possession of the room assigned to her, subject only to such proper intrusions by the defendants and their servants as may have been necessary in the regular and orderly conduct of the inn, or under some commanding emergency. Had such an emergency arisen, calling for immediate and unpremeditated action on the part of the defendants or their servants, in conserving the safety or protection of the plaintiff or of other guests, or of the building in which they were housed, the usual rules of decency, propriety, convenience or comfort might have been disregarded without subjecting the defendants to liability for mistake of judgment or delinquency in conduct; but for all other purposes their occasional or regular entries into the plaintiff's room were subject to the fundamental consideration that it was for the time being her room, and that she was entitled to respectful and considerate treatment at their hands. Such treatment necessarily implied an observance by the defendants of the proprieties as to the time and manner of entering the plaintiff's room, and of civil deportments towards her when such an entry was either necessary or proper. Instead of acting according to these simple rules the servant of the defendants forced his way into the plaintiff's room, under conditions which would have caused any woman, except the most shameless harlot, a degree of humiliation and suffering that only a pure and modest woman can properly describe. Not content with that, the servant castigated the plaintiff with opprobrious and offensive epithets, imputing to her immorality and unchastity, and, as a fitting climax to such an episode, ordered the plaintiff to leave the inn.

The majority opinion handed down by the Appellate Division, in which the dismissal of the complaint was sustained, seems to be based upon the theory that under the common law the innkeeper is not responsible for the safety of his guest for hire, and as authority for that view it cites Calye's Case, 8 Coke's Rep. 63. All that appears to have been decided in that case is that the innkeeper is under an absolute duty to safely keep the chattels brought to the inn and intrusted to him by his guest. There is a dictum in the opinion to the effect that if the guest be beaten in the inn, the innkeeper shall not answer for it; but under no reasonable construction could that language be held to mean that an innkeeper and his servants might assault a guest and yet not be liable. There may doubtless be many conditions under which a guest at an inn may be assaulted or insulted by another guest or by an outsider without subjecting the innkeeper to liability, but if it ever was thought to be the law that an innkeeper and his servants have the right to wilfully assault, abuse or maltreat a guest, we think the time has arrived when it may very properly and safely be changed to accord with a more modern conception of the relation of innkeeper and guest. We think it would be startling, to say the least, to announce it as the law of this state that an innkeeper and his male servants may invade the room of a female guest at any hour of the day or night without her consent, in utter disregard of every law of decency and modesty, and that the necessity for such an extraordinary right lies in the rule that an innkeeper must be permitted to control every part of his inn for the protection of all his guests. Such a doctrine, so far from holding an innkeeper to a reasonable responsibility in the quasi public business which he is permitted to carry on, would clothe him with dangerous prerogatives permitted to no other class of men.

We conclude, therefore, that the invasion of the plaintiff's room in the defendants' inn and the treatment to which she was there subjected under the circumstances described in the complaint constituted a violation of the duty which the defendants owed to the plaintiff and for which they may be held liable if the facts alleged are established by proof. The complaint, although somewhat in artificial in form, sets forth all the facts necessary to such a cause of action. The measure of liability, if any, will be purely compensatory and not punitive, the plaintiff's right to recover being confined to such injury to her feelings and such personal humiliation as she may have suffered. Gillespie v. Brooklyn Heights R. Co., 178 N.Y. 347, 102 Am.St.Rep. 503, 66 L.R.A. 618. That is the extent to which the defendants' liability may fairly be said to spring from their breach of duty. Any remedy beyond that which the plaintiff may seek to assert must be invoked in a different form of action. The gravamen of the action at bar is not the alleged slanderous defamation of the plaintiff, but the defendants' breach of the duty which it owed to the plaintiff and the injury which was directly caused thereby.

■ CULLEN, C.J., and GRAY, VANN, WILLARD BARTLETT, HISCOCK, and CHASE, JJ., concur.

QUESTIONS

1. Is the harm caused by the insulting behavior of a railroad employee any less abstract and ill-defined than the harm caused by the insulting behavior of a neighbor?

2. Why does it make a difference if the person causing the emotional harm is in a special relationship, such as that of a common carrier or an inn-keeper, with the plaintiff?

3. In *Gillespie,* the majority cited *Palmeri v. Manhattan R. Co.* in support of the liability of the railroad for "acts of injury and insult" committed by its employee in the course of his employment. Judge Gray was the author of the *Palmeri* decision. Yet he dissented in *Gillespie.* Why, do you suppose?

4. In *Gillespie,* the New York Court of Appeals divided 4–3. A mere four years later, in *De Wolf v. Ford*, the court was unanimous, including Judge Gray. Why?

c.   CLAIM SUSTAINED IF THE WILLFUL CONDUCT CAUSING THE EMOTIONAL DISTRESS WAS INDEPENDENTLY WRONGFUL

Garrison v. Sun Printing & Publishing Ass'n

Court of Appeals of New York, 1912.
207 N.Y. 1, 100 N.E. 430.

■ HISCOCK, J. By demurrer to one of the purported causes of action set forth in the complaint, the question is presented whether a husband may recover for loss of services of his wife caused by her sickness resulting from mental distress, which in turn was caused by the defendant's willful and malicious publication concerning her of defamatory words actionable per se. There is no question but that the published words are libelous per se, and, whatever facts may be established on a trial, we must assume for the purposes of this appeal, in accordance with defendant's admissions, concededly to be implied from its demurrer, that the defendant not only published them of and concerning plaintiff's wife, but that it did so "wickedly and maliciously and intentionally and willfully," for thus it is alleged in the complaint.

Inasmuch as plaintiff's right to recover, if at all under the circumstances, must in effect be derived through his wife, it will be important in the first place to inquire whether the wife herself might recover for mental distress and physical sufferings resulting from the willful and malicious publication of such libelous words.

It was early established in this state, by decisions which do not appear to have been overruled or limited, that an action to recover for the utterance of defamatory words, not actionable in themselves, could not be sustained by proof of mental distress and physical pain suffered by the complainant as a result thereof. Terwilliger v. Wands, 17 N.Y. 54, 72 Am.Dec. 420; Wilson v. Goit, 17 N.Y. 442. And the same doctrine seems to have prevailed in England. Alsop v. Alsop, 5 H. & N. 534, 539; Lynch v. Knight, 9 H. of L. Cases, 577, 592.

On a superficial examination of the opinion in Terwilliger v. Wands, and on which rested the decision in Wilson v. Goit, it would seem to be founded on reasons which would be as applicable to a case of defamatory words actionable in themselves as to one where the words were not thus in themselves actionable and required proof of special damages. It was held that special damages of the kind stated and of which recovery was there being sought were not such natural, immediate, and legal consequences of the words spoken as to sustain the action. A more careful examination, however, discloses that the real and full theory on which a recovery was refused was that an action for slander or libel is brought to recover fundamentally for injury to character, and that the special damages necessary to sustain such an action must flow from disparaging and injuring it; that illness "was not, in a legal view, a natural, ordinary one (consequence), as it does not prove that the plaintiff's character was injured. The slander may not have been credited by or had the slightest influence upon any one unfavorable to the plaintiff." It was further remarked that "this element of an action for slander in a case of words not actionable of themselves"—that the special damages must flow from impaired reputation—had been overlooked in several cases, but that, nevertheless, "where there is *no proof that the character has suffered* from the words, if sickness results it must be attributed to apprehension of loss of character, and such fear of harm to character, with resulting sickness and bodily prostration, cannot be such special damage as the law requires for the action. The loss of character must be a substantive loss, one which has actually taken place." 17 N.Y. 62, 63, 72 Am.Dec. 420.

Both the Terwilliger and the Wilson Cases took pains to limit their effect to cases of defamatory words not actionable in themselves. Their plain intent was to declare that an action of libel or slander involves as its very foundation an injury to character; that where the language complained of is not of such a character that the law presumes an injury, but requires proof of special damages, this requirement cannot be satisfied by simply proving that the plaintiff had been made sick, there being no proof whatever of injury to the character, which involves the effect of the defamatory words on third persons rather than on the complainant himself. Hamilton v. Eno, 16 Hun. 599, 601. It will be seen that this reasoning does not apply to a case where the words are actionable in themselves because there the law presumes an injury to character which of itself will sustain an action, and proof of mental or physical suffering is presented as an element of additional or special damages accompanying or resulting from the injury to character thus presumed.

While the further proposition does not appear to have been specifically decided in this state, I have no doubt that a plaintiff, being entitled to recover compensatory damages for mental distress resulting from the publication of defamatory words actionable in themselves, may likewise recover for physical sufferings brought about by or attending such mental distress. It is true that the physical sufferings as in this case may be removed one step further from the wrong than the mental disturbance which gives rise to it; but this fact of itself does not prevent a recovery provided these damages otherwise come within the rules applicable to such a subject. . . .

I think the rule must be regarded as well recognized that in an action brought for the redress of a wrong intentionally, willfully, and maliciously committed, the wrongdoer will be held responsible for the injuries which he has directly caused, even though they lie beyond the limit of natural and apprehended results as established in cases where the injury was unintentional. [Citation.]

In Spade v. Lynn, etc., R.R. Co., supra, the court, after affirming the rule that in an action for negligence there could be no recovery for physical sufferings resulting from mere fright and mental disturbance, said: "It is hardly necessary to add that this decision does not reach those classes of action where an intention to cause mental distress or to hurt the feelings is shown or is reasonably to be inferred, as for example in cases of * * * slander."

In Burt v. McBain, supra, which was an action to recover damages for the utterance of words similar to those alleged in this case and like the latter made actionable per se by statute, it was held that injury in mind and health were such natural results of such an utterance that they might be shown as an element of damages without even a special declaration thereof.

In Swift v. Dickerman, supra, it was held that a plaintiff might recover damages for physical sufferings caused by the utterance of words actionable per se.

In the *Terwilliger* and *Wilson* cases, already quoted from, it is fairly to be inferred from the pains with which those decisions were limited to cases of words not actionable per se that a different rule would apply and a recovery be allowed for physical sufferings and mental distress resulting from the defamatory utterance of words actionable in themselves.

Reaching the conclusion, as I therefore do, that the wife might have recovered damages for the mental distress and physical sufferings caused by the publication of defendant's libel, it follows that plaintiff as her husband may maintain this action for loss of society and services. He had a right to these. The services were presumably of pecuniary value to him, and any wrong by which he was deprived thereof was a wrong done to his rights and interests for which he may recover damages. [Citation.] . . .

■ CULLEN, C.J., HAIGHT, VANN, CHASE, and COLLIN, JJ, concur. WILLARD BARTLETT, J., not sitting.

QUESTIONS

1. Has *Garrison* followed *Terwilliger,* or quietly overruled it?
2. What is the basis of the husband's claim?

Beck v. Libraro

Supreme Court, Appellate Division, Second Department, 1927.
220 App.Div. 547, 221 N.Y.S. 737.

■ KAPPER, J. The action is for damages for alleged personal injuries attributable to the defendant's act in discharging a loaded gun from the window of his [home] into and through a window of plaintiff's apartment while she was at home. The defendant was successful in his motion, made under rule 106 of the Rules of Civil Practice, to dismiss the complaint for failure to state a cause of action.

The complaint charges that the defendant "assaulted" plaintiff. This conclusion of fact is followed by allegations showing that the defendant fired this gun into the plaintiff's apartment several times, in doing which the windows were broken; the bullets struck various parts of a room in which the plaintiff was, and broke household articles therein. Plaintiff also alleged that, while the defendant did this shooting, she was lying in bed, having but a few moments before given birth to a child. The plaintiff was not shot, but alleged that defendant's act or acts caused her extreme fright, nervous shock, and hysteria, and resulted in serious illness to her. The complaint also sets forth the conclusion that the defendant's conduct was wanton, reckless, unlawful, and mischievous, and was committed without regard for plaintiff's safety, when the defendant knew, from the lighted apartment in which plaintiff was, that she was therein at the time, or that he should have known that an occupant was therein. . . .

Ignoring the allegation of assault, the other acts charged in the complaint are sufficient to constitute a cause of action, in my opinion. The defendant relies on the well-known case of Mitchell v. Rochester Railway Co., 151 N.Y. 107, 45 N.E. 354, 34 L.R.A. 781, 56 Am.St.Rep. 604, where it was held that a recovery of damages may not be had for injuries sustained by fright occasioned by the negligence of another, where there is no immediate personal injury. In that case, while the plaintiff was standing upon a street crosswalk, awaiting an opportunity to board an approaching street car drawn by horses, the approaching horses turned to the right and so close to the plaintiff as to result in her finding herself standing between the horses' heads when they were stopped, and her testimony was that, from the fright and excitement caused by the approach and proximity of the team, she became unconscious and ill, and that a miscarriage followed.

That case obviously was one of negligence in the want of ordinary prudence, as ordinarily understood and accepted in law, and involved no element of wantonness or willfulness. Here, however, there is a great deal more. The defendant's act of shooting this gun through the lighted windows of plaintiff's apartment was so wanton, reckless, and mischievous as to constitute an apparent disregard of human safety. This is shown by a mere recital of the facts set forth in the complaint, even without the conclusion alleged that such was the character of the defendant's wrongdoing. We have held (Preiser v. Wielandt, 48 App.Div. 569, 570, 62 N.Y.S. 890) that the doctrine of the Mitchell Case, supra, applies only to actions based on negligence, and not to cases of willful tort, and that, where the defendant's act was in and of itself wrongful, the fact that the injury started in fright is not a ground for denying a recovery of damages. Our decision in the case cited was followed by the First Department in Williams v. Underhill, 63 App.Div. 223, 226, 71

N.Y.S. 291. In this view, I think the complaint states a cause of action, and that its dismissal was error.

■ KELLY, P.J., and MANNING, YOUNG, and LAZANSKY, JJ, concur.

QUESTION

Why should it make a difference that the wrongful conduct underpinning the claim for emotional distress was intentional rather than negligent? We will return to this issue when we consider *Battalla v. State*, the decision which overruled the *Mitchell* case, *infra* subsection II.B.2.

d.   CLAIM SUSTAINED EVEN IF THE WILLFUL CONDUCT CAUSING THE EMOTIONAL DISTRESS WAS NOT OTHERWISE WRONGFUL

Flamm v. Van Nierop
Supreme Court, Westchester County, 1968.
56 Misc.2d 1059, 291 N.Y.S.2d 189.

■ DILLON, J.

The defendant moves to dismiss the first two causes of action alleged in the complaint for insufficiency in law. It is alleged in the first cause of action that on numerous occasions since October, 1966, the defendant has done the following: Dashed at the plaintiff in a threatening manner in various public places, with "threatening gestures, grimaces, leers, distorted faces and malign looks," accompanied by "ridiculous utterances and laughs"; driven his automobile behind that of the plaintiff at a dangerously close distance; walked closely behind, or beside, or in front of the plaintiff on the public streets; and constantly telephoned the plaintiff at his home and place of business and either hung up or remained on the line in silence. It is alleged further that all of this has been done maliciously and for the purpose of causing physical and mental damage, and that the plaintiff has suffered severe mental and emotional distress, sleeplessness and physical debilitation.

It seems probable that the complaint states a cause of action for assault (Brown v. Yaspan, 256 App.Div. 991, 10 N.Y.S.2d 502), but the plaintiff does not urge the point. He claims to have stated a cause of action for the intentional infliction of emotional and physical harm. This is a relatively new and unfamiliar cause of action, which requires some discussion.

The law cannot be expected to provide a civil remedy for every personal conflict in this crowded world. Physical injuries to the person, inflicted either intentionally or through negligence, are actionable under familiar principles. Acts causing mental distress are in a different category. Oral or written statements which are false and defamatory, and which upon publication tend to deprive the victim of his good name, may be remedied in actions for libel and slander. . . .

On the other hand, offenses of a minor nature, such as name-calling or angry looks, are not actionable though they may wound the feelings of the victim and cause some degree of emotional upset. This is because the law has no cure for trifles.

But when the actor's conduct is extraordinarily vindictive, it may be regarded as so extreme and so outrageous as to give rise to a cause of action for emotional distress. This is the test laid down in the Restatement 2d, Torts, § 46 (1966). An example of extreme and outrageous conduct may be found in Halio v. Lurie, 15 A.D.2d 62, 222 N.Y.S.2d 759, where the defendant, having jilted his fiancee and married another, addressed a taunting and insulting letter to the forsaken female. The complaint in that case was held to state a cause of action for the intentional infliction of serious mental distress. . . .

In the court's opinion the complaint in this case states a similar cause of action. If a man finds himself perpetually haunted by an enemy; if he is greeted at every turn by baleful looks, sudden sorties which fall short of physical contact, and derisive laughter; if he cannot drive his car without the imminent threat of a collision from the rear; and if he is troubled at all hours by telephone calls followed only by silence, then it can hardly be doubted that he is being subjected to the extreme and outrageous conduct which gives rise to a cause of action in tort. An analogy may be found in the concept of cruelty in a matrimonial action. In holding that such cruelty is not limited to physical injury, the Court of Appeals has said that "if it were, a husband might constantly and without cause publicly call his wife a vile and shameless bawd so long as he did not strike her or threaten to strike her, and might thus intentionally break down her health and destroy her reason without giving her a claim on him for separate maintenance" (Pearson v. Pearson, 230 N.Y. 141, 146, 129 N.E. 349, 350). Conceivably a similar result might follow if the plaintiff can prove what is alleged in this complaint.

Of course, whether the proof can be furnished at the trial is another question. It would seem that evidence connecting the defendant with the speechless telephone calls will be difficult to produce; and whether the plaintiff can prove the remaining allegations to a sufficient degree to establish the cause of action is a question to be determined by the trier of the facts. Upon this motion the court must assume the truth of what is stated in the complaint, and upon that assumption this complaint states a cause of action.

The second cause of action is a repetition of the first, with the additional allegation that the defendant's conduct still continues and will continue in the future, resulting in irreparable injury to the plaintiff. Under that cause of action the plaintiff demands injunctive relief, in addition to the money damages demanded in the first cause of action. The court is of the opinion that both forms of relief are available upon proper proof. The motion is therefore denied as to both causes of action.

Howell v. New York Post Co., Inc.

Court of Appeals of New York, 1993.
81 N.Y.2d 115, 612 N.E.2d 699.

■ CHIEF JUDGE KAYE.

This appeal, involving a newspaper's publication of plaintiff's photograph without her consent, calls upon us to consider the relationship between two separate but potentially overlapping torts: intentional infliction of emotional distress, and invasion of the right to privacy.

In early September 1988, plaintiff Pamela J. Howell was a patient at Four Winds Hospital, a private psychiatric facility in Westchester County. Her complaint and affidavit (accepted as true on this appeal) allege that it was imperative to her recovery that the hospitalization remain a secret from all but her immediate family.

Hedda Nussbaum was also at that time a patient at Four Winds. Nussbaum was the "adoptive" mother of six-year-old Lisa Steinberg, whose November 1987 death from child abuse generated intense public interest. [Citation.]

On September 1, 1988, a New York Post photographer trespassed onto Four Winds' secluded grounds and, with a telephoto lens, took outdoor pictures of a group that included Nussbaum and plaintiff. That night, the hospital's medical director telephoned a Post editor requesting that the paper not publish any patient photographs. Nevertheless, on the front page of next days' edition two photographs appeared—one of Nussbaum taken in November 1987, shortly after her arrest in connection with Lisa's death, and another of Nussbaum walking with plaintiff, taken the previous day at Four Winds.

In the earlier photograph, Nussbaum's face is bruised and disfigured, her lips split and swollen, and her matted hair is covered with a scarf. By contrast, in the photograph taken at Four Winds, Nussbaum's facial wounds have visibly healed, her hair is coiffed, and she is neatly dressed in jeans, a sweater and earrings. Plaintiff, walking alongside her, smiling, is in tennis attire and sneakers. The caption reads: "The battered face above belongs to the Hedda Nussbaum people remember— the former live-in lover of accused child-killer, Joel Steinberg. The serene woman in jeans at left is the same Hedda, strolling with a companion in the grounds of the upstate psychiatric center where her face and mind are healing from the terrible wounds Steinberg inflicted."

The accompanying article centers on Nussbaum's physical and mental rehabilitation and quotes her as saying: "I feel good. I'm healthy . . . They're good to me here. The People are nice and I do my photography." The article concludes by noting that several issues still haunt Nussbaum, including whether she should cooperate with the prosecution and testify against Steinberg.

Although plaintiff's name was not mentioned in the caption or article, her face is readily discernible. Alleging she experienced emotional distress and humiliation, plaintiff commenced an action against the Post, the photographer and two writers, seeking multimillion dollar damages for alleged violations of Civil Rights Law § 50 and 51, intentional and negligent infliction of emotional distress, trespass, harassment and prima facie tort. Plaintiff's husband, by the same complaint, brought a derivative claim for loss of consortium.

Supreme Court granted in part defendants' CPLR 3211(a)(7) motion by dismissing all causes of action except for intentional infliction of emotional distress and the derivative claim, and denied plaintiff's motion for summary judgment. On the parties' cross appeals, the Appellate Division modified by dismissing the entire complaint. This Court granted plaintiff's motion for leave to appeal to consider the dismissal of her claims for violation of the right to privacy and intentional infliction of emotional distress. We now affirm.

The Legal Backdrop

This appeal brings together two separate bodies of tort law, each with a long history that is relevant to resolution of the issues before us.

Intentional Infliction of Emotional Distress

Historically, the common law of this State did not recognize emotional injury—even with physical manifestations—as an independent basis for recovery. In Mitchell v. Rochester Ry. Co. (151 NY 107 [1896]), for example, a pregnant woman nearly hit by defendant's horses suffered a miscarriage. The Court noted that since there was no cause of action for fright, "it is obvious that no recovery can be had for injuries resulting therefrom. That the result may be nervous disease, blindness, insanity, or even a miscarriage, in no way changes the principle." (151 NY, at 109–110.) The Court expressed two concerns, present even today, with permitting emotional distress damages: (i) the potential "flood of litigation," and (ii) the ease with which emotional injury "may be . . . feigned without detection" (id., at 110).

Nevertheless, emotional distress damages as an adjunct, or "parasitic," to recognized torts were allowed (see, e.g., Garrison v. Sun Print. & Publ. Assn., 207 NY 1, 8 [1912] [defamation]). Indeed, courts often struggled to find an established cause of action upon which to base an award of emotional distress damages to a deserving plaintiff. This is exemplified by a line of cases allowing victims of unacceptable behavior to recover under a breach of contract theory (see, e.g., Boyce v. Greeley Sq. Hotel Co., 228 NY 106; Aaron v. Ward, 203 NY 351; de Wolf v. Ford, 193 NY 397).

The Restatement of Torts, first adopted in 1934, generally insulated an actor from liability for causing solely emotional distress: "conduct which is intended or which though not so intended is likely to cause only a mental or emotional disturbance to another does not subject the actor to liability . . . for emotional distress resulting therefrom" (Restatement of Torts § 46 [a]). Shortly thereafter, in an influential article surveying the field—including the New York cases—Calvert Magruder concluded that courts were already giving extensive protection to feelings and emotions, showing an "adaptability of technique" in redressing the more serious invasions (Magruder, *Mental and Emotional Disturbance in the Law of Torts*, 49 Harv L Rev 1033, 1067 [1936]).

Building on the Magruder article, Professor Prosser argued that, without expressly saying so, courts had actually created a new tort consisting of the intentional, outrageous infliction of mental suffering in an extreme form (Prosser, *Intentional Infliction of Mental Suffering: A New Tort*, 37 Mich L Rev 874, 874 [1939]). "Out of the array of technical assaults, batteries, imprisonments, trespasses, 'implied contracts,' invasions of 'privacy' or of doubtful 'property rights,' the real interest which is being protected stands forth very clearly." (Id., at 886–887.) Prosser suggested that there was no longer a reason or necessity for resorting to such "subterfuges," and that it was "high time to abandon them, and to rest the action upon its real ground." (Id., at 881.)

Responding to these and similar importunings, the Restatement in 1948 abandoned its earlier position and declared that "[o]ne who, without a privilege to do so, intentionally causes severe emotional distress to another is liable . . . for such emotional distress" (Restatement of Torts § 46 [a] [1948 Supp]).

While working on the Second Restatement of Torts, its Reporter, Dean Prosser, noted that the 1948 version was so broad as to suggest the need for further limitation (Prosser, Insult and Outrage, 44 Cal L Rev 40, 41 [1956]). The requirement of "extreme and outrageous conduct" was the apparent solution. As the Second Restatement reads: "One who by extreme and outrageous conduct intentionally or recklessly causes severe emotional distress to another is subject to liability for such emotional distress" (Restatement [Second] of Torts § 46 [1] [1965]). This Court subsequently adopted the Restatement formulation (see, Fischer v. Maloney, 43 NY2d 553, 557; Murphy v. American Home Prods. Corp., 58 NY2d 293, 303; Freihofer v. Hearst Corp., 65 NY2d 135, 143).

The tort has four elements: (i) extreme and outrageous conduct; (ii) intent to cause, or disregard of a substantial probability of causing, severe emotional distress; (iii) a causal connection between the conduct and injury; and (iv) severe emotional distress. The first element— outrageous conduct—serves the dual function of filtering out petty and trivial complaints that do not belong in court, and assuring that plaintiff's claim of severe emotional distress is genuine (see, Prosser, Insult and Outrage, 44 Cal L Rev, at 44–45; compare, Mitchell v. Rochester Ry Co., 151 NY, at 110). In practice, courts have tended to focus on the outrageousness element, the one most susceptible to determination as a matter of law (see, Restatement [Second] of Torts § 46, comment h; Givelber, *The Right to Minimum Social Decency and the Limits of Evenhandedness: Intentional Infliction of Emotional Distress by Outrageous Conduct* ["Social Decency"], 82 Colum L Rev 42, 42–43 [1982]).

Unlike other intentional torts, intentional infliction of emotional distress does not proscribe specific conduct (compare, e.g., Restatement [Second] of Torts § 18 [battery]; id., § 35 [false imprisonment]), but imposes liability based on after-the-fact judgments about the actor's behavior. Accordingly, the broadly defined standard of liability is both a virtue and a vice. The tort is as limitless as the human capacity for cruelty. The price for this flexibility in redressing utterly reprehensible behavior, however, is a tort that, by its terms, may overlap other areas of the law, with potential liability for conduct that is otherwise lawful. Moreover, unlike other torts, the actor may not have notice of the precise conduct proscribed (see, Givelber, Social Decency, 82 Colum L Rev, at 51–52).

Consequently, the "requirements of the rule are rigorous, and difficult to satisfy" (Prosser and Keeton, Torts § 12, at 60–61 [5th ed]; see also, Murphy, 58 NY2d, at 303 [describing the standard as "strict"]). Indeed, of the intentional infliction of emotional distress claims considered by this Court, every one has failed because the alleged conduct was not sufficiently outrageous (see, Freihofer v. Hearst Corp., 65 NY2d, at 143–144; Burlew v. American Mut. Ins. Co., 63 NY2d 412, 417–418; Murphy, 58 NY2d, at 303; Fischer v. Maloney, 43 NY2d, at 557). " 'Liability has been found only where the conduct has been so outrageous in character, and so extreme in degree, as to go beyond all possible bounds of decency, and to be regarded as atrocious, and utterly intolerable in a civilized community' " (*Murphy*, 58 NY2d, at 303, *quoting* Restatement [Second] of Torts § 46, comment d).

The Right to Privacy

While legal scholarship has been influential in the development of a tort for intentional infliction of emotional distress, it has had less success in the development of a right to privacy in this State. In a famous law review article written more than a century ago, Samuel Warren and Louis Brandeis advocated a tort for invasion of the right to privacy (Warren and Brandeis, *The Right to Privacy*, 4 Harv L Rev 193 [1890]). Relying in part on this article, Abigail Marie Roberson sued a flour company for using her picture, without consent, in the advertisement of its product (Roberson v. Rochester Folding Box Co., 171 NY 538). Finding a lack of support for the thesis of the Warren-Brandeis study, this Court, in a four to three decision, rejected plaintiff's claim.

The *Roberson* decision was roundly criticized[, citation]. The Legislature responded by enacting the Nation's first statutory right to privacy (L 1903, Ch 132), now codified as sections 50 and 51 of the Civil Rights Law. Section 50 prohibits the use of a living person's name, portrait or picture for "advertising" or "trade" purposes without prior written consent (Civil Rights Law § 50). Section 50 provides criminal penalties and section 51 a private right of action for damages and injunctive relief.

Although the statute itself does not define the terms "advertising" or "trade" purposes, courts have consistently held that the statute should not be construed to apply to publications concerning newsworthy events or matters of public interest (Finger v. Omni Publs. Intl., 77 NY2d 138, 141–142; Stephano v. News Group Publs., 64 NY2d 174, 184). This is both a matter of legislative intent and a reflection of constitutional values in the area of free speech and free press (*Stephano*, 64 NY2d, at 184; Arrington v. New York Times Co., 55 NY2d 433, 440). Thus, a " 'picture illustrating an article on a matter of public interest is not considered used for the purpose of trade or advertising within the prohibition of the statute . . . unless it has no real relationship to the article . . . or unless the article is an advertisement in disguise' " (Murray v. New York Mag. Co., 27 NY2d 406, 409, *quoting* Dallesandro v. Holt & Co., 4 AD2d 470, 471, *appeal dismissed* 7 NY2d 735; see also, *Finger*, 77 NY2d, at 142; *Stephano*, 64 NY2d, at 185; *Arrington*, 55 NY2d, at 440).

At least three other "privacy" torts have been recognized elsewhere (see, Prosser, Privacy, 48 Cal L Rev 383; Restatement [Second] of Torts § 652A–652E): unreasonable publicity given to another's private life (Restatement [Second] of Torts § 652D); unreasonable intrusion upon seclusion (id., § 652B); and publicity that unreasonably places another in a false light (id., § 652E). While the courts of other jurisdictions have adopted some or all of these torts, in this State the right to privacy is governed exclusively by sections 50 and 51 of the Civil Rights Law; we have no common law of privacy (*Stephano*, 64 NY2d, at 182; *Arrington*, 55 NY2d, at 439–440; Cohen v. Hallmark Cards, 45 NY2d 493, 497, n. 2; Flores v. Mosler Safe Co., 7 NY2d 276, 280). Balancing the competing policy concerns underlying tort recovery for invasion of privacy is best left to the Legislature, which in fact has rejected proposed bills to expand New York law to cover all four categories of privacy protection (see, *Arrington*, 55 NY2d, at 440; Savell, *Right of Privacy-Appropriation*, 48 Alb L Rev, at 3, n 4).

Application of the Law to the Present Appeal

The core of plaintiff's grievance is that, by publishing her photograph, defendants revealed to her friends, family and business associates that she was undergoing psychiatric treatment—a personal fact she took pains to keep confidential. There is, of course, no cause of action in this State for publication of truthful but embarrassing facts. Thus, a claim grounded in the right to privacy must fall within Civil Rights Law § 50 and 51.

The statutory right to privacy is not transgressed unless defendants used plaintiff's photograph in connection with trade or advertising. Accordingly, if plaintiff's picture accompanied a newspaper article on a matter of public interest, to succeed she must demonstrate that the picture bore no real relationship to the article, or that the article was an advertisement in disguise (see, *Stephano*, 64 NY2d, at 185; *Arrington*, 55 NY2d, at 440; Murray v. New York Mag. Co., 27 NY2d, at 409). Plaintiff concedes that, in the aftermath of Lisa Steinberg's death, articles about Hedda Nussbaum were a matter of public interest. Additionally, the Post article plainly was not a veiled advertisement. Thus, analysis of the civil rights claim centers on the "no real relationship" requirement.

We have been reluctant to intrude upon reasonable editorial judgments in determining whether there is a real relationship between an article and photograph (*Finger*, 77 NY2d, at 143; see also, Gaeta v. New York News, 62 NY2d 340, 349). In *Finger*, for example, a magazine without consent used a photograph of plaintiffs and their six children to illustrate a segment about caffeine-enhanced fertility. Although none of the children had been conceived in the manner suggested by the article, we concluded that the requisite nexus between the article and photograph was established because the article's theme—having a large family—was fairly reflected in the picture (see, *Finger*, 77 NY2d, at 142–143).

In the present case, similarly, plaintiff has failed to meet her burden. The subject of the article was Hedda Nussbaum's physical and emotional recovery from the beatings allegedly inflicted by Joel Steinberg. The photograph of a visibly healed Nussbaum, interacting with her smiling, fashionably clad "companion" offers a stark contrast to the adjacent photograph of Nussbaum's disfigured face. The visual impact would not have been the same had the Post cropped plaintiff out of the photograph, as she suggests was required. Thus, there is a real relationship between the article and the photograph of plaintiff, and the civil rights cause of action was properly dismissed.

Defendants would have our analysis end here—without considering whether plaintiff has stated a cause of action for intentional infliction of emotional distress—arguing that the tort may not be used as an end run around a failed right to privacy claim. Insofar as plaintiff's claim is based on the publication of her photograph, we agree, for the publication was qualifiedly privileged—meaning that defendants acted within their legal right—and no circumstances are present that would defeat the privilege.

The distinction between privileged and nonprivileged conduct as it relates to infliction of emotional distress is implicit in our cases and explicit in the Restatement. In Murphy v. American Home Prods. Corp. (58 NY2d, at 303), an employment case, we held that plaintiff could not "subvert the traditional at-will contract rule by casting his cause of action in terms of a tort of intentional infliction of emotional distress." If an employer has the right to discharge an employee, the exercise of that right cannot lead to a claim for infliction of emotional distress, however distressing the discharge may be to the employee. In the course of discharging the employee, however, an employer's deliberate reprehensible conduct intentionally or recklessly causing severe emotional distress is not within the employer's right, and may support a claim for intentional infliction of emotional distress.

The 1948 Restatement expressly provided that privileged conduct could not be the basis for liability (Restatement of Torts § 46 [1948 Supp]), and the comments to the current version signify an intent to continue the privileged-conduct exception: "The conduct, although it would otherwise be extreme and outrageous, may be privileged under the circumstances. The actor is never liable, for example, where [the actor] has done no more than to insist upon his [or her] legal rights in a permissible way, even though he [or she] is well aware that such insistence is certain to cause emotional distress." (Restatement [Second] of Torts § 46, comment g.)

A newspaper's publication of a newsworthy photograph is an act within the contemplation of the "privileged-conduct" exception (compare, Hustler Mag. v. Falwell, 485 US 46, 56). Thus, even if defendants were aware that publication would cause plaintiff emotional distress (see, Restatement [Second] of Torts § 46, comment f), publication—without more—could not ordinarily lead to liability for intentional infliction of emotional distress. We do not mean to suggest, however, that a plaintiff could never defeat the privilege and state a claim for intentional infliction of emotional distress. But because plaintiff's allegations offer no basis for concluding that the privilege has been abused, we need not explore today what circumstances might overcome the privilege.

That does not conclude our analysis, for plaintiff additionally complains that the manner in which her photograph was obtained constituted extreme and outrageous conduct contemplated by the tort of intentional infliction of emotional distress.

Courts have recognized that newsgathering methods may be tortious (see, e.g., Galella v. Onassis, 487 F2d 986, 995 [2d Cir]) and, to the extent that a journalist engages in such atrocious, indecent and utterly despicable conduct as to meet the rigorous requirements of an intentional infliction of emotional distress claim, recovery may be available. The conduct alleged here, however—a trespass onto Four Winds' grounds—does not remotely approach the required standard. That plaintiff was photographed outdoors and from a distance diminishes her claim even further.

Accordingly, the order of the Appellate Division, insofar as it pertains to the individual defendants, should be affirmed, with costs.

■ SIMONS, TITONE, HANCOCK, JR., and BELLACOSA concur; SMITH, J., taking no part.

NOTES AND QUESTIONS

1.   In light of the Court of Appeals' decision in *Howell*, what acts, do you suppose, would satisfy the standard? Have the New York courts ended up recognizing a claim for intentional infliction of emotional distress in

principle, but not in fact? Does it make sense for courts to have adopted a theory of liability, if in practice no facts have fulfilled the elements of the claim? On the other hand, does it make sense to allow a claim for intentional infliction of emotional distress if the conduct is otherwise lawful or even privileged?

2. Other common law jurisdictions have proved less reluctant to redress a claim for intentional infliction of emotional distress and have allowed recovery in a number of different circumstances. For example, in Burgess v. Taylor, 44 S.W.3d 806 (Ky. Ct. App. 2001), the Kentucky Court of Appeals considered whether the tort applied to the slaughter of pet horses. Judy Taylor was the owner of two much-loved Appaloosa horses, nicknamed Poco and P.J. After she began to suffer from ill-health, she sought someone with a farm who could care for the horses, in exchange for the pleasure of having them around, without Judy having to sell them. Lisa and Jeff Burgess, who had a small farm with their own horses, assured Taylor they would care for Poco and P.J. and that she could visit them anytime. Within the next several days, however, the Burgesses sold Poco and P.J. off for slaughter. Taylor begged the Burgesses to let her see her horses, but they refused and repeatedly misled her about their whereabouts. Poco and P.J. were killed before Taylor could locate them. Taylor sued for intentional infliction of emotional distress, and the jury awarded her $126,000. The Burgesses appealed, and the Kentucky Court of Appeals upheld the award:

> In order to recover under the tort . . . a plaintiff must prove: 1) the wrongdoer's conduct must be intentional or reckless; 2) the conduct must be outrageous and intolerable in that it offends against the generally accepted standards of decency and morality; 3) there must be a causal connection between the wrongdoer's conduct and the emotional distress; and 4) the emotional distress must be severe. . . .

> First, it is clear that the Burgesses' conduct was reckless . . . Lisa Burgess admitted that she never had any intentions of keeping Poco and P.J. . . . There was significant evidence that the Burgesses were aware of Taylor's feelings for Poco and P.J., and hence, knew or should have known that emotional distress would result from their selling them to a slaughter-buyer.

> Second, the Burgesses' conduct clearly rises to the level of being outrageous and intolerable. . .The jury heard evidence of subsequent phone calls by a distraught and frightened Taylor to Lisa Burgess and Kenny Randolph, begging to know where her horses were. . . . The Burgesses knew that Poco and P.J. were heading to slaughter, and that Taylor was, in reality, pleading for their lives. Yet, in the face of Taylor's pleas for the horses she loved like children, the Burgesses continued to lie and refuse to tell her where they were. This Court cannot characterize this emotional torment inflicted by the Burgesses upon Taylor as anything other than "heartless, flagrant, and outrageous."

Third, the sale of Poco and P.J. by the Burgesses to a known slaughter-buyer satisfies the requirement of a causal connection. . . . Further, the Burgesses' subsequent lies precluded Taylor from locating and saving her horses before they were slaughtered. . . .

Finally, the evidence indicates that Taylor suffered severe emotional distress. Taylor testified that when she learned what had happened to Poco and P.J., she broke down, knowing that "my babies were dead." Since then she has suffered from many panic attacks, and has had major problems with high blood pressure for which she must receive medical care. She suffers from anxiety and depression, for which she takes medication, and has had many thoughts of suicide. She described overwhelming feelings of loss and failure. She testified she has trouble sleeping and has recurring nightmares in which she hears Poco's scream in her head. . . .

2. OVERRULING

It is a maxim among these lawyers, that whatever hath been done before may legally be done again: and therefore they take special care to record all the decisions formerly made against common justice and the general reason of mankind. These, under the name of precedents, they produce as authorities, to justify the most iniquitous opinions; and the judges never fail of directing accordingly.

J. Swift, *Gulliver's Travels* 275 (1726) (The Novel Library 1947), *quoted in* James C. Rehnquist, The Power That Shall Be Vested in a Precedent: *Stare Decisis*, the Constitution, and the Supreme Court, 66 B.U.L.Rev. 345 (1986).

In England, before 1966, the House of Lords (in its judicial capacity) took the position that it could not overrule prior decisions. Whether this position was as rigid as it purported to be is a matter for some argument. However, it is true that the doctrine of *stare decisis* was more strictly applied in England than in the United States, where it has always been accepted that a court could overrule its prior decisions.*

A court's option, in the last analysis, to overrule a prior decision makes the concept of "holding" even more elusive than it might otherwise be. What, you may ask, is all of the fuss about "binding decisions" if they aren't really binding? Consider the rationale behind adherence to precedent. It has often been argued that *stare decisis* promotes certainty, impartiality, efficiency, and the appearance of justice in the legal system. Nonetheless, there are legitimate reasons to overrule precedent. In addition to asking *why* a decision has been overruled, you might also ask yourself *how* the decision was overruled. Did the court explicitly overrule precedent? Did it recognize that, in practice, the old ruling had ceased to have legal relevance? How much of the "old rule" survives? How much of a difference is there between an outright overruling and a progressive distinguishing of contrary precedent?

---

* Before judgments were given in the House of Lords on July 26, 1966, Lord Gardiner, L.C., made the following statement on behalf of himself and the Lords of Appeal in Ordinary:

> Their lordships regard the use of precedent as an indispensable foundation upon which to decide what is the law and its application to individual cases. It provides at least some degree of certainty upon which individuals can rely in the conduct of their affairs, as well as a basis for orderly development of legal rules.

> Their lordships nevertheless recognise that too rigid adherence to precedent may lead to injustice in a particular case and also unduly restrict the proper development of the law. They propose therefore to modify their present practice and, while treating former decisions of this House as normally binding, to depart from a previous decision when it appears right to do so.

> In this connexion they will bear in mind the danger of disturbing retrospectively the basis on which contracts, settlements of property and fiscal arrangements have been entered into and also the especial need for certainty as to the criminal law.

> This announcement is not intended to affect the use of precedent elsewhere than in this House.

3 All E.R. Ch. D. 77.

Battalla v. State

Court of Appeals of New York, 1961.
10 N.Y.2d 237, 219 N.Y.S.2d 34, 176 N.E.2d 729.

■ BURKE, JUDGE.

The question presented is whether the claim states a cause of action when it alleges that claimant was negligently caused to suffer "severe emotional and neurological disturbances with residual physical manifestations".

The appellant avers that in September of 1956, at Bellayre Mountain Ski Center, the infant plaintiff was placed in a chair lift by an employee of the State who failed to secure and properly lock the belt intended to protect the occupant. As a result of this alleged negligent act, the infant plaintiff became frightened and hysterical upon the descent, with consequential injuries.

The Court of Claims, on a motion to dismiss the complaint, held that a cause of action does lie. The Appellate Division found itself constrained to follow Mitchell v. Rochester Ry. Co., 151 N.Y. 107, 45 N.E. 354, 34 L.R.A. 781 [1896] and, therefore, reversed and dismissed the claim. The Mitchell case decided that there could be no recovery for injuries, physical or mental, incurred by fright negligently induced.

It is our opinion that Mitchell should be overruled. It is undisputed that a rigorous application of its rule would be unjust, as well as opposed to experience and logic. On the other hand, resort to the somewhat inconsistent exceptions would merely add further confusion to a legal situation which presently lacks that coherence which precedent should possess. "We act in the finest common-law tradition when we adapt and alter decisional law to produce common-sense justice. * * * Legislative action there could, of course, be, but we abdicate our own function, in a field peculiarly nonstatutory, when we refuse to reconsider an old and unsatisfactory court-made rule." Woods v. Lancet, 303 N.Y. 349, 355, 102 N.E.2d 691, 694, 27 A.L.R.2d 1250.

Before passing to a résumé of the evolution of the doctrine in this State, it is well to note that it has been thoroughly repudiated by the English courts which initiated it, rejected by a majority of American jurisdictions, abandoned by many which originally adopted it, and diluted, through numerous exceptions, in the minority which retained it. Moreover, it is the opinion of scholars that *the right* to bring an action should be enforced.[1]

---

[1] For excellent studies see 1936 Report of N.Y.Law Rev.Comm., pp. 379–450; McNiece, *Psychic Injury and Tort Liability in New York*, 24 St. John's L.Rev. 1; see also, Smith, *Relation of Emotions to Injury and Disease; Legal Liability for Psychic Stimuli*, 30 Va.L.Rev. 193 (1944); Magruder, *Mental and Emotional Disturbance in the Law of Torts*, 49 Harv.L.Rev. 1033 (1936); Throckmorton, *Damages for Fright*, 34 Harv.L.Rev. 260 (1921); Wilson, *The New York Rule as to Nervous Shock*, 11 Cornell L.Q. 512 (1926); Edgar, *Foreseeability and Recovery in Tort*, 9 St. John's L.Rev. 84 (1934); Prosser, *Torts* (2d ed.), pp. 38–47, 178, 192; for others, see 1936 Report

It is fundamental to our common-law system that one may seek redress for every substantial wrong. "The best statement of the rule is that a wrong-doer is responsible for the natural and proximate consequences of his misconduct; and what are such consequences must generally be left for the determination of the jury." Ehrgott v. Mayor of City of New York, 96 N.Y. 264, 281. A departure from this axiom was introduced by Mitchell (supra), wherein recovery was denied to plaintiff, a pregnant woman, who, although not physically touched, was negligently caused to abort her child. Defendant's horses were driven in such a reckless manner that, when finally restrained, plaintiff was trapped between their heads. The court indicated essentially three reasons for dismissing the complaint. It stated first that, since plaintiff could not recover for mere fright, there could be no recovery for injuries resulting therefrom. It was assumed, in addition, that the miscarriage was not the proximate result of defendant's negligence, but rather was due to an accidental or unusual combination of circumstances. Finally, the court reasoned that a recovery would be contrary to public policy because that type of injury could be feigned without detection and it would result in a flood of litigation where damages must rest on speculation.

With the possible exception of the last, it seems "[a]ll these objections have been demolished many times, and it is threshing old straw to deal with them." (Prosser, Torts [2d ed.], § 37, pp. 176–177.) Moreover, we have stated that the conclusions of the *Mitchell* case (supra) "cannot be tested by pure logic". Comstock v. Wilson, 1931, 257 N.Y. 231, 234, 177 N.E. 431, 432, 76 A.L.R. 676. Although finding impact and granting recovery, the unanimous court in *Comstock* rejected all but the public policy arguments of the *Mitchell* decision.

We presently feel that even the public policy argument is subject to challenge. Although fraud, extra litigation and a measure of speculation are, of course, possibilities, it is no reason for a court to eschew a measure of its jurisdiction. "The argument from mere expediency cannot commend itself to a Court of justice, resulting in the denial of a logical legal right and remedy in *all* cases because in *some* a fictitious injury may be urged as a real one." Green v. T.A. Shoemaker & Co., 111 Md. 69, 81, 73 A. 688, 692, 23 L.R.A., N.S., 667.

---

of N.Y.Law Rev.Comm., p. 448; see, also, 15 Am.Jur., Damages, § 188; 25 C.J.S. Damages § 70; Restatement, Torts, § 436, subds. (1), (2).

In any event, it seems that fraudulent accidents and injuries are just as easily feigned in the slight-impact cases[2] and other exceptions[3] wherein New York permits a recovery, as in the no-impact cases which it has heretofore shunned.[4] As noted by the Law Revision Commission: "The exceptions to the rule cannot be said to insure recovery to any substantial number of meritorious claimants and there is good ground for believing that they breed dishonest attempts to mold the facts so as to fit them within the grooves leading to recovery." (1936 Report of N.Y.Law Rev.Comm., p. 450.) The ultimate result is that the honest claimant is penalized for his reluctance to fashion the facts within the framework of the exceptions.

Not only, therefore, are claimants in this situation encouraged by the Mitchell disqualification to perjure themselves, but the constant attempts to either come within an old exception, or establish a new one, lead to excess appellate litigation (see Gulf, C. & S.F. Ry. Co. v. Hayter, 93 Tex. 239, 54 S.W. 944, 47 L.R.A. 325). In any event, even if a flood of litigation were realized by abolition of the exception, it is the duty of the courts to willingly accept the opportunity to settle these disputes.

The only substantial policy argument of Mitchell is that the damages or injuries are somewhat speculative and difficult to prove. However, the question of proof in individual situations should not be the arbitrary basis upon which to bar all actions, and "it is beside the point * * * in determining sufficiency of a pleading". Woods v. Lancet, 303 N.Y. 349, 356, 102 N.E.2d 691, 695, supra. In many instances, just as in impact cases, there will be no doubt as to the presence and extent of the damage and the fact that it was proximately caused by defendant's negligence. In the difficult cases, we must look to the quality and genuineness of proof, and rely to an extent on the contemporary sophistication of the medical profession and the ability of the court and jury to weed out the dishonest claims. Claimant should, therefore, be given an opportunity to prove that her injuries were proximately caused by defendant's negligence.

---

[2] For example, Jones v. Brooklyn Heights R.R. Co., 23 App.Div. 141, 48 N.Y.S. 914, wherein plaintiff was hit on the head by a small incandescent light bulb which fell from a lamp attached to the roof of defendant's car in which plaintiff was a passenger. Plaintiff was allowed to recover for a miscarriage brought on *by the shock* stimulated by the injury. See, also, Buckbee v. Third Ave. R.R. Co., 64 App.Div. 360, 72 N.Y.S. 217 (slight electric shock); Powell v. Hudson Valley Ry. Co., 88 App.Div. 133 (slight burn); Comstock v. Wilson, 257 N.Y. 231, 177 N.E. 431, supra (fright induced by prior collision caused passenger to faint and fracture skull); Sawyer v. Dougherty, 286 App.Div. 1061, 144 N.Y.S.2d 746 (blast of air filled with glass).

[3] Injuries from fright are also recoverable generally in: "the burial right cases, the contract relationship cases [innkeeper and common carrier cases], the immediate physical injury cases * * *, the Workmen's Compensation cases, the food cases, the wilful or wanton injury cases, and the right of privacy cases" (brackets mine; McNiece, 24 St. John's L.Rev., pp. 33–65).

[4] No recovery: Newton v. New York, N.H. & H.R.R. Co., 106 App.Div. 415, 94 N.Y.S. 825 (plaintiff passenger in train collision); Hutchinson v. Stern, 115 App.Div. 791, 101 N.Y.S. 145 (plaintiff could not recover for loss of wife's services when she gave birth to a stillborn child while witnessing an attack on plaintiff); O'Brien v. Moss, 220 App.Div. 464, 221 N.Y.S. 621 (passenger in car collision).

Accordingly, the judgment should be reversed and the claim reinstated, with costs.

■ VAN VOORHIS, JUDGE (dissenting).

In following the Massachusetts rule, which corresponded to that enunciated in this State by Mitchell v. Rochester Ry. Co., 151 N.Y. 107, 45 N.E. 354, Mr. Justice Holmes described it as "an arbitrary exception, based upon a notion of what is practicable, that prevents a recovery for visible illness resulting from nervous shock alone. [Citation.]" [Citation.] Illogical as the legal theoreticians acknowledge this rule to be, it was Justice Holmes who said that the life of the law has not been logic but experience. Experience has produced this rule to prevent the ingenuity of special pleaders and paid expert witnesses from getting recoveries in negligence for nervous shock without physical injury, which was stated as well as possible in Mitchell v. Rochester Ry. Co., supra, 151 N.Y. at page 110, 45 N.E. at page 354 as follows: "If the right of recovery in this class of cases should be once established, it would naturally result in a flood of litigation in cases where the injury easily feigned without detection, and where the damages must rest upon mere conjecture or speculation. The difficulty which often exists in cases of alleged physical injury, in determining whether they exist, and if so, whether they were caused by the negligent act of the defendant, would not only be greatly increased, but a wide field would be opened for fictitious or speculative claims. To establish such a doctrine would be contrary to principles of public policy."

The opinion likewise points out (151 N.Y. at page 109, 45 N.E. at page 354) the speculative nature of the usual evidence of causation where it is contended that mere fright has resulted in "nervous disease, blindness, insanity, or even a miscarriage".

These statements in the Mitchell opinion are not archaic or antiquated, but are even more pertinent today than when they were first stated. At a time like the present, with constantly enlarging recoveries both in scope and amount in all fields of negligence law, and when an influential portion of the Bar is organized as never before to promote ever-increasing recoveries for the most intangible and elusive injuries, little imagination is required to envision mental illness and psychosomatic medicine as encompassed by the enlargement of the coverage of negligence claims to include this fertile field. In Comstock v. Wilson, 257 N.Y. 231, 177 N.E. 431, Mitchell v. Rochester Ry. Co. (supra) is not overruled, but the opinion by Judge Lehman (257 N.Y. at page 238, 177 N.E. at page 433) cites it as well as the Massachusetts rule of Spade v. Lynn & Boston R.R. Co., 168 Mass. 285, 47 N.E. 88, as holding that "for practical reasons there is ordinarily no duty to exercise care to avert causing mental disturbance, and no legal right to mental security." Judge Lehman's opinion continues: "Serious consequences from mere mental disturbance unaccompanied by physical shock cannot be anticipated, and no person is bound to be alert to avert a danger that foresight does not disclose. The conclusion is fortified by the practical consideration that where there has been no physical contact there is danger that fictitious claims may be fabricated. Therefore, where no wrong was claimed other than a mental disturbance, the courts refuse to sanction a recovery for the consequence of that disturbance" (257 N.Y. at pages 238–239, 177 N.E. at page 433).

The problem involved in enlarging the scope of recovery in negligence, even in instances where, as here, an enlargement might be justified on purely theoretical grounds, is that, when once the door has been opened, the new and broader rule is in practice pressed to its extreme conclusion. Courts and juries become prone to accept as established fact that fright has been the cause of mental or physical consequences which informed medical men of balanced judgment find too complicated to trace. Once a medical expert has been found who, for a consideration, expresses an opinion that the relationship of cause and effect exists, courts and juries tend to lay aside critical judgment and accept the fact as stated.

This is the practical reason mentioned by Judges Holmes and Lehman. The Pennsylvania Supreme Court has recently decided that to hold otherwise "would open a Pandora's box." Bosley v. Andrews, 393 Pa. 161, 168, 142 A.2d 263, 266.

In my view the judgment dismissing the claim should be affirmed.

■ FULD, FROESSEL and FOSTER, JJ., concur with BURKE, J.

■ VAN VOORHIS, J., dissents in an opinion in which DESMOND, C.J., and DYE, J., concur.

Judgment reversed and order of the Court of Claims reinstated, with costs in this court and in the Appellate Division.

NOTES AND QUESTIONS

1. What reasons does the court give for overruling precedent? Are these more important than the doctrine of *stare decisis*?

2. When and how does a court decide that a rule has become "unjust" and "opposed to experience and logic," as argued in *Battalla*?

3. Consider Justice Brandeis' dissent in Burnet v. Coronado Oil & Gas, 285 U.S. 393, 406 (1932):

> *Stare decisis* is usually the wise policy, because in most matters it is more important that the applicable rule of law be settled than that it be settled right.

4. In **Planned Parenthood of Southeastern Pa. v. Casey**, 505 U.S. 833 (1992). A plurality of the Court offered the following framework for analyzing whether it is appropriate to overrule a prior decision:

> The obligation to follow precedent begins with necessity, and a contrary necessity marks its outer limit. With Cardozo, we recognize that no judicial system could do society's work if it eyed

each issue afresh in every case that raised it. See B. Cardozo, The Nature of the Judicial Process 149 (1921). Indeed, the very concept of the rule of law underlying our own Constitution requires such continuity over time that a respect for precedent is, by definition, indispensable. See Powell, *Stare Decisis* and Judicial Restraint, 1991 Journal of Supreme Court History 13, 16. At the other extreme, a different necessity would make itself felt if a prior judicial ruling should come to be seen so clearly as error that its enforcement was for that very reason doomed.

Even when the decision to overrule a prior case is not, as in the rare, latter instance, virtually foreordained, it is common wisdom that the rule of *stare decisis* is not an "inexorable command," and certainly it is not such in every constitutional case, see Burnet v. Coronado Oil Gas Co., 285 U.S. 393, 405–411 (1932) (Brandeis, J., dissenting). Rather, when this Court reexamines a prior holding, its judgment is customarily informed by a series of prudential and pragmatic considerations designed to test the consistency of overruling a prior decision with the ideal of the rule of law, and to gauge the respective costs of reaffirming and overruling a prior case. Thus, for example, we may ask whether the rule has proved to be intolerable simply in defying practical workability; whether the rule is subject to a kind of reliance that would lend a special hardship to the consequences of overruling and add inequity to the cost of repudiation; whether related principles of law have so far developed as to have left the old rule no more than a remnant of abandoned doctrine; or whether facts have so changed or come to be seen so differently, as to have robbed the old rule of significant application or justification. [citations omitted]

Is the New York Court of Appeals' reasoning in *Battalla* consistent with this framework? Is the reasoning of the Supreme Court in the following decision? Does it matter?

Lawrence v. Texas

Supreme Court of the United States, 2003.
539 U.S. 558, 123 S.Ct. 2472, 156 L.Ed.2d 508.

■ JUSTICE KENNEDY delivered the opinion of the Court[, in which JUSTICE STEVENS, JUSTICE SOUTER, JUSTICE GINSBURG, and JUSTICE BREYER joined].

Liberty protects the person from unwarranted government intrusions into a dwelling or other private places. In our tradition the State is not omnipresent in the home. And there are other spheres of our lives and existence, outside the home, where the State should not be a dominant presence. Freedom extends beyond spatial bounds. Liberty presumes an autonomy of self that includes freedom of thought, belief, expression, and certain intimate conduct. The instant case involves liberty of the person both in its spatial and more transcendent dimensions.

I

The question before the Court is the validity of a Texas statute making it a crime for two persons of the same sex to engage in certain intimate sexual conduct.

In Houston, Texas, officers of the Harris County Police Department were dispatched to a private residence in response to a reported weapons disturbance. They entered an apartment where one of the petitioners, John Geddes Lawrence, resided. The right of the police to enter does not seem to have been questioned. The officers observed Lawrence and another man, Tyron Garner, engaging in a sexual act. The two petitioners were arrested, held in custody over night, and charged and convicted before a Justice of the Peace.

The complaints described their crime as "[d]eviate sexual intercourse, namely anal sex, with a member of the same sex (man)." App. to Pet. for Cert. 127a, 139a. The applicable state law is Tex. Penal Code Ann. § 21.06(a) (2003). It provides: "A person commits an offense if he engages in deviate sexual intercourse with another individual of the same sex." The statute defines "deviate sexual intercourse" as follows:

"(A) any contact between any part of the genitals of one person and the mouth or anus of another person; or

"(B) the penetration of the genitals or the anus of another person with an object." § 21.01(1).

The petitioners exercised their right to a trial *de novo* in Harris County Criminal Court. They challenged the statute as a violation of the Equal Protection Clause of the Fourteenth Amendment and of a like provision of the Texas Constitution. Tex. Const., Art. 1, § 3a. Those contentions were rejected. The petitioners, having entered a plea of *nolo contendere*, were each fined $200 and assessed court costs of $141.25. App. to Pet. for Cert. 107a–110a.

The Court of Appeals for the Texas Fourteenth District considered the petitioners' federal constitutional arguments under both the Equal Protection and Due Process Clauses of the Fourteenth Amendment. After hearing the case en banc the court, in a divided opinion, rejected the constitutional arguments and affirmed the convictions. 41 S. W. 3d 349 (Tex. App. 2001). The majority opinion indicates that the Court of Appeals considered our decision in *Bowers* v. *Hardwick,* 478 U.S. 186, 92 L. Ed. 2d 140, 106 S.Ct. 2841 (1986), to be controlling on the federal due process aspect of the case. *Bowers* then being authoritative, this was proper.

We granted certiorari, 537 U.S. 1044, 154 L. Ed. 2d 514, 123 S.Ct. 661 (2002), to consider [among the] questions:

". . . Whether *Bowers* v. *Hardwick*, 478 U.S. 186, 92 L. Ed. 2d 140, 106 S.Ct. 2841 (1986), should be overruled?"

The petitioners were adults at the time of the alleged offense. Their conduct was in private and consensual.

II

We conclude the case should be resolved by determining whether the petitioners were free as adults to engage in the private conduct in the exercise of their liberty under the Due Process Clause of the Fourteenth Amendment to the Constitution. For this inquiry we deem it necessary to reconsider the Court's holding in *Bowers*. . . .

The facts in *Bowers* had some similarities to the instant case. A police officer, whose right to enter seems not to have been in question, observed Hardwick, in his own bedroom, engaging in intimate sexual conduct with another adult male. The conduct was in violation of a Georgia statute making it a criminal offense to engage in sodomy. One difference between the two cases is that the Georgia statute prohibited the conduct whether or not the participants were of the same sex, while the Texas statute, as we have seen, applies only to participants of the same sex. Hardwick was not prosecuted, but he brought an action in federal court to declare the state statute invalid. He alleged he was a practicing homosexual and that the criminal prohibition violated rights guaranteed to him by the Constitution. The Court, in an opinion by Justice White, sustained the Georgia law. Chief Justice Burger and Justice Powell joined the opinion of the Court and filed separate, concurring opinions. Four Justices dissented. 478 U.S., at 199 (opinion of BLACKMUN, J., joined by BRENNAN, MARSHALL, and STEVENS, JJ.); *id.*, at 214 (opinion of STEVENS, J., joined by BRENNAN and MARSHALL, JJ.).

The Court began its substantive discussion in *Bowers* as follows: "The issue presented is whether the Federal Constitution confers a fundamental right upon homosexuals to engage in sodomy and hence invalidates the laws of the many States that still make such conduct illegal and have done so for a very long time." *Id.*, at 190. That statement, we now conclude, discloses the Court's own failure to appreciate the extent of the liberty at stake. To say that the issue in *Bowers* was simply the right to engage in certain sexual conduct demeans the claim the individual put forward, just as it would demean a married couple were it to be said marriage is simply about the right to have sexual intercourse. The laws involved in *Bowers* and here are, to be sure, statutes that purport to do no more than prohibit a particular sexual act. Their penalties and purposes, though, have more far-reaching consequences, touching upon the most private human conduct, sexual behavior, and in the most private of places, the home. The statutes do seek to control a personal relationship that, whether or not entitled to formal recognition in the law, is within the liberty of persons to choose without being punished as criminals.

This, as a general rule, should counsel against attempts by the State, or a court, to define the meaning of the relationship or to set its boundaries absent injury to a person or abuse of an institution the law protects. It suffices for us to acknowledge that adults may choose to enter upon this relationship in the confines of their homes and their own private lives and still retain their dignity as free persons. When sexuality finds overt expression in intimate conduct with another person, the conduct can be but one element in a personal bond that is more enduring. The liberty protected by the Constitution allows homosexual persons the right to make this choice.

Having misapprehended the claim of liberty there presented to it, and thus stating the claim to be whether there is a fundamental right to engage in consensual sodomy, the *Bowers* Court said: "Proscriptions against that conduct have ancient roots." *Id.*, at 192. In academic writings, and in many of the scholarly *amicus* briefs filed to assist the Court in this case, there are fundamental criticisms of the historical premises relied upon by the majority and concurring opinions in *Bowers*. Brief for Cato Institute as *Amicus Curiae* 16–17; Brief for American Civil Liberties Union et al. as *Amici Curiae* 15–21; Brief for Professors of History et al. as *Amici Curiae* 3–10. We need not enter this debate in the attempt to reach a definitive historical judgment, but the following considerations counsel against adopting the definitive conclusions upon which *Bowers* placed such reliance.

At the outset it should be noted that there is no longstanding history in this country of laws directed at homosexual conduct as a distinct matter. Beginning in colonial times there were prohibitions of sodomy derived from the English criminal laws passed in the first instance by the Reformation Parliament of 1533. The English prohibition was understood to include relations between men and women as well as relations between men and men. See, *e.g., King* v. *Wiseman*, 92 Eng. Rep. 774, 775 (K. B. 1718) (interpreting "mankind" in Act of 1533 as including women and girls). Nineteenth-century commentators similarly read American sodomy, buggery, and crime-against-nature statutes as criminalizing certain relations between men and women and between men and men. See, *e.g.*, 2 J. Bishop, Criminal Law § 1028 (1858); 2 J. Chitty, Criminal Law 47–50 (5th Am. ed. 1847); R. Desty, A Compendium of American Criminal Law 143 (1882); J. May, The Law of Crimes § 203 (2d ed. 1893). The absence of legal prohibitions focusing on homosexual conduct may be explained in part by noting that according to some scholars the concept of the homosexual as a distinct category of person did not emerge until the late 19th century. See, *e.g.*, J. Katz, The Invention of Heterosexuality 10 (1995); J. D'Emilio & E. Freedman, Intimate Matters: A History of Sexuality in America 121 (2d ed. 1997) ("The modern terms *homosexuality* and *heterosexuality* do not apply to an era that had not yet articulated these distinctions"). Thus early American sodomy laws were not directed at homosexuals as such but instead sought to prohibit nonprocreative sexual activity more generally. This does not suggest approval of homosexual conduct. It does tend to show that this particular form of conduct was not thought of as a separate category from like conduct between heterosexual persons.

Laws prohibiting sodomy do not seem to have been enforced against consenting adults acting in private. A substantial number of sodomy prosecutions and convictions for which there are surviving records were for predatory acts against those who could not or did not consent, as in the case of a minor or the victim of an assault. As to these, one purpose for the prohibitions was to ensure there would be no lack of coverage if a predator committed a sexual assault that did not constitute rape as defined by the criminal law. Thus the model sodomy indictments presented in a 19th-century treatise, see 2 Chitty, *supra,* at 49, addressed the predatory acts of an adult man against a minor girl or minor boy. Instead of targeting relations between consenting adults in private, 19th-century sodomy prosecutions typically involved relations between men and minor girls or minor boys, relations between adults involving force, relations between adults implicating disparity in status, or relations between men and animals.

To the extent that there were any prosecutions for the acts in question, 19th-century evidence rules imposed a burden that would make a conviction more difficult to obtain even taking into account the problems always inherent in prosecuting consensual acts committed in private. Under then-prevailing standards, a man could not be convicted of sodomy based upon testimony of a consenting partner, because the partner was considered an accomplice. A partner's testimony, however, was admissible if he or she had not consented to the act or was a minor, and therefore incapable of consent. See, *e.g.,* F. Wharton, Criminal Law 443 (2d ed. 1852); 1 F. Wharton, Criminal Law 512 (8th ed. 1880). The rule may explain in part the infrequency of these prosecutions. In all events that infrequency makes it difficult to say that society approved of a rigorous and systematic punishment of the consensual acts committed in private and by adults. The longstanding criminal prohibition of homosexual sodomy upon which the *Bowers* decision placed such reliance is as consistent with a general condemnation of nonprocreative sex as it is with an established tradition of prosecuting acts because of their homosexual character.

The policy of punishing consenting adults for private acts was not much discussed in the early legal literature. We can infer that one reason for this was the very private nature of the conduct. Despite the absence of prosecutions, there may have been periods in which there was public criticism of homosexuals as such and an insistence that the criminal laws be enforced to discourage their practices. But far from possessing "ancient roots," *Bowers*, 478 U.S., at 192, American laws targeting same-sex couples did not develop until the last third of the 20th century. The reported decisions concerning the prosecution of consensual, homosexual sodomy between adults for the years 1880–1995 are not always clear in the details, but a significant number involved conduct in a public place. See Brief for American Civil Liberties Union et al. as *Amici Curiae* 14–15, and n. 18.

It was not until the 1970's that any State singled out same-sex relations for criminal prosecution, and only nine States have done so. See 1977 Ark. Gen. Acts no. 828; 1983 Kan. Sess. Laws p. 652; 1974 Ky. Acts p. 847; 1977 Mo. Laws p. 687; 1973 Mont. Laws p. 1339; 1977 Nev. Stats. p. 1632; 1989 Tenn. Pub. Acts ch. 591; 1973 Tex. Gen. Laws ch. 399; see also *Post* v. *State*, 1986 OK CR 30, 715 P.2d 1105 (Okla. Crim. App. 1986) (sodomy law invalidated as applied to different-sex couples). Post-*Bowers* even some of these States did not adhere to the policy of suppressing homosexual conduct. Over the course of the last decades, States with same-sex prohibitions have moved toward abolishing them. See, *e.g.*, *Jegley* v. *Picado*, 349 Ark. 600, 80 S. W. 3d 332 (2002); *Gryczan* v. *State*, 283 Mont. 433, 942 P.2d 112 (1997); *Campbell* v. *Sundquist*, 926 S.W.2d 250 (Tenn. App. 1996); *Commonwealth* v. *Wasson*, 842 S.W.2d 487 (Ky. 1992); see also 1993 Nev. Stats. p. 518 (repealing Nev. Rev. Stat. § 201.193).

In summary, the historical grounds relied upon in *Bowers* are more complex than the majority opinion and the concurring opinion by Chief Justice Burger indicate. Their historical premises are not without doubt and, at the very least, are overstated.

It must be acknowledged, of course, that the Court in *Bowers* was making the broader point that for centuries there have been powerful voices to condemn homosexual conduct as immoral. The condemnation has been shaped by religious beliefs, conceptions of right and acceptable behavior, and respect for the traditional family. For many persons these are not trivial concerns but profound and deep convictions accepted as ethical and moral principles to which they aspire and which thus determine the course of their lives. These considerations do not answer the question before us, however. The issue is whether the majority may use the power of the State to enforce these views on the whole society through operation of the criminal law. "Our obligation is to define the liberty of all, not to mandate our own moral code." *Planned Parenthood of Southeastern Pa.* v. *Casey,* 505 U.S. 833, 850, 112 S.Ct. 2791, 120 L. Ed. 2d 674 (1992).

Chief Justice Burger joined the opinion for the Court in *Bowers* and further explained his views as follows: "Decisions of individuals relating to homosexual conduct have been subject to state intervention throughout the history of Western civilization. Condemnation of those practices is firmly rooted in Judeao-Christian moral and ethical standards." 478 U.S., at 196. As with Justice White's assumptions about history, scholarship casts some doubt on the sweeping nature of the statement by Chief Justice Burger as it pertains to private homosexual conduct between consenting adults. See, *e.g.,* Eskridge, Hardwick and

Historiography, 1999 U. Ill. L. Rev. 631, 656. In all events we think that our laws and traditions in the past half century are of most relevance here. These references show an emerging awareness that liberty gives substantial protection to adult persons in deciding how to conduct their private lives in matters pertaining to sex. . . .

This emerging recognition should have been apparent when *Bowers* was decided. In 1955 the American Law Institute promulgated the Model Penal Code and made clear that it did not recommend or provide for "criminal penalties for consensual sexual relations conducted in private." ALI, Model Penal Code § 213.2, Comment 2, p. 372 (1980). It justified its decision on three grounds: (1) The prohibitions undermined respect for the law by penalizing conduct many people engaged in; (2) the statutes regulated private conduct not harmful to others; and (3) the laws were arbitrarily enforced and thus invited the danger of blackmail. ALI, Model Penal Code, Commentary 277–280 (Tent. Draft No. 4, 1955). In 1961 Illinois changed its laws to conform to the Model Penal Code. Other States soon followed. Brief for Cato Institute as *Amicus Curiae* 15–16.

In *Bowers* the Court referred to the fact that before 1961 all 50 States had outlawed sodomy, and that at the time of the Court's decision 24 States and the District of Columbia had sodomy laws. 478 U.S., at 192–193. Justice Powell pointed out that these prohibitions often were being ignored, however. Georgia, for instance, had not sought to enforce its law for decades. *Id.*, at 197–198, n. 2 ("The history of nonenforcement suggests the moribund character today of laws criminalizing this type of private, consensual conduct").

The sweeping references by Chief Justice Burger to the history of Western civilization and to Judeo-Christian moral and ethical standards did not take account of other authorities pointing in an opposite direction. A committee advising the British Parliament recommended in 1957 repeal of laws punishing homosexual conduct. The Wolfenden Report: Report of the Committee on Homosexual Offenses and Prostitution (1963). Parliament enacted the substance of those recommendations 10 years later. Sexual Offences Act 1967, § 1.

Of even more importance, almost five years before *Bowers* was decided the European Court of Human Rights considered a case with parallels to *Bowers* and to today's case. An adult male resident in Northern Ireland alleged he was a practicing homosexual who desired to engage in consensual homosexual conduct. The laws of Northern Ireland forbade him that right. He alleged that he had been questioned, his home had been searched, and he feared criminal prosecution. The court held that the laws proscribing the conduct were invalid under the European Convention on Human Rights. *Dudgeon* v. *United Kingdom*, 45 Eur. Ct. H. R. (1981) ¶52. Authoritative in all countries that are members of the Council of Europe (21 nations then, 45 nations now), the decision is at odds with the premise in *Bowers* that the claim put forward was insubstantial in our Western civilization.

In our own constitutional system the deficiencies in *Bowers* became even more apparent in the years following its announcement. The 25 States with laws prohibiting the relevant conduct referenced in the *Bowers* decision are reduced now to 13, of which 4 enforce their laws only against homosexual conduct. In those States where sodomy is still proscribed, whether for same-sex or heterosexual conduct, there is a pattern of nonenforcement with respect to consenting adults acting in private. The State of Texas admitted in 1994 that as of that date it had not prosecuted anyone under those circumstances. *State* v. *Morales*, 869 S.W.2d 941, 943, 37 Tex. Sup. Ct. J. 390.

Two principal cases decided after *Bowers* cast its holding into even more doubt. In *Planned Parenthood of Southeastern Pa.* v. *Casey,* 505 U.S. 833, 120 L. Ed. 2d 674, 112 S.Ct. 2791 (1992), the Court reaffirmed the substantive force of the liberty protected by the Due Process Clause. The *Casey* decision again confirmed that our laws and tradition afford constitutional protection to personal decisions relating to marriage, procreation, contraception, family relationships, child rearing, and education. . . .

Persons in a homosexual relationship may seek autonomy for these purposes, just as heterosexual persons do. The decision in Bowers would deny them this right.

The second post-*Bowers* case of principal relevance is *Romer* v. *Evans,* 517 U.S. 620, 134 L. Ed. 2d 855, 116 S.Ct. 1620 (1996). There the Court struck down class-based legislation directed at homosexuals as a violation of the Equal Protection Clause. *Romer* invalidated an amendment to Colorado's constitution which named as a solitary class persons who were homosexuals, lesbians, or bisexual either by "orientation, conduct, practices or relationships," *id.,* at 624 (internal quotation marks omitted), and deprived them of protection under state antidiscrimination laws. We concluded that the provision was "born of animosity toward the class of persons affected" and further that it had no rational relation to a legitimate governmental purpose. *Id.,* at 634. . . .

The foundations of *Bowers* have sustained serious erosion from our recent decisions in *Casey* and *Romer.* When our precedent has been thus weakened, criticism from other sources is of greater significance. In the United States criticism of *Bowers* has been substantial and continuing, disapproving of its reasoning in all respects, not just as to its historical assumptions. See, *e.g.,* C. Fried, Order and Law: Arguing the Reagan Revolution—A Firsthand Account 81–84 (1991); R. Posner, Sex and Reason 341–350 (1992). The courts of five different States have declined to follow it in interpreting provisions in their own state constitutions parallel to the Due Process Clause of the Fourteenth Amendment, see *Jegley* v. *Picado*, 349 Ark. 600, 80 S. W. 3d 332 (2002); *Powell* v. *State*, 270 Ga. 327, 510 S. E. 2d 18, 24 (1998); *Gryczan* v. *State*, 283 Mont. 433, 942 P.2d 112 (1997); *Campbell* v. *Sundquist*, 926 S.W.2d 250 (Tenn. App. 1996); *Commonwealth* v. *Wasson*, 842 S.W.2d 487 (Ky. 1992).

To the extent *Bowers* relied on values we share with a wider civilization, it should be noted that the reasoning and holding in *Bowers* have been rejected elsewhere. The European Court of Human Rights has followed not *Bowers* but its own decision in *Dudgeon* v. *United Kingdom.* See *P. G. & J. H.* v. *United Kingdom*, App. No. 00044787/98, P56 (Eur. Ct. H. R., Sept. 25, 2001); *Modinos* v. *Cyprus*, 259 Eur. Ct. H. R. (1993); *Norris* v. *Ireland*, 142 Eur. Ct. H. R. (1988). Other nations, too, have taken action consistent with an affirmation of the protected right of homosexual adults to engage in intimate, consensual conduct. See Brief for Mary Robinson et al. as *Amici Curiae* 11–12. The right the petitioners seek in this case has been accepted as an integral part of human freedom in many other countries. There has been no showing that in this country the governmental interest in circumscribing personal choice is somehow more legitimate or urgent.

The doctrine of *stare decisis* is essential to the respect accorded to the judgments of the Court and to the stability of the law. It is not, however, an inexorable command. *Payne* v. *Tennessee*, 501 U.S. 808, 828, 115 L. Ed. 2d 720, 111 S.Ct. 2597 (1991) ("*Stare decisis* is not an inexorable command; rather, it 'is a principle of policy and not a mechanical formula of adherence to the latest decision'") (quoting *Helvering* v. *Hallock*, 309 U.S. 106, 119, 84 L. Ed. 604, 60 S.Ct. 444 (1940)). In *Casey* we noted that when a Court is asked to overrule a precedent recognizing a constitutional liberty interest, individual or societal reliance on the existence of that liberty cautions with particular strength against reversing course. 505 U.S., at 855–856; see also *id.*, at 844 ("Liberty finds no refuge in a jurisprudence of doubt"). The holding in *Bowers*, however, has not induced detrimental reliance comparable to some instances where recognized individual rights are involved. Indeed, there has been no individual or societal reliance on *Bowers* of the sort that could counsel against overturning its holding once there are compelling reasons to do so. *Bowers* itself causes uncertainty, for the precedents before and after its issuance contradict its central holding.

The rationale of *Bowers* does not withstand careful analysis. In his dissenting opinion in *Bowers* JUSTICE STEVENS came to these conclusions:

"Our prior cases make two propositions abundantly clear. First, the fact that the governing majority in a State has traditionally viewed a particular practice as immoral is not a sufficient reason for upholding a law prohibiting the practice; neither history nor tradition could save a law prohibiting miscegenation from constitutional attack. Second, individual decisions by married persons, concerning the intimacies of their physical relationship, even when not intended to produce offspring, are a form of 'liberty' protected by the Due Process Clause of the Fourteenth Amendment. Moreover, this protection extends to intimate choices by unmarried as well as married persons." 478 U.S., at 216 (footnotes and citations omitted).

Justice Stevens' analysis, in our view, should have been controlling in *Bowers* and should control here.

Bowers was not correct when it was decided, and it is not correct today. It ought not to remain binding precedent. *Bowers* v. *Hardwick* should be and now is overruled. . . .

[The concurring opinion of JUSTICE O'CONNOR has been omitted.]

■ JUSTICE SCALIA, with whom CHIEF JUSTICE [REHNQUIST] and JUSTICE THOMAS join, dissenting.

"Liberty finds no refuge in a jurisprudence of doubt." *Planned Parenthood of Southeastern Pa.* v. *Casey*, 505 U.S. 833, 844, 120 L. Ed. 2d 674, 112 S.Ct. 2791 (1992). That was the Court's sententious response, barely more than a decade ago, to those seeking to overrule *Roe* v. *Wade*, 410 U.S. 113, 35 L. Ed. 2d 147, 93 S.Ct. 705 (1973). The Court's response today, to those who have engaged in a 17-year crusade to overrule *Bowers* v. *Hardwick*, 478 U.S. 186, 106 S.Ct. 2841, 92 L. Ed. 2d 140 (1986), is very different. The need for stability and certainty presents no barrier.

Most of the rest of today's opinion has no relevance to its actual holding—that the Texas statute "furthers no legitimate state interest which can justify" its application to petitioners under rational-basis review. *Ante*, (overruling *Bowers* to the extent it sustained Georgia's antisodomy statute under the rational-basis test). Though there is discussion of "fundamental proposition[s]," and "fundamental decisions," *ibid*. nowhere does the Court's opinion declare that homosexual sodomy is a "fundamental right" under the Due Process Clause; nor does it subject the Texas law to the standard of review that would be appropriate (strict scrutiny) if homosexual sodomy *were* a "fundamental right." Thus, while overruling the *outcome* of *Bowers*, the Court leaves strangely untouched its central legal conclusion: "Respondent would have us announce . . . a fundamental right to engage in homosexual sodomy. This we are quite unwilling to do." 478 U.S., at 191. Instead the Court simply describes petitioners' conduct as "an exercise of their liberty" . . . .

I begin with the Court's surprising readiness to reconsider a decision rendered a mere 17 years ago in *Bowers* v. *Hardwick*. I do not myself believe in rigid adherence to *stare decisis* in constitutional cases; but I do believe that we should be consistent rather than manipulative in invoking the doctrine. Today's opinions in support of reversal do not bother to distinguish—or indeed, even bother to mention—the paean to *stare decisis* coauthored by three Members of today's majority in *Planned Parenthood* v. *Casey*. There, when *stare decisis* meant preservation of judicially invented abortion rights, the widespread criticism of *Roe* was strong reason to *reaffirm* it:

"Where, in the performance of its judicial duties, the Court decides a case in such a way as to resolve the sort of intensely divisive controversy reflected in *Roe*[,] . . . its decision has a dimension that the resolution of the normal case does not carry. . . . To overrule under fire in the absence of the most compelling reason . . . would subvert the Court's legitimacy beyond any serious question." 505 U.S., at 866–867.

Today, however, the widespread opposition to *Bowers*, a decision resolving an issue as "intensely divisive" as the issue in *Roe*, is offered as a reason in favor of *overruling* it. See *ante*. Gone, too, is any "enquiry" (of the sort conducted in *Casey*) into whether the decision sought to be overruled has "proven 'unworkable,' " *Casey, supra*, at 855.

Today's approach to *stare decisis* invites us to overrule an erroneously decided precedent (including an "intensely divisive" decision) *if:* (1) its foundations have been "ero[ded]" by subsequent decisions, *ante*; (2) it has been subject to "substantial and continuing" criticism, *ibid.*; and (3) it has not induced "individual or societal reliance" that counsels against overturning. The problem is that *Roe* itself—which today's majority surely has no disposition to overrule—satisfies these conditions to at least the same degree as *Bowers*. . . .

I do not quarrel with the Court's claim that *Romer* v. *Evans*, 517 U.S. 620, 134 L. Ed. 2d 855, 116 S.Ct. 1620 (1996), "eroded" the "foundations" of *Bowers*' rational-basis holding. See *Romer, supra*, at 640–643 (SCALIA, J., dissenting). But *Roe* and *Casey* have been equally "eroded" by *Washington* v. *Glucksberg*, 521 U.S. 702, 721, 138 L. Ed. 2d 772, 117 S.Ct. 2258, 117 S.Ct. 2302 (1997), which held that *only* fundamental rights which are " 'deeply rooted in this Nation's history and tradition' " qualify for anything other than rational basis scrutiny under the doctrine of "substantive due process." *Roe* and *Casey*, of course, subjected the restriction of abortion to heightened scrutiny without even attempting to establish that the freedom to abort *was* rooted in this Nation's tradition.

(2) *Bowers*, the Court says, has been subject to "substantial and continuing [criticism], disapproving of its reasoning in all respects, not just as to its historical assumptions." Exactly what those nonhistorical criticisms are, and whether the Court even agrees with them, are left unsaid, although the Court does cite two books. See *ibid.* (citing C. Fried, Order and Law: Arguing the Reagan Revolution—A Firsthand Account 81–84 (1991); R. Posner, Sex and Reason 341–350 (1992)).[1] Of course, *Roe* too (and by extension *Casey*) had been (and still is) subject to unrelenting criticism, including criticism from the two commentators cited by the Court today. See Fried, *supra*, at 75 ("Roe was a prime example of twisted judging"); Posner, *supra*, at 337 ("[The Court's] opinion in *Roe* . . . fails to measure up to professional expectations regarding judicial opinions"); Posner, Judicial Opinion Writing, 62 U. Chi. L. Rev. 1421, 1434 (1995) (describing the opinion in *Roe* as an "embarrassing performanc[e]").

(3) That leaves, to distinguish the rock-solid, unamendable disposition of *Roe* from the readily overrulable *Bowers*, only the third

---

[1]   This last-cited critic of *Bowers* actually writes: "*[Bowers]* is correct nevertheless that the right to engage in homosexual acts is not deeply rooted in America's history and tradition." Posner, Sex and Reason, at 343.

factor. "[T]here has been," the Court says, "no individual or societal reliance on *Bowers* of the sort that could counsel against overturning its holding. . . . " It seems to me that the "societal reliance" on the principles confirmed in *Bowers* and discarded today has been overwhelming. Countless judicial decisions and legislative enactments have relied on the ancient proposition that a governing majority's belief that certain sexual behavior is "immoral and unacceptable" constitutes a rational basis for regulation. See, *e.g.*, *Williams* v. *Pryor*, 240 F.3d 944, 949 (CA11 2001) (citing *Bowers* in upholding Alabama's prohibition on the sale of sex toys on the ground that "[t]he crafting and safeguarding of public morality . . . indisputably is a legitimate government interest under rational basis scrutiny"); *Milner* v. *Apfel*, 148 F.3d 812, 814 (CA7 1998) (citing *Bowers* for the proposition that "[l]egislatures are permitted to legislate with regard to morality . . . rather than confined to preventing demonstrable harms"); *Holmes* v. *California Army National Guard* 124 F.3d 1126, 1136 (CA9 1997) (relying on *Bowers* in upholding the federal statute and regulations banning from military service those who engage in homosexual conduct); *Owens* v. *State*, 352 Md. 663, 683, 724 A.2d 43, 53 (1999) (relying on *Bowers* in holding that "a person has no constitutional right to engage in sexual intercourse, at least outside of marriage"); *Sherman* v. *Henry*, 928 S.W.2d 464, 469–473 (Tex. 1996) (relying on *Bowers* in rejecting a claimed constitutional right to commit adultery). We ourselves relied extensively on *Bowers* when we concluded, in *Barnes* v. *Glen Theatre, Inc.*, 501 U.S. 560, 569, 115 L. Ed. 2d 504, 111 S.Ct. 2456 (1991), that Indiana's public indecency statute furthered "a substantial government interest in protecting order and morality," *ibid.*, (plurality opinion); see also *id.*, at 575 (SCALIA, J., concurring in judgment). State laws against bigamy, same-sex marriage, adult incest, prostitution, masturbation, adultery, fornication, bestiality, and obscenity are likewise sustainable only in light of *Bowers*' validation of laws based on moral choices. . . .[2]

---

[2]   While the Court does not overrule *Bowers*' holding that homosexual sodomy is not a "fundamental right," it is worth noting that the "societal reliance" upon that aspect of the decision has been substantial as well. See 10 U.S.C. § 654(b)(1) ("A member of the armed forces shall be separated from the armed forces . . . if . . . the member has engaged in . . . a homosexual act or acts"); *Marcum* v. *McWhorter*, 308 F.3d 635, 640–642 (CA6 2002) (relying on *Bowers* in rejecting a claimed fundamental right to commit adultery); *Mullins* v. *Oregon*, 57 F.3d 789, 793–794 (CA9 1995) (relying on *Bowers* in rejecting a grandparent's claimed "fundamental liberty interest" in the adoption of her grandchildren); *Doe* v. *Wigginton*, 21 F.3d 733, 739–740 (CA6 1994) (relying on *Bowers* in rejecting a prisoner's claimed "fundamental right" to on-demand HIV testing); *Schowengerdt* v. *United States*, 944 F.2d 483, 490 (CA9 1991) (relying on *Bowers* in upholding a bisexual's discharge from the armed services); *Charles* v. *Baesler*, 910 F.2d 1349, 1353 (CA6 1990) (relying on *Bowers* in rejecting fire department captain's claimed "fundamental" interest in a promotion); *Henne* v. *Wright*, 904 F.2d 1208, 1214–1215 (CA8 1990) (relying on *Bowers* in rejecting a claim that state law restricting surnames that could be given to children at birth implicates a "fundamental right"); *Walls* v. *Petersburg*, 895 F.2d 188, 193 (CA4 1990) (relying on *Bowers* in rejecting substantive-due-process challenge to a police department questionnaire that asked prospective employees about homosexual activity); *High Tech Gays* v. *Defense Industrial Security Clearance Office*, 895 F.2d 563, 570–571 (CA9 1990) (relying on *Bowers*' holding that homosexual activity is not a fundamental right in rejecting—on the basis of the rational-basis standard—an equal-protection challenge to the Defense

What a massive disruption of the current social order, therefore, the overruling of *Bowers* entails. Not so the overruling of *Roe*, which would simply have restored the regime that existed for centuries before 1973, in which the permissibility of and restrictions upon abortion were determined legislatively State-by-State. *Casey*, however, chose to base its *stare decisis* determination on a different "sort" of reliance. "[P]eople," it said, "have organized intimate relationships and made choices that define their views of themselves and their places in society, in reliance on the availability of abortion in the event that contraception should fail." 505 U.S., at 856. This falsely assumes that the consequence of overruling *Roe* would have been to make abortion unlawful. It would not; it would merely have *permitted* the States to do so. Many States would unquestionably have declined to prohibit abortion, and others would not have prohibited it within six months (after which the most significant reliance interests would have expired). Even for persons in States other than these, the choice would not have been between abortion and childbirth, but between abortion nearby and abortion in a neighboring State.

To tell the truth, it does not surprise me, and should surprise no one, that the Court has chosen today to revise the standards of *stare decisis* set forth in *Casey*. It has thereby exposed *Casey*'s extraordinary deference to precedent for the result-oriented expedient that it is. . . .

[The dissenting opinion of JUSTICE THOMAS has been omitted.]

QUESTIONS

1. The *Lawrence* majority criticizes the majority opinion in *Bowers v. Hardwick* for asking the wrong question, or, more precisely, for asking the question at the wrong level of generality. The Georgia Supreme Court in *Pavesich* leveled a similar criticism at the analytic approach of the *Roberson* court. To what extent does rephrasing the issue at a higher level of generality make the ensuing analysis more persuasive? To what extent does it simply mask the court's determination to reach a different outcome?

2. Justice Scalia indicates that *Roe v. Wade* should have been at least "readily overrulable" as *Bowers* because the "societal reliance" on *Bowers* was at least as great as on *Roe*. What is the nature of the reliance in each case? What sanctions may the State impose if *Roe* is overruled? If *Bowers* is not?

3. Note the *Lawrence* majority's invocation of decisions by non-U.S. jurisdictions. What role does reference to those authorities play? How is it akin to or different from the Massachusetts Supreme Judicial Court's investigation of English precedent in *Baker v. Libbie*?

4. At several points, the *Lawrence* majority cites *amici curiae*, briefs filed as "friends of the court" by individuals or groups asserting a special interest in or knowledge about the issues to be resolved. *Amici* do not represent

---

Department's policy of conducting expanded investigations into backgrounds of gay and lesbian applicants for secret and top-secret security clearance).

parties but may be given leave to file briefs in support of one, or neither, party. The special expertise of some *amici* (for example, the Brief for Professors of History) may illuminate particular issues, or even the entire controversy.

5. *Lawrence* is but one example of the Supreme Court overruling its own prior decisions, principles of *stare decisis* notwithstanding. Several years after the Court decided *Lawrence*, it unanimously overturned another of its precedents—Saucier v. Katz, 533 U.S. 194 (2001)—in Pearson v. Callahan, 555 U.S. 223 (2009). In *Pearson*, Justice Alito, writing for a unanimous court, set out general criteria for when it may be appropriate for the Court to overrule its own precedent:

> In considering whether the *Saucier* procedure should be modified or abandoned, we must begin with the doctrine of *stare decisis*. *Stare decisis* "promotes the evenhanded, predictable, and consistent development of legal principles, fosters reliance on judicial decisions, and contributes to the actual and perceived integrity of the judicial process." [Citation.] Although "[w]e approach the reconsideration of [our] decisions . . . with the utmost caution," "[s]tare decisis is not an inexorable command." [Citation.] Revisiting precedent is particularly appropriate where, as here, a departure would not upset expectations, the precedent consists of a judge-made rule that was recently adopted to improve the operation of the courts, and experience has pointed up the precedent's shortcomings.

> "Considerations in favor of *stare decisis* are at their acme in cases involving property and contract rights, where reliance interests are involved; the opposite is true in cases . . . involving procedural and evidentiary rules" that do not produce such reliance. [Citation.] Like rules governing procedures and the admission of evidence in the trial courts, *Saucier*'s two-step protocol does not affect the way in which parties order their affairs. Withdrawing from *Saucier*' s categorical rule would not upset settled expectations on anyone's part. [Citation.]

> Nor does this matter implicate "the general presumption that legislative changes should be left to Congress." [Citation.] We recognize that "considerations of *stare decisis* weigh heavily in the area of statutory construction, where Congress is free to change this Court's interpretation of its legislation." [Citation.] But the *Saucier* rule is judge made and implicates an important matter involving internal Judicial Branch operations. Any change should come from this Court, not Congress.

Consider whether these criteria would call for, or caution against, overruling precedent in *Battalla* and *Lawrence*, *supra*. Consider also whether the Court's statement in *Pearson* is at odds with the plurality's discussion of *stare decisis* in *Casey*, *supra*. Keep *Pearson*'s *stare decisis* presumption concerning the interpretation of statutes in mind when you read Part III.

Queensland v. The Commonwealth*

High Court of Australia.
[1977] HCA 60; (1977) 139 CLR 585.

[In 1975 the Australian Parliament enacted legislation providing for the election of Territory representatives to the Australian Senate. Some of the States challenged the constitutionality of the Act. A 4:3 majority of the High Court of Australia (Australia's Supreme Court) rejected the States' arguments and upheld the validity of the legislation. Shortly after, one of the judges in the majority retired and a new judge, thought to be against the Territory Senators, was appointed. The State of Queensland brought another challenge to the legislation, on essentially the same grounds.]

■ GIBBS, J.

9. . . . It has been said, too, that since this Court has the duty of maintaining the constitution, it has a duty to overrule an earlier decision if convinced that it is plainly wrong. In the case already cited, Isaacs J. went on to say [1913] HCA 41; (1913) 17 CLR 261, at p 278: "Our sworn loyalty is to the law itself, and to the organic law of the Constitution first of all. If, then, we find the law to be plainly in conflict with what we or any of our predecessors erroneously thought it to be, we have, as I conceive, no right to choose between giving effect to the law, and maintaining an incorrect interpretation. It is not, in my opinion, better that the Court should be persistently wrong than that it should be ultimately right." But like most generalizations, this statement can be misleading. No Justice is entitled to ignore the decisions and reasoning of his predecessors, and to arrive at his own judgment as though the pages of the law reports were blank, or as though the authority of a decision did not survive beyond the rising of the Court. A Justice, unlike a legislator, cannot introduce a programme of reform which sets at nought decisions formerly made and principles formerly established. It is only after the most careful and respectful consideration of the earlier decision, and after giving due weight to all the circumstances, that a Justice may give effect to his own opinions in preference to an earlier decision of the Court.

10. It would be futile to attempt to state any succinct general principle by which the Court should be guided in deciding whether to overrule an earlier decision of its own. Some cases may be clear enough. On the one hand the Court would be slow to disturb a decision which applied a principle that had been carefully worked out in a succession of cases, and had been more than once reaffirmed. On the other hand, a judgment which had been given per incuriam, and was in conflict with some other decision of the Court, or with some well-established principle, might be readily reviewed. However the present case does not lie at either of these

---

*   Thanks to Simona Gory, Associate-in-Law, Columbia University School of Law 2007–08, Barrister, Victoria, Australia, for contributing and editing this excerpt.

extremes, and I have had much difficulty in deciding what course my duty requires. As the plaintiffs have urged, the decision in Western Australia v. The Commonwealth [1975] HCA 46; (1975) 134 CLR 201 was recently given, and by a narrow majority. It has not been followed in any other case. It involves a question of grave constitutional importance. But when it is asked what has occurred to justify the reconsideration of a judgment given not two years ago, the only possible answer is that one member of the Court has retired, and another has succeeded him. It cannot be suggested that the majority in Western Australia v. The Commonwealth failed to advert to any relevant consideration, or overlooked any apposite decision or principle. The arguments presented in the present case were in their essence the same as those presented in the earlier case. No later decision has been given that conflicts with Western Australia v. The Commonwealth. Moreover, the decision has been acted on; senators for the Territories have been elected under the legislation there held valid. To reverse the decision now would be to defeat the expectations of the people of the Territories that they would be represented, as many of them believed that they ought to be represented, by senators entitled to vote—expectations and beliefs that were no less understandable because in my view they were constitutionally erroneous, and that were encouraged by the decision of this Court.

11. When, in The Tramways Case (No. 1) [1914] HCA 15; (1914) 18 CLR 54, at p 69, Barton J. said that "Changes in the number of appointed Justices can ... never of themselves furnish a reason for review" of a previous decision, it may be that not all who had become his brethren agreed with him, but his statement in my respectful opinion ought to be regarded as, in general, correct, having regard to "the need for continuity and consistency in judicial decision" to which he there referred. Still less should the replacement of one Justice by another in itself justify the review of an earlier decision. Having considered all the circumstances that I have mentioned I have reached the conclusion that it is my duty to follow Western Australia v. The Commonwealth, although in my view it was wrongly decided.

[The separate concurring opinions of BARWICK, C.J., and STEPHEN, MASON, JACOBS, MURPHY, and AICKIN, JJ., have been omitted.]

QUESTIONS

1. Was Justice Gibbs in the majority or the minority in the First Territory Senator's case (*Western Australia v. The Commonwealth*)?

2. Did Justice Gibbs change his mind?

3. Do you think it made a difference (or should have made a difference) that the Territory Senators had already been elected by the time the second challenge was brought?

4. Why is it problematic for a differently-composed court of last resort to overrule precedent developed by judges whose political or social views the current occupants of that court do not share? How persuasive is the following?

> The root of American governmental power is revealed most clearly in the instance of the power conferred by the Constitution upon the Judiciary of the United States and specifically upon this Court. As Americans of each succeeding generation are rightly told, the Court cannot buy support for its decisions by spending money and, except to a minor degree, it cannot independently coerce obedience to its decrees. The Court's power lies, rather, in its legitimacy, a product of substance and perception that shows itself in the people's acceptance of the Judiciary as fit to determine what the Nation's law means and to declare what it demands. . . .

> The need for principled action to be perceived as such is implicated to some degree whenever this, or any other appellate court, overrules a prior case. . . . [T]he country can accept some correction of error without necessarily questioning the legitimacy of the Court. . . . [H]owever, the Court would almost certainly fail to receive the benefit of the doubt in overruling prior cases [if it crossed the] point beyond which frequent overruling would overtax the country's belief in the Court's good faith. . . . If that limit should be exceeded, disturbance of prior rulings would be taken as evidence that justifiable reexamination of principle had given way to drives for particular results in the short term. The legitimacy of the Court would fade with the frequency of its vacillation.

Planned Parenthood of Southeastern Pa. v. Casey, 505 U.S. 833 (1992) (declining to overrule *Roe v. Wade*'s protection of a woman's liberty interest to decide whether to carry a pregnancy to term). Is a court more likely to ensure its legitimacy if, instead of overruling a prior decision, the differently-composed court simply ignores or distinguishes inconvenient precedent away? See Gonzales v. Carhart, 550 U.S. 124 (2007) (sustaining legislation banning "partial-birth abortion").

3. RETROACTIVITY

When a judicial decision announces a new rule of law, or overrules an old one, to what events does it apply? In addition to determining the rights and/or responsibilities of the parties to the case decided, does the ruling apply forward and/or backward in time as well? Consider the following possibilities:

The Court announces a new rule in response to a new question, *e.g.* the Georgia Supreme Court recognizes the right of privacy, and holds that the unauthorized publication of a person's photograph for commercial purposes violates that right.

Possibility #1. All unauthorized publications occurring in Georgia from the date of decision (1905) forward are subject to the rule.

Possibility #2. In addition, all unauthorized publications occurring in Georgia before 1905 are also covered (assuming the statute of limitations has not run).

The Court announces a new rule that overrules a prior rule, *e.g.*, the New York Court of Appeals overturns its precedent that barred a claim for negligent infliction of emotional distress.

Possibility #1. All claims alleging emotional distress resulting from negligent conduct occurring as of the decision (1961) are actionable, but the new rule does not apply to the parties in the overruling case.

Possibility #2. All claims alleging emotional distress resulting from negligent conduct occurring as of the decision are actionable, and the new rule applies to the parties in the overruling case.

Possibility #3. In addition, all claims alleging emotional distress resulting from negligent conduct occurring before the decision are also covered (assuming the statute of limitations has not run), so long as such a claim had not already been brought and finally adjudicated under the old rule.

Possibility #4. In addition, old claims may be reopened and readjudicated under the new rule.

As a general matter, judicial decisions in fact do apply to events that occurred before the new or changed rule was declared. However, where prior decisions have been overruled, the parties to those cases are not free to reopen the case, if it has already been the object of a final judgment.

Why do judicial decisions operate in this retroactive way? Should they? Could it, or should it, be otherwise? The materials in this section introduce some of the considerations involved in these and related questions.

The problem of retroactivity, along with *stare decisis* and *res judicata* (the rule that prohibits relitigating a claim that has gone to final judgment), is one of the forces promoting stability and predictability in the judicial process. People act—or are thought to act—in reliance on existing rules, including judge-made rules. Where there was no pre-existing rule, as in the first example above, retroactive application of judicial response to a "new question" unsettles no expectations. But when a court has overruled its precedent, retroactive application of its decision can undermine the expectations of those who acted in accordance with the prior rule, particularly if in cases preceding the overruling the court has not signaled a disposition to change the law. This concern may present a substantial argument for continued adherence to precedent. *See, e.g., Cullings v. Goetz, supra*, p. 149.

As a result, courts may seek to limit the retroactive impact of a changed rule, so that the change does not prejudice prior actors who were not parties to the case. However, this technique too, encounters criticism. With retroactivity as the baseline rule, courts will hesitate to make abrupt changes in the law. Without the constraint of retroactivity, judges might be inclined to rule on more than the parties' dispute requires. Thus, were courts free to limit their decisions' retroactive effect, some critics fear courts might be tempted to usurp the legislature's functions. Recall that even in a common law system, courts, unlike legislatures, are not constituted as "lawmakers." Rather, judge-made law is the product of the dispute-settling process. Judges, at least in theory, assess and adjust the law in the limited context of the parties and controversy before them; they do not announce sweeping rules of general and abstract application. (Consider the accuracy of that proposition in light of the materials you have studied up till now.)

Fitzgerald v. Meissner & Hicks, Inc.

Supreme Court of Wisconsin, 1968.
38 Wis.2d 571, 157 N.W.2d 595.

This appeal involves application of this court's decision in Moran v. Quality Aluminum Casting Co. (1967), 34 Wis.2d 542, 150 N.W.2d 137, which held a wife could bring an action for loss of consortium.

The plaintiff-appellant, Marie E. Fitzgerald, commenced this action on September 18, 1966, to recover for loss of consortium of her husband, Richard T. Fitzgerald. The complaint alleged that on August 7, 1964, Fitzgerald had been seriously injured when he fell from a scaffolding while engaged in his employment at a construction site in the city of Milwaukee. Each of the defendants were owners of the site at the time of the accident.

The defendants demurred to the complaint contending it did not state facts sufficient to constitute a cause of action. The trial court sustained the demurrers. The trial court's reasoning does not appear of record but the parties agree the decision was based upon a prior rule that a wife could not maintain an action for loss of consortium. The demurrers were argued on February 6, 1967. The trial court sustained the demurrers and granted judgment dismissing the complaint on February 15, 1967.

On February 22, 1967, the plaintiff filed a notice of appeal. Five days later the Moran case was argued before this court and on April 28, 1967, the court overruled its previous decision in Nickel v. Hardware Mut. Casualty Co. (1955), 269 Wis. 647, 70 N.W.2d 205, and held that a wife could maintain an action for loss of consortium of her husband who has been injured by the negligent acts of a third person.

■ BEILFUSS, JUSTICE.

The [issue] presented on this appeal [is]:

1.   Does the rule of law recognizing a wife's right to maintain a cause of action for loss of consortium as set forth in Moran v. Quality Aluminum Casting Co., supra, have prospective or retrospective application? . . .

The general rule adhered to by this court is the "Blackstonian Doctrine." This doctrine provides that a decision which overrules or repudiates an earlier decision is retrospective in operation.*

There are, however, exceptions to this rule which have long been recognized by this court:

> "While there would seem to be no middle ground in logic, between a complete adherence to or a complete repudiation of the Blackstonian doctrine, the courts nevertheless have established certain exceptions to it for the purpose of mitigating hardships created by its literal application. Without attempting to deal exhaustively with the subject, it may be said that, generally speaking, courts adhering to the rule that a later decision operates retrospectively, have created the following exceptions: (1) Where contracts have been entered into in reliance upon a legislative enactment as construed by the earlier decisions. (2) Where a legislative enactment has been declared valid by earlier decisions. and contracts have been entered into in reliance upon the statute and decisions. [Cases cited.] (3) Where a criminal statute, which has received a limited construction by earlier decisions, has been so expanded in meaning by the later overruling decision as to make acts criminal which were not such under the earlier decisions, and the later decision is sought to be applied to one whose acts were committed before the statute was given the enlarged construction." [Citation.]

Generally, throughout the various American jurisdictions, other exceptions to the Blackstonian doctrine have been utilized. Retroactive operation has been sometimes denied where there has been great reliance on an overruled decision by a substantial number of persons and considerable harm or detriment could result to them. It has also been denied where the purpose of the new ruling cannot be served by retroactivity, and where retroactivity would tend to thrust an excessive burden on the administration of justice. 10 A.L.R.3d 1384.

In this jurisdiction the "reliance" and "administration of justice" considerations have been recognized. In relatively recent years the court has applied exceptions to the Blackstonian doctrine in the tort area of the law where it has determined a compelling judicial reason exists. The reliance factor has been a most prominent consideration in the prospective only abrogation of the various tort immunities.[3] [Citation.]

---

*   Editors' Note: The doctrine is founded on the idea that judges discover rather than make law. According to Blackstone, a court overruling a prior decision does not announce a new law, but "vindicate[s] the old one from misrepresentation. . . . [I]t is declared, not that such a sentence was bad law, but that it was not law." 1 Blackstone, Commentaries on the Laws of England, Introduction, section p. 46 (New York 1827).

[3]   The decisions cited were limited to prospective application with the exception that it was determined they would apply to the parties involved in the actual case.

Recently in Dupuis v. General Casualty Co. (1967), 36 Wis.2d 42, 45, 152 N.W.2d 884, 885, the court emphasized the importance of the reliance factor in its decisions to limit application of the foregoing list of cases:

> "Inherent in a court declaring that a decision should apply prospectively only is a determination that a compelling judicial reason exists for doing so. In many of the cases previously decided which apply this principle, one of the important compelling judicial reasons which has been considered is what has been referred to as the reliance factor, *i.e.*, that the parties involved had relied upon the immunity doctrine and that to make a decision effective retroactive would manifestly adversely affect great numbers of individuals and institutions that had correctly relied upon their expressed immunity in the conduct of their affairs."

Obviously the court was not suggesting a great number of individuals and institutions had committed torts relying upon the immunity. The reason for the prospective application of these decisions . . . was because the court was concerned about the failure of those affected to purchase insurance coverage in reliance upon the immunity.

The possibility of imposing an excessive burden on the administration of justice was a compelling judicial reason for the limitation placed on the retrospective application of this court's decision in Bielski v. Schulze (1962), 16 Wis.2d 1, 114 N.W.2d 105, which changed our contribution rule and discarded the concept of gross negligence. This is best described by former Mr. Justice THOMAS E. FAIRCHILD in his article in 46 Marquette L.Rev. 1, 15:

> "In Bielski the court limited the retrospective application of the change in law with respect to contribution and gross negligence. Here again were elements of law which are ordinarily not relied upon by people who are about to engage in tortious conduct. Yet the court was mindful of the fact that if full retrospective application were given, burdens of further litigation would probably be imposed on litigants and the public in cases where claims had been substantially disposed of by litigation or settlement. Such burdens would seem to be wasteful."

The compelling judicial reason for the prospective limitation placed on this court's decision abrogating the doctrine of parental immunity, Goller v. White (1963), 20 Wis.2d 402, 122 N.W.2d 193, contained consideration both for the reliance placed on the doctrine and for the [e]ffect retroactive operation would have on the administration of justice. Our statute controlling limitations of actions of minors (sec. 893.33) provides that a child has until one year after he attains majority to bring suit for injuries sustained during his minority. Conceivably, retroactive application of Goller could have resulted in suits for injuries sustained by minors for a period of more than 20 years previous to that decision. There was not only concern over the possibility of overburdening the courts with litigation, but also concern for those who in reliance on the immunity doctrine failed to preserve essential evidence. Dupuis v. General Casualty Co., supra.

In the case at bar none of the considerations presented by the foregoing are present to any significant degree. Obviously the contract and criminal considerations are not present. The degree of reliance a tortfeasor might have placed on a wife's inability to recover consortium damages would be insignificant if existent. Certainly the tort was not committed with this in mind and the degree to which it may have influenced the decision whether or not to purchase liability insurance would be less than minimal. Nor will it [a]ffect the monetary limits of liability of the insurance carrier.

The respondents vigorously contend the reliance factor is present because insurance companies have relied on this court's position prior to *Moran* in the calculation of their insurance rates. The degree to which the premiums charged by insurance companies would have differed had a wife always been accorded the right to recover consortium damages is speculative and probably relatively insignificant. In any event, it is not of such proportion to be recognized as a compelling judicial reason.

Mr. Justice Fairchild's statement setting forth the reasons for this court's retroactive application of its decisions abolishing the defense of assumption of risk is apropos:

"In *McConville* and *Colson,* abrogating the defense of assumption of risk, the court did not limit the application of the change in law. The existence of the defense becomes important to most people only in retrospect. A prospective host probably does not consciously rely upon it, either in offering an automobile ride to his guest or deciding whether or not to carry liability insurance. The degree to which the existence of the defense might affect the premiums charged by insurance companies is not clear. Nor is it clear that a farmer would rely on the doctrine in deciding against insurance. In any event, the concurring opinions in Baird v. Cornelius ((1961), 12 Wis.2d 284, 107 N.W.2d 278), decided one year before *McConville,* had very clearly signalled the probability that the defense was likely to be abrogated." 46 Marquette L.Rev. 1, 15.

The retroactive operation of *Moran* will not unduly burden the administration of justice. With our three-year statute of limitation on such actions (sec. 893.205), retroactive application, considered at this point in time, will only affect those actions arising a little more than two years prior to *Moran*.

Finally, in consideration of the issue it should be noted that the actual monetary amount involved will probably not be substantial. The largest item in loss of consortium damages, no doubt, is the support item. The inability to maintain a wife's support has always been an item for which the husband has been allowed to recover. Consequently, the only items Moran makes recoverable that were not recoverable before are loss of society, affection, and sexual companionship.

Although several of the cases referred to above provide for prospective application for the reasons stated therein, we adhere to the concept that a decision that overrules or changes a rule of law is to be applied retrospectively unless it is established there are compelling judicial reasons for not doing so. No sufficient compelling judicial reasons are apparent nor established to warrant an exception to the rule of retrospective application of the *Moran* decision, which recognizes the right of a wife to assert a claim for loss of consortium. *Moran* is, therefore, to be applied retrospectively. . . .

Judgment reversed, and remanded for further proceedings.

Darrow v. Hanover Township
Supreme Court of New Jersey, 1971.
58 N.J. 410, 278 A.2d 200.

The opinion of the Court was delivered by

■ PROCTOR, J.

In Immer v. Risko, 267 A.2d 481, decided July 10, 1970, we abrogated the doctrine of interspousal immunity in automobile negligence cases. Prior to *Immer* the immunity rule barred negligence actions between spouses. Orr v. Orr, 176 A.2d 241 (N.J. 1961); Koplik v. C.P. Trucking Corp., 141 A.2d 34 (N.H. 1958); Kennedy v. Camp, 102 A.2d 595 (N.J. 1954). Although we applied the new rule permitting such suits to the parties in *Immer*, we purposely left open the question of whether it should be fully retrospective. . . .

The present case arose out of an accident in the defendant Hanover Township when an automobile operated by plaintiff Gerald Darrow hit a tree, causing injuries to himself and his wife Herma, who was a passenger at the time. The Darrows brought suit against Hanover Township and the County of Morris, alleging that the tree projected into the road and that there was no warning of the danger. At the pretrial conference plaintiffs voluntarily dismissed their action against the County of Morris.

The accident occurred on April 13, 1967, and the suit was filed on April 14, 1969. (April 13, 1969, was a Sunday.) Our decision in *Immer* was rendered on July 10, 1970, as noted above, and on September 9, 1970, defendant Township was permitted to file a counterclaim for contribution against plaintiff Gerald Darrow. He answered, raising the defense of interspousal immunity[, citation,] and moved for summary judgment on the counterclaim. The trial court, after hearing oral argument, denied the motion and permitted the counterclaim to stand holding that *Immer* was retrospective and that interspousal immunity could no longer be pleaded. Thereafter, plaintiff Gerald Darrow sought and was granted leave to appeal. . . .

Plaintiff Gerald Darrow contends that the trial court erred in applying *Immer* retrospectively and urges us to reverse and give that decision prospective effect only. It can no longer be doubted that this Court has the power to give a decision solely prospective application . . . Although we have the power to make our decisions solely prospective, our courts have generally followed the traditional view that the overruling of a judicial decision is retrospective in nature. [Citation.] We have not done so on the basis of the old common law notion that overruling decisions do not "pretend to make a new law, but to vindicate the old one from misrepresentation," [1 William Blackstone, Commentaries *70], but rather because we believed that a weighing of the various policies involved called for retrospectivity. [Citation.] Thus, the question involved in this case is whether there are sound policy reasons for limiting our decision in *Immer* to prospective effect.

Plaintiff urges several reasons for doing so. First, he contends that retrospective application of *Immer* will result in an undue burden on the court system. While we recognize fully that court congestion may work a substantial prejudice to litigants, we would never exclude from our courts persons having just causes of action on this basis. The court system was designed to serve the needs of the people and it would hardly be fulfilling its purpose if it excluded litigants because of inconvenience to lawyers and judges. As we said in Falzone v. Busch, 214 A.2d 12 (N.J. 1965) in response to an argument that abrogation of the impact rule in negligence actions would open a "flood of litigations": "[T]he fear of an expansion of litigation should not deter courts from granting relief in meritorious cases; the proper remedy is an expansion of the judicial machinery, not a decrease in the availability of justice."

Next plaintiff contends that *Immer* should not be given retrospective effect because our decision there was predicated on the availability of insurance, and prior to January 1, 1967, coverage for "any member of the family of the insured" was excluded from the Standard Family Automobile Policy in New Jersey; consequently, allowing recovery for interspousal torts prior to that date would not further the purpose of *Immer* to place the risk of loss on insurers so as not to disturb the spousal relationship. We cannot accept the argument. While the presence of insurance was an important factor in our decision in *Immer*, we never held or meant to imply that the absence of insurance would be a bar to suits between spouses. . . .

Although we cannot agree with the above arguments in favor of prospectivity, we find persuasive appellants' main point—that there has been justifiable reliance on our earlier decisions upholding interspousal immunity. It is, of course, true that reliance has very little place in the field of torts so far as it affects the negligence itself; persons do not generally regulate their conduct because they believe they will or will not be liable in negligence. [Citation.] This is particularly true in automobile accidents where negligence may be equally harmful to the wrongdoer. However, it is entirely conceivable that persons would rely on the state of the law in determining what financial protection they need, or that the insurance institutions providing that protection would rely thereon in determining the degree of risk entailed and the rates of premiums to charge, and in deciding whether to investigate accidents involving their insureds or to settle claims at an early date.

Reliance has been the primary factor which has led courts in other jurisdictions to limit decisions abrogating immunities to prospective effect. [Citation.]

Defendant points out, however, that many of the above decisions which held abrogation of an immunity to be prospective dealt with charitable immunity and that this Court took the opposite position in its decision overruling that doctrine. Dalton v. St. Luke's Catholic Church, [141 A.2d 273 (N.J. 1958)]. In *Dalton*, we held that Collopy v. Newark Eye and Ear Infirmary, 141 A.2d 276 (N.J. 1958), which abrogated charitable immunity, should be retrospective. But we think that the situation in *Dalton* is entirely different from that in the present case. In *Dalton*, we expressly found that there had been no reasonable basis for reliance on the continuance of the charitable immunity doctrine. Charitable institutions had been repeatedly warned over a considerable period of time that their status of immunity was imperiled. Prior to *Dalton* the most recent decision of this Court discussing the issue showed that three of the six participating justices affirmatively voiced their opposition to the doctrine. Lokar v. Church of the Sacred Heart, 133 A.2d 12 (N.J. 1957). Even before *Lokar* it was apparent to commentators that the doctrine "was clearly in full retreat," Prosser, Law of Torts 787, 789 (2d ed. 1955), and that its demise in New Jersey was imminent. [Citation.]

In contradistinction to the charitable immunity doctrine, we think that there was a reasonable basis for reliance on the continued viability of the doctrine of interspousal immunity. Although it is true that this Court was sharply divided on the issue for a number of years, there was no indication that the balance would change. It was only because the writer of this opinion changed his views on the subject that the majority shifted, and I had given no indication of my rethinking prior to *Immer*. [Citation.] In fact, recent decisions of this Court, two of which were decided after the accident in the present case, would have led readers reasonably to believe that all members of the majority were steadfast in their opinion that the doctrine of interspousal immunity should stand. See Franco v. Davis, 239 A.2d 1, 3 (N.J. 1968) ("[W]e remain sharply divided in the whole field of intra-family tort immunity."); Patusco v. Prince Macaroni, Inc., 235 A.2d 465, 467 (N.J. 1967) ("It must be kept in mind that under the existing policy in our State a wife may not sue her husband as a tortfeasor.").

Accordingly, we think there was a reasonable basis for reliance on the existing state of the law. But defendant Township urges that even if there was a basis for reliance, there was no actual reliance because torts are not ordinarily committed in reliance on a substantive doctrine of law. We agree with that premise. As we stated earlier, we do not mean to suggest that drivers are less cautious because they may be immune from suit by their spouses. However, we do believe that their insurance carriers had a reasonable basis to rely on the immunity. As we pointed out in *Immer*, it is they who are most frequently the real parties in interest.

The primary area of reliance by carriers is the investigation of accidents. While this Court was firmly split, insurers had no reason to promptly investigate accidents involving the possibility of interspousal claims. It is crucial to an adequate determination of liability that an insurer have the opportunity to gather evidence as soon as possible after the accident. To effectively protect its interests, a carrier must ordinarily identify the witnesses and take their statements while memories are fresh; it must also make prompt physical examinations of prospective claimants. As time passes, witnesses disappear, memories fade and claimants may have intervening physical difficulties; investigations can be pursued only with great difficulty and little promise of success. When we spoke in *Immer* of the ability of trial judges and juries to weed out collusive and fraudulent claims, we were thinking of claims which could be adequately defended through an independent investigation of the facts. If insurance carriers are reduced to relying entirely upon statements by the litigant spouses, without further investigation, the task may prove too onerous.

We note that the majority of other courts faced with the problem of whether to apply their decisions abrogating intrafamily immunities have done so prospectively primarily because they have found justified reliance by defendants or their insurers. [Citation.]

Aside from protecting those who justifiably relied on interspousal immunity, prospective application of *Immer* will serve yet another purpose. It will foster stability since it will avoid the necessity of opening claims which might have gone stale because of a failure to promptly investigate. Prospectivity permits the Court to introduce an important change in the law with minimal disruption; it will not affect past conduct or relationships. The fear of disrupting what had been regarded as settled has sometimes restrained our courts from adopting a new and more just rule. [Citation.] Prospectivity can avoid unsettling the past and serve as an encouragement for judicial creativity. See generally Levy, Realist Jurisprudence and Prospective Overruling, 109 U. Pa. L. Rev. 1 (1960).

For the above reasons we hold that *Immer* is prospective only and that defendant Township's counterclaim is barred. The *Immer* rule will be available only to persons suffering injuries in automobile accidents occurring after July 10, 1970, the date *Immer* was decided. We applied *Immer* retrospectively to the parties in that case because we believed that the plaintiff and cross-claimant should have been rewarded for their efforts in challenging the immunity doctrine; purely prospective rulings do not provide any inducement for litigants to challenge common law doctrines.

The judgment of the trial court is reversed and the cause is remanded to that court for disposition consistent with this opinion. . . .

NOTES AND QUESTIONS

1. As the *Fitzgerald* opinion notes, courts depart from the traditional Blackstonian doctrine in certain situations. For instance, when parties such as charitable, governmental, and religious entities relied on accepted doctrines granting them immunity, they did not purchase liability insurance. Some believe that to impose liability retrospectively on such parties would be unfair. Therefore, in such limited cases, the general rule is to apply the changed law prospectively only, although there is not uniform agreement on this point.

2. In its *Immer* and *Darrow* opinions, the New Jersey Supreme Court departed from the traditional rule of retroactively, but only after applying *Immer* retroactively to the parties in that case. A similar approach was taken in Molitor v. Kaneland Comm. Unit Dist. No. 302, 163 N.E.2d 89 (Ill. 1959), which abolished the rule that a school district is immune from tort liability. (The plaintiff sued the district after he was injured in a school bus accident.) The majority made the new rule prospective but applied it to the parties in the case; otherwise, the court reasoned, plaintiffs would have no incentive to appeal the upholding of an "unjust" precedent since they would not benefit from a reversal. The majority did not decide whether the new rule would apply to other children injured in the same accident. Compare Holytz v. City of Milwaukee, 115 N.W.2d 618 (Wis. 1962) (making the new rule effective 40 days after the date of the decision); Jones v. State Highway Comm., 557 S.W.2d 225 (Mo. banc 1977) (making the new rule effective almost a year later than the decision); Spanel v. Mounds View School Dist. No. 621, 118 N.W.2d 795 (Minn. 1962) (making the new rule apply only to torts committed after the adjournment of the next session of the state legislature).

3. More recently, Texas courts have announced rules running the gamut of combinations of retrospective and prospective effect. See Lohec v. Galveston County Com'rs Court, 841 S.W.2d 361, 366 n.4 (Tex. 1992) (decision retroactive to date of the district court's judgment). In State Farm Fire and Cas. Co. v. Gandy, 925 S.W.2d 696, 720 (Tex. 1996), and Elbaor v. Smith, 845 S.W.2d 240, 250 (Tex. 1992), the Texas Supreme Court limited the application of these decisions only to pending cases; First Int'l Bank in San Antonio v. Roper Corp., 686 S.W.2d 602, 603 (Tex. 1985) (procedural change in comparative fault cases applied only to cases tried after the decision was handed down); Minyard Food Stores v. Newman, 612 S.W.2d 198, 198–199 (Tex. 1980) (rule permitting recovery by a spouse for negligent

impairment of consortium applied only in that case and causes of action arising after the date of the decision); Whittlesey v. Miller, 572 S.W.2d 665, 669 (Tex. 1978) (announcement that spouse can recover for negligent impairment of consortium applies only in the case and to causes of action arising after the date of the case). See 6 McDonald & Carlson Tex. Civ. Prac. App. Prac. § 45:7 (2d ed.).

4.   Does the practice of choosing an effective date other than the date of decision seem more "legislative"? Does that trouble you?

5.   What, in your view, are the relative merits and demerits of (a) making the overruling wholly prospective as in *Spanel*; making the overruling prospective except as to the plaintiff in the immediate case, as in *Immer, Darrow* and *Molitor*; or (c) making the overruling prospective except as to those involved in the same accident, as was advocated by the dissent in *Molitor*?

6.   Who is disadvantaged by the failure to apply *Immer* retrospectively? How do their interests compare to the spouses who would not have been able to recover for loss of consortium had *Fitzgerald* not applied *Moran* retrospectively?

7.   In a footnote in *Darrow*, the New Jersey Supreme Court refers to an affidavit from a claims manager at Gerald Darrow's liability insurer, stating that the insurer had relied on the interspousal immunity doctrine in not investigating the Darrows' accident. The court then quoted the affidavit:

> During my entire claims career, in which I have had substantial contact with many other claims people at Liberty Mutual and with claims men of other insurance companies, I know of no situation where any insurance carrier has investigated or prepared to defend itself in regard to claims that might be asserted by a wife against her husband as a result of the commission of a tort in New Jersey. This is so because we had understood that the Supreme Court of New Jersey had consistently reaffirmed its position that interspousal and interfamilial immunity was the law of the State of New Jersey.

Darrow, 278 A.2d at 203 n.4.

Does this specific claim of reliance help explain the difference in result between *Darrow* and *Fitzgerald*? Do you see any problems with giving weight to insurers' claims of reliance on the prior state of the law?

8.   In both *Fitzgerald* and *Darrow* the courts refer to signals their prior decisions may have sent regarding the strength or infirmity of the old common law rule. How strong need these signals be to put litigants and others potentially affected on notice of an impending change in the rule?

9.   The *Darrow* opinion distinguishes other decisions that had retroactively revoked immunity. What does *Darrow* mean when it refers to a "reasonable basis for reliance" on the continuation of a doctrine? What factors weigh for finding reasonable reliance, and which against? Does *Darrow* do a convincing job of drawing the line between reasonable and unreasonable reliance on the existing state of the law in these cases?

At this point in the reading, you may find particular resonance in the following observations of Justice Cardozo:

> Our survey of judicial methods teaches us, I think, the lesson that the whole subject matter of jurisprudence is more plastic, more malleable, the molds less definitively cast, the bounds of right and wrong less preordained and constant, than most of us, without the aid of some such analysis, have been accustomed to believe. We like to picture ourselves the field of the law as accurately mapped and plotted. We draw our little lines, and they are hardly down before we blur them. As in time and space, so here. Divisions are working hypotheses, adopted for our convenience. We are tending more and more toward an appreciation of the truth that, after all, there are few rules; there are chiefly standards and degrees. It is a question of degree whether I have been negligent. It is a question of degree whether in the use of my own land, I have created a nuisance which may be abated by my neighbor. It is a question of degree whether the law which takes my property and limits my conduct impairs my liberty unduly. So also the duty of a judge becomes a question of degree, and he is a useful judge or a poor one as he estimates the measure accurately or loosely. He must balance all his ingredients, his philosophy, his logic, his analogies, his history, his customs, his sense of right, and all the rest, and adding a little here and taking out a little there, must determine, as wisely as he can, which weight shall tip the scales.

Benjamin Nathan Cardozo, The Nature of the Judicial Process 161–62 (Yale Univ. Press. 1921).

PART III

THE INTERPRETATION OF STATUTES

A. STATING AND RESOLVING STATUTORY ISSUES

1. FINDING AND STATING ISSUES OF STATUTORY LAW

To interpret and apply a statute, you must work with its precise language. This proposition may seem obvious, but it marks an essential change of emphasis as the beginning law student moves from legal methods in the use of case-law analysis to legal methods in the interpretation of statutes. After even a few weeks of case law analysis and synthesis, the first-year law student has discovered that the rule of law derived from a case or from a line of cases can be stated in many different forms of language, each of which may constitute an acceptable statement. But a statutory rule of law is cast in an exclusively textual form. The beginning law student finds it difficult—as, for that matter, do many members of the profession—to work comfortably with a legal principle of which there is only one authorized version. Inevitably the beginner wants to handle statutes with the freedom to paraphrase in the manner she has found permissible in stating case law principles.

Moreover, confronting statutes after acquiring some facility with common-law reasoning can be jarring. Recounted in or underlying every case is a story; the judges' opinions offer at the same time examples from which a legal rule can be derived and applied to a concrete problem (thus giving both the story and its moral). Statutes, by contrast, are embodied in fixed text unrelieved by anecdote (though the legislative process that produced the text can sometimes prove picaresque). Accordingly, the interpretive technique calls not for telling a tale, but for perceiving a problem. What problem does the statutory text respond to? How does it address the problem? Does it satisfactorily solve the problem? Does the text create new problems, perhaps inadvertently? You might, at least at first, liken statutory text to pieces of a puzzle: you can't solve the puzzle by redesigning the pieces, you have to work to fit together the pieces you're given.

The Problem Cases in this Section are designed to give you practice in statutory analysis and in the statement of statutory issues. The vital lesson to derive from the preparation and discussion of these Problem Cases is this: *The issue in a case of statutory interpretation must be so stated as to include an exact quotation of the precise term of the statute with respect to which the question of statutory applicability arises*: DO NOT PARAPHRASE THE STATUTE! As to each Problem Case—and, later, as to each statute examined in this Part—you must be prepared to give an accurate and precise answer to the question: "What does the statute *say,* exactly, with respect to the legal problem at hand?" Accordingly, you should analyze and discuss the following Problem Cases solely on the basis of the words of the statutes at issue. If you are studying a judicial opinion that construes a statute, first practice reading and rereading the text of the statute itself. Only after you are familiar with the precise statutory language on its own terms should you turn to its judicial exposition.

NOTE: THE IMPORTANCE OF THE TEXT

The remarks of Erwin N. Griswold, then Solicitor General of the United States, in his discussion on "Appellate Advocacy," 26 The Record of the Association of the Bar of the City of New York 342 (1971), underscore the importance to lawyers of finding and precisely stating statutory issues. Solicitor General Griswold urged that advocates "orient the court" at the beginning of any oral argument on appeal. As a part of "orienting" the court, he recommended that counsel focus the issue for the judges, commenting as follows:

> [L]et the court see—and I mean "see"—the exact language with which they have to deal. Tell them, right at the beginning: "The statutory language involved appears at page 4 of my brief. Though the clause is a somewhat long one, the issue turns, I believe, on the proper construction or effect of words in two lines near the top of the page." Give the court time to find the two lines, and then read the words to them. At this point, the eye can be as important as the

ear in oral argument, and the court will follow all of the rest of your argument much better if you have taken pains to tell them exactly what it is about, and where to find the words if they want to look at them again.

In the years when I was a law teacher, I suppose that my most famous classroom remark was "Look at the statute"—or "What does the statute say?" Over the years, I have had literally hundreds of my former students write me and say that this was the most important thing they learned in law school. There is something about the student, and some oral advocates, too, which leads them to think great thoughts without ever taking the time and care to see just exactly what they are thinking about. Now I would not suggest that the court would make such a mistake. But courts are accustomed to think in terms of concrete, rather specific cases. The oral advocate takes a great step in advancing his cause, I think, if, right at the beginning of his argument, after the procedural setting has been established, he tells the court exactly what the case is about, including specific reference to any statutory language which must be construed or evaluated in bringing the case to a decision. With orientation, the court finds moorings. It is no longer cast adrift on the great sea of all the law. If you can get the court moored to the question as you see it, and so that they see it clearly and distinctly, you may be off to a good start towards leading them to decide the case your way.

PROBLEM CASES

Problem Case No. 1

Humphrey Hume was born in England of English parents in 1940 and came to the United States in 1960. He has never become a naturalized citizen of the United States.

In 1969, Hume was indicted on a charge of willfully destroying valuable federal property (Selective Service files) earlier in that year in the course of militant anti-war protest activity. He was tried shortly afterward and found guilty by a jury and then sentenced to imprisonment for a year and a day. He served his sentence as required.

Two and a half years ago, Hume drove a motor vehicle on behalf of a labor union engaged in demonstrations against certain West Coast grape growers. In the course of one demonstration his vehicle struck and killed a bystander. Hume was thereafter indicted for manslaughter, based on negligent and reckless operation (without intent to injure the victim) of a motor vehicle in violation of state law. On his plea of guilty he was sentenced to imprisonment by state authorities for a term of two years. He served his sentence and was recently released from the penitentiary. Thereupon deportation proceedings were commenced against him under Section 241(a) of the Immigration and Nationality Act of 1952, 66 Stat. 204, 8 U.S.C.A. Sec. 1251(a).

Section 241(a) of the Immigration and Nationality Act of 1952 (as modified for the purpose of this Problem Case) provides as follows:

> (a)   Any alien in the United States shall, upon the order of the Attorney General, be deported who—
>
> * * *
>
> (4)   is hereafter convicted of a crime involving moral turpitude committed within five years after entry and either sentenced to confinement or confined therefor in a prison or corrective institution for a year or more, or who hereafter at any time after entry is more than once convicted of a crime involving moral turpitude.

After a procedurally correct deportation hearing, Hume has now been ordered deported and taken into custody for that purpose. He seeks *habeas corpus* in a District Court of the United States on the ground that Section 241(a) does not authorize his deportation.

State the issue or issues of statutory interpretation raised by this case, noting as to each issue the precise language of the statute with respect to which the question of statutory applicability arises.

Problem Case No. 2

The Growers' Irrigation Company (hereinafter called the "Company") owns, maintains and operates within the State of New Coda an irrigation system consisting of four large storage reservoirs and 400 miles of irrigation canals. More than 100,000 acres of New Coda farm land, owned by many different farmers, are irrigated with water furnished by the Company. The water distributed by the Company is diverted from streams in New Coda during the non-irrigation season and runs through canals into the Company's reservoirs. During the irrigation season, this water is released from the reservoirs, carried through the Company's canals, and delivered to the lateral irrigation ditches of the farmers.

Sugar beets, corn, peas and beans are grown on the land irrigated. Virtually all of the sugar beets are processed into refined sugar in plants operated within New Coda, and large amounts of the corn, peas, and beans are canned in factories within New Coda. More than 75% of the refined sugar and canned vegetables is shipped in interstate commerce to purchasers outside New Coda.

There are 1,000 shares of authorized capital stock in the Company, all of which shares are owned by farmers in the irrigation area of New Coda. Each share of stock entitles the owner thereof to a 1/1,000th share of the property of the Company and of the total supply of water available during the irrigation season. The expenses necessary to the operation of the irrigation system are borne by annual assessments levied on the Company's stockholders, and the proceeds of the assessments constitute the Company's sole source of income. Payment of the assessment on his shares of stock is a condition precedent to the right of a stockholder to receive water for his farm during the irrigation season. The Company does not sell water to persons other than stockholders.

The Company employs 16 reservoir tenders, who take care of the diverting and storage of water during the non-irrigation season and attend the conduct of water through the Company's canals and into the lateral ditches of the farmers during the irrigation season. These reservoir tenders do not look after the lateral ditches of the farmers; in fact, they do not go at all on to the farmers' property. The Company pays its reservoir tenders a flat wage rate of $3 per hour, irrespective of the number of hours worked during any week. During the irrigation season, the 16 reservoir tenders work considerably more than 40 hours a week.

The Administrator of the Wage and Hour Division of the Department of Labor has now filed a complaint in the United States District Court for the State of New Coda, charging that the Company is violating the federal Fair Labor Standards Act by failing to pay the 16 reservoir tenders time-and-a-half for overtime. The Administrator's complaint asks that the District Court issue an injunction against the Company restraining continued violation of the Act.

The Fair Labor Standards Act (as modified and renumbered for the purposes of this Problem Case) provides, in pertinent part, as follows:

Section 1: *Declaration of Policy.* The Congress finds that the existence, in industries engaged in commerce, of labor conditions detrimental to the maintenance of minimum standards of living causes commerce and the channels of commerce to be used to spread such detrimental labor conditions among the workers of the several States.

Section 2: No employer shall employ any employee who is engaged in commerce or in the production of goods for commerce for a workweek longer than 40 hours unless such employee receives compensation for his employment in excess of the hours above specified at a rate not less than one and one-half times the regular pay rate at which he is employed.

Section 3: The provisions of Section 2 of this Act shall not apply with respect to: (1) any employee employed in a bona fide executive, administrative, or professional capacity; (2) any employee engaged in any retail or service establishment the greater part of whose selling or servicing is done within the State; (3) any employee employed in agriculture; or (4) any individual employed in handling, packing, storing, or canning agricultural commodities for market.

Section 4: *Definitions.*

(a) "Commerce" means trade, commerce, transportation, transmission, or communication among the several States or from any State to any place outside thereof.

(b) "Employer" includes any person acting directly or indirectly in the interest of an employer in relation to an employee but shall not include the United States or any State or political subdivision of a State.

(c) "Employee" includes any individual employed by an employer.

(d) "Agriculture" includes farming and all its branches and includes any practices performed by a farmer or on a farm as incident to or in conjunction with farming operations, including preparation for market and delivery to storage or to market.

(e) "Goods" means wares, products, commodities, merchandise or articles or subjects of commerce of any character whatsoever.

(f) "Produced" means produced, manufactured, mined, handled, or in any other manner worked on in any State; and for the purposes of this Act an employee shall be deemed to have been engaged in the production of goods if such employee was employed in any process or occupation necessary to the production of goods in any State.

The Growers' Irrigation Company moves to dismiss the Administrator's injunction action on the ground that the Company's activities are not within the area of coverage of the Fair Labor Standards Act.

State the issues of statutory interpretation raised by this case, noting as to each issue the *precise language* of the statute with respect to which the question of statutory applicability arises.

Problem Case No. 3

Prior to 1949, no anti-discrimination legislation had ever been enacted in the State of New Coda. During its 1949 session, the State Legislature passed the following statute, which was approved by the Governor and became effective June 1, 1949:

An Act to protect all citizens in the enjoyment of their civil rights.

Be it enacted by the Legislature of the State of New Coda:

Section 1: This statute may be cited as "The Anti-Discrimination Act of 1949."

Section 2: All persons within the jurisdiction of this State shall be entitled to the full and equal accommodations, advantages, facilities and privileges of inns, restaurants, hotels, eating-houses, bath-houses, barber shops, theatres, music halls, public conveyances on land and water, and all other places of public accommodation or amusement, subject only to conditions and limitations applicable alike to all citizens.

Section 3: Any person who shall violate any of the provisions of the foregoing section by denying to any citizen, except for reasons applicable alike to all citizens of every race, creed or color, and regardless of race, creed or color, the full enjoyment of any of the accommodations, advantages, facilities or privileges in said section enumerated, or by aiding or inciting such denial, shall for every such offense be subject to a fine of not more than $5,000, or to imprisonment for not more than one year, or to both such fine and such imprisonment.

The facts of this Problem Case are as follows: Dr. Claudius Smythe, a retired physician, is the sole owner of a rest home for persons recovering from major operations or from severe illnesses. The rest home is situated in one of the rural counties of the State of New Coda, and there are usually about fifteen convalescents in residence there. For some time, all financial and other business details have been handled by Rufus DeLong, who serves as the rest home's resident manager. Recently, DeLong wrote and had printed certain circulars describing the rest home, copies of which circulars were sent to all physicians in New Coda. At the specific direction of Dr. Smythe, DeLong included in the printed circulars the following statement:

> *Admission Policy:* It is the policy of the Smythe Rest Home to admit *white* patients only. Applications from non-white persons will not be considered.

No non-white person was ever actually turned away by the Smythe Rest Home; in fact, there is no record of any application to the rest home ever having been received from a non-white person.

Early this year, copies of the Smythe Rest Home's circular were called to the attention of the prosecuting attorney of the county in which the rest home is situated. Dr. Smythe was promptly indicted for violation of the Anti-Discrimination Act of 1949. After trial before a jury, Dr. Smythe was convicted and fined $1,500. He appeals to the appropriate appellate court of the State of New Coda.

State the issue or issues of statutory interpretation raised by Dr. Smythe's appeal, noting as to each issue the *precise language* of the statute with respect to which the question of statutory applicability arises.

Problem Case No. 4

A. A sign posted at the entry to a public path by order of the New Coda City Council states: "Pedestrians only. No bikes." Which of the following are prohibited from or permitted on the path? Why?

1. A cyclist dismounts and walks her bicycle.

2. A roller skater.

3. A skate boarder.

4. A pedestrian pushing a baby carriage.

5. A jogger pushing a high-tech 3-wheeled high-speed baby stroller.

6. A jogger.

B. Uncertainty about the meaning of the 'Pedestrians only. No bikes.' sign has prompted the New Coda City Council to try again. This time, it has added pictograms to its revision of the prohibition.

Photo by Zach Horton, Columbia Law School Class of 2021. Used with permission.

Has the revised version resolved the ambiguities of the prior sign? Has it introduced new ambiguities?

Problem Case No. 5: California Civil Code 3344.1 (as amended 2007)

(a) (1)   Any person who uses a deceased personality's name, voice, signature, photograph, or likeness, in any manner, on or in products, merchandise, or goods, or for purposes of advertising or selling, or soliciting purchases of, products, merchandise, goods, or services, without prior consent from the [heirs], shall be liable for any damages sustained by the person or persons injured as a result thereof. . . .

(2)   For purposes of this subdivision, a play, book, magazine, newspaper, musical composition, audiovisual work, radio or television program, single and original work of art, work of political or newsworthy value, or an advertisement or commercial announcement for any of these works, shall not be considered a product, article of merchandise, good, or service if it is fictional or nonfictional entertainment, or a dramatic, literary, or musical work.

       . . .

(b)   The rights recognized under this section are property rights, freely transferable or descendible, in whole or in part, by contract or by means of any trust or any other testamentary instrument, ... and . . . shall vest in the persons entitled to these property rights under the testamentary instrument of the deceased personality effective as of the date of his or her death. In the absence of an express transfer in a testamentary instrument of the deceased personality's rights in his or her name, voice, signature, photograph, or likeness, a provision in the testamentary instrument that provides for the disposition of the residue of the deceased personality's assets shall be effective to transfer the rights recognized under this section in accordance with the terms of that provision. The rights established by this section shall also be freely transferable or descendible by contract, trust, or any other testamentary instrument by any subsequent owner of the deceased personality's rights as recognized by this section. Nothing in this section shall be construed to render invalid or unenforceable any contract entered into by a deceased personality during his or her lifetime by which the deceased personality assigned the rights, in whole or in part, to use his or her name, voice, signature, photograph or likeness . . .

(g) No action shall be brought under this section by reason of any use of a deceased personality's name, voice, signature, photograph, or likeness occurring after the expiration of 70 years after the death of the deceased personality.

(h) As used in this section, "deceased personality" means any natural person whose name, voice, signature, photograph, or likeness has commercial value at the time of his or her death, whether or not during the lifetime of that natural person the person used his or her name, voice, signature, photograph, or likeness on or in products, merchandise or goods, or for purposes of advertising or selling, or solicitation of purchase of, products, merchandise, goods, or services. A "deceased personality" shall include, without limitation, any such natural person who has died within 70 years prior to January 1, 1985.

(i) As used in this section, "photograph" means any photograph or photographic reproduction, still or moving, or any video tape or live television transmission, of any person, such that the deceased personality is readily identifiable. A deceased personality shall be deemed to be readily identifiable from a photograph when one who views the photograph with the naked eye can reasonably determine who the person depicted in the photograph is.

(j) For purposes of this section, a use of a name, voice, signature, photograph, or likeness in connection with any news, public affairs, or sports broadcast or account, or any political campaign, shall not constitute a use for which consent is required under subdivision (a). . . .

(m) The remedies provided for in this section are cumulative and shall be in addition to any others provided for by law.

(n) This section shall apply to the adjudication of liability and the imposition of any damages or other remedies in cases in which the liability, damages, and other remedies arise from acts occurring directly in this state. . . .

QUESTIONS

Your client, Edsel Parsley, Jr., is the son and sole heir of the deceased famous eponymous rock star. He asks you to explain what the statute means, and how it works. For example:

1.   Pablita Metisse made a series of cubist portraits of Parsley in the 1960s. She has for many years, been licensing the images for reproduction and sale on a variety of products, including posters, wall calendars, and t-shirts. What, if any, claims might Parsley Jr. have against Metisse?

2.   Of all Parsley's hit songs, "Red Leather Boots" has proven the most loved and most enduring. Nick Nack Emporium has been producing and selling a novelty item, a red leather key chain in the form of a boot, with a microchip that plays a digitally remastered clip of Parsley singing the opening bars of "Red Leather Boots." Does Parsley Jr. have a claim under this statute?

3.   During Parsley's lifetime, his business manager, Sergeant Sanders, handled all Parsley's affairs, including concert and club appearances and endorsements. He has contacted Parsley Jr. to inform him that, in light of his relationship with Parsley Sr., Sergeant Sanders has sole authority to exercise Parsley's post-mortem rights. What is the basis of Sanders' claim, and is it valid?

4.   Andy Varhol is a famous artist who creates silk screens of dead celebrities, including Parsley. He mass produces these silk screens and sells them to art dealers. The Varhol images have received extensive press coverage, and have come to be considered current cultural icons. Andy has never sought permission from Parsley Jr. Does the latter have a claim under the statute?

5.   Parsley Sr.'s brother, Syd, was also a famous singer, and in fact, he was probably a better musician and more famous than Parsley Sr. at one point. However, a series of personal scandals left Syd unpopular and broke, and by the time he passed away, not many people remembered Syd or his music. A few years ago, Syd's music was rediscovered by the underground music community, and now it has regained popularity among mainstream music fans. Vendors have followed suit, and now t-shirts and posters are being sold in California with Syd's face on them. Are these vendors liable to Syd's heirs under the statute?

Problem Case No. 6: California and New York State Eavesdropping Statutes

Cal. Penal Code

§ 632. Eavesdropping on or recording confidential communications

(a) A person who, intentionally and without the consent of all parties to a confidential communication, uses an electronic amplifying or recording device to eavesdrop upon or record the confidential communication, whether the communication is carried on among the parties in the presence of one another or by means of a telegraph, telephone, or other device, except a radio, shall be punished by a fine not exceeding two thousand five hundred dollars ($2,500) per violation, or imprisonment in a county jail not exceeding one year, or in the state prison, or by both that fine and imprisonment.

(b) For the purposes of this section, "person" means an individual, business association, partnership, corporation, limited liability company, or other legal entity, and an individual acting or purporting to act for or on behalf of any government or subdivision thereof, whether federal, state, or local, but excludes an individual known by all parties to a confidential communication to be overhearing or recording the communication.

(c) For the purposes of this section, "confidential communication" means any communication carried on in circumstances as may reasonably indicate that any party to the communication desires it to be confined to the parties thereto, but excludes a communication made in a public gathering or in any legislative, judicial, executive, or administrative proceeding open to the public, or in any other circumstance in which the parties to the communication may reasonably expect that the communication may be overheard or recorded.

§ 637. Disclosure of telegraphic or telephonic message; punishment; exception

Every person not a party to a telegraphic or telephonic communication who willfully discloses the contents of a telegraphic or telephonic message, or any part thereof, addressed to another person, without the permission of that person, unless directed so to do by the lawful order of a court, is punishable by imprisonment . . . , or in a county jail not exceeding one year, or by fine not exceeding five thousand dollars ($5,000), or by both that fine and imprisonment.

§ 637.2. Civil action by person injured; injunction

(a) Any person who has been injured by a violation of this chapter may bring an action against the person who committed the violation for the greater of the following amounts:

(1) Five thousand dollars ($5,000) per violation.

(2) Three times the amount of actual damages, if any, sustained by the plaintiff. . . .

New York Penal Law

§ 250.00 Eavesdropping; definitions of terms

The following definitions are applicable to this article:

1. "Wiretapping" means the intentional overhearing or recording of a telephonic or telegraphic communication by a person other than a sender or receiver thereof, without the consent of either the sender or receiver, by means of any instrument, device or equipment. The normal operation of a telephone or telegraph corporation and the normal use of the services and facilities furnished by such corporation pursuant to its tariffs or necessary to protect the rights or property of said corporation shall not be deemed "wiretapping."

2. "Mechanical overhearing of a conversation" means the intentional overhearing or recording of a conversation or discussion, without the consent of at least one party thereto, by a person not present thereat, by means of any instrument, device or equipment.

3. "Telephonic communication" means any aural transfer made in whole or in part through the use of facilities for the transmission of communications by the aid of wire, cable or other like connection between the point of origin and the point of reception (including the use of such connection in a switching station) furnished or operated by any person engaged in providing or operating such facilities for the transmission of communications and such term includes any electronic storage of such communications.

4. "Aural transfer" means a transfer containing the human voice at any point between and including the point of origin and the point of reception.

5. "Electronic communication" means any transfer of signs, signals, writing, images, sounds, data, or intelligence of any nature transmitted in whole or in part by a wire, radio, electromagnetic, photoelectronic or photo-optical system, but does not include:

(a) any telephonic or telegraphic communication; or

(b) any communication made through a tone only paging device; or

(c) any communication made through a tracking device consisting of an electronic or mechanical device which permits the tracking of the movement of a person or object; or

(d) any communication that is disseminated by the sender through a method of transmission that is configured so that such communication is readily accessible to the general public.

6. "Intercepting or accessing of an electronic communication" and "intentionally intercepted or accessed" mean the intentional acquiring, receiving, collecting, overhearing, or recording of an electronic communication, without the consent of the sender or intended receiver thereof, by means of any instrument, device or equipment, except when used by a telephone company in the ordinary course of its business or when necessary to protect the rights or property of such company.

7. "Electronic communication service" means any service which provides to users thereof the ability to send or receive wire or electronic communications.

8. "Unlawfully" means not specifically authorized pursuant to article seven hundred or seven hundred five of the criminal procedure law for the purposes of this section and sections 250.05, 250.10 . . . of this article.

§ 250.05 Eavesdropping

A person is guilty of eavesdropping when he unlawfully engages in wiretapping, mechanical overhearing of a conversation, or intercepting or accessing of an electronic communication.

Eavesdropping is a . . . felony.

§ 250.10 Possession of eavesdropping devices

A person is guilty of possession of eavesdropping devices when, under circumstances evincing an intent to use or to permit the same to be used in violation of section 250.05, he possesses any instrument, device or equipment designed for, adapted to or commonly used in wiretapping or mechanical overhearing of a conversation.

Possession of eavesdropping devices is a . . . misdemeanor.

Please consider whether the following situations are covered by either the California or New York Eavesdropping Statutes.

1. Online retailer Amaze-on sells a voice-controlled Gotcha speaker that, when turned on, listens and records all ambient sounds nearby it. Gotcha's sound recordings are uploaded to Amaze-on's cloud server, though the recordings are inaccessible to the owner of the device that recorded them. A homeowner who keeps a Gotcha on at all times in her living room invites a friend over, and the Gotcha listens to their conversation. The friend is unaware of the Gotcha's presence. Has either Amaze-on or the host violated either statute? Does it matter whether the host is aware of, and consented to, Gotcha's background recording and storage practices?

2. A parent keeps a baby monitor that looks like a teddy bear in his child's bedroom; the monitor records both video and audio in the room. While the parent is out at dinner, a babysitter puts the child to bed by reading her a bedtime story in the child's bedroom. Has the parent violated either statute if he fails to inform the babysitter about the baby monitor's recording?

3. A police officer pulls over a driver whose car has one taillight out. An observer nearby, concerned about possible police brutality, surreptitiously records the police officer's interactions with the driver of the car. The observer feels the driver was treated very rudely (and possibly verbally abusively) by the police officer, so unbeknownst to both the driver and officer, she posts the recording to her Facepalm social media account to expose the local police department. Has she violated either statute by either recording and/or posting the interaction?

4. A group of policymakers meet to discuss important current affairs issues under "Chatham House Rules" (where the broad contents of the meeting can be disclosed but nothing can be attributed to any particular participant). Unbeknownst to the group, one participant records the conversation. He later plays it for a journalist, who posts the recording online. Has either the recording participant or the leaking journalist violated either statute? Would it matter if the recording was of a conference call rather than an in-person gathering?

5. Three individuals are on a Swype video chat. One of the participants, who is recording the video chat without the knowledge of the other two participants, leaves the room for another meeting midway through the call, and does not return. Nevertheless, he secretly keeps the recording going; the recording captures a conversation between the other two about how unlikeable he is. Has he violated either statute by keeping the recording going?

6. A wife secretly records her deaf husband's sign language conversations over Swype video chat with a deaf ex-girlfriend who lives overseas. Has the wife violated either statute? Does it matter if at any point during the conversation either the husband or the ex-girlfriend speaks?

7. A celebrity gossip website gains access to a celebrity's cellular text messages without his permission and posts excerpts of the text messages online. Has the gossip website violated either statute?

2. RESOLVING STATUTORY ISSUES—A GENERAL VIEW

Heydon's Case

Court of Exchequer, 1584.
3 Coke 7a, 76 Eng.Rep. 637.

[The technique of identifying the problem to which the statutory text responds is usually traced back to this case. Sir Edward Coke (later Lord Chief Justice of England and Wales) stated the much quoted "Doctrine of Heydon's Case" as follows:]

And it was resolved by them [the judges], that for the sure and true interpretation of all statutes in general (be they penal or beneficial, restrictive or enlarging of the common law) four things are to be discerned and considered—

1st. What was the common law before the making of the Act.

2nd. What was the mischief and defect for which the common law did not provide.

3rd. What remedy the Parliament hath resolved and appointed to cure the disease of the commonwealth.

And 4th. The true reason of the remedy, and then the office of all the Judges is always to make such construction as shall suppress the mischief, and advance the remedy, and to suppress subtle inventions of evasion for continuance of the mischief, and *pro privato commodo*, and to add force and life to the cure and remedy, according to the true intent of the makers of the Act, *pro bono publico*. . . .

QUESTION

What assumptions about sources of law underlie the "Doctrine of Heydon's Case"? How valid are these assumptions today, especially when interpreting federal statutes?

———

In applying statutes, courts have traditionally looked to "the intent of the legislature" to resolve doubts as to the meaning or legal effect of statutory language, as *Heydon's Case* articulates. In your study of the cases in this Part, you will find that the effort to ascertain the "legislative intent" is, on many occasions, quite as difficult and subtle an operation as is the parallel case law job of arriving at the "holding" of a case.

Consider the range of problems that may arise when deciding particular cases by reference to the general commands of statutes. A legislative direction must be expressed in words, and words are notoriously inexact and imperfect symbols for the communication of ideas. In addition, one must reckon with the inexhaustible variety of the facts to which such words could be applied. To determine from the language of an enactment the "legislative intent," in the sense of a pre-existing understanding of the lawmakers as to the statute's construction in relation to a particular issue, may involve semantic problems of very great difficulty.

Even more difficult are the cases in which the interpretive issue before the court is one which was not, and perhaps could not have been, foreseen, even in the most general outline, by the legislators responsible for the enactment. In such cases, the "interpreting" judge must perform the originative function of assigning to the statute a meaning or legal effect which it did not possess before the court's decision. Cardozo saw this with his characteristic clarity when he wrote:*

> Interpretation is often spoken of as if it were nothing but the search and the discovery of a meaning which, however obscure and latent, had none the less a real and ascertainable pre-existence in the legislator's mind. The process is, indeed, that at times, but it is often something more.

There are a number of other questions or considerations related to the methods of statutory interpretation which you should keep in mind in analyzing the materials to come. What light do these cases and other materials shed on the nature and application of legislative intent or other basic approaches to interpretation? What, if anything, does this case or material reveal as to the types and causes of statutory ambiguity? What, if any, intrinsic and extrinsic aids to interpretation, or interpretative rules or maxims, are employed in this case and what conclusions may be drawn as to their value and use? What lessons emerge from these materials for purposes of advocacy in statutory cases? Note, incidentally, that the materials provide many illustrations of the different types of statutory enactments one may expect to encounter in law practice.

a.   A TYPOLOGY OF LEGAL METHODS FOR STATUTORY INTERPRETATION

One approach to questions of statutory interpretation is to scrutinize prevailing legal methods of interpretation *as methods*, and examine the (both stated and unstated) justifications for their application. One may

---

*   The Nature of the Judicial Process 14 (1921).

typologize legal methods of interpretation on the basis of three broad sources of authority:

i.   *The Drafter's Intended Meaning*

First, some interpretive methods identify the drafters' *intended* meaning of the statute. These methods' legitimacy derives from the concept of legislative supremacy. Since democratically elected legislative bodies enact statutes on the basis of popular mandate, the interpreter should endeavor to understand what that popular will—as manifested through the legislature—sought to accomplish in enacting the statute. "Intended meaning" subdivides into two further categories:

(a) *Drafters' Purpose or* Objective *Intent:* This approach examines the goals of the statute, often evidenced by the statute's "findings" or "purpose" section. This may take the form of a holistic reading of the statutory scheme in order to identify the "evil" or "mischief" sought to be remedied—as articulated above in *Heydon's Case*—or to ascertain the regulatory scheme the legislature sought to put in place.

(b) *Drafters' Intentions or* Subjective *Intent:* A second, related approach focuses on specific drafters' intentions as articulated by individual legislators or in documents prepared by the legislative committee(s) responsible for drafting the statute. As you will see throughout this Part, these materials, which document the "legislative history" of the bill on its way to becoming a statute, purport to elucidate the drafters' specific intention(s) as to how the statute should operate. These materials include comments made in committee reports, floor statements, and committee testimony. Non-drafting legislators (and their staffs) also rely on these materials to understand how the bills they are voting on are intended to alter the law.

ii.   *The Reasonable Reader's Understanding*

By contrast, many interpretive methods instead key in on the meaning of the statute as the statute's *reasonable reader* might understand it. These methods generally purport to identify the "ordinary" meaning of the statutory term or phrase at issue, drawing on evidence of customary linguistic usage, syntax, and semantics. Many judicial "canons of construction" derive from broadly applicable syntactic and semantic rules for deriving meaning from text, as you will see in the next subsection. These methods derive much of their legitimacy from the public availability of the text and the presumption that the law's texts must communicate effectively to those whom the law regulates. "Textualist" jurists like Justice Robert Jackson and Justice Antonin Scalia have often remarked that "[w]e do not inquire what the *legislature* meant; we ask only what the *statute* means."[*] For a variety of jurisprudential and methodological reasons discussed throughout this Part, these jurists are skeptical of the value of ascertaining drafters' intentions, and prefer instead to focus on the meaning of the drafters' words.

Interpretive methods grounded in the reasonable reader's understanding align along two further axes, those of temporality and sophistication:

Temporality

(a) *The* Original *Reasonable Reader's Understanding:* This is the meaning of the statutory term or phrase as it would have been understood by the reasonable reader at the time of the statute's enactment.

(b) *The* Present-Day *Reasonable Reader's Understanding:* This is the meaning of the statutory term or phrase as understood by the *present-day* reasonable reader of the statute at the time the interpretive problem arises.

As with all linguistic usage, the meaning commonly attributed to a statutory term or phrase may change over time. These contrasting approaches highlight the choice between giving the term or phrase its commonly understood meaning at the time of the statute's enactment or instead its contemporary meaning at the time the interpretive question arises.

The statute *itself* may indicate whether to interpret its meaning historically or dynamically: for example, in Business Electronics Corp. v. Sharp Electronics Corp., 485 U.S. 717, 732 (1988), the Supreme Court recognized that "[t]he Sherman Act adopted the term 'restraint of trade' along with its dynamic potential. It invokes the common law itself, and not merely the static content that the common law had assigned to the term in 1890. . . . The changing content of the term 'restraint of trade' was well recognized at the time the Sherman Act was enacted." Thus, the present-day reasonable reader's understanding of a "restraint of trade" might prevail over the common understanding of a "restraint of trade" at the time the statute was enacted.

Sophistication

A second axis concerns the reasonable reader's presumed degree of sophistication or specialization:

(a) *The Reasonable* Generalist *Reader's Understanding:* This is commonly referred to as the "ordinary" meaning that a member of the general public might attribute to the term or phrase in question. Judges often turn to dictionaries or other

---

[*]   Antonin Scalia, A Matter of Interpretation: Federal Courts and the Law 23 (Amy Gutmann ed., 1997) (emphasis added).

depositories of general linguistic usage to ascertain the "ordinary" meaning of a term.

(b) The Reasonable Specialist *Reader's Understanding:* As you will see, while the audience for many statutes is presumed to be members of the general public, some statutory provisions address a more specialized audience. In those circumstances, interpretive methods may seek to ascertain the meaning of a word or phrase as understood by a specialized community of readers, such as lawyers. Interpretive methods such as *Black's Law Dictionary* may identify the meaning of a legal term of art that may differ from that term's ordinary meaning. In other circumstances, judges have sought evidence of the linguistic usage of specialists in fields such as intellectual property or bankruptcy.

Thus, when drawing on methods that seek the reasonable reader's understanding, the interpreter will assume (either tacitly or expressly) *both* a temporality *and* a level of sophistication of the presumed reader.

Note that if methods that yield the reasonable reader's interpretation are to be *dispositive*, there can be only *one* reasonable reading of the statute. Otherwise, if the statute is susceptible to multiple reasonable understandings, then the reasonable reader approach will not, *on its own*, resolve the interpretive question. Thus, in some instances interpreters who employ the reasonable reader approach may beg the question: what makes one particular hypothetical reader's understanding *reasonable*, and another's *unreasonable*? As you will see throughout this Part, in many cases judges disagree about a statute's "ordinary" or "plain" meaning. Sometimes they also disagree about whether the presumed reader should be a generalist reader or a specialist reader.

If presumptively reasonable *judges* often disagree about the "ordinary" or "plain" meaning of a statutory term or phrase, one may wonder how often only one single, reasonable "ordinary" or "plain" meaning can be found for a statutory term or phrase. To that end, prevailing practices in administrative law anticipate the possibility of multiple reasonable interpretations: in certain circumstances, *any* reasonable reading may suffice when courts review an administrative agency's proposed interpretation. However, if two readers can arrive at distinct yet reasonable understandings of the statute's meaning outside of the context of agency interpretations of statutes, then what makes one reader's understanding more legally persuasive than another's?

iii. Rule-of-Law-Based Methods for Interpretation

Perhaps because judges often disagree about what the legislature intended, or what a reasonable reader might understand the statute to mean, a third set of interpretive methods may prove useful. Some "canons of construction" thus draw on jurisprudential tenets that guide the interpreter in deciding on a *legal* meaning or effect of a statutory text. Importantly, the legal meaning may not reflect either the drafters' intended meaning or (one or more) reasonable reader's understandings of the meaning of the term or phrase. These methods derive their legitimacy primarily from long-standing rule-of-law principles that undergird our legal system.

Indeed, many "substantive" canons of interpretation you will encounter in this Part do not necessarily purport to reflect either the drafters' intended meaning or the reasonable reader's understanding. Canons such as the "clear notice rule," the "rule of lenity," the doctrine of "constitutional avoidance," and the "presumption against retroactive application" are primarily grounded in fundamental legal principles like fair notice, reasonable reliance, and separation of powers. For this reason, substantive canons sometimes come under attack because they are hard to justify on faithful agency grounds: they may appear in tension with both legislative supremacy and popular understanding. Nevertheless, these methods prove to be remarkably enduring (and well received) among judges across the interpretive spectrum. Perhaps for this reason, judges generally do not disagree about *whether* to apply these substantive methods in at least some circumstances; instead, disagreements arise concerning *when* and *how* they apply. (And the principles undergirding these canons may be familiar to the reader who has already worked her way through Part II, for they often function similarly to the judicially developed, prudentially oriented common-law legal methods surveyed in that part.)

b.   APPLYING LEGAL METHODS OF STATUTORY INTERPRETATION

Of course, courts regularly draw on all three sets of methods to arrive at a chosen interpretation, often shoring up the weaknesses in reasoning of one set of methods with support from another. As you read the cases in this Part, look for instances in which judges either expressly or implicitly rely on rule-of-law methods as a form of tie-breaker for deciding between competing potential drafters' intended meanings or reasonable readers' understandings of the statute.

For instance, the opinions rendered in the appellate and Supreme Court decisions in *Johnson v. Southern Pacific Co.* below expose many different varieties of statutory interpretation. As you study the opinions, try to identify the different interpretive techniques and devices employed.

BUT, before you read any of the judicial analysis, concentrate first on the facts of the case and on the language of the statute:

— What happened in this case?

— What does the statute say (verbatim)?

— How does the statute apply to these facts?

Consider how *you* would rule on Johnson's claim under the statute. Only then should you turn to the courts' treatment of his claim.

Johnson v. Southern Pacific Co.

Circuit Court of Appeals for the Eighth Circuit, 1902.
117 Fed. 462, reversed 196 U.S. 1, 25 S.Ct. 158, 49 L.Ed. 363 (1904).

The Southern Pacific Co. was operating passenger trains between San Francisco and Ogden, Utah. It habitually drew a dining car in these trains. Such a car formed a part of a train leaving San Francisco, and ran through to Ogden, where it was ordinarily turned and put into a train going west to San Francisco. On August 5, 1900, the east-bound train was so late that it was not practicable to get the dining car into Ogden in time to place it in the next west-bound train, and it was therefore left on a side track at Promontory, Utah, to be picked up by the west-bound train when it arrived. While it was standing on this track the conductor of an interstate freight train which arrived there was directed to take this dining car to a turntable, turn it, and place it back upon the side track so that it would be ready to return to San Francisco. The conductor instructed his crew to carry out this direction. The plaintiff, Johnson, the head brakeman, undertook to couple the freight engine to the dining car for the purpose of carrying out the conductor's order. The freight engine and the eight-wheel dining car involved were the property of defendant railroad company. The freight engine, regularly used in interstate hauling of standard eight-wheel freight cars, was equipped with a Janney coupler, which would couple automatically with another Janney coupler, and the dining car was provided with a Miller automatic hook; but the Miller hook would not couple automatically with the Janney coupler, because it was on the same side, and would pass over it. Johnson knew this, and undertook to make the coupling by means of a link and pin. He knew that it was a difficult coupling to make, and that it was necessary to go between the engine and the car to accomplish it, and that it was dangerous to do so. Nevertheless, he went in between the engine and the car without objection or protest and tried three times to make the coupling. He failed twice; the third time his hand was caught and crushed so that it became necessary to amputate his hand above the wrist.

Johnson brought an action for damages for personal injury against the railroad. The case was tried in the Circuit Court of the United States for the District of Utah. At the trial, Southern Pacific, after the plaintiff had rested, moved the court to instruct the jury to find in defendant's favor. The motion was granted and the jury found a verdict accordingly on which judgment was entered. Plaintiff carried the case to the Circuit Court of Appeals for the Eighth Circuit.

Defendant contended in the district and circuit courts that it was not liable for the injury on the ground that plaintiff, under the rules of the common law, had "assumed the risk" involved in coupling the dining car and locomotive. Plaintiff Johnson, on the other hand, contended that at the time of the injury defendant was violating a federal statute (*infra*) in respect to the dining car and locomotive concerned, and that by reason of such violation plaintiff, under this statute, was not to be deemed to have assumed the risk. It was acknowledged that the locomotive possessed a power driving-wheel brake, that there were train brakes and appliances for operating a train brake system as required and that there was no failure, as to either vehicle, to provide the requisite grab irons or drawbars.

The text of the federal statute relied on by plaintiff, which was in effect at the time of the injury and at all times pertinent to this problem, is set out herewith as it appears in the Statutes at Large (27 Stat. 531):

> Chap. 196.—An act to promote the safety of employees and travelers upon railroads by compelling common carriers engaged in interstate commerce to equip their cars with automatic couplers and continuous brakes and their locomotives with driving-wheel brakes, and for other purposes.
>
> Sec. 1. *Be it enacted by the Senate and House of Representatives of the United States of America in Congress assembled,* That from and after the first day of January, eighteen hundred and ninety-eight, it shall be unlawful for any common carrier engaged in interstate commerce by railroad to use on its line any locomotive engine in moving interstate traffic not equipped with a power driving-wheel brake and appliances for operating the train-brake system, or to run any train in such traffic after said date that has not a sufficient number of cars in it so equipped with power or train brakes that the engineer on the locomotive drawing such train can control its speed without requiring brakemen to use the common hand brake for that purpose.
>
> Sec. 2. That on and after the first day of January, eighteen hundred and ninety-eight, it shall be unlawful for any such common carrier to haul or permit to be hauled or used on its line any car used in moving interstate traffic not equipped with couplers coupling automatically by impact, and which can be uncoupled without the necessity of men going between the ends of the cars.
>
> Sec. 3. That when any person, firm, company, or corporation engaged in interstate commerce by railroad shall have equipped a sufficient number of its cars so as to comply with the provisions of section one of this act, it may lawfully refuse to receive from connecting lines of road or shippers any cars not equipped sufficiently, in accordance with the first section of this act, with such power or train brakes as will work and readily interchange with the brakes in use on its own cars, as required by this act.

Sec. 4.   That from and after the first day of July, eighteen hundred and ninety-five, until otherwise ordered by the Interstate Commerce Commission, it shall be unlawful for any railroad company to use any car in interstate commerce that is not provided with secure grab irons or handholds in the ends and sides of each car for greater security to men in coupling and uncoupling cars.

Sec. 5.   That within ninety days from the passage of this act the American Railway Association is authorized hereby to designate to the Interstate Commerce Commission the standard height of drawbars for freight cars, measured perpendicular from the level of the tops of the rails to the centers of the drawbars, for each of the several gauges of railroads in use in the United States, and shall fix a maximum variation from such standard height to be allowed between the drawbars of empty and loaded cars. Upon their determination being certified to the Interstate Commerce Commission, said Commission shall at once give notice of the standard fixed upon to all common carriers, owners, or lessees engaged in interstate commerce in the United States by such means as the Commission may deem proper. But should said association fail to determine a standard as above provided, it shall be the duty of the Interstate Commerce Commission to do so, before July first, eighteen hundred and ninety-four, and immediately to give notice thereof as aforesaid. And after July first, eighteen hundred and ninety-five, no cars, either loaded or unloaded, shall be used in interstate traffic which do not comply with the standard above provided for.

Sec. 6.   That any such common carrier using any locomotive engine, running any train, or hauling or permitting to be hauled or used on its line any car in violation of any of the provisions of this act, shall be liable to a penalty of one hundred dollars for each and every such violation, to be recovered in a suit or suits to be brought by the United States district attorney in the district court of the United States having jurisdiction in the locality where such violation shall have been committed, and it shall be the duty of such district attorney to bring such suits upon duly verified information being lodged with him of such violation having occurred. And it shall also be the duty of the Interstate Commerce Commission to lodge with the proper district attorneys information of any such violations as may come to its knowledge: *Provided,* that nothing in this act contained shall apply to trains composed of four-wheel cars or to locomotives used in hauling such trains.

Sec. 7.   That the Interstate Commerce Commission may from time to time upon full hearing and for good cause extend the period within which any common carrier shall comply with the provisions of this act.

Sec. 8. That any employee of any such common carrier who may be injured by any locomotive, car, or train in use contrary to the provision of this act shall not be deemed thereby to have assumed the risk thereby occasioned, although continuing in the employment of such carrier after the unlawful use of such locomotive, car, or train had been brought to his knowledge.

Approved, March 2, 1893.

■ SANBORN, CIRCUIT JUDGE [joined by LOCHREN, DISTRICT JUDGE], after stating the case . . .

Under the common law the plaintiff assumed the risks and dangers of the coupling which he endeavored to make, and for that reason he is estopped from recovering the damages which resulted from his undertaking. He was an intelligent and experienced brakeman, familiar with the couplers he sought to join, and with their condition, and well aware of the difficulty and danger of his undertaking, so that he falls far within the familiar rules that the servant assumes the ordinary risk and dangers of the employment upon which he enters, so far as they are known to him, and so far as they would have been known to one of his age, experience, and capacity by the use of ordinary care, and that the risks and dangers of coupling cars provided with different kinds of well-known couplers, bumpers, brakeheads and deadwoods are the ordinary risks and dangers of a brakeman's service. [Citations.]

This proposition is not seriously challenged, but counsel base their claim for a reversal of the judgment below upon the position that the plaintiff was relieved of this assumption of risk, and of its consequences, by the provisions of the act of Congress of March 2, 1893 (27 Stat. c. 196, p. 531). The title of that act, and the parts of it that are material to the consideration of this contention are these: [see *supra*]

The first thought that suggests itself to the mind upon a perusal of this law, and a comparison of it with the facts of this case, is that this statute has no application here, because both the dining car and the engine were equipped as this act directs. The car was equipped with Miller couplers which would couple automatically with couplers of the same construction upon cars in the train in which it was used to carry on interstate commerce, and the engine was equipped with a power driving wheel brake such as this statute prescribes. To overcome this difficulty, counsel for the plaintiff persuasively argues that this is a remedial statute; that laws for the prevention of fraud, the suppression of a public wrong, and the bestowal of a public good are remedial in their nature, and should be liberally construed, to prevent the mischief and to advance the remedy, notwithstanding the fact that they may impose a penalty for their violation; and that this statute should be so construed as to forbid the use of a locomotive as well as a car which is not equipped with an automatic coupler. In support of this contention he cites Suth. St. Const. § 360; Wall v. Platt, 169 Mass. 398, 48 N.E. 270; Taylor v. U.S., 3 How. 197, 11 L.Ed. 559; and other cases of like character. The general propositions which counsel quote may be found in the opinions in these cases, and in some of them they were applied to the particular facts which those actions presented. But the interpolation in this act of Congress by construction of an ex post facto provision that it is, and ever since January 1, 1898, has been unlawful for any common carrier to use any engine in interstate traffic that is or was not equipped with couplers coupling automatically, and that any carrier that has used or shall use an engine not so equipped has been and shall be liable to a penalty of $100 for every violation of this provision, is too abhorrent to the sense of justice and fairness, too rank and radical a piece of judicial legislation, and in violation of too many established and salutary rules of construction, to commend itself to the judicial reason or conscience. The primary rule for the interpretation of a statute or a contract is to ascertain, if possible, and enforce, the intention which the legislative body that enacted the law, or the parties who made the agreement, have expressed therein. But it is the intention expressed in the law or contract, and that only, that the courts may give effect to. They cannot lawfully assume or presume secret purposes that are not indicated or expressed by the statute itself and then enact provisions to accomplish these supposed intentions. While ambiguous terms and doubtful expressions may be interpreted to carry out the intention of a legislative body which a statute fairly evidences, a secret intention cannot be interpreted into a statute which is plain and unambiguous, and which does not express it. The legal presumption is that the legislative body expressed its intention, that it intended what is expressed, and that it intended nothing more. [Citation.] Construction and interpretation have no place or office where the terms of a statute are clear and certain, and its meaning is plain. In such a case they serve only to create doubt and to confuse the judgment. When the language of a statute is unambiguous, and its meaning evident, it must be held to mean what it plainly expresses, and no room is left for construction [Citations.]

This statute clearly prohibits the use of any engine in moving interstate commerce not equipped with a power driving wheel brake, and the use of any car not equipped with automatic couplers, under a penalty of $100 for each offense; and it just as plainly omits to forbid, under that or any penalty, the use of any car which is not equipped with a power driving wheel brake, and the use of any engine that is not equipped with automatic couplers. This striking omission to express any intention to prohibit the use of engines unequipped with automatic couplers raises the legal presumption that no such intention existed, and prohibits the courts from importing such a purpose into the act, and enacting provisions to give it effect. The familiar rule that the expression of one thing is the exclusion of others points to the same conclusion. Section 2 of the act does not declare that it shall be unlawful to use any engine or car not equipped with automatic couplers, but that it shall be unlawful only to use any car lacking this equipment. This clear and concise definition of the unlawful act is a cogent and persuasive argument against the contention that the use without couplers of locomotives, hand cars, or other means of conducting interstate traffic, was made a misdemeanor by this act. Where the statute enumerates the persons, things, or acts affected by it, there is an implied exclusion of all others. Suth. St. Const. § 227. And when the title of this statute and its first section are again read; when it is perceived that it was not from inattention, thoughtlessness, or forgetfulness; that it was not because locomotives were overlooked or out of mind, but that it was advisedly and after careful consideration of the equipment which they should have, that Congress forbade the use of cars alone without automatic couplers; when it is seen that the title of the act is to compel common carriers to "equip their cars with automatic couplers . . . and their locomotives with driving wheel brakes"; that the first section makes it unlawful to use locomotives not equipped with such brakes, and the second section declares it to be illegal to use cars without automatic couplers,—the argument becomes unanswerable and conclusive.

Again, this act of Congress changes the common law. Before its enactment, servants coupling cars used in interstate commerce without automatic couplers assumed the risk and danger of that employment, and carriers were not liable for injuries which the employés suffered in the discharge of this duty. Since its passage the employés no longer assume this risk, and, if they are free from contributory negligence, they may recover for the damages they sustain in this work. A statute which thus changes the common law must be strictly construed. The common or the general law is not further abrogated by such a statute than the clear import of its language necessarily requires. Shaw v. Railroad Co., 101 U.S. 557, 565, 25 L.Ed. 892; Fitzgerald v. Quann, 109 N.Y. 441, 445, 17 N.E. 354; Brown v. Barry, 3 Dall. 365, 367, 1 L.Ed. 638. The language of this statute does not require the abrogation of the common law that the servant assumes the risk of coupling a locomotive without automatic couplers with a car which is provided with them.

Moreover, this is a penal statute, and it may not be so broadened by judicial construction as to make it cover and permit the punishment of an act which is not denounced by the fair import of its terms. The acts which this statute declares to be unlawful, and for the commission of which it imposes a penalty, were lawful before its enactment, and their performance subjected to no penalty or liability. It makes that unlawful which was lawful before its passage, and it imposes a penalty for its performance. Nor is this penalty a mere forfeiture for the benefit of the party aggrieved or injured. It is a penalty prescribed by the statute, and recoverable by the government. It is, therefore, under every definition of the term, a penal statute. The act which lies at the foundation of this suit—the use of a locomotive which was not equipped with a Miller hook to turn a car which was duly equipped with automatic couplers—was therefore unlawful or lawful as it was or was not forbidden by this statute. That act has been done. When it was done it was neither forbidden nor declared to be unlawful by the express terms of this law. There is no language in it which makes it unlawful to use in interstate commerce a locomotive engine which is not equipped with automatic couplers. The argument of counsel for the plaintiff is, however, that it falls within the mischief which congress was seeking to remedy, and hence it should be construed to make this act unlawful because it falls within the mischief which congress was seeking to remedy, and hence it should be presumed that the legislative body intended to denounce this act as much as that which it forbade by the terms of the law. An ex post facto statute which would make such an innocent act a crime would be violative of the basic principles of Anglo-Saxon jurisprudence. An ex post facto construction which has the same effect is equally abhorrent to the sense of justice and of reason. The mischief at which a statute was leveled, and the fact that other acts which it does not denounce are within the mischief, and of equal atrocity with those which it forbids, do not raise the presumption that the legislative body which enacted it had the intention, which the law does not express, to prohibit the performance of the acts which it does not forbid. Nor will they warrant a construction which imports into the statute such a prohibition. The intention of the legislature and the meaning of a penal statute must be found in the language actually used, interpreted according to its fair and usual meaning, and not in the evils which it was intended to remedy, nor in the assumed secret intention of the lawmakers to accomplish that which they did not express. [Citation.] The decision and opinion of the Supreme Court in U.S. v. Harris, 177 U.S. 305, 309, 20 S.Ct. 609, 44 L.Ed. 780, is persuasive—nay, it is decisive—in the case before us. The question there presented was analogous to that here in issue. It was whether Congress intended to include receivers managing a railroad among those who were prohibited from confining cattle, sheep, and other animals in cars more than 28 consecutive hours without unloading them for rest, water, and feeding, under "An act to prevent cruelty to animals while in transit by railroad or other means of transportation," approved March 3, 1873, and published in the Revised Statutes as sections 4386, 4387, 4388, and 4389. This statute forbids the confinement of stock in cars by any railroad company engaged in interstate commerce more than 28 consecutive hours, and prescribes a penalty of $500 for a violation of its provisions. The plain purpose of the act was to prohibit the confinement of stock while in transit for an unreasonable length of time. The confinement of cattle by receivers operating a railroad was as injurious as their confinement by a railroad company, and the argument for the United States was that, as such acts committed by receivers were plainly within the mischief Congress was seeking to remedy, the conclusion should be that it intended to prohibit receivers, as well as railroad companies, from the commission of the forbidden acts, and hence that receivers were subject to the provisions of the law. The Supreme Court conceded that the confinement of stock in transit was within the mischief that Congress sought to remedy. But it held that as the act did not, by its terms, forbid such acts when committed by receivers, it could not presume the intention of Congress to do so, and import such a provision into the plain terms of the law. Mr. Justice Shiras, who delivered the unanimous opinion of the court, said:

> "Giving all proper force to the contention of the counsel for the government, that there has been some relaxation on the part of the courts in applying the rule of strict construction to such statutes, it still remains that the intention of a penal statute must be found in the language actually used, interpreted according to its fair and obvious meaning. It is not permitted to courts, in this class of cases, to attribute inadvertence or oversight to the legislature when enumerating the classes of persons who are subjected to a penal enactment, nor to depart from the settled meaning of words or phrases in order to bring persons not named or distinctly described within the supposed purpose of the statute."

He cited with approval the decision of the Supreme Court in Sarlls v. United States, 152 U.S. 570, 575, 14 S.Ct. 720, 38 L.Ed. 556, to the effect that lager beer was not included within the meaning of the term "spirituous liquors" in the penal statute found in section 2139 of the Revised Statutes, and closed the discussion with the following quotation from the opinion of Chief Justice Marshall in United States v. Wiltberger, 5 Wheat. 76, 5 L.Ed. 37:

> "The rule that penal statutes are to be construed strictly is perhaps not much less old than construction itself. It is founded on the tenderness of the law for the rights of individuals, and on the plain principle that the power of punishment is vested in the legislative, and not in the judicial, department. It is the legislature, not the court, which is to define a crime and ordain its punishment. It is said that, notwithstanding this rule, the intention of the lawmaker must govern in the construction of penal as well as other statutes. But this is not a new, independent rule, which subverts the old. It is a modification of the ancient maxim, and amounts to this: that, though penal statutes are to be construed strictly, they are not to be construed so strictly as to defeat the obvious intention of the legislature. The maxim is not to be applied so as to narrow the words of the statute, to the exclusion of cases which those words, in their ordinary acceptation, or in that sense in which the legislature ordinarily used them, would comprehend. The intention of the legislature is to be collected from the words they employ. Where there is no ambiguity in the words, there is no room for construction. The case must be a strong one, indeed, which

would justify a court in departing from the plain meaning of words,—especially in a penal act,—in search of an intention which the words themselves did not suggest. To determine that a case is within the intention of a statute, its language must authorize us to say so. It would be dangerous, indeed, to carry the principle that a case which is within the reason or mischief of a statute is within its provisions, so far as to punish a crime not enumerated in the statute, because it is of equal atrocity or of a kindred character with those which are enumerated. If this principle has ever been recognized in expounding criminal law, it has been in cases of considerable irritation, which it would be unsafe to consider as precedents forming a general rule in other cases."

The act of March 2, 1893, is a penal statute, and it changes the common law. It makes that unlawful which was innocent before its enactment, and imposes a penalty, recoverable by the government. Its terms are plain and free from doubt, and its meaning is clear. It declares that it is unlawful for a common carrier to use in interstate commerce a car which is not equipped with automatic couplers, and it omits to declare that it is illegal for a common carrier to use a locomotive that is not so equipped. As Congress expressed in this statute no intention to forbid the use of locomotives which were not provided with automatic couplers, the legal presumption is that it had no such intention, and provisions to import such an intention into the law and to effectuate it may not be lawfully enacted by judicial construction. The statute does not make it unlawful to use locomotives that are not equipped with automatic couplers in interstate commerce, and it did not modify the rule of the common law under which the plaintiff assumed the known risk of coupling such an engine to the dining car.

There are other considerations which lead to the same result. If we are in error in the conclusion already expressed, and if the word "car," in the second section of this statute, means locomotive, still this case does not fall under the law, (1) because both the locomotive and the dining car were equipped with automatic couplers; and (2) because at the time of the accident they were not "used in moving interstate traffic."

For the reasons which have been stated, this statute may not be lawfully extended by judicial construction beyond the fair meaning of its language. There is nothing in it which requires a common carrier engaged in interstate commerce to have every car on its railroad equipped with the same kind of coupling, or which requires it to have every car equipped with a coupler which will couple automatically with every other coupler with which it may be brought into contact in the usual course of business upon a great transcontinental system of railroads. If the lawmakers had intended to require such an equipment, it would have been easy for them to have said so, and the fact that they made no such requirement raises the legal presumption that they intended to make none. Nor is the reason for their omission to do so far to seek or difficult to perceive. There are several kinds or makes of practical and efficient automatic couplers. Some railroad companies use one kind; others have adopted other kinds. Couplers of each kind will couple automatically with others of the same kind or construction. But some couplers will not couple automatically with couplers of different construction. Railroad companies engaged in interstate commerce are required to haul over their roads cars equipped with all these couplers. They cannot relieve themselves from this obligation or renounce this public duty for the simple reason that their cars or locomotives are not equipped with automatic couplers which will couple with those with which the cars of other roads are provided, and which will couple with equal facility with those of their kind. These facts and this situation were patent to the congress when it enacted this statute. It must have known the impracticability of providing every car with as many different couplers as it might meet upon a great system of railroads, and it made no such requirement. It doubtless knew the monopoly it would create by requiring every railroad company to use the same coupler, and it did not create this monopoly. The prohibition of the statute goes no farther than to bar the handling of a car "not equipped with couplers coupling automatically by impact and which can be uncoupled without the necessity of men going between the ends of the car." It does not bar the handling and use of a car which will couple automatically with couplers of its kind because it will not also couple automatically with couplers of all kinds, and it would be an unwarrantable extension of the terms of this law to import into it a provision to this effect. A car equipped with practical and efficient automatic couplers, such as the Janney couplers or the Miller hooks, which will couple automatically with those of their kind, fully and literally complies with the terms of the law, although these couplers will not couple automatically with automatic couplers of all kinds or constructions. The dining car and the locomotive were both so equipped. Each was provided with an automatic coupler which would couple with those of its kind, as provided by the statute, although they would not couple with each other. Each was accordingly equipped as the statute directs, and the defendant was guilty of no violation of it by their use.

Again, the statute declares it to be unlawful for a carrier "to haul or permit to be hauled or used on its line any car used in moving interstate traffic not equipped," etc. It is not, then, unlawful, under this statute, for a carrier to haul a car not so equipped which is either used in intrastate traffic solely, or which is not used in any traffic at all. It would be no violation of the statute for a carrier to haul an empty car not used to move any interstate traffic from one end of its railroad to the other. It would be no violation of the law for it to haul such a car in its yards, on its side track, to put it into its trains, to move it in any manner it chose. It is only when a car is "used in moving interstate traffic" that it becomes unlawful to haul it unless it is equipped as the statute prescribes. On the day of this accident the dining car in this case was standing empty on the side track. The defendant drew it to a turntable, turned it, and placed it back upon the side track. The accident occurred during the performance of this act. The car was vacant when it went to the turntable, and vacant when it returned. It moved no traffic on its way. How could it be said to have been "used in moving interstate traffic" either while it was standing on the side track, or while it was going to and returning from the turntable? . . .

[In a part of the opinion omitted here, the court argues that its conclusion that the dining car was not "used in moving interstate traffic" is dictated not only by rules of construction earlier referred to, but by limitations on the power of Congress.]

The fact that such cars have been or will be so used does not constitute their use in moving interstate traffic, because the prohibition is not of the hauling of cars that have been or will be used in such traffic, but only of those used in moving that traffic. . . . Neither the empty dining car standing upon the side track, nor the freight engine which was used to turn it at the little station in Utah, was then used in moving interstate traffic, within the meaning of this statute, and this case did not fall within the provisions of this law.

The judgment below must accordingly be affirmed, and it is so ordered.

■ THAYER, CIRCUIT JUDGE[, concurring in part and concurring in the judgment]. I am unable to concur in the conclusion, announced by the majority of the court, that the act of Congress of March 2, 1893 (27 Stat. 531, c. 196), does not require locomotive engines to be equipped with automatic couplers; and I am equally unable to concur in the other conclusion announced by my associates that the dining car in question at the time of the accident was not engaged or being used in moving interstate traffic.

In my judgment, it is a very technical interpretation of the provisions of the act in question, and one which is neither in accord with its spirit nor with the obvious purpose of the lawmaker, to say that Congress did not intend to require engines to be equipped with automatic couplers. The statute is remedial in its nature; it was passed for the protection of human life; and there was certainly as much, if not greater, need that engines should be equipped to couple automatically, as that ordinary cars should be so equipped, since engines have occasion to make couplings more frequently. In my opinion, the true view is that engines are included by the words "any car," as used in the second section of the act. The word "car" is generic, and may well be held to comprehend a locomotive or any other similiar [sic] vehicle which moves on wheels; and especially should it be so held in a case like the one now in hand, where no satisfactory reason has been assigned or can be given which would probably have influenced Congress to permit locomotives to be used without automatic coupling appliances.

I am also of opinion that, within the fair intent and import of the act, the dining car in question at the time of the accident was being hauled or used in interstate traffic. The reasoning by which a contrary conclusion is reached seems to me to be altogether too refined and unsatisfactory to be of any practical value. It was a car which at the time was employed in no other service than to furnish meals to passengers between Ogden and San Francisco. It had not been taken out of that service, even for repairs or for any other use, when the accident occurred, but was engaged therein to the same extent that it would have been if it had been hauled through to Ogden, and if the accident had there occurred while it was being turned to make the return trip to San Francisco. The cars composing a train which is regularly employed in interstate traffic ought to be regarded as used in that traffic while the train is being made up with a view to an immediate departure on an interstate journey as well as after the journey has actually begun. I accordingly dissent from the conclusion of the majority of the court on this point.

While I dissent on the foregoing propositions, I concur in the other view which is expressed in the opinion of the majority, to the effect that the case discloses no substantial violation of the provisions of the act of Congress, because both the engine and the dining car were equipped with automatic coupling appliances. In this respect the case discloses a compliance with the law, and the ordinary rule governing the liability of the defendant company should be applied. The difficulty was that the car and engine were equipped with couplers of a different pattern, which would not couple, for that reason, without a link. Janney couplers and Miller couplers are in common use on the leading railroads of the country, and Congress did not see fit to command the use of either style of automatic coupler to the exclusion of the other, while it must have foreseen that, owing to the manner in which cars were ordinarily handled and exchanged, it would sometimes happen, as in the case at bar, that cars having different styles of automatic couplers would necessarily be brought in contact in the same train. It made no express provision for such an emergency, but declared generally that, after a certain date, cars should be provided with couplers coupling automatically. The engine and dining car were so equipped in the present instance, and there was no such violation of the provisions of the statute as should render the defendant company liable to the plaintiff by virtue of the provisions contained in the eighth section of the act. In other words, the plaintiff assumed the risk of making the coupling in the course of which he sustained the injury. On this ground I concur in the order affirming the judgment below.

Johnson v. Southern Pacific Co.

Supreme Court of the United States, 1904.
196 U.S. 1, 25 S.Ct. 158, 49 L.Ed. 363.

Error and Certiorari to the Circuit Court of Appeals for the Eighth Circuit.

■ Statement by MR. CHIEF JUSTICE FULLER:

Johnson brought this action in the district court of the first judicial district of Utah against the Southern Pacific Company to recover damages for injuries received while employed by that company as a brakeman. The case was removed to the circuit court of the United States for the district of Utah by defendant on the ground of diversity of citizenship.

The facts were briefly these: August 5, 1900, Johnson was acting as head brakeman on a freight train of the Southern Pacific Company, which was making its regular trip between San Francisco, California, and Ogden, Utah. On reaching the town of Promontory, Utah, Johnson was directed to uncouple the engine from the train and couple it to a dining car, belonging to the company, which was standing on a side track, for the purpose of turning the car around preparatory to its being picked up and put on the next westbound passenger train. The engine and the dining car were equipped, respectively, with the Janney coupler and the Miller hook, so called, which would not couple together automatically by impact, and it was, therefore, necessary for Johnson, and he was ordered, to go between the engine and the dining car, to accomplish the coupling. In so doing Johnson's hand was caught between the engine bumper and the dining car bumper, and crushed, which necessitated amputation of the hand above the wrist.

On the trial of the case, defendant, after plaintiff had rested, moved the court to instruct the jury to find in its favor, which motion was granted, and the jury found a verdict accordingly, on which judgment was entered. Plaintiff carried the case to the circuit court of appeals for the eighth circuit, and the judgment was affirmed. [54 C.C.A. 508, 117 Fed. 462.]

■ MR. CHIEF JUSTICE FULLER delivered the [unanimous] opinion of the court:

. . . The plaintiff claimed that he was relieved of assumption of risk under common-law rules by the act of Congress of March 2, 1893 (27 Stat. at L. 531, chap. 196, U.S.Comp.Stat.1901, p. 3174), entitled "An Act to Promote the Safety of Employees and Travelers upon Railroads by Compelling Common Carriers Engaged in Interstate Commerce to Equip their Cars with Automatic Couplers and Continuous Brakes and their Locomotives with Driving-Wheel Brakes, and for Other Purposes."

The issues involved questions deemed of such general importance that the government was permitted to file a brief and be heard at the bar.

The act of 1893 provided: [see *supra*]

The circuit court of appeals held, in substance, Sanborn, J., delivering the opinion and Lochren, J., concurring, that the locomotive and car were both equipped as required by the act, as the one had a power driving-wheel brake and the other a coupler; that § 2 did not apply to locomotives; that at the time of the accident the dining car was not "used in moving interstate traffic;" and, moreover, that the locomotive, as well as the dining car, was furnished with an automatic coupler, so that each was equipped as the statute required if § 2 applied to both. Thayer, J., concurred in the judgment on the latter ground, but was of opinion that locomotives were included by the words "any car" in the 2d section, and that the dining car was being "used in moving interstate traffic."

We are unable to accept these conclusions, notwithstanding the able opinion of the majority, as they appear to us to be inconsistent with the plain intention of Congress, to defeat the object of the legislation, and to be arrived at by an inadmissible narrowness of construction.

The intention of Congress, declared in the preamble and in §§ 1 and 2 of the act, was "to promote the safety of employees and travelers upon railroads by compelling common carriers engaged in interstate commerce to equip their cars with automatic couplers and continuous brakes and their locomotives with driving-wheel brakes," those brakes to be accompanied with "appliances for operating the train-brake system;" and every car to be "equipped with couplers coupling automatically by impact, and which can be uncoupled without the necessity of men going between the ends of the cars," whereby the danger and risk consequent on the existing system was averted as far as possible.

The present case is that of an injured employee, and involves the application of the act in respect of automatic couplers, the preliminary question being whether locomotives are required to be equipped with such couplers. And it is not to be successfully denied that they are so required if the words "any car" of the 2d section were intended to embrace, and do embrace, locomotives. But it is said that this cannot be so because locomotives were elsewhere, in terms, required to be equipped with power driving-wheel brakes, and that the rule that the expression of one thing excludes another applies. That, however, is a question of intention, and as there was special reason for requiring locomotives to be equipped with power driving-wheel brakes, if it were also necessary that locomotives should be equipped with automatic couplers, and the word "car" would cover locomotives, then the intention to limit the equipment of locomotives to power driving-wheel brakes, because they were separately mentioned, could not be imputed. Now it was as necessary for the safety of employees in coupling and uncoupling that locomotives should be equipped with automatic couplers as it was that freight and passenger and dining cars should be; perhaps more so, as Judge Thayer suggests, "since engines have occasion to make couplings more frequently."

And manifestly the word "car" was used in its generic sense. There is nothing to indicate that any particular kind of car was meant. Tested by context, subject-matter, and object, "any car" meant all kinds of cars running on the rails, including locomotives. And this view is supported by the dictionary definitions and by many judicial decisions, some of them having been rendered in construction of this act. [Citations.]

The result is that if the locomotive in question was not equipped with automatic couplers, the company failed to comply with the provisions of the act. It appears, however, that this locomotive was in fact equipped with automatic couplers, as well as the dining car; but that the couplers on each, which were of different types, would not couple with each other automatically, by impact, so as to render it unnecessary for men to go between the cars to couple and uncouple.

Nevertheless, the circuit court of appeals was of opinion that it would be an unwarrantable extension of the terms of the law to hold that where the couplers would couple automatically with couplers of their own kind, the couplers must so couple with couplers of different kinds. But we think that what the act plainly forbade was the use of cars which could not be coupled together automatically by impact, by means of the couplers actually used on the cars to be coupled. The object was to protect the lives and limbs of railroad employees by rendering it unnecessary for a man operating the couplers to go between the ends of the cars; and that object would be defeated, not necessarily by the use of automatic couplers of different kinds, but if those different kinds would not automatically couple with each other. The point was that the railroad companies should be compelled, respectively, to adopt devices, whatever they were, which would act so far uniformly as to eliminate the danger consequent on men going between the cars.

If the language used were open to construction, we are constrained to say that the construction put upon the act by the circuit court of appeals was altogether too narrow.

This strictness was thought to be required because the common-law rule as to the assumption of risk was changed by the act, and because the act was penal.

The dogma as to the strict construction of statutes in derogation of the common law only amounts to the recognition of a presumption against an intention to change existing law; and as there is no doubt of that intention here, the extent of the application of the change demands at least no more rigorous construction than would be applied to penal laws. And, as Chief Justice Parker remarked, conceding that statutes in derogation of the common law are to be construed strictly, "They are also to be construed sensibly, and with a view to the object aimed at by the legislature." Gibson v. Jenney, 15 Mass. 205.

The primary object of the act was to promote the public welfare by securing the safety of employees and travelers; and it was in that aspect remedial; while for violations a penalty of $100, recoverable in a civil action, was provided for, and in that aspect it was penal. But the design to give relief was more dominant than to inflict punishment, and the act might well be held to fall within the rule applicable to statutes to prevent fraud upon the revenue, and for the collection of customs,—that rule not requiring absolute strictness of construction. [Citations.]

Moreover, it is settled that "though penal laws are to be construed strictly, yet the intention of the legislature must govern in the construction of penal as well as other statutes; and they are not to be construed so strictly as to defeat the obvious intention of the legislature." [Citation.] . . .

Tested by these principles, we think the view of the circuit court of appeals, which limits the 2d section to merely providing automatic couplers, does not give due effect to the words "coupling automatically by impact, and which can be uncoupled without the necessity of men going between the cars," and cannot be sustained.

We dismiss, as without merit, the suggestion which has been made, that the words "without the necessity of men going between the ends of the cars," which are the test of compliance with § 2, apply only to the act of uncoupling. The phrase literally covers both coupling and uncoupling; and if read, as it should be, with a comma after the word "uncoupled," this becomes entirely clear. [Citations.]

The risk in coupling and uncoupling was the evil sought to be remedied, and that risk was to be obviated by the use of couplers actually coupling automatically. True, no particular design was required, but, whatever the devices used, they were to be effectively interchangeable. Congress was not paltering in a double sense. And its intention is found "in the language actually used, interpreted according to its fair and obvious meaning." United States v. Harris, 177 U.S. 309, 44 L.Ed. 782, 20 Sup.Ct.Rep. 609.

That this was the scope of the statute is confirmed by the circumstances surrounding its enactment, as exhibited in public documents to which we are at liberty to refer. [Citations.]

President Harrison, in his annual messages of 1889, 1890, 1891, and 1892, earnestly urged upon Congress the necessity of legislation to obviate and reduce the loss of life and the injuries due to the prevailing method of coupling and braking. In his first message he said: "It is competent, I think, for Congress to require uniformity in the construction of cars used in interstate commerce, and the use of improved safety appliances upon such trains. Time will be necessary to make the needed changes, but an earnest and intelligent beginning should be made at once. It is a reproach to our civilization that any class of American workmen should, in the pursuit of a necessary and useful vocation, be subjected to a peril of life and limb as great as that of a soldier in time of war."

And he reiterated his recommendation in succeeding messages, saying in that for 1892: "Statistics furnished by the Interstate Commerce Commission show that during the year ending June 30, 1891, there were forty-seven different styles of car couplers reported to be in use, and that during the same period there [were] 2,660 employees killed and 26,140 injured. Nearly 16 per cent of the deaths occurred in the coupling and uncoupling of cars, and over 36 per cent of the injuries had the same origin."

The Senate report of the first session of the Fifty-second Congress (No. 1049) and the House report of the same session (No. 1678) set out the numerous and increasing casualties due to coupling, the demand for protection, and the necessity of automatic couplers, coupling interchangeably. The difficulties in the case were fully expounded and the result reached to require an automatic coupling by impact so as to render it unnecessary for men to go between the cars; while no particular device or type was adopted, the railroad companies being left free to work out the details for themselves, ample time being given for that purpose. The law gave five years, and that was enlarged, by the Interstate Commerce Commission as authorized by law, two years, and subsequently seven months, making seven years and seven months in all.

The diligence of counsel has called our attention to changes made in the bill in the course of its passage, and to the debates in the Senate on the report of its committee. 24 Cong.Rec., pt. 2, pp. 1246, 1273 et seq. These demonstrate that the difficulty as to interchangeability was fully in the mind of Congress, and was assumed to be met by the language which was used. The essential degree of uniformity was secured by providing that the couplings must couple automatically by impact without the necessity of men going between the ends of the cars.

In the present case the couplings would not work together; Johnson was obliged to go between the cars; and the law was not complied with.

March 2, 1903, 32 Stat. 943, c. 976, an act in amendment of the act of 1893 was approved, which provided, among other things, that the provisions and requirements of the former act "shall be held to apply to common carriers by railroads in the Territories and the District of Columbia and shall apply in all cases, whether or not the couplers brought together are of the same kind, make, or type;" and "shall be held to apply to all trains, locomotives, tenders, cars, and similar vehicles used on any railroad engaged in interstate commerce."

This act was to take effect September first, nineteen hundred and three, and nothing in it was to be held or construed to relieve any common carrier "from any of the provisions, powers, duties, liabilities, or requirements" of the act of 1893, all of which should apply except as specifically amended.

As we have no doubt of the meaning of the prior law, the subsequent legislation cannot be regarded as intended to operate to destroy it. Indeed, the latter act is affirmative, and declaratory, and, in effect, only construed and applied the former act. [Citations.] This legislative recognition of the scope of the prior law fortifies and does not weaken the conclusion at which we have arrived.

Another ground on which the decision of the circuit court of appeals was rested remains to be noticed. That court held by a majority that, as the dining car was empty and had not actually entered upon its trip, it was not used in moving interstate traffic, and hence was not within the act. The dining car had been constantly used for several years to furnish meals to passengers between San Francisco and Ogden, and for no other purpose. On the day of the accident the eastbound train was so late that it was found that the car could not reach Ogden in time to return on the next westbound train according to intention, and it was therefore dropped off at Promontory, to be picked up by that train as it came along that evening. . . .

Confessedly this dining car was under the control of Congress while in the act of making its interstate journey, and in our judgment it was equally so when waiting for the train to be made up for the next trip. It was being regularly used in the movement of interstate traffic, and so within the law.

Finally, it is argued that Johnson was guilty of such contributory negligence as to defeat recovery, and that, therefore, the judgment should be affirmed. But the circuit court of appeals did not consider this question, nor apparently did the circuit court, and we do not feel constrained to inquire whether it could have been open under § 8, or, if so, whether it should have been left to the jury, under proper instructions.

The judgment of the Circuit Court of Appeals is reversed; the judgment of the Circuit Court is also reversed, and the cause remanded to that court with instructions to set [aside] the verdict, and award a new trial.

NOTES AND QUESTIONS

1. While *Johnson* arose at the beginning of the twentieth century, the same statutory provisions at issue in *Johnson* continue to demand judicial construction. Consider the following more recent decision:

Porter v. Bangor & Aroostook Railroad Co., 75 F.3d 70 (1st Cir. 1996)

■ ALDRICH, SENIOR CIRCUIT JUDGE.

Mark J. Porter, an experienced brakeman employed by defendant Bangor & Aroostook Railroad Co., injured his back on October 1, 1992, while adjusting a rusty car coupler device that had previously failed to couple automatically with another car. He seeks recovery under the Federal Safety Appliance Act

(FSAA), 45 U.S.C. § 2,¹ a statute that has been ruled to impose liability without fault, San Antonio & Aransas Pass Railway Company v. Wagner, 241 U.S. 476, 36 S.Ct. 626, 60 L.Ed. 1110 (1916), when a violation contributed in any degree to an employee's injuries. Carter v. Atlantic & St. Andrews Bay Ry. Co., 338 U.S. 430, 434–35, 70 S.Ct. 226, 94 L.Ed. 236 (1949). . . . In response to special questions the jury found that defendant had violated the FSAA but that the failure was not a cause of plaintiff's injury. . . . After denial of plaintiff's motion for new trial . . . , the court entered judgment for defendant. Plaintiff appeals. We affirm.

Plaintiff . . . faces the substantial obstacle of a jury finding of no causal connection between the violation and the injury. Recognizing this burden, he takes the bull by the horns and argues that, the violation and injury having been established, the jury not merely should have found, but was required to find a causal connection between them as matter of law.

Plaintiff's contention takes two forms. First, he says the jury's finding that defendant violated the FSAA means that the coupling equipment was defective. Thus plaintiff strained his back working on defective coupler equipment; hence he was within the statute. We do not agree. There is nothing especially dangerous in coupling devices themselves, the statutory reach is the coupling maneuver. As the Court said in the early case of Johnson v. Southern Pacific Co., 196 U.S. 1, 19, 25 S.Ct. 158, 49 L.Ed. 363 (1904), "The risk in coupling and uncoupling was the evil sought to be remedied. . . . " Although plaintiff speaks about having to go between the ends of the cars, it was not for coupling, but in preparation for coupling. One must go behind, viz., between the cars, to align the drawbars before commencing the coupling operation.² If, as here, the cars are safely separated and not in motion, readying is not coupling, and does not involve the special coupling risks. What could be the reason, or purpose, for requiring special protection for this isolated activity? It is true that other circuits appear to have read the FSAA more broadly, see Clark v. Kentucky & Indiana Terminal Railroad, 728 F.2d 307 (6th Cir.1984) (collecting cases), but they give no answer to our question. We can think of none. Plaintiff had no FSAA case.

In light of the prior decision, *Johnson,* is the First Circuit's analysis persuasive? Is the court's distinction between going between railroad cars in order to couple them, and going between the cars in order to *prepare* to couple them, a convincing interpretation of the statutory language? Of the statute's "intent"?

2.   Note that the previous question asked if, *in light of a prior decision,* a subsequent court (bound by the prior court's authority) correctly interpreted the statute. While many different individuals and entities may engage in

---

¹ "It shall be unlawful for any common carrier engaged in interstate commerce by railroad to haul or permit to be hauled or used on its line any car . . . not equipped with couplers coupling automatically by impact, and which can be uncoupled without the necessity of men going between the ends of the cars." 45 U.S.C. § 2 (1893) (repealed 1994) (current version at 49 U.S.C. § 20302).

² Plaintiff himself testified that the drawbars can swing, and must sometimes be lined up in order to meet, a procedure he performed routinely every day. See Goedel v. Norfolk & Western Railway Co., 13 F.3d 807, 809 (4th Cir.1994).

statutory interpretation, the *authoritative* interpreters of statutes are almost always courts. (For the interpretations of administrative agencies, see *infra,* Section III.F, and for other audiences, see *infra,* subsection III.D.3.) As a result, many of the concepts you learned in Part II (Analysis and Synthesis of Judicial Decisions) continue to apply, even for the interpretation of statutes. For example, under the doctrine of precedent, when a court has interpreted a statute, it and dependent lower courts are bound by that interpretation. Hence, should a case like *Johnson* arise in a federal district court after the Supreme Court's decision, the judge would not be free to rule that the statute tolerates equipment of cars with automatic couplers that do not in fact couple automatically to each other. By the same token, distinguishing cases on their facts—another technique with which you became familiar in the common-law context—remains a tool in analyzing whether a prior judicial interpretation of a statute determines the case at hand. Thus, the First Circuit was able to rule that *Johnson* did not control the application of the FSAA to brakeman Porter, because *Johnson* involved an injury sustained in the act of coupling; by contrast, Porter was hurt not while coupling railroad cars, but merely while preparing to engage in the act of coupling railroad cars.

The materials in later subsections of this Part will afford you further opportunity to consider statutory interpretation in the context of prior judicial decisions (see *infra* subsection III.G.2).

3. For another controversy involving application of the Federal Safety Appliance Act to an accident involving misaligned drawbars, as well as a pictorial catalogue of automatic couplers, see Goedel v. Norfolk & Western Railway Co., 13 F.3d 807 (4th Cir.1994).

3. CANONS OF STATUTORY CONSTRUCTION

Both the Eighth Circuit and the Supreme Court in *Johnson* invoked a variety of maxims to aid their interpretation of the Railway Safety Appliance Act. Sometimes these principles, known as "canons of construction"—which often take the form of maxims, or even Latin phrases—appear to be opposed. For example, the canon favoring narrow interpretation of a "penal" statute and the canon counseling expansive interpretation of a "remedial" statute are both canons that are brought to bear on a statute designed to remedy a problem by imposing sanctions on those who violate the new norm. Sometimes different courts appear to apply the *same* canon of construction, yet reach different conclusions.

How helpful *are* canons of construction? What is their relationship to statutory text? Should we assume that legislatures enact statutes against the backdrop of the canons, and thus take into account, or are at least aware of, the interpretive lenses through which judges will study the statutory language? Is there an accepted repertory of canons?* Is

---

* Professors William Eskridge and Philip Frickey have catalogued canons of construction extracted from Supreme Court decisions from the 1986 through 1993 Terms. Their illuminating listing is set out in *Appendix: The Rehnquist Court's Canons of Statutory Construction,* in WILLIAM N. ESKRIDGE, JR., PHILIP P. FRICKEY AND ELIZABETH GARRETT, LEGISLATION AND

there an accepted hierarchy of canons? Do we need an answer to both of those questions before we can attribute to a legislature an understanding or an expectation of how courts will interpret the language it enacts? Does it make any difference whether canons of construction are implicitly part of the legislative package, or instead are imposed by judges as a reasonable or "ordinary" way of understanding language or resolving legal ambiguity? In the latter event, are canons any more reliable or useful than other extratextual aids to interpretation? Consider the Harvard Law School Dean John Manning's discussion of the role of canons of construction:

> Karl Llewellyn largely persuaded two generations of academics that the canons of construction were not to be taken seriously. His point was simple: The canons are indeterminate, and judges use them to justify reasoning by other means. . . . [But] a large and growing number of academics (and academics-turned-judges) now believe in the utility of canons of construction. . . . Modern textualists, who tend to be formalist in orientation, understandably favor the use of canons, particularly the traditional linguistic canons. Justice Scalia, for instance, argue[d] that many such canons are "so commonsensical that, were [they] not couched in Latin, you would find it hard to believe that anyone could criticize them." And Judge Easterbrook, a formalist with a law and economics twist, defends canons "as off-the-rack provisions that spare legislators the costs of anticipating all possible interpretive problems and legislating solutions for them." . . . [T]hese scholars . . . have sought to revive . . . the idea that a system of established rules of construction might make the process of statutory interpretation more predictable, effective, and even legitimate.

> This intellectual development raises two questions. First, why have canons of construction recently gone from laughingstock to the subject of serious academic inquiry? And why do textualists and pragmatists, who think so differently about most questions of statutory interpretation, now share enthusiasm for the once maligned idea of such canons of construction? . . . Although he is not usually identified with this trend, Llewellyn's view of the canons nicely complemented an emerging scholarly consensus that, contrary to prior realist scholarship, judges could meaningfully resolve textual ambiguity by consulting the legislature's intent or purpose, to be derived in no small part from legislative history. Conversely, his impact began to wane in the 1980s, when influential textualist and pragmatist scholars revived (for quite different reasons) broader realist

STATUTORY INTERPRETATION, 375–83 (Foundation Press, Concepts and Insights series, 2000). More recently, Justice Antonin Scalia and lexicographer Bryan Garner produced a comprehensive compendium of canons in their treatise, *Reading Law*. See ANTONIN SCALIA & BRYAN GARNER, READING LAW: THE INTERPRETATION OF LEGAL TEXTS (2012).

claims about the inaccessibility and unreliability of legislative intent and purpose as organizing principles in statutory construction. . . .

In economists' terms, canons of construction and intent or purpose are substitutes, rather than complements. . . . Textualists believe that the statutory text will often be determinate and decisive, and that intent or purpose derived from the legislative history are unreliable guides for resolving statutory doubts. They want clearly established background rules of construction to guide legislators and interpreters in decoding textual commands. Pragmatists have less faith in the statutory text, but also question whether intent and purpose can effectively address its deficiencies. They favor the rationalization and harmonization of rules of construction to provide judges with guidelines for addressing indeterminacy and for doing so in ways that promote socially and institutionally beneficial outcomes. . . . In short, the canons' revival may be the flip side of a growing perception that the early realists were correct in arguing that it is hard to get inside "Congress's mind."

John F. Manning, *Legal Realism & the Canons' Revival*, 5 Green Bag 283, 283–85 (2002).

Canons of construction generally fall into two broad categories: (a) "linguistic" canons, which purport to explain how meaning follows from prevailing linguistic usage; and (b) "substantive" canons, which purport to set out legal rules or first principles for arriving at a legal meaning of a statutory provision. While linguistic canons chiefly aid in identifying the reasonable reader's understanding of the statutory term or phrase in question, the application of many linguistic canons will also depend on claims or assumptions about the legislative drafters' intentions. By contrast, substantive canons often yield statutory meanings that may conflict with either the drafters' seeming intended meaning or the reasonable reader's understanding. Some examples of each:

a. EXAMPLES OF LINGUISTIC CANONS

Ejusdem Generis: This linguistic canon, named for the Latin phrase meaning "of the same kind," instructs that "[w]here general words follow specific words in a statutory enumeration, the general words are construed to embrace only objects similar in nature to those objects enumerated by the preceding specific words." Circuit City Stores, Inc. v. Adams, 532 U.S. 105, 114–15 (2001). In *Circuit City Stores*, for instance, the Court interpreted a portion of the Federal Arbitration Act (FAA) that excludes from the FAA's coverage "contracts of employment of seamen, railroad employees, or any other class of workers engaged in foreign or interstate commerce." 9 U.S.C. § 1. In deciding whether this exclusion applied to *all* workers engaged in foreign and interstate commerce, or only to those workers engaged in the transportation industry, a majority of the Supreme Court drew on the *ejusdem generis* canon to conclude that the inclusion of "seamen" and "railroad employees"—workers engaged in transportation industries—narrowed the meaning of the term "other class of workers" to those workers who are also engaged in transportation industries. Whether this canon should have dispositive effect is often open to debate; as the dissent in *Circuit City Stores* cautioned, "Like many interpretive canons, . . . *ejusdem generis* is a fallback, and if there are good reasons not to apply it, it is [to be] put aside." *Id.* at 138 (Stevens, J., dissenting).

Expressio Unius est Exclusio Alterius: This linguistic canon, named for the Latin phrase meaning "the explicit mention of one (thing) is the exclusion of another," provides that "when the items expressed are members of an 'associated group or series,' [the interpreter may] infer[ ] that items not mentioned were excluded by deliberate choice, not inadvertence." Barnhart v. Peabody Coal Co., 537 U.S. 149, 168 (2003). Although a linguistic canon grounded in the reasonable reader's understanding of the text of the statute, the application of *expressio unius* may be limited to circumstances in which its application conforms to evidence of the legislative drafters' intent. For example in *Barnhart*, and more recently in *Marx v. General Revenue Corp.*, the U.S. Supreme Court noted that the "*expressio unius* canon does not apply 'unless it is fair to suppose that Congress considered the unnamed possibility and meant to say no to it.'" 568 U.S. 371, 381 (2013) (quoting *Barnhart*, 537 U.S. at 168).

Whether such a supposition is "fair" will often depend on other evidence of the drafters' intended meaning or purpose in enacting the statute, including whether there is evidence they "considered the unnamed possibility." Recall, for example, that in *Johnson v. Southern Pacific Co.*, *supra*, the Eighth Circuit and the Supreme Court reached opposite conclusions about whether the absence of an *express* requirement for the use of automatic couplers shed light on whether the statute as a whole required their use. Consider the degree to which different views about the relevance of the statute's broad purpose and the drafters' specific intent influenced the courts' conflicting intuitions about the application of *expressio unius*.

Rule Against Superfluities: Also known as the "surplusage canon" or the "antiredundancy canon," this rule reflects the judicial assumption, as articulated in *Bailey v. United States*, *infra*, that when a legislative body uses multiple terms to modify a noun, or sets out multiple action verbs that trigger liability or culpability, "Congress use[d] [different] terms because it intended each term to have a particular, nonsuperfluous meaning." 516 U.S. 137, 146 (1995). That is, where two competing interpretations of a term or phrase are plausible, but one interpretation would render its meaning redundant or "mere surplusage" in light of other provisions in the same statute, the surplusage canon instructs the interpreter to select the meaning that would avoid the redundancy. As with many other linguistic canons, the U.S. Supreme Court has added the proviso that "our hesitancy to construe statutes to render language superfluous does not require us to avoid surplusage at all costs. It is appropriate to tolerate a degree of surplusage rather than adopt a textually dubious construction that threatens to render the entire provision a nullity." United States v. Atl. Research Corp., 551 U.S. 128, 137 (2007).

The surplusage canon's legitimacy rests in no small part on the assumption that legislators (and their aides) aspire to avoid redundancy in drafting. However, when Professors Abbe Gluck and Lisa Schultz Bressman surveyed congressional drafters, they reported that redundancy is often not only inevitable, but *intentional*:

> . . . [Drafters] pointed out that the political interests of the audience often demand redundancy. They told us, for example, that "sometimes politically for compromise they must include certain words in the statute—that senator, that constituent, that lobbyist wants to see that word"; similarly, they said that "sometimes the lists are in there to satisfy groups, certain phrases are needed to satisfy political interests and they might overlap" or that "sometimes you have it in there because someone had to see their phrase in the bill to get it passed."

> Common sense tells us that, despite the popularity of this rule with judges, there is likely to be redundancy, especially in exceedingly long statutes. (We have seen no evidence, however, that judges take the length of statutes into account when applying the rule.) But what respondents told us was different from that common-sense assumption: namely, that even in short statutes—indeed, even within single sections of statutes—that terms are often purposefully redundant to satisfy audiences other than courts. . . .

Abbe R. Gluck & Lisa Schultz Bressman, *Statutory Interpretation from the Inside: An Empirical Study of Congressional Drafting, Delegation, and the Canons: Part I*, 65 Stan. L. Rev. 901 (2013).

Last Antecedent Rule: This linguistic canon instructs that where a statutory provision "include[s] a list of terms or phrases followed by a limiting clause, the limiting clause or phrase should ordinarily be read as modifying only the noun or phrase that it immediately follows." Lockhart v. United States, 136 S.Ct. 958, 962 (2016) (citation omitted). In *Lockhart*, for example, the majority concluded that in a list of prior convictions "related to aggravated sexual assault, sexual abuse, or abusive sexual conduct *involving a minor or ward*," the modifier "involving a minor or ward" applied only to the last antecedent—a prior conviction for abusive sexual conduct. *Id.* at 963–64. However, structural or contextual evidence may "rebut the last antecedent inference." *Id.* at 962.

Series-Qualifier Canon: The series-qualifier canon yields the opposite inference of the last antecedent rule. This canon holds that in circumstances where the modifying clause appears at the end of a *single, integrated list*, "the exact opposite is usually true: . . . the modifying phrase refers alike to each of the list's terms." *Lockhart*, 136 S.Ct. at 970 (Kagan, J., dissenting). Whether a list can be said to be a "single, integrated list" that calls for the series-qualifier canon, or simply "a list of terms or phrases" that calls for the last antecedent rule, is not always clear. In *Lockhart*, the majority applied the last antecedent rule to reach one meaning, while the dissent applied the series-qualifier canon to yield the other meaning. (One could view the disagreement in *Lockhart* as a tailor-made example of Professor Llewelyn's skepticism that the canons of construction do much more than provide a plausible basis for confirming the interpreter's pre-existing interpretive inclinations.)

b.   EXAMPLES OF SUBSTANTIVE CANONS

Rule of Lenity: This substantive canon instructs that "when there are two rational readings of a criminal statute, one harsher than the other, [the interpreter is] to choose the harsher only when [the legislature] has spoken in clear and definite language." McNally v. United States, 483 U.S. 350, 359–60 (1987). The lenity rule has an esteemed normative basis: as articulated by the dissent in *Muscarello v. United States*, *infra*, "[t]his policy embodies the instinctive distaste against men languishing in prison unless the lawmaker has clearly said they should." 524 U.S. at 150 (Ginsburg, J., dissenting) (citation omitted). This rule does not purport to reveal the conduct that the legislative drafters *intended* to prohibit, nor what the drafters *thought* their language would convey, but instead provides a rule-of-law basis for deciding between "two rational readings" of a statutory provision. In this way, the rule of lenity functions as a kind of tie-breaker in circumstances where two reasonable readers of a criminal statute could reach opposite conclusions as to the meaning of the prohibition at issue.

While judges seem to be in near-unanimous agreement that the rule applies in at least some circumstances, they often disagree vigorously about *when* it should apply. The lenity rule's application depends in large part on (a) the degree of ambiguity necessary for it to trigger; and (b) whether the interpreter must exhaust all other methods of interpretation before triggering it. For example, the majority in *Muscarello* bluntly rejected the rule's application because "[t]he simple existence of some statutory ambiguity . . . is not sufficient to warrant application of that rule, for most statutes are ambiguous to some degree." *Id.* at 138. What degree of ambiguity is necessary? One scholar has suggested that the Supreme Court has provided at least *four* arguably meaningfully distinct articulations of the degree of ambiguity necessary to trigger the rule: (1) where it is not "unambiguously correct" that the statute penalizes the defendant's conduct; (2) where "reasonable doubt" remains after exhausting other methods; (3) where a court is left with "no more than a guess" as to the provision's meaning; and (4) where "grievous ambiguity" remains.*

Clear Notice Rule: An analog to the rule of lenity for the interpretation of civil statutes, the clear notice rule applies to the interpretation of statutes in which Congress sets particular terms for the disbursal of federal money to the States. The U.S. Supreme Court has said, as in *Arlington Central School District Board of Education v. Murphy, infra,* that "when Congress attaches conditions to a State's acceptance of federal funds, the conditions must be set out 'unambiguously.'" 548 U.S. 291, 296 (2006) (citation omitted). Like its criminal-law cousin the rule of lenity, the clear notice rule's application risks begging the question of the extent or degree of ambiguity that the interpreter may tolerate before employing the rule as a tie-breaker. The clear notice rule thus raises questions about the relative clarity one may expect from legislative drafters—after all, as the *Muscarello* majority noted, many statutes are ambiguous *to some degree.* The clear notice rule may also raise questions of audience: if the statute must furnish clear notice to state officials, what level of sophistication should those officials be presumed to have such that the provision in question is clear *to them*? The same level of sophistication as judges? As laypeople? As state officials with more expertise than laypeople but less expertise than judges?

Presumption Against Statutory Retroactivity: This longstanding presumption instructs courts to "decline[ ] to give retroactive effect to statutes burdening private rights unless Congress had made clear its intent." Landgraf v. USI Film Prod., 511 U.S. 244, 270 (1994). As noted in *Landgraf,* this presumption "has consistently been explained by reference to the unfairness of imposing new burdens on persons after the fact," particularly where new provisions affect contractual or property rights, "matters in which predictability and stability are of prime importance." *Id.* at 270–71. As you will see in *Martin v. Hadix, Vartelas v. Holder,* and *Noreen Hulteen v. AT&T, infra,* this presumption often requires identifying the "retroactivity event" or action whose legal consequences would change unfavorably for the actor were the statute to apply to acts completed before the statute's enactment. As with the clear notice rule, this presumption also raises difficult questions about precisely how "clear" Congress must be.

Constitutional Avoidance: Among the Supreme Court's preferred substantive canons, the canon of constitutional avoidance instructs that "[w]hen the validity of an act of the Congress is drawn in question, and even if a serious doubt of constitutionality is raised, it is a cardinal principle that this Court will first ascertain whether a construction of the statute is fairly possible by which the question may be avoided." Crowell

---

* See Daniel Ortner, *The Merciful Corpus: The Rule of Lenity, Ambiguity and Corpus Linguistics,* 25 B.U. Pub. Int. L.J. 101, 103–04 (2016).

v. Benson, 285 U.S. 22, 62 (1932). Like other substantive canons, this presumption serves an important rule-of-law function—in this case, reducing the likelihood that the Court will be required to reach a constitutional question in order to resolve the statutory interpretation problem. As with other substantive canons, it is almost universally accepted in theory; controversy arises concerning when and how it should apply. In recent years, some members of the Court have argued that the constitutional avoidance canon should "come[ ] into play only when, after the application of ordinary textual analysis, the statute is found to be susceptible of more than one construction. In the absence of more than one plausible construction, the canon simply has no application." Jennings v. Rodriguez, 138 S.Ct. 830, 842 (2018) (citations omitted). A skeptic might contend that this articulation of the rule simply begs the question of deciding whether multiple "plausible" constructions are possible.

Presumption Against Ineffectiveness: This canon stands for the principle that an interpretation of a statutory provision that would hinder the manifest purpose of the statute should be avoided where the statute is amenable to an alternative interpretation. Or, as articulated by the Texas Supreme Court, "It is recognized that a statute is to be construed with reference to its manifest object, and if the language is susceptible of two constructions, one of which will carry out and the other defeat such manifest object, it should receive the former construction." Citizens Bank of Bryan v. First State Bank, Hearne, 580 S.W.2d 344, 348 (Tex. 1979). In his academic writing, Justice Antonin Scalia endorsed this canon on the following grounds: "This canon follows inevitably from the facts that (1) interpretation always depends on context, (2) context always includes evident purpose, and (3) evident purpose always includes effectiveness." Antonin Scalia & Bryan Garner, Reading Law: The Interpretation of Legal Texts 63 (2012). As discussed in subsection III.C.2, *infra*, a close cousin of this canon is the anti-self-destruction principle, which cautions against a literal interpretation of a provision that would cause the statutory scheme to self-destruct.

Absurd Results Canon: As articulated in *Holy Trinity Church, infra*, the absurd results canon recognizes that "frequently words of general meaning are used in a statute, words broad enough to include an act in question, and yet a consideration of . . . the absurd results which follow from giving such broad meaning to the words, makes it unreasonable to believe that the legislator intended to include the particular act." 143 U.S. at 459. To some degree, this canon depends on the (perhaps questionable) assumption that legislative drafters always seek to avoid the possibility of producing results that some might consider to be "absurd." The absurdity doctrine is sometimes justified on the basis that a criminal prohibition whose interpretation yields an absurd result is unlikely to have provided sufficient notice to members of the general public. Of course, whether a given result is "absurd" may itself be a matter of vigorous disagreement. E.g., Public Citizen v. U.S. Dep't of Justice, 491 U.S. 440, 470–74 (1989) (Kennedy, J., concurring in the judgment).

QUESTION

The Eighth Circuit and Supreme Court opinions in *Johnson* employ a variety of canons both "linguistic" and "substantive." They also invoke other sources of statutory meaning (see the "Typology" of approaches, *supra*). Go back through the *Johnson* decisions to identify where in the opinions the various canons appear. What other kinds of statutory interpretation methods and sources figure in each opinion? What can you infer about the consequences of resorting to some methods or sources, as opposed to others? Do you find some interpretive devices more persuasive than others? Why?

B. TWO PREVAILING APPROACHES TO INTERPRETATION: PURPOSIVISM AND TEXTUALISM

John Manning endorses application of the canons of statutory construction as a means to illuminate ambiguous text without recourse to the extratextual aid of legislative history. Dictionaries offer another preferred "textualist" interpretative aid. (Several of the decisions you will soon encounter in the casebook make varying use of the dictionary.) As the *Johnson* case itself illustrates, however, strict textualism risks producing robotic results that rankle common sense (at least the common sense that some judges intuit, and that they, perhaps wishfully, attribute to legislators).

Of course, not every case presents such a stark disagreement between the seeming purpose of the statute and the strict construction of the relevant statutory text as in *Johnson*. Nevertheless, these two approaches, respectively known as purposivism and textualism, are the prevailing theories of contemporary statutory interpretation. As Dean Manning has helpfully explained, debates about purposivism and textualism operate on two levels: the first concerns a disagreement about the methods judges should prioritize when interpreting statutes, and the second concerns a disagreement about the role common-law judges should play in a constitutional system of legislative supremacy in which the legislature, not the judiciary, makes the law:

> For a not inconsiderable part of our history, the Supreme Court held that the "letter" (text) of a statute must yield to its "spirit" (purpose) when the two conflicted. Traditionally, the Court's "purposivism" rested on the following intuitions: In our constitutional system, federal courts act as faithful agents of Congress; accordingly, they must ascertain and enforce Congress's commands as accurately as possible. Statutes are active instruments of policy, enacted to serve some background purpose or goal. Ordinarily, a statutory text will adequately reflect its intended purpose. Sometimes, however, the text of a particular provision will seem incongruous with the statutory purpose reflected in various contextual cues—such as the overall tenor of the statute, patterns of policy judgments made in related legislation, the "evil" that inspired Congress to act, or express statements found in the legislative history. Since legislators act under the constraints of limited resources, bounded foresight, and inexact human language, unanticipated problems of fit have long been viewed as unavoidable. It is said that just as individuals sometimes inadvertently misstate their intended meaning, so too does Congress. Accordingly, the Court long assumed that when the clear import of a statute's text deviated sharply from its purpose, (1) Congress must have expressed its true intentions imprecisely, and (2) a judicial faithful agent could properly adjust the enacted text to capture what Congress would have intended had it expressly confronted the apparent mismatch between text and purpose.

> Near the close of the twentieth century, however, the "new textualism" challenged the prevailing judicial orthodoxy by arguing that the Constitution, properly understood, requires judges to treat the clear import of an enacted text as conclusive, even when the text fits poorly with its apparent background purposes. The textualist critique—which took shape largely in judicial opinions written by Justice Scalia and Judge Easterbrook—initially stressed two related themes: First, textualists emphasized that the statutory text alone has survived the constitutionally prescribed process of bicameralism and presentment. Accordingly, they argued that when a statute is clear in context, purposivist judges disrespect the legislative

process by relying upon unenacted legislative intentions or purposes to alter the meaning of a duly enacted text.

Second, building upon the intent skepticism of the legal realists, the new textualists contended that the purposivist judge's aspiration to identify and rely upon the actual intent of any multimember lawmaking body is fanciful. In brief, textualists have contended that the final wording of a statute may reflect an otherwise unrecorded legislative compromise, one that may—or may not—capture a coherent set of purposes. A statute's precise phrasing depends, moreover, on often untraceable procedural considerations, such as the sequence of alternatives presented (agenda manipulation) or the effect of strategic voting (including logrolling). Given the opacity, complexity, and path dependency of this process, textualists believe that it is unrealistic for judges ever to predict with accuracy what Congress would have "intended" if it had expressly confronted a perceived mismatch between the statutory text and its apparent purpose. In place of traditional conceptions of "actual" legislative intent, modern textualists urge judges to focus on what they consider the more realistic—and objective—measure of how "a skilled, objectively-reasonable user of words" would have understood the statutory text in context.' . . .

The distinction between textualism and purposivism is not, as is often assumed, cut-and-dried. Properly understood, textualism is not and could not be defined either by a strict preference for enacted text over unenacted context, or by a wholesale rejection of the utility of purpose. Because the meaning of language depends on the way a linguistic community uses words and phrases in context, textualists recognize that meaning can never be found exclusively within the enacted text. This feature of textualism, moreover, goes well beyond the often subconscious process of reading words in context in order to pinpoint the "ordinary" meaning of a word that may mean several things in common parlance. Rather, because legal communication often entails the use of specialized conventions, textualists routinely consult unenacted sources of context whose contents might be obscure to the ordinary reader without further inquiry. Moreover, because textualists understand that speakers use language purposively, they recognize that evidence of purpose (if derived from sources other than the legislative history) may also form an appropriate ingredient of the context used to define the text.

Conversely, certain features of purposivism reflect textualist practices and assumptions more deeply than textualists sometimes acknowledge. . . . . [M]any important conceptual similarities were already present in the (now canonical) mid-twentieth-century account of purposivism developed in the Legal Process materials of Professors Hart and Sacks. Although Legal Process purposivists believe that interpretation entails the attribution of purpose, they do not deny that semantic meaning of the text casts light—perhaps the most important light—on the purposes to be attributed. Nor do they deny that, in such a pursuit, the judge should carefully consult the technical conventions that distinctively pertain to legalese. Perhaps most important, much like modern textualists, Hart-and-Sacks-style purposivists recognize that a judge's task, properly conceived, is not to seek actual legislative intent; rather, their method of interpretation poses the objective question of how a hypothetical "reasonable legislator" (as opposed to a real one) would have resolved the problem addressed by the statute. . . .

[Nevertheless, s]ignificant practical and theoretical differences persist between textualists and purposivists. Why? Each side gives priority to different elements of statutory context. Textualists give primacy to the semantic context—evidence about the way a reasonable person conversant with relevant social and linguistic practices would have used the words. Purposivists give precedence to policy context—evidence that goes to the way a reasonable person conversant with the circumstances underlying enactment would suppress the mischief and advance the remedy. This difference accounts for the distinct questions that each methodology poses for the hypothetical reasonable interpreter. As noted, textualists ask how "a skilled, objectively reasonable user of words" would have understood the text, in the circumstances in which it was uttered. Legal Process purposivists ask how "reasonable persons pursuing reasonable purposes reasonably" would have resolved the policy issue addressed by the words.

Ultimately, the justifications for their disparate preferences are rooted in competing understandings of the legislative process as it relates to the constitutional ideal of legislative supremacy. Purposivists in the Legal Process tradition think it unrealistic and arbitrary to suppose that Congress collectively knows or cares about the semantic detail of often complex statutes. For them, enforcing the overarching policy of a statute rather than the minutiae of its semantic detail better serves legislative supremacy while also promoting the independently valuable aims of policy coherence and adaptability of the law to unforeseen circumstances.

Textualists (again, myself included) believe that the purposivist approach disregards the central place of legislative compromise embedded in both the constitutional structure and the corresponding congressional rules of legislative procedure. Textualists contend that once one gives up the idea of ascertaining subjective legislative intent, as Legal Process purposivists do, legislative supremacy is most meaningfully served by attributing to legislators the understanding that a reasonable person conversant with applicable conventions would attach to the enacted text in context. From that starting point, textualists argue that purposivism cannot deal adequately with legislative compromise because semantic detail, in the end, is the only effective means that legislators possess to specify the limits of an agreed-upon legislative bargain. When interpreters disregard clear contextual clues about semantic detail, it becomes surpassingly difficult for legislative actors to agree reliably upon terms that give half a loaf. . . .

John F. Manning, *What Divides Textualists from Purposivists?*, 106 Colum. L. Rev. 70, 71–92 (2006).

The degree of agreement or disagreement among legislators may vary depending on the statute they seek to enact; this, naturally, will influence the degree of specificity of the statutory enactment. To this end, Judge Pierre N. Leval of the U.S. Court of Appeals for the Second Circuit has endeavored to identify the kinds of statutes that properly call for purely textualist interpretations, and those that demand a more wide-ranging and purposivist analysis. In his view, textual ambiguity need not be seen as a shortcoming to be overcome by reference to static text-fillers, whether lexicographic or drawn from legislative history. Rather, ill-defined terms might instead be deemed invitations to judicial elaboration, in a dynamic process of partnership between legislators who design the frame, and judges who fill in the picture.

A View from the Bench

How should these statutes be understood? How far-reaching are the rights they establish? What is the pertinence to them of the old common law decisions? To answer those questions, it is useful to divide statutes into two admittedly oversimplified categories.

1. Micromanager Statutes

One category is what I shall call a *micromanager* statute. In passing a micromanager statute, the legislature undertakes not only to establish policies, but to make the rules that will govern all the questions that will arise in the enforcement of these policies. Such statutes are generally quite lengthy and detailed. The best example of such a statute is probably the Internal Revenue Code. The passage of a micromanager statute may well, depending on the legislature's intent, relegate to the dustbin all prior decisional law in the area, which may be seen as superseded.

It is fashionable in speaking of statutory interpretation to say that the only interpretive source a court should use is a dictionary. That maxim is most appropriate for micromanager statutes, because, at least in theory, the text undertakes to answer all the questions that may arise. Thus, an understanding of the words used in the text of the statute will produce an answer to the problem in litigation.

2.   Delegating Statutes

The other category is what I shall call a *delegating* statute. The legislature states its policy in generalized terms but intentionally delegates to the courts a considerable interpretive role. Delegating statutes can be of two basic types.

a.   *Statutes Adopting Common Law*

At the furthest remove from the micromanager statute is the statute which does nothing more than give statutory recognition to a body of law previously developed by the courts. Such statutes neither establish new rules nor set new policies. They do not change the law, even in the smallest degree. Their sole purpose is a highly respectable one—to place a reference to the particular body of doctrine in statute books so as to enable those searching for law to discover there at least a reference to that body of rules which previously could be found only by a common law search through the volumes of court opinions. Such statutes often express themselves circumspectly. A single word— murder, larceny, embezzlement, for example—may stand for the full complexity of the doctrine's development. Alternatively, the statute may undertake a fairly detailed summary of the law, or of some of its provisions. Regardless, however, of whether the text is detailed or consists of only a vague generalized reference to the body of doctrine, if the intention of the statute was not to make law but to give recognition in statutory form to a previously developed body of court-made law, proper interpretation of the statute demands that it be so understood.

Furthermore, as the enactment of such a statute is not intended to, and should not, alter the future development of doctrine, such a statute preserves in the court the function by which it developed the body of rules newly given statutory recognition. The court's dynamic function, by which it previously created and shaped the law, is not superseded; it continues to operate, notwithstanding that the law is now expressed in statutory form. As new questions arise, the courts' answers to these questions should be derived from the same considerations that governed the development of the doctrine, rather than from the words chosen by the legislature to summarize or represent that doctrine. Those words were not intended as exercises of the legislature's power to create law.

b.   *New Policy*

The second class of *delegating* statute falls somewhere between the micromanager statute and the statute adopting common law. Such a statute, which I shall call a *new policy* statute, is created when the legislature enacts a new policy but does so in vague, imprecise terms. The legislature recognizes that innumerable questions of interpretation will arise as experience unfolds and delegates to the courts the task of answering those questions in the light of experience and the legislative objective for which the statute was passed. A paradigm example is the Sherman Act. Such an enactment has, on the one hand, some similarity to the micromanager statute in that court interpretations should seek to advance the policy enacted by the legislature. In this respect such statutes are quite unlike enactments of common law, as to which the legislature expresses no policy objective other than to give statutory recognition to a court-developed doctrine, so that future court decisions should be guided by the same principles which guided the courts prior to the enactment. On the other hand, statutes of the *new policy* type are similar to common law adopting statutes and unlike micromanager statutes in that they are delegating. Rather than undertaking to answer the problems expected to arise, the legislature refrains from trying to anticipate and solve such problems; it formulates vague policy statements and delegates responsibility to the courts to work out the problems as they arise.

The proposition that courts should approach the task of interpretation armed only with a dictionary is wholly inappropriate to delegating statutes. The words of the statute simply will not provide the answers and were not intended by the legislature to do so. In passing delegating statutes, legislatures recognize that they function together with courts in a law-making partnership, each having its proper role. As to delegating statutes of the new policy type, the legislature relies on the courts, as experience unfolds, to use their good judgment to do the fine-tuning, to establish contours and boundaries to achieve the legislature's objective. The courts' interpretive rulings, of course, are always subject to legislative correction. As to delegating statutes of the type adopting common law, the legislature delegates to the courts the continued exercise of the function they always performed: the continued development of the common law doctrine in the light of the policies that always drove its development, without regard for the particular words chosen by the legislature to summarize the development.

Needless to say, statutes can be and often are hybrids—partially micromanaging while partially delegating, partially preserving a common law tradition while partially superseding it.

Pierre N. Leval, *Trademark: Champion of Free Speech*, 27 Colum. J. L. & The Arts 187, 196–98 (2004).

QUESTIONS

1. Consider the *Johnson* case: Would you call the Federal Railway Safety Appliance Act a "Micromanager" or a "Delegating" statute? Some of both? Which, if any, portions call for development of judge-made standards in tandem with the statutory rules? As you work through the statutory language in the other cases in this Part, consider the extent to which the micromanager/delegating distinction helps you analyze the statute's application to the controversy at hand.

2. Are Dean Manning's and Judge Leval's approaches to statutory interpretation reconcilable? How would a strict textualist interpret a "delegating statute" adopting the common law? One adopting a new policy?

United States v. Church of the Holy Trinity

United States Circuit Court for the Southern District of New York, 1888.
36 Fed. 303, reversed, 143 U.S. 457, 12 S.Ct. 511, 36 L.Ed. 226 (1892).

■ WALLACE, J. This suit is brought to recover a penalty of $1,000 imposed by the act of congress of February 26, 1885, (23 St. at Large, 332,) upon every person or corporation offending against its provisions by knowingly encouraging the migration of any alien into the United States "to perform labor or service of any kind under contract or agreement, express or implied," previously made with such alien. The defendant, a religious corporation, engaged one Warren, an alien residing in England, to come here and take charge of its church as a pastor. The act makes it the duty of the United States district attorney to bring suit to enforce the penalty prescribed. The demurrer interposed to the complaint raises the single question whether such a contract as was made in this case is within the terms of the act. In other words, the question is whether congress intended to prohibit the migration here of an alien who comes pursuant to a contract with a religious society to perform the functions of a minister of the gospel, and to subject to the penalty the religious society making the contract and encouraging the migration of the alien minister. The act is entitled "An act to prohibit the importation and migration of foreigners and aliens under contract or agreement to perform labor in the United States." It was, no doubt, primarily the object of the act to prohibit the introduction of assisted immigrants, brought here under contracts previously made by corporations and capitalists to prepay their passage and obtain their services at low wages for limited periods of time. It was a measure introduced and advocated by the trades union and labor associations, designed to shield the interests represented by such organizations from the effects of the competition in the labor market of foreigners brought here under contracts having a tendency to stimulate immigration and reduce the rates of wages. Except from the language of the statute there is no reason to suppose a contract like the present to be within the evils which the law was designed to suppress; and, indeed, it would not be indulging a violent supposition to assume that no legislative body in this country would have advisedly enacted a law framed so as to cover a case like the present. Nevertheless, where the terms of a statute are plain, unambiguous, and explicit, the courts are not at liberty to go outside of the language to search for a meaning which it does not reasonably bear in the effort to ascertain and give effect to what may be imagined to have been or not to have been the intention of congress. Whenever the will of congress is declared in ample and unequivocal language, that will must be absolutely followed, and it is not admissible to resort to speculations of policy, nor even to the views of members of congress in debate, to find reasons to control or modify the statute. U.S. v. Railroad Co., 91 U.S. 72. If it were permissible to narrow the provisions of the act to correspond with the purport of the title, and restrain its operation to cases in which the alien is assisted to come here under contract "to perform labor," there might be room for interpretation; and the restricted meaning might possibly be given to the word "labor" which signifies the manual work of the laborer, as distinguished from the work of the skilled artisan, or the professional man. But no rule in the construction of statutes is more familiar than the one to the effect that the title cannot be used to extend or restrain positive provisions in the body of the act. In Hadden v. Collector, 5 Wall. 107, it is said: "The title of an act furnishes little aid in the construction of its provisions." The encouragement of migration prohibited by the first section is of aliens under contract or agreement previously made "to perform labor or service of any kind in the United States." The contracts which are declared to be void by the second section are contracts "having reference to the performance of labor or service by any person in the United States" previous to the migration of the alien. The penalty imposed by the third section is imposed on the person or corporation encouraging the migration of the alien under a contract or agreement previously made "to perform labor or service of any kind." No more comprehensive terms could have been employed to include every conceivable kind of labor or avocation, whether of the hand or brain, in the class of prohibited contracts; and, as if to emphasize and make more explicit the intention that the words "labor or service" should not be taken in any restricted sense, they are followed by the words "of any kind." Every kind of industry, and every employment, manual or intellectual, is embraced within the language used. If it were possible to import a narrower meaning than the natural and ordinary one to the language of these sections, the terms of the fifth section would forbid the attempt. That section is a proviso withdrawing from the operation of the act several classes of persons and contracts. Foreigners residing here temporarily, who may engage private secretaries; persons desirous of establishing a new industry not then existing in the United States, who employ skilled workmen therein; domestic servants; and a limited professional class, are thereby exempted from its provisions. The last clause of the proviso is: "Nor shall the provisions of this act apply to professional actors, artists, lecturers, or singers, nor to persons employed strictly as personal or domestic servants." If, without this exemption, the act would apply to this class of persons, because such persons come here under contracts for labor or service, then clearly it must apply to ministers, lawyers, surgeons, architects, and all others who labor in any professional calling. Unless congress supposed the act to apply to the excepted classes, there was no necessity for the proviso. The office of a proviso is generally to restrain an enacting clause, and to except something which would otherwise have been within it. Wayman v. Southard, 10 Wheat. 30; Minis v. U.S., 15 Pet. 423. In the language of the authorities: "A proviso carves special exemptions only out of the enacting clauses." U.S. v. Dickson, 15 Pet. 165; Ryan v. Carter, 93 U.S. 83. Giving effect to this well-settled rule of statutory interpretation, the proviso is equivalent to a declaration that contracts to perform professional services except those of actors, artists, lecturers, or singers, are within the prohibition of the preceding sections.

The argument based upon the fourth section of the act has not been overlooked. That section subjects to fine and imprisonment any master of a vessel who knowingly brings within the United States any alien "laborer, mechanic, or artisan," who has previously entered into any contract to perform labor or service in the United States. This section is wholly independent of the others, and the difference in the persons described may reasonably be referred to an intention to mitigate the severity of the act in its application to masters of vessels. The demurrer is overruled.

Holy Trinity Church v. United States

Supreme Court of the United States, 1892.
143 U.S. 457, 12 S.Ct. 511, 36 L.Ed. 226.

In error to the circuit court of the United States for the southern district of New York.

■ MR. JUSTICE BREWER delivered the [unanimous] opinion of the court.

Plaintiff in error is a corporation duly organized and incorporated as a religious society under the laws of the state of New York. E. Walpole Warren was, prior to September, 1887, an alien residing in England. In that month the plaintiff in error made a contract with him, by which he was to remove to the city of New York, and enter into its service as rector and pastor; and, in pursuance of such contract, Warren did so remove and enter upon such service. It is claimed by the United States that this contract on the part of the plaintiff in error was forbidden by chapter 164, 23 St. p. 332; and an action was commenced to recover the penalty prescribed by that act. The circuit court held that the contract was within the prohibition of the statute, and rendered judgment accordingly, (36 Fed.Rep. 303,) and the single question presented for our determination is whether it erred in that conclusion.

The first section describes the act forbidden, and is in these words:

"Be it enacted by the senate and house of representatives of the United States of America, in congress assembled, that from and after the passage of this act it shall be unlawful for any person, company, partnership, or corporation, in any manner whatsoever, to prepay the transportation, or in any way assist or encourage the importation or migration, of any alien or aliens, any foreigner or foreigners, into the United States, its territories, or the District of Columbia, under contract or agreement, parol or special, express or implied, made previous to the importation or migration of such alien or aliens, foreigner or foreigners, to perform labor or service of any kind in the United States, its territories, or the District of Columbia."

It must be conceded that the act of the corporation is within the letter of this section, for the relation of rector to his church is one of service, and implies labor on the one side with compensation on the other. Not only are the general words "labor" and "service" both used, but also, as it were to guard against any narrow interpretation and emphasize a breadth of meaning, to them is added "of any kind;" and, further, as noticed by the circuit judge in his opinion, the fifth section, which makes specific exceptions, among them professional actors, artists, lecturers, singers, and domestic servants, strengthens the idea that every other kind of labor and service was intended to be reached by the first section. While there is great force to this reasoning, we cannot think congress intended to denounce with penalties a transaction like that in the present case. It is a familiar rule that a thing may be within the letter of the statute and yet not within the statute, because not within its spirit nor within the intention of its makers. This has been often asserted, and the Reports are full of cases illustrating its application. This is not the substitution of the will of the judge for that of the legislator; for frequently words of general meaning are used in a statute, words broad enough to include an act in question, and yet a consideration of the whole legislation, or of the circumstances surrounding its enactment, or of the absurd results which follow from giving such broad meaning to the words, makes it unreasonable to believe that the legislator intended to include the particular act. . . .

In U.S. v. Kirby, 7 Wall. 482, 486, the defendants were indicted for the violation of an act of congress providing "that if any person shall knowingly and willfully obstruct or retard the passage of the mail, or of any driver or carrier, or of any horse or carriage carrying the same, he shall, upon conviction, for every such offense, pay a fine not exceeding one hundred dollars." The specific charge was that the defendants knowingly and willfully retarded the passage of one Farris, a carrier of the mail, while engaged in the performance of his duty, and also in like manner retarded the steam-boat Gen. Buell, at that time engaged in carrying the mail. To this indictment the defendants pleaded specially that Farris had been indicted for murder by a court of competent authority in Kentucky; that a bench-warrant had been issued and placed in the hands of the defendant Kirby, the sheriff of the county, commanding him to arrest Farris, and bring him before the court to answer to the indictment; and that, in obedience to this warrant, he and the other defendants, as his posse, entered upon the steam-boat Gen. Buell and arrested Farris, and used only such force as was necessary to accomplish that arrest. The question as to the sufficiency of this plea was certified to this court, and it was held that the arrest of Farris upon the warrant from the state court was not an obstruction of the mail, or the retarding of the passage of a carrier of the mail, within the meaning of the act. In its opinion the court says: "All laws should receive a sensible construction. General terms should be so limited in their application as not to lead to injustice, oppression, or an absurd consequence. It will always, therefore, be presumed that the legislature intended exceptions to its language which would avoid results of this character. The reason of the law in such cases should prevail over its letter. The common sense of man approves the judgment mentioned by Puffendorf, that the Bolognian law which enacted 'that whoever drew blood in the streets should be punished with the utmost severity,' did not extend to the surgeon who opened the vein of a person that fell down in the street in a fit. The same common sense accepts the ruling, cited by Plowden, that the statute of 1 Edw. II., which enacts that a prisoner who breaks prison shall be guilty of felony, does not extend to a prisoner who breaks out when the prison is on fire, 'for he is not to be hanged because he would not stay to be burnt.' And we think that a like common sense will sanction the ruling we make, that the act of congress which punishes the obstruction or retarding of the passage of the mail, or of its carrier, does not apply to a case of temporary detention of the mail caused by the arrest of the carrier upon an indictment for murder." . . .

Among other things which may be considered in determining the intent of the legislature is the title of the act. We do not mean that it may be used to add to or take from the body of the statute, (Hadden v. Collector, 5 Wall. 107) but it may help to interpret its meaning. In the case of U.S. v. Fisher, 2 Cranch 358, 386, Chief Justice MARSHALL said: "On the influence which the title ought to have in construing the enacting clauses, much has been said, and yet it is not easy to discern the point of difference between the opposing counsel in this respect. Neither party contends that the title of an act can control plain words in the body of the statute; and neither denies that, taken with other parts, it may assist in removing ambiguities. Where the intent is plain, nothing is left to construction. Where the mind labors to discover the design of the legislature, it seizes everything from which aid can be derived; and in such case the title claims a degree of notice, and will have its due share of consideration." . . .

It will be seen that words as general as those used in the first section of this act were by that decision limited, and the intent of congress with respect to the act was gathered partially, at least, from its title. Now, the title of this act is, "An act to prohibit the importation and migration of foreigners and aliens under contract or agreement to perform labor in the United States, its territories, and the District of Columbia." Obviously the thought expressed in this reaches only to the work of the manual laborer, as distinguished from that of the professional man. No one reading such a title would suppose that congress had in its mind any purpose of staying the coming into this country of ministers of the gospel, or, indeed, of any class whose toil is that of the brain. The common understanding of the terms "labor" and "laborers" does not include preaching and preachers, and it is to be assumed that words and phrases are used in their ordinary meaning. So whatever of light is thrown upon the statute by the language of the title indicates an exclusion from its penal provisions of all contracts for the employment of ministers, rectors, and pastors.

Again, another guide to the meaning of a statute is found in the evil which it is designed to remedy; and for this the court properly looks at contemporaneous events, the situation as it existed, and as it was pressed upon the attention of the legislative body. U.S. v. Railroad Co., 91 U.S. 72, 79. The situation which called for this statute was briefly but fully stated by Mr. Justice Brown when, as district judge, he decided the case of U.S. v. Craig, 28 Fed.Rep. 795, 798: "The motives and history of the act are matters of common knowledge. It had become the practice for large capitalists in this country to contract with their agents abroad for the shipment of great numbers of an ignorant and servile class of foreign laborers, under contracts by which the employer agreed, upon the one hand, to prepay their passage, while, upon the other hand, the laborers agreed to work after their arrival for a certain time at a low rate of wages. The effect of this was to break down the labor market, and to reduce other laborers engaged in like occupations to the level of the assisted immigrant. The evil finally became so flagrant that an appeal was made to congress for relief by the passage of the act in question, the design of which was to raise the standard of foreign immigrants, and to discountenance the migration of those who had not sufficient means in their own hands, or those of their friends, to pay their passage."

It appears, also, from the petitions, and in the testimony presented before the committees of congress, that it was this cheap, unskilled labor which was making the trouble, and the influx of which congress sought to prevent. It was never suggested that we had in this country a surplus of brain toilers, and, least of all, that the market for the services of

Christian ministers was depressed by foreign competition. Those were matters to which the attention of congress, or of the people, was not directed. So far, then, as the evil which was sought to be remedied interprets the statute, it also guides to an exclusion of this contract from the penalties of the act.

A singular circumstance, throwing light upon the intent of congress, is found in this extract from the report of the senate committee on education and labor, recommending the passage of the bill: "The general facts and considerations which induce the committee to recommend the passage of this bill are set forth in the report of the committee of the house. The committee report the bill back without amendment, although there are certain features thereof which might well be changed or modified, in the hope that the bill may not fail of passage during the present session. Especially would the committee have otherwise recommended amendments, substituting for the expression, 'labor and service,' whenever it occurs in the body of the bill, the words 'manual labor' or 'manual service,' as sufficiently broad to accomplish the purposes of the bill, and that such amendments would remove objections which a sharp and perhaps unfriendly criticism may urge to the proposed legislation. The committee, however, believing that the bill in its present form will be construed as including only those whose labor or service is manual in character, and being very desirous that the bill become a law before the adjournment, have reported the bill without change." Page 6059, Congressional Record, 48th Cong. And, referring back to the report of the committee of the house, there appears this language: "It seeks to restrain and prohibit the immigration or importation of laborers who would have never seen our shores but for the inducements and allurements of men whose only object is to obtain labor at the lowest possible rate, regardless of the social and material well-being of our own citizens, and regardless of the evil consequences which result to American laborers from such immigration. This class of immigrants care nothing about our institutions, and in many instances never even heard of them. They are men whose passage is paid by the importers. They come here under contract to labor for a certain number of years. They are ignorant of our social condition, and, that they may remain so, they are isolated and prevented from coming into contact with Americans. They are generally from the lowest social stratum, and live upon the coarsest food, and in hovels of a character before unknown to American workmen. They, as a rule, do not become citizens, and are certainly not a desirable acquisition to the body politic. The inevitable tendency of their presence among us is to degrade American labor, and to reduce it to the level of the imported pauper labor." Page 5359, Congressional Record, 48th Cong.

We find, therefore, that the title of the act, the evil which was intended to be remedied, the circumstances surrounding the appeal to congress, the reports of the committee of each house, all concur in affirming that the intent of congress was simply to stay the influx of this cheap, unskilled labor. . . .

The judgment will be reversed, and the case remanded for further proceedings in accordance with this opinion.

NOTES AND QUESTIONS

1. How clear was it that the words of the statute encompassed the services of the Rev. E. Walpole Warren? Consider that, when the contract labor statute was enacted, in 1885, the predominant meaning of the word "labor" was "physical toil," and "service" generally was understood to mean "domestic service," rather than professional services (referred to in the plural). On the other hand, contemporary dictionaries also included broader meanings for these terms. See William N. Eskridge, Jr., *Textualism: The Unknown Ideal?*, 96 Mich. L. Rev. 1509, 1518, 1533 (1998). Does the exemption clause's coverage of "persons employed strictly as personal or domestic servants" suggest what meaning should apply to "service of any kind"?

2. Is it relevant that the meaning of the word "lecturer" has evolved from its 16th-century meaning of "preacher" to its current secular connotation?* If, as the Oxford English Dictionary suggests, both meanings were still current in the late-nineteenth century, how should we interpret the contract labor statute's clause excluding "lecturers" from the statute's coverage? As a general matter, if judges are to consult dictionaries in aid of interpretation, should they not ensure that the dictionary they peruse offers definitions contemporaneous with the statute under scrutiny? Keep these questions in mind as you read *MCI Telecommunications v. AT&T*, and *New Prime Inc. v. Oliveira*, *infra*.

3. For an account of the history of the contract labor statute and the prosecution of the Holy Trinity Church under it, as well as different approaches to the Supreme Court's use of legislative history, *compare* Carol Chomsky, *Unlocking the Mysteries of Holy Trinity: Spirit, Letter, and History in Statutory Interpretation*, 100 Colum. L. Rev. 901 (2000), *with* Adrian Vermeule, *Legislative History and the Limits of Judicial Competence: the Story of Holy Trinity Church*, 50 Stan. L. Rev. 1833 (1998).

4. Contrast the nature of the problem posed for the Court in the principal case with that posed in *United States v. Kirby* (discussed in the *Holy Trinity Church* case *supra*) and consider the result reached in the *Kirby* decision and the quoted justifications offered for that result. What other reasonable justifications, if any, might have been given? What are the implications of *Kirby* for the judicial function in interpretation?

5. Compare Riggs v. Palmer, 115 N.Y. 506, 22 N.E. 188 (1889). In that case, the beneficiary under a will had murdered the testator and then claimed the property pursuant to the will's provisions. The question was whether the beneficiary could have the property in such circumstances. It was

---

* Thanks to Prof. William Eskridge and to Josephine Coakley, Columbia JD 2004, for direction concerning the etymology of the words "lecturer," "lectureship," and "lecture."

acknowledged that the statute regulating the making, proof and effect of wills and the devolution of property did not deal with "murdering heirs." If literally construed, the statute would award the property to the murderer.

The relevant statute provided:

N.Y. Rev. Stat § 3.1.42 (1882): No will in writing, except in the cases herein after mentioned, nor any part thereof, shall be revoked, or altered, otherwise than by some other will in writing, or some other writing of the testator, declaring such revocation or alteration, and executed with the same formalities with which the will itself was required by law to be executed; or unless such will be burnt, torn, cancelled, obliterated or destroyed, with the intent and for the purpose of revoking the same, by the testator himself, or by another person in his presence, by his direction and consent; and when so done by another person, the direction and consent of the testator, and the fact of such injury or destruction, shall be proved by at least two witnesses.

The Court however ruled that the murderer was not entitled to the property. Inter alia, the Court stated:

The purpose of [the statutes concerned] was to enable testators to dispose of their estates to the objects of their bounty at death, and to carry into effect their final wishes legally expressed; and in considering and giving effect to them this purpose must be kept in view. It was the intention of the law-makers that the donees in a will should have the property given to them. But it never could have been their intention that a donee who murdered the testator to make the will operative should have any benefit under it. . . .

What could be more unreasonable than to suppose that it was the legislative intention in the general laws passed for the orderly, peaceable and just devolution of property, that they should have operation in favor of one who murdered his ancestor that he might speedily come into the possession of his estate? Such an intention is inconceivable. We need not, therefore, be much troubled by the general language contained in the laws.

Besides, all laws as well as all contracts may be controlled in their operation and effect by general, fundamental maxims of the common law. No one shall be permitted to profit by his own fraud, or to take advantage of his own wrong, or to found any claim upon his own iniquity, or to acquire property by his own crime. These maxims are dictated by public policy, have their foundation in universal law administered in all civilized countries, and have nowhere been superseded by statutes.

United States v. Marshall

United States Court of Appeals for Seventh Circuit, 1990.
908 F.2d 1312, *aff'd sub nom.* Chapman v. U.S., 500 U.S. 453,
111 S.Ct. 1919, 114 L.Ed.2d 524 (1991).

[Argued In Banc May 30, 1990, before BAUER, CHIEF JUDGE, and
CUMMINGS, WOOD, JR., CUDAHY, POSNER, COFFE, FLAUM, EASTERBROOK,
RIPPLE, MANION, and KANNE, CIRCUIT JUDGES.]

■ EASTERBROOK, CIRCUIT JUDGE.

. . . [W]e must resolve . . . [w]hether 21 U.S.C. § 841(b)(1)(A)(v) and (B)(v),
which set mandatory minimum terms of imprisonment—five years for
selling more than one gram of a "mixture or substance containing a
detectable amount" of LSD, ten years for more than ten grams—exclude
the weight of a carrier medium. . . .

I

According to the Sentencing Commission, the LSD in an average
dose weighs 0.05 milligrams. Twenty thousand pure doses are a gram.
But 0.05 mg is almost invisible, so LSD is distributed to retail customers
in a carrier. Pure LSD is dissolved in a solvent such as alcohol and
sprayed on paper or gelatin; alternatively the paper may be dipped in the
solution. After the solvent evaporates, the paper or gel is cut into one-
dose squares and sold by the square. Users swallow the squares or may
drop them into a beverage, releasing the drug. Although the gelatin and
paper are light, they weigh much more than the drug. Marshall's 11,751
doses weighed 113.32 grams; the LSD accounted for only 670.72 mg of
this, not enough to activate the five-year mandatory minimum sentence,
let alone the ten-year minimum. The ten sheets of blotter paper carrying
the 1,000 doses Chapman and confederates sold weighed 5.7 grams; the
LSD in the paper did not approach the one-gram threshold for a
mandatory minimum sentence. This disparity between the weight of the
pure LSD and the weight of LSD-plus-carrier underlies the defendants'
arguments.

A

If the carrier counts in the weight of the "mixture or substance
containing a detectable amount" of LSD, some odd things may happen.
Weight in the hands of distributors may exceed that of manufacturers
and wholesalers. Big fish then could receive paltry sentences or small
fish draconian ones. Someone who sold 19,999 doses of pure LSD (at 0.05
mg per dose) would escape the five-year mandatory minimum of
§ 841(b)(1)(B)(v) and be covered by § 841(b)(1)(C), which lacks a
minimum term and has a maximum of "only" 20 years. Someone who sold
a single hit of LSD dissolved in a tumbler of orange juice could be exposed
to a ten-year mandatory minimum. Retailers could fall in or out of the
mandatory terms depending not on the number of doses but on the
medium: sugar cubes weigh more than paper, which weighs more than
gelatin. One way to eliminate the possibility of such consequences is to

say that the carrier is not a "mixture or substance containing a detectable amount" of the drug. Defendants ask us to do this. . . .

It is not possible to construe the words of § 841 to make the penalty turn on the net weight of the drug rather than the gross weight of carrier and drug. The statute speaks of "mixture or substance containing a detectable amount" of a drug. "Detectable amount" is the opposite of "pure"; the point of the statute is that the "mixture" is not to be converted to an equivalent amount of pure drug. . . .

[The 7th Circuit *en banc* majority concluded that despite these arguably anomalous results, the LSD carrier came within the statutory term "mixture or substance containing a detectable amount."]

■ POSNER, CIRCUIT JUDGE, joined by BAUER, CHIEF JUDGE, and WOOD, JR., and CUDAHY, CIRCUIT JUDGES, dissenting.

. . . LSD is a potentially dangerous drug, especially for psychotics (whom it can drive to suicide). Hoffman, LSD: My Problem Child 67–71 (1983). But many things are dangerous for psychotics. No one believes that LSD is a more dangerous drug than heroin or cocaine (particularly crack cocaine). The general view is that it is *much* less dangerous. Cox, *et al.,* Drugs and Drug Abuse: A Reference Text 313–15 (1983). There is no indication that Congress believes it to be more dangerous, or more difficult to control. The heavy sentences that the law commands for minor traffickers in LSD are the inadvertent result of the interaction among a statutory procedure for measuring weight, adopted without understanding how LSD is sold; a decision to specify harsh mandatory minimum sentences for drug traffickers, based on the weight of the drug sold; and a decision (gratuitous and unreflective, as far as I can see) by the framers of the Guidelines to key punishment to the statutory measure of weight, thereby amplifying Congress's initial error and ensuring that the big dealer who makes or ships the pure drug will indeed receive a shorter sentence than the small dealer who handles the stuff in its street form. As the wholesale value of LSD may be as little as 35 cents a dose (Report 1988: The Supply of Illicit Drugs to the United States 52 (National Narcotics Intelligence Consumers Comm.1989)), a seller of five sugar cubes could be subject to a mandatory minimum prison term of ten years for selling $2 worth of illegal drugs. Dean received six years (no parole, remember) for selling $73 worth. The irrationality is quite bad enough if we confine our attention to LSD sold on blotter paper, since the weight of blotter paper varies considerably, making punishment turn on a factor that has no relation to the dosages or market values of LSD.

Well, what if anything can we judges do about this mess? The answer lies in the shadow of a jurisprudential disagreement that is not less important by virtue of being unavowed by most judges. It is the disagreement between the severely positivistic view that the content of law is exhausted in clear, explicit, and definite enactments by or under express delegation from legislatures, and the natural lawyer's or legal pragmatist's view that the practice of interpretation and the general terms of the Constitution (such as "equal protection of the laws") authorize judges to enrich positive law with the moral values and practical concerns of civilized society. Judges who in other respects have seemed quite similar, such as Holmes and Cardozo, have taken opposite sides of this issue. Neither approach is entirely satisfactory. The first buys political neutrality and a type of objectivity at the price of substantive injustice, while the second buys justice in the individual case at the price of considerable uncertainty and, not infrequently, judicial willfulness. It is no wonder that our legal system oscillates between the approaches. The positivist view, applied unflinchingly to this case, commands the affirmance of prison sentences that are exceptionally harsh by the standards of the modern Western world, dictated by an accidental, unintended scheme of punishment nevertheless implied by the words (taken one by one) of the relevant enactments. The natural law or pragmatist view leads to a freer interpretation, one influenced by norms of equal treatment; and let us explore the interpretive possibilities here. One is to interpret "mixture or substance containing a detectable amount of [LSD]" to exclude the carrier medium—the blotter paper, sugar or gelatin cubes, and orange juice or other beverage. That is the course we rejected in *United States v. Rose, supra,* 881 F.2d at 388, as have the other circuits. I wrote *Rose,* but I am no longer confident that its literal interpretation of the statute, under which the blotter paper, cubes, etc. are "substances" that "contain" LSD, is inevitable. The blotter paper, etc. are better viewed, I now think, as carriers, like the package in which a kilo of cocaine comes wrapped or the bottle in which a fifth of liquor is sold.

Interpreted to exclude the carrier, the punishment schedule for LSD would make perfectly good sense; it would not warp the statutory design. The comparison with heroin and cocaine is again illuminating. The statute imposes the five-year mandatory minimum sentence on anyone who sells a substance or mixture containing a hundred grams of heroin, equal to 10,000 to 20,000 doses. One gram of pure LSD, which also would trigger the five-year minimum, yields 20,000 doses. The comparable figures for cocaine are 3250 to 50,000 doses, placing LSD in about the middle. So Congress may have wanted to base punishment for the sale of LSD on the weight of the pure drug after all, using one and ten grams of the pure drug to trigger the five-year and ten-year minima (and corresponding maxima—twenty years and forty years). This interpretation leaves "substance or mixture containing" without a referent, so far as LSD is concerned. But we must remember that Congress used the identical term in each subsection that specifies the quantity of a drug that subjects the seller to the designated minimum and maximum punishments. In thus automatically including the same term in each subsection, Congress did not necessarily affirm that, for each and every drug covered by the statute, a substance or mixture containing the drug *must* be found. . . .

[The dissent of JUDGE CUMMINGS, joined by CHIEF JUDGE BAUER and CIRCUIT JUDGES WOOD, JR., CUDAHY, and POSNER, has been omitted.]

NOTES

1. In Chapman v. United States, 500 U.S. 453 (1991), the Supreme Court adopted the position of the Seventh Circuit majority in *Marshall* that the mandatory minimum prison term statute should be interpreted to include the weight of the LSD carrier in calculating the weight of the "mixture or substance containing a detectable amount" of the drug.

2. The two broad trends in statutory interpretation that Judge Posner recognizes in *United States v. Marshall* are by no means limited to the construction of criminal statutes. The sequence of decisions in this book, from *Johnson v. Southern Pacific* to *Holy Trinity Church* and onward, also demonstrate courts' "jurisprudential disagreement" over the interpretation of statutes.

C. INTERPRETING A STATUTE "ON ITS FACE"

The Statute on its Face

1. THE "PLAIN MEANING RULE"

Cases like *Holy Trinity Church* concern tensions between a literal interpretation of the statutory text, which could lead to potentially undesirable results seemingly at odds with the purpose behind the statute's enactment, and a purposivist interpretation of the statute, which would avoid the undesirable result, but at the expense of the statute's seemingly literal meaning. For many statutory interpretation controversies, however, the distinction between the literal meaning and the legislative intent are not so clear.

In many such cases, the statutory interpreter must decide which sources and methods of interpretation to prioritize, and the reasons for doing so. The predominant judicial approach to statutory interpretation has long sought guidance from extrinsic as well intrinsic sources of interpretation. For example, in the course of interpreting the ordinary meanings of the statutory words at issue, courts often consult extratextual aids like legislative history and inquire into the social context that gave rise to the legislation. By contrast, some of the older cases, and a strain of more recent decisions in the mode of "the new textualism" popularized by jurists like Justice Scalia, reject the resort to extratextual aids *on principle* in circumstances where they perceive that the "plain meaning" of the words alone suffices to ascertain the statutory meaning. According to this view, for all intents and purposes, the legislature "meant what [it] said, and said what [it] meant."* (And—as some of the decisions imply—if the legislature did not mean what it said, it is for the legislature, and not the courts, to correct its misstatement.)

When courts exclude evidence of statutory purpose because the text itself conveys a plain meaning, they often do so on the basis of the "Plain Meaning Rule." This rule rests on the premise that the meaning of a statutory term is indeed "plain." But plainness may be in the eye of the beholder; what may seem clear to one reader may appear ambiguous to another. The context in which a statement is made, however, can clarify—or change—the meaning. For example, in some parts of the English-speaking world, when people meet, they simply say:

Q.: "How are you?"

A.: "How are you?"

And they will leave it at that. They do not expect an answer. The words, through custom, have lost their plain meaning and are now used as greetings. The same question asked by a physician in an examination room will get a different answer. Once again, custom and context supply the "meaning," as even textualists—per Dean Manning, *supra*—acknowledge.

Context can also fill the gaps in meaning when a statement, taken literally, appears incomplete. Many statements leave much to

---

* Theodor Seuss Geisel (Dr. Seuss), Horton Hatches the Egg (1940).

assumption. For example, if one office-worker asks her co-worker if he has a stapler, it is usually not because the inquirer seeks to compile an inventory of the co-worker's equipment, but because she wishes to borrow the stapler. Moreover, the asker also assumes that the loaned stapler will include staples. To supply an empty stapler would respond literally to the request, but would "clearly" not offer what the borrower sought.

In order to understand a statement, we often need to know its purpose. Consider a sign posted in a classroom: "NO COFFEE." What is this supposed to mean? If a student brings in a sealed can of ground coffee, has she violated the rule indicated by the sign? What if she brings in a cup of tea? What do we know about this rule? Is it intended to keep classrooms clean? If so, one can infer that it prohibits bringing in cups of the coffee beverage. If that is the purpose of the rule, should one infer by extension a prohibition on other beverages? All other beverages? What about other potential sources of classroom untidiness, such as candy bars? Loose notebook paper? Eraser shavings—erasers?

What if the classroom at issue were located in the Macrobiotic Institute of America, an institution whose creed bans artificial stimulants, such as caffeine? Does the prohibition take on a different meaning now? What purpose do you now infer? What meaning follows from it?

* * *

The Plain Meaning Rule has venerable roots, and variable applications. The following oft-cited judicial statement indicates the function and effect of this approach to statutory interpretation:

> The general rule is perfectly well settled that, where a statute is of doubtful meaning and susceptible upon its face of two constructions, the court may look into prior and contemporaneous acts, the reasons which induced the act in question, the mischiefs intended to be remedied, the extraneous circumstances, and the purpose intended to be accomplished by it, to determine its proper construction. But where the act is clear upon its face, and when standing alone it is fairly susceptible of but one construction, that construction must be given to it. * * * The whole doctrine applicable to the subject may be summed up in the single observation that prior acts may be referred to *solve* but not to *create* an ambiguity.

Brown, J., in Hamilton v. Rathbone, 175 U.S. 414 (1899).

In the following case, the majority and dissent disagree on the plainness of the meaning of the term in question. Consider what methods they apply to decide whether the term is plain, as well as what the significance of such a finding is.

Yates v. United States

Supreme Court of the United States, 2015.
574 U.S. 528, 135 S.Ct. 1074, 1919 L.Ed.2d 64.

■ JUSTICE GINSBURG announced the judgment of the Court and delivered an opinion, in which . . . CHIEF JUSTICE [ROBERTS], JUSTICE BREYER, and JUSTICE SOTOMAYOR join.

John Yates, a commercial fisherman, caught undersized red grouper in federal waters in the Gulf of Mexico. To prevent federal authorities from confirming that he had harvested undersized fish, Yates ordered a crew member to toss the suspect catch into the sea. For this offense, he was charged with, and convicted of, violating 18 U.S.C. § 1519, which provides:

> "Whoever knowingly alters, destroys, mutilates, conceals, covers up, falsifies, or makes a false entry in any record, document, or tangible object with the intent to impede, obstruct, or influence the investigation or proper administration of any matter within the jurisdiction of any department or agency of the United States or any case filed under title 11, or in relation to or contemplation of any such matter or case, shall be fined under this title, imprisoned not more than 20 years, or both."

Yates was also indicted and convicted under § 2232(a), which provides:

> "DESTRUCTION OR REMOVAL OF PROPERTY TO PREVENT SEIZURE.—Whoever, before, during, or after any search for or seizure of property by any person authorized to make such search or seizure, knowingly destroys, damages, wastes, disposes of, transfers, or otherwise takes any action, or knowingly attempts to destroy, damage, waste, dispose of, transfer, or otherwise take any action, for the purpose of preventing or impairing the Government's lawful authority to take such property into its custody or control or to continue holding such property under its lawful custody and control, shall be fined under this title or imprisoned not more than 5 years, or both."

Yates does not contest his conviction for violating § 2232(a), but he maintains that fish are not trapped within the term "tangible object," as that term is used in § 1519.

Section 1519 was enacted as part of the Sarbanes-Oxley Act of 2002 [citation], legislation designed to protect investors and restore trust in financial markets following the collapse of Enron Corporation. A fish is no doubt an object that is tangible; fish can be seen, caught, and handled, and a catch, as this case illustrates, is vulnerable to destruction. But it would cut § 1519 loose from its financial-fraud mooring to hold that it encompasses any and all objects, whatever their size or significance, destroyed with obstructive intent. Mindful that in Sarbanes-Oxley,

Congress trained its attention on corporate and accounting deception and cover-ups, we conclude that a matching construction of § 1519 is in order: A tangible object captured by § 1519, we hold, must be one used to record or preserve information.

I

On August 23, 2007, the Miss Katie, a commercial fishing boat, was six days into an expedition in the Gulf of Mexico. . . . Engaged in a routine offshore patrol to inspect both recreational and commercial vessels, Officer John Jones . . . decided to board the Miss Katie to check on the vessel's compliance with fishing rules. . . .

Upon boarding the Miss Katie, Officer Jones noticed three red grouper that appeared to be undersized hanging from a hook on the deck. At the time, federal conservation regulations required immediate release of red grouper less than 20 inches long. Violation of those regulations is a civil offense punishable by a fine or fishing license suspension. [Citation.]

Suspecting that other undersized fish might be on board, Officer Jones proceeded to inspect the ship's catch, setting aside and measuring only fish that appeared to him to be shorter than 20 inches. After separating the fish measuring below 20 inches from the rest of the catch by placing them in wooden crates, Officer Jones directed Yates[, the captain,] to leave the fish, thus segregated, in the crates until the Miss Katie returned to port. . . .

Four days later, after the Miss Katie had docked in Cortez, Florida, Officer Jones measured the fish contained in the wooden crates. This time, however, the measured fish, although still less than 20 inches, slightly exceeded the lengths recorded on board. Jones surmised that the fish brought to port were not the same as those he had detected during his initial inspection. Under questioning, one of the crew members admitted that, at Yates's direction, he had thrown overboard the fish Officer Jones had measured at sea, and that he and Yates had replaced the tossed grouper with fish from the rest of the catch.

. . . On May 5, 2010, [Yates] was indicted for destroying property to prevent a federal seizure, in violation of § 2232 (a), and for destroying, concealing, and covering up undersized fish to impede a federal investigation, in violation of § 1519.[1] By the time of the indictment, the minimum legal length for Gulf red grouper had been lowered from 20 inches to 18 inches. See 50 C.F.R. § 622.37(d)(2)(iv) (effective May 18, 2009). No measured fish in Yates's catch fell below that limit. The record does not reveal what civil penalty, if any, Yates received for his possession of fish undersized under the 2007 regulation. See 16 U.S.C. § 1858(a).

---

[1] Yates was also charged with making a false statement to federal law enforcement officers, in violation of 18 U.S.C. § 1001(a)(2). That charge, on which Yates was acquitted, is not relevant to our analysis.

Yates was tried on the criminal charges in August 2011. . . . For violating § 1519 and § 2232(a), the court sentenced Yates to imprisonment for 30 days, followed by supervised release for three years. For life, he will bear the stigma of having a federal felony conviction. . . .

II

The Sarbanes-Oxley Act, all agree, was prompted by the exposure of Enron's massive accounting fraud and revelations that the company's outside auditor, Arthur Andersen LLP, had systematically destroyed potentially incriminating documents. The Government acknowledges that § 1519 was intended to prohibit, in particular, corporate document-shredding to hide evidence of financial wrongdoing. . . .

In the Government's view, § 1519 extends beyond the principal evil motivating its passage. The words of § 1519, the Government argues, support reading the provision as a general ban on the spoliation of evidence, covering all physical items that might be relevant to any matter under federal investigation.

Yates urges a contextual reading of § 1519, tying "tangible object" to the surrounding words, the placement of the provision within the Sarbanes-Oxley Act, and related provisions enacted at the same time, in particular § 1520 and § 1512(c)(1). Section 1519, he maintains, targets not all manner of evidence, but records, documents, and tangible objects used to preserve them, e.g., computers, servers, and other media on which information is stored.

We agree with Yates and reject the Government's unrestrained reading. "Tangible object" in § 1519, we conclude, is better read to cover only objects one can use to record or preserve information, not all objects in the physical world.

A

The ordinary meaning of an "object" that is "tangible," as stated in dictionary definitions, is "a discrete . . . thing," Webster's Third New International Dictionary 1555 (2002), that "possess[es] physical form," Black's Law Dictionary 1683 (10th ed. 2014). From this premise, the Government concludes that "tangible object," as that term appears in § 1519, covers the waterfront, including fish from the sea.

Whether a statutory term is unambiguous, however, does not turn solely on dictionary definitions of its component words. Rather, "[t]he plainness or ambiguity of statutory language is determined [not only] by reference to the language itself, [but as well by] the specific context in which that language is used, and the broader context of the statute as a whole." *Robinson v. Shell Oil Co.*, 519 U.S. 337, 34 (1997). [Citation.] Ordinarily, a word's usage accords with its dictionary definition. In law as in life, however, the same words, placed in different contexts, sometimes mean different things.

We have several times affirmed that identical language may convey varying content when used in different statutes, sometimes even in different provisions of the same statute. . . .

. . . [A]lthough dictionary definitions of the words "tangible" and "object" bear consideration, they are not dispositive of the meaning of "tangible object" in § 1519.

Supporting a reading of "tangible object," as used in § 1519, in accord with dictionary definitions, the Government points to the appearance of that term in Federal Rule of Criminal Procedure 16. That Rule requires the prosecution to grant a defendant's request to inspect "tangible objects" within the Government's control that have utility for the defense.

Rule 16's reference to "tangible objects" has been interpreted to include any physical evidence. [Citation.] Rule 16 is a discovery rule designed to protect defendants by compelling the prosecution to turn over to the defense evidence material to the charges at issue. In that context, a comprehensive construction of "tangible objects" is fitting. In contrast, § 1519 is a penal provision that refers to "tangible object" not in relation to a request for information relevant to a specific court proceeding, but rather in relation to federal investigations or proceedings of every kind, including those not yet begun. See *Commissioner v. National Carbide Corp.*, 167 F.2d 304, 306 (C.A.2 1948) (Hand, J.) ("words are chameleons, which reflect the color of their environment"). Just as the context of Rule 16 supports giving "tangible object" a meaning as broad as its dictionary definition, the context of § 1519 tugs strongly in favor of a narrower reading.

B

Familiar interpretive guides aid our construction of the words "tangible object" as they appear in § 1519.

We note first § 1519's caption: "Destruction, alteration, or falsification of records in Federal investigations and bankruptcy." That heading conveys no suggestion that the section prohibits spoliation of any and all physical evidence, however remote from records. Neither does the title of the section of the Sarbanes-Oxley Act in which § 1519 was placed, § 802: "Criminal penalties for altering documents." [Citation.] Furthermore, § 1520, the only other provision passed as part of § 802, is titled "Destruction of corporate audit records" and addresses only that specific subset of records and documents. While these headings are not commanding, they supply cues that Congress did not intend "tangible object" in § 1519 to sweep within its reach physical objects of every kind, including things no one would describe as records, documents, or devices closely associated with them. [Citation.] If Congress indeed meant to make § 1519 an all-encompassing ban on the spoliation of evidence, as the dissent believes Congress did, one would have expected a clearer indication of that intent. . . .

The contemporaneous passage of § 1512(c)(1), which was contained in a section of the Sarbanes-Oxley Act discrete from the section embracing § 1519 and § 1520, is also instructive. Section 1512(c)(1) provides:

"(c) Whoever corruptly—

"(1) alters, destroys, mutilates, or conceals a record, document, or other object, or attempts to do so, with the intent to impair the object's integrity or availability for use in an official proceeding

"shall be fined under this title or imprisoned not more than 20 years, or both."

The legislative history reveals that § 1512(c)(1) was drafted and proposed after § 1519. [Citation.] The Government argues, and Yates does not dispute, that § 1512(c)(1)'s reference to "other object" includes any and every physical object. But if § 1519's reference to "tangible object" already included all physical objects, as the Government and the dissent contend, then Congress had no reason to enact § 1512(c)(1): Virtually any act that would violate § 1512(c)(1) no doubt would violate § 1519 as well, for § 1519 applies to "the investigation or proper administration of any matter within the jurisdiction of any department or agency of the United States . . . or in relation to or contemplation of any such matter," not just to "an official proceeding."

The Government acknowledges that, under its reading, § 1519 and § 1512(c)(1) "significantly overlap." [Citation.] Nowhere does the Government explain what independent function § 1512(c)(1) would serve if the Government is right about the sweeping scope of § 1519. We resist a reading of § 1519 that would render superfluous an entire provision passed in proximity as part of the same Act. [Citation.]

The words immediately surrounding "tangible object" in § 1519—"falsifies, or makes a false entry in any record [or] document"—also cabin the contextual meaning of that term. As explained in *Gustafson v. Alloyd Co.*, 513 U.S. 561, 575 (1995), we rely on the principle of *noscitur a sociis*—a word is known by the company it keeps—to "avoid ascribing to one word a meaning so broad that it is inconsistent with its accompanying words, thus giving unintended breadth to the Acts of Congress." [Citation.] . . .

"Tangible object" is the last in a list of terms that begins "any record [or] document." The term is therefore appropriately read to refer, not to any tangible object, but specifically to the subset of tangible objects involving records and documents, i.e., objects used to record or preserve information. [Citation.]

This moderate interpretation of "tangible object" accords with the list of actions § 1519 proscribes. The section applies to anyone who "alters, destroys, mutilates, conceals, covers up, falsifies, or makes a false entry in any record, document, or tangible object" with the requisite obstructive intent. The last two verbs, "falsif[y]" and "mak[e] a false entry in," typically take as grammatical objects records, documents, or things used to record or preserve information, such as logbooks or hard drives. [Citation.] It would be unnatural, for example, to describe a killer's act of wiping his fingerprints from a gun as "falsifying" the murder weapon. But it would not be strange to refer to "falsifying" data stored on a hard drive as simply "falsifying" a hard drive. Furthermore, Congress did not include on § 1512(c)(1)'s list of prohibited actions "falsifies" or "makes a false entry in." [Citation.] That contemporaneous omission also suggests that Congress intended "tangible object" in § 1519 to have a narrower scope than "other object" in § 1512(c)(1).

A canon related to *noscitur a sociis*, *ejusdem generis*, counsels: "Where general words follow specific words in a statutory enumeration, the general words are [usually] construed to embrace only objects similar in nature to those objects enumerated by the preceding specific words." [Citation.] . . . Just so here. Had Congress intended "tangible object" in § 1519 to be interpreted so generically as to capture physical objects as dissimilar as documents and fish, Congress would have had no reason to refer specifically to "record" or "document." The Government's unbounded reading of "tangible object" would render those words misleading surplusage.

Having used traditional tools of statutory interpretation to examine markers of congressional intent within the Sarbanes-Oxley Act and § 1519 itself, we are persuaded that an aggressive interpretation of "tangible object" must be rejected. It is highly improbable that Congress would have buried a general spoliation statute covering objects of any and every kind in a provision targeting fraud in financial record-keeping. . . .

C

Finally, if our recourse to traditional tools of statutory construction leaves any doubt about the meaning of "tangible object," as that term is used in § 1519, we would invoke the rule that "ambiguity concerning the ambit of criminal statutes should be resolved in favor of lenity." [Citation.] That interpretative principle is relevant here, where the Government urges a reading of § 1519 that exposes individuals to 20-year prison sentences for tampering with *any* physical object that *might* have evidentiary value in *any* federal investigation into *any* offense, no matter whether the investigation is pending or merely contemplated, or whether the offense subject to investigation is criminal or civil. . . .

For the reasons stated, we resist reading § 1519 expansively to create a coverall spoliation of evidence statute, advisable as such a measure might be. Leaving that important decision to Congress, we hold that a "tangible object" within § 1519's compass is one used to record or preserve information. The judgment of the U.S. Court of Appeals for the Eleventh Circuit is therefore reversed, and the case is remanded for further proceedings.

It is so ordered.

■ JUSTICE ALITO, concurring in the judgment.

This case can and should be resolved on narrow grounds. And though the question is close, traditional tools of statutory construction confirm that John Yates has the better of the argument. Three features of 18 U.S.C. § 1519 stand out to me: the statute's list of nouns, its list of verbs, and its title. Although perhaps none of these features by itself would tip the case in favor of Yates, the three combined do so.

Start with the nouns. Section 1519 refers to "any record, document, or tangible object." The *noscitur a sociis* canon instructs that when a statute contains a list, each word in that list presumptively has a "similar" meaning. [Citation.] A related canon, *ejusdem generis*, teaches that general words following a list of specific words should usually be read in light of those specific words to mean something "similar." [Citation.] Applying these canons to § 1519's list of nouns, the term "tangible object" should refer to something similar to records or documents. A fish does not spring to mind—nor does an antelope, a colonial farmhouse, a hydrofoil, or an oil derrick. All are "objects" that are "tangible." But who wouldn't raise an eyebrow if a neighbor, when asked to identify something similar to a "record" or "document," said "crocodile"?

This reading, of course, has its shortcomings. For instance, this is an imperfect *ejusdem generis* case because "record" and "document" are themselves quite general. And there is a risk that "tangible object" may be made superfluous—what is similar to a "record" or "document" but yet is not one? An e-mail, however, could be such a thing. [Citation.] An e-mail, after all, might not be a "document" if, as was "traditionally" so, a document was a "piece of paper with information on it," not "information stored on a computer, electronic storage device, or any other medium." Black's Law Dictionary 587–588 (10th ed. 2014). E-mails might also not be "records" if records are limited to "minutes" or other formal writings "designed to memorialize [past] events." *Id.*, at 1465. A hard drive, however, is tangible and can contain files that are precisely akin to even these narrow definitions. Both "record" and "document" can be read more expansively, but adding "tangible object" to § 1519 would ensure beyond question that electronic files are included. . . .

Next, consider § 1519's list of verbs: "alters, destroys, mutilates, conceals, covers up, falsifies, or makes a false entry in." Although many of those verbs could apply to nouns as far-flung as salamanders, satellites, or sand dunes, the last phrase in the list—"makes a false entry in"—makes no sense outside of filekeeping. How does one make a false entry in a fish? "Alters" and especially "falsifies" are also closely associated with filekeeping. . . .

Again, the Government is not without a response. One can imagine Congress trying to write a law so broadly that not every verb lines up with every noun. But failure to "line up" may suggest that something has gone awry in one's interpretation of a text. Where, as here, each of a statute's verbs applies to a certain category of nouns, there is some reason to think that Congress had that category in mind. . . .

Finally, my analysis is influenced by § 1519's title: "Destruction, alteration, or falsification of records in Federal investigations and bankruptcy." This too points toward filekeeping, not fish. . . . The title is especially valuable here because it reinforces what the text's nouns and verbs independently suggest—that no matter how other statutes might be read, this particular one does not cover every noun in the universe with tangible form.

Titles, of course, are also not dispositive. Here, if the list of nouns did not already suggest that "tangible object" should mean something similar to records or documents, especially when read in conjunction with § 1519's peculiar list of verbs with their focus on filekeeping, then the title would not be enough on its own. In conjunction with those other two textual features, however, the Government's argument, though colorable, becomes too implausible to accept.

■ JUSTICE KAGAN, with whom JUSTICE SCALIA, JUSTICE KENNEDY, and JUSTICE THOMAS join, dissenting.

. . . This case raises the question whether the term "tangible object" means the same thing in § 1519 as it means in everyday language—any object capable of being touched. The answer should be easy: Yes. The term "tangible object" is broad, but clear. Throughout the U.S. Code and many States' laws, it invariably covers physical objects of all kinds. And in § 1519, context confirms what bare text says: All the words surrounding "tangible object" show that Congress meant the term to have a wide range. That fits with Congress's evident purpose in enacting § 1519: to punish those who alter or destroy physical evidence—any physical evidence—with the intent of thwarting federal law enforcement. . . .

I

When Congress has not supplied a definition, we generally give a statutory term its ordinary meaning. [Citation.] As the plurality must acknowledge, the ordinary meaning of "tangible object" is "a discrete thing that possesses physical form. A fish is, of course, a discrete thing that possesses physical form. *See generally* Dr. Seuss, *One Fish Two Fish Red Fish Blue Fish* (1960). So the ordinary meaning of the term "tangible object" in § 1519, as no one here disputes, covers fish (including too-small red grouper).

That interpretation accords with endless uses of the term in statute and rule books as construed by courts. Dozens of federal laws and rules of procedure (and hundreds of state enactments) include the term "tangible object" or its first cousin "tangible thing"—some in association with documents, others not. [Citation.] To my knowledge, no court has ever read any such provision to exclude things that don't record or preserve data; rather, all courts have adhered to the statutory language's ordinary (i.e., expansive) meaning. . . .

That is not necessarily the end of the matter; I agree with the plurality (really, who does not?) that context matters in interpreting statutes. We interpret particular words "in their context and with a view to their place in the overall statutory scheme." [Citation.] And sometimes that means, as the plurality says, that the dictionary definition of a disputed term cannot control. [Citation.] But this is not such an occasion, for here the text and its context point the same way. Stepping back from the words "tangible object" provides only further evidence that Congress said what it meant and meant what it said.

Begin with the way the surrounding words in § 1519 reinforce the breadth of the term at issue. Section 1519 refers to "any" tangible object, thus indicating (in line with that word's plain meaning) a tangible object "of whatever kind." Webster's Third New International Dictionary 97 (2002). This Court has time and again recognized that "any" has "an expansive meaning," bringing within a statute's reach all types of the item (here, "tangible object") to which the law refers. And the adjacent laundry list of verbs in § 1519 ("alters, destroys, mutilates, conceals, covers up, falsifies, or makes a false entry") further shows that Congress wrote a statute with a wide scope. Those words are supposed to ensure—just as "tangible object" is meant to—that § 1519 covers the whole world of evidence-tampering, in all its prodigious variety. . . .

The words "record, document, or tangible object" in § 1519 also track language in 18 U.S.C. § 1512, the federal witness-tampering law covering (as even the plurality accepts) physical evidence in all its forms. Section 1512, both in its original version (preceding § 1519) and today, repeatedly uses the phrase "record, document, or other object"—most notably, in a provision prohibiting the use of force or threat to induce another person to withhold any of those materials from an official proceeding. [Citation.] That language encompasses no less the bloody knife than the incriminating letter, as all courts have for decades agreed. [Citation.] And typically "only the most compelling evidence" will persuade this Court that Congress intended "nearly identical language" in provisions dealing with related subjects to bear different meanings. [Citation.] Context thus again confirms what text indicates.

And legislative history, for those who care about it, puts extra icing on a cake already frosted. Section 1519, as the plurality notes, was enacted after the Enron Corporation's collapse, as part of the Sarbanes-Oxley Act of 2002. [Citation.] But the provision began its life in a separate bill, and the drafters emphasized that Enron was "only a case study exposing the shortcomings in our current laws" relating to both "corporate and criminal" fraud. . . .

As Congress recognized in using a broad term, giving immunity to those who destroy non-documentary evidence has no sensible basis in penal policy. A person who hides a murder victim's body is no less culpable than one who burns the victim's diary. A fisherman, like John Yates, who dumps undersized fish to avoid a fine is no less blameworthy than one who shreds his vessel's catch log for the same reason. Congress thus treated both offenders in the same way. It understood, in enacting § 1519, that destroying evidence is destroying evidence, whether or not that evidence takes documentary form.

II

. . . The plurality's analysis starts with § 1519's title: "Destruction, alteration, or falsification of records in Federal investigations and bankruptcy." That's already a sign something is amiss. I know of no other case in which we have begun our interpretation of a statute with the title, or relied on a title to override the law's clear terms. Instead, we have followed "the wise rule that the title of a statute and the heading of a section cannot limit the plain meaning of the text."

The reason for that "wise rule" is easy to see: A title is, almost necessarily, an abridgment. Attempting to mention every term in a statute "would often be ungainly as well as useless"; accordingly, "matters in the text . . . are frequently unreflected in the headings." [Citation.] Section 1519's title refers to "destruction, alteration, or falsification" but not to mutilation, concealment, or covering up, and likewise mentions "records" but not other documents or objects. Presumably, the plurality would not refuse to apply § 1519 when a person only conceals evidence rather than destroying, altering, or falsifying it;

instead, the plurality would say that a title is just a title, which cannot "undo or limit" more specific statutory text. [Citation.] The same holds true when the evidence in question is not a "record" but something else whose destruction, alteration, etc., is intended to obstruct justice. . . .

The plurality's third argument, relying on the surplusage canon, at least invokes a known tool of statutory construction—but it too comes to nothing. Says the plurality: If read naturally, § 1519 "would render superfluous" § 1512(c)(1), which Congress passed "as part of the same act." But that is not so: Although the two provisions significantly overlap, each applies to conduct the other does not. The key difference between the two is that § 1519 protects the integrity of "matter[s] within the jurisdiction of any [federal] department or agency" whereas § 1512(c)(1) safeguards "official proceeding[s]" as defined in § 1515(a)(1)(A). Section 1519's language often applies more broadly than § 1512(c)(1)'s, as the plurality notes. For example, an FBI investigation counts as a matter within a federal department's jurisdiction, but falls outside the statutory definition of "official proceeding" as construed by courts. [Citation.] But conversely, § 1512(c)(1) sometimes reaches more widely than § 1519. For example, because an "official proceeding" includes any "proceeding before a judge or court of the United States," § 1512(c)(1) prohibits tampering with evidence in federal litigation between private parties. [Citation.] By contrast, § 1519 wouldn't ordinarily operate in that context because a federal court isn't a "department or agency." So the surplusage canon doesn't come into play. Overlap—even significant overlap—abounds in the criminal law. . . .

Getting nowhere with surplusage, the plurality switches canons, hoping that *noscitur a sociis* and *ejusdem generis* will save it. . . . But understood as this Court always has, the canons have no such transformative effect on the workaday language Congress chose.

As an initial matter, this Court uses *noscitur a sociis* and *ejusdem generis* to resolve ambiguity, not create it. . . . [w]hen words have a clear definition, and all other contextual clues support that meaning, the canons cannot properly defeat Congress's decision to draft broad legislation. [Citation.]

Anyway, assigning "tangible object" its ordinary meaning comports with *noscitur a sociis* and *ejusdem generis* when applied, as they should be, with attention to § 1519's subject and purpose. Those canons require identifying a common trait that links all the words in a statutory phrase. [Citation.] In responding to that demand, the plurality characterizes records and documents as things that preserve information—and so they are. But just as much, they are things that provide information, and thus potentially serve as evidence relevant to matters under review. And in a statute pertaining to obstruction of federal investigations, that evidentiary function comes to the fore. The destruction of records and documents prevents law enforcement agents from gathering facts relevant to official inquiries. And so too does the destruction of tangible objects—of whatever kind. Whether the item is a fisherman's ledger or an undersized fish, throwing it overboard has the identical effect on the administration of justice. [Citation.] For purposes of § 1519, records, documents, and (all) tangible objects are therefore alike.

Indeed, even the plurality can't fully credit its *noscitur /ejusdem* argument. The same reasoning would apply to every law placing the word "object" (or "thing") after "record" and "document." But as noted earlier, such statutes are common[.] . . . The plurality accepts that in those laws "object" means object; its argument about superfluity positively depends on giving § 1512(c)(1) that broader reading. What, then, is the difference here? The plurality proposes that some of those statutes describe less serious offenses than § 1519. How and why that distinction affects application of the *noscitur a sociis* and *ejusdem generis* canons is left obscure: Count it as one more of the plurality's never-before-propounded, not-readily-explained interpretive theories. [Citation.] But in any event, that rationale cannot support the plurality's willingness to give "object" its natural meaning in § 1512, which (like § 1519) sets out felonies with penalties of up to 20 years. [Citation.] The canons, in the plurality's interpretive world, apparently switch on and off whenever convenient.

And the plurality's invocation of § 1519's verbs does nothing to buttress its canon-based argument. The plurality observes that § 1519 prohibits "falsif[ying]" or "mak[ing] a false entry in" a tangible object, and no one can do those things to, say, a murder weapon (or a fish). But of course someone can alter, destroy, mutilate, conceal, or cover up such a tangible object, and § 1519 prohibits those actions too. The Court has never before suggested that all the verbs in a statute need to match up with all the nouns. [Citation.] And for good reason. It is exactly when Congress sets out to draft a statute broadly—to include every imaginable variation on a theme—that such mismatches will arise. To respond by narrowing the law, as the plurality does, is thus to flout both what Congress wrote and what Congress wanted. . . .

III

If none of the traditional tools of statutory interpretation can produce today's result, then what accounts for it? The plurality offers a clue when it emphasizes the disproportionate penalties § 1519 imposes if the law is read broadly. . . . That brings to the surface the real issue: overcriminalization and excessive punishment in the U.S. Code.

. . . The plurality omits from its description of § 1519 the requirement that a person act "knowingly" and with "the intent to impede, obstruct, or influence" federal law enforcement. And in highlighting § 1519's maximum penalty, the plurality glosses over the absence of any prescribed minimum. (Let's not forget that Yates's sentence was not 20 years, but 30 days.) Congress presumably enacts laws with high maximums and no minimums when it thinks the prohibited conduct may run the gamut from major to minor. . . . Most district judges, as Congress knows, will recognize differences between such cases . . . and will try to make the punishment fit the crime. Still and all, I tend to think, for the reasons the plurality gives, that § 1519 is a bad law—too broad and undifferentiated, with too-high maximum penalties, which give prosecutors too much leverage and sentencers too much discretion. And I'd go further: In those ways, § 1519 is unfortunately not an outlier, but an emblem of a deeper pathology in the federal criminal code.

But whatever the wisdom or folly of § 1519, this Court does not get to rewrite the law. . . . If judges disagree with Congress's choice, we are perfectly entitled to say so—in lectures, in law review articles, and even in dicta. But we are not entitled to replace the statute Congress enacted with an alternative of our own design.

I respectfully dissent.

QUESTIONS

1. How do the plurality and the dissent use the statute's context to illuminate the meaning of the phrase "tangible object"?

2. Compare the use of the statutes' titles to limit the scope of their operative language in *Holy Trinity Church* and in *Yates*. Which, if any, treatment seems to you more persuasive and why?

3. The dissent claims that its interpretation "fits with Congress's evident purpose in enacting § 1519: to punish those who alter or destroy physical evidence—any physical evidence—with the intent of thwarting federal law enforcement." *Is* it so evident that that was Congress's purpose? Recall that § 1519 was enacted as part of the Sarbanes-Oxley Act, with the heading "Destruction, alteration, or falsification *of records* in Federal investigations and bankruptcy" (emphasis added). What methods does the dissent employ to conclude that its broader reading of Congress's purpose was "evident?" Do those methods yield a meaning that is any more evident than the methods employed by the plurality or concurrence?

4. Under the plurality and concurrence's approaches, must the information that the defendant "knowingly alters, destroys, mutilates, conceals, covers up, falsifies, or makes a false entry in any record, document, or tangible object with the intent to impede, obstruct, or influence the investigation [of]" relate to financial records? What if Captain Yates had cast overboard together with the grouper the ledger recording their size?

5. If the plurality and concurring opinions allow fish and other tangible objects not "used to record or preserve information" to escape § 1519's net, are they rewriting the statute?

6. Does it matter that § 1519 was passed as part of Sarbanes-Oxley, a statute seeking to deter white-collar financial crimes, but codified into the U.S. Code alongside other provisions related to the general obstruction of justice, 18 U.S.C. §§ 1501–21? Which context do you find more illuminating, and why?

NOTE: IS THE PLAIN MEANING RULE "PLAIN"?

From the standpoint of method, the Plain Meaning Rule limits the resort to certain methods or sources of statutory meaning. The dissent's primary rationale in *Yates* was that the ordinary meaning of the term "tangible object" was "plain," and so the Court should have followed "the wise rule that the title of a statute and the heading of a section cannot limit the plain meaning of the text." What makes this rule so wise? Because the invocation of the Plain Meaning Rule has legal significance only when it functions to exclude otherwise illuminating interpretive sources, Professors William Baude and Ryan Doerfler have questioned the circumstances where courts, invoking the Plain Meaning Rule, can justify excluding information that would tend to help clarify the meaning of a statute:

> The plain meaning rule says that otherwise-relevant information about statutory meaning is forbidden when the statutory text is plain or unambiguous. To see the rule in action, we need not look far. Consider one of the Court's recent and entertaining statutory interpretation cases, *Yates v United States*, in which [the dissent] invoked "the wise rule that the title of a statute and the heading of a section cannot limit the plain meaning of the text. . . ."
>
> Upon closer examination, there is something puzzling about the plain meaning rule. There are reasons to consider all pertinent information. There are reasons to categorically discard certain kinds of pertinent information. But why consider it only *sometimes*? . . .
>
> [W]hy make otherwise-relevant information only *conditionally* admissible? If legislative history is truly bad evidence of statutory meaning, shouldn't it be ignored both when the meaning is plain and when it is less than clear? Conversely, if it is good evidence, shouldn't we always at least *look* at it, even when the text seems pretty clear on its own? Why should legislative history's admissibility depend on the evidence we get from another source, like the text? . . .
>
> [O]ne might be able to construct a justification for considering pertinent information only sometimes—but such a limit makes sense only if that "sometimes" is connected to some epistemic or other practical end. What makes little sense is a blanket prohibition against considering pertinent nontextual information if statutory language is "clear." This is especially so if the courts' main concern is interpretive *accuracy*—that is, getting it right. Courts justify adherence to the plain meaning rule as a way to avoid interpretive mistakes, but the rule seems ill-suited to the task. . . .
>
> ### A. Cost Efficiency
>
> The plain meaning rule might make sense for evidence that is probative but also expensive to collect or consider.

Note that a cost-efficiency story for the plain meaning rule is still a little tricky. . . . [T]he cost-efficiency justification for the plain meaning rule would have to justify the *conditional* exclusion of evidence. Some scholars have argued, for example, that most nontextual evidence should be *categorically* excluded in part on cost-efficiency grounds. That kind of categorical argument, of course, is too strong to yield the plain meaning rule. Rather, a cost-efficiency justification for the plain meaning rule would require a particular ratio of costs and accuracies such that the extra evidence is too costly when A is clear, but not *so* costly that it is prohibitive when A is unclear. Again, this is *possible*, but would require a more precise quantification of the decision costs of considering different kinds of evidence than we have seen.

A cost-efficiency justification for the plain meaning rule is at least conceivable for some classes of evidence . . . . Legislative history, for example, might be time-consuming for courts to consider. . . . In this respect, legislative history contrasts sharply with, say, titles or section headings, which are easy for courts to consider. It is hard for us to imagine any cost-exclusion justification for excluding those kinds of materials.

B. Bias

Perhaps the plain meaning rule could make sense for certain kinds of evidence that have both potential value but also a hard-to-assess sort of bias. . . .

It seems at least conceivable to us that something like the practical consequences of a statutory interpretation might fit this model. Judges might well be committed to the view that practical consequences are relevant but of secondary importance to more standard legal materials like text and so on. On the other hand, judges might also worry that once they take into account practical considerations, it is hard to think clearly about anything else, and hard to resist the urge to start reinterpreting the standard materials to match the consequences the judges want to see. . . .

C. Legal Convention

An alternative justification, of sorts, might proceed in a more legalistic way: judges should follow the plain meaning rule because it is a rule, and judges should follow the rules. We recognize that this argument sounds hilariously circular—where did the rule *come from*?—but we think a version of it can be made to work.

One way is by focusing on the "law of interpretation." This argument requires us first to accept that rules of statutory interpretation can be set by law, in which case they need not be justified on first-order normative grounds. . . .

Under this argument, maybe the plain meaning rule is simply a common-law rule of statutory interpretation.

Perhaps Congress knows about the plain meaning rule and intends (or means) that its work should be interpreted through the rule. . . .

[R]ecent empirical research by Professors Abbe Gluck and Lisa Schultz Bressman has suggested that Congress does not know very much about the Supreme Court's statutory interpretation rules, suggesting that we should be hesitant to justify interpretive rules purely on the basis of expectations. . . .

D. Public-Facing Explanation

It is also possible that there is a difference between a court's own reasoning process and the reasoning process it presents to the audience of its opinions. Or, to put a finer point on it, maybe the plain meaning doctrine is a public lie or, more generously, an oversimplification. . . .

Under this justification, then, it is not actually true that outside information is ignored when the meaning is plain. Rather, judges think that the outside information will change the purely textual result only in an unusual case, and when the information does not change the result, it is better to pretend that it *could not* have changed the result. . . .

Why might a court do this? Perhaps it does not fully trust its audience. When presenting its textual argument to nonjudges and even lay people, who are not as steeped in the court's conventions of statutory interpretation, it makes sense to speak in accessible shorthand. . . .

E. Predictability and Consistency

Additionally, the plain meaning rule might make sense— under certain extremely specific assumptions—if one were willing to trade *accuracy* for *predictability*. Suppose, for example, that a regulated private party cares not very much about whether she has the meaning of the statute "right" in the abstract, but cares a great deal about whether she correctly guesses how a judge will interpret the statute. That party might prefer that the range of considerations for a judge be limited in cases in which one consideration—the text—points clearly in one direction. . . .

[T]his justification requires some tricky assumptions. It is not enough to argue—as many have—that text is a useful coordinating point. That argument would be more likely to point toward textualism across the board. Rather, it requires an argument that text is only *sometimes* useful as a coordinating point. The underlying intuition seems to be that when the text is plain, the coordinating function is strong and the loss in accuracy is weak, but when the text is less plain, we should flip to emphasizing accuracy over coordination.

Maybe that argument could work, but it rests on several empirical assumptions. . . .

The first required assumption is that the plain meaning *threshold* is itself reasonably plain—in other words, that most interpreters can agree on which textual meanings are plain. . . . The current evidence suggests that this assumption is false—that is, the plain meaning threshold is highly vulnerable to dispute (good faith and otherwise). . . .

CONCLUSION

[W]e come neither to praise the plain meaning rule nor to bury it. Our main aim is to challenge those who use the rule to consider and explain why they think nontextual evidence is relevant at some times but not at others—and to show all readers that the challenge is harder to answer than they might have first thought.

William Baude & Ryan D. Doerfler, *The (Not So) Plain Meaning Rule*, 84 U. Chi. L. Rev. 539 (2017) (excerpt).

2.   LITERALISM AND ITS LIMITS

The previous materials should have illustrated that few statutes reveal a truly "plain" meaning; more often, courts look to a variety of aids to interpretation. And even when two judges both seek the "ordinary meaning" of the statutory term or phrase in question, they may disagree about which of several plausible meanings is the "ordinary" one.

The interpretative techniques discussed above, as well as the use of dictionaries, canons of construction, and corpus linguistics surveyed in subsection III.C.4, below, are often called "textual" methods because they seek to resolve interpretive questions by looking to the common meanings and linguistic usage of the words and phrases in the statutory text. In many circumstances, however, there may be practical impediments to giving the words or phrases in the statute their "literal" meaning.

Indeed, in most circumstances, a court will seek to understand the statutory provision at issue by reference to any number of legal methods, many of which look beyond the meaning of the words or phrases in the text of the contested provision itself, including by reference to:

a.   a statutory definitions section, an intra-statutory solution (*see, e.g., McBoyle v. US* and *Lozman v. City of Riviera Beach, Fla, infra*);

b.   related provisions in the same statute, an intra-statutory canon known as the "whole statute" canon (*see, e.g., Holy Trinity Church, supra; King v. Burwell* and *Peacock v. Lubbock Compress Co., infra*);

c.   related provisions in *other* statutes, an inter-statutory canon known as the "whole code" canon, which draws on materials from other related statutes (*see, e.g., Alaska Steamship Co., infra*);

d.   dictionaries, corpus linguistics, and other evidence of linguistic usage, which are extra-statutory sources of linguistic meaning that examine statutory text against the backdrop of ordinary usage and which attribute to the legislature an intent, or at least an imputed practice, of using words according to their commonly-understood meanings (*see infra* subsection III.C.4, "Sources of Ordinary Meaning");

e.   canons of construction, some of which, like the plain meaning rule, discussed *supra* in *Yates v. United States*, or the clear notice rule, discussed *infra* in *Arlington Central School District v. Board of Education v. Murphy*, are substantive canons developed by *courts*, not by elected legislators;

f.   context stated in or inferable from the statute, for example from titles and purpose clauses, a technique which may be implicit in b. and c. (as discussed in *Yates, supra*); and/or

g.   context supplied by extra-statutory sources such as the legislative history of the statute's enactment (*see, e.g., Johnson v. Southern Pacific Co. and Holy Trinity Church, supra*).

Finally, courts sometimes consider not only methods of interpretation, but also the *consequences* of interpretation. Chief Justice Marshall long ago recognized that limits may exist to the application of the literal meaning of the statute:

> Where words conflict with each other, where the different clauses of an instrument bear upon each other, and would be inconsistent unless the natural and common import of words be varied, construction becomes necessary, and a departure from the obvious meaning of words is justifiable. But if, in any case, the plain meaning of a provision, not contradicted by any other provision in the same instrument, is to be disregarded, because we believe the framers of that instrument could not intend what they say, it must be one in which the absurdity and injustice of applying the provision to the case would be so monstrous that all mankind would, without hesitation, unite in rejecting the application.

Marshall, Ch. .J., in Sturges v. Crowninshield, 4 Wheat. 122, 202, 4 L.Ed. 529, 550 (1819).

In some circumstances, courts may choose to depart from the "obvious meaning of words" where such meaning may effectively lead to the statute "self-destructing." In other circumstances, courts have applied the "absurd results" canon to avoid a bizarre application of the statute in a particular case. While similar in ethos, these two approaches arise from distinct concerns. The "anti-self-destruction" canon, a variation on the presumption against ineffectiveness (see *supra* subsection III.A.3.b), cautions against interpreting a statute in such a manner as to destroy the evident or core purpose of the statute *generally*. By contrast, the absurd results canon applies in circumstances in which the statute's application may yield an absurd or bizarre result *in the particular case*. The interpreter typically applies the absurd results canon only in fringe cases where the overarching statutory scheme itself is not implicated, regardless of the outcome in the case. Recall the interpretive inquiry in *Holy Trinity Church*: even though the Supreme Court declined to apply the statutory prohibition in question to the Episcopal priest because it would have yielded an "absurd" result, no doubt remained that the statute applied to a core set of cases—manual laborers, for example.

In these next cases, consider the reasons why it may (or may not) be appropriate for courts to look beyond the "literal" meaning of the text itself, as well as the other methods and sources, if any, that courts should prioritize instead. For the statutes in question, consider whether the literal meaning urged upon the statutory text is indeed "plain," and if you think it is, whether its application in those cases would meet Chief Justice Marshall's "absurdity and injustice" test.

King v. Burwell

Supreme Court of the United States, 2015.
135 S.Ct. 2480, 192 L.Ed.2d 483.

■ CHIEF JUSTICE ROBERTS delivered the opinion of the Court[, in which JUSTICE KENNEDY, JUSTICE GINSBURG, JUSTICE BREYER, JUSTICE SOTOMAYOR, and JUSTICE KAGAN joined].

The Patient Protection and Affordable Care Act adopts a series of interlocking reforms designed to expand coverage in the individual health insurance market. First, the Act bars insurers from taking a person's health into account when deciding whether to sell health insurance or how much to charge. Second, the Act generally requires each person to maintain insurance coverage or make a payment to the Internal Revenue Service. And third, the Act gives tax credits to certain people to make insurance more affordable.

In addition to those reforms, the Act requires the creation of an "Exchange" in each State—basically, a marketplace that allows people to compare and purchase insurance plans. The Act gives each State the opportunity to establish its own Exchange, but provides that the Federal Government will establish the Exchange if the State does not. . . .

An Exchange may be created in one of two ways. First, the Act provides that "[e]ach State shall . . . establish an American Health Benefit Exchange . . . for the State." *Ibid.* Second, if a State nonetheless chooses not to establish its own Exchange, the Act provides that the Secretary of Health and Human Services "shall . . . establish and operate such Exchange within the State." § 18041(c)(1).

The issue in this case is whether the Act's tax credits are available in States that have a Federal Exchange rather than a State Exchange. The Act initially provides that tax credits "shall be allowed" for any "applicable taxpayer." 26 U.S.C. § 36B(a). The Act then provides that the amount of the tax credit depends in part on whether the taxpayer has enrolled in an insurance plan through "an Exchange *established by the State* under section 1311 of the Patient Protection and Affordable Care

Act [hereinafter 42 U.S.C. § 18031]." 26 U.S.C. §§ 36B(b)–(c) (emphasis added). . . .

[T]he [relevant] IRS Rule provides that a taxpayer is eligible for a tax credit if he enrolled in an insurance plan through "an Exchange," [citation], which is defined as "an Exchange serving the individual market . . . regardless of whether the Exchange is established and operated by a State . . . or by HHS," [citation]. . . .

When analyzing an agency's interpretation of a statute, we often apply the two-step framework announced in *Chevron* [citation]. Under that framework, we ask whether the statute is ambiguous and, if so, whether the agency's interpretation is reasonable. [Citation.] This approach "is premised on the theory that a statute's ambiguity constitutes an implicit delegation from Congress to the agency to fill in the statutory gaps." [Citation.] "In extraordinary cases, however, there may be reason to hesitate before concluding that Congress has intended such an implicit delegation." [Citation.]

This is one of those cases. The tax credits are among the Act's key reforms, involving billions of dollars in spending each year and affecting the price of health insurance for millions of people. Whether those credits are available on Federal Exchanges is thus a question of deep "economic and political significance" that is central to this statutory scheme; had Congress wished to assign that question to an agency, it surely would have done so expressly. [Citation.] It is especially unlikely that Congress would have delegated this decision to the *IRS,* which has no expertise in crafting health insurance policy of this sort. [Citation.] This is not a case for the IRS.

It is instead our task to determine the correct reading of Section 36B. If the statutory language is plain, we must enforce it according to its terms. [citation] But oftentimes the "meaning—or ambiguity—of certain words or phrases may only become evident when placed in context." [citation] So when deciding whether the language is plain, we must read the words "in their context and with a view to their place in the overall statutory scheme." [Citation.] Our duty, after all, is "to construe statutes, not isolated provisions." [Citation.]

We begin with the text of Section 36B. As relevant here, Section 36B allows an individual to receive tax credits only if the individual enrolls in an insurance plan through "an Exchange established by the State under [42 U.S.C. § 18031]." In other words, three things must be true: First, the individual must enroll in an insurance plan through "an Exchange." Second, that Exchange must be "established by the State." And third, that Exchange must be established "under [42 U.S.C. § 18031]." We address each requirement in turn.

First, all parties agree that a Federal Exchange qualifies as "an Exchange" for purposes of Section 36B. [Citation.] Section 18031 provides that "[e]ach State shall . . . establish an American Health Benefit

Exchange ... for the State." § 18031(b)(1). Although phrased as a requirement, the Act gives the States "flexibility" by allowing them to "elect" whether they want to establish an Exchange. § 18041(b). If the State chooses not to do so, Section 18041 provides that the Secretary "shall ... establish and operate *such Exchange* within the State." § 18041(c)(1) (emphasis added).

By using the phrase "such Exchange," Section 18041 instructs the Secretary to establish and operate the *same* Exchange that the State was directed to establish under Section 18031. See Black's Law Dictionary 1661 (10th ed. 2014) (defining "such" as "That or those; having just been mentioned"). In other words, State Exchanges and Federal Exchanges are equivalent—they must meet the same requirements, perform the same functions, and serve the same purposes. Although State and Federal Exchanges are established by different sovereigns, Sections 18031 and 18041 do not suggest that they differ in any meaningful way. A Federal Exchange therefore counts as "an Exchange" under Section 36B.

Second, we must determine whether a Federal Exchange is "established by the State" for purposes of Section 36B. At the outset, it might seem that a Federal Exchange cannot fulfill this requirement. After all, the Act defines "State" to mean "each of the 50 States and the District of Columbia"—a definition that does not include the Federal Government. 42 U.S.C. § 18024(d). But when read in context, "with a view to [its] place in the overall statutory scheme," the meaning of the phrase "established by the State" is not so clear. [Citation.]

After telling each State to establish an Exchange, Section 18031 provides that all Exchanges "shall make available qualified health plans to qualified individuals." 42 U.S.C. § 18031(d)(2)(A). Section 18032 then defines the term "qualified individual" in part as an individual who "resides in the State that established the Exchange." § 18032(f)(1)(A). And that's a problem: If we give the phrase "the State that established the Exchange" its most natural meaning, there would be *no* "qualified individuals" on Federal Exchanges. But the Act clearly contemplates that there will be qualified individuals on *every* Exchange. As we just mentioned, the Act requires all Exchanges to "make available qualified health plans to qualified individuals"—something an Exchange could not do if there were no such individuals. § 18031(d)(2)(A). And the Act tells the Exchange, in deciding which health plans to offer, to consider "the interests of qualified individuals ... in the State or States in which such Exchange operates"—again, something the Exchange could not do if qualified individuals did not exist. § 18031(e)(1)(B). This problem arises repeatedly throughout the Act. See, *e.g.,* § 18031(b)(2) (allowing a State to create "one Exchange ... for providing ... services to both qualified individuals and qualified small employers," rather than creating separate Exchanges for those two groups).[1]

These provisions suggest that the Act may not always use the phrase "established by the State" in its most natural sense. Thus, the meaning of that phrase may not be as clear as it appears when read out of context.

Third, we must determine whether a Federal Exchange is established "under [42 U.S.C. § 18031]." This too might seem a requirement that a Federal Exchange cannot fulfill, because it is Section 18041 that tells the Secretary when to "establish and operate such Exchange." But here again, the way different provisions in the statute interact suggests otherwise.

The Act defines the term "Exchange" to mean "an American Health Benefit Exchange established under section 18031." § 300gg–91(d)(21). If we import that definition into Section 18041, the Act tells the Secretary to "establish and operate such 'American Health Benefit Exchange established under section 18031.'" That suggests that Section 18041 authorizes the Secretary to establish an Exchange under Section 18031, not (or not only) under Section 18041. Otherwise, the Federal Exchange, by definition, would not be an "Exchange" at all. [Citation.]

This interpretation of "under [42 U.S.C. § 18031]" fits best with the statutory context. All of the requirements that an Exchange must meet are in Section 18031, so it is sensible to regard all Exchanges as established under that provision. In addition, every time the Act uses the word "Exchange," the definitional provision requires that we substitute the phrase "Exchange established under section 18031." If Federal Exchanges were not established under Section 18031, therefore, literally none of the Act's requirements would apply to them. Finally, the Act repeatedly uses the phrase "established under [42 U.S.C. § 18031]" in situations where it would make no sense to distinguish between State and Federal Exchanges. See, *e.g.,* 26 U.S.C. § 125(f)(3)(A) (2012 ed., Supp. I) ("The term 'qualified benefit' shall not include any qualified health plan . . . offered through an Exchange established under [42 U.S.C. § 18031]"); 26 U.S.C. § 6055(b)(1)(B)(iii)(I) (2012 ed.) (requiring insurers to report whether each insurance plan they provided "is a qualified health plan offered through an Exchange established under [42 U.S.C. § 18031]"). A Federal Exchange may therefore be considered one established "under [42 U.S.C. § 18031]."

The upshot of all this is that the phrase "an Exchange established by the State under [42 U.S.C. § 18031]" is properly viewed as ambiguous. The phrase may be limited in its reach to State Exchanges. But it is also

---

[1] The dissent argues that one would "naturally read instructions about qualified individuals to be inapplicable to the extent a particular Exchange has no such individuals." [Citation.] But the fact that the dissent's interpretation would make so many parts of the Act "inapplicable" to Federal Exchanges is precisely what creates the problem. It would be odd indeed for Congress to write such detailed instructions about customers on a State Exchange, while having nothing to say about those on a Federal Exchange.

possible that the phrase refers to *all* Exchanges—both State and Federal—at least for purposes of the tax credits. If a State chooses not to follow the directive in Section 18031 that it establish an Exchange, the Act tells the Secretary to establish "such Exchange." § 18041. And by using the words "such Exchange," the Act indicates that State and Federal Exchanges should be the same. But State and Federal Exchanges would differ in a fundamental way if tax credits were available only on State Exchanges—one type of Exchange would help make insurance more affordable by providing billions of dollars to the States' citizens; the other type of Exchange would not.[2]

The conclusion that Section 36B is ambiguous is further supported by several provisions that assume tax credits will be available on both State and Federal Exchanges. . . .

Petitioners and the dissent respond that the words "established by the State" would be unnecessary if Congress meant to extend tax credits to both State and Federal Exchanges. [Citation.] But "our preference for avoiding surplusage constructions is not absolute." [Citation.] And specifically with respect to this Act, rigorous application of the canon does not seem a particularly useful guide to a fair construction of the statute.

The Affordable Care Act contains more than a few examples of inartful drafting. (To cite just one, the Act creates three separate Section 1563s. *See* 124 Stat. 270, 911, 912.) Several features of the Act's passage contributed to that unfortunate reality. Congress wrote key parts of the Act behind closed doors, rather than through "the traditional legislative process." [Citation.] And Congress passed much of the Act using a complicated budgetary procedure known as "reconciliation," which limited opportunities for debate and amendment, and bypassed the Senate's normal 60-vote filibuster requirement. [Citation.] As a result, the Act does not reflect the type of care and deliberation that one might expect of such significant legislation. [Citation.]

Anyway, we "must do our best, bearing in mind the fundamental canon of statutory construction that the words of a statute must be read in their context and with a view to their place in the overall statutory scheme." [Citation.] After reading Section 36B along with other related provisions in the Act, we cannot conclude that the phrase "an Exchange established by the State under [Section 18031]" is unambiguous. . . .

---

[2]   The dissent argues that the phrase "such Exchange" does not suggest that State and Federal Exchanges "are in all respects equivalent." In support, it quotes the Constitution's Elections Clause, which makes the state legislature primarily responsible for prescribing election regulations, but allows Congress to "make or alter such Regulations." Art. I, § 4, cl. 1. No one would say that state and federal election regulations are in all respects equivalent, the dissent contends, so we should not say that State and Federal Exchanges are. But the Elections Clause does not precisely define what an election regulation must look like, so Congress can prescribe regulations that differ from what the State would prescribe. The Affordable Care Act does precisely define what an Exchange must look like, however, so a Federal Exchange cannot differ from a State Exchange.

Given that the text is ambiguous, we must turn to the broader structure of the Act to determine the meaning of Section 36B. "A provision that may seem ambiguous in isolation is often clarified by the remainder of the statutory scheme ... because only one of the permissible meanings produces a substantive effect that is compatible with the rest of the law." [Citation.] Here, the statutory scheme compels us to reject petitioners' interpretation because it would destabilize the individual insurance market in any State with a Federal Exchange, and likely create the very "death spirals" that Congress designed the Act to avoid. [Citation.][3] ...

It is implausible that Congress meant the Act to operate in this manner. [Citation.] Congress made the guaranteed issue and community rating requirements applicable in every State in the Nation. But those requirements only work when combined with the coverage requirement and the tax credits. So it stands to reason that Congress meant for those provisions to apply in every State as well.[4]

Petitioners respond that Congress was not worried about the effects of withholding tax credits from States with Federal Exchanges because "Congress evidently believed it was offering states a deal they would not refuse.". . . Section 18041 refutes the argument . . . . [and] provides that, if a State elects not to establish an Exchange, the Secretary "shall . . . establish and operate such Exchange within the State." 42 U.S.C. § 18041(c)(1)(A). The whole point of that provision is to create a federal fallback in case a State chooses not to establish its own Exchange. Contrary to petitioners' argument, Congress did not believe it was offering States a deal they would not refuse—it expressly addressed what would happen if a State *did* refuse the deal. . . .

Petitioners' arguments about the plain meaning of Section 36B are strong. But while the meaning of the phrase "an Exchange established

---

[3]   The dissent notes that several other provisions in the Act use the phrase "established by the State," and argues that our holding applies to each of those provisions. [citation] But "the presumption of consistent usage readily yields to context," and a statutory term may mean different things in different places. [citation] That is particularly true when, as here, "the Act is far from a chef d'oeuvre of legislative draftsmanship." [citation] Because the other provisions cited by the dissent are not at issue here, we do not address them.

[4]   The dissent argues that our analysis "show[s] only that the statutory scheme contains a flaw," one "that appeared as well in other parts of the Act." For support, the dissent notes that the guaranteed issue and community rating requirements might apply in the federal territories, even though the coverage requirement does not. The confusion arises from the fact that the guaranteed issue and community rating requirements were added as amendments to the Public Health Service Act, which contains a definition of the word "State" that includes the territories, 42 U.S.C. § 201(f), while the later-enacted Affordable Care Act contains a definition of the word "State" that excludes the territories, § 18024(d). The predicate for the dissent's point is therefore uncertain at best.

The dissent also notes that a different part of the Act "established a long-term-care insurance program with guaranteed-issue and community-rating requirements, but without an individual mandate or subsidies." True enough. But the fact that Congress was willing to accept the risk of adverse selection in a comparatively minor program does not show that Congress was willing to do so in the general health insurance program—the very heart of the Act. Moreover, Congress said expressly that it wanted to avoid adverse selection in the *health* insurance markets. § 18091(2)(I).

by the State under [42 U.S.C. § 18031]" may seem plain "when viewed in isolation," such a reading turns out to be "untenable in light of [the statute] as a whole." [Citation.] In this instance, the context and structure of the Act compel us to depart from what would otherwise be the most natural reading of the pertinent statutory phrase.

Reliance on context and structure in statutory interpretation is a "subtle business, calling for great wariness lest what professes to be mere rendering becomes creation and attempted interpretation of legislation becomes legislation itself." [Citation.] For the reasons we have given, however, such reliance is appropriate in this case, and leads us to conclude that Section 36B allows tax credits for insurance purchased on any Exchange created under the Act. Those credits are necessary for the Federal Exchanges to function like their State Exchange counterparts, and to avoid the type of calamitous result that Congress plainly meant to avoid. . . .

■ JUSTICE SCALIA, with whom JUSTICE THOMAS and JUSTICE ALITO joins, dissenting. . . .

Perhaps sensing the dismal failure of its efforts to show that "established by the State" means "established by the State or the Federal Government," the Court tries to palm off the pertinent statutory phrase as "inartful drafting." This Court, however, has no free-floating power "to rescue Congress from its drafting errors." [Citation.] Only when it is patently obvious to a reasonable reader that a drafting mistake has occurred may a court correct the mistake. The occurrence of a misprint may be apparent from the face of the law, as it is where the Affordable Care Act "creates three separate Section 1563s." But the Court does not pretend that there is any such indication of a drafting error on the face of § 36B. The occurrence of a misprint may also be apparent because a provision decrees an absurd result—a consequence "so monstrous, that all mankind would, without hesitation, unite in rejecting the application." [Citation.] But § 36B does not come remotely close to satisfying that demanding standard. It is entirely plausible that tax credits were restricted to state Exchanges deliberately—for example, in order to encourage States to establish their own Exchanges. We therefore have no authority to dismiss the terms of the law as a drafting fumble.

The Court's decision reflects the philosophy that judges should endure whatever interpretive distortions it takes in order to correct a supposed flaw in the statutory machinery. That philosophy ignores the American people's decision to give *Congress* "[a]ll legislative Powers" enumerated in the Constitution. Art. I, § 1. They made Congress, not this Court, responsible for both making laws and mending them. This Court holds only the judicial power—the power to pronounce the law as Congress has enacted it. We lack the prerogative to repair laws that do not work out in practice, just as the people lack the ability to throw us out of office if they dislike the solutions we concoct. We must always remember, therefore, that "[o]ur task is to apply the text, not to improve upon it." [Citation.]

Trying to make its judge-empowering approach seem respectful of congressional authority, the Court asserts that its decision merely ensures that the Affordable Care Act operates the way Congress "meant [it] to operate." First of all, what makes the Court so sure that Congress "meant" tax credits to be available everywhere? Our only evidence of what Congress meant comes from the terms of the law, and those terms show beyond all question that tax credits are available only on state Exchanges. More importantly, the Court forgets that ours is a government of laws and not of men. That means we are governed by the terms of our laws, not by the unenacted will of our lawmakers. "If Congress enacted into law something different from what it intended, then it should amend the statute to conform to its intent[Citation.] In the meantime, this Court "has no roving license . . . to disregard clear language simply on the view that . . . Congress 'must have intended' something broader." [Citation.]

Even less defensible, if possible, is the Court's claim that its interpretive approach is justified because this Act "does not reflect the type of care and deliberation that one might expect of such significant legislation." It is not our place to judge the quality of the care and deliberation that went into this or any other law. A law enacted by voice vote with no deliberation whatever is fully as binding upon us as one enacted after years of study, months of committee hearings, and weeks of debate. Much less is it our place to make everything come out right when Congress does not do its job properly. It is up to Congress to design its laws with care, and it is up to the people to hold them to account if they fail to carry out that responsibility.

Rather than rewriting the law under the pretense of interpreting it, the Court should have left it to Congress to decide what to do about the Act's limitation of tax credits to state Exchanges. If Congress values above everything else the Act's applicability across the country, it could make tax credits available in every Exchange. If it prizes state involvement in the Act's implementation, it could continue to limit tax credits to state Exchanges while taking other steps to mitigate the economic consequences predicted by the Court. If Congress wants to accommodate both goals, it could make tax credits available everywhere while offering new incentives for States to set up their own Exchanges. And if Congress thinks that the present design of the Act works well enough, it could do nothing. Congress could also do something else altogether, entirely abandoning the structure of the Affordable Care Act. The Court's insistence on making a choice that should be made by Congress both aggrandizes judicial power and encourages congressional lassitude. . . .

NOTE

In his review of *Reading Law*, a book by Justice Antonin Scalia and lawyer and lexicographer Bryan A. Garner, Judge Posner expressed skepticism regarding whether textualism furthers either political neutrality or judicial objectivity in the interpretation of statutory language. As you read the following excerpt, ask yourself how the views expressed in the book review are related to the reasoning of Judge Posner's dissent in *Marshall* and Justice Scalia's dissent in *King v. Burwell*:

> The passive view of the judicial role is aggressively defended in a new book by Justice Antonin Scalia and the legal lexicographer Bryan Garner. They advocate what is best described as textual originalism, because they want judges to "look for meaning in the governing text, ascribe to that text the meaning that it has borne from its inception, and reject judicial speculation about both the drafters' extra-textually derived purposes and the desirability of the fair reading's anticipated consequences." This austere interpretive method leads to a heavy emphasis on dictionary meanings, in disregard of a wise warning issued by Judge Frank Easterbrook, who though himself a self-declared textualist advises that "the choice among meanings [of words in statutes] must have a footing more solid than a dictionary—which is a museum of words, an historical catalog rather than a means to decode the work of legislatures." . . . [T]ext as such may be politically neutral, but textualism is conservative.

> A legislature is thwarted when a judge refuses to apply its handiwork to an unforeseen situation that is encompassed by the statute's aim but is not a good fit with its text. Ignoring the limitations of foresight, and also the fact that a statute is a collective product that often leaves many questions of interpretation to be answered by the courts because the legislators cannot agree on the answers, the textual originalist demands that the legislature think through myriad hypothetical scenarios and provide for all of them explicitly rather than rely on courts to be sensible. In this way, textualism hobbles legislation—and thereby tilts toward "small government" and away from "big government," which in modern America is a conservative preference.

> Scalia and Garner insist that legal terms be given their original meaning lest the intent of the legislators or the constitution-makers be subverted by unforeseen linguistic changes. . . .

> The decisive objection to the quest for original meaning, even when the quest is conducted in good faith, is that judicial historiography rarely dispels ambiguity. Judges are not competent historians. Even real historiography is frequently indeterminate, as real historians acknowledge. To put to a judge a question that he cannot answer is to evoke "motivated thinking," the form of cognitive delusion that consists of credulously accepting the

evidence that supports a preconception and of peremptorily rejecting the evidence that contradicts it. . . .

It is possible to glean from judges who actually are loose constructionists the occasional paean to textualism, but it is naïve to think that judges believe everything they say, especially when speaking *ex cathedra* (that is, in their judicial opinions). Judges tend to deny the creative—the legislative—dimension of judging, important as it is in our system, because they do not want to give the impression that they are competing with legislators, or engaged in anything but the politically unthreatening activity of objective, literal-minded interpretation, using arcane tools of legal analysis. The fact that loose constructionists sometimes publicly endorse textualism is evidence only that judges are, for strategic reasons, often not candid.

Richard A. Posner, *The Spirit Killeth, But the Letter Giveth Life*, New Republic, Sept. 13, 2012, at 18 (reviewing Antonin Scalia & Brian A. Garner, Reading Law: The Interpretation of Legal Texts (2012)).

Posner alleges that textualism calls for "austere" and "conservative" interpretive methods that "hobble" legislation. Is this necessarily always so? For example, as you will see in *Commonwealth v. Welosky* in subsection III.E.1, *infra*, sometimes the literal interpretation of the statutory text yields the *broader* application, and extratextual methods yield the *narrower*, more conservative result.

Certainly, Posner's critique appears to apply in at least some circumstances: in *King*, for example, the dissent's textually driven approach would seem to cause the statute to self-destruct. (Notably, Scalia and Garner, in *Reading Law*, include the presumption against ineffectiveness among the "fundamental principles" of statutory interpretation). The majority, by contrast, suggests that where a statutory phrase is susceptible to multiple reasonable interpretations of the phrase's "ordinary" meaning, a court should avoid interpreting the statute in a way that produces a "death spiral," the very "calamitous result" the statute was enacted to avoid.

Consider how concerns about statutory self-destruction and absurd results arise in *In re Adamo* and related cases, below. Under what circumstances is it appropriate for courts to "fix" legislative errors?

In re Adamo

United States Court of Appeals for the Second Circuit, 1980.
619 F.2d 216.

■ BARTELS, DISTRICT JUDGE[, joined by LUMBARD and MANSFIELD, CIRCUIT JUDGES]:

This is an appeal from a judgment of the United States District Court for the Western District of New York, Burke, J., affirming the discharge by the Bankruptcy Court of certain student loan obligations in proceedings brought on by twenty-one voluntary petitions in bankruptcy. The sole question for review is the effect of the repeal by Congress of Section 439A of the Higher Education Act of 1965, as amended, 20 U.S.C. § 1087–3, pertaining to dischargeability of student loans, on petitions in bankruptcy commenced but not disposed of prior to the date of such repeal.

The pertinent facts are undisputed. Each of the loans here involved is either owed to or guaranteed by appellant New York State Higher Education Services Corporation ("NYSHESC"), and each was reinsured to appellant by the United States Office of Education by agreements entered into pursuant to the Higher Education Act of 1965, as amended, 20 U.S.C. §§ 1071 et seq. At the time the twenty-one voluntary petitions in bankruptcy were filed, § 1087–3 of Title 20 provided, in part, as follows:

(a) A debt which is a loan insured or guaranteed under the authority of this part may be released by a discharge in bankruptcy under the Bankruptcy Act only if such discharge is granted after the five-year period . . . beginning on the date of commencement of the repayment period of such loan, except that prior to the expiration of that five-year period, such loan may be released only if the court in which the proceeding is pending determines that payment from future income or other wealth will impose an undue hardship on the debtor or his dependents.

(b) Subsection (a) of this section shall be effective with respect to any proceedings begun under the Bankruptcy Act on or after September 30, 1977.

This provision was subsequently repealed effective November 6, 1978, however, by Section 317 of the Bankruptcy Reform Act of 1978 ("BRA"), Pub.L. 95–598,[2] and was replaced . . . by Section 523(a)(8), as amended by Pub.L. 96–56, [which] provides:

(a) A discharge under section 727, 1141, or 1328(b) of this title does not discharge an individual debtor from any debt . . .

(8) for an educational loan made, insured, or guaranteed by a governmental unit, or made under any program funded in whole or in part by a governmental unit or a nonprofit institution of higher education, unless—

(A) such loan first became due before five years . . . before the date of the filing of the petition; or

---

[2] Section 317 of the Bankruptcy Reform Act of 1978 ("BRA") provides that "Section 439A of part B of title IV of the Higher Education Act of 1965 (20 U.S.C. § 1087–3) is repealed." The effective date of this section appears in section 402(d) of the BRA, which provides that "(t)he amendments made by sections 217, 218, 230, 247, 302, 314(j), 317, 327, 328, 338, and 411 of this Act shall take effect on the date of enactment of this Act."

(B) excepting such debt from discharge under this paragraph will impose an undue hardship on the debtor and the debtor's dependents; . . .

Under section 402(a) of the BRA, this replacement provision did not become effective until October 1, 1979, approximately eleven months after the effective date of the repeal of its predecessor, 20 U.S.C. § 1087–3.[3] According to appellant, this interruption in the rule of nondischargeability of student loans constitutes a loophole through which certain student loan debtors now attempt to escape their repayment obligations.

The Bankruptcy Court disposed of all of the twenty-one petitions by two identical memorandum decisions and orders dated March 16 and April 5, 1979, respectively, holding that because the petitions were considered and resolved after the repeal of 20 U.S.C. § 1087–3 but before the effective date of 11 U.S.C. § 523(a)(8), the Bankruptcy Court no longer had jurisdiction "to determine that the subject bankrupts are not entitled to a discharge, since the law which exists at the time of this decision has no provision for the denial of the discharge of student loans." Accordingly, Bankruptcy Judge Hayes ordered that the student loan debts in question be discharged. His decision was affirmed by the district court in a brief order on September 27, 1979, and this appeal followed. . . .

We conclude that the hiatus between the repeal of section 1087–3 of Title 20 and the effective date of its successor provision, 11 U.S.C. § 523(a)(8), was purely a manifestation of congressional inadvertence and that to follow blindly the plain meaning of the statute without regard to the obvious intention of Congress would create an absurd result in accord with neither established principles of statutory construction nor common sense. Accordingly, the decisions of the district court and the bankruptcy court below must be reversed.

Analysis of the legislative history of the BRA supports appellant's contention that the failure of the effective dates of the repeal and replacement statutes to coincide resulted from a mistake of Congress. Section 1087–3 of Title 20 of the United States Code was enacted in 1976 to prevent abuse of the bankruptcy laws by students petitioning for bankruptcy immediately upon graduation without attempting to realize the potential increased earning capacity which education may provide. [Citation.] By creating a special exception from discharge for education loans, Congress hoped to insure a more realistic view of a student's ability to repay the debt.

During the 95th Congress, however, bankruptcy reform legislation was introduced in the House of Representatives which included the repeal of section 1087–3 in order to "restore the law to where it had been before the 1976 amendment . . . " H.Rep. 95–595, 95th Cong., 1st Sess.,

---

[3]   Section 402(a) of the BRA provides that "[e]xcept as otherwise provided in this title, this Act shall take effect on October 1, 1979."

132, *reprinted in* [1978] U.S.Code Cong. & Admin.News, pp. 5787, 6093. This repeal provision, which was to take effect on the date of enactment of the legislation, was predicated upon the view that student abuses were not as widespread as had been thought and, therefore, did not warrant special treatment under the bankruptcy laws. This sentiment did not prevail, however, and when the legislation H.R. 8200 was reintroduced for further consideration in early 1978, the House, by amendment to section 523(a)(8) of the bill, adopted a replacement provision making nondischargeable educational loans insured or guaranteed under Part B of Title IV of the Higher Education Act of 1965, *supra.*

Similar bankruptcy reform legislation was introduced in the Senate in October 1977 as S. 2266. While § 317 of S. 2266 also provided for the repeal of 20 U.S.C. § 1087–3, the bill contained a more comprehensive replacement provision in section 523(a)(8) excepting from discharge any debt for an educational loan. The effective date of both sections 317 and 523(a)(8) was October 1, 1979. The differences between the House and Senate versions of the relevant provisions were resolved by the conference committee in September 1978. Because the Senate members would not acquiesce to the limited nondischargeability provision contained in H.R. 8200, the committee amended the House bill by broadening the scope of section 523(a)(8) to make nondischargeable all educational loans owing to or insured or guaranteed by a governmental unit or a nonprofit institution of higher education. The committee failed, however, to notice that the section repealing 20 U.S.C. § 1087–3 as of the date of enactment remained in the House bill. Thus, as subsequently approved by Congress and signed into law by the President, the BRA contained the House repeal provision and, due to the insistence of the Senate conferees, a broad replacement provision, the effective dates of which did not coincide. There is no indication in the history of the BRA that Congress intended to legislate such an inconsistency or that it sought for some unexpressed reason to create an approximately eleven-month hiatus for the benefit of student loan debtors.

The inadvertence of this action was subsequently acknowledged by the Senate Committee on the Judiciary . . . :

> The gap in coverage of a prohibition on the discharge in bankruptcy of loans made under the Guaranteed Student Loan Program resulting from the early repeal of section 349A (sic) is very undesirable and totally inadvertent. . . . [An] inadvertent "gap" [was] created when the applicable section of the Higher Education Act of 1965 prohibiting discharge of student loans was repealed as of November 6, 1978, and its replacement section in Title II was not made effective until October 1, 1979. Congress obviously did not mean to create a gap and at all times held to the principle of nondischargeability of student loans. . . .[7]

---

[7] . . . The remarks of various members of Congress . . . confirm the conclusion of the Senate Judiciary Committee quoted above. Senator DeConcini (D.Ariz.), principal sponsor and

Although such an interpretation by a subsequent Congress is not necessarily controlling, it may be useful in determining the intention of an earlier Congress. [Citation.]

The language of the BRA gives further credence to this interpretation. In addition to the obvious significance of the inclusion of a more comprehensive exception provision in section 523(a)(8) of the BRA than had existed previously in section 1087–3 of Title 20 U.S.C., the BRA also includes a "savings" provision in section 403(a) which preserves the substantive rights of the parties to actions commenced prior to the effective date of the BRA. Section 403(a) provides as follows:

> A case commenced under the Bankruptcy Act, and all matters and proceedings in or relating to any such case, shall be conducted and determined under such Act as if this Act had not been enacted, and the substantive rights of parties in connection with any such bankruptcy case, matter or proceeding shall continue to be governed by the law applicable to such case, matter or proceeding as if the Act had not been enacted.

Because this section, together with the BRA as a whole, did not become effective until October 1, 1979, it is not dispositive of this appeal. However, we consider it persuasive evidence of Congress' desire not to impair the rights of parties to actions commenced under the old Bankruptcy Act.

Finally, we note the apparent absurdity of a construction of the BRA which, for no discernible reason, would permit the discharge of student loans by debtors who, by sheer chance, have their bankruptcy petitions adjudicated during the eleven-month gap. Both before and after this period, nondischargeability has been and will continue to be the rule; absent an explicit statement of intent by Congress to provide a period of "amnesty" for student loan debtors, to recognize the repeal of section 1087–3 before giving effect to either section 523(a)(8) of the BRA or the savings provision in section 403(a) would, it seems to us, effectuate a legislative mistake prejudicial to the substantive rights of appellant.

The result of an obvious mistake should not be enforced, particularly when it "overrides common sense and evident statutory purpose." . . . It is a well established principle of statutory construction that a statute should not be applied strictly in accord with its literal meaning where to

---

floor manager for the BRA in the Senate, explained the intent of Congress with respect to . . . the BRA:

> . . . [T]he Bankruptcy Reform Act . . . inadvertently created a "gap" in provisions of existing law concerning nondischargeability of student loans in a bankruptcy case. Public Law 95–598 repealed provisions in the Higher Education Act making student loans nondischargeable. It was the intent to merely shift the location of the nondischargeability provision from the Higher Education Act to the Bankruptcy Code, 11 U.S.C. However, . . . a "gap" was created between November 6, 1978, and October 1, 1979, when it can be argued that there is no nondischargeability provision in the law although it clearly was not the intent of Congress to have created such a gap.

125 Cong.Rec. S. 9160 (daily ed. July 11, 1979). . . .

do so would pervert its manifest purpose. Nowhere has this principle been expressed more eloquently than by Judge Learned Hand in his concurring opinion in *Guiseppi v. Walling,* 144 F.2d 608, 624 (2d Cir.1944), where he stated:

> There is no surer way to misread any document than to read it literally; in every interpretation we must pass between Scylla and Charybdis; and I certainly do not wish to add to the barrels of ink that have been spent in logging the route. As nearly as we can, we must put ourselves in the place of those who uttered the words, and try to divine how they would have dealt with the unforeseen situation; and, although their words are by far the most decisive evidence of what they would have done, they are by no means final. [Citation.]

In this case, a literal application of the effective date of section 317 of the BRA, repealing 20 U.S.C. § 1087–3, would require us to disregard its intended purpose.[9] We hold, therefore, that the premature repeal of section 1087–3 is of no effect with respect to proceedings commenced prior to the effective date of the BRA on October 1, 1979. Accordingly, the decision of the district court is hereby reversed, and the petitions at bar are remanded to the bankruptcy court for further proceedings in accordance with this opinion.

---

[9]   "[F]or the letter killeth but the spirit giveth life." 2 Corinthians 3.6.

NOTES AND QUESTIONS

1. In re Hogan, 707 F.2d 209, 210 n.2 (5th Cir. 1983), also concerned the "inadvertent gap" created by the repeal and effective dates of the Bankruptcy Reform Act:

> The disposition of this case is compelled by *In the Matter of Williamson.* To preserve our institutional integrity, we must adhere to the precedent established by a prior panel. We cannot do so, however, without expressing our concern that in following the lead of our colleagues of the other circuits we have used a rule of statutory construction to effectively enact a law the Congress did not adopt. There is no ambiguity in the two statutes. The courts have strained to rectify congressional inadvertence by saying, in effect, that one statute is effective 11 months longer than Congress said it was. *See, e.g.,* Carnegia v. Georgia Higher Educ. Assistance Corp., 691 F.2d 482 (11th Cir. 1982); *In the Matter of Williamson*; Wisconsin Higher Educ. Aids Bd. v. Lipke, 630 F.2d 1225 (7th Cir. 1980); *In re Adamo, cert. denied sub nom* Williams v. New York State Higher Educ. Servs. Corp., 449 U.S. 843 (1980); In re Hawes, No. B78–28 (D.N.J. 1979), *aff'd per curiam,* 633 F.2d 210 (3d Cir. 1980).
>
> The result of these cases comports with one's sense of fairness, and would draw our votes if we were operating in a legislative setting. But we are not. In underscoring our concern, we highlight our apprehension that the course we have chosen to pursue has taken us over the line which separates legislative interpretation from legislating. We therefore caution those who would read this opinion to signal that such interpretative glossing will come easily in the future. It will not.

2. Independent Ins. Agents v. Clarke, 955 F.2d 731 (D.C. Cir. 1992), involved the inadvertent repeal of § 92 of the National Bank Act. Section 92 permitted any national bank, or its branch, located in a community of not more than 5,000 inhabitants to sell insurance to customers outside that community. Although early provisions of Title 12 of the United States Code included § 92, the 1952 U.S.C. and subsequent editions omitted it, with a note indicating that Congress had repealed the section in 1918. The parties in the case did not raise the issue of the validity of § 92, but, assuming the section to be applicable, differed as to its interpretation.

The Court of Appeals, acting *sua sponte,* held that § 92 had been repealed in 1918, notwithstanding the perception of Congress, other courts, and the Comptroller of the Currency that the section remained in effect. The court rejected arguments that the deletion of § 92 was the result of mistake in punctuation (in this case, the misplacement of quotation marks around restated text of the statute, which excluded the language at issue) and that its repeal should therefore be ignored. The court stated:

> We recognize that, in order to give effect to a clear congressional intent, federal courts have assumed a rather broad responsibility for correcting flaws in the language and punctuation of federal

statutes. There is a point, however, beyond which a court cannot go without trespassing on the exclusive prerogatives of the legislative branch.

We believe we are at that point. It is one thing for a court to bend statutory language to make it achieve a clearly stated congressional purpose; it is quite another for a court to reinstate a law that, intentionally or unintentionally, Congress has stricken from the statute books. If the deletion of section 92 was a mistake, it is one for Congress to correct, not the courts. *Id.* at 739.

The Supreme Court reversed, holding that § 92 was not repealed in 1918. Writing for a unanimous Court, Justice Souter concluded that the deletion of the section "was a simple scrivener's error, a mistake made by someone unfamiliar with the law's object and design. . . . The true meaning of the . . . Act is clear beyond question, and so we repunctuate." United States National Bank of Oregon v. Independent Ins. Agents, 508 U.S. 439, 462 (1993).

3. Can you reconcile the different approaches of the Second Circuit and the D.C. Circuit in *In re Adamo* and *Independent Insurance Agents v. Clarke*?

Correcting "plain" errors in statutory text

If the meaning is indeed "plain," why *shouldn't* a court "countenance" applying the plain meaning to the statute even where it leads to "absurd or futile results plainly at variance with the policy of the legislation as a whole"? How does a court know what is "the policy of the legislation as a whole," and which application of the statute is "plainly at variance" with that policy? As we have seen (and will see again), discerning a coherent policy underlying legislation is not always an easy task, though it is usually possible to ascertain *some* policy objective. In some circumstances, however, the statutory text is so flawed that one cannot articulate *any* policy under which the wording would make sense. The following is an example of an error in legislative drafting ascribable only to inadvertence.

Amalgamated Transit Union Local 1309 v. Laidlaw Transit Services, Inc., 435 F.3d 1140 (9th Cir.), rehearing en banc denied, 448 F.3d 1092 (9th Cir. 2006), involved the interpretation of a provision of the Class Action Fairness Act.

The statute, 28 USC 1453(c)(1), provides:

[A] court of appeals may accept an appeal from an order of a district court granting or denying a motion to remand a class action to the State court from which it was removed if application is made to the court of appeals not less than 7 days after entry of the order.

The three-judge panel held that the "not less than" provision in the statute must mean "not more than."

We remain somewhat troubled that, in contrast to most statutory construction cases where we are usually asked to construe the meaning of an ambiguous phrase or word, we are here faced with the task of striking a word passed on by both Houses of Congress and approved by the President, and replacing it with a word of the exact opposite meaning. We nonetheless agree with the Tenth Circuit, the only other circuit to address this issue, that there is no apparent logical reason for the choice of the word "less" in the statute, use of the word "less" is, in fact, illogical and contrary to the stated purpose of the provision, and the statute should therefore be read to require that an application to appeal under § 1453(c)(1) must be filed-in accordance with the requirements of FRAP 5—not more than 7 days after the district court's order.

The Circuit Court denied rehearing en banc, with 6 dissenters discussing and rejecting both the "scrivener's error" and "absurd results" doctrines.

Which approach shows more deference to Congress: judicial correction of inadvertent errors in a law in accordance with congressional intent, or application of the law as enacted by Congress?

For a comparative law perspective, consider, **France, Cassation Chambre Criminelle, decision of March 8, 1930**, D.1930.I.101, note Voirin.

The law in question forbade descending from a train "*when* it has completely stopped" (emphasis supplied). Apparently, the legislature intended to forbid descending from a train *before* it has completely stopped. The defendant descended from a still-moving train, and was fined for this conduct. He claimed that he had not violated the law, but had in fact obeyed it to the letter (though it is doubtful he knew of the drafting error in the penal code at the time he got off the train). The Cour de cassation rejected the appeal from the lower court's decision upholding the fine, on the ground that the lower court was entitled to interpret the text as forbidding defendant's act.

The commentary of Professor Pierre Voirin justifies the result on the ground that there was evidence "intrinsic" to the text of the law to indicate that the legislature intended to prohibit descent from still-moving trains. (It appears that other provisions of the same law must have supported that interpretation, though he does not quote them.) He distinguishes judicial error-correction based on "intrinsic" evidence of statutory intent from "extrinsic" evidence of legislative error. He finds the latter illegitimate.

He evokes a then-recent High Court decision in which the Cour de cassation ruled as if a provision of the civil code concerning the guardians of minors had not been repealed, when in fact it had: "Even if it occurred unintentionally and unbeknown to the legislature, the repeal nonetheless occurred in fact, and nothing in the current text of the civil code permits one to avoid that result, for the general principle, from which the repealed provision derogated, remaining in effect, barred any room for interpretation."

Professor Voirin then explores the consequences of allowing "extrinsic" considerations, such as the judges' conviction that the legislature made a mistake, to justify courts' error-correction:

> If the interpreter could correct texts that are enacted, promulgated, and published in the regular fashion, on the pretext of giving effect to the true will of the legislature, when this intent is discerned exclusively by extrinsic information, that would be the end of the guarantees that the formalities of legislative or administrative procedure assure to citizens. And once embarked on this slope, no doubt we will manage to declare without effect the formulation of some laws whose terms each Assembly will have voted, by giving a very different meaning to those words, for in fact there will have been no "legislative intent."

Do these criticisms sound familiar? Should it make a difference to the defendant's criminal liability in the train case that the textual error could be corrected based on other provisions of the same statute, even though defendant's conduct comported perfectly with the precisely applicable provision? Would your answer be the same if defendant faced only civil liability?

3. STATUTORY DEFINITIONS

Rather than leave problems with the definitions of statutory terms entirely to their readers, many statutes include a section that provides definitions of some of the key statutory terms. Often, however, definitions sections can lead to ambiguities of their own.

McBoyle v. United States

Supreme Court of the United States, 1931.
283 U.S. 25, 51 S.Ct. 340, 75 L.Ed. 816.

■ MR. JUSTICE HOLMES delivered the [unanimous] opinion of the Court.

The petitioner was convicted of transporting from Ottawa, Illinois, to Guymon, Oklahoma, an airplane that he knew to have been stolen, and was sentenced to serve three years' imprisonment and to pay a fine of $2,000. The judgment was affirmed by the Circuit Court of Appeals for the Tenth Circuit. 43 F.(2d) 273. A writ of certiorari was granted by this Court on the question whether the National Motor Vehicle Theft Act applies to aircraft. Act of October 29, 1919, c. 89; 41 Stat. 324; U.S.Code, Title 18, § 408. That Act provides: "Sec. 2. That when used in this Act: (a) The term 'motor vehicle' shall include an automobile, automobile truck, automobile wagon, motor cycle, or any other self-propelled vehicle not designed for running on rails; . . . Sec. 3. That whoever shall transport or cause to be transported in interstate or foreign commerce a motor vehicle, knowing the same to have been stolen, shall be punished by a fine of not more than $5,000, or by imprisonment of not more than five years, or both."

Section 2 defines the motor vehicles of which the transportation in interstate commerce is punished in § 3. The question is the meaning of the word "vehicle" in the phrase "any other self-propelled vehicle not designed for running on rails." No doubt etymologically it is possible to use the word to signify a conveyance working on land, water or air, and sometimes legislation extends the use in that direction, e.g., land and air, water being separately provided for, in the Tariff Act, September 22, 1922, c. 356, § 401(b), 42 Stat. 858, 948. But in everyday speech "vehicle" calls up the picture of a thing moving on land. Thus in Rev.Stats. § 4, intended, the Government suggests, rather to enlarge than to restrict the definition, vehicle includes every contrivance capable of being used "as a means of transportation on land." And this is repeated, expressly excluding aircraft, in the Tariff Act, June 17, 1930, c. 997, § 401(b); 46 Stat. 590, 708. So here, the phrase under discussion calls up the popular picture. For after including automobile truck, automobile wagon and motor cycle, the words "any other self-propelled vehicle not designed for running on rails" still indicate that a vehicle in the popular sense, that is a vehicle running on land, is the theme. It is a vehicle that runs, not something, not commonly called a vehicle, that flies. Airplanes were well known in 1919, when this statute was passed; but it is admitted that they were not mentioned in the reports or in the debates in Congress. It is impossible to read words that so carefully enumerate the different forms of motor vehicles and have no reference of any kind to aircraft, as including airplanes under a term that usage more and more precisely confines to a different class. The counsel for the petitioner have shown that the phraseology of the statute as to motor vehicles follows that of earlier statutes of Connecticut, Delaware, Ohio, Michigan and Missouri, not to mention the late Regulations of Traffic for the District of Columbia, Title 6, c. 9, § 242, none of which can be supposed to leave the earth.

Although it is not likely that a criminal will carefully consider the text of the law before he murders or steals, it is reasonable that a fair warning should be given to the world in language that the common world will understand, of what the law intends to do if a certain line is passed. To make the warning fair, so far as possible the line should be clear. When a rule of conduct is laid down in words that evoke in the common mind only the picture of vehicles moving on land, the statute should not be extended to aircraft, simply because it may seem to us that a similar policy applies, or upon the speculation that, if the legislature had thought of it, very likely broader words would have been used. United States v. Thind, 261 U.S. 204, 209.

Judgment reversed.

Lozman v. City of Riviera Beach, Fla.

Supreme Court of the United States, 2013.
568 U.S. 115, 133 S.Ct. 735, 184 L.Ed.2d 604.

■ JUSTICE BREYER delivered the opinion of the Court[, joined by CHIEF JUSTICE ROBERTS, JUSTICE SCALIA, JUSTICE THOMAS, JUSTICE GINSBURG, JUSTICE ALITO, and JUSTICE KAGAN].

The Rules of Construction Act defines a "vessel" as including "every description of watercraft or other artificial contrivance used, or capable of being used, as a means of transportation on water." 1 U.S.C. § 3. The question before us is whether petitioner's floating home (which is not self-propelled) falls within the terms of that definition.

In answering that question we focus primarily upon the phrase "capable of being used." This term encompasses "practical" possibilities, not "merely . . . theoretical" ones. Stewart v. Dutra Constr. Co., 543 U.S. 481, 496 (2005). We believe that a reasonable observer, looking to the home's physical characteristics and activities, would not consider it to be designed to any practical degree for carrying people or things on water. And we consequently conclude that the floating home is not a "vessel."

I

In 2002 Fane Lozman, petitioner, bought a 60-foot by 12-foot floating home. The home consisted of a house-like plywood structure with French doors on three sides. It contained a sitting room, bedroom, closet, bathroom, and kitchen, along with a stairway leading to a second level with office space. An empty bilge space underneath the main floor kept it afloat. After buying the floating home, Lozman had it towed about 200 miles to North Bay Village, Florida, where he moored it and then twice more had it towed between nearby marinas. In 2006 Lozman had the home towed a further 70 miles to a marina owned by the city of Riviera Beach (City), respondent, where he kept it docked.

After various disputes with Lozman and unsuccessful efforts to evict him from the marina, the City brought this federal admiralty lawsuit *in rem* against the floating home. It sought a maritime lien for dockage fees and damages for trespass. [Citation.]

Lozman, acting *pro se,* asked the District Court to dismiss the suit on the ground that the court lacked admiralty jurisdiction. After summary judgment proceedings, the court found that the floating home was a "vessel" and concluded that admiralty jurisdiction was consequently proper. The judge then conducted a bench trial on the merits and awarded the City $3,039.88 for dockage along with $1 in nominal damages for trespass. On appeal the Eleventh Circuit affirmed. It agreed with the District Court that the home was a "vessel." In its view, the home was "capable" of movement over water and the owner's subjective intent to remain moored "indefinitely" at a dock could not show the contrary.

Lozman sought certiorari. In light of uncertainty among the Circuits about application of the term "capable" we granted his petition. Compare De La Rosa v. St. Charles Gaming Co., 474 F.3d 185, 187 (C.A.5 2006) (structure is not a "vessel" where "physically," but only "theoretical[ly]," "capable of sailing," and owner intends to moor it indefinitely as floating casino), with Board of Comm'rs of Orleans Levee Dist. v. M/V Belle of Orleans, 535 F.3d 1299, 1311–1312 (C.A.11 2008) (structure is a "vessel" where capable of moving over water under tow, "albeit to her detriment," despite intent to moor indefinitely). See also 649 F.3d, at 1267 (rejecting views of Circuits that " 'focus on the intent of the shipowner' "). . . .

III

A

We focus primarily upon the statutory phrase "capable of being used . . . as a means of transportation on water." 1 U.S.C. § 3. The Court of Appeals found that the home was "capable" of transportation because it could float, it could proceed under tow, and its shore connections (power cable, water hose, rope lines) did not " 'rende[r]' " it "practically incapable of transportation or movement." 649 F.3d, at 1266 (quoting Belle of Orleans, supra, at 1312). At least for argument's sake we agree with the Court of Appeals about the last-mentioned point, namely that Lozman's shore connections did not " 'render' " the home " 'practically incapable of transportation.' " But unlike the Eleventh Circuit, we do not find these considerations (even when combined with the home's other characteristics) sufficient to show that Lozman's home was a "vessel."

The Court of Appeals recognized that it had applied the term "capable" broadly. Indeed, it pointed with approval to language in an earlier case, Burks v. American River Transp. Co., 679 F.2d 69 (C.A.5 1982), in which the Fifth Circuit said:

" 'No doubt the three men in a tub would also fit within our definition, and one probably could make a convincing case for Jonah inside the whale.' " 649 F.3d, at 1269 (brackets omitted) (quoting Burks, supra, at 75).

But the Eleventh Circuit's interpretation is too broad. Not *every* floating structure is a "vessel." To state the obvious, a wooden washtub, a plastic dishpan, a swimming platform on pontoons, a large fishing net, a door taken off its hinges, or Pinocchio (when inside the whale) are not "vessels," even if they are "artificial contrivance[s]" capable of floating, moving under tow, and incidentally carrying even a fair-sized item or two when they do so. Rather, the statute applies to an "artificial contrivance . . . capable of being used . . . *as a means of transportation on water*." 1 U.S.C. § 3 (emphasis added). "[T]ransportation" involves the "conveyance (of things or persons) from one place to another." 18 Oxford English Dictionary 424 (2d ed. 1989) (OED). [Citation.] And we must apply this definition in a "practical," not a "theoretical," way. Stewart, supra, at 496, 125 S.Ct. 1118. Consequently, in our view a structure does not fall within the scope of this statutory phrase unless a reasonable observer, looking to the home's physical characteristics and activities, would consider it designed to a practical degree for carrying people or things over water.

B

. . . But for the fact that it floats, nothing about Lozman's home suggests that it was designed to any practical degree to transport persons or things over water. It had no rudder or other steering mechanism. Its hull was unraked, and it had a rectangular bottom 10 inches below the water. It had no special capacity to generate or store electricity but could obtain that utility only through ongoing connections with the land. Its small rooms looked like ordinary nonmaritime living quarters. And those inside those rooms looked out upon the world, not through watertight portholes, but through French doors or ordinary windows. . . .

Lozman's home differs significantly from an ordinary houseboat in that it has no ability to propel itself. Cf. 33 CFR § 173.3 (2012) ("Houseboat means a *motorized* vessel . . . designed primarily for multi-purpose accommodation spaces with low freeboard and little or no foredeck or cockpit" (emphasis added)). Lozman's home was able to travel over water only by being towed. Prior to its arrest, that home's travel by tow over water took place on only four occasions over a period of seven years. And when the home was towed a significant distance in 2006, the towing company had a second boat follow behind to prevent the home from swinging dangerously from side to side. . . .

In a word, we can find nothing about the home that could lead a reasonable observer to consider it designed to a practical degree for "transportation on water."

C

. . . The Court's reasoning in Stewart also supports our conclusion. We there considered the application of the statutory definition to a dredge. 543 U.S., at 494. The dredge was "a massive floating platform" from which a suspended clamshell bucket would "remov[e] silt from the ocean floor," depositing it "onto one of two scows" floating alongside the dredge. *Id.*, at 484. Like more traditional "seagoing vessels," the dredge had, *e.g.,* "a captain and crew, navigational lights, ballast tanks, and a crew dining area." Ibid. Unlike more ordinary vessels, it could navigate only by "manipulating its anchors and cables" or by being towed. Ibid. Nonetheless it did move. In fact it moved over water "every couple of hours." *Id.*, at 485.

We held that the dredge was a "vessel." We wrote that § 3's definition "merely codified the meaning that the term 'vessel' had acquired in general maritime law." *Id.*, at 490. We added that the question of the "watercraft's use 'as a means of transportation on water' is . . . practical," and not "merely . . . theoretical." *Id.*, at 496. And we pointed to cases holding that dredges ordinarily "served a waterborne transportation function," namely that "in performing their work they carried machinery, equipment, and crew over water." *Id.*, at 491–492 (citing, *e.g.,* Butler v. Ellis, 45 F.2d 951, 955 (C.A. 4th 1930)).

As the Court of Appeals pointed out, in Stewart we also wrote that § 3 "does not require that a watercraft be used *primarily* for that [transportation] purpose," 543 U.S., at 495; that a "watercraft need not be in motion to qualify as a vessel," ibid.; and that a structure may qualify as a vessel even if attached—but not "permanently" attached—to the land or ocean floor. *Id.*, at 493–494. We did not take these statements, however, as implying a universal set of sufficient conditions for application of the definition. Rather, they say, and they mean, that the statutory definition *may* (or may not) apply—not that it *automatically must* apply—where a structure has some other *primary* purpose, where it is stationary at relevant times, and where it is attached—but not permanently attached—to land.

After all, a washtub is normally not a "vessel" though it does not have water transportation as its primary purpose, it may be stationary much of the time, and it might be attached—but not permanently attached—to land. . . .

IV

Although we have focused on the phrase "*capable* of being used" for transportation over water, the statute also includes as a "vessel" a structure that is *actually* "used" for that transportation. 1 U.S.C. § 3 (emphasis added). And the City argues that, irrespective of its design, Lozman's floating home was *actually* so used. We are not persuaded by its argument.

We are willing to assume for argument's sake that sometimes it is possible actually to use for water transportation a structure that is in no practical way designed for that purpose. But even so, the City cannot show the actual use for which it argues. Lozman's floating home moved only under tow. Before its arrest, it moved significant distances only twice in seven years. And when it moved, it carried, not passengers or cargo, but at the very most (giving the benefit of any factual ambiguity to the City) only its own furnishings, its owner's personal effects, and personnel present to assure the home's safety. This is far too little *actual* "use" to bring the floating home within the terms of the statute. See Evansville, 271 U.S., at 20–21 (wharfboat not a "vessel" even though "[e]ach winter" it "was towed to [a] harbor to protect it from ice"); see also Roper v. United States, 368 U.S. 20, 23 (1961) ("Unlike a barge, the S.S. *Harry Lane* was not moved in order to transport commodities from one location to another").

V

For these reasons, the judgment of the Court of Appeals is reversed.

It is so ordered.

■ JUSTICE SOTOMAYOR, with whom JUSTICE KENNEDY joins, dissenting.

I agree with much of the Court's reasoning. Our precedents fully support the Court's reasoning that the Eleventh Circuit's test is overinclusive; that the subjective intentions of a watercraft's owner or designer play no role in the vessel analysis of 1 U.S.C. § 3; and that an objective assessment of a watercraft's purpose or function governs whether that structure is a vessel. The Court, however, creates a novel and unnecessary "reasonable observer" reformulation of these principles and errs in its determination, under this new standard, that the craft before us is not a vessel. Given the underdeveloped record below, we should remand. Therefore, I respectfully dissent.

I

The relevant statute, 1 U.S.C. § 3, "sweeps broadly." Stewart v. Dutra Constr. Co., 543 U.S. 481, 494 (2005). It provides that "[t]he word 'vessel' includes every description of watercraft or other artificial contrivance used, or capable of being used, as a means of transportation on water." This broad phrasing flows from admiralty law's long recognition that vessels come in many shapes and sizes. See E. Benedict, American Admiralty § 218, p. 121 (1870 ed.) ("[V]essel, is a general word, many times used for any kind of navigation"); M. Cohen, Admiralty Jurisdiction, Law, and Practice 232 (1883) ("[T]he term 'vessel' shall be understood to comprehend every description of vessel navigating on any sea or channel, lake or river . . . ").

Our test for vessel status has remained the same for decades: "Under § 3, a 'vessel' is any watercraft practically capable of maritime transportation. . . ." Stewart, 543 U.S., at 497. At its core, vessel status has always rested upon the objective physical characteristics of a vessel (such as its structure, shape, and materials of construction), as well as its usage history. But over time, several important principles have guided both this Court and the lower courts in determining what kinds of watercraft fall properly within the scope of admiralty jurisdiction.

Consider the most basic of requirements. For a watercraft to be "practically capable" of maritime transportation, it must first be "capable" of such transportation. Only those structures that can simultaneously float and carry people or things over water are even presumptively within § 3's reach. Stopping here, as the Eleventh Circuit essentially did, results in an overinclusive test. Section 3, after all, does not drag every bit of floating and towable flotsam and jetsam into admiralty jurisdiction. Rather, the terms "capable of being used" and "practical" have real significance in our maritime jurisprudence.

"[A] water craft is not 'capable of being used' for maritime transport in any meaningful sense if it has been permanently moored." Stewart, 543 U.S., at 494. So, . . . a watercraft whose objective physical connections to land "evidence a permanent location" does not fall within § 3's ambit. [Citation.] Put plainly, structures "permanently affixed to shore or resting on the ocean floor," Stewart, 543 U.S., at 493–494, have never been treated as vessels for the purposes of § 3.

Our precedents have also excluded from vessel status those watercraft "rendered practically incapable of transportation or movement." Id., at 494. Take the easiest case, a vessel whose physical characteristics have been so altered as to make waterborne transportation a practical impossibility. [Citation.] The longstanding admiralty exception for "dead ships," those watercraft that "require a major overhaul" for their "reactivation," also falls into this category. [Citation.] Likewise, ships that "have been withdrawn from the water for extended periods of time" in order to facilitate repairs and reconstruction may lose their status as vessels until they are rendered capable of maritime transport. Stewart, 543 U.S., at 496, 125 S.Ct. 1118. . . . Finally, our maritime jurisprudence excludes from vessel status those floating structures that, based on their physical characteristics, do not "transport people, freight, or cargo from place to place" as one of their purposes. Stewart, 543 U.S., at 493. "Purpose," in this context, is determined solely by an objective inquiry into a craft's function. "[N]either size, form, equipment nor means of propulsion are determinative factors upon the question of [vessel status]," though all may be considered. The Robert W. Parsons, 191 U.S. 17, 30 (1903). Moreover, in assessing a particular structure's function, we have consistently examined its past and present activities. Of course, a seaborne craft is not excluded from vessel status simply because its "primary purpose" is not maritime transport. Stewart, 543 U.S., at 497. We held as much in Stewart when we concluded that a dredge was a vessel notwithstanding that its "primary purpose" was "dredging rather than transportation." Id., at 486, 495. So long as one purpose of a craft is transportation, whether of cargo or people or both, § 3's practical capability requirement is satisfied. . . .

In sum, our precedents offer substantial guidance for how objectively to determine whether a watercraft is practically capable of maritime transport and thus qualifies as a § 3 vessel. First, the capacity to float and carry things or people is an obvious prerequisite to vessel status. Second, structures or ships that are permanently moored or fixed in place are not § 3 vessels. Likewise, structures that are practically incapable of maritime transport are not vessels . . . [e.g., dead ships]. Third, those watercraft whose physical characteristics and usage history reveal no maritime transport purpose or use are not § 3 vessels.

II

. . . The majority errs . . . in concluding that the purpose component of the § 3 test is whether "a reasonable observer, looking to the [craft]'s physical characteristics and activities, would not consider it to be designed to any practical degree for carrying people or things on water." This phrasing has never appeared in any of our cases and the majority's use of it, despite its seemingly objective gloss, effectively (and erroneously) introduces a subjective component into the vessel-status inquiry.

For one thing, in applying this test the majority points to some characteristics of Lozman's craft that have no relationship to maritime transport, such as the style of the craft's rooms or that "those inside those rooms looked out upon the world, not through water-tight portholes, but through French doors or ordinary windows." The majority never explains why it believes these particular esthetic elements are important for determining vessel status. In fact, they are not. Section 3 is focused on whether a structure is "used, or capable of being used, as a means of transportation on water." By importing windows, doors, room style, and other esthetic criteria into the § 3 analysis, the majority gives our vessel test an "I know it when I see it" flavor. [Citation.] But that has never been nor should it be the test . . . .

The majority's treatment of the craft's past voyages is also strange. The majority notes that Lozman's craft could be and was, in fact, towed over long distances, including over 200 miles at one point. But the majority determines that, given the design of Lozman's craft, this is "far too little *actual* 'use' to bring the floating home within the terms of the statute." This is because "when it moved, it carried, not passengers or cargo, but at the very most (giving the benefit of any factual ambiguity to the City) only its own furnishings, its owner's personal effects, and personnel present to assure the home's safety."

I find this analysis confusing. The majority accepts that the record indicates that Lozman's craft traveled hundreds of miles while "carrying people or things." But then, in the same breath, the majority concludes that a "reasonable observer" would nonetheless conclude that the craft was not "designed to any practical degree for carrying people or things on water." The majority fails to explain how a craft that apparently did carry people and things over water for long distances was not "practically capable" of maritime transport.

This is not to say that a structure capable of such feats is necessarily a vessel. A craft like Lozman's might not be a vessel, for example, if it could only carry its owner's clothes and personal effects, or if it is only capable of transporting itself and its appurtenances. [Citation.] But if such a craft can carry large appliances (like an oven or a refrigerator) and all of the other things we might find in a normal home in addition to the occupants of that home, as the existing record suggests Lozman's craft may have done, then it would seem to be much more like a mobile home . . . . The simple truth is that we know very little about the craft's capabilities and what did or did not happen on its various trips. By focusing on the little we do know for certain about this craft (*i.e.,* its windows, doors, and the style of its rooms) in determining whether it is a vessel, the majority renders the § 3 inquiry opaque and unpredictable.

Indeed, the little we do know about Lozman's craft suggests only that it was an unusual structure. A surveyor was unable to find any comparable craft for sale in the State of Florida. Lozman's home was neither obviously a houseboat, as the majority describes such ships, nor clearly a floating home. The only clear difference that the majority identifies between these two kinds of structures is that the former are self-propelled, while the latter are not. But even the majority recognizes that self-propulsion has never been a prerequisite for vessel status. Consequently, it is unclear why Lozman's craft is a floating home, why all floating homes are not vessels, or why Lozman's craft is not a vessel. If windows, doors, and other esthetic attributes are what take Lozman's craft out of vessel status, then the majority's test is completely malleable. If it is the craft's lack of self-propulsion, then the majority's test is unfaithful to our longstanding precedents. [Citation.] If it is something else, then that something is not apparent from the majority's opinion. . . .

III

With a more developed record, Lozman's craft might be distinguished from the houseboats in those lower court cases just discussed. For example, if Lozman's craft's previous voyages caused it serious damage, then that would strongly suggest that it lacked a maritime transportation purpose or function. There is no harm in remanding the case for further factfinding along the lines described above, cautioning the lower courts to be aware that features of Lozman's "incomparable" craft, may distinguish it from previous precedents. At most, such a remand would introduce a relatively short delay before finally ending the years-long battle between Lozman and the city of Riviera Beach.

. . . [N]umerous maritime industries rely heavily on clear and predictable legal rules for determining which ships are vessels. The majority's distorted application of our settled law to the facts of this case frustrates these ends. . . .

IV

It is not clear that Lozman's craft is a § 3 vessel. It is clear, however, that we are not in a good position to make such a determination based on the limited record we possess. The appropriate response is to remand the case for further proceedings in light of the proper legal standard. The Court resists this move and in its haste to christen Lozman's craft a nonvessel delivers an analysis that will confuse the lower courts and upset our longstanding admiralty precedent. I respectfully dissent.

QUESTIONS

As the majority acknowledged, the meaning of the term "vessel" might, depending on the circumstances, include everything from a wooden washtub to a plastic dishpan to a door taken off its hinges. How should judges decide what the proper context should be?

In particular, are any of the following "vessels"?

— A surfboard

— A swimming pool raft

— An inflatable life raft

— A non self-propelled barge used for transporting goods

— Boats used for amusement park rides such as "Splash Mountain"

4. SOURCES OF ORDINARY MEANING

Concepts like "literal purview" or "plain meaning" are not self-evident. They conceal the predicate question of how to determine whether the language of the statute is indeed "plain," or whether a particular phrase has a "literal" meaning at all. Legislators sometimes simplify that inquiry by including a definitions section (although as we have seen, statutory definitions do not always dispel interpretive doubt). Otherwise, courts must look elsewhere to determine the meaning of the ambiguous term or phrase in question. Courts often use "plain meaning" and "ordinary meaning" interchangeably; note, for example, how the dissent in *Yates*, *supra*, suggested that if the ordinary meaning of the term "tangible object" was readily apparent, then that meaning was "plain," and no deeper inquiry was warranted. However, if the meaning is not "plain," to what should the interpreter turn?

Federal Communications Commission
v. AT & T Inc.

Supreme Court of the United States, 2011.
562 U.S. 397, 131 S.Ct. 1177, 179 L.Ed.2d 132.

■ CHIEF JUSTICE ROBERTS delivered the opinion of the Court[, in which all other Members joined, except JUSTICE KAGAN, who took no part in the consideration or decision of the case.]

The Freedom of Information Act requires federal agencies to make records and documents publicly available upon request, unless they fall within one of several statutory exemptions. One of those exemptions covers law enforcement records, the disclosure of which "could reasonably be expected to constitute an unwarranted invasion of personal privacy."

5 U.S.C. § 552(b)(7)(C).* The question presented is whether corporations have "personal privacy" for the purposes of this exemption.

I

The Freedom of Information Act request at issue in this case relates to an investigation of respondent AT&T Inc., conducted by the Federal Communications Commission. AT&T participated in an FCC-administered program—the E-Rate (or Education-Rate) program—that was created to enhance access for schools and libraries to advanced telecommunications and information services. In August 2004, AT&T voluntarily reported to the FCC that it might have overcharged the Government for services it provided as part of the program.

The FCC's Enforcement Bureau launched an investigation. As part of that investigation, AT&T provided the Bureau various documents, including responses to interrogatories, invoices, emails with pricing and billing information, names and job descriptions of employees involved, and AT&T's assessment of whether those employees had violated the company's code of conduct. The FCC and AT&T resolved the matter in December 2004 through a consent decree in which AT&T—without conceding liability—agreed to pay the Government $ 500,000 and to institute a plan to ensure compliance with the program.

Several months later, CompTel—"a trade association representing some of AT&T's competitors"—submitted a FOIA request seeking " '[a]ll pleadings and correspondence' " in the Bureau's file on the AT&T

---

*   Editors' Note: 5 U.S.C. § 552 provides:

Public information; agency rules, opinions, orders, records, and proceedings

(a) Each agency shall make available to the public information as follows: . . .

(b) This section does not apply to matters that are—

. . .

(4) trade secrets and commercial or financial information obtained from a person and privileged or confidential; . . .

(6) personnel and medical files and similar files the disclosure of which would constitute a clearly unwarranted invasion of personal privacy;

(7) records or information compiled for law enforcement purposes, but only to the extent that the production of such law enforcement records or information

(A) could reasonably be expected to interfere with enforcement proceedings,

(B) would deprive a person of a right to a fair trial or an impartial adjudication,

(C) could reasonably be expected to constitute an unwarranted invasion of personal privacy,

(D) could reasonably be expected to disclose the identity of a confidential source, including a State, local, or foreign agency or authority or any private institution which furnished information on a confidential basis, and, in the case of a record or information compiled by criminal law enforcement authority in the course of a criminal investigation or by an agency conducting a lawful national security intelligence investigation, information furnished by a confidential source,

(E) would disclose techniques and procedures for law enforcement investigations or prosecutions, or would disclose guide-lines for law enforcement investigations or prosecutions if such disclosure could reasonably be expected to risk circumvention of the law, or

(F) could reasonably be expected to endanger the life or physical safety of any individual; . . .

investigation. AT&T opposed CompTel's request, and the Bureau issued a letter-ruling in response.

The Bureau concluded that some of the information AT&T had provided (including cost and pricing data, billing-related information, and identifying information about staff, contractors, and customer representatives) should be protected from disclosure under FOIA Exemption 4, which relates to "trade secrets and commercial or financial information," 5 U.S.C. § 552(b)(4). The Bureau also decided to withhold other information under FOIA Exemption 7(C). Exemption 7(C) exempts "records or information compiled for law enforcement purposes" that "could reasonably be expected to constitute an unwarranted invasion of personal privacy." § 552(b)(7)(C). The Bureau concluded that "individuals identified in [AT&T's] submissions" have "privacy rights" that warrant protection under Exemption 7(C). The Bureau did not, however, apply that exemption to the corporation itself, reasoning that "businesses do not possess 'personal privacy' interests as required" by the exemption.

On review the FCC agreed with the Bureau. The Commission found AT&T's position that it is "a 'private corporate citizen' with personal privacy rights that should be protected from disclosure that would 'embarrass' it . . . within the meaning of Exemption 7(C) . . . at odds with established [FCC] and judicial precedent." It therefore concluded that "Exemption 7(C) has no applicability to corporations such as [AT&T]."

AT&T sought review in the Court of Appeals for the Third Circuit, and that court rejected the FCC's reasoning. Noting that Congress had defined the word "person" to include corporations as well as individuals, 5 U.S.C. § 551(2), the court held that Exemption 7(C) extends to the "personal privacy" of corporations, since "the root from which the statutory word [personal] . . . is derived" is the defined term "person." 582 F.3d at 497. As the court explained, "[i]t would be very odd indeed for an adjectival form of a defined term not to refer back to that defined term." The court accordingly ruled "that FOIA's text unambiguously indicates that a corporation may have a 'personal privacy' interest within the meaning of Exemption 7(C)."

The FCC petitioned this Court for review of the Third Circuit's decision and CompTel filed as a respondent supporting petitioners. We granted certiorari, and now reverse.

II

Like the Court of Appeals below, AT&T relies on the argument that the word "personal" in Exemption 7(C) incorporates the statutory definition of the word "person." The Administrative Procedure Act defines "person" to include "an individual, partnership, corporation, association, or public or private organization other than an agency." 5 U.S.C. § 551(2). Because that definition applies here, the argument goes, "personal" must mean relating to those "person[s]": namely, corporations and other entities as well as individuals. This reading, we are told, is dictated by a "basic principle of grammar and usage." [Citation.] According to AT&T, "[b]y expressly defining the noun 'person' to include corporations, Congress *necessarily* defined the adjective form of that noun—'personal'—also to include corporations."

We disagree. Adjectives typically reflect the meaning of corresponding nouns, but not always. Sometimes they acquire distinct meanings of their own. The noun "crab" refers variously to a crustacean and a type of apple, while the related adjective "crabbed" can refer to handwriting that is "difficult to read," Webster's Third New International Dictionary 527 (2002); "corny" can mean "using familiar and stereotyped formulas believed to appeal to the unsophisticated," *id.,* at 509, which has little to do with "corn," *id.,* at 507 ("the seeds of any of the cereal grasses used for food"); and while "crank" is "a part of an axis bent at right angles," "cranky" can mean "given to fretful fussiness," *id.,* at 530.

Even in cases such as these there may well be a link between the noun and the adjective. "Cranky" describes a person with a "wayward" or "capricious" temper, see 3 Oxford English Dictionary 1117 (2d ed. 1989) (OED), which might bear some relation to the distorted or crooked angular shape from which a "crank" takes its name. That is not the point. What is significant is that, in ordinary usage, a noun and its adjective form may have meanings as disparate as any two unrelated words. The FCC's argument that "personal" does not, in fact, derive from the English word "person," but instead developed along its own etymological path, simply highlights the shortcomings of AT&T's proposed rule.

"Person" is a defined term in the statute; "personal" is not. When a statute does not define a term, we typically "give the phrase its ordinary meaning." *Johnson* v. *United States*, 559 U.S. 133, ___, 130 S.Ct. 1265, 176 L. Ed. 2d 1, 8 (2010). "Personal" ordinarily refers to individuals. We do not usually speak of personal characteristics, personal effects, personal correspondence, personal influence, or personal tragedy as referring to corporations or other artificial entities. This is not to say that corporations do not have correspondence, influence, or tragedies of their own, only that we do not use the word "personal" to describe them.

Certainly, if the chief executive officer of a corporation approached the chief financial officer and said, "I have something personal to tell you," we would not assume the CEO was about to discuss company business. Responding to a request for information, an individual might say, "that's personal." A company spokesman, when asked for information about the company, would not. In fact, we often use the word "personal" to mean precisely the *opposite* of business-related: We speak of personal expenses and business expenses, personal life and work life, personal opinion and a company's view.

Dictionaries also suggest that "personal" does not ordinarily relate to artificial "persons" such as corporations. See, *e.g.,* 7 OED 726 (1933) ("[1] [o]f, pertaining to . . . the individual person or self," "individual;

private; one's own," "[3] [o]f or pertaining to one's person, body, or figure," "[5] [o]f, pertaining to, or characteristic of a person or self-conscious being, as opposed to a thing or abstraction"); 11 OED at 599–600 (2d ed. 1989) (same); Webster's Third New International Dictionary 1686 (1976) ("[3] relating to the person or body"; "[4] relating to an individual, his character, conduct, motives, or private affairs"; "[5] relating to or characteristic of human beings as distinct from things"); *ibid.* (2002) (same).

AT&T dismisses these definitions, correctly noting that "personal"— at its most basic level—simply means "[o]f or pertaining to a particular person." Webster's New International Dictionary 1828 (2d ed. 1954). The company acknowledges that "in non-legal usage, where a 'person' is a human being, it is entirely unsurprising that the word 'personal' is used to refer to human beings." But in a watered-down version of the "grammatical imperative" argument, AT&T contends that "person"—in common *legal* usage—is understood to include a corporation. "Personal" in the same context therefore can and should have the same scope, especially here in light of the statutory definition.

The construction of statutory language often turns on context, see, *e.g., Johnson, supra,* at ___, 130 S.Ct. 1265, 176 L. Ed. 2d 1 (slip op., at 5), which certainly may include the definitions of related words. But here the context to which AT&T points does not dissuade us from the ordinary meaning of "personal." We have no doubt that "person," in a legal setting, often refers to artificial entities. The Dictionary Act makes that clear. 1 U.S.C. § 1 (defining "person" to include "corporations, companies, associations, firms, partnerships, societies, and joint stock companies, as well as individuals"). But AT&T's effort to ascribe a corresponding legal meaning to "personal" again elides the difference between "person" and "personal."

When it comes to the word "personal," there is little support for the notion that it denotes corporations, even in the legal context. AT&T notes that corporations are "protected by the doctrine of 'personal' jurisdiction," but that phrase refers to jurisdiction *in personam,* as opposed to *in rem,* not the jurisdiction "of a person." The only other example AT&T cites is an 1896 case that referred to the " 'personal privilege' " of a corporation. (quoting *Mercantile Bank* v. *Tennessee ex rel. Memphis,* 161 U.S. 161, 171, 16 S.Ct. 461, 40 L. Ed. 656 (1896) (emphasis deleted)). These examples fall far short of establishing that "personal" here has a legal meaning apart from its ordinary one, even if "person" does. [Citation.]

Regardless of whether "personal" can carry a special meaning in legal usage, "when interpreting a statute . . . we construe language . . . in light of the terms surrounding it." *Leocal* v. *Ashcroft,* 543 U.S. 1, 9, 125 S.Ct. 377, 160 L. Ed. 2d 271 (2004). Exemption 7(C) refers not just to the word "personal," but to the term "personal privacy." § 552(b)(7)(C); [citation]. AT&T's effort to attribute a special legal meaning to the word "personal" in this particular context is wholly unpersuasive.

AT&T's argument treats the term "personal privacy" as simply the sum of its two words: the privacy of a person. Under that view, the defined meaning of the noun "person," or the asserted specialized legal meaning, takes on greater significance. But two words together may assume a more particular meaning than those words in isolation. We understand a golden cup to be a cup made of or resembling gold. A golden boy, on the other hand, is one who is charming, lucky, and talented. A golden opportunity is one not to be missed. "Personal" in the phrase "personal privacy" conveys more than just "of a person." It suggests a type of privacy evocative of human concerns—not the sort usually associated with an entity like, say, AT&T.

Despite its contention that "[c]ommon legal usage" of the word "person" supports its reading of the term "personal privacy," AT&T does not cite a single instance in which this Court or any other (aside from the Court of Appeals below) has expressly referred to a corporation's "personal privacy." Nor does it identify any other statute that does so. See Tr. of Oral Arg. 26. On the contrary, treatises in print around the time that Congress drafted the exemptions at hand reflect the understanding that the specific concept of "personal privacy," at least as a matter of common law, did not apply to corporations. [Citation.] AT&T contends that this Court has recognized "privacy" interests of corporations in the Fourth Amendment and double jeopardy contexts, and that the term should be similarly construed here. But this case does not call upon us to pass on the scope of a corporation's "privacy" interests as a matter of constitutional or common law. The discrete question before us is instead whether Congress used the term "personal privacy" to refer to the privacy of artificial persons in FOIA Exemption 7(C); the cases AT&T cites are too far afield to be of help here.

AT&T concludes that the FCC has simply failed to demonstrate that the phrase "personal privacy" "necessarily *excludes* the privacy of corporations." [AT&T Brief], at 31–32 (emphasis added). But construing statutory language is not merely an exercise in ascertaining "the outer limits of [a word's] definitional possibilities," *Dolan* v. *Postal Service*, 546 U.S. 481, 486, 126 S.Ct. 1252, 163 L. Ed. 2d 1079 (2006). AT&T has given us no sound reason in the statutory text or context to disregard the ordinary meaning of the phrase "personal privacy."

III

The meaning of "personal privacy" in Exemption 7(C) is further clarified by the rest of the statute. Congress enacted Exemption 7(C) against the backdrop of pre-existing FOIA exemptions, and the purpose and scope of Exemption 7(C) becomes even more apparent when viewed in this context. See *Nken* v. *Holder*, 556 U.S. 418, ___, 129 S.Ct. 1749, 173 L. Ed. 2d 550, 561 (2009) ("statutory interpretation turns on 'the language itself, the specific context in which that language is used, and the broader context of the statute as a whole' " (quoting *Robinson* v. *Shell*

Oil Co., 519 U.S. 337, 341, 117 S.Ct. 843, 136 L. Ed. 2d 808 (1997)). Two of those other exemptions are particularly relevant here.

The phrase "personal privacy" first appeared in the FOIA exemptions in Exemption 6, enacted in 1966, eight years before Congress enacted Exemption 7(C). See 80 Stat. 250, codified as amended at 5 U.S.C. § 552(b)(6). Exemption 6 covers "personnel and medical files and similar files the disclosure of which would constitute a clearly unwarranted invasion of personal privacy." § 552(b)(6). Not only did Congress choose the same term in drafting Exemption 7(C), it also used the term in a nearly identical manner.

Although the question whether Exemption 6 is limited to individuals has not come to us directly, we have regularly referred to that exemption as involving an "individual's right of privacy." *Department of State* v. *Ray*, 502 U.S. 164, 175, 112 S.Ct. 541, 116 L. Ed. 2d 526 (1991) (quoting *Department of Air Force* v. *Rose*, 425 U.S. 352, 372, 96 S.Ct. 1592, 48 L. Ed. 2d 11 (1976) (internal quotation marks omitted)); see also *Department of State* v. *Washington Post Co.*, 456 U.S. 595, 599, 102 S.Ct. 1957, 72 L. Ed. 2d 358 (1982).

AT&T does not dispute that "identical words and phrases within the same statute should normally be given the same meaning," *Powerex Corp.* v. *Reliant Energy Services, Inc.*, 551 U.S. 224, 232, 127 S.Ct. 2411, 168 L. Ed. 2d 112 (2007), but contends that "if Exemption 6 does not protect corporations, it is because [it] applies only to 'personnel and medical files and similar files,'" not because of the term "personal privacy." Yet the significance of the pertinent phrase—"the disclosure of which would constitute a clearly unwarranted invasion of personal privacy," § 552(b)(6)—cannot be so readily dismissed. Without it, Exemption 6 would categorically exempt "personnel and medical files" as well as any "similar" file. Even if the scope of Exemption 6 is also limited by the types of files it protects, the "personal privacy" phrase importantly defines the particular subset of that information Congress sought to exempt. See *Washington Post Co., supra,* at 599, 102 S.Ct. 1957, 72 L. Ed. 2d 358. And because Congress used the same phrase in Exemption 7(C), the reach of that phrase in Exemption 6 is pertinent in construing Exemption 7(C).

In drafting Exemption 7(C), Congress did not, on the other hand, use language similar to that in Exemption 4. Exemption 4 pertains to "trade secrets and commercial or financial information obtained from a person and privileged or confidential." 5 U.S.C. § 552(b)(4). This clearly applies to corporations—it uses the defined term "person" to describe the source of the information—and we far more readily think of corporations as having "privileged or confidential" documents than personally private ones. So at the time Congress enacted Exemption 7(C), it had in place an exemption that plainly covered a corporation's commercial and financial information, and another that we have described as relating to "individuals." The language of Exemption 7(C) tracks the latter.

* * *

    We reject the argument that because "person" is defined for purposes of FOIA to include a corporation, the phrase "personal privacy" in Exemption 7(C) reaches corporations as well. The protection in FOIA against disclosure of law enforcement information on the ground that it would constitute an unwarranted invasion of personal privacy does not extend to corporations. We trust that AT&T will not take it personally.

    The judgment of the Court of Appeals is reversed.

IT IS SO ORDERED.

NOTE

    The Court's approach in *FCC v. AT&T* exemplifies a common method courts employ when seeking the "ordinary meaning" of a statutory term: the resort to dictionary definitions of the term in question. Indeed, the Court fairly readily dismissed AT&T's argument that the Court should look to the statute's definitions section, which defined "person" to include *corporate* persons, in order to divine the statutory meaning of "personal." Rather, the Court emphasized that the meaning of the adjective "personal" had "acquire[d a] distinct meaning[ ] of [its] own." Would it always be unreasonable for a related statutory definition to inform the interpretation of an ambiguous term?

    The Court also reached its conclusion by centering the interpretive inquiry on the meaning of the statutory phrase "*personal privacy*"—not the word "personal" as defined or used in isolation. As you will see later in this subsection, that phrase is an example of a linguistic "collocation" in which two words that frequently appear together may take on a more specific or contextual meaning than when either word is used on its own. As you read the next subsection, consider whether dictionary definitions are as useful when interpreting a statutory *phrase* as opposed to an individual word, given that most dictionary definitions provide definitions only of individual words. Consider also whether a central task for an interpreter is to decide whether the interpretive inquiry should be to define a *word* or a *phrase*. For example, as you will see in *Muscarello v. U.S., infra*, the majority focused its interpretive inquiry primarily on the meaning of the statutory word "carries," while the dissent focused instead on the statutory phrase "carries *a firearm*." Thus, whether an interpreter chooses to "zoom in" or "zoom out" may itself be dispositive in deciding which meaning to give to a statutory provision in question.

a. DICTIONARY DEFINITIONS

Dictionaries may be a useful source of "ordinary" meaning because they are generally widely available (including online), and they seek to reflect how "ordinary" members of the general public commonly use and understand language. At a minimum, then, dictionaries might be said to capture how the reasonable reader would understand the meaning of the statute in question. Nevertheless, dictionaries are not themselves neutral depositaries of word meanings and usages. The editors of dictionaries make conscious choices about whether to exclude, include, or prioritize one meaning or usage of a word over another—or even to include a word at all. As essayist David Foster Wallace once famously documented in a 2001 article in *Harper's*, lexicographic Usage Wars have in recent decades become as heated as judicial debates about textualism and purposivism:

> Did you know that probing the seamy underbelly of U.S. lexicography reveals ideological strife and controversy and intrigue and nastiness and fervor . . . ? For instance, did you know that some modern dictionaries are notoriously liberal and others notoriously conservative, and that certain conservative dictionaries were actually conceived and designed as corrective responses to the "corruption" and "permissiveness" of certain liberal dictionaries? That the oligarchic device of having a special "Distinguished Usage Panel . . . of outstanding professional speakers and writers" is an attempted compromise between the forces of egalitarianism and traditionalism in English, but that most linguistic liberals dismiss the Usage Panel as mere sham-populism . . . ? Did you know that U.S. lexicography even *had* a seamy underbelly? . . .
>
> We regular citizens tend to go to The Dictionary for authoritative guidance. Rarely, however, do we ask ourselves who decides what gets in The Dictionary or what words or spellings or pronunciations get deemed "substandard" or "incorrect." Whence the authority of dictionary-makers to decide what's OK and what isn't? Nobody elected them, after all. And simply appealing to precedent or tradition won't work, because what's considered correct changes over time. In the 1600s, for

instance, the second-singular pronoun took a singular conjugation—"You is." . . . English itself changes over time; if it didn't, we'd all still be talking like Chaucer. Who's to say which changes are natural and which are corruptions? . . .

You'd sure know lexicography had an underbelly if you read the little introductory essays in modern dictionaries . . . . They're salvos in the Usage Wars that have been under way ever since editor Philip Gove first sought to apply the value-neutral principles of structural linguistics to lexicography in *Webster's Third*. Gove's famous response to conservatives who howled when *Webster's Third* endorsed *OK* and described *ain't* as "used orally in most parts of the U.S. by many cultivated speakers [*sic*]" was this: "A dictionary should have no traffic with . . . artificial notions of correctness or superiority. It should be descriptive and not prescriptive." These terms stuck and turned epithetic, and linguistic conservatives are now formally known as Prescriptivists and linguistic liberals as Descriptivists.

Descriptivists . . . . tend to be hard-core academics, mostly linguists or Comp theorists. Loosely organized under the banner of structural (or "descriptive") linguistics, they are doctrinaire positivists . . . . In this age of technology, [some] Descriptivists contend, it's the Scientific Method—clinically objective, value-neutral, based on direct observation and demonstrable hypothesis—that should determine both the content of dictionaries and the standards of "correct" English. Because language is constantly evolving, such standards will always be fluid. Gove's now classic introduction to *Webster's Third* outlines this type of Descriptivism's five basic edicts:

"1—Language changes constantly;

2—Change is normal;

3—Spoken language is the language;

4—Correctness rests upon usage;

5—All usage is relative."

These principles look *prima facie* OK—commonsensical and couched in the bland simple s.-v.-o. prose of dispassionate Science—but in fact they're vague and muddled and it takes about three seconds to think of reasonable replies to each one of them, viz.:

1—OK, but how much and how fast?

2—Same thing. Is Heraclitean flux as normal or desirable as gradual change? Do some changes actually serve the language's overall pizzazz better than others? And how many people have to deviate from how many conventions before we say the language has actually changed? Fifty percent? Ten percent? Where do you draw the line? Who draws the line?

3—This is an old claim, at least as old as Plato's *Phaedrus*. And it's specious. If Derrida and the infamous Deconstructionists have done nothing else, they've debunked the idea that speech is language's primary instantiation. Plus consider the weird arrogance of Gove's (3) [with respect to] correctness. Only the most mullahlike Prescriptivists care very much about spoken English; most Prescriptive usage guides concern Standard *Written* English.

4—Fine, but whose usage? Gove's (4) begs the whole question. What he wants to suggest here, I think, is a reversal of the traditional entailment-relation between abstract rules and concrete usage: Instead of usage ideally corresponding to a rigid set of regulations, the regulations ought to correspond to the way real people are actually using the language. Again, fine, but which people? Urban Latinos? Boston Brahmins? Rural Midwesterners? Appalachian Neogaelics?

5—*Huh?* If this means what it seems to mean, then it ends up biting Gove's whole argument in the ass. (5) appears to imply that the correct answer to the above "which people?" is: "All of them!" And it's easy to show why this will not stand up as a lexicographical principle. The most obvious problem with [Descriptivist ambitions] is that not everything can go in The Dictionary. Why not? Because you can't observe every last bit of every last native speaker's "language behavior," and even if you could, the resultant dictionary would weigh 4 million pounds and have to be updated hourly. The fact is that any lexicographer is going to have to make choices about what gets in and what doesn't. And these choices are based on . . . what? And now we're right back where we started. . . .

There's an even more important way Descriptivists are wrong in thinking that the Scientific Method is appropriate to the study of language: . . . [Language] is both *human* and fundamentally *normative*. . . . To understand this, you have only to accept the proposition that language is by its very nature public. [Norms, after all, are just practices people have agreed on as optimal ways of doing things for certain purposes. They're not laws, but they're not laissez-faire, either.] Norms-wise, let's keep in mind that language didn't come into being because our hairy ancestors were sitting around the veldt with nothing better to do. Language was invented to serve certain specific purposes: "That mushroom is poisonous"; "Knock these two rocks together and you can start a fire"; "This shelter is mine!" And so on. Clearly, as linguistic communities evolve over time, they discover that some ways of using language are "better" than others—meaning better with respect to the community's purposes. . . . The whole point of norms is to help us evaluate our actions (including utterances) according to what we as a community have decided our real interests and purposes are. . . .

David Foster Wallace, Tense Present, Harper's (April 2001).

The question of whether usage authorities are, or should be, engaged in "value judgment" is not a uniquely English-language phenomenon, either. Consider this recent controversy:

[Ghent U]niversity in Belgium has refused demands to "immediately" strip its website of Flemish sign-language videos displaying stereotypical and anti-Semitic symbols for Jews, saying it was merely hosting a dictionary of signs without adding "value judgment." . . .

According to the Flemish dictionary, there are four ways to sign the word "Jewish": by stroking the chin; by stroking an imagined goatee; by mimicking bilateral pipe curls with the fingers; and by moving a hooked finger over the face— symbolizing a hooked nose. . . .

But the university . . . . said that it had discussed the complaints with the researchers who created the dictionary [and] in a statement on Friday . . . , the university described the controversy as a purely "scientific issue."

It said that in creating the dictionary, researchers merely "register and describe the signs that are used in the Flemish sign language." It added: "They don't take position on these signs, and don't cast a value judgment on them. This is what lexicographers do." . . .

The Flemish Sign Language Center, which helped create the dictionary in 1999 and is responsible for updating its content, said in a statement that . . . "We don't decide ourselves whether or not a sign has its place in the dictionary[.]" . . .

But in many dictionaries of sign languages around the world, including of American Sign Language in the United States, the sign for "Jewish" is simply a stroke under the chin. . . .

Milan Schreuer, University Denounced for Showing Sign Language for 'Jewish' as a Hooked Nose, New York Times (Sept. 20, 2019), available at https://www.nytimes.com/2019/09/20/world/europe/belgium-sign-language-jews.html.

Keep these debates about the proper place of dictionaries—and the authorities who develop them—in mind as you read the following case, as well as the cases in the next sections of this Part.

MCI Telecommunications Corp.
v. American Tel. & Tel. Co.

Supreme Court of the United States, 1994.
512 U.S. 218, 114 S.Ct. 2223, 129 L.Ed.2d 182.

■ JUSTICE SCALIA delivered the opinion of the Court[, in which CHIEF JUSTICE REHNQUIST, JUSTICE KENNEDY, JUSTICE THOMAS, and JUSTICE GINSBURG joined].

Section 203(a) of Title 47 of the United States Code requires communications common carriers to file tariffs with the Federal Communications Commission, and § 203(b) authorizes the Commission to "modify" any requirement of § 203. These cases present the question whether the Commission's decision to make tariff filing optional for all nondominant long-distance carriers is a valid exercise of its modification authority.

I

. . . When Congress created the Commission in 1934, AT & T, through its vertically integrated Bell system, held a virtual monopoly over the Nation's telephone service. The Communications Act of 1934, 48 Stat. 1064, as amended, authorized the Commission to regulate the rates charged for communication services to ensure that they were reasonable and nondiscriminatory. The requirements of § 203 that common carriers file their rates with the Commission and charge only the filed rate were the centerpiece of the Act's regulatory scheme.

. . . By 1979, competition in the provision of long-distance service was well established, and some urged that the continuation of extensive tariff filing requirements served only to impose unnecessary costs on new entrants and to facilitate collusive pricing. The Commission held hearings on the matter, see *Competitive Carrier Notice of Inquiry and Proposed Rulemaking,* 77 F.C.C.2d 308 (1979), following which it issued a series of rules that have produced this litigation.

The *First Report and Order,* 85 F.C.C.2d 1, 20–24 (1980), distinguished between dominant carriers (those with market power) and nondominant carriers—in the long-distance market, this amounted to a distinction between AT & T and everyone else—and relaxed some of the filing procedures for nondominant carriers, *id.,* at 30–49. In the *Second Report and Order,* 91 F.C.C.2d 59 (1982), the Commission entirely eliminated the filing requirement for resellers of terrestrial common carrier services. This policy of optional filing, or permissive detariffing, was extended to all other resellers, and to specialized common carriers, including petitioner MCI Telecommunications Corp., by the *Fourth Report and Order,* 95 F.C.C.2d 554 (1983), and to virtually all remaining categories of nondominant carriers by the *Fifth Report and Order,* 98 F.C.C.2d 1191 (1984). . . .

On August 7, 1989, AT & T filed a complaint, pursuant to the third-party complaint provision of the Communications Act, 47 U.S.C. § 208(a), which alleged that MCI's collection of unfiled rates violated §§ 203(a) and (c). MCI responded that the *Fourth Report* was a substantive rule, and so MCI had no legal obligation to file rates. AT & T rejoined that . . . if the *Fourth Report and Order* established a substantive rule, it was in excess of statutory authority. The Commission . . . refused to address . . . AT & T's contention that the rule was ultra vires, announcing instead a proposed rulemaking to consider that question. [Citation.] . . .

[T]he Commission released a Report and Order from the rulemaking proceeding commenced in response to AT & T's complaint. See *In re Tariff Filing Requirements for Interstate Common Carriers,* 7 FCC Rcd 8072 (1992), stayed pending further notice, 7 FCC Rcd 7989 (1992). That is the Report and Order at issue in this case. The Commission, relying upon the § 203(b) authority to "modify" . . . determined that its permissive detariffing policy was within its authority under the Communications Act. AT & T filed a motion with the District of Columbia Circuit seeking summary reversal of the Commission's order. . . . We granted the petitions and consolidated them.

II

Section 203 of the Communications Act contains both the filed rate provisions of the Act and the Commission's disputed modification authority. It provides in relevant part:

"(a) Filing; public display.

"Every common carrier, except connecting carriers, shall, within such reasonable time as the Commission shall designate, file with the Commission and print and keep open for public inspection schedules showing all charges . . ., whether such charges are joint or separate, and showing the classifications, practices, and regulations affecting such charges. . . .

"(b) Changes in schedule; discretion of Commission to *modify* requirements. . . .

"(2) The Commission may, in its discretion and for good cause shown, *modify* any requirement made by or under the authority of this section either in particular instances or by general order applicable to special circumstances or conditions except that the Commission may not require the notice period specified in paragraph (1) to be more than one hundred and twenty days. . . . " [emphasis added]

The dispute between the parties turns on the meaning of the phrase "modify any requirement" in § 203(b)(2). Petitioners argue that it gives the Commission authority to make even basic and fundamental changes in the scheme created by that section. We disagree. The word "modify"— like a number of other English words employing the root "mod-" (deriving from the Latin word for "measure"), such as "moderate," "modulate," "modest," and "modicum"—has a connotation of increment or limitation. Virtually every dictionary we are aware of says that "to modify" means to change moderately or in minor fashion. See, *e.g.,* Random House

Dictionary of the English Language 1236 (2d ed. 1987) ("to change somewhat the form or qualities of; alter partially; amend"); Webster's Third New International Dictionary 1452 (1981) ("to make minor changes in the form or structure of: alter without transforming"); 9 Oxford English Dictionary 952 (2d ed. 1989) ("[t]o make partial changes in; to change (an object) in respect of some of its qualities; to alter or vary without radical transformation"); Black's Law Dictionary 1004 (6th ed. 1990) ("[t]o alter; to change in incidental or subordinate features; enlarge; extend; amend; limit; reduce").

In support of their position, petitioners cite dictionary definitions contained in, or derived from, a single source, Webster's Third New International Dictionary 1452 (1981) (Webster's Third), which includes among the meanings of "modify," "to make a basic or important change in."[2] Petitioners contend that this establishes sufficient ambiguity to entitle the Commission to deference in its acceptance of the broader meaning, which in turn requires approval of its permissive detariffing policy. [Citation.] In short, they contend that the courts must defer to the agency's choice among available dictionary definitions, citing *National Railroad Passenger Corporation v. Boston & Maine Corp.,* 503 U.S. 407, 418, 112 S.Ct. 1394, 1402, 118 L.Ed.2d 52 (1992).

But *Boston & Maine* does not stand for that proposition. That case involved the question whether the statutory term "required" could only mean "demanded as essential" or could also mean "demanded as appropriate." In holding that the latter was a permissible interpretation, to which [judicial] deference was owed, the opinion did not rely exclusively upon dictionary definitions, but also upon contextual indications, see 503 U.S., at 417–419, 112 S.Ct., at 1401–1402,—which in the present cases, as we shall see, contradict petitioners' position. Moreover, when the *Boston & Maine* opinion spoke of "alternative dictionary definitions," *ibid.,* it did not refer to what we have here: one dictionary whose suggested meaning contradicts virtually all others. It referred to alternative definitions *within the dictionary cited* (Webster's Third, as it happens), which was not represented to be the *only* dictionary giving those alternatives. To the contrary, the Court said "these alternative interpretations are as old as the jurisprudence of this Court," *id.,* at 419, 112 S.Ct., at 1402, citing *McCulloch v. Maryland,* 4 Wheat. 316, 4 L.Ed. 579 (1819). See also Webster's New International Dictionary

---

[2] Petitioners also cite Webster's Ninth New Collegiate Dictionary 763 (1991), which includes among its definitions of "modify," "to make basic or fundamental changes in often to give a new orientation to or to serve a new end." They might also have cited the eighth version of Webster's New Collegiate Dictionary 739 (1973), which contains that same definition; and Webster's Seventh New Collegiate Dictionary 544 (1963), which contains the same definition as Webster's Third New International Dictionary quoted in text. The Webster's New Collegiate Dictionaries, published by G. & C. Merriam Company of Springfield, Massachusetts, are essentially abridgments of that company's Webster's New International Dictionaries, and recite that they are based upon those lengthier works. The last New Collegiate to be based upon Webster's Second New International, rather than Webster's Third, does not include "basic or fundamental change" among the accepted meanings of "modify." See Webster's New Collegiate Dictionary 541 (6th ed. 1949).

2117 (2d ed. 1934); 2 New Shorter Oxford English Dictionary 2557 (1993) (giving both alternatives).

Most cases of verbal ambiguity in statutes involve, as *Boston & Maine* did, a selection between accepted alternative meanings shown as such by many dictionaries. One can envision (though a court case does not immediately come to mind) having to choose between accepted alternative meanings, one of which is so newly accepted that it has only been recorded by a single lexicographer. (Some dictionary must have been the very first to record the widespread use of "projection," for example, to mean "forecast.") But what petitioners demand that we accept as creating an ambiguity here is a rarity even rarer than that: a meaning set forth in a single dictionary (and, as we say, its progeny) which not only *supplements* the meaning contained in all other dictionaries, but *contradicts* one of the meanings contained in virtually all other dictionaries. Indeed, contradicts one of the alternative meanings contained in the out-of-step dictionary itself—for as we have observed, Webster's Third itself defines "modify" to connote *both* (specifically) major change *and* (specifically) minor change. It is hard to see how that can be. When the word "modify" has come to mean *both* "to change in some respects" *and* "to change fundamentally" it will in fact mean *neither* of those things. It will simply mean "to change," and some adverb will have to be called into service to indicate the great or small degree of the change.

If that is what the peculiar Webster's Third definition means to suggest has happened—and what petitioners suggest by appealing to Webster's Third—we simply disagree. "Modify," in our view, connotes moderate change. It might be good English to say that the French Revolution "modified" the status of the French nobility—but only because there is a figure of speech called understatement and a literary device known as sarcasm. And it might be unsurprising to discover a 1972 White House press release saying that "the Administration is modifying its position with regard to prosecution of the war in Vietnam"—but only because press agents tend to impart what is nowadays called "spin." Such intentional distortions, or simply careless or ignorant misuse, must have formed the basis for the usage that Webster's Third, and Webster's Third alone, reported.[3] It is perhaps gilding the lily to add this: In 1934, when the Communications Act became law—the most relevant time for determining a statutory term's meaning, [citation], Webster's Third was not yet even contemplated. To our knowledge *all* English dictionaries provided the narrow definition of "modify," including those published by

---

[3] That is not an unlikely hypothesis. Upon its long-awaited appearance in 1961, Webster's Third was widely criticized for its portrayal of common error as proper usage. See, e.g., Follett, Sabotage in Springfield, 209 Atlantic 73 (Jan. 1962); Barzun, What is a Dictionary? 32 The American Scholar 176, 181 (spring 1963); Macdonald, The String Unwound, 38 The New Yorker 130, 156–157 (Mar. 1962). An example is its approval (without qualification) of the use of "infer" to mean "imply": "infer" "5: to give reason to draw an inference concerning: HINT <did not take part in the debate except to ask a question inferring that the constitution must be changed— Manchester Guardian Weekly >." Webster's Third New International Dictionary 1158 (1961).

G. & C. Merriam Company. See Webster's New International Dictionary 1577 (2d ed. 1934); Webster's Collegiate Dictionary 628 (4th ed. 1934). We have not the slightest doubt that is the meaning the statute intended.

Beyond the word itself, a further indication that the § 203(b)(2) authority to "modify" does not contemplate fundamental changes is the sole exception to that authority which the section provides. One of the requirements of § 203 is that changes to filed tariffs can be made only after 120 days' notice to the Commission and the public. § 203(b)(1). The *only* exception to the Commission's § 203(b)(2) modification authority is as follows: "except that the Commission may not require the notice period specified in paragraph (1) to be more than one hundred and twenty days." Is it conceivable that the statute is indifferent to the Commission's power to eliminate the tariff-filing requirement entirely for all except one firm in the long-distance sector, and yet strains out the gnat of extending the waiting period for tariff revision beyond 120 days? We think not. The exception is not as ridiculous as a Lilliputian in London only because it is to be found in Lilliput: in the small-scale world of "modifications," it is a big deal. . . .

[T]he Commission's permissive detariffing policy can be justified only if it makes a less than radical or fundamental change in the Act's tariff-filing requirement. The Commission's attempt to establish that no more than that is involved greatly understates the extent to which its policy deviates from the filing requirement, and greatly undervalues the importance of the filing requirement itself.

To consider the latter point first: For the body of a law, as for the body of a person, whether a change is minor or major depends to some extent upon the importance of the item changed to the whole. Loss of an entire toenail is insignificant; loss of an entire arm tragic. The tariff-filing requirement is, to pursue this analogy, the heart of the common-carrier section of the Communications Act. In the context of the Interstate Commerce Act, which served as its model, [citation,] this Court has repeatedly stressed that rate filing was Congress's chosen means of preventing unreasonableness and discrimination in charges. . . .

Bearing in mind, then, the enormous importance to the statutory scheme of the tariff-filing provision, we turn to whether what has occurred here can be considered a mere "modification." The Commission stresses that its detariffing policy applies only to nondominant carriers, so that the rates charged to over half of all consumers in the long-distance market are on file with the Commission. It is not clear to us that the proportion of customers affected, rather than the proportion of carriers affected, is the proper measure of the extent of the exemption (of course *all* carriers in the long-distance market are exempted, except AT & T). But even assuming it is, we think an elimination of the crucial provision of the statute for 40% of a major sector of the industry is much too extensive to be considered a "modification." What we have here, in reality, is a fundamental revision of the statute, changing it from a scheme of rate regulation in long-distance common-carrier communications to a scheme of rate regulation only where effective competition does not exist. That may be a good idea, but it was not the idea Congress enacted into law in 1934. . . .

The judgment of the Court of Appeals is

Affirmed.

■ JUSTICE O'CONNOR took no part in the consideration or decision of [this case].

■ JUSTICE STEVENS, with whom JUSTICE BLACKMUN and JUSTICE SOUTER join, dissenting.

. . . According to the Court, the term "modify," as explicated in all but the most unreliable dictionaries, rules out the Commission's claimed authority to relieve nondominant carriers of the basic obligation to file tariffs. Dictionaries can be useful aids in statutory interpretation, but they are no substitute for close analysis of what words mean as used in a particular statutory context. *Cf. Cabell v. Markham,* 148 F.2d 737, 739 (CA2 1945) (Hand, J.). Even if the sole possible meaning of "modify" were to make "minor" changes, further elaboration is needed to show why the detariffing policy should fail. The Commission came to its present policy through a series of rulings that gradually relaxed the filing requirements for nondominant carriers. Whether the current policy should count as a cataclysmic or merely an incremental departure from the § 203(a) baseline depends on whether one focuses on particular carriers' obligations to file (in which case the Commission's policy arguably works a major shift) or on the statutory policies behind the tariff-filing requirement (which remain satisfied because market constraints on nondominant carriers obviate the need for rate filing). When § 203 is viewed as part of a statute whose aim is to constrain monopoly power, the Commission's decision to exempt nondominant carriers is a rational and "measured" adjustment to novel circumstances—one that remains faithful to the core purpose of the tariff-filing section. See Black's Law Dictionary 1198 (3d ed. 1933) (defining "modification" as "A change; an alteration which introduces new elements into the details, or cancels some of them, but leaves *the general purpose and effect of the subject-matter* intact").

The Court seizes upon a particular sense of the word "modify" at the expense of another, long-established meaning that fully supports the Commission's position. That word is first defined in Webster's Collegiate Dictionary 628 (4th ed. 1934) as meaning "to limit or reduce in extent or degree."[5] The Commission's permissive detariffing policy fits comfortably

---

[5] See also 9 Oxford English Dictionary 952 (2d ed. 1989) ("2. To alter in the direction of moderation or lenity; to make less severe, rigorous, or decided; to qualify, tone down. . . . 1610 Donne *Pseudomartyr* 184 'For so Mariana modefies his Doctrine, that the Prince should not execute any Clergy man, though hee deser[v]e it' "); Random House Dictionary of the English Language 1236 (2d ed. 1987) ("5. to reduce or lessen in degree or extent; moderate; soften; *to modify one's demands* "); Webster's Third New International Dictionary 1452 (1981) ("1: to make

within this common understanding of the term. The FCC has in effect adopted a general rule stating that "if you are dominant you must file, but if you are nondominant you need not." The Commission's partial detariffing policy—which excuses nondominant carriers from filing *on condition that* they remain nondominant—is simply a relaxation of a costly regulatory requirement that recent developments had rendered pointless and counterproductive in a certain class of cases.

. . . Whatever the best reading of § 203(b)(2), the Commission's reading cannot in my view be termed unreasonable. It is informed (as ours is not) by a practical understanding of the role (or lack thereof) that filed tariffs play in the modern regulatory climate and in the telecommunications industry. . . . We should sustain its eminently sound, experience-tested, and uncommonly well-explained judgment.

I respectfully dissent.

NOTE

In **United States v. Costello**, 666 F.3d 1040, 1043–45 (7th Cir. 2012), Judge Posner considered whether the defendant, who allowed her boyfriend to live with her while knowing he was in the United States without authorization, had violated a statute criminalizing the knowing "harboring" of an unauthorized alien. The government's argument relied heavily on dictionary definitions:

> The actual definition of "to harbor" that the government has found in these dictionaries and urges us to adopt is "to shelter," which is not synonymous with "to provide a place to stay." "To shelter" has an aura of protectiveness, as in taking "shelter" from a storm. To shelter is to provide a refuge. "Sheltering" doesn't seem the right word for letting your boyfriend live with you. . . .
>
> [D]ictionaries must be used as sources of statutory meaning only with great caution. "Of course it is true that the words used, even in their literal sense, are the primary, and ordinarily the most reliable, source of interpreting the meaning of any writing: be it a statute, a contract, or anything else. But it is one of the surest indexes of a mature and developed jurisprudence not to make a fortress out of the dictionary; but to remember that statutes always have some purpose or object to accomplish, whose sympathetic and imaginative discovery is the surest guide to their meaning." *Cabell v. Markham,* 148 F.2d 737, 739 (2d Cir. 1945) (L. Hand, J.). . . .
>
> Dictionary definitions are acontextual, whereas the meaning of sentences depends critically on context, including all sorts of

more temperate and less extreme: lessen the severity of; . . . 'traffic rules were *modified* to let him pass' "); Webster's New Collegiate Dictionary 739 (1973) ("1. to make less extreme; MODERATE"); Webster's Seventh New Collegiate Dictionary 544 (1963) (same); Webster's Seventh New International Dictionary 1577 (2d ed. 1934) ("2. To reduce in extent or degree; to moderate; qualify; lower; as, to *modify* heat, pain, punishment"); N. Webster, American Dictionary of the English Language (1828) ("To moderate; to qualify; to reduce in extent or degree. Of his grace\He *modifies* his first severe decree. *Dryden*").

background understandings. . . . We doubt that the government would argue that a hospital emergency room that takes in a desperately ill person whom the hospital staff knows to be an illegal alien would be guilty of harboring, although it fits the government's definition of the word.

A Google search . . . of several terms in which the word "harboring" appears—a search based on the supposition that the number of hits per term is a rough index of the frequency of its use—reveals the following:

"harboring fugitives": 50,800 hits

"harboring enemies": 4,730 hits

"harboring refugees": 4,820 hits

"harboring victims": 114 hits

"harboring flood victims": 0 hits

"harboring victims of disasters": 0 hits . . .

"harboring Jews": 19,100 hits

"harboring guests": 184 hits

"harboring victims of persecution": 0 hits

It is apparent from these results that "harboring," as the word is actually used, has a connotation—which "sheltering," and *a fortiori* "giving a person a place to stay"—does not, of deliberately safeguarding members of a specified group from the authorities, whether through concealment, movement to a safe location, or physical protection. This connotation enables one to see that the emergency staff at the hospital may not be "harboring" an alien when it renders emergency treatment even if he stays in the emergency room overnight, that giving a lift to a gas station to an alien with a flat tire may not be harboring, that driving an alien to the local office of the Department of Homeland Security to apply for an adjustment of status to that of lawful resident may not be harboring, that inviting an alien for a "one night stand" may not be attempted harboring, that placing an illegal alien in a school may not be harboring (cf. *Plyler v. Doe,* 457 U.S. 202 (1982)), and finally that allowing your boyfriend to live with you may not be harboring, even if you know he shouldn't be in the United States.

Judge Manion disagreed with Judge Posner's conclusion as to the ordinary meaning of the term "harboring," and dissented:

[T]he court rejects the ordinary definition of the term "harboring" and asserts that the facts cannot support Costello's conviction even when considering a more exacting definition of "harboring"; thus, the court would reverse Costello's conviction. I disagree, and conclude that the plain language of the statute and the stipulated facts support the conviction of harboring. . . .

Contrary to the court's assertion, the ordinary meaning of "harboring" certainly includes "providing shelter to." This was a common understanding of the term when the term "harbor" was first added to the statute in 1917, and when the statute was amended and the term retained in 1952. See Webster's New International Dictionary of the English Language 981 (1917) ("harbor" defined as "[t]o afford lodging to; to entertain as a guest; to shelter; to receive; to give refuge to"); Webster's New Collegiate Dictionary 376 (John P. Bethel et al., eds.1953) ("harbor" defined as "to entertain as a guest; to shelter; to give a refuge to"). . . .

As we [have] noted [previously], " 'conceal,' 'harbor,' and 'shield from detection' have independent meanings, and thus a conviction can result from committing (or attempting to commit) any one of the three acts." Perhaps if Costello had shooed her boyfriend out the back door when the police were approaching from the front, she could be accused of shielding. Or if she had hidden him in the basement under a pile of laundry when federal agents showed up with a search warrant, she could also be charged with concealing. But she neither shielded nor concealed; instead, she provided shelter to her boyfriend, and nothing more is required to charge her with harboring under the statute.

QUESTIONS

1. Do you agree with Judge Posner's critique of the relative utility of dictionaries? Does his use of Google search results reveal more or less about the contextual meaning of the word "harbor"? What sources are legitimate for a judge to consult when seeking the meaning of a word in a statute? Should there be any limits placed on how many, and what kinds of, sources judges can consult? Would your answer be different for criminal statutes than for technical, regulatory statutes? Remember this last point when you read *Muscarello v U.S., infra.*

2. Recall David Foster Wallace's description of the notable role that *Webster's Third* played in leading to a split among descriptive and prescriptive lexicographers. In preparing *Webster's Third*, its editor sought to capture language as actually used in present-day communication, rather than as it had been used in the past, or as prescribed as appropriate by lexicographers. When a court turns to a dictionary in search of the definition of a statutory term, does it matter whether that dictionary's editor has primarily sought to capture language as actually used, as compared to providing acceptable usage guidelines drawn from a subset of experts in linguistic usage? Would it matter whether one seeks the "ordinary" or "specialized" meaning of a word or phrase? Do these choices depend on assumptions about legislative drafters' intentions when drafting statutes?

3. What kind of authority do dictionaries have as sources of *legal* knowledge? After all, lexicographers are not elected by the public, nor delegated lawmaking authority by legislatures. Recall the typology of interpretive methods from subsection III.A.2.a, *supra.* In theory, the use of dictionaries could be justified on at least several grounds, including that: (a) they reveal the intended meaning of a term *as used by legislative drafters*;

(b) they reveal the meaning *that members of the public* most frequently associate with a term; and/or (c) they reveal a meaning that the interpreter believes would most satisfactorily resolve the *legal* dispute at issue, whether or not it purports to represent either the legislature's intention or the public's understanding. What kind of empirical or normative assumptions are necessary to justify each of these claims to authority?

4. Dictionaries may not always resolve problems of linguistic ambiguity. After all, dictionary definitions, like statutory definitions sections, often use vague or ambiguous words. As Judge Raymond Randolph of the U.S. Court of Appeals for the District of Columbia has observed:

> [C]iting to dictionaries creates a sort of optical illusion, conveying the existence of certainty—or "plainness"—when appearance may be all there is. Lexicographers define words with words. Words in the definition are defined by more words, as are those words. The trail may be endless; sometimes, it is circular. Using a dictionary definition simply pushes the problem back. . . .

> Dictionary citing in judicial opinions, and the plain meaning rule itself, imply that the meanings of the words used in a statute equal the meaning of the statute. This is demonstrably false . . . . Of course, one must comprehend the words in a statute in order to comprehend the statute, just as one must comprehend the letters in a word in order to comprehend the word. A statute, however, cannot be understood merely by understanding the words in it. Judge Easterbrook thinks dictionaries are like "word museums." I think they are also like "word zoos." One can observe an animal's features in the zoo, but one still cannot be sure how the animal will behave in its native surroundings. The same is true of words in a text.

A. Raymond Randolph, *Dictionaries, Plain Meaning, and Context in Statutory Interpretation*, 17 Harv. J.L. & Pub. Pol'y 71 (1994).

5. If dictionaries are thought to aid in revealing the intended meaning of a term as used by legislative drafters, should it matter whether legislative drafters themselves rely on dictionaries when drafting? In surveying dozens of legislative drafters, Abbe Gluck and Lisa Schultz Bressman found that dictionaries do not play a significant role in most legislative drafting:

> "No one uses a freaking dictionary"

> More than 50% of our respondents said that dictionaries are never or rarely used when drafting. This finding stands in stark juxtaposition with the frequent and increasing use of dictionaries by the Supreme Court in statutory interpretation cases. Although the Court has always looked to dictionaries in some statutory cases, scholars have documented that the Court's use of this interpretive tool recently has risen dramatically: the Court used dictionaries in 225 opinions from 2000 to 2010, compared to just sixteen opinions in the 1960s.

> Our respondents were aware of this judicial trend, but told us that it nevertheless did not affect their practice. Several specifically

referenced Justice Scalia—acknowledging that the Court frequently uses dictionaries but noting that they remain mostly irrelevant to the drafting process. As one respondent put it (while laughing): "Scalia is a bright guy, but no one uses a freaking dictionary." Another noted more delicately: "This question presumes that legislative staff have dictionaries. I have tried to get an OED but people over at finance say we aren't spending money to buy you a dictionary. And no Black's Law Dictionary either."

The Court's rationale for dictionary consultation, however, may assume that Congress does use dictionaries or at least would welcome their use by judges. . . .

Abbe R. Gluck & Lisa Schultz Bressman, *Statutory Interpretation from the Inside: An Empirical Study of Congressional Drafting, Delegation, and the Canons: Part I*, 65 Stan. L. Rev. 901 (2013).

b.   OTHER SOURCES OF ORDINARY MEANING

Muscarello v. United States

Supreme Court of the United States, 1998.
524 U.S. 125, 118 S.Ct. 1911, 141 L.Ed.2d 111.

■ JUSTICE BREYER delivered the opinion of the Court[, joined by JUSTICE STEVENS, JUSTICE O'CONNOR, JUSTICE KENNEDY, and JUSTICE THOMAS].

A provision in the firearms chapter of the federal criminal code imposes a 5-year mandatory prison term upon a person who "uses or carries a firearm" "during and in relation to" a "drug trafficking crime." 18 U.S.C. § 924(c)(1). The question before us is whether the phrase "carries a firearm" is limited to the carrying of firearms on the person. We hold that it is not so limited. Rather, it also applies to a person who knowingly possesses and conveys firearms in a vehicle, including in the locked glove compartment or trunk of a car, which the person accompanies.

The question arises in two cases, which we have consolidated for argument. [The defendant] in the first case, Frank J. Muscarello, unlawfully sold marijuana, which he carried in his truck to the place of sale. Police officers found a handgun locked in the truck's glove compartment. During plea proceedings, Muscarello admitted that he had "carried" the gun "for protection in relation" to the drug offense, though he later claimed to the contrary, and added that, in any event, his "carrying" of the gun in the glove compartment did not fall within the scope of the statutory word "carries."

[The defendants] in the second case, Donald Cleveland and Enrique Gray-Santana, placed several guns in a bag, put the bag in the trunk of a car, and then traveled by car to a proposed drug-sale point, where they intended to steal drugs from the sellers. Federal agents at the scene stopped them, searched the cars, found the guns and drugs, and arrested them.

In both cases the Courts of Appeals found that [the defendants] had "carried" the guns during and in relation to a drug trafficking offense. [Citation.] We granted certiorari to determine whether the fact that the guns were found in the locked glove compartment, or the trunk, of a car, precludes application of § 924(c)(1). We conclude that it does not.

A.

We begin with the statute's language. The parties vigorously contest the ordinary English meaning of the phrase "carries a firearm." Because they essentially agree that Congress intended the phrase to convey its ordinary, and not some special legal, meaning, and because they argue the linguistic point at length, we too have looked into the matter in more than usual depth. Although the word "carry" has many different meanings, only two are relevant here. When one uses the word in the first, or primary, meaning, one can, as a matter of ordinary English, "carry firearms" in a wagon, car, truck, or other vehicle that one accompanies. When one uses the word in a different, rather special, way, to mean, for example, "bearing" or (in slang) "packing" (as in "packing a gun"), the matter is less clear. But, for reasons we shall set out below, we believe Congress intended to use the word in its primary sense and not in this latter, special way.

Consider first the word's primary meaning. The Oxford English Dictionary gives as its first definition "convey, originally by cart or wagon, hence in any vehicle, by ship, on horseback, etc." 2 Oxford English Dictionary 919 (2d ed. 1989); see also Webster's Third New International Dictionary 343 (1986) (first definition: "move while supporting (as in a vehicle or in one's hands or arms)"); The Random House Dictionary of the English Language Unabridged 319 (2d ed. 1987) (first definition: "to take or support from one place to another; convey; transport").

The origin of the word "carries" explains why the first, or basic, meaning of the word "carry" includes conveyance in a vehicle. See The Barnhart Dictionary of Etymology 146 (1988) (tracing the word from Latin "carum," which means "car" or "cart"); 2 Oxford English Dictionary, *supra*, at 919 (tracing the word from Old French "carier" and the late Latin "carricare," which meant to "convey in a car"); The Oxford Dictionary of English Etymology 148 (C. Onions ed.1966) (same); The Barnhart Dictionary of Etymology, *supra*, at 143 (explaining that the term "car" has been used to refer to the automobile since 1896).

The greatest of writers have used the word with this meaning. See, e.g., the King James Bible, 2 Kings 9:28 ("His servants carried him in a chariot to Jerusalem"); *id.*, Isaiah 30:6 ("They will carry their riches upon the shoulders of young asses"). Robinson Crusoe says, "with my boat, I carry'd away every Thing." D. Defoe, Robinson Crusoe 174 (J. Crowley ed. 1972). And the owners of Queequeg's ship, Melville writes, "had lent him a [wheelbarrow], in which to carry his heavy chest to his boarding-house." H. Melville, Moby Dick 43 (U. Chicago 1952). . . .

These examples do not speak directly about carrying guns. But there is nothing linguistically special about the fact that weapons, rather than drugs, are being carried. Robinson Crusoe might have carried a gun in his boat; Queequeg might have borrowed a wheelbarrow in which to carry, not a chest, but a harpoon. And, to make certain that there is no special ordinary English restriction (unmentioned in dictionaries) upon the use of "carry" in respect to guns, we have surveyed modern press usage, albeit crudely, by searching computerized newspaper databases—both the New York Times database in Lexis/Nexis, and the "US News" database in Westlaw. We looked for sentences in which the words "carry," "vehicle," and "weapon" (or variations thereof) all appear. We found thousands of such sentences, and random sampling suggests that many, perhaps more than one third, are sentences used to convey the meaning at issue here, i.e., the carrying of guns in a car. . . .

Now consider a different, somewhat special meaning of the word "carry"—a meaning upon which the linguistic arguments of petitioners and the dissent must rest. The Oxford English Dictionary's twenty-sixth definition of "carry" is "bear, wear, hold up, or sustain, as one moves about; habitually to bear about with one." 2 Oxford English Dictionary, *supra*, at 921. Webster's defines "carry" as "to move while supporting," not just in a vehicle, but also "in one's hands or arms." Webster's Third New International Dictionary, *supra*, at 343. And Black's Law Dictionary defines the entire phrase "carry arms or weapons" as

"To wear, bear or carry them upon the person or in the clothing or in a pocket, for the purpose of use, or for the purpose of being armed and ready for offensive or defensive action in case of a conflict with another person." Black's Law Dictionary 214 (6th ed. 1990).

These special definitions, however, do not purport to limit the "carrying of arms" to the circumstances they describe. No one doubts that one who bears arms on his person "carries a weapon." But to say that is not to deny that one may also "carry a weapon" tied to the saddle of a horse or placed in a bag in a car.

Nor is there any linguistic reason to think that Congress intended to limit the word "carries" in the statute to any of these special definitions. To the contrary, all these special definitions embody a form of an important, but secondary, meaning of "carry," a meaning that suggests support rather than movement or transportation, as when, for example, a column "carries" the weight of an arch. 2 Oxford English Dictionary, *supra*, at 919, 921. In this sense a gangster might "carry" a gun (in colloquial language, he might "pack a gun") even though he does not move from his chair. It is difficult to believe, however, that Congress intended to limit the statutory word to this definition—imposing special punishment upon the comatose gangster while ignoring drug lords who drive to a sale carrying an arsenal of weapons in their van.

We recognize, as the dissent emphasizes, that the word "carry" has other meanings as well. But those other meanings, (e.g., "carry all he knew," "carries no colours") are not relevant here. And the fact that speakers often do not add to the phrase "carry a gun" the words "in a car" is of no greater relevance here than the fact that millions of Americans did not see Muscarello carry a gun in his truck. The relevant linguistic facts are that the word "carry" in its ordinary sense includes carrying in a car and that the word, used in its ordinary sense, keeps the same meaning whether one carries a gun, a suitcase, or a banana.

Given the ordinary meaning of the word "carry," it is not surprising to find that the Federal Courts of Appeals have unanimously concluded that "carry" is not limited to the carrying of weapons directly on the person but can include their carriage in a car. [Citation.]

B.

[The Court then] conclude[d] that neither the statute's basic purpose nor its legislative history support circumscribing the scope of the word "carry" by applying an "on the person" limitation.

This Court has described the statute's basic purpose broadly, as an effort to combat the "dangerous combination" of "drugs and guns." [Citation.] . . .

From the perspective of any such purpose (persuading a criminal "to leave his gun at home") what sense would it make for this statute to penalize one who walks with a gun in a bag to the site of a drug sale, but to ignore a similar individual who, like defendant Gray-Santana, travels to a similar site with a similar gun in a similar bag, but instead of walking, drives there with the gun in his car? How persuasive is a punishment that is without effect until a drug dealer who has brought his gun to a sale (indeed has it available for use) actually takes it from the trunk (or unlocks the glove compartment) of his car? It is difficult to say that, considered as a class, those who prepare, say, to sell drugs by placing guns in their cars are less dangerous, or less deserving of punishment, than those who carry handguns on their person. . . .

C.

We are not convinced by petitioners' remaining arguments to the contrary. First, they say that our definition of "carry" makes it the equivalent of "transport." Yet, Congress elsewhere in related statutes used the word "transport" deliberately to signify a different, and broader, statutory coverage. The immediately preceding statutory subsection, for example, imposes a different set of penalties on one who, with an intent to commit a crime, "ships, transports, or receives a firearm" in interstate commerce. 18 U.S.C. § 924(b). Moreover, § 926A specifically "entitles" a person "not otherwise prohibited . . . from transporting, shipping, or receiving a firearm" to "transport a firearm . . . from any place where he may lawfully possess and carry" it to "any other place" where he may do so. Why, petitioners ask, would Congress have used the word "transport," or used both "carry" and "transport" in the same provision, if it had intended to obliterate the distinction between the two?

The short answer is that our definition does not equate "carry" and "transport." "Carry" implies personal agency and some degree of possession, whereas "transport" does not have such a limited connotation and, in addition, implies the movement of goods in bulk over great distances. [Citation.] If Smith, for example, calls a parcel delivery service, which sends a truck to Smith's house to pick up Smith's package and take it to Los Angeles, one might say that Smith has shipped the package and the parcel delivery service has transported the package. But only the truck driver has "carried" the package in the sense of "carry" that we believe Congress intended. Therefore, "transport" is a broader category that includes "carry" but also encompasses other activity.

The dissent refers to § 926A and to another statute where Congress used the word "transport" rather than "carry" to describe the movement of firearms. 18 U.S.C. §§ 925(a)(2)(B). According to the dissent, had Congress intended "carry" to have the meaning we give it, Congress would not have needed to use a different word in these provisions. But as we have discussed above, we believe the word "transport" is broader than the word "carry."

And, if Congress intended "carry" to have the limited definition the dissent contends, it would have been quite unnecessary to add the proviso in § 926A requiring a person, to be exempt from penalties, to store her firearm in a locked container not immediately accessible. See § 926A (exempting from criminal penalties one who transports a firearm from a place where "he may lawfully possess and carry such firearm" but not exempting the "transportation" of a firearm if it is "readily accessible or is directly accessible from the passenger compartment of such transporting vehicle"). The statute simply could have said that such a person may not "carry" a firearm. But, of course, Congress did not say this because that is not what "carry" means.

As we interpret the statutory scheme, it makes sense. Congress has imposed a variable penalty with no mandatory minimum sentence upon a person who "transports" (or "ships" or "receives") a firearm knowing it will be used to commit any "offense punishable by imprisonment for [more than] one year," § 924(b), and it has imposed a 5-year mandatory minimum sentence upon one who "carries" a firearm "during and in relation to" a "drug trafficking crime," § 924(c). The first subsection imposes a less strict sentencing regime upon one who, say, ships firearms by mail for use in a crime elsewhere; the latter subsection imposes a mandatory sentence upon one who, say, brings a weapon with him (on his person or in his car) to the site of a drug sale. . . .

. . . [P]etitioners say that our reading of the statute would extend its coverage to passengers on buses, trains, or ships, who have placed a firearm, say, in checked luggage. . . . In our view, this argument does not take adequate account of other limiting words in the statute—words that make the statute applicable only where a defendant "carries" a gun *both* "during *and* in relation to" a drug crime. § 924(c)(1) (emphasis added). Congress added these words in part to prevent prosecution where guns "played" no part in the crime. [Citation.]

Once one takes account of the words "during" and "in relation to," it no longer seems beyond Congress' likely intent, or otherwise unfair, to interpret the statute as we have done. If one carries a gun in a car "during" and "in relation to" a drug sale, for example, the fact that the gun is carried in the car's trunk or locked glove compartment seems not only logically difficult to distinguish from the immediately accessible gun, but also beside the point.

At the same time, the narrow interpretation creates its own anomalies. The statute, for example, defines "firearm" to include a "bomb," "grenade," "rocket having a propellant charge of more than four ounces," or "missile having an explosive or incendiary charge of more than one-quarter ounce," where such device is "explosive," "incendiary," or delivers "poison gas." 18 U.S.C. § 921(a)(4)(A). On petitioners' reading, the "carry" provision would not apply to instances where drug lords, engaged in a major transaction, took with them "firearms" such as these, which most likely could not be carried on the person.

. . . [P]etitioners [also] argue that we should construe the word "carry" to mean "immediately accessible." And, as we have said, they point out that several Circuit Courts of Appeals have limited the statute's scope in this way. [Citations.] That interpretation, however, is difficult to square with the statute's language, for one "carries" a gun in the glove compartment whether or not that glove compartment is locked. Nothing in the statute's history suggests that Congress intended that limitation. And, for reasons pointed out above, we believe that the words "during" and "in relation to" will limit the statute's application to the harms that Congress foresaw.

Finally, petitioners and the dissent invoke the "rule of lenity." The simple existence of some statutory ambiguity, however, is not sufficient to warrant application of that rule, for most statutes are ambiguous to some degree. Cf. *Smith*, 508 U.S. at 239 ("The mere possibility of articulating a narrower construction . . . does not by itself make the rule of lenity applicable"). " 'The rule of lenity applies only if, "after seizing everything from which aid can be derived," . . . we can make "no more than a guess as to what Congress intended." ' " [Citation.] To invoke the rule, we must conclude that there is a " ' "grievous ambiguity or uncertainty" ' in the statute." [Citation.] Certainly, our decision today is based on much more than a "guess as to what Congress intended," and there is no "grievous ambiguity" here. The problem of statutory interpretation in this case is indeed no different from that in many of the criminal cases that confront us. Yet, this Court has never held that the rule of lenity automatically permits a defendant to win. . . .

For these reasons, we conclude that [defendants]' conduct falls within the scope of the phrase "carries a firearm." The decisions of the Courts of Appeals are affirmed.

It is so ordered.

■ JUSTICE GINSBURG, with whom . . . CHIEF JUSTICE [REHNQUIST], JUSTICE SCALIA, and JUSTICE SOUTER join, dissenting.

. . . It is uncontested that § 924(c)(1) applies when the defendant bears a firearm, i.e., carries the weapon on or about his person "for the purpose of being armed and ready for offensive or defensive action in case of a conflict." Black's Law Dictionary 214 (6th ed. 1990) (defining the phrase "carry arms or weapons"). The Court holds that, in addition, "carries a firearm," in the context of § 924(c)(1), means personally transporting, possessing, or keeping a firearm in a vehicle, anyplace in a vehicle.

Without doubt, "carries" is a word of many meanings, definable to mean or include carting about in a vehicle. But that encompassing definition is not a ubiquitously necessary one. Nor, in my judgment, is it a proper construction of "carries" as the term appears in § 924(c)(1). In line with . . . the principle of lenity the Court has long followed, I would confine "carries a firearm," for § 924(c)(1) purposes, to the undoubted meaning of that expression in the relevant context. I would read the words to indicate not merely keeping arms on one's premises or in one's vehicle, but bearing them in such manner as to be ready for use as a weapon.

I

A

I note first what is at stake for petitioners. The question before the Court "is not whether possession of a gun [on the drug offender's premises or in his car, during and in relation to commission of the offense,] means a longer sentence for a convicted drug dealer. It most certainly does. . . . Rather, the question concerns which sentencing statute governs the precise length of the extra term of punishment," § 924(c)(1)'s "blunt 'mandatory minimum'" five-year sentence, or the more finely tuned "sentencing guideline statutes, under which extra punishment for drug-related gun possession varies with the seriousness of the drug crime." United States v. McFadden, 13 F.3d 463, 466 (C.A.1 1994) (Breyer, C. J., dissenting).

Accordingly, there would be no "gap," no relevant conduct "ignored," were the Court to reject the Government's broad reading of § 924(c)(1). To be more specific, as cogently explained on another day by today's opinion writer:

"The special 'mandatory minimum' sentencing statute says that anyone who 'uses or carries' a gun 'during and in relation to any . . . drug trafficking crime' must receive a mandatory five-year prison term added on to his drug crime sentence. 18 U.S.C. § 924(c). At the same time, the Sentencing Guidelines, promulgated under the authority of a different statute, 28 U.S.C. § 994, provide for a two-level (i.e., a 30% to 40%) sentence enhancement where a 'firearm . . . was possessed' by a drug offender, U.S. S. G. § 2D1.1(b)(1), unless the possession clearly was not 'connected with the [drug] offense.' " *McFadden*, 13 F.3d at 467 (Breyer, C. J., dissenting).

In Muscarello's case, for example, the underlying drug crimes involved the distribution of 3.6 kilograms of marijuana, and therefore carried a base offense level of 12. See United States Sentencing Commission, Guidelines Manual § 2D1.1(a)(3) (Nov. 1995). After adjusting for Muscarello's acceptance of responsibility, see *id.*, § 3E1.1(a), his final offense level was 10, placing him in the 6-to-12 month sentencing range. See *id.*, ch. 5, pt. A. The two-level enhancement for possessing a firearm, *id.*, § 2D1.1(b)(1), would have increased his final offense level to 12 (a sentencing range of 10 to 16 months). In other words, the less rigid (tailored to "the seriousness of the drug crime," *McFadden*, 13 F.3d at 466) Guidelines regime would have added four months to Muscarello's prison time, in contrast to the five-year minimum addition the Court's reading of § 924(c)(1) mandates.

In sum, drug traffickers will receive significantly longer sentences if they are caught traveling in vehicles in which they have placed firearms. The question that divides the Court concerns the proper reference for enhancement in the cases at hand, the Guidelines or § 924(c)(1).

B

Unlike the Court, I do not think dictionaries,[2] surveys of press reports,[3] or the Bible[4] tell us, dispositively, what "carries" means

---

[2] I note, however, that the only legal dictionary the Court cites, Black's Law Dictionary, defines "carry arms or weapons" restrictively.

[3] Many newspapers, the New York Times among them, have published stories using "transport," rather than "carry," to describe gun placements resembling petitioners'. See, e.g., Atlanta Constitution, Feb. 27, 1998, p. 9D, col. 2 ("House members last week expanded gun laws by allowing weapons to be *carried into restaurants or transported anywhere in cars*."); Chicago Tribune, June 12, 1997, sports section, p. 13 ("Disabled hunters with permission to hunt from a standing vehicle would be able to *transport a shotgun in an all-terrain vehicle* as long as the gun is unloaded and the breech is open."); Colorado Springs Gazette Telegraph, Aug. 4, 1996, p. C10 (British gun laws require "locked steel cases bolted onto a car for *transporting guns from home to shooting range*."); Detroit News, Oct. 26, 1997, p. D14 ("It is unlawful to *carry afield or transport a rifle* . . . or shotgun if you have buckshot, slug, ball loads, or cut shells in possession except while traveling directly to deer camp or target range with firearm not readily available to vehicle occupants."); N. Y. Times, July 4, 1993, p. A21, col. 2 ("The gun is supposed to be *transported unloaded*, in a locked box in the trunk."); Santa Rosa Press Democrat, Sept. 28, 1996, p. B1 ("Police and volunteers ask that participants . . . *transport [their guns] to the fairgrounds* in the trunks of their cars."); Worcester Telegram & Gazette, July 16, 1996, p. B3 ("Only one gun can be turned in per person. *Guns transported in a vehicle* should be locked in the trunk.") (emphasis added in all quotations).

[4] The translator of the Good Book, it appears, bore responsibility for determining whether the servants of Ahaziah "carried" his corpse to Jerusalem. Compare ante, with, e.g., The New

embedded in § 924(c)(1). On definitions, "carry" in legal formulations could mean, inter alia, transport, possess, have in stock, prolong (carry over), be infectious, or wear or bear on one's person. At issue here is not "carries" at large but "carries a firearm." The Court's computer search of newspapers is revealing in this light. Carrying guns in a car showed up as the meaning "perhaps more than one third" of the time. One is left to wonder what meaning showed up some two thirds of the time. Surely a most familiar meaning is, as the Constitution's Second Amendment ("keep and *bear* Arms") (emphasis added) and Black's Law Dictionary, at 214, indicate: "wear, bear, or carry . . . upon the person or in the clothing or in a pocket, for the purpose . . . of being armed and ready for offensive or defensive action in a case of conflict with another person."

On lessons from literature, a scan of Bartlett's and other quotation collections shows how highly selective the Court's choices are. If "the greatest of writers" have used "carry" to mean convey or transport in a vehicle, so have they used the hydra-headed word to mean, inter alia, carry in one's hand, arms, head, heart, or soul, sans vehicle. Consider, among countless examples:

> "He shall gather the lambs with his arm, and carry them in his bosom." The King James Bible, Isaiah 40:11.

> "And still they gaz'd, and still the wonder grew, That one small head could carry all he knew." O. Goldsmith, The Deserted Village, ll. 215–216, in The Poetical Works of Oliver Goldsmith 30 (A. Dobson ed. 1949).

> "There's a Legion that never was 'listed, That carries no colours or crest." R. Kipling, The Lost Legion, st. 1, in Rudyard Kipling's Verse, 1885–1918, p. 222 (1920).

> "There is a homely adage which runs, 'Speak softly and carry a big stick; you will go far.'" T. Roosevelt, Speech at Minnesota State Fair, Sept. 2, 1901, in J. Bartlett, Familiar Quotations 575:16 (J. Kaplan ed. 1992).[6]

These and the Court's lexicological sources demonstrate vividly that "carry" is a word commonly used to convey various messages. Such

---

English Bible, 2 Kings 9:28 ("His servants *conveyed* his body to Jerusalem."); Saint Joseph Edition of the New American Bible ("His servants *brought* him in a chariot to Jerusalem."); Tanakh: The Holy Scriptures ("His servants *conveyed* him in a chariot to Jerusalem."); see also *id.*, Isaiah 30:6 ("They *convey* their wealth on the backs of asses."); The New Jerusalem Bible ("They *bear* their riches on donkeys' backs.") (emphasis added in all quotations).

6 Popular films and television productions provide corroborative illustrations. In "The Magnificent Seven," for example, O'Reilly (played by Charles Bronson) says: "You think I am brave because I carry a gun; well, your fathers are much braver because they carry responsibility, for you, your brothers, your sisters, and your mothers." See http://us.imdb.com/M/search_quotes?for=carry. And in the television series "M*A*S*H," Hawkeye Pierce (played by Alan Alda) presciently proclaims: "I will not carry a gun. . . . I'll carry your books, I'll carry a torch, I'll carry a tune, I'll carry on, carry over, carry forward, Cary Grant, cash and carry, carry me back to Old Virginia, I'll even 'hari-kari' if you show me how, but I will not carry a gun!" See http://www.geocities.com/Hollywood/8915/mashquotes.html.

references, given their variety, are not reliable indicators of what Congress meant, in § 924(c)(1), by "carries a firearm."

C

Noting the paradoxical statement, " 'I use a gun to protect my house, but I've never had to use it,' " the Court in *Bailey*, 516 U.S. at 143, emphasized the importance of context—the statutory context. Just as "uses" was read to mean not simply "possession," but "active employment," so "carries," correspondingly, is properly read to signal the most dangerous cases—the gun at hand, ready for use as a weapon. It is reasonable to comprehend Congress as having provided mandatory minimums for the most life-jeopardizing gun-connection cases (guns in or at the defendant's hand when committing an offense), leaving other, less imminently threatening, situations for the more flexible guidelines regime.[8] As the Ninth Circuit suggested, it is not apparent why possession of a gun in a drug dealer's moving vehicle would be thought more dangerous than gun possession on premises where drugs are sold: "A drug dealer who packs heat is more likely to hurt someone or provoke someone else to violence. A gun in a bag under a tarp in a truck bed [or in a bedroom closet] poses substantially less risk." [Citation.][9]

For indicators from Congress itself, it is appropriate to consider word usage in other provisions of Title 18's chapter on "Firearms." . . . Section 925(a)(2)(B), for example, provides that no criminal sanction shall attend "the transportation of [a] firearm or ammunition carried out to enable a person, who lawfully received such firearm or ammunition from the Secretary of the Army, to engage in military training or in competitions." . . . In describing when and how a person may travel in a vehicle that contains his firearm without violating the law, §§ 925(a)(2)(B) and 926A use "transport," not "carry," to "imply personal agency and some degree of possession."[10] . . . [U]nder § 925(a)(2)(B), one could carry his gun to a car, transport it to the shooting competition, and use it to shoot targets. Under the conditions of § 926A, one could transport her gun in a car, but under no circumstances could the gun be

---

[8] The Court reports that the Courts of Appeals "have unanimously concluded that 'carry' is not limited to the carrying of weapons directly on the person." In *Bailey*, however, the Government's argument based on a similar observation did not carry the day. . . .

[9] The "Firearms" statutes indicate that Congress, unlike the Court, recognizes that a gun in the hand is indeed more dangerous than a gun in the trunk. See, e.g., 18 U.S.C. § 926A (permitting the transportation of firearms in a vehicle, but only if "neither the firearm nor any ammunition being transported is readily accessible or is directly accessible from the passenger compartment of such transporting vehicle").

[10] The Court asserts that " 'transport' is a broader category that includes 'carry' but encompasses other activity." "Carry," however, is not merely a subset of "transport" A person seated at a desk with a gun in hand or pocket is carrying the gun, but is not transporting it. Yes, the words "carry" and "transport" often can be employed interchangeably, as can the words "carry" and "use." . . . Without doubt, Congress is alert to the discrete meanings of "transport" and "carry" in the context of vehicles, as the Legislature's placement of each word in § 926A illustrates. The narrower reading of "carry" preserves discrete meanings for the two words, while in the context of vehicles the Court's interpretation of "carry" is altogether synonymous with "transport." Tellingly, when referring to firearms traveling in vehicles, the "Firearms" statutes routinely use a form of "transport"; they never use a form of "carry."

readily accessible while she travels in the car. "Courts normally try to read language in different, but related, statutes, so as best to reconcile those statutes, in light of their purposes and of common sense." *McFadden*, 13 F.3d at 467 (Breyer, C. J., dissenting). So reading the "Firearms" statutes, I would not extend the word "carries" in § 924(c)(1) to mean transports out of hand's reach in a vehicle.

II

Section 924(c)(1), as the foregoing discussion details, is not decisively clear one way or another. The sharp division in the Court on the proper reading of the measure confirms, "at the very least, . . . that the issue is subject to some doubt. Under these circumstances, we adhere to the familiar rule that, 'where there is ambiguity in a criminal statute, doubts are resolved in favor of the defendant.'" [Citation.] . . . "Carry" bears many meanings, as the Court and the "Firearms" statutes demonstrate. The narrower "on or about [one's] person" interpretation is hardly implausible nor at odds with an accepted meaning of "carries a firearm."

Overlooking that there will be an enhanced sentence for the gun-possessing drug dealer in any event, the Court asks rhetorically: "How persuasive is a punishment that is without effect until a drug dealer who has brought his gun to a sale (indeed has it available for use) actually takes it from the trunk (or unlocks the glove compartment) of his car?" Correspondingly, the Court defines "carries a firearm" to cover "a person who knowingly possesses and conveys firearms [anyplace] in a vehicle . . . which the person accompanies." Congress, however, hardly lacks competence to select the words "possesses" or "conveys" when that is what the Legislature means.[14] Notably in view of the Legislature's capacity to speak plainly, and of overriding concern, the Court's inquiry pays scant attention to a core reason for the rule of lenity: "Because of the seriousness of criminal penalties, and because criminal punishment usually represents the moral condemnation of the community, legislatures and not courts should define criminal activity. This policy embodies 'the instinctive distaste against men languishing in prison unless the lawmaker has clearly said they should.'" [Citation.]

* * *

The narrower "on or about [one's] person" construction of "carries a firearm" . . . respects the Guidelines system by resisting overbroad readings of statutes that deviate from that system." [Citation.] It fits plausibly with other provisions of the "Firearms" chapter, and it adheres to the principle that, given two readings of a penal provision, both consistent with the statutory text, we do not choose the harsher

---

[14] See, e.g., 18 U.S.C.A. § 924(a)(6)(B)(ii) (Supp. 1998) ("if the person sold . . . a handgun . . . to a juvenile knowing . . . that the juvenile intended to *carry or otherwise possess* . . . the handgun . . . in the commission of a crime of violence"); 18 U.S.C. § 926A ("may lawfully *possess and carry* such firearm to any other place where he may lawfully *possess and carry* such firearm"); § 929(a)(1) ("uses or *carries a firearm and is in possession* of armor piercing ammunition"); § 2277 ("brings, *carries, or possesses* any dangerous weapon") (emphasis added in all quotations).

construction. The Court, in my view, should leave it to Congress to speak " 'in language that is clear and definite' " if the Legislature wishes to impose the sterner penalty. [Citation.] . . .

QUESTIONS

1. Do you agree with the majority that the "primary" meaning of "carry" means to " 'carry . . . ' in a wagon, car, truck, or other vehicle"? When interpreting a statutory phrase, should the "primary" meaning of one word in that phrase be dispositive if there are alternative plausible meanings? How should the interpreter decide which, if any, of these plausible meanings is the "plain" meaning? To be "plain," must the word's meaning be "ubiquitously necessary"? What difference should the "rule of lenity" make in deciding whether to interpret the term broadly or narrowly?

2. To what extent is the plain meaning of a term determined by which dictionary or other sources of linguistic usage the interpreter chooses as his reference? If leading dictionaries provide competing definitions, or if the term is commonly used to convey different ideas, could the interpreter reasonably conclude that a "plain" meaning exists at all? Would a judge applying the plain meaning rule in this manner be said to be more or less deferential to the legislature?

3. The dissent points out that "Congress . . . hardly lacks the competence to select the words 'possess' or 'conveys' when that is what the legislature means." What inference should one draw from Congress's use of related but distinct words across a single statute? Recall the typology of interpretive methods in subsection III.A.2.a, *supra*. Does this evidence of nuanced and varied word selection shed light on what *the legislative drafters' intended* the statutory phrase in question to mean, or what the *reasonable reader* should infer the statute to mean? Note that the latter method attributes to the "reasonable reader" the capacity to parse an entire statute carefully in order to understand the meaning of a single term or phrase. (And recall this Part's opening salvo that one must always *read* the statute closely, and not paraphrase it!)

NOTE: "CORPUS LINGUISTICS"

As discussed, dictionaries have inherent limits as sources of ordinary meaning. An emerging alternative method, known as "corpus linguistics," seeks to capture more holistically the contextual ordinary meanings and usage of words. Justice Thomas R. Lee of the Utah Supreme Court is a leading advocate of this method, and has argued that compared to dictionary definitions written by a small number of experts, corpus linguistics analysis provides a more systematic survey of linguistic usage and a more representative account of "ordinary" meaning in contemporary practice:

> When we speak of *ordinary* meaning, we are asking an empirical question—about the sense of a word or phrase that is most likely implicated in a given linguistic context. Linguists have developed computer-aided means of answering such questions. We propose to import those methods into the modern theory and practice of

interpretation, and we identify problems in the methods that the law has been using to address these issues.

Our proposed methodology is a set of tools utilized in a field called corpus linguistics. Corpus linguists study language through data derived from large bodies—corpora—of naturally occurring language. They look for patterns in meaning and usage in large databases of actual written language. And we think their methods may easily be adapted in a manner that will allow us to conceptualize and measure the "standard picture" in a much more careful way. . . .

Is a woman who allows her boyfriend—an undocumented immigrant—to sleep at her apartment guilty of harboring an alien under a federal statute criminalizing that act? . . . *Costello* involved a statutory term broad enough to encompass both parties' positions. Sometimes harbor refers to the mere act of providing shelter, but it may also indicate the sort of sheltering that is aimed at concealment. How is the court to decide which sense is the ordinary one? Writing for the majority, Judge Posner recognized the deficiencies of standard methods—principally, dictionaries—in answering that question. So he proceeded to a search for data, and he did so using the tool that is perhaps most familiar to us today. He performed a Google search.

Is this the best we can do? . . . [There are] theoretical and operational deficiencies in the law's search for ordinary meaning. . . .

The case law embraces a startlingly broad range of senses of ordinary meaning. When judges speak of ordinary meaning, they often seem to be speaking to a question of relative frequency—as in a point on the following continuum:

POSSIBLE→COMMON→MOST FREQUENT→EXCLUSIVE

At the left end of the continuum is the idea of a possible or linguistically permissible meaning—a sense of a word or phrase that is attested in a known body of written or spoken language. A meaning is a possible one if we can say that "you can use that word in that way" (as attested by evidence that other people have used the word in that way in the past). Yet a possible meaning may be an uncommon or unnatural sense of a given term. In that case, we might note that a given sense of a term is not common in a given linguistic setting, even if it is possible to speak that way. And even a common sense of a term might not be the most frequent use of it in a certain context.

The notion of plain meaning adds the final point to the continuum. When courts speak of plain meaning (as a concept distinct from ordinary meaning) they generally mean to "denote obvious meaning" or "meaning that is clear." A plain—obvious or clear—meaning would be more than most frequent. It would be nearly exclusive. . . .

Judge Posner rejects a dictionary-based approach to ordinary meaning in Costello. . . . Judge Posner turns to Google to get a "rough index of the frequency of [harboring's] use." This approach is innovative. But it is far from perfect.

Google might seem to be a good source for data-driven analysis of language usage. "The World Wide Web is enormous, free, immediately available, and largely linguistic." And it is "appealing to use the Web as a data source" because "language analysis and generation benefit from big data." Google has low entry costs, moreover. Even the most Luddite lawyer or judge is likely to be able to perform a basic Google search. Yet we still see a range of problems in Judge Posner's approach.

First is the black box of the Google algorithm. Google searches "are sorted according to a complex and unknown algorithm (with full listings of all results usually not permitted) so we do not know what biases are being introduced." Google returns can vary by geography, by time of day, and from day to day. Google search results are thus rather unscientific, if we understand good science as including replicability.

Second are problems with the Google search engine: the fact that it does not allow us to search only for verb forms of harbor and that it will not allow us to look at a particular speech community or period of time (only contemporary web pages, even if their content was first published in the past). If we are interested in knowing the ordinary use of harbor as a verb among ordinary English speakers at the time of the enactment of the statute at issue (1917), Google cannot give us that kind of parsed data.

In light of these search engine problems, Judge Posner formulated his own set of search terms—comparing hit counts for phrases like "harboring fugitives" and "harboring guests." But this innovation introduces a third set of problems: Judge Posner gives no basis for his chosen set of search terms, and the terms he chose seem likely to affect the outcome.

Finally, even setting aside the problems discussed above, the hit counts that Judge Posner relies on may not be indicative of ordinariness in the sense of frequency of usage. Judge Posner implies that relative hit counts are an indication of frequency of usage in our ordinary language. But that may not hold. Google hit counts are based on the total number of web pages, not the total number of occurrences of a given phrase. A single web page may have tens, hundreds, or thousands of uses of an individual word or phrase that would only register in a Google search as a single hit. So hit counts may not be a reliable indication of ordinariness, even if we could overcome the other problems identified here.

We think Judge Posner was onto something in seeking an empirical method of measurement, but we also think his Google search was inadequate. . . .

Corpus linguistic tools can be employed to measure ordinary meaning as conceptualized in this Article. . . . Linguistic corpora come in a number of varieties, each tailored to suit the needs of a particular set of empirical questions about language use. . . .

Linguistic corpora can perform a variety of tasks that cannot be performed by human linguistic intuition alone. . . . [C]orpora can be used to measure the statistical frequency of words and word senses in a given speech community and over a given time period. Whether we regard the ordinary meaning of a given word to be the possible, common, or the most common sense of that word in a given context, linguistic corpora allows us to determine empirically where a contested sense of a term falls on that continuum.

Corpora can also show collocation, "which is the tendency of words to be biased in the way they co-occur." As we have seen, words are often interpreted according to the semantic environment in which they are found. A collocation program can show the possible range of linguistic contexts in which a word typically appears and can provide useful information about the range of possible meanings and sense divisions.

Corpora also have a concordance or key word in context ("KWIC") function, which allows their users to review a particular word or phrase in hundreds of contexts, all on the same page of running text. This allows a corpus user to evaluate words in context systematically. . . .

[The authors then ran the term "harbor" through several prominent corpora databases:]

[W]e examined 140 concordance lines in which harbor occurred in the same environment as fugitives, terrorists, criminals, aliens, and refugees. Of these, twenty-three instances of harbor referred to concealment while thirty-two referred to shelter. In an additional eighty-three instances, the distinction could not be determined by context. There were also three instances of unrelated senses of harbor. In the COHA, there were only three clear-cut cases of the shelter sense. The remaining five instances of harbor could not be determined by context. . . .

This data raises more questions than it answers. With respect to frequency, we would be hard-pressed to say that either the shelter meaning or the conceal meaning of harbor are the most common. We might say that both are common meanings, and they are both certainly possible and attested meanings. But where more than half of the instances of harbor are unclear as to whether they include shelter or concealment or both, it is hard to state from the standpoint of frequency what the ordinary meaning actually is. . . .

Such are the data. But what to make of them? Do corpus data yield means of measuring ordinary meaning? We think the answer is a resounding yes—with a few caveats. Certainly, the answer is yes by comparison with existing means of measurement. If ordinary meaning is an empirical construct—and we think it is—then corpus analysis is superior to an intuitive guess (or, worse, crediting a dictionary or a word's etymology). . . .

Thomas R. Lee & Stephen C. Mouritsen, *Judging Ordinary Meaning*, 127 Yale L.J. 788 (2018)

———————

The authors acknowledge that corpus linguistics will not always yield a "most frequent," let alone "exclusive," ordinary meaning of a statutory term or phrase. Does this suggest an inherent problem with their proposed approach? Or, alternatively, might it suggest that many statutory terms and phrases simply do not have a "most frequent" or "exclusive" ordinary meaning? Perhaps corpus linguistics may be more useful when the interpreter seeks the "prototypical" meaning of a term or phrase. For example, just as the dissent in *Muscarello* suggested, when one hears *"carry a firearm,"* the prototypical image that the phrase evokes is carriage on the person—*i.e.*, "pack[ing] heat"—even if one could permissibly, and even commonly, use the phrase *"carry* a firearm" to refer to transporting a firearm in one's truck. If so, might corpus linguistics be most usefully employed as a way to rule out the Plain Meaning Rule in circumstances where an analysis of various corpora turn up no such single "plain" meaning, but rather several common or plausible meanings?

As a method of legal interpretation, corpus linguistics also raises questions about source selection and access, and thus also the notion of objectivity. Adherents such as Lee and Mouritsen argue, perhaps rightly, that the resort to corpus linguistics is at least as objective as the resort to dictionaries, and is more likely to yield a useful "ordinary meaning." Yet whereas any ordinary reader of English can (relatively) easily resort to a dictionary (online or otherwise), corpus linguistics requires access to sophisticated databases—or "corpora"—of evidence of common usage. It also requires knowledge of how to derive meaning correctly from these vast corpora. (And we should not forget the potential selection bias in the composition of the corpora.) However accurate corpus linguistics may be as a method of obtaining the ordinary meaning of a word or phrase, might its costs outweigh its benefits for all but the most diligent and sophisticated statutory readers?

Other scholars are less sanguine about the possibility that corpus linguistics can bring greater objectivity to the interpretation of statutes, given issues of access and selection bias:

> Just as a legal interpreter resorting to a dictionary must choose a particular dictionary to use, so too must the user of corpus linguistics techniques choose a corpus to search. The choice of corpus is subjective because it is not constrained by any principle that suggests why one corpus rather than another should be chosen. . . . [T]here is nothing internal to a particular

corpus that requires its use in certain circumstances. Likewise, there is nothing about a particular term or phrase that tells the interpreter which corpus to use when searching for its meaning. As a result, simply by opting for a corpus search, the user of corpus linguistics techniques introduces a subjective element into the interpretive process.

Corpus usage confirms that the choice of corpus is subjective: corpus users rely on multiple or different corpora without articulating a standard for determining when one corpus would be appropriate and another would not be appropriate. Take Lee and Mouritsen's searches for the terms "vehicle," "carry," and "interpreter" in their work advocating the adoption of corpus techniques. Lee and Mouritsen rely on searches in the News on the Web (NOW) Corpus and the Corpus of Historical American English (COHA) without describing why either or both of these corpora are appropriate for their searches and despite the significant differences between the texts found in these corpora. The NOW Corpus, for example, contains not only news sources, but also online magazines with subjects as diverse as video games, cricket, and fashion. And the origin of these web sources? The NOW Corpus includes texts that come not only from the United States, but, unless specifically excluded by the researcher, texts from markedly different linguistic communities, like India, Nigeria, Singapore, Kenya, Pakistan, and the Philippines, among others. The COHA, by contrast, includes different kinds of texts, including movie scripts and poetry.

Some proponents of corpus linguistics techniques acknowledge that they must choose a corpus, but minimize the significance of the choice by suggesting that it is driven by a distinction between "ordinary" words and legal terms of art. If the word under consideration is an "ordinary" one, they search for it in a general corpus, like the COHA, the COCA, or the NOW Corpus; by contrast, if it is a legal term of art, some intimate that interpreters should use a still-hypothetical specialized legal corpus. However, framing the choice of corpus as a choice between an ordinary term and a legal term of art does not eliminate its subjectivity; it merely substitutes one subjective decision for another. The determination that a word is ordinary itself reflects a subjective decision because there is not an objective way to distinguish between ordinary words and legal terms of art. As linguists have noted, the line between legal terms of art and ordinary words is indistinct at best. David Mellinkoff notes that not every word "that has the sound of the law is a term of art." Conversely, many words that sound ordinary, because they are used in nonlegal settings, also have specialized legal meanings. For these reasons, the "difference between legal terms and words of ordinary language is relative and hard to define." Even linguists who are more optimistic about the possibility of identifying legal terms of art recognize the significant disagreement over what constitutes a legal term. Because choosing to designate a statutory term ordinary rather than legal does not appear to be "reliably constrained," the choice between a general corpus and a still-hypothetical specialized legal corpus is subjective.

Evan C. Zoldan, *Corpus Linguistics and the Dream of Objectivity*, 50 Seton Hall L. Rev. 401 (2019).

D. THE CONTEXTS OF STATUTES AND THEIR INTERPRETATION

In contrast to textualism, which calls for deriving statutory meaning primarily from the statutory text alone, purposivism as a method of interpretation prioritizes contextual evidence that sheds light on the statute's purpose and meaning, sometimes even over the "literal" meaning of a specific word or phrase when taken out of context. Purposivists proceed from the premise that Congress enacts statutes in response to a societal problem; ascertaining "the evil to be remedied" can provide the key to understanding Congress' solution. The context of a statute's passage, then, may shed important light on its meaning. To supply that context, courts might look to the state of the law before passage of the statute in question to discern what the new law was enacted to change. Recall Sir Edward Coke's inquiries in *Heydon's Case, supra*: "What was the common law before the making of the Act? What was the mischief and defect for which the common law did not provide?"

More controversial, at least for some jurists, is "legislative history," that is, "extratextual sources" generated through the legislative process—such as prior versions of the bill that became a law, as well as the committee reports, hearings, floor statements, and other documentation of the bill's journey from proposal to passage. The following cases will address these and other sources of context for legislative enactments.

1. INTERPRETING A STATUTE IN LIGHT OF . . . THE "EVIL SOUGHT TO BE REMEDIED"

As discussed above, courts may seek to uncover either (a) the specific intent of the legislators regarding the particular statutory provision in question, and/or (b) whether the problem before the court appears to fall within the scope of the broader purpose the legislation sought to accomplish through its enactment.

As you read the Indian Child Welfare Act of 1978 and the case of *Adoptive Couple v. Baby Girl*, consider the grounds for disagreement about the broad purpose of the legislation, as well as the different methods the majority and dissent draw on to determine that purpose.

The Indian Child Welfare Act of 1978
United States Code, Title 25, Chapter 21.

§ 1901. Congressional findings

Recognizing the special relationship between the United States and the Indian tribes and their members and the Federal responsibility to Indian people, the Congress finds—

(1) that clause 3, section 8, article I of the United States Constitution provides that "The Congress shall have Power . . . To regulate Commerce . . . with Indian tribes" and, through this and other constitutional authority, Congress has plenary power over Indian affairs;

(2) that Congress, through statutes, treaties, and the general course of dealing with Indian tribes, has assumed the responsibility for the protection and preservation of Indian tribes and their resources;

(3) that there is no resource that is more vital to the continued existence and integrity of Indian tribes than their children and that the United States has a direct interest, as trustee, in protecting Indian children who are members of or are eligible for membership in an Indian tribe;

(4) that an alarmingly high percentage of Indian families are broken up by the removal, often unwarranted, of their children from them by nontribal public and private agencies and that an alarmingly high percentage of such children are placed in non-Indian foster and adoptive homes and institutions; and

(5) that the States, exercising their recognized jurisdiction over Indian child custody proceedings through administrative and judicial bodies, have often failed to recognize the essential tribal relations of Indian people and the cultural and social standards prevailing in Indian communities and families.

§ 1902. Congressional declaration of policy

The Congress hereby declares that it is the policy of this Nation to protect the best interests of Indian children and to promote the stability and security of Indian tribes and families by the establishment of minimum Federal standards for the removal of Indian children from their families and the placement of such children in foster or adoptive homes which will reflect the unique values of Indian culture, and by providing for assistance to Indian tribes in the operation of child and family service programs.

§ 1903. Definitions

For the purposes of this chapter, except as may be specifically provided otherwise, the term—

(1) "child custody proceeding" shall mean and include—

(i) "foster care placement" which shall mean any action removing an Indian child from its parent or Indian custodian for temporary placement in a foster home or institution or the home of a guardian or conservator where the parent or Indian custodian cannot have the child returned upon demand, but where parental rights have not been terminated;

(ii) "termination of parental rights" which shall mean any action resulting in the termination of the parent-child relationship;

(iii) "preadoptive placement" which shall mean the temporary placement of an Indian child in a foster home or institution after the termination of parental rights, but prior to or in lieu of adoptive placement; and

(iv) "adoptive placement" which shall mean the permanent placement of an Indian child for adoption, including any action resulting in a final decree of adoption.

Such term or terms shall not include a placement based upon an act which, if committed by an adult, would be deemed a crime or upon an award, in a divorce proceeding, of custody to one of the parents.

(2) "extended family member" shall be as defined by the law or custom of the Indian child's tribe or, in the absence of such law or custom, shall be a person who has reached the age of eighteen and who is the Indian child's grandparent, aunt or uncle, brother or sister, brother-in-law or sister-in-law, niece or nephew, first or second cousin, or stepparent;

(3) "Indian" means any person who is a member of an Indian tribe, or who is an Alaska Native and a member of a Regional Corporation as defined in 1606 of title 43;

(4) "Indian child" means any unmarried person who is under age eighteen and is either (a) a member of an Indian tribe or (b) is eligible for membership in an Indian tribe and is the biological child of a member of an Indian tribe;

(5) "Indian child's tribe" means (a) the Indian tribe in which an Indian child is a member or eligible for membership or (b), in the case of an Indian child who is a member of or eligible for membership in more than one tribe, the Indian tribe with which the Indian child has the more significant contacts;

(6) "Indian custodian" means any Indian person who has legal custody of an Indian child under tribal law or custom or under State

law or to whom temporary physical care, custody, and control has been transferred by the parent of such child; . . .

(8) "Indian tribe" means any Indian tribe, band, nation, or other organized group or community of Indians recognized as eligible for the services provided to Indians by the Secretary because of their status as Indians, including any Alaska Native village as defined in section 1602(c) of title 43;

[Editors' Note: ICWA does not further define "Indian." Nor does ICWA further define Indian "status" through enrollment in an Indian Tribe. The list of the 573 Federally-recognized Indian Tribes is published at Federal Register / Vol. 84, No. 22 p. 1200/ Friday, Feb. 1, 2019/ Notices. Indian tribes determine their own rules for tribal membership. According to the Department of the Interior:

> Tribal enrollment criteria are set forth in tribal constitutions, articles of incorporation or ordinances. The criterion varies from tribe to tribe, so uniform membership requirements do not exist.

> Two common requirements for membership are lineal decendency from someone named on the tribe's base roll or relationship to a tribal member who descended from someone named on the base roll. (A "base roll" is the original list of members as designated in a tribal constitution or other document specifying enrollment criteria.) Other conditions such as tribal blood quantum, tribal residency, or continued contact with the tribe are common.

U.S. Department of the Interior, "Tribal enrollment process," http://www. doi.gov/tribes/enrollment.cfm]

(9) "parent" means any biological parent or parents of an Indian child or any Indian person who has lawfully adopted an Indian child, including adoptions under tribal law or custom. It does not include the unwed father where paternity has not been acknowledged or established; . . .

(11) "Secretary" means the Secretary of the Interior; and

(12) "tribal court" means a court with jurisdiction over child custody proceedings and which is either a Court of Indian Offenses, a court established and operated under the code or custom of an Indian tribe, or any other administrative body of a tribe which is vested with authority over child custody proceedings.

§ 1911. Indian tribe jurisdiction over Indian child custody proceedings . . .

(b) Transfer of proceedings; declination by tribal court

In any State court proceeding for the foster care placement of, or termination of parental rights to, an Indian child not domiciled or residing within the reservation of the Indian child's tribe, the court, in the absence of good cause to the contrary, shall transfer such proceeding to the jurisdiction of the tribe, absent objection by either parent, upon the petition of either parent or the Indian custodian or the Indian child's tribe: *Provided,* That such transfer shall be subject to declination by the tribal court of such tribe.

(c) State court proceedings; intervention

In any State court proceeding for the foster care placement of, or termination of parental rights to, an Indian child, the Indian custodian of the child and the Indian child's tribe shall have a right to intervene at any point in the proceeding. . . .

§ 1912. Pending court proceedings

(a) Notice; time for commencement of proceedings; additional time for preparation

In any involuntary proceeding in a State court, where the court knows or has reason to know that an Indian child is involved, the party seeking the foster care placement of, or termination of parental rights to, an Indian child shall notify the parent or Indian custodian and the Indian child's tribe, by registered mail with return receipt requested, of the pending proceedings and of their right of intervention. If the identity or location of the parent or Indian custodian and the tribe cannot be determined, such notice shall be given to the Secretary in like manner, who shall have fifteen days after receipt to provide the requisite notice to the parent or Indian custodian and the tribe. No foster care placement or termination of parental rights proceeding shall be held until at least ten days after receipt of notice by the parent or Indian custodian and the tribe or the Secretary: *Provided,* That the parent or Indian custodian or the tribe shall, upon request, be granted up to twenty additional days to prepare for such proceeding.

(b) Appointment of counsel

In any case in which the court determines indigency, the parent or Indian custodian shall have the right to court-appointed counsel in any removal, placement, or termination proceeding. The court may, in its discretion, appoint counsel for the child upon a finding that such appointment is in the best interest of the child. Where State law makes no provision for appointment of counsel in such proceedings, the court shall promptly notify the Secretary upon appointment of counsel, and the Secretary, upon certification of the presiding judge, shall pay reasonable fees and expenses out of funds which may be appropriated pursuant to section 13 of this title.

(c) Examination of reports or other documents

Each party to a foster care placement or termination of parental rights proceeding under State law involving an Indian child shall have the right to examine all reports or other documents filed with the court upon which any decision with respect to such action may be based.

(d) Remedial services and rehabilitative programs; preventive measures

Any party seeking to effect a foster care placement of, or termination of parental rights to, an Indian child under State law shall satisfy the court that active efforts have been made to provide remedial services and rehabilitative programs designed to prevent the breakup of the Indian family and that these efforts have proved unsuccessful.

(e) Foster care placement orders; evidence; determination of damage to child

No foster care placement may be ordered in such proceeding in the absence of a determination, supported by clear and convincing evidence, including testimony of qualified expert witnesses, that the continued custody of the child by the parent or Indian custodian is likely to result in serious emotional or physical damage to the child.

(f) Parental rights termination orders; evidence; determination of damage to child

No termination of parental rights may be ordered in such proceeding in the absence of a determination, supported by evidence beyond a reasonable doubt, including testimony of qualified expert witnesses, that the continued custody of the child by the parent or Indian custodian is likely to result in serious emotional or physical damage to the child.

§ 1913. Parental rights; voluntary termination

(a) Consent; record; certification matters; invalid consents

Where any parent or Indian custodian voluntarily consents to a foster care placement or to termination of parental rights, such consent shall not be valid unless executed in writing and recorded before a judge of a court of competent jurisdiction and accompanied by the presiding judge's certificate that the terms and consequences of the consent were fully explained in detail and were fully understood by the parent or Indian custodian. The court shall also certify that either the parent or Indian custodian fully understood the explanation in English or that it was interpreted into a language that the parent or Indian custodian understood. Any consent given prior to, or within ten days after, birth of the Indian child shall not be valid.

(b) Foster care placement; withdrawal of consent

Any parent or Indian custodian may withdraw consent to a foster care placement under State law at any time and, upon such withdrawal, the child shall be returned to the parent or Indian custodian.

(c) Voluntary termination of parental rights or adoptive placement; withdrawal of consent; return of custody

In any voluntary proceeding for termination of parental rights to, or adoptive placement of, an Indian child, the consent of the parent may be withdrawn for any reason at any time prior to the entry of a final decree of termination or adoption, as the case may be, and the child shall be returned to the parent.

(d) Collateral attack; vacation of decree and return of custody; limitations

After the entry of a final decree of adoption of an Indian child in any State court, the parent may withdraw consent thereto upon the grounds that consent was obtained through fraud or duress and may petition the court to vacate such decree. Upon a finding that such consent was obtained through fraud or duress, the court shall vacate such decree and return the child to the parent. No adoption which has been effective for at least two years may be invalidated under the provisions of this subsection unless otherwise permitted under State law. . . .

§ 1915. Placement of Indian children

(a) Adoptive placements; preferences

In any adoptive placement of an Indian child under State law, a preference shall be given, in the absence of good cause to the contrary, to a placement with (1) a member of the child's extended family; (2) other members of the Indian child's tribe; or (3) other Indian families.

(b) Foster care or preadoptive placements; criteria; preferences

Any child accepted for foster care or preadoptive placement shall be placed in the least restrictive setting which most approximates a family and in which his special needs, if any, may be met. The child shall also be placed within reasonable proximity to his or her home, taking into account any special needs of the child. In any foster care or preadoptive placement, a preference shall be given, in the absence of good cause to the contrary, to a placement with—

(i)   a member of the Indian child's extended family;

(ii) a foster home licensed, approved, or specified by the Indian child's tribe;

(iii) an Indian foster home licensed or approved by an authorized non-Indian licensing authority; or

(iv) an institution for children approved by an Indian tribe or operated by an Indian organization which has a program suitable to meet the Indian child's needs.

(c) Tribal resolution for different order of preference; personal preference considered; anonymity in application of preferences

In the case of a placement under subsection (a) or (b) of this section, if the Indian child's tribe shall establish a different order of preference by resolution, the agency or court effecting the placement shall follow such order so long as the placement is the least restrictive setting appropriate to the particular needs of the child, as provided in subsection (b) of this section. Where appropriate, the preference of the Indian child or parent shall be considered: *Provided,* That where a consenting parent evidences a desire for anonymity, the court or agency shall give weight to such desire in applying the preferences.

(d) Social and cultural standards applicable

The standards to be applied in meeting the preference requirements of this section shall be the prevailing social and cultural standards of the Indian community in which the parent or extended family resides or with which the parent or extended family members maintain social and cultural ties.

(e) Record of placement; availability

A record of each such placement, under State law, of an Indian child shall be maintained by the State in which the placement was made, evidencing efforts to comply with the order of preference specified in this section. Such record shall be made available at any time upon the request of the Secretary or the Indian child's tribe. . . .

§ 1921. Higher State or Federal standard applicable to protect rights of parent or Indian custodian of Indian child

In any case where State or Federal law applicable to a child custody proceeding under State or Federal law provides a higher standard of protection to the rights of the parent or Indian custodian of an Indian child than the rights provided under this subchapter, the State or Federal court shall apply the State or Federal standard. . . .

§ 1931. Grants for on or near reservation programs and child welfare codes

(a) Statement of purpose; scope of programs

The Secretary is authorized to make grants to Indian tribes and organizations in the establishment and operation of Indian child and family service programs on or near reservations and in the preparation and implementation of child welfare codes. The objective of every Indian child and family service program shall be to prevent the breakup of Indian families and, in particular, to insure that the permanent removal of an Indian child from the custody of his parent or Indian custodian shall be a last resort. Such child and family service programs may include, but are not limited to—

    (1) a system for licensing or otherwise regulating Indian foster and adoptive homes;

    (2) the operation and maintenance of facilities for the counseling and treatment of Indian families and for the temporary custody of Indian children;

    (3) family assistance, including homemaker and home counselors, day care, afterschool care, and employment, recreational activities, and respite care;

    (4) home improvement programs;

(5) the employment of professional and other trained personnel to assist the tribal court in the disposition of domestic relations and child welfare matters;

(6) education and training of Indians, including tribal court judges and staff. in skills relating to child and family assistance and service programs;

(7) a subsidy program under which Indian adoptive children may be provided support comparable to that for which they would be eligible as foster children, taking into account the appropriate State standards of support for maintenance and medical needs; and

(8) guidance, legal representation, and advice to Indian families involved in tribal, State, or Federal child custody proceedings. . . .

§ 1932. Grants for off-reservation programs for additional services

The Secretary is also authorized to make grants to Indian organizations to establish and operate off-reservation Indian child and family service programs which may include, but are not limited to—

(1) a system for regulating, maintaining, and supporting Indian foster and adoptive homes, including a subsidy program under which Indian adoptive children may be provided support comparable to that for which they would be eligible as Indian foster children, taking into account the appropriate State standards of support for maintenance and medical needs;

(2) the operation and maintenance of facilities and services for counseling and treatment of Indian families and Indian foster and adoptive children;

(3) family assistance, including homemaker and home counselors, day care, afterschool care, and employment, recreational activities, and respite care; and

(4) guidance, legal representation, and advice to Indian families involved in child custody proceedings.

QUESTIONS

1. If you were advising an unrelated, non-Indian couple looking to adopt an Indian child, what sections of ICWA would be most relevant? What information would you need in order to advise the couple of the steps necessary to undertake the adoption?

2. What aspects of your answer will vary between States? Between Indian Tribes? What information will be generally applicable to all adoptions from a particular Tribe in a particular State, and what will depend on the circumstances of the particular Indian child?

3. Once an adoption has taken place, when, if ever, could you assure your clients that it is irrevocable? If an adoption is complete under state law,

under what circumstances could it still be revoked under ICWA, and who would have the right or opportunity to do so?

4. Look at the declaration of policy in § 1902. Could the policies it expresses ever be in tension? If so, does ICWA accommodate one policy more than another?

Adoptive Couple v. Baby Girl

Supreme Court of the United States, 2013.
570 U.S. 637, 133 S.Ct. 2552, 186 L.Ed.2d 729.

■ JUSTICE ALITO delivered the opinion of the Court[, in which CHIEF JUSTICE ROBERTS, JUSTICE KENNEDY, JUSTICE THOMAS, and JUSTICE BREYER joined].

This case is about a little girl (Baby Girl) who is classified as an Indian because she is 1.2% (3/256) Cherokee. Because Baby Girl is classified in this way, the South Carolina Supreme Court held that certain provisions of the federal Indian Child Welfare Act of 1978 required her to be taken, at the age of 27 months, from the only parents she had ever known and handed over to her biological father, who had attempted to relinquish his parental rights and who had no prior contact with the child. The provisions of the federal statute at issue here do not demand this result.

Contrary to the State Supreme Court's ruling, we hold that 25 U. S. C. § 1912(f)—which bars involuntary termination of a parent's rights in the absence of a heightened showing that serious harm to the Indian child is likely to result from the parent's "continued custody" of the child—does not apply when, as here, the relevant parent never had custody of the child. We further hold that § 1912(d)—which conditions involuntary termination of parental rights with respect to an Indian child on a showing that remedial efforts have been made to prevent the "breakup of the Indian family"—is inapplicable when, as here, the parent abandoned the Indian child before birth and never had custody of the child. Finally, we clarify that § 1915(a), which provides placement preferences for the adoption of Indian children, does not bar a non-Indian family like Adoptive Couple from adopting an Indian child when no other eligible candidates have sought to adopt the child. We accordingly reverse the South Carolina Supreme Court's judgment and remand for further proceedings.

I

"The Indian Child Welfare Act of 1978 (ICWA), 92 Stat.3069, 25 U. S. C. §§ 1901–1963, was the product of rising concern in the mid-1970's over the consequences to Indian children, Indian families, and Indian tribes of abusive child welfare practices that resulted in the separation of large numbers of Indian children from their families and tribes through adoption or foster care placement, usually in non-Indian homes." *Mississippi Band of Choctaw Indians v. Holyfield*, 490 U.S. 30, 32 (1989).

Congress found that "an alarmingly high percentage of Indian families [were being] broken up by the removal, often unwarranted, of their children from them by nontribal public and private agencies." § 1901(4). This "wholesale removal of Indian children from their homes" prompted Congress to enact the ICWA, which establishes federal standards that govern state-court child custody proceedings involving Indian children. *Id.*, at 32, 36 (internal quotation marks omitted); see also § 1902 (declaring that the ICWA establishes "minimum Federal standards for the removal of Indian children from their families").

Three provisions of the ICWA are especially relevant to this case. First, "[a]ny party seeking" an involuntary termination of parental rights to an Indian child under state law must demonstrate that "active efforts have been made to provide remedial services and rehabilitative programs designed to prevent the breakup of the Indian family and that these efforts have proved unsuccessful." § 1912(d). Second, a state court may not involuntarily terminate parental rights to an Indian child "in the absence of a determination, supported by evidence beyond a reasonable doubt, including testimony of qualified expert witnesses, that the continued custody of the child by the parent or Indian custodian is likely to result in serious emotional or physical damage to the child." § 1912(f). Third, with respect to adoptive placements for an Indian child under state law, "a preference shall be given, in the absence of good cause to the contrary, to a placement with (1) a member of the child's extended family; (2) other members of the Indian child's tribe; or (3) other Indian families." § 1915(a).

II

In this case, Birth Mother (who is predominantly Hispanic) and Biological Father (who is a member of the Cherokee Nation) became engaged in December 2008. One month later, Birth Mother informed Biological Father, who lived about four hours away, that she was pregnant. . . . The couple's relationship deteriorated, and Birth Mother broke off the engagement in May 2009. In June, Birth Mother sent Biological Father a text message asking if he would rather pay child support or relinquish his parental rights. Biological Father responded via text message that he relinquished his rights.

Birth Mother then decided to put Baby Girl up for adoption. Because Birth Mother believed that Biological Father had Cherokee Indian heritage, her attorney contacted the Cherokee Nation to determine whether Biological Father was formally enrolled. The inquiry letter misspelled Biological Father's first name and incorrectly stated his birthday, and the Cherokee Nation responded that, based on the information provided, it could not verify Biological Father's membership in the tribal records.

Working through a private adoption agency, Birth Mother selected Adoptive Couple, non-Indians living in South Carolina, to adopt Baby Girl. . . . [After the birth,] Adoptive Couple initiated adoption proceedings in South Carolina a few days later, and returned there with Baby Girl. After returning to South Carolina, Adoptive Couple allowed Birth Mother to visit and communicate with Baby Girl.

It is undisputed that, for the duration of the pregnancy and the first four months after Baby Girl's birth, Biological Father provided no financial assistance to Birth Mother or Baby Girl, even though he had the ability to do so. Indeed, Biological Father "made no meaningful attempts to assume his responsibility of parenthood" during this period.

Approximately four months after Baby Girl's birth, Adoptive Couple served Biological Father with notice of the pending adoption. (This was the first notification that they had provided to Biological Father regarding the adoption proceeding.) Biological Father signed papers stating that he accepted service and that he was "not contesting the adoption." But Biological Father later testified that, at the time he signed the papers, he thought that he was relinquishing his rights to Birth Mother, not to Adoptive Couple.

Biological Father contacted a lawyer the day after signing the papers, and subsequently requested a stay of the adoption proceedings. In the adoption proceedings, Biological Father sought custody and stated that he did not consent to Baby Girl's adoption. Moreover, Biological Father took a paternity test, which verified that he was Baby Girl's biological father.

A trial took place in the South Carolina Family Court in September 2011, by which time Baby Girl was two years old. The Family Court concluded that Adoptive Couple had not carried the heightened burden under § 1912(f) of proving that Baby Girl would suffer serious emotional or physical damage if Biological Father had custody. The Family Court therefore denied Adoptive Couple's petition for adoption and awarded custody to Biological Father. On December 31, 2011, at the age of 27 months, Baby Girl was handed over to Biological Father, whom she had never met.

The South Carolina Supreme Court affirmed the Family Court's denial of the adoption and the award of custody to Biological Father. . . .

III

It is undisputed that, had Baby Girl not been 3/256 Cherokee, Biological Father would have had no right to object to her adoption under South Carolina law. . . .

A

Section 1912(f) addresses the involuntary termination of parental rights with respect to an Indian child. Specifically, § 1912(f) provides that "[n]o termination of parental rights may be ordered in such proceeding in the absence of a determination, supported by evidence beyond a reasonable doubt, . . . that the *continued* custody of the child by the parent or Indian custodian is likely to result in serious emotional or physical damage to the child." (Emphasis added.) The South Carolina Supreme Court held that Adoptive Couple failed to satisfy § 1912(f) because they did not make a heightened showing that Biological Father's "prospective legal and physical custody" would likely result in serious damage to the child. [Citation.] That holding was error.

Section 1912(f) conditions the involuntary termination of parental rights on a showing regarding the merits of "*continued* custody of the child by the parent." (Emphasis added.) The adjective "continued" plainly refers to a pre-existing state. As Justice SOTOMAYOR concedes, "continued" means "[c]arried on or kept up without cessation" or "[e]xtended in space without interruption or breach of conne[ct]ion." Compact Edition of the Oxford English Dictionary 909 (1981 reprint of 1971 ed.) (Compact OED); see also American Heritage Dictionary 288 (1981) (defining "continue" in the following manner: "1. To go on with a particular action or in a particular condition; persist. . . . 3. To remain in the same state, capacity, or place"); Webster's Third New International Dictionary 493 (1961) (Webster's) (defining "continued" as "stretching out in time or space esp. without interruption"); Aguilar v. FDIC, 63 F. 3d 1059, 1062 (CA11 1995) (per curiam) (suggesting that the phrase "continue an action" means "go on with . . . an action" that is "preexisting"). The term "continued" also can mean "resumed after interruption." Webster's 493; see American Heritage Dictionary 288. The phrase "continued custody" therefore refers to custody that a parent already has (or at least had at some point in the past). As a result, § 1912(f) does not apply in cases where the Indian parent never had custody of the Indian child. . . .

Our reading of § 1912(f) comports with the statutory text demonstrating that the primary mischief the ICWA was designed to counteract was the unwarranted removal of Indian children from Indian families due to the cultural insensitivity and biases of social workers and state courts. The statutory text expressly highlights the primary problem that the statute was intended to solve: "an alarmingly high percentage of Indian families [were being] broken up by the removal, often unwarranted, of their children from them by nontribal public and private agencies." § 1901(4)(emphasis added); see also § 1902 (explaining that the ICWA establishes "minimum Federal standards for the removal of Indian children from their families" (emphasis added)); *Holyfield*, 490 U. S., at 32–34. And if the legislative history of the ICWA is thought to be relevant, it further underscores that the Act was primarily intended to stem the unwarranted removal of Indian children from intact Indian families. See, e.g., H. R. Rep. No. 95–1386, p. 8 (1978) (explaining that, as relevant here, "[t]he purpose of [the ICWA] is to protect the best interests of Indian children and to promote the stability and security of Indian tribes and families by establishing minimum Federal standards for the removal of Indian children from their families and the placement of such children in foster or adoptive homes" (emphasis added)); *id.*, at 9 (decrying the "wholesale separation of Indian children" from their Indian families); *id.*, at 22 (discussing "the removal" of Indian children from their parents pursuant to §§ 1912(e) and (f)). In sum, when, as here, the adoption of an Indian child is voluntarily and lawfully initiated by a non-Indian parent with sole custodial rights, the ICWA's primary goal of preventing the unwarranted removal of Indian children and the dissolution of Indian families is not implicated. . . .

B

Section 1912(d) provides that "[a]ny party" seeking to terminate parental rights to an Indian child under state law "shall satisfy the court that active efforts have been made to provide remedial services and rehabilitative programs designed to prevent the breakup of the Indian family and that these efforts have proved unsuccessful." (Emphasis added.) The South Carolina Supreme Court found that Biological Father's parental rights could not be terminated because Adoptive Couple had not demonstrated that Biological Father had been provided remedial services in accordance with § 1912(d). [Citation.] We disagree.

Consistent with the statutory text, we hold that § 1912(d) applies only in cases where an Indian family's "breakup" would be precipitated by the termination of the parent's rights. The term "breakup" refers in this context to "[t]he discontinuance of a relationship," American Heritage Dictionary 235 (3d ed. 1992), or "an ending as an effective entity," Webster's 273 (defining "breakup" as "a disruption or dissolution into component parts: an ending as an effective entity"). See also Compact OED 1076 (defining "break-up" as, inter alia, a "disruption, separation into parts, disintegration"). But when an Indian parent abandons an Indian child prior to birth and that child has never been in the Indian parent's legal or physical custody, there is no "relationship" that would be "discontinu[ed]"—and no "effective entity" that would be "end[ed]"—by the termination of the Indian parent's rights. In such a situation, the "breakup of the Indian family" has long since occurred, and § 1912(d) is inapplicable.

Our interpretation of § 1912(d) is, like our interpretation of § 1912(f), consistent with the explicit congressional purpose of providing certain "standards for the removal of Indian children from their families." § 1902 (emphasis added); see also, e.g., § 1901(4); *Holyfield*, 490 U. S., at 32–34. In addition, the B[ureau of] I[ndian] A[ffairs]'s Guidelines confirm that remedial services under § 1912(d) are intended "to alleviate the need to remove the Indian child from his or her parents or Indian custodians," not to facilitate a transfer of the child to an Indian parent. See 44 Fed. Reg., at 67592 (emphasis added). . . .

The Indian Child Welfare Act was enacted to help preserve the cultural identity and heritage of Indian tribes, but under the State Supreme Court's reading, the Act would put certain vulnerable children at a great disadvantage solely because an ancestor—even a remote one—was an Indian. As the State Supreme Court read §§ 1912(d) and (f), a

[handwritten margin notes: There was no family to begin with] as in no relationship since the biological father relinquished his parental rights from the start]

biological Indian father could abandon his child in utero and refuse any support for the birth mother—perhaps contributing to the mother's decision to put the child up for adoption—and then could play his ICWA trump card at the eleventh hour to override the mother's decision and the child's best interests. If this were possible, many prospective adoptive parents would surely pause before adopting any child who might possibly qualify as an Indian under the ICWA. Such an interpretation would raise equal protection concerns, but the plain text of §§ 1912(f) and (d) makes clear that neither provision applies in the present context. Nor do § 1915(a)'s rebuttable adoption preferences apply when no alternative party has formally sought to adopt the child. We therefore reverse the judgment of the South Carolina Supreme Court and remand the case for further proceedings not inconsistent with this opinion.

It is so ordered.

[The concurring opinions of JUSTICE THOMAS and JUSTICE BREYER have been omitted.]

■ JUSTICE SOTOMAYOR, with whom JUSTICE GINSBURG and JUSTICE KAGAN join, and with whom JUSTICE SCALIA joins in part, dissenting.

A casual reader of the Court's opinion could be forgiven for thinking this an easy case, one in which the text of the applicable statute clearly points the way to the only sensible result. In truth, however, the path from the text of the Indian Child Welfare Act of 1978 (ICWA) to the result the Court reaches is anything but clear, and its result anything but right.

The reader's first clue that the majority's supposedly straightforward reasoning is flawed is that not all Members who adopt its interpretation believe it is compelled by the text of the statute (Thomas, J., concurring); nor are they all willing to accept the consequences it will necessarily have beyond the specific factual scenario confronted here. The second clue is that the majority begins its analysis by plucking out of context a single phrase from the last clause of the last subsection of the relevant provision, and then builds its entire argument upon it. That is not how we ordinarily read statutes. The third clue is that the majority openly professes its aversion to Congress' explicitly stated purpose in enacting the statute. The majority expresses concern that reading the Act to mean what it says will make it more difficult to place Indian children in adoptive homes, but the Congress that enacted the statute announced its intent to stop "an alarmingly high percentage of Indian families [from being] broken up" by, among other things, a trend of "plac[ing][Indian children] in non-Indian . . . adoptive homes." 25 U. S. C. § 1901(4). Policy disagreement with Congress' judgment is not a valid reason for this Court to distort the provisions of the Act. Unlike the majority, I cannot adopt a reading of ICWA that is contrary to both its text and its stated purpose. I respectfully dissent.

I

. . .

A

Better to start at the beginning and consider the operation of the statute as a whole. ICWA commences with express findings. Congress recognized that "there is no resource that is more vital to the continued existence and integrity of Indian tribes than their children," 25 U. S. C. § 1901(3), and it found that this resource was threatened. State authorities insufficiently sensitive to "the essential tribal relations of Indian people and the cultural and social standards prevailing in Indian communities and families" were breaking up Indian families and moving Indian children to non-Indian homes and institutions. See §§ 1901(4)–(5). As § 1901(4) makes clear, and as this Court recognized in *Mississippi Band of Choctaw Indians v. Holyfield*, 490 U. S. 30, 33 (1989), adoptive placements of Indian children with non-Indian families contributed significantly to the overall problem. See § 1901(4) (finding that "an alarmingly high percentage of [Indian] children are placed in non-Indian . . . adoptive homes").Consistent with these findings, Congress declared its purpose "to protect the best interests of Indian children and to promote the stability and security of Indian tribes and families by the establishment of minimum Federal standards" applicable to child custody proceedings involving Indian children. § 1902. Section 1903 then goes on to establish the reach of these protections through its definitional provisions. . . .

II

The majority's textually strained and illogical reading of the statute might be explicable, if not justified, if there were reason to believe that it avoided anomalous results or furthered a clear congressional policy. But neither of these conditions is present here. . . .

B

On a more general level, the majority intimates that ICWA grants Birth Father an undeserved windfall: in the majority's words, an "ICWA trump card" he can "play . . . at the eleventh hour to override the mother's decision and the child's best interests." The implicit argument is that Congress could not possibly have intended to recognize a parent-child relationship between Birth Father and Baby Girl that would have to be legally terminated (either by valid consent or involuntary termination) before the adoption could proceed.

But this supposed anomaly is illusory. In fact, the law of at least 15 States did precisely that at the time ICWA was passed. And the law of a number of States still does so. The State of Arizona, for example, requires that notice of an adoption petition be given to all "potential father[s]"and that they be informed of their "right to seek custody." Ariz. Rev. Stat. §§ 8–106(G)–(J) (West Supp. 2012). In Washington, an "alleged father['s]" consent to adoption is required absent the termination of his parental rights, Wash. Rev. Code §§ 26.33.020(1), 26.33.160(1)(b) (2012); and those rights may be terminated only "upon a showing by clear, cogent, and convincing evidence" not only that termination is in the best interest of the child and that the father is withholding his consent to adoption contrary to child's best interests, but also that the father "has failed to perform parental duties under circumstances showing a substantial lack of regard for his parental obligations," § 26.33.120(2).

Without doubt, laws protecting biological fathers' parental rights can lead—even outside the context of ICWA—to outcomes that are painful and distressing for both would be adoptive families, who lose a much wanted child, and children who must make a difficult transition. See, e.g., *In re Adoption of Tobias D.*, 2012 Me. 45, ¶ 27, 40 A. 3d 990, 999 (recognizing that award of custody of 2½-year-old child to biological father under applicable state law once paternity is established will result in the "difficult and painful" necessity of "removing the child from the only home he has ever known"). On the other hand, these rules recognize that biological fathers have a valid interest in a relationship with their child. And children have a reciprocal interest in knowing their biological parents. See *Santosky*, 455 U. S., at 760–761, n. 11 (describing the foreclosure of a newborn child's opportunity to "ever know his natural parents" as a "los[s] [that] cannot be measured"). These rules also reflect the understanding that the biological bond between a parent and a child is a strong foundation on which a stable and caring relationship may be built. Many jurisdictions apply a custodial preference for a fit natural parent over a party lacking this biological link. [Citations] Cf. *Smith v. Organization of Foster Families For Equality & Reform*, 431 U. S. 816, 845 (1977) (distinguishing a natural parent's "liberty interest in family privacy," which has its source "in intrinsic human rights," with a foster parent's parallel interest in his or her relationship with a child, which has its "origins in an arrangement in which the State has been a partner from the outset"). This preference is founded in the "presumption that fit parents act in the best interests of their children." *Troxel v. Granville*, 530 U. S. 57, 68 (2000) (plurality opinion). " '[H]istorically [the law] has recognized that natural bonds of affection [will] lead parents' " to promote their child's well-being. Ibid. (quoting Parham v. J. R., 442 U. S. 584, 602 (1979)).

Balancing the legitimate interests of unwed biological fathers against the need for stability in a child's family situation is difficult, to be sure, and States have, over the years, taken different approaches to the problem. Some States, like South Carolina, have opted to hew to the constitutional baseline established by this Court's precedents and do not require a biological father's consent to adoption unless he has provided financial support during pregnancy. [Citation.] Other States, how-ever, have decided to give the rights of biological fathers more robust protection and to afford them consent rights on the basis of their biological link to the child. At the time that ICWA was passed, as noted, over one-fourth of States did so.

ICWA, on a straightforward reading of the statute, is consistent with the law of those States that protected, and protect, birth fathers' rights more vigorously. This reading can hardly be said to generate an anomaly. ICWA, as all acknowledge, was "the product of rising concern . . . [about] abusive child welfare practices that resulted in the separation of large numbers of Indian children from their families." *Holyfield*, 490 U. S., at 32. It stands to reason that the Act would not render the legal status of an Indian father's relationship with his biological child fragile, but would instead grant it a degree of protection commensurate with the more robust state-law standards.

C

The majority also protests that a contrary result to the one it reaches would interfere with the adoption of Indian children. This claim is the most perplexing of all. A central purpose of ICWA is to "promote the stability and security of Indian . . . families," 25 U. S. C. § 1902, in part by countering the trend of placing "an alarmingly high percentage of [Indian] children . . . in non-Indian foster and adoptive homes and institutions." § 1901(4). The Act accomplishes this goal by, first, protecting the familial bonds of Indian parents and children; and, second, establishing placement preferences should an adoption take place, see § 1915(a). ICWA does not interfere with the adoption of Indian children except to the extent that it attempts to avert the necessity of adoptive placement and makes adoptions of Indian children by non-Indian families less likely. The majority may consider this scheme unwise. But no principle of construction licenses a court to interpret a statute with a view to averting the very consequences Congress expressly stated it was trying to bring about. Instead, it is the " 'judicial duty to give faithful meaning to the language Congress adopted in the light of the evident legislative purpose in enacting the law in question.' " [Citation.]

The majority further claims that its reading is consistent with the "primary" purpose of the Act, which in the majority's view was to prevent the dissolution of "intact" Indian families. We may not, however, give effect only to congressional goals we designate "primary" while casting aside others classed as "secondary"; we must apply the entire statute Congress has written. While there are indications that central among Congress' concerns in enacting ICWA was the removal of Indian children from homes in which Indian parents or other guardians had custody of them, see, e.g., §§ 1901(4), 1902, Congress also recognized that "there is no resource that is more vital to the continued existence and integrity of Indian tribes than their children," § 1901(3). As we observed in *Holyfield*, ICWA protects not only Indian parents' interests but also those of Indian tribes. See 490 U. S., at 34, 52. A tribe's interest in its next generation of citizens is adversely affected by the placement of Indian children in homes with no connection to the tribe, whether or not those children were initially in the custody of an Indian parent.

Moreover, the majority's focus on "intact" families begs the question of what Congress set out to accomplish with ICWA. In an ideal world, perhaps all parents would be perfect. They would live up to their parental responsibilities by providing the fullest possible financial and emotional support to their children. They would never suffer mental health problems, lose their jobs, struggle with substance dependency, or encounter any of the other multitudinous personal crises that can make it difficult to meet these responsibilities. In an ideal world parents would never become estranged and leave their children caught in the middle. But we do not live in such a world. Even happy families do not always fit the custodial-parent mold for which the majority would reserve IWCA's substantive protections; unhappy families all too often do not. They are families nonetheless. Congress understood as much. ICWA's definitions of "parent" and "termination of parental rights" provided in § 1903 sweep broadly. They should be honored. . . .

The majority opinion turns § 1912 upside down, reading it from bottom to top in order to reach a conclusion that is manifestly contrary to Congress' express purpose in enacting ICWA: preserving the familial bonds between Indian parents and their children and, more broadly, Indian tribes' relationships with the future citizens who are "vital to [their] continued existence and integrity." § 1901(3). The majority casts Birth Father as responsible for the painful circumstances in this case, suggesting that he intervened "at the eleventh hour to override the mother's decision and the child's best interests." I have no wish to minimize the trauma of removing a 27-month old child from her adoptive family. It bears remembering, however, that Birth Father took action to assert his parental rights when Baby Girl was four months old, as soon as he learned of the impending adoption. As the South Carolina Supreme Court recognized, " '[h]ad the mandate of . . . ICWA been followed [in 2010], . . . much potential anguish might have been avoided[;] and in any case the law cannot be applied so as automatically to "reward those who obtain custody, whether lawfully or otherwise, and maintain it during any ensuing (and protracted) litigation.' " [Citation.]

The majority's hollow literalism distorts the statute and ignores Congress' purpose in order to rectify a perceived wrong that, while heartbreaking at the time, was a correct application of federal law and that in any case cannot be undone. Baby Girl has now resided with her father for 18 months. However difficult it must have been for her to leave Adoptive Couple's home when she was just over 2 years old, it will be equally devastating now if, at the age of 3½, she is again removed from her home and sent to live halfway across the country. Such a fate is not foreordained, of course. But it can be said with certainty that the anguish this case has caused will only be compounded by today's decision.

I believe that the South Carolina Supreme Court's judgment was correct, and I would affirm it. I respectfully dissent.

NOTES AND QUESTIONS

1. The majority and dissent identify different principal evils to be remedied by the statute. Recall the typology of interpretive methods in subsection III.A.2.a, *supra*. Which methods do the majority and dissent draw upon to determine what those evils were?

2. What relevance, if any, is the percentage (1/256th) of Baby Veronica's Cherokee heritage to the application of the statute?

3. To what extent do you think normative objectives informed the majority's textualist interpretation? Would the majority's textualist-based methods of interpretation reach the same result even if one did not share the majority's view that Congress's "primary" goal was to preserve only *intact* Indian families?

4. For further information about ICWA and the families embroiled in the "Baby Veronica" controversy, listen to this podcast: https://www.wnyc studios.org/story/more-perfect-presents-adoptive-couple-v-baby-girl.

Moskal v. United States

Supreme Court of the United States, 1990.
498 U.S. 103, 111 S.Ct. 461, 112 L.Ed.2d 449.

■ JUSTICE MARSHALL delivered the opinion of the Court[, in which CHIEF JUSTICE REHNQUIST, JUSTICE WHITE, JUSTICE BLACKMUN, and JUSTICE STEVENS joined].

The issue in this case is whether a person who knowingly procures genuine vehicle titles that incorporate fraudulently tendered odometer readings receives those titles "knowing [them] to have been *falsely made*." 18 U.S.C. § 2314 (emphasis added). We conclude that he does.

[Editors' Note: the statute at issue, 18 U.S.C. § 2314, provided in part:

"Whoever, with unlawful or fraudulent intent, transports in interstate or foreign commerce any falsely made, forged, altered, or counterfeited securities or tax stamps, knowing the same to have been falsely made, forged, altered, or counterfeited; . . . .

Shall be fined not more than $10,000 or imprisoned not more than ten years, or both."

For purposes of § 2314, "securities" are defined to include any "valid . . . motor vehicle title."]

I

Petitioner Raymond Moskal participated in a "title-washing" scheme. Moskal's confederates purchased used cars in Pennsylvania, rolled back the cars' odometers, and altered their titles to reflect those lower mileage figures. The altered titles were then sent to an accomplice in Virginia, who submitted them to Virginia authorities. Those officials, unaware of the alterations, issued Virginia titles incorporating the false mileage figures. The "washed" titles were then sent back to Pennsylvania, where they were used in connection with car sales to unsuspecting buyers. Moskal played two roles in this scheme: He sent altered titles from Pennsylvania to Virginia; he received "washed" titles when they were returned.

The Government indicted and convicted Moskal under 18 U.S.C. § 2314 for receiving two washed titles, each recording a mileage figure that was 30,000 miles lower than the true number. Section 2314 imposes fines or imprisonment on anyone who, "with unlawful or fraudulent intent, transports in interstate . . . commerce any falsely made, forged, altered, or counterfeited securities . . . , knowing the same to have been falsely made, forged, altered or counterfeited." On appeal, Moskal maintained that the washed titles were nonetheless genuine and thus not "falsely made." The Court of Appeals disagreed, finding that "the purpose of the term 'falsely made' was to . . . prohibit the fraudulent introduction into commerce of falsely made documents regardless of the precise method by which the introducer or his confederates effected their lack of authenticity." [Citation.]

Notwithstanding the narrowness of this issue, we granted certiorari to resolve a divergence of opinion among the Courts of Appeals. [Citation]. We now affirm petitioner's conviction.

II

As indicated, § 2314 prohibits the knowing transportation of "falsely made, forged, altered, or counterfeited securities" in interstate commerce. Moskal acknowledges that he could have been charged with violating this provision when he sent the Pennsylvania titles to Virginia, since those titles were "altered" within the meaning of § 2314. But he insists that he did not violate the provision in subsequently receiving the washed titles from Virginia because, although he was participating in a fraud (and thus no doubt had the requisite intent under § 2314), the washed titles themselves were not "falsely made." He asserts that when a title is issued by appropriate state authorities who do not know of its falsity, the title is "genuine" or valid as the state document it purports to be and therefore not "falsely made."

Whether a valid title that contains fraudulently tendered odometer readings may be a "falsely made" security for purposes of § 2314 presents a conventional issue of statutory construction, and we must therefore determine what scope Congress intended § 2314 to have. Moskal, however, suggests a shortcut in that inquiry. Because it is *possible* to read the statute as applying only to forged or counterfeited securities, and because *some* courts have so read it, Moskal suggests we should simply resolve the issue in his favor under the doctrine of lenity. [citation].

In our view, this argument misconstrues the doctrine. We have repeatedly "emphasized that the 'touchstone' of the rule of lenity 'is statutory ambiguity.'" [Citation.] Stated at this level of abstraction, of course, the rule "provides little more than atmospherics, since it leaves open the crucial question—almost invariably present—of *how much* ambiguousness constitutes . . . ambiguity." [Citation].

Because the meaning of language is inherently contextual, we have declined to deem a statute "ambiguous" for purposes of lenity merely because it was *possible* to articulate a construction more narrow than that urged by the Government. [Citation.] Nor have we deemed a division of judicial authority automatically sufficient to trigger lenity. [Citation]. If that were sufficient, one court's unduly narrow reading of a criminal statute would become binding on all other courts, including this one. Instead, we have always reserved lenity for those situations in which a reasonable doubt persists about a statute's intended scope even *after* resort to "the language and structure, legislative history, and motivating policies" of the statute. [Citation.] Examining these materials, we conclude that § 2314 unambiguously applies to Moskal's conduct.

A

"In determining the scope of a statute, we look first to its language," [citation], giving the "words used" their "ordinary meaning," [citation]. We think that the words of § 2314 are broad enough, on their face, to encompass washed titles containing fraudulently tendered odometer readings. Such titles are "falsely made" in the sense that they are made to contain false, or incorrect, information.

Moskal resists this construction of the language on the ground that the state officials responsible for issuing the washed titles did not know that they were incorporating false odometer readings. We see little merit in this argument. As used in § 2314, "falsely made" refers to the character of the securities being transported. In our view, it is perfectly consistent with ordinary usage to speak of the security as *being* "falsely made" regardless of whether the party responsible for the physical production of the document *knew* that he was making a security in a manner that incorporates false information. Indeed, we find support for this construction in the nexus between the *actus reus* and *mens rea* elements of § 2314.* Because liability under the statute depends on *transporting* the "falsely made" security with unlawful or fraudulent intent, there is no reason to infer a scienter requirement for the act of falsely making itself.[2]

Short of construing "falsely made" in this way, we are at a loss to give *any* meaning to this phrase independent of the other terms in § 2314, such as "forged" or "counterfeited." By seeking to exclude from § 2314's scope any security that is "genuine" or valid, Moskal essentially equates "falsely made" with "forged" or "counterfeited." His construction therefore violates the established principle that a court should " 'give effect, if possible, to every clause and word of a statute.' " [Citation.]

Our conclusion that "falsely made" encompasses genuine documents containing false information is supported by Congress' purpose in enacting § 2314. Inspired by the proliferation of interstate schemes for passing counterfeit securities, [citation], Congress in 1939 added the clause pertaining to "falsely made, forged, altered or counterfeited securities" as an amendment to the National Stolen Property Act. 53 Stat. 1178. Our prior decisions have recognized Congress' "general intent" and "broad purpose" to curb the type of trafficking in fraudulent securities that often depends for its success on the exploitation of interstate commerce. In *United States v. Sheridan,* 329 U.S. 379 (1946), we explained that Congress enacted the relevant clause of § 2314 in order to "com[e] to the aid of the states in detecting and punishing criminals whose offenses are complete under state law, but who utilize the

---

*   Editors' Note: *Actus reus* and *mens rea* are terms of art in criminal law: *actus reus* refers to the conduct that is an element of the crime, whereas *mens rea* refers to the mental state of the accused when engaged in the conduct at issue.

[2]   Indeed, we offer no view on how we would construe "falsely made" in a statute that punished the *act* of false making and that specified no scienter requirement. [Citation.]

channels of interstate commerce to make a successful getaway and thus make the state's detecting and punitive processes impotent." *Id.,* at 384. This, we concluded, "was indeed one of the most effective ways of preventing further frauds." *Ibid.*; see also *McElroy v. United States,* 455 U.S. 642, 655 (1982) (rejecting a narrow reading of § 2314 that was at odds with Congress' "broad purpose" and that would "undercut sharply . . . federal prosecutors in their effort to combat crime in interstate commerce").

We think that "title-washing" operations are a perfect example of the "further frauds" that Congress sought to halt in enacting § 2314. As Moskal concedes, his title-washing scheme is a clear instance of fraud involving securities. And as the facts of this case demonstrate, title washes involve precisely the sort of fraudulent activities that are dispersed among several States in order to elude state detection.

Moskal draws a different conclusion from this legislative history. Seizing upon the references to counterfeit securities, petitioner finds no evidence that "the 1939 amendment had anything at all to do with odometer rollback schemes." We think petitioner misconceives the inquiry into legislative purpose by failing to recognize that Congress sought to attack a category of fraud. At the time that Congress amended the National Stolen Property Act, counterfeited securities no doubt constituted (and may still constitute) the most prevalent form of such interstate fraud. The fact remains, however, that Congress did not limit the statute's reach to "counterfeit securities" but instead chose the broader phrase "falsely made, forged, altered, *or* counterfeited securities," which was consistent with its purpose to reach a class of frauds that exploited interstate commerce.

This Court has never required that every permissible application of a statute be expressly referred to in its legislative history. . . .

Our precedents concerning § 2314 specifically reject constructions of the statute that limit it to *instances* of fraud rather than the *class* of fraud encompassed by its language. For example, in *United States v. Sheridan,* the defendant cashed checks at a Michigan bank, drawn on a Missouri account, with a forged signature. The Court found that such conduct was proscribed by § 2314. In reaching that conclusion, the Court noted Congress' primary objective of reaching counterfeiters of corporate securities but nonetheless found that the statute covered check forgeries "done by 'little fellows' who perhaps were not the primary aim of the congressional fire." 329 U.S., at 390. "Whether or not Congress had in mind primarily such small scale transactions as Sheridan's," we held, "his operation was covered literally and we think purposively. Had this not been intended, appropriate exception could easily have been made." *Ibid.* In explaining that conclusion, we stated further:

"Drawing the [forged] check upon an out-of-state bank, knowing it must be sent there for presentation, is an obviously facile way to delay and often to defeat apprehension, conviction and restoration of the ill-gotten gain. There are sound reasons therefore why Congress would wish not to exclude such persons [from the statute's reach], among them the very ease with which they may escape the state's grasp." *Id.,* at 391.

In *McElroy v. United States,* we similarly rejected a narrow construction of § 2314. The defendant used blank checks that had been stolen in Ohio to buy a car and a boat in Pennsylvania. Defendant conceded that the checks he had thus misused constituted "forged securities" but maintained his innocence under the federal statute because the checks were not yet forged when they were transported across state boundaries. The Court acknowledged that "Congress could have written the statute to produce this result," *id.,* 455 U.S. at 656, but rejected such a reading as inconsistent with Congress' "broad purpose" since it would permit "a patient forger easily [to] evade the reach of federal law," *id.,* at 655. Moreover, because we found the defendant's interpretation to be contradicted by Congress' intent in § 2314 and its predecessors, we also rejected the defendant's plea for lenity: "[A]lthough 'criminal statutes are to be construed strictly . . . this does not mean that every criminal statute must be given the narrowest possible meaning in complete disregard of the purpose of the legislature.'" *Id.,* at 658, [citation.] We concluded that the defendant had failed to "raise significant questions of ambiguity, for the statutory language and legislative history . . . indicate that Congress defined the term 'interstate commerce' more broadly than the petitioner contends." 455 U.S., at 658.

Thus, in both *Sheridan* and *McElroy,* defendants who admittedly circulated fraudulent securities among several States sought to avoid liability by offering a reading of § 2314 that was narrower than the scope of its language and of Congress' intent, and in each instance we rejected the proffered interpretation. Moskal's interpretation in the present case rests on a similarly cramped reading of the statute's words, and we think it should likewise be rejected as inconsistent with Congress' general purpose to combat interstate fraud. "[F]ederal criminal statutes that are intended to fill a void in local law enforcement should be construed broadly." [Citation.]

To summarize our conclusions as to the meaning of "falsely made" in § 2314, we find both in the plain meaning of those words and in the legislative purpose underlying them ample reason to apply the law to a fraudulent scheme for washing vehicle titles.

B

Petitioner contends that such a reading of § 2314 is nonetheless precluded by a further principle of statutory construction. "[W]here a federal criminal statute uses a common-law term of established meaning without otherwise defining it, the general practice is to give that term its common-law meaning." United States v. Turley, 352 U.S. 407, 411 (1957). Petitioner argues that, at the time Congress enacted the relevant clause of § 2314, the term "falsely made" had an established common-law meaning equivalent to forgery. As so defined, "falsely made" excluded authentic or genuine documents that were merely false in content. Petitioner maintains that Congress should be presumed to have adopted this common-law definition when it amended the National Stolen Property Act in 1939 and that § 2314 therefore should be deemed not to cover washed vehicle titles that merely contain false odometer readings. We disagree for two reasons.

First, . . . [the Court concluded that the common-law meaning of "false made" was not universally agreed upon].

Our second reason for rejecting Moskal's reliance on the "common-law meaning" rule is that, as this Court has previously recognized, Congress' general purpose in enacting a law may prevail over this rule of statutory construction. In *Taylor v. United States,* 495 U.S. 575 (1990), we confronted the question whether "burglary," when used in a sentence enhancement statute, was intended to take its common-law meaning. We declined to apply the "common-law meaning" rule, in part, because the common-law meaning of burglary was inconsistent with congressional purpose. "The arcane distinctions embedded in the common-law definition [of burglary]," we noted, "have little relevance to modern law-enforcement concerns." *Id.,* at 593 (footnote omitted). [Citations].

We reach a similar conclusion here. The position of those common-law courts that defined "falsely made" to exclude documents that are false only in content does not accord with Congress' broad purpose in enacting § 2314—namely, to criminalize trafficking in fraudulent securities that exploits interstate commerce. We conclude, then, that it is far more likely that Congress adopted the common-law view of "falsely made" that encompasses "genuine" documents that are false in content.

Affirmed.

■ JUSTICE SOUTER took no part in the consideration or decision of this case.

■ JUSTICE SCALIA, with whom JUSTICE O'CONNOR and JUSTICE KENNEDY join, dissenting.

Today's opinion succeeds in its stated objective of "resolv[ing] a divergence of opinion among the Courts of Appeals." It does that, however, in a manner that so undermines generally applicable principles of statutory construction that I fear the confusion it produces will far exceed the confusion it has removed.

I

The Court's decision rests ultimately upon the proposition that, pursuant to "ordinary meaning," a "falsely made" document includes a document which is genuinely what it purports to be, but which contains information that the maker knows to be false, or even information that the maker does not know to be false but that someone who causes him to insert it knows to be false. It seems to me that such a meaning is quite *extra*-ordinary. Surely the adverb preceding the word "made" naturally refers to the manner of making, rather than to the nature of the product made. An inexpensively made painting is not the same as an inexpensive painting. A forged memorandum is "falsely made"; a memorandum that contains erroneous information is simply "false."

One would not expect general-usage dictionaries to have a separate entry for "falsely made," but some of them do use precisely the phrase "to make falsely" to define "forged." See, *e.g.,* Webster's New International Dictionary 990 (2d ed. (1945); Webster's Third New International Dictionary 891 (1961). The Court seeks to make its interpretation plausible by the following locution: "Such titles are 'falsely made' in the sense that they are made to contain false, or incorrect, information." This sort of word-play can transform virtually anything into "falsely made." Thus: "The building was falsely made in the sense that it was made to contain a false entrance." This is a far cry from "ordinary meaning."

That "falsely made" refers to the manner of making is also evident from the fifth clause of § 2314, which forbids the interstate transportation of "any tool, implement, or thing used or fitted to be used in falsely making, forging, altering, or counterfeiting any security or tax stamps." This obviously refers to the tools of counterfeiting, and not to the tools of misrepresentation.

The Court maintains, however, that giving "falsely made" what I consider to be its ordinary meaning would render the term superfluous, offending the principle of construction that if possible each word should be given some effect. [Citation.] The principle is sound, but its limitation ("if possible") must be observed. It should not be used to distort ordinary meaning. Nor should it be applied to the obvious instances of iteration to which lawyers, alas, are particularly addicted—such as "give, grant, bargain, sell, and convey," "aver and affirm," "rest, residue, and remainder," or "right, title, and interest." See generally B. Garner, A Dictionary of Modern Legal Usage 197–200 (1987). The phrase at issue here, "falsely made, forged, altered, or counterfeited," is, in one respect at least, uncontestedly of that sort. As the United States conceded at oral argument, and as any dictionary will confirm, "forged" and "counterfeited" mean the same thing. See, *e.g.,* Webster's 2d, *supra,* at 607 (defining to "counterfeit" as to "forge," and listing "forged" as a synonym of the adjective "counterfeit"), *id.,* at 990 (defining to "forge" as to "counterfeit," and listing "counterfeit" as a synonym of "forge"). Since iteration is obviously afoot in the relevant passage, there is no justification for extruding an unnatural meaning out of "falsely made" simply in order to avoid iteration. The entire phrase "falsely made, forged, altered, or counterfeited" is self-evidently not a listing of differing and precisely calibrated terms, but a collection of near synonyms which describes the product of the general crime of forgery.

II

Even on the basis of a layman's understanding, therefore, I think today's opinion in error. But in declaring that understanding to be the governing criterion, rather than the specialized legal meaning that the term "falsely made" has long possessed, the Court makes a mistake of greater consequence. The rigid and unrealistic standard it prescribes for establishing a specialized legal meaning, and the justification it announces for ignoring such a meaning, will adversely affect many future cases.

The Court acknowledges, as it must, the doctrine that when a statute employs a term with a specialized legal meaning relevant to the matter at hand, that meaning governs. As Justice Jackson explained for the Court in *Morissette v. United States,* 342 U.S. 246, 263, 72 S.Ct. 240, 250, 96 L.Ed. 288 (1952):

"[W]here Congress borrows terms of art in which are accumulated the legal tradition and meaning of centuries of practice, it presumably knows and adopts the cluster of ideas that were attached to each borrowed word in the body of learning from which it was taken and the meaning its use will convey to the judicial mind unless otherwise instructed. In such a case, absence of contrary direction may be taken as satisfaction with widely accepted definitions, not as departure from them."

Or as Justice Frankfurter more poetically put it: "[I]f a word is obviously transplanted from another legal source, whether the common law or other legislation, it brings its soil with it." *Some Reflections on the Reading of Statutes,* 47 Colum. L. Rev. 527, 537 (1947).

We have such an obvious transplant before us here. Both Black's Law Dictionary and Ballentine's Law Dictionary contain a definition of the term "false making." The former reads as follows:

"False making. An essential element of forgery, where material alteration is not involved. Term has reference to manner in which writing is made or executed rather than to its substance or effect. A falsely made instrument is one that is fictitious, not genuine, or in some material particular something other than it purports to be and without regard to truth or falsity of facts stated therein." Black's Law Dictionary 602 (6th ed. 1990).

Ballentine's is to the same effect. See Ballentine's Law Dictionary 486 (2d ed. 1948). "Falsely made" is, in other words, a term laden with meaning in the common law, because it describes an essential element of the crime of forgery. Blackstone defined forgery as "the *fraudulent making* or alteration of a writing to the prejudice of another man's right." 4 W. Blackstone, Commentaries 245 (1769) (emphasis added). The most prominent 19th-century American authority on criminal law wrote that "[f]orgery, at the common law, is the *false making* or materially altering, with intent to defraud, of any writing which, if genuine, might apparently be of legal efficacy or the foundation of a legal liability." 2 J. Bishop, Criminal Law § 523, p. 288 (5th ed. 1872) (emphasis added). The distinction between "falsity in execution" (or "false making") and "falsity of content" was well understood on both sides of the Atlantic as marking the boundary between forgery and fraud.

"The definition of forgery is not, as has been suggested in argument, that every instrument containing false statements fraudulently made is a forgery; but . . . that every instrument which fraudulently purports to be that which it is not is a forgery. . . ." *Queen v. Ritson,* L.R. 1 Cr.Cas.Res. 200, 203 (1869).

"The term *falsely,* as applied to making or altering a writing in order to make it forgery, has reference not to the contracts or tenor of the writing, or to the fact stated in the writing . . . but it implies that the paper or writing is false, not genuine, fictitious, not a true writing, without regard to the truth or falsity of the statement it contains." *State v. Young,* 46 N.H. 266, 270 (1865) (emphasis in original).

In 1939, when the relevant portion of § 2314 was enacted, the States and the Federal Government had been using the "falsely made" terminology for more than a century in their forgery statutes. [Citations.] More significantly still, the most common statutory definition of forgery had been a formulation employing precisely the four terms that appear in § 2314: falsely make, alter, forge, and counterfeit. [Citations.] By 1939, several federal courts and eight States had held that the formula "falsely make, alter, forge or counterfeit" did not encompass the inclusion of false information in a genuine document. [Citations.]

Commentators in 1939 were apparently unanimous in their understanding that "false making" was an element of the crime of forgery, and that the term did not embrace false contents. . . .

I think it plain that "falsely made" had a well-established common-law meaning at the time the relevant language of § 2314 was enacted—indeed, that the entire formulary phrase "falsely made, forged, altered, or counterfeited" had a well-established common-law meaning; and that that meaning does not support the present conviction. . . .

[Part III, discussing prior federal cases interpreting the term "falsely made" in related statutes, has been omitted.]

IV

The Court acknowledges the principle that common-law terms ought to be given their established common-law meanings, but asserts that the principle is inapplicable here because the meaning of "falsely made" I have described above "was not universal." For support it cites three cases and an A.L.R. annotation. . . . If such minimal "divergence"—by States with statutes that did not include the term "falsely made" (see *supra,* at 473)—is sufficient to eliminate a common-law meaning long accepted by virtually all the courts and by apparently all the commentators, the principle of common-law meaning might as well be frankly abandoned.

The Court's second reason for refusing to give "falsely made" its common-law meaning is that "Congress' general purpose in enacting a law may prevail over this rule of statutory construction." That is undoubtedly true in the sense that an explicitly stated statutory purpose that contradicts a common-law meaning (and that accords with another, "ordinary" meaning of the contested term) will prevail. The Court, however, means something quite different. What displaces normal principles of construction here, according to the Court, is "Congress' broad purpose in enacting § 2314—namely, to criminalize trafficking in fraudulent securities that exploits interstate commerce." *Ibid.* But that analysis does *not* rely upon any explicit language, and is simply question-begging. The whole issue before us here is how "broad" Congress' purpose in enacting § 2314 was. Was it, as the Court simply announces, "to criminalize trafficking in fraudulent securities"? Or was it to exclude trafficking in *forged* securities? The answer to that question is best sought by examining the language that Congress used—here, language that Congress has used since 1790 to describe not fraud but forgery, and that we reaffirmed bears that meaning as recently as 1962 . . . . . It is perverse to find the answer by assuming it, and then to impose that answer upon the text.

The "Congress' broad purpose" approach is not supported by the authorities the Court cites. . . . .

We should have rejected the argument in precisely those terms today. Instead, the Court adopts a new principle that can accurately be described as follows: "Where a term of art has a plain meaning, the Court will divine the statute's purpose and substitute a meaning more appropriate to that purpose."

NOTES AND QUESTIONS

1.   The majority invokes the "rule against superfluities," a canon that counsels the interpreter to give, where possible, each statutory term an independent (non-redundant) meaning. The dissent contends that the "where possible" proviso excludes the rule's application when giving the term a non-redundant meaning would contradict the term's ordinary meaning. In indulging the legal fiction that Congress drafts statutes concisely, the "rule against superfluities" may impose a counter-factual coherence on the text. Recall the findings of Professors Gluck and Bressman, discussed in subsection III.A.3 *supra*, that legislative drafters often *purposefully* introduce superfluous language into legislation. Redundancy can supply the "belt and suspenders" to understanding a provision even when the rest of the text is (sometimes deliberately) opaque. By contrast, the rule against superfluities may enable courts, in the guise of finding independent meaning, to read the statute to say what they think it "ought" to say.

2.   The majority dismisses the defendant's argument that the common-law meaning of "falsely made" at the time of the statute's enactment was the defendant's preferred narrower meaning. Does evidence of the enacting-era's common-law (as opposed to ordinary) meaning reveal the drafters' intent, the reasonable (law-literate) reader's understanding, or both? Would it

matter if the narrower meaning was also the reasonable (generalist) reader's "ordinary" meaning at the time of the statute's enactment? Keep these questions in mind as you read *New Prime, Inc. v. Oliveira*, in subsection III.E.1, *infra*.

2.   INTERPRETING A STATUTE IN LIGHT OF LEGISLATIVE HISTORY

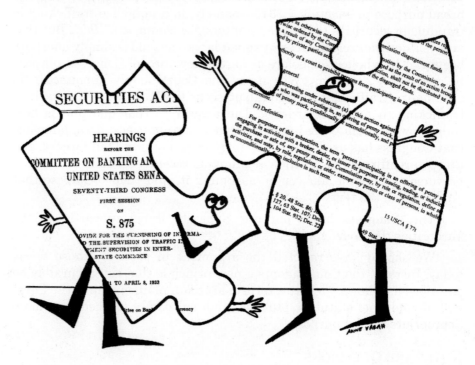

When courts speak of "legislative history," they generally refer to materials produced during a statute's drafting process—the committee reports, floor debates, proposed alterations and amendments, and legislator statements—that may collectively shed light on the specific intent of Congress in enacting legislation. The cases below highlight the potential benefits and risks of relying on these materials when interpreting statutes.

Securities and Exchange Commission
v. Robert Collier & Co.

United States Court of Appeals for the Second Circuit, 1935.
76 F.2d 939.

Appeal from the District Court of the United States for the Southern District of New York.

Suit by the Securities & Exchange Commission against Robert Collier & Co., Inc., and others, to enjoin the defendants under the Securities Act of 1933. From a decree dismissing the bill (10 F.Supp. 95), plaintiff appeals.

■ Before L. HAND, SWAN, and AUGUSTUS N. HAND, CIRCUIT JUDGES.

■ L. HAND, CIRCUIT JUDGE. The single question presented by this appeal is whether the Securities and Exchange Commission, created under section 4(a) of title 1 of the Securities Exchange Act of 1934, section 78d, tit. 15, U.S.Code, 15 U.S.C.A. § 78d, may appear in the District Court by its own solicitor and file a bill under section 20(b)† of the Securities Act (15 U.S.C.A. § 77t, subd. (b)), or whether it must appear by the Attorney General, or a district attorney. The defendants and the judge thought that the situation fell within our decision in Sutherland v. International Insurance Co., 43 F.2d 969; the Commission insists that section 20(b) is an exception to the general rule. Though we had before us section 20(b) without any knowledge of its amendments in committee, we might still have held that the contrast between the diction of the two clauses was enough to turn the scale against a tradition of even such long standing as that on which the defendants rely. There would have been strong reasons for supposing that so striking a change in expression could only have proceeded from a deliberate difference of intent, no matter how inveterate the contrary usage. But if that be doubtful, the change in the section on its way through Congress makes the intent entirely plain. When first introduced, the two clauses were in identical language. "Whenever it shall appear to the Commission" (at that time the Federal Trade Commission), "that the practices investigated constitute a fraud . . . it shall transmit such evidence as may be available" to "the Attorney General who may in his discretion bring an action. . . . The Commission may transmit such evidence as may be available concerning such acts and practices to the Attorney General who may, in his discretion institute the necessary criminal proceedings under this sub-chapter." Hearings on H.R. 4314, 73d Congress, 1st Session, p. 6; Hearings on S.R. 875, p. 7. As the bill then stood, its intent was therefore to follow the ancient custom and deny to the Commission control over civil, as well as criminal, prosecutions. During the hearings before the committees, the chief counsel of the Federal Trade Commission, Robert E. Healey, testified; we quote the relevant passages in the margin.* It was after this that the first

---

† Editors' Note:

(b) Whenever it shall appear to the Commissioner that any person is engaged or about to engage in any acts or practices which constitute or will constitute a violation of the provisions of this subchapter, or of any rule or regulation prescribed under the authority thereof, it may in its discretion, bring an action in any district court of the United States, United States court of any Territory, or the Supreme Court of the District of Columbia to enjoin such acts or practices, and upon a proper showing a permanent or temporary injunction or restraining order shall be granted without bond. The Commission may transmit such evidence as may be available concerning such acts or practices to the Attorney General who may, in his discretion, institute the necessary criminal proceedings under this sub-chapter. * * *

* "This bill provides that if the Commission discovers fraud and misrepresentation in connection with the sale of securities, it shall bring that information to the attention of the Attorney General, who shall proceed by injunction to stop that fraud and also to prosecute the guilty person criminally. My suggestion is where there is such a condition existing that Congress by this bill should say to the Attorney General, 'Punish them,' and then say to the Federal Trade Commission, 'Stop them.' I would amend this bill to provide for giving the power to apply for injunctions to the Commission. It is not wise to leave it to us to submit the information to the

clause was changed to its present form. We cannot see how any one can doubt what was the purpose of both committees in this amendment, though it is quite true that they said nothing about it in their reports. Healey was not a casual interloper; he was the person chiefly responsible for the prosecution of the new functions about to be conferred, at least so far as they touched legal questions. There cannot be the least question that in fact it was at his suggestion that the change was made and that it was intended to allow the Commission complete autonomy in civil prosecutions. The committees' intent may be irrelevant in construing the section, but the evidence of it as a fact is incontrovertible.

The defendants suggest that the purpose may have been limited to giving power to the Commission to decide when suits should be begun, but yet to require district attorneys to conduct them. Congress has indeed done just that on occasion. Section 12(1) tit. 49, U.S.Code, 49 U.S.C.A. § 12(1); section 413, tit. 33, U.S.Code (33 U.S.C.A. § 413); section 486, tit. 28, U.S.Code (28 U.S.C.A. § 486). But the resulting situation is certainly undesirable administratively, and whenever it has been prescribed, the language has been express. It is extremely unlikely that such a halfway measure should have been here intended. The original bill gave power to the Attorney General not only to decide when to sue, but necessarily to conduct the suit. The amendment was in form at least a transfer of the total power; unless some good reason to the contrary appears, it ought to be construed as total, not as leaving the Commission subject to a public officer whom they could not control. . . .

Finally, it is said that we should not regard the testimony of a witness before the committees; that it is not even as relevant as speeches on the floor of either house, which courts will not consider at all. [Citation.] It would indeed be absurd to suppose that the testimony of a witness by itself could be used to interpret an act of Congress; we are not so using it. The bill was changed in a most significant way; we are concerned to learn why this was done; we find that it can most readily be

---

Attorney General. If we get the information why should we not use it and go after the fellow right then and there and get the injunction against him continuing to sell the stock? Why should we tell the Attorney General about it so he can seek the injunction? We should tell the Attorney General about it so that he can punish them, but why divide the responsibility? Why create such a magnificent buck-passing opportunity as that?

"Now if this Commission is competent to go out and get these facts,—and I will tell you I think that we are,—and if not, there are two vacancies down there, two vacancies that are just yearning to be filled, by some deserving Democrats,—I tell you I believe that we should be allowed to stop the practice. I submit to you gentlemen, first, if this Commission is on to its job and it finds these fellows selling stock by fraud or misrepresentation, we should be given the power to apply to the courts for an injunction and the prosecuting power should be left to the Attorney General where it belongs." [Hearings on H.R. 4312, 73rd Cong., 1st Sess. pp. 240, 241].

"I wish to offer the suggestion that in the section of this bill which provides that the power of injunction shall be given, that provision be made that if the Commission which is charged with the administration of the bill finds people acting contrary to law or in defiance of the Act, that Commission and not the Attorney General will proceed to ask for an injunction. I would suggest that it is unwise to divide the responsibility and to encounter the delay that would come if we have to send our stuff to the Attorney General. Let him prosecute criminally, let us proceed to stop them." [Hearings on S. 875, 73rd Cong., 1st Sess. p. 226.]

explained, and indeed cannot naturally be explained on any other assumption than by supposing that the committees assented to a request from the very agency to whom the new functions were to be committed. To close our eyes to this patent and compelling argument would be the last measure of arid formalism. The amendments of a bill in committee are fertile sources of interpretation, [citation]. It is of course true that members who vote upon a bill do not all know, probably very few of them know, what has taken place in committee. On the most rigid theory possibly we ought to assume that they accept the words just as the words read, without any background of amendment or other evidence as to their meaning. But courts have come to treat the facts more really; they recognize that while members deliberately express their personal position upon the general purposes of the legislation, as to the details of its articulation they accept the work of the committees; so much they delegate because legislation could not go on in any other way.

Decree reversed.

QUESTIONS

1. How did the change in the Section in the course of its enactment make the Congressional intent "entirely plain"? Is this meaning of intent the subjective intent of individual drafters, the objective intent evident in the statutory purpose, or both? Does it, or should it, matter?

2. In what respect does the contrast in diction of the two clauses indicate a deliberate difference of intent?

3. Under what theory did the court solve the problem of the transference of the committee intent to Congress?

4. As the court noted, the change in the legislation was due to "a request from the very agency to whom the new functions were to be committed," and that same agency, the SEC, was involved in the subsequent case at hand. As the discussion of legislative history in *Robert Collier & Co.* reflects, agencies are often involved in drafting statutes that later give rise to interpretive disputes in which they are parties. Where this is the case, should a court treat an agency statement about the interpretation of such a statute with greater authority? Keep this question in mind in Section III.F, *infra*.

5. In Zuber v. Allen, 396 U.S. 168 (1969), quoted favorably in Garcia v. United States, 469 U.S. 70, 76 (1984), the Supreme Court stated, per Justice Harlan: "We consider our conclusions in no way undermined by the colloquy on the floor between Senator Copeland and Senator Murphy upon which the dissent places such emphasis. A committee report represents the considered and collective understanding of those Congressmen involved in drafting and studying proposed legislation. Floor debates reflect at best the understanding of individual Congressmen. It would take extensive and thoughtful debate to detract from the plain thrust of a committee report in this instance." 396 U.S. at 186. In a dissenting opinion, Justice Black took issue with the majority's treatment of the floor debates, observing that "anyone acquainted with the realities of the United States Senate knows that the remarks of the floor manager [Senator Murphy] are taken by other Senators as reflecting the views of the committee itself." Justice Rehnquist, dissenting in the case of Simpson v. United States, 435 U.S. 6, 17–18 (1978), made the following statement about this matter more broadly:

> The decisions of this Court have established that some types of legislative history are substantially more reliable than others. The report of a joint conference committee of both Houses of Congress, for example, or the report of a Senate or a House committee, is accorded a good deal more weight than the remarks even of the sponsor of a particular portion of a bill on the floor of the chamber. (Citations omitted.) It is a matter of common knowledge that at any given time during the debate, particularly a prolonged debate, of a bill the members of either House in attendance on the Floor may not be great, and it is only these members or those who later read the remarks in the Congressional Record, who will have the benefit of the Floor remarks. In the last analysis, it is the statutory language embodied in the enrolled bill which Congress enacts, and that must be our first reference point in interpreting its meaning.

The Court has also noted that "oral testimony of . . . individual Congressmen, unless very precisely directed to the intended meaning of particular words in a statute, can seldom be expected to be as precise as the enacted language itself." Regan v. Wald, 468 U.S. 222, 237 (1984).

In Chrysler Corp. v. Brown, 441 U.S. 281, 311 (1979), Justice Rehnquist's opinion for a virtually unanimous Court went still further, arguing that "[t]he remarks of a single legislator, even the sponsor, are not controlling in analyzing legislative history . . . [such remarks] must be considered with the Reports of both Houses and the statements of other Congressmen" as well as with the statute in question.

Subsequently, in Barnhart v. Sigmon Coal Company, 534 U.S. 438 (2002), Justice Thomas writing for a majority of six Justices wrote:

> Floor statements from two Senators cannot amend the clear and unambiguous language of a statute. We see no reason to give greater weight to the views of two Senators than to the collective votes of both Houses, which are memorialized in the unambiguous statutory text. Moreover, were we to adopt this form of statutory interpretation, we would be placing an obligation on Members of Congress not only to monitor their colleague's floor statements but to read every word of the Congressional Record including written explanations inserted into the record. This we will not do. The only "evidence" that we need rely on is the clear statutory text.

Although these statements reflect a growing disfavor of relying on Floor Statements among members of the Court, that view has not been entirely shared. Justice Stevens, writing in dissent in *Barnhart*, argued that ignoring Floor Statements that provide convincing evidence of Congressional intent may lead to arbitrary results:

> This case raises the question whether clear evidence of coherent congressional intent should inform the Court's construction of a

statutory provision that seems, at first blush, to convey an
incoherent message. Today a majority of the Court chooses to
disregard that evidence and instead, adheres to an interpretation
of the statute that produces absurd results. Two Members of
Congress—both sponsors of the legislation at issue—have
explained that the statute does not mandate such results, and the
agency charged with administering the statute agrees. As a partner
of the other two branches of Government, we should heed their
more reasonable interpretation of Congress' objectives.

Note that Justice Stevens' dissent refers to the Court's role in interpreting
legislation as one of "partnership" with the other branches of government.
Based on the decisions you have studied so far, does this characterization
accurately capture the approach of the current Supreme Court? Of its
predecessors? How would you describe the Court's role? Keep these inquiries
in mind as you work through the other materials in this Part.

For a summary of the use of legislative intent in statutory interpretation
and a discussion of what weight to give floor statements in particular, see
Lori L. Outzs, A Principled Use of Congressional Floor Speeches in Statutory
Interpretation, 28 Colum. J.L. & Soc. Probs. 297 (1995).

NOTE

The ongoing debate over the misuses of legislative history received
particularly sharp treatment in **Bank One Chicago, N.A. v. Midwest
Bank & Trust Company,** 516 U.S. 264 (1996), in which Justices Scalia and
Stevens offered strongly contrasting assessments:

■ JUSTICE SCALIA, concurring in part and concurring in the judgment.

I agree with the Court's opinion, except that portion of it which enters
into a discussion of the drafting history of § 4010. In my view a law means
what its text most appropriately conveys, whatever the Congress that
enacted it might have "intended." The law is what the law says, and we
should content ourselves with reading it rather than psychoanalyzing those
who enacted it. See United States v. Public Util. Comm'n of Cal., 345 U.S.
295, 319, 73 S.Ct. 706, 97 L.Ed. 1020 (1953) (Jackson, J., concurring).
Moreover, even if subjective intent rather than textually expressed intent
were the touchstone, it is a fiction of Jack-and-the-Beanstalk proportions to
assume that more than a handful of those Senators and Members of the
House who voted for the final version of the Expedited Funds Availability
Act, and the President who signed it, were, when they took those actions,
aware of the drafting evolution that the Court describes; and if they were,
that their actions in voting for or signing the final bill show that they had
the same "intent" which that evolution suggests was in the minds of the
drafters.

Justice STEVENS acknowledges that this is so, but asserts that the intent
of a few committee members is nonetheless dispositive because legislators
are "busy people," and "most members [of Congress] are content to endorse
the views of the responsible committees." I do not know the factual basis for
that assurance. Many congressional committees tend not to be

representative of the full house, but are disproportionately populated by Members whose constituents have a particular stake in the subject matter—agriculture, merchant marine and fisheries, science and technology, etc. I think it quite unlikely that the House of Representatives would be "content to endorse the views" that its Agriculture Committee would come up with if that committee knew (as it knows in drafting Committee Reports) that those views need not be moderated to survive a floor vote. And even more unlikely that the Senate would be "content to endorse the views" of the House Agriculture Committee. But assuming Justice Stevens is right about this desire to leave details to the committees, the very first provision of the Constitution forbids it. Article I, Section 1 provides that "all legislative Powers herein granted shall be vested in a Congress of the United States, which shall consist of a Senate and a House of Representatives." It has always been assumed that these powers are nondelegable—or, as John Locke put it, that legislative power consists of the power "to make laws, . . . not to make legislators." J. Locke, Second Treatise of Government 87 (R. Cox ed. 1982). No one would think that the House of Representatives could operate in such fashion that only the broad outlines of bills would be adopted by vote of the full House, leaving minor details to be written, adopted, and voted upon, only by the cognizant committees. Thus, if legislation consists of forming an "intent" rather than adopting a text (a proposition with which I do not agree), Congress cannot leave the formation of that intent to a small band of its number, but must, as the Constitution says, form an intent of the Congress. There is no escaping the point: Legislative history that does not represent the intent of the whole Congress is nonprobative; and legislative history that does represent the intent of the whole Congress is fanciful.

Our opinions using legislative history are often curiously casual, sometimes even careless, in their analysis of what "intent" the legislative history shows. [Citation.] Perhaps that is because legislative history is in any event a make-weight; the Court really makes up its mind on the basis of other factors. Or perhaps it is simply hard to maintain a rigorously analytical attitude, when the point of departure for the inquiry is the fairyland in which legislative history reflects what was in "the Congress's mind."

In any case, it seems to me that if legislative history is capable of injecting into a statute an "intent" that its text alone does not express, the drafting history alluded to in today's opinion should have sufficed to win this case for respondent. It shows that interbank liability was not merely omitted from subsection (a), entitled "Civil liability." It was removed from that subsection, simultaneously with the addition of subsection (f), 12 U.S.C. § 4010(f), which gave the Federal Reserve Board power to "impose on or allocate among depository institutions the risks of loss and liability in connection with any aspect of the payment system" (language that is at least as compatible with adjudication as with rulemaking). Now if the only function of this new subsection (f) had been to give the Board rulemaking power, there would have been no logical reason to eliminate interbank disputes from the "Civil liability" subsection, whose basic prescription (banks are civilly liable for violations of the statute or of rules issued under the statute)[1] applies no less in the interbank than in the bank-customer context. Nor can the removal of interbank disputes from subsection (a) be explained on the ground that Congress had decided to apply different damages limits to those disputes. The former subsection (a), in both House and Senate versions, already provided varying damages limits for individual suits and class actions, see S. 790, 100th Cong., 1st Sess., § 609(a) (1987); H.R.Rep. No. 100–52, pp. 10–11 (1987), and it would have been logical to set forth the newly desired interbank variation there as well, leaving to the new subsection (f) only the conferral of rulemaking authority. Or, if it were thought essential to "consolidate" all the details of interbank disputes in subsection (f), it would still not have been necessary to specifically exclude interbank disputes from the general "civil liability" pronouncement of subsection (a). The prologue of that subsection, "except as otherwise provided in this section," would have made it clear that interbank civil liability was limited as set forth in subsection (f). The most plausible explanation for specifically excluding interbank disputes from the "Civil liability" subsection when subsection (f) was added—and for avoiding any reference to "civil liability" in subsection (f) itself—is an intent to commit those disputes to a totally different regime, i.e., to Board adjudication rather than the normal civil-liability regime of the law courts.[2]

Today's opinion does not consider this argument, but nonetheless refutes it (in my view) conclusively. After recounting the drafting history, the Court states that *"nothing in § 4010(f)'s text* suggests that Congress meant the Federal Reserve Board to function as both regulator and adjudicator in interbank controversies." (emphasis added). Quite so. The text's the thing. We should therefore ignore drafting history without discussing it, instead of after discussing it.

■ JUSTICE STEVENS, concurring.

Given the fact that the Expedited Funds Availability Act was a measure that easily passed both houses of Congress, Justice SCALIA is quite right that it is unlikely that more than a handful of legislators were aware of the Act's drafting history. He is quite wrong, however, to conclude from that observation that the drafting history is not useful to conscientious and disinterested judges trying to understand the statute's meaning.

---

[1]   The Senate version of subsection (a) did not refer to violations of rules, see S. 790, 100th Cong., 1st Sess., § 609(a) (1987), but it was the House version of subsection (a), see H.R.Rep. No. 100–52, p. 10 (1987), which did specifically mention rules, that was retained.

[2]   I have explained why the "consolidation" explanation developed by Justice Stevens, does not ring true. Even if it did, however, it would not be accurate to say that the legislative history thus provides "the answer to an otherwise puzzling aspect of the statutory text," ibid. What Justice Stevens calls "the answer" (viz., the wish to consolidate all the interbank provisions in one section) is no more evident from the legislative history than it is from the face of the statute itself. Nothing in the legislative history says "we will consolidate interbank matters in a new subsection (f)"; Justice Stevens simply surmises, from the fact that the final text contains such consolidation, that consolidation was the reason for excluding interbank disputes from subsection (a). What investigation of legislative history has produced, in other words, is not an answer (that, if there is one, is in the text), but rather the puzzlement to which an answer is necessary: why were interbank disputes eliminated from subsection (a) when subsection (f) was adopted? Being innocent of legislative history, I would not have known of that curious excision if the Court's opinion had not told me. Thus, legislative history has produced what it usually produces: more questions rather than more answers.

Legislators, like other busy people, often depend on the judgment of trusted colleagues when discharging their official responsibilities. If a statute such as the Funds Availability Act has bipartisan support and has been carefully considered by committees familiar with the subject matter, Representatives and Senators may appropriately rely on the views of the committee members in casting their votes. In such circumstances, since most members are content to endorse the views of the responsible committees, the intent of those involved in the drafting process is properly regarded as the intent of the entire Congress.

In this case, as the Court and Justice SCALIA agree, the statutory text of § 4010 supports petitioner's construction of the Act. However, the placement of the authorization for interbank litigation in subsection (f) rather than subsection (a) lends some support to the Court of Appeals' interpretation. When Congress creates a cause of action, the provisions describing the new substantive rights and liabilities typically precede the provisions describing enforcement procedures; subsection (f) does not conform to this pattern. The drafting history, however, provides a completely satisfactory explanation for this apparent anomaly in the text.

Justice SCALIA nevertheless views the Court's reference to this history as unwise. As he correctly notes, the simultaneous removal of the provision for interbank liability from subsection (a) and the addition of a new subsection (f) support another inference favoring the Court of Appeals' construction of the statute: that the drafters intended to relegate the resolution of interbank disputes to a different tribunal. Justice SCALIA is mistaken, however, in believing that this inference provides the "most plausible explanation" for the change. In my judgment the Court has correctly concluded that the most logical explanation for the change is a decision to consolidate the aspects of § 4010 that relate to interbank disputes—liability limits and rulemaking authority—in the same subsection. Thus, the net result of the inquiry into drafting history is to find the answer to an otherwise puzzling aspect of the statutory text.

I must also take exception to Justice SCALIA's psychoanalysis of judges who examine legislative history when construing statutes. He confidently asserts that we use such history as a make-weight after reaching a conclusion on the basis of other factors. I have been performing this type of work for more than 25 years and have never proceeded in the manner Justice SCALIA suggests. It is quite true that I have often formed a tentative opinion about the meaning of a statute and thereafter examined the statute's drafting history to see whether the history supported my provisional conclusion or provided a basis for revising it. In my judgment, a reference to history in the Court's opinion in such a case cannot properly be described as a "make-weight." That the history could have altered my opinion is evidenced by the fact that there are significant cases, such as Green v. Bock Laundry Machine Co., 490 U.S. 504, 109 S.Ct. 1981, 104 L.Ed.2d 557 (1989), in which the study of history did alter my original analysis. In any event, I see no reason why conscientious judges should not feel free to examine all public records that may shed light on the meaning of a statute.

Finally, I would like to suggest that Justice SCALIA may be guilty of the transgression that he ascribes to the Court. He has confidently asserted that the legislative history in this case and in Wisconsin Public Intervenor v. Mortier, 501 U.S. 597, 111 S.Ct. 2476, 115 L.Ed.2d 532 (1991), supports a result opposite to that reached by the Court. While I do not wish to reargue the *Mortier* case, I will say that I remain convinced that a disinterested study of the entire legislative history supports the conclusion reached by the eight-member majority of the Court. Even if his analysis in both cases is plausible, it is possible that Justice SCALIA's review of the history in *Mortier* and in this case may have been influenced by his zealous opposition to any reliance on legislative history in any case. In this case, as in *Mortier*, his opinion is a fine example of the work product of a brilliant advocate.[2] It is the Court's opinion, however, that best sets forth the reasons for reversing the judgment of the Court of Appeals.

Justice BREYER has authorized me to say that he agrees with the foregoing views.

QUESTIONS

1. Recall Question 3 following *S.E.C. v. Robert Collier & Co., supra,* asking you to articulate the theory underlying Judge Hand's transference of the House Committee's intent to the entire enacting Congress. What are the views of the opinion writers in *Bank One* concerning transference of intent? Whose views do you find most persuasive?

2. Inquiries into legislative history are not usually clear-cut, but instead require balancing the evidence in support of conflicting interpretations. In Justice Scalia's view, one can characterize "the use of legislative history as the equivalent of entering a crowded cocktail party and looking over the heads of the guests for one's friends. . . . The legislative history of [the Act in question] contains a variety of diverse personages, a selected few of whom—its 'friends'—the Court has introduced to us in support of its result. But there are many other faces in the crowd, most of which, I think, are set against today's result." Conroy v. Aniskoff, 507 U.S. 511 (1993) (Scalia, J., concurring in the judgment). Does this critique discredit legislative history per se, or simply its selective citation? Is there a difference? Could the same accusation be made when selecting from among dictionary definitions or canons of construction?

NOTE

Chief Judge Robert A. Katzmann of the U.S. Court of Appeals for the Second Circuit has written extensively about the relationship between Congress and the Courts. In particular, he has advocated that the judiciary enhance its understanding of the process through which legislation is drafted

---

[2] Justice Jackson, whose opinion in United States v. Public Util. Comm'n of Cal., 345 U.S. 295, 73 S.Ct. 706, 97 L.Ed. 1020 (1953), Justice Scalia cites, was also a brilliant advocate. Like Justice Scalia, he recognized the danger of indiscriminate use of legislative history, but unlike Justice Scalia he also recognized that it can be helpful in appropriate cases. See Schwegmann Brothers v. Calvert Distillers Corp., 341 U.S. 384, 395–396, 71 S.Ct. 745, 95 L.Ed. 1035 (1951).

and enacted. Drawn from his book, *Judging Statutes*, this excerpt identifies some of the important dynamics legislators face when drafting legislation, and in particular the important role that legislative history plays *for legislators* when shepherding a drafted bill to passage:

> Since the early nineteenth century, congressional committees have been central to lawmaking. Without committees, Congress could not function. . . . Congressional staffs, on committees or in the personal offices of legislators, assist members in their legislative work in every facet of activity. Today there are some 130 standing committees and subcommittees of various kinds in the House and 98 in the Senate. Some committees are authorizing committees, charged with making substantive policy as well as recommending spending levels to fund programs in their jurisdiction. . . .

> In the 111th Congress, 383 public bills were enacted, with a total of 7,617 pages, averaging 19.89 pages per statute. In the House of Representatives, 6,677 bills were introduced (including joint resolutions), and 861 passed, with a .129 ratio of bills passed to bills introduced. In the Senate, 4,101 bills were introduced and 176 bills passed, with a ratio of .043 bills passed to bills introduced.31 Additionally, the Senate held 2,374 committee and subcommittee hearings. . . . In recent decades, Congress has more frequently enacted legislation through large omnibus bills or resolutions, packing together a wide range of disparate issues. The omnibus mechanism is a departure from the traditional approach of handling individual pieces of legislation. In part, Congress uses omnibus bills to facilitate passage of overdue measures. For example, in 2009, 2010, 2011, and 2014, Congress packaged appropriations bills into a single omnibus bill, reducing opportunities for further delay as opposed to considering each bill individually. Because it is generally subject to an up-and-down vote, the massive omnibus bill masks differences over contentious measures included in the legislation that might not have passed if considered individually as stand-alone bills.

> Congressional life is marked by incredible pressure—such as the pressures of the permanent campaign for reelection, raising funds, balancing work in Washington and time in the district, balancing committee and floor work in an environment of increasing polarization, and balancing work and family responsibilities. It is also now more intense than in the past. Consider these statistics: In 1955, the number of recorded votes in the House was 147; in the 111th Congress (2009–2010), it was 991 and 664 respectively . . . . In 1955, the number of recorded votes in the Senate was 88; in the 111th Congress (2009–2010), it was 400 and 307, respectively . . . . At times, these votes take place in the dead of night, especially as the legislative session moves at a frenetic pace to recess or end of the session. In 1955–1956, Congress was in session 227 days; from 2007 to 2012, the average was 323 days. In the House, the session day consisted of an average of 7.4

and 5.3 hours per day in the 111th and 112th Congress, respectively, as compared to 4.1 hours per day in 1955–1956. In the Senate, the session day consisted of 7.1 and 6.3 hours per day in the 111th and 112th Congress, respectively, as compared to 6.1 hours per day in 1955–1956. In 1955–1956, the average total of committee assignments for members of the House was 3.0; in 2011–2012, it was 5.3 (1.7 standing committee assignments, 3.4 subcommittee assignments, and .20 other committee assignments). Similarly, in the Senate, the average number of committee assignments was 7.9 in 1955–1956; in 2011–2012, it was 12.9 (3.4 standing committee assignments, 8.6 subcommittee assignments, and .9 other committee assignments).

The key point is that the expanding, competing demands on legislators' time reduce opportunities for reflection and deliberation. In that circumstance, beyond the work of their own committees of which legislators have direct knowledge, members operate in a system in which they rely on the work of colleagues on other committees. Members of Congress accept the trustworthiness of statements made by their colleagues on other committees, especially those charged with managing the bill, about what the proposed legislation means. They cannot read every word of the bills they vote upon, and, indeed, reading every word is often not particularly instructive, to the degree bills contain language amending the United States Code or enacted statutes. For example, a legislator unfamiliar with the Hobby Protection Act in its codified or statutory version might have a hard time understanding this provision in a bill that the House adopted in July 2013:

The Hobby Protection Act (15 U.S.C. § 2101 et seq.) is amended—

(1) in section 2—

(A) in subsection (b), by inserting ", or the sale in commerce" after "distribution in commerce";

(B) by redesignating subsection (d) as subsection (e) and inserting after subsection (c) the following: "(d) Provision of Assistance or Support—It shall be a violation of subsection (a) or (b) for a person to provide substantial assistance or support to any manufacturer, importer, or seller if that person knows or should have known that the manufacturer, importer, or seller is engaged in any act or practice that violates subsection (a) or (b)."; and

(C) in subsection (e) (as so redesignated), by striking "and (b)" and inserting "(b), and (d)";

(2) in section 3—

(A) by striking "If any person" and inserting "(a) In General—If any person";

(B) by striking "or has an agent" and inserting ", has an agent, transacts business, or wherever venue is proper under section 1391 of title 28, United States Code"; and

(C) by adding at the end the following:

"(b) Trademark Violations—If the violation of section 2 (a) or (b) or a rule under section 2(c) also involves unauthorized use of registered trademarks belonging to a collectibles certification service, the owner of such trademarks shall have, in addition to the remedies provided in subsection (a), all rights provided under sections 34, 35, and 36 of the Trademark Act of 1946 (15 U.S.C. 1116, 1117, and 1118) for violations of such Act.";

. . .

Legislators and their staffs become educated about the bill by reading the materials produced by the committees and conference committees from which the proposed legislation emanates. These materials include, for example, committee reports, conference committee reports, and the joint statements of conferees who drafted the final bill.

Committee reports accompanying bills have long been important means of informing the whole chamber about proposed legislation; they are often the primary means by which staffs brief their principals before voting on a bill. To facilitate deliberation, Congress was concerned from its earliest days that its proceedings be published, consistent with the constitutional requirement that a journal be kept. With the advent of the committee system, reports of committee activity were delivered orally, but, in the House by the period 1830–1860, and in the Senate by 1900, it was also commonplace for committee reports accompanying proposed legislation to be disseminated to the full chamber so that members could have a fuller appreciation of the bills on which they were called on to vote. Committee reports are generally circulated at least two calendar days before legislation is considered on the floor. Those reports provide members and their staffs with explanatory material about a bill's context, purposes, policy implications, and details, as well as information about who the committee supporters of a particular bill are and about possible minority views. Conference committee reports represent the views of legislators from both chambers who are charged with reconciling bills that have passed both the House and the Senate and presenting them for final legislative consideration. Members and their staffs will also hear from interest groups—including groups they find credible—and the executive branch about particular bills. The system works because committee members and their staffs will lose influence with their colleagues as to future bills if they do not accurately represent the bills under consideration within their jurisdiction. Indeed, staffers would risk losing their jobs if they were to mislead legislators as to the details of legislation and accompanying reports.

Although any legislator can introduce a bill, it is the committee of jurisdiction that generally processes the proposed measure. In drafting bills, legislators look to multiple sources. In his memoir, the late Senator Edward M. Kennedy wrote that "[n]inety-five percent of the nitty-gritty work of drafting and even negotiating is now done by staff," marking "an enormous shift of responsibility over the past forty or fifty years." Ninety-five percent, observed veteran journalist Robert Kaiser, the author of a rich saga of the passage of the Dodd-Frank Act, "might underestimate staff members' share of the work." Committees are aided by professional drafters in each chamber's office of legislative counsel; these drafters are trained in the nuances of statute writing. Although legislators and their staffs are not required to consult with legislative counsel, doing so is prudent because a poorly drafted bill can lead to all manner of problems for agencies and courts charged with interpreting the statute. Typically, a committee staffer will contact the office for assistance in framing the bill so that it is technically correct. Those who work as legislative counsel think of the committees as clients. Their role is not to offer views about the merits of a particular proposal; it is to determine how best to commit the bill's purposes to writing.

Not all bills originate from the committees themselves. Some originate with the executive branch; others from interest groups, lobbyists, businesses, and state and local governments. These various interests may assist in drafting bills as well, but not necessarily with the care that each chamber's office of legislative counsel provides. Not all bills are drafted in the committee; bills can also be drafted, or at least substantially revised, on the floor and in conference committee. In the Senate, flexible procedures allow senators to draft bills in the course of debate. When bills are drafted on the floor, for example, the pressures of time mean that legislators do not generally check with the legislative counsel, and thus there is more likely to be problematic drafting language. In conference committee, the pressure to come to closure and pass a bill can compromise technical precision.

. . . The statutemaking process, as legislators and staffs understand it, involves not just the text of legislation, but also quite importantly legislative history—such as the reports and debates associated with the legislative text. As I described earlier, committee reports and conference committee reports accompanying bills can provide guidance to legislators in the enactment process. Legislative history accompanying legislation can also be helpful by providing direction to agencies as to how to interpret and implement legislation. Scholars . . . have more recently shown how Congress operates within a milieu of rules, norms, and practices—including importantly the applicability of legislative history. The degree to which these norms and practices shape both the drafting process and also legislative expectations about how laws should be understood is not commonly known within the judiciary—a matter to which I return later in this book when I discuss judicial interpretation of statutes.

* * *

What relevance does this whirlwind survey of Congress and lawmaking have for the interpretation of statutes? The point is a simple one. The laws of Congress are the product of often complex institutional processes, which engage legislators, staff, and other interests with stakes in the outcome. Having a basic understanding of legislative lawmaking can only better prepare judges to undertake their interpretive responsibilities. . . .

Robert A. Katzmann, Judging Statutes (2014).

3.   INTERPRETING A STATUTE IN LIGHT OF ITS AUDIENCES

Chief Judge Katzmann's discussion of the role that legislative history can play as an aid for legislators voting on pending legislation raises important related questions: who are the audiences of a statute, and how do those audiences determine what the statute means? Chief Judge Katzmann has suggested that an important and underexamined audience for a bill's legislative history is the non-drafting legislators who must understand what the drafted bill accomplishes before deciding whether to vote for it. Yet other audiences may look primarily to the enacted statutory text, rather than the legislative history. And some audiences—such as the administrative agency tasked with implementing the legislation—are likely to focus on *both*.

One of us has written about precisely this issue: depending on the audience of the statute in question, and the circumstances in which that audience may be called upon to interpret it, the selection and prioritization of interpretive methods may (and in practice does) reasonably vary:

> "IDENTIFY THE AUDIENCE.—Decide who is supposed to get the message." So instructs the U.S. House of Representatives' legislative drafting manual. This advice is common to many statutory drafting guides, which emphasize that a statute's audience should influence a statute's structure, style, and terminology. Different audiences have varied levels of legal fluency and background knowledge, and distinct audiences have very different modes of interacting with a given statutory scheme. It would be foolish to draft a playground ordinance in the same manner as a multinational corporate tax provision. For statutory drafting, at least, audience considerations appear to be a central concern.

> When it comes to the interpretation of statutes, however, important considerations of audience often go overlooked in statutory interpretation debates. In using the term "audience," I mean to focus on the range of legal actors whose behavior may be altered as a result of a statutory enactment. These include audiences that are actively engaged in understanding statutory meaning, as well as those passively affected by statutory rules, and also include the many third parties whom the law conscripts to transmit legal knowledge to the affected audience(s). Not all statutes communicate to their respective audiences in the same manner: some statutes establish specific rules that regulate the conduct of lay audiences like the general public, while other statutes set out broad mandates to specialized government audiences, who implement them through subsequent regulation and enforcement.

> Despite these differences, when it comes to methods of interpretation (*i.e.*, semantic and syntactic canons of construction, evidence of linguistic usage, and extratextual sources of statutory meaning), judges often treat all statutes, and all statutory audiences, homogeneously. They deploy the same tools and rules of interpretation to decipher a firearms carriage rule with direct application to the general public as

they do to decode technical statutory language directing federal agencies to implement the Affordable Care Act.[7]

A common trope in discussions of statutory interpretation theory is that American judges lack a principled method of interpreting statutes .... [and] judges tend to apply interpretive methods inconsistently such that even sophisticated litigants cannot predict which canons of construction, dictionaries, or sources of meaning may apply in any given case. And the prevailing dialogue seems to offer no obvious path forward; Abbe Gluck recently concluded that debates between textualism and purposivism have "taken us as far as they can go."

An important reason that these debates have largely run aground, I argue, is that the leading theories of statutory interpretation, textualism and purposivism, are as much theories about how *judges* should behave vis-à-vis the legislatures as they are theories about the interpretation and implementation of statutory texts. Textualist and purposivist theories are largely motivated by faithful-agent concerns that arise due to the inherent tension of common-law judges interpreting statutes enacted by democratically accountable legislatures. Anxiety about legislative supremacy has been called "a shibboleth in discourse about statutory interpretation." A core disagreement between these approaches is not just about the meaning and interpretation of text but also a debate about how to *judge* it: textualism and purposivism *both* "seek to provide a superior way for federal judges to fulfill their presumed duty as Congress's faithful agents." Indeed, it has been said that the "fundamental question" for statutory interpretation is "whether courts should view themselves as faithful agents of the legislature or as independent cooperative partners."

Problematically, judges tend to disagree just as much about theories of judging as they do about theories of interpretation. Many debates ostensibly about how to interpret statutes (i.e., which canons of construction and sources of statutory meaning to prioritize) thus transform into debates about how to judge

---

[7] *Compare* Muscarello v. United States, 524 U.S. 125 (1998) (majority and dissent employing, among other methods and canons: consistent usage presumption, dictionary definitions, legislative history, legislative intent, ordinary meaning, plain meaning, rule against superfluity, statutory context, statutory purpose, statutory scheme/structure, whole act, whole code, and the legal significance of semantic ambiguity), *with* King v. Burwell, 135 S.Ct. 2480 (2015) (majority and dissent employing, among other methods and canons: dictionary definitions, legislative history, legislative intent, ordinary meaning, plain meaning, rule against superfluity, statutory context, statutory purpose, statutory scheme/structure, whole act, whole code, and the legal significance of semantic ambiguity).

statutes, fixating on separation-of-powers concerns related to the proper rule of the courts vis-à-vis legislatures. . . .

Debates about judicial faithful agency often overshadow other equally pressing aspects of statutory interpretation theory. These include providing an account of how statutes communicate meaning to, and alter the behavior of, relevant audiences, and the proper role of judicial interpretive theory in enhancing a statute's capacity to ensure its relevant audiences get (and effectuate) the statutory message. . . . Scott Shapiro has helpfully analogized laws to specific social plans. On this account, the individuals and/or entities subject to laws—what I call statutory audiences—give functional meaning to these statutory plans through implementation and practice. This, of course, is why many legislative drafters are mindful of the intended audience when they draft statutes—for the social plan to be effective, the audience must be able to get the message.

Inherent in the nature of statutory enactments is that they will inevitably be incomplete social plans—the communication can only be completed through responsive action. This is because statutory texts communicate in a manner distinct from other forms of linguistic communication. In contrast to the speech acts of individual speakers, legislation constitutes a form of collective speech act that is typically the result of one or more compromises. Legislative compromises often result in incomplete decisions about the precise legal content of the enacted legislation.

In addition, statutory plans as a form of communication may be strategically and intentionally under-specified. As a result, cooperative assumptions in ordinary conversation about how speakers conventionally convey information—for example, that the speaker intends to convey her message with specificity and precision—often does not apply in the case of legislative speech acts. The unique dynamics associated with the production of legislative "speech" are especially important when making assumptions about the sufficiency of the communicative content conveyed by legislative texts. In many conversational contexts, the audience may assume the speaker seeks, through choice of language, intentional omission or ambiguity, and implicatures that suggest something different is meant than what was literally said, to provide the sufficient quality and quantity of information necessary to convey her meaning.

In legislative contexts, however, textual underspecification, redundancy, and contradiction—both intentional and unintentional—are common features of legislative texts, in single statutes and across them. Among other things, this may diminish just how much implied content can be reasonably derived from legislative speech acts, with semantically enriched content subject to debatable and competing inferences about how broadly or narrowly to read the statutory text. Despite this, legislated "speech" often necessitates that the audience—those implementing legislative plans—must fill larger gaps as compared to instructions given in interpersonal communication between individuals.

Moreover, in contrast to most conversational communicative contexts between speaker and audience, the legislative context is inherently impersonal. Legislators address an audience comprised largely of those not personally known (or sometimes even anticipated) by the legislature. Thus, both the precise execution of the plans themselves, as well as those who implement them, may be unknown at the time the broad plan is enacted. . . .

The upshot of this is twofold. First, notions of judicial "faithful agency" may often have limited utility when courts are tasked with attributing legal meaning to ambiguous statutory texts—there may simply not be an objective answer as to what either the legislature "intended" or what the text "means." Rather, the legal meaning of statutes will often have to be developed through post-enactment implementation and interpretation, or what Scott Soames calls "precisifying." To the degree this is so, then judicial choices about which substantive canons and interpretive methods to prioritize function to provide a legal grammar for how statutory audiences are expected to engage with statutes, at least as much as these choices function as an act of discovering the "plain" or "objective" meaning of the text itself.

A second upshot is that while courts and government officials play an important role in precisifying statutory meaning, statutes are also directed at other audiences, who also play an important role in precisfying statutory meaning. Thus, for statutes to function in their essential capacity as a means to implement social plans and coordinate societal behavior, in at least some circumstances the uncertainty about statutory meaning must also be resolved (and resolvable) by [those] statutory audiences. . . .

Of course, not all statutory provisions seek to communicate or alter behavior in the same manner, nor with respect to the same audiences. . . . [Professor] Meir Dan-Cohen [ha]s observ[ed] that an "acoustic separation" often exists between conduct rules and decision rules embedded in the criminal law. Whereas conduct rules are specific statutory provisions that directly address (and seek to expressly alter) the actions of lay audiences, decision rules are aimed at guiding the (often discretionary) enforcement decisions of government officials, and thus may have little to say directly to the public at large.

This distinction—between statutory provisions that delegate authority to government officials and those that directly regulate the conduct of members of the public more broadly—is essential to my theory of statutory audience. As [Professor] Ed Rubin has described, statutes have both "transitive" and "intransitive" modes of communication and application. Transitive statutes state the precise rule to be applied, which means that the relevant statutory audiences might be thought to be put on notice simply by the enactment of the rule itself. Given their direct application, transitive statutory provisions may raise heightened concerns about notice and the possibility of textual ambiguity or vagueness.[71] These kinds of statutory provisions may also require judges to treat the statutory communication as "complete," for rule of law reasons [related to due process and fair notice] . . .

By contrast, intransitive statutes merely set out the mechanism by which subsequent rules shall be developed— usually by government officials, such as administrative agencies. As a practical matter, "the ultimate target of the [intransitive] statute cannot know what behavior the statute will require." In these circumstances, the capacity for the affected audience to derive notice from the statutory text itself may be of less concern, because no such notice can be derived from the text alone since the legislative communication is incomplete. The legal rule that will modify the audience's behavior will instead derive from an administrative adjudication, regulation, or guidance document promulgated by the agency in accordance with administrative law and in furtherance of the intransitive statutory delegation. So long as the statute provides a sufficient textually-enriched basis to guide the officials addressed with implementing it, whether the statutory text alone provides clear notice, or gives specific instructions to the audiences it seeks to regulate, may be of less concern than for transitive provisions. . . . [T]here may be good reasons to prioritize different interpretive methods depending

---

[71] Drawing a clear distinction between ambiguity and vagueness is essential to understanding how statutes can give notice to relevant audiences. Whereas a term is ambiguous if it is susceptible to two different, but potentially overlapping meanings (such as the word "blue" conveying both the color and the mood), a term is vague if among the range of normal applications of the term are borderline cases separating instances in which the term clearly applies and when it clearly doesn't (such as the word "tall"). . . . Statutory ambiguity is an unavoidable aspect of many statutes, but statutory vagueness can raise essential rule-of-law concerns, at least for criminal statutes directed at the general public. In other circumstances, intentionally vague regulatory plans may provide an agency with a wide berth in which to implement a range of potential policymaking objectives.

on whether the relevant audience is regulated by a direct conduct rule or an instransitive statutory delegation.

. . . Because statutes address distinct audiences in different ways, courts play a crucial role in helping statutory audiences (and their interpreters) translate and derive meaning from underspecified and often-ambiguous statutory enactments. How a judge chooses to interpret a legal text will affect that text's legal meaning just as much as the semantic meaning of the text itself. The semantic meaning derived from "bare" text is not always synonymous with the legal meaning a judge may attribute to it. A statute's legal meaning can be derived not only from the statute's semantic content, but also from contextual content associated with that statute, such as evidence of the enacting legislature's intentions—collectively, its communicative content.

Most crucially, the legal content of a statute is also not synonymous with its communicative content. When judges apply substantive canons like the rule of lenity, clear notice rules, or the plain meaning rule, they specify the legal meaning that shall be derived from the statutory text. That meaning may not be the meaning that one or more of its drafters intended, nor the semantic meaning most commonly associated with the term or phrase in question (to the degree one can be clearly ascertained). In this sense, judicial interpretation provides the authoritative lens through which to view the statutory text, framing and shaping the meaning(s) that others may permissibly derive from that text.

Understood this way, judicial rules of interpretation function as a kind of legal grammar: they provide guidance for deriving legal meaning from oft-underspecified statutory text. [J]udges['] . . . opinions not only resolve particular . . . interpretive disputes, but also provide interpretive rules and rationales that can have secondary effects for future cases. (This, of course, assumes such rules are justified on the basis of more than the mere ad-hoc whims of the particular judge(s).) Most canons of construction seem to derive their authority from the presumption that they apply across statutes. If so, then their application will necessarily have the effect of altering how future audiences may be expected to understand and interpret legal texts that present similar ambiguities. . . .

My thesis . . . is that statutes communicate in distinct ways and to varied audiences, and so different tools of interpretation may be more appropriate for transitive statutes than for intransitive ones, and for statutes addressed primarily at somes kinds of audience than others. Moreover, most statutes are directed at multiple audiences, so a central task for many statutory interpretation questions should be to identify the principal audience at issue, which will often clarify what the statute means, how it applies, and which normative concerns should prevail when they conflict. . . .

David S. Louk, *The Audiences of Statutes*, 105 Cornell L. Rev. 137 (2019).

QUESTIONS

1. Consider the distinctions between transitive conduct rules and intransitive decision rules raised in the excerpt. Although this distinction may be purely descriptive, it also has potential normative significance. For example, are the practical concerns about ambiguity the same for criminal prohibitions as they are for legislative delegations to administrative agencies? If not, should ambiguity be more (or less) tolerated for statutes directed primary at one audience than for statutes directed primarily at another?

2. Chief Judge Katzmann has observed that ambiguity can be the "solvent of disagreement, at least temporarily,"[*] for legislators often draft statutory language imprecisely on purpose, in order to facilitate the bill's passage. Thus a statute may be *intentionally* ambiguous, either because legislators cannot agree on the precise range of possible applications, or because legislators would prefer to "pass the buck" to the law's enforcers to help refine the statute's meaning across a range of reasonable applications over time. In these circumstances, should courts prioritize different methods of interpretation than they might when interpreting a statute for which they believe a "true" meaning of the statutory text exists? When the statutory text appears intentionally ambiguous or open-ended, should judges give more weight to the interpretations of the enforcing agency? Consider how, if at all, such a possibility may alter the normative force of interpretive canons such as the "plain meaning rule," the "evil sought to be remedied," or the "clear notice rule," as discussed *infra* in *Arlington Central School District v. Murphy*.

a.   THE MULTIPLE AUDIENCES OF A SINGLE STATUTE

Statutes are often directed at several distinct audiences, each of which has its own interests, capacities, and concerns. Given this, it is possible—and sometimes probable—that different audiences may encounter a statute in a very different light. Consider a question of statutory interpretation raised by an amendment to the Individuals with Disabilities Education Act (IDEA) as part of the Handicapped Children's Protection Act of 1986. How might you approach this problem of statutory interpretation differently depending on the audience of which you are a member?

---

[*]   *See* Robert A. Katzmann, Judging Statutes 47 (2014) (citing Herbert Kaufman, The Administrative Behavior of Federal Bureau Chiefs (1981)).

i.   A Legislator Voting Whether to Enact the Statute

Imagine that you are a member of the U.S. House of Representatives who has no particular experience with, or strong views about, education issues—your campaign platform, and the chief concerns of your district, lie elsewhere. Last summer, you and your colleagues approved amendments to the Individuals with Disabilities Education Act (IDEA)* as part of the Handicapped Children's Protection Act (HCPA)—one of over 500 votes you cast that year. The amendments respond to your colleagues' concerns that although the IDEA guarantees an adequate education to all special needs children at no cost to parents or guardians, parents and guardians have often had to pay out of pocket for costs associated with demonstrating their children's special education needs. These costs include hiring expensive qualified experts who can attest, if necessary in court, to a child's special education needs.

Prior to the vote, sponsors of the bill indicated that the HCPA would amend the IDEA to ensure that the attorney's fee award provided under the IDEA would "include[ ] expenses of expert witnesses [and] the reasonable costs of any study, report, test, or project which is found to be necessary for the preparation of the parents' or guardian's due process hearing, state administrative review or civil action; as well as traditional costs and expenses incurred in the course of litigating a case." H.R. REP. No. 99–296, at 6 (1985) (Comm. Rep.). This amendment would ensure that a parent or guardian with a legitimate claim would not have to pay out of pocket for an expert to vouch for their child's special education needs. After adoption by unanimous consent, the bill was then sent to conference, where members of both houses resolved the remaining differences between the House and Senate versions of the bill.

The conference has reconciled the two bills and provided a Conference Report clarifying the changes ahead of a final vote on the HCPA. Your legislative aid has provided you with the Conference Report, which contains both the revised bill and the joint committee's statement about the reconciled bill. Your chief of staff has indicated that you have roughly 10 minutes to read the materials and decide whether to support the revised HCPA before you must attend a meeting with constituents who have flown all the way to D.C. from your faraway district.

The Statute as Drafted:

SHORT TITLE

SECTION 1. This Act may be cited as the "Handicapped Children's Protection Act of 1986".

---

*   Editors' Note: At the time the legislation was enacted, the act now known as the IDEA was referred to as the "Education for All Handicapped Children Act." For simplicity's sake, it will be referred to as the IDEA throughout.

AWARD OF ATTORNEYS' FEES

SEC. 2. Section 615(e)(4) of the Education of the Handicapped Act is amended by inserting "(A)" after the paragraph designation and by adding at the end thereof the following new subparagraphs:

"(B) In any action or proceeding brought under this subsection, the court, in its discretion, may award reasonable attorneys' fees as part of the costs to the parents or guardian of a handicapped child or youth who is the prevailing party.

"(C) For the purpose of this subsection, fees awarded under this subsection shall be based on rates prevailing in the community in which the action or proceeding arose for the kind and quality of services furnished. No bonus or multiplier may be used in calculating the fees awarded under this subsection.

"(D) No award of attorneys' fees and related costs may be made in any action or proceeding under this subsection for services performed subsequent to the time of a written offer of settlement to a parent or guardian, if—

"(i) the offer is made within the time prescribed by Rule 68 of the Federal Rules of Civil Procedure or, in the case of an administrative proceeding, at any time more than ten days before the proceeding begins;

"(ii) the offer is not accepted within ten days; and

"(iii) the court or administrative officer finds that the relief finally obtained by the parents or guardian is not more favorable to the parents or guardian than the offer of settlement.

"(E) Notwithstanding the provisions of subparagraph (D), an award of attorneys' fees and related costs may be made to a parent or guardian who is the prevailing party and who was substantially justified in rejecting the settlement offer.

"([F]) Whenever the court finds that—

"(i) the parent or guardian, during the course of the action or proceeding, unreasonably protracted the final resolution of the controversy;

"(ii) the amount of the attorneys' fees otherwise authorized to be awarded unreasonably exceeds the hourly rate prevailing in the community for similar services by attorneys of reasonably comparable skill, experience, and reputation; or

"(iii) the time spent and legal services furnished were excessive considering the nature of the action or proceeding,

the court shall reduce, accordingly, the amount of the attorneys' fees awarded under this subsection.

"(G) The provisions of subparagraph (F) shall not apply in any action or proceeding if the court finds that the State or local

educational agency unreasonably protracted the final resolution of the action or proceeding or there was a violation of section 615 of this Act." . . .

GAO STUDY OF ATTORNEYS' FEES PROVISION

SEC. 4. (a) The Comptroller General of the United States, through the General Accounting Office, shall conduct a study of the impact of the amendments to the Education of the Handicapped Act made by section 2 of this Act. Not later than June 30, 1989, the Comptroller General shall submit a report containing the findings of such study to the Committee on Education and Labor of the House of Representatives and the Committee on Labor and Human Resources of the Senate. The Comptroller General shall conduct a formal briefing for such Committees on the status of the study not later than March 1, 1988. Such report shall include the information described in subsection (b).

(b) The report authorized under subsection (a) shall include the following information:

(1) The number, in the aggregate and by State, of written decisions under sections "615(b)(2) and (c) transmitted to State advisory panels under section 615(d)(4) for fiscal years 1984 through 1988, the prevailing party in each such decision, and the type of complaint. For fiscal year 1986, the report shall designate which decisions concern complaints filed after the date of the enactment of this Act.

(2) The number, in the aggregate and by State, of civil actions brought under section 615(e)(2), the prevailing party in each action, and the type of complaint for fiscal years 1984 through 1988. For fiscal year 1986 the report shall designate which decisions concern complaints filed after the date of enactment.

(3) Data, for a geographically representative selective sample of States, indicating (A) the specific amount of attorneys' fees, costs, and expenses awarded to the prevailing party, in each action and proceeding under section 615(e)(4)(B) from the date of the enactment of this Act through fiscal year 1988, and the range of such fees, costs, and expenses awarded in the actions and proceedings under such section, categorized by type of complaint and (B) for the same sample as in (A) the number of hours spent by personnel, including attorneys and consultants, involved in the action or proceeding, and expenses incurred by the parents and the State educational agency and local educational agency.

(4) Data, for a geographically representative sample of States, on the experience of educational agencies in resolving complaints informally under section 615(b)(2), from the date of the enactment of this Act through fiscal year 1988. . . .

The Accompanying Conference Report*:

JOINT EXPLANATORY STATEMENT OF THE COMMITTEE OF CONFERENCE

The managers on the part of the House and the Senate at the conference on the disagreeing votes of the two Houses on the amendment of the House to the bill (S. 415) . . . . The differences between the Senate bill and the House amendment and the substitute agreed to in the conference, are noted below, except for clerical corrections, conforming changes made necessary by agreements reached by the conferees, and minor drafting and clarifying changes.

1.   The Senate bill provides for "a reasonable attorney's fee."

The House amendment provides for "reasonable attorneys' fees."

The Senate recedes.

2.   With slightly different wording, both the Senate bill and the House amendment provide for the awarding of attorneys' fees in addition to costs.

The Senate recedes to the House and the House recedes to the Senate with an amendment clarifying that "the court, in its discretion, may award reasonable attorneys' fees as part of the costs . . ." This change in wording incorporates the Supreme Court *Marek v. Chesny* decision (87 L. Ed. 2d 1).

The conferees intend that the term "attorneys' fees as part of the costs" include reasonable expenses and fees of expert witnesses and the reasonable costs of any test or evaluation which is found to be necessary for the preparation of the parent or guardian's case in the action or proceeding, as well as traditional costs incurred in the course of litigating a case.

3.   The Senate bill provides for the award of attorney's fees "to a parent or legal representative."

The House amendment provides for the award of attorneys' fees "to the parents or guardian."

The Senate recedes. . . .

6.   The House amendment, but not the Senate bill, provides for a GAO study of the impact of the bill authorizing the awarding of fees and costs.

The Senate recedes to the House with an amendment expanding the data collection requirements of the GAO study to include information regarding the amount of funds expended by local

---

*   H.R. REP. NO. 99–687 (1986) (Conf. Rep.).

educational agencies and state educational agencies on civil actions and administrative proceedings. . . .

11. The House amendment, but not the Senate bill, includes an anti-retaliation provision.

The House recedes. It is the conferees' intent that no person may discharge, intimidate, retaliate, threaten, coerce, or otherwise take an adverse action against any person because such person has filed a complaint, testified, furnished information, assisted or participated in any manner in a meeting, hearing, review, investigation, or other activity related to the administration of, exercise of authority under, or right secured by part B of EHA. The term "person" the first time it is used means a state educational agency, local educational agency, intermediate educational unit or any official or employee thereof. . . .

QUESTIONS

1. The revised bill does not expressly identify the aspects the Committee altered from the version that the House approved last year. To identify the salient changes to the bill since you last voted on it, how useful do you find the text of the revised bill as compared to the conference report's explanation of the changes?

2. For the purposes of deciding whether you would continue to support the bill, which portions of the above texts, if any, would you find most useful in identifying what the revised bill seeks to achieve?

3. Do you think you would be more likely to consult a dictionary to understand the meaning of an ambiguous term in the amended bill, or would you refer to the Committee Report's explanation as to what that term means?

ii.   A Beneficiary Seeking Relief Under the Statute

Suppose you are the parent of a special needs child who is not receiving an adequate education in his traditional classroom. You know that your son is entitled to a free and appropriate education under federal law, but after discussions with both your child's teacher and his principal, the school has declined to accommodate your son's needs, and the district will not transfer him to a special education classroom in another school.

In considering your options, you speak to a local attorney who tells you that you may initiate an administrative action against the district, which could lead to your filing a federal civil lawsuit if the district proves obstinate. The attorney offers to take your case for free on a contingency basis, for she will be awarded attorney's fees if you prevail in an action brought against the district. However, she requires a retainer of $10,000 to cover the costs of an early childhood development consultant whose needs assessment of your child will be critical for you to prevail. The attorney indicates that if you win, it is probable that a judge may ultimately award you the costs of the expert's assessment. After some internet research, you discover that parents and guardians of special needs children who are represented by an attorney and an expert witness are almost twice as likely to prevail in IDEA actions brought against school districts. See U.S. Gov't Accountability Office, GAO/HRD–90–22BR, Special Education: The Attorney Fees Provision of Public Law 99–372 26 (1990).

Below is an excerpted portion of New York State's Procedural Safeguards Notice, a notice that the IDEA requires each state to furnish on an annual basis to every parent or guardian of a disabled child. See New York State Education Department, Procedural Safeguards Notice, July 2017, available at http://www.p12.nysed.gov/specialed/formsnotices/documents/NYSEDProceduralSafeguardsNoticeJuly2017v2.pdf. Among other rights, the Procedural Safeguards Notice informs parents about their rights to an independent educational evaluation for their child, at no cost to the parent:

... INDEPENDENT EDUCATIONAL EVALUATIONS

34 CFR section 300.502; 8 NYCRR section 200.5(g)

General

As described below, you have the right to obtain an independent educational evaluation (IEE) of your child if you disagree with the evaluation of your child that was obtained by your school district.

If you request an IEE, the school district must provide you with information about where you may obtain one and about the school district's criteria that apply to IEEs.

Definitions

Independent educational evaluation means an evaluation conducted by a qualified examiner who is not employed by the school district responsible for the education of your child.

Public expense means that the school district either pays for the full cost of the evaluation or ensures that the evaluation is otherwise provided at no cost to you, consistent with the provisions of Part B of IDEA, which allow each state to use whatever State, local, federal and private sources of support are available in the State to meet the requirements of Part B of IDEA.

Parent right to evaluation at public expense

You have the right to an IEE of your child at public expense if you disagree with an evaluation of your child obtained by your school district, subject to [certain] conditions. . . .

You are entitled to only one IEE of your child at public expense each time your school district conducts an evaluation of your child with which you disagree. . . .

Requests for evaluations by impartial hearing officers

If an impartial hearing officer requests an IEE of your child as part of a due process hearing, the cost of the evaluation must be at public expense. . . .

* * *

While it is clear that as a parent you are entitled to the initial IEE of your child at public expense in preparing for the administrative hearing, the Notice is silent as to whether you can expect the district to cover the costs of the expert's participation in a possible federal civil suit.

QUESTIONS

1. As a parent, how likely would you be to press your child's case in court if you would have to cover the costs of the expert's fees yourself?

2. The statute's purpose—to ensure an adequate education for special needs children at no cost to their parent or guardian—seems undermined if an expert assessment and involvement in the civil suit doubles your likelihood of success, and yet the costs associated are not covered under the statute's fee and cost-shifting provision. As a parent, what reasons would you have to think the assessment should be covered? What methods of interpretation, if any, would support your conclusion?

iii. A State Official Implementing the Statute

Imagine that you are the Deputy General Counsel of the New York State Education Department. Your responsibilities include overseeing the State's compliance with federal education laws, including the IDEA. Under the IDEA, New York State has received at least $1.2 billion in grant allocations from the federal government during each of the past five years. In exchange for the grant funding, New York State and its subdivisions must comply with a number of IDEA procedural requirements, including the provision of an administrative hearing for any parent or guardian who brings an action alleging that their local school district has failed to provide their child with a free and appropriate special education. Such an administrative proceeding can be costly and time-consuming, especially if it fails to resolve the dispute, leading to an even more costly federal lawsuit. It also usually requires the involvement of an expensive special education consultant who assesses the child's needs. While the IDEA requires the local school district to cover the costs of the consultant's assessment and testimony as part of the administrative proceeding, the district need not cover the costs of further assessments (or testimony) undertaken as part of any subsequent federal lawsuit.

The U.S. Supreme Court has just granted cert in a case that will decide whether prevailing parents in federal suits may include expert witness fees among "reasonable attorneys' fees as part of the costs" that may be awarded to prevailing parents under the statutes. These fees can range from between $5,000 and $20,000, depending on the case, and thus far most federal district courts have included them in the fee awards they have granted.

The Governor has asked your opinion on whether New York State should join either of two competing *amicus curiae* briefs to be filed before the Court. One brief argues that expert witness fees should be included among the "reasonable attorneys' fees as part of the costs," the other argues that they should not be included. In addition, the Governor has also asked whether you think New York should continue to accept IDEA grants if the Supreme Court holds that the IDEA fee-shifting provision includes expert witness fees. Although the state does not gather data on the total annual costs the state incurs in paying for the attorney's fee and expert witness fee awards of prevailing parents, you know that last year, parents in New York State prevailed in approximately 200 administrative actions and in 1 civil action brought under the IDEA. See GAO Special Education: The Attorney Fees Provision of Public Law 99–372, GAO/HRD–90–22BR, at 63. In each, it is probable that an award of expert witness fees would be in the $5,000–$20,000 range. Should you decline to accept IDEA fees, the state would lose at least $1.2 billion in federal grants per year.

QUESTIONS

1. What factors do you consider, and how would you decide? How great would the costs of covering expert witness fees in IDEA litigation in your state have be before you would advise the Governor to decline IDEA grants altogether?

2. If you were uncertain about the statute's meaning, to what would you turn? The text of the statute? The legislative history? Guidance from the U.S. Department of Education? The term's use in other federal statutes? Judicial decisions in the lower federal courts?

iv. A Judge Interpreting the Statute

You are a busy district court judge on the Southern District of New York, with a docket of over 500 cases filed per year. See Comparison of Districts Within the Second Circuit—12-Month Period Ending September 30, 2019, available at https://www.uscourts.gov/sites/default/files/data_tables/fcms_na_distcomparison0930.2019.pdf. You and your three law clerks each work at least 60 hours a week just to maintain your docket load. Every judge in your district receives monthly statistics indicating the number of active cases on each judge's docket, so you are especially motivated to ensure you are not one of the judges with the largest active dockets in your district. The cases on your docket require you to resolve complicated merits questions on the papers, conduct trials, sentencing federal criminals, adjudicate discovery disputes between highly contentious corporate commercial litigants, and you also sit by designation on the U.S. Court of Appeals for the Second Circuit several times per year. Among these cases on your docket are a number of motions to shift attorney's fees to prevailing parties under several dozen federal statutes that awards a reasonable attorney's fee to the prevailing party.

Such fee award petitions are usually presented in the form of a separate motion filed at the end of what is often protracted litigation, just as the case is otherwise ready to be closed and removed from your docket. In your decade on the bench, you have repeatedly encountered statutory provisions that grant you the discretion to "award reasonable attorneys' fees as part of the costs" to the prevailing party, and in nearly every instance in your experience, such an award has *excluded* expert witness fees.

In the instant case, the attorney for the prevailing petitioner contends that the legislative history of *this* statute—the IDEA—suggests that "reasonable attorneys' fees as part of the costs" should include expert witness fees. The district has opposed this position, arguing that the U.S. Supreme Court has on several occasions considered an almost identical phrase in other federal fee-shifting statutes and each time has held that the term of art excludes expert witness fees.

QUESTION

How likely are you to credit this legislative history, considering that: (a) several Supreme Court precedents have adopted the contrary interpretation when applied to similar provisions in other federal statutes; and (b) to carefully consider the legislative history will require a special first-impression merits opinion that will take at least a week of one of your law clerk's time to research, write, and edit?

Arlington Central School District
Board of Education v. Murphy

Supreme Court of the United States, 2006.
548 U.S. 291, 126 S.Ct. 2455, 165 L.Ed.2d 526.

■ JUSTICE ALITO delivered the opinion of the Court[, in which CHIEF JUSTICE ROBERTS, JUSTICE SCALIA, JUSTICE KENNEDY, and JUSTICE THOMAS joined].

The Individuals with Disabilities Education Act (IDEA or Act) provides that a court "may award reasonable attorneys' fees as part of the costs" to parents who prevail in an action brought under the Act. 111 Stat. 92, 20 U.S.C. § 1415(i)(3)(B). We granted certiorari to decide whether this fee-shifting provision authorizes prevailing parents to recover fees for services rendered by experts in IDEA actions. We hold that it does not.

I

Respondents Pearl and Theodore Murphy filed an action under the IDEA on behalf of their son, Joseph Murphy, seeking to require petitioner Arlington Central School District Board of Education to pay for their son's private school tuition for specified school years. Respondents prevailed in the District Court, and the Court of Appeals for the Second Circuit affirmed.

As prevailing parents, respondents then sought . . . fees for the services of an educational consultant, Marilyn Arons, who assisted respondents throughout the IDEA proceedings. The District Court . . . held that only the value of Arons' time spent between the hearing request and the ruling in respondents' favor could properly be considered charges incurred in an "action or proceeding brought" under the Act, [citation]. This reduced the maximum recovery to $8,650. The District Court also held that Arons, a nonlawyer, could be compensated only for time spent on expert consulting services, not for time spent on legal representation, but it concluded that all the relevant time could be characterized as falling within the compensable category, and thus allowed compensation for the full $8,650.

The Court of Appeals for the Second Circuit affirmed. [Citation.] Acknowledging that other Circuits had taken the opposite view, the Court of Appeals for the Second Circuit held that "Congress intended to and did authorize the reimbursement of expert fees in IDEA actions." [Citation.] The court began by discussing two decisions of this Court holding that expert fees could not be recovered as taxed costs under particular cost- or fee-shifting provisions. See *Crawford Fitting Co. v. J.T. Gibbons, Inc.*, 482 U.S. 437 (1987) (interpreting Fed. Rule Civ. Proc. 54(d) and 28 U.S.C. § 1920); *West Virginia Univ. Hospitals, Inc. v. Casey*, 499 U.S. 83 (1991) (interpreting 42 U.S.C. § 1988 (1988 ed.)). According to these decisions, the court noted, a cost- or fee-shifting provision will not be read to permit a prevailing party to recover expert fees without " 'explicit statutory authority' indicating that Congress intended for that sort of fee-shifting." [Citation.]

Ultimately, though, the court was persuaded by a statement in the Conference Committee Report relating to 20 U.S.C. § 1415(i)(3)(B) and by a footnote in *Casey* that made reference to that Report. [Citation.] Based on these authorities, the court concluded that it was required to interpret the IDEA to authorize the award of the costs that prevailing parents incur in hiring experts. . . . We now reverse.

II

Our resolution of the question presented in this case is guided by the fact that Congress enacted the IDEA pursuant to the Spending Clause. [Citation.] Like its statutory predecessor, the IDEA provides federal funds to assist state and local agencies in educating children with disabilities "and conditions such funding upon a State's compliance with extensive goals and procedures." [Citation.]

Congress has broad power to set the terms on which it disburses federal money to the States, [citation], but when Congress attaches conditions to a State's acceptance of federal funds, the conditions must be set out "unambiguously," [citations]. "[L]egislation enacted pursuant to the spending power is much in the nature of a contract," and therefore, to be bound by "federally imposed conditions," recipients of federal funds must accept them "voluntarily and knowingly." [Citation.] States cannot knowingly accept conditions of which they are "unaware" or which they are "unable to ascertain." Thus, in the present case, we must view the IDEA from the perspective of a state official who is engaged in the process of deciding whether the State should accept IDEA funds and the obligations that go with those funds. We must ask whether such a state official would clearly understand that one of the obligations of the Act is the obligation to compensate prevailing parents for expert fees. In other words, we must ask whether the IDEA furnishes clear notice regarding the liability at issue in this case.

III

A

In considering whether the IDEA provides clear notice, we begin with the text. We have "stated time and again that courts must presume that a legislature says in a statute what it means and means in a statute what it says there." [Citation.] When the statutory "language is plain, the sole function of the courts—at least where the disposition required by the text is not absurd—is to enforce it according to its terms."[Citations.]

The governing provision of the IDEA, 20 U.S.C. § 1415(i)(3)(B), provides that "[i]n any action or proceeding brought under this section, the court, in its discretion, may award reasonable attorneys' fees as part of the costs" to the parents of "a child with a disability" who is the "prevailing party." While this provision provides for an award of "reasonable attorneys' fees," this provision does not even hint that acceptance of IDEA funds makes a State responsible for reimbursing prevailing parents for services rendered by experts.

Respondents contend that we should interpret the term "costs" in accordance with its meaning in ordinary usage and that § 1415(i)(3)(B) should therefore be read to "authorize reimbursement of all costs parents incur in IDEA proceedings, including expert costs."

This argument has multiple flaws. For one thing, as the Court of Appeals in this case acknowledged, " 'costs' is a term of art that generally does not include expert fees." [Citation.] The use of this term of art, rather than a term such as "expenses," strongly suggests that § 1415(i)(3)(B) was not meant to be an open-ended provision that makes participating States liable for all expenses incurred by prevailing parents in connection with an IDEA case—for example, travel and lodging expenses or lost wages due to time taken off from work. Moreover, contrary to respondents' suggestion, § 1415(i)(3)(B) does not say that a court may award "costs" to prevailing parents; rather, it says that a court may award reasonable attorney's fees "as part of the costs" to prevailing parents. This language simply adds reasonable attorney's fees incurred by prevailing parents to the list of costs that prevailing parents are otherwise entitled to recover. This list of otherwise recoverable costs is obviously the list set out in 28 U.S.C. § 1920, the general statute governing the taxation of costs in federal court, and the recovery of witness fees under § 1920 is strictly limited by § 1821, which authorizes travel reimbursement and a $40 per diem. Thus, the text of 20 U.S.C. § 1415(i)(3)(B) does not authorize an award of any additional expert fees, and it certainly fails to provide the clear notice that is required under the Spending Clause.

Other provisions of the IDEA point strongly in the same direction. While authorizing the award of reasonable attorney's fees, the Act contains detailed provisions that are designed to ensure that such awards are indeed reasonable. See §§ 1415(i)(3)(C)–(G). The absence of any comparable provisions relating to expert fees strongly suggests that recovery of expert fees is not authorized. Moreover, the lack of any reference to expert fees in § 1415(d)(2) gives rise to a similar inference. This provision, which generally requires that parents receive "a full explanation of the procedural safeguards" available under § 1415 and refers expressly to "attorneys' fees," makes no mention of expert fees.

B

Respondents contend that their interpretation of § 1415(i)(3)(B) is supported by a provision of the Handicapped Children's Protection Act of 1986 that required the General Accounting Office (GAO) to collect certain data [citation] (hereinafter GAO study provision), but this provision is of little significance for present purposes. The GAO study provision directed the Comptroller General, acting through the GAO, to compile data on, among other things: "(A) the specific amount of attorneys' fees, costs, and expenses awarded to the prevailing party" in IDEA cases for a particular period of time, and (B) "the number of hours spent by personnel, including attorneys and consultants, involved in the action or proceeding, and expenses incurred by the parents and the State educational agency and local educational agency. [Citation.]

Subparagraph (A) would provide some support for respondents' position if it directed the GAO to compile data on awards to prevailing parties of the expense of hiring consultants, but that is not what subparagraph (A) says. Subparagraph (A) makes no mention of consultants or experts or their fees.[11]

---

[1] Because subparagraph (A) refers to both "costs" and "expenses" awarded to prevailing parties and because it is generally presumed that statutory language is not superfluous, it could be argued that this provision manifests the expectation that prevailing parties would be awarded certain "expenses" not included in the list of "costs" set out in 28 U.S.C. § 1920 and

Subparagraph (B) similarly does not help respondents. Subparagraph (B), which directs the GAO to study "the number of hours spent [in IDEA cases] by personnel, including . . . consultants," says nothing about the award of fees to such consultants. Just because Congress directed the GAO to compile statistics on the hours spent by consultants in IDEA cases, it does not follow that Congress meant for States to compensate prevailing parties for the fees billed by these consultants.

Respondents maintain that "Congress' direction to the GAO would be inexplicable if Congress did not anticipate that the expenses for 'consultants' would be recoverable," [citation,] but this is incorrect. There are many reasons why Congress might have wanted the GAO to gather data on expenses that were not to be taxed as costs. Knowing the costs incurred by IDEA litigants might be useful in considering future procedural amendments (which might affect these costs) or a future amendment regarding fee shifting. And, in fact, it is apparent that the GAO study provision covered expenses that could not be taxed as costs. . . .

In sum, the terms of the IDEA overwhelmingly support the conclusion that prevailing parents may not recover the costs of experts or consultants. Certainly the terms of the IDEA fail to provide the clear notice that would be needed to attach such a condition to a State's receipt of IDEA funds.

IV

Thus far, we have considered only the text of the IDEA, but perhaps the strongest support for our interpretation of the IDEA is supplied by our decisions and reasoning in *Crawford Fitting*, [citation,] and *Casey*, [citation]. In light of those decisions, we do not see how it can be said that the IDEA gives a State unambiguous notice regarding liability for expert fees.

In *Crawford Fitting*, the Court rejected an argument very similar to respondents' argument that the term "costs" in § 1415(i)(3)(B) should be construed as an open-ended reference to prevailing parents' expenses. It was argued in *Crawford Fitting* that Federal Rule of Civil Procedure 54(d), which provides for the award of "costs" to a prevailing party, authorizes the award of costs not listed in 28 U.S.C. § 1821. [Citation.] The Court held, however, that Rule 54(d) does not give a district judge

---

that expert fees were intended to be among these unenumerated "expenses." This argument fails because, whatever expectation this language might seem to evidence, the fact remains that neither 20 U.S.C. § 1415 nor any other provision of the IDEA authorizes the award of any "expenses" other than "costs." Recognizing this, respondents argue not that they are entitled to recover "expenses" that are not "costs," but that expert fees *are* recoverable "costs." As a result, the reference to awards of both "expenses" and "costs" does not support respondents' position. The reference to "expenses" may relate to IDEA actions brought in state court, § 1415(i)(2)(A), where "expenses" other than "costs" might be receivable. Or the reference may be surplusage. While it is generally presumed that statutes do not contain surplusage, instances of surplusage are not unknown.

"discretion to tax whatever costs may seem appropriate"; rather, the term "costs" in Rule 54(d) is defined by the list set out in § 1920. [Citation.] Because the recovery of witness fees, see § 1920(3), is strictly limited by § 1821, the Court observed, a broader interpretation of Rule 54(d) would mean that the Rule implicitly effected a partial repeal of those provisions. [Citation.] But, the Court warned, "[w]e will not lightly infer that Congress has repealed §§ 1920 and 1821, either through Rule 54(d) or any other provision not referring explicitly to witness fees." [Citation.]

The reasoning of *Crawford Fitting* strongly supports the conclusion that the term "costs" in 20 U.S.C. § 1415(i)(3)(B), like the same term in Rule 54(d), is defined by the categories of expenses enumerated in 28 U.S.C. § 1920. This conclusion is buttressed by the principle, recognized in *Crawford Fitting,* that no statute will be construed as authorizing the taxation of witness fees as costs unless the statute "refer[s] explicitly to witness fees." [Citation.] ("[A]bsent explicit statutory or contractual authorization for the taxation of the expenses of a litigant's witness as costs, federal courts are bound by the limitations set out in 28 U.S.C. § 1821 and § 1920").

Our decision in *Casey* confirms even more dramatically that the IDEA does not authorize an award of expert fees. In *Casey,* as noted above, we interpreted a fee-shifting provision, 42 U.S.C. § 1988, the relevant wording of which was virtually identical to the wording of 20 U.S.C. § 1415(i)(3)(B). Compare *ibid.* (authorizing the award of "reasonable attorneys' fees as part of the costs" to prevailing parents) with 42 U.S.C. § 1988 (1988 ed.) (permitting prevailing parties in certain civil rights actions to be awarded "a reasonable attorney's fee as part of the costs"). We held that § 1988 did not empower a district court to award expert fees to a prevailing party. [Citation.] To decide in favor of respondents here, we would have to interpret the virtually identical language in 20 U.S.C. § 1415 as having exactly the opposite meaning. Indeed, we would have to go further and hold that the relevant language in the IDEA *unambiguously means* exactly the opposite of what the nearly identical language in 42 U.S.C. § 1988 was held to mean in *Casey.*

The Court of Appeals, as noted above, was heavily influenced by a *Casey* footnote, [citation,] but the court misunderstood the footnote's meaning. The text accompanying the footnote argued, based on an analysis of several fee-shifting statutes, that the term "attorney's fees" does not include expert fees. [Citation.] In the footnote, we commented on petitioners' invocation of the Conference Committee Report relating to 20 U.S.C. § 1415(i)(3)(B), which stated: " 'The conferees intend[ed] that the term "attorneys' fees as part of the costs" include reasonable expenses and fees of expert witnesses and the reasonable costs of any test or evaluation which is found to be necessary for the preparation of the . . . case.' " [Citation.] This statement, the footnote commented, was "an apparent effort to *depart* from ordinary meaning and to define a term of art." [Citation.] The footnote did not state that the Conference Committee

Report set out the correct interpretation of § 1415(i)(3)(B), much less that the Report was sufficient, despite the language of the statute, to provide the clear notice required under the Spending Clause. The thrust of the footnote was simply that the term "attorneys' fees," standing alone, is generally not understood as encompassing expert fees. Thus, *Crawford Fitting* and *Casey* strongly reinforce the conclusion that the IDEA does not unambiguously authorize prevailing parents to recover expert fees.

V

Respondents make several arguments that are not based on the text of the IDEA, but these arguments do not show that the IDEA provides clear notice regarding the award of expert fees.

Respondents argue that their interpretation of the IDEA furthers the Act's overarching goal of "ensur[ing] that all children with disabilities have available to them a free appropriate public education," 20 U.S.C. § 1400(d)(1)(A), as well as the goal of "safeguard[ing] the rights of parents to challenge school decisions that adversely affect their child." These goals, however, are too general to provide much support for respondents' reading of the terms of the IDEA. The IDEA obviously does not seek to promote these goals at the expense of all other considerations, including fiscal considerations. Because the IDEA is not intended in all instances to further the broad goals identified by respondents at the expense of fiscal considerations, the goals cited by respondents do little to bolster their argument on the narrow question presented here.[3]

Finally, respondents vigorously argue that Congress clearly intended for prevailing parents to be compensated for expert fees. They rely on the legislative history of § 1415 and in particular on the following statement in the Conference Committee Report, discussed above: "The conferees intend that the term 'attorneys' fees as part of the costs' include reasonable expenses and fees of expert witnesses and the reasonable costs of any test or evaluation which is found to be necessary for the preparation of the . . . case." [Citation.]

Whatever weight this legislative history would merit in another context, it is not sufficient here. Putting the legislative history aside, we see virtually no support for respondents' position. Under these circumstances, where everything other than the legislative history overwhelmingly suggests that expert fees may not be recovered, the legislative history is simply not enough. In a Spending Clause case, the key is not what a majority of the Members of both Houses intend but what the States are clearly told regarding the conditions that go along with the acceptance of those funds. Here, in the face of the unambiguous text of the IDEA and the reasoning in *Crawford Fitting* and *Casey*, we

---

[3] Respondents note that a GAO report stated that expert witness fees are reimbursable expenses. But this passing reference in a report issued by an agency not responsible for implementing the IDEA is plainly insufficient to provide clear notice regarding the scope of the conditions attached to the receipt of IDEA funds.

cannot say that the legislative history on which respondents rely is sufficient to provide the requisite fair notice. . . .

We reverse the judgment of the Court of Appeals for the Second Circuit and remand the case for further proceedings consistent with this opinion.

It is so ordered.

■ JUSTICE GINSBURG, concurring in part and concurring in the judgment.

I agree, in the main, with the Court's resolution of this case, but part ways with the Court's opinion in one respect. The Court extracts from *Pennhurst State School and Hospital v. Halderman,* 451 U.S. 1, 17 (1981), a "clear notice" requirement, and deems it applicable in this case because Congress enacted the Individuals with Disabilities Education Act (IDEA), as it did the legislation at issue in *Pennhurst,* pursuant to the Spending Clause. That extraction, in my judgment, is unwarranted. *Pennhurst's* "clear notice" requirement should not be unmoored from its context. The Court there confronted a plea to impose "an unexpected condition for compliance—a new [programmatic] obligation for participating States." [Citation.] The controversy here is lower key: It concerns not the educational programs IDEA directs school districts to provide, but "the remedies available against a noncomplying [district]."

The Court's repeated references to a Spending Clause derived "clear notice" requirement are questionable on other grounds as well. For one thing, IDEA was enacted not only pursuant to Congress' Spending Clause authority, but also pursuant to § 5 of the Fourteenth Amendment. [Citation.] Furthermore, no "clear notice" prop is needed in this case given the twin pillars on which the Court's judgment securely rests. First, as the Court explains, the specific, attorneys'-fees-oriented, provisions of IDEA, [citation,] overwhelmingly support the conclusion that prevailing parents may not recover the costs of experts or consultants." Those provisions place controls on fees recoverable for attorneys' services, without mentioning costs parents might incur for other professional services and controls geared to those costs. Second, as the Court develops, prior decisions closely in point "strongly suppor[t]," even "confir[m] . . . dramatically," today's holding that IDEA trains on attorneys' fees and does not authorize an award covering amounts paid or payable for the services of an educational consultant. [Citations.]

For the contrary conclusion, Justice BREYER's dissent relies dominantly on a Conference Report stating the conferees' view that the term "attorneys' fees as part of the costs" includes "expenses and fees of expert witnesses" and payments for tests necessary for the preparation of a case. [Citation.] Including costs of consultants and tests in § 1415(i)(3)(B) would make good sense in light of IDEA's overarching goal, *i.e.,* to provide a "free appropriate public education" to children with disabilities, § 1400(d)(1)(A). But Congress did not compose

§ 1415(i)(3)(B)'s text,[2] as it did the texts of other statutes too numerous and varied to ignore, to alter the common import of the terms "attorneys' fees" and "costs" in the context of expense-allocation legislation. [Citations.] Given the constant meaning of the formulation "attorneys' fees as part of the costs" in federal legislation, we are not at liberty to rewrite "the statutory text adopted by both Houses of Congress and submitted to the President," [citation,] to add several words Congress wisely might have included. The ball, I conclude, is properly left in Congress' court to provide, if it so elects, for consultant fees and testing expenses beyond those IDEA and its implementing regulations already authorize,[3] along with any specifications, conditions, or limitations geared to those fees and expenses Congress may deem appropriate. Cf. § 1415(i)(3)(B)–(G); § 1415(d)(2)(L) (listing only attorneys' fees, not expert or consulting fees, among the procedural safeguards about which school districts must inform parents).

In sum, although I disagree with the Court's rationale to the extent that it invokes a "clear notice" requirement tied to the Spending Clause, I agree with the Court's discussion of IDEA's terms, and of our decisions in *Crawford* and *Casey.* Accordingly, I concur in part in the Court's opinion, and join the Court's judgment.

[The dissenting opinion of JUSTICE SOUTER has been omitted.]

■ JUSTICE BREYER, with whom JUSTICE STEVENS and JUSTICE SOUTER join, dissenting.

. . . Unlike the Court, I believe that the word "costs" includes, and authorizes payment of, the costs of experts. The word "costs" does not define its own scope. Neither does the phrase "attorneys' fees as part of costs." But Members of Congress did make clear their intent by, among other things, approving a Conference Report that specified that "the term 'attorneys' fees as part of the costs' include[s] reasonable expenses and fees of expert witnesses and the reasonable costs of any test or evaluation which is found to be necessary for the preparation of the parent or guardian's case in the action or proceeding." [Citation.] No Senator or

---

[2]   At the time the Conference Report was submitted to the Senate and House, sponsors of the legislation did not mention anything on the floor about expert or consultant fees. They were altogether clear, however, that the purpose of the legislation was to "reverse" this Court's decision in Smith v. Robinson, 468 U.S. 992, 104 S.Ct. 3457, 82 L.Ed.2d 746 (1984). In Smith, the Court held that, under the statute as then designed, prevailing parents were not entitled to attorneys' fees. See 132 Cong. Rec. 16823 (1986) (remarks of Sen. Weicker) ("In adopting this legislation, we are rejecting the reasoning of the Supreme Court in Smith versus Robinson."); *id.,* at 16824 (remarks of Sen. Kerry) ("This vital legislation reverses a U.S. Supreme Court decision Smith versus Robinson [.]"); *id.,* at 17608–17609 (remarks of Rep. Bartlett) ("I support those provisions in the conference agreement that, in response to the Supreme Court decision in . . . Smith versus Robinson, authoriz[e] the awarding of reasonable attorneys' fees to parents who prevail in special education court cases."); *id.,* at 17609 (remarks of Rep. Biaggi) ("This legislation clearly supports the intent of Congress back in 1975 and corrects what I believe was a gross misinterpretation of the law. Attorneys' fees should be provided to those individuals who are being denied access to the educational system.").

[3]   Under 34 CFR § 300.502(b)(1) (2005), a "parent has the right to an independent educational evaluation at public expense if the parent disagrees with an evaluation obtained by the public agency."

Representative voiced *any* opposition to this statement in the discussion preceding the vote on the Conference Report—the last vote on the bill before it was sent to the President. I can find no good reason for this Court to interpret the language of this statute as meaning the precise opposite of what Congress told us it intended.

I

There are two strong reasons for interpreting the statutory phrase to include the award of expert fees. First, that is what Congress said it intended by the phrase. Second, that interpretation furthers the IDEA's statutorily defined purposes.

A

Congress added the IDEA's cost-shifting provision when it enacted the Handicapped Children's Protection Act of 1986 (HCPA), 100 Stat. 796. Senator Lowell Weicker introduced the relevant bill in 1985. [Citation.] As introduced, it sought to overturn this Court's determination that the then-current version of the IDEA (and other civil rights statutes) did not authorize courts to award attorney's fees to prevailing parents in IDEA cases. [Citation.] The bill provided that " '[i]n any action or proceeding brought under this subsection, the court, in its discretion, may award a reasonable attorney's fee as part of the costs to a parent or legal representative of a handicapped child or youth who is the prevailing party.' " [Citation.]

After hearings and debate, several Senators introduced a new bill in the Senate that would have put a cap on attorney's fees for legal services lawyers, but at the same time would have explicitly authorized the award of "a reasonable attorney's fee, reasonable witness fees, and *other reasonable expenses of the civil action,* in addition to the costs to a parent . . . who is the prevailing party." [Citation.] While no Senator objected to the latter provision, some objected to the cap. [Citation.] A bipartisan group of Senators, led by Senators Hatch and Weicker, proposed an alternative bill that authorized courts to award " 'a reasonable attorney's fee in addition to the costs to a parent' " who prevailed. [Citations.]

Senator Weicker explained that the bill

"will enable courts to compensate parents for *whatever reasonable costs they had to incur to fully secure what was guaranteed to them by the [Education of the Handicapped Act].* As in other fee shifting statutes, it is our intent that such awards will include, at the discretion of the court, reasonable attorney's fees, *necessary expert witness fees, and other reasonable expenses which were necessary for parents to vindicate their claim to a free appropriate public education for their handicapped child."* [Citation] (emphasis added).

Not a word of opposition to this statement (or the provision) was voiced on the Senate floor, and S. 415 passed without a recorded vote. [Citation.]

The House version of the bill also reflected an intention to authorize recovery of expert costs. Following the House hearings, the Committee on Education and Labor produced a substitute bill that authorized courts to " 'award reasonable attorneys' fees, *expenses, and costs*' " to prevailing parents. [Citation.] The House Report stated:

"The phrase 'expenses and costs' includes *expenses of expert witnesses; the reasonable costs of any study, report, test, or project which is found to be necessary for the preparation of the parents' or guardian's due process hearing, state administrative review or civil action;* as well as traditional costs and expenses incurred in the course of litigating a case (*e.g.,* depositions and interrogatories)." [Citation (emphasis added).]

No one objected to this statement. By the time H.R. 1523 reached the floor, another substitute bill was introduced. [Citation.] This new bill did not change in any respect the text of the authorization of expenses and costs. It did add a provision, however, that directed the General Accounting Office (GAO)—now known as the Government Accountability Office, see note following 31 U.S.C. § 731 (2000 ed., Supp.IV)—to study and report to Congress on the fiscal impact of the cost-shifting provision. [Citation.] The newly substituted bill passed the House without a recorded vote. [Citation.]

Members of the House and Senate (including all of the primary sponsors of the HCPA) then met in conference to work out certain differences. At the conclusion of those negotiations, they produced a Conference Report, which contained the text of the agreed-upon bill and a "Joint Explanatory Statement of the Committee of Conference." [Editors' Note: a portion of this statement has been excerpted, *supra.*] The Conference accepted the House bill's GAO provision with "an amendment expanding the data collection requirements of the GAO study to include information regarding the amount of funds expended by local educational agencies and state educational agencies on civil actions and administrative proceedings." [Citation.] And it accepted (with minor changes) the cost-shifting provisions provided in both the Senate and House versions. The conferees explained:

. . . *"The conferees intend that the term 'attorneys' fees as part of the costs' include reasonable expenses and fees of expert witnesses and the reasonable costs of any test or evaluation which is found to be necessary for the preparation of the parent or guardian's case in the action or proceeding, as well as traditional costs incurred in the course of litigating a case."* [Citation.]

The Conference Report was returned to the Senate and the House. A motion was put to each to adopt the Conference Report, and both the Senate and the House agreed to the Conference Report by voice votes. [Citation.] No objection was raised to the Conference Report's statement that the cost-shifting provision was intended to authorize expert costs. I concede that "sponsors of the legislation did not mention anything on the floor about expert or consultant fees" at the time the Conference Report was submitted. But I do not believe that silence is significant in light of the fact that *every* Senator and *three of the five* Representatives who spoke on the floor had previously *signed his name* to the Conference Report—a Report that made Congress' intent clear on the first page of its explanation. [Citation.] And every Senator and Representative who took the floor preceding the votes voiced his strong support for the Conference Report. [Citation.] The upshot is that Members of both Houses of Congress voted to adopt both the statutory text before us and the Conference Report that made clear that the statute's words include the expert costs here in question.

B

The Act's basic purpose further supports interpreting the provision's language to include expert costs. The IDEA guarantees a "free" and "appropriate" public education for "all" children with disabilities. 20 U.S.C. § 1400(d)(1)(A) (2000 ed., Supp.V); see also § 1401(9)(A) (defining "free appropriate public education" as one "provided at public expense," "without charge"); § 1401(29) (defining "special education" as "specially designed instruction, at *no cost* to parents, to meet the unique needs of a child with a disability" (emphasis added)).

Parents have every right to become involved in the Act's efforts to provide that education; indeed, the Act encourages their participation. § 1400(c)(5)(B) (IDEA "ensur[es] that families of [disabled] children have meaningful opportunities to participate in the education of their children at school"). It assures parents that they may question a school district's decisions about what is "appropriate" for their child. And in doing so, they may secure the help of experts. § 1415(h)(1) (parents have "the right to be accompanied and advised by counsel and by individuals with special knowledge or training with respect to the problems of children with disabilities"); [citations.]

The practical significance of the Act's participatory rights and procedural protections may be seriously diminished if parents are unable to obtain reimbursement for the costs of their experts. In IDEA cases, experts are necessary. [Citation] (detailing findings of study showing high correlation between use of experts and success of parents in challenging school district's plan); [citations].

Experts are also expensive. [Citation] (collecting District Court decisions awarding expert costs ranging from $200 to $7,600, and noting three reported cases in which expert awards exceeded $10,000). The costs of experts may not make much of a dent in a school district's budget, as many of the experts they use in IDEA proceedings are already on the staff. [Citation.] But to parents, the award of costs may matter enormously. Without potential reimbursement, parents may well lack the services of experts entirely. [Citations.]

In a word, the Act's statutory right to a "free" and "appropriate" education may mean little to those who must pay hundreds of dollars to obtain it. That is why this Court has previously avoided interpretations that would bring about this kind of result. . . . [W]e [have] explained: "IDEA was intended to ensure that children with disabilities receive an education that is both appropriate and free. To read the provisions of § 1401(a)(18) to bar reimbursement in [such] circumstances . . . would defeat this statutory purpose." [Citation.]

To read the word "costs" as requiring successful parents to bear their own expenses for experts suffers from the same problem. Today's result will leave many parents and guardians "without an expert with the firepower to match the opposition," [citation], a far cry from the level playing field that Congress envisioned.

II

The majority makes essentially three arguments against this interpretation. It says that the statute's purpose and "legislative history is simply not enough" to overcome: (1) the fact that this is a Spending Clause case; (2) the text of the statute; and (3) our prior cases which hold that the term "costs" does not include expert costs. I do not find these arguments convincing.

A

At the outset the majority says that it "is guided by the fact that Congress enacted the IDEA pursuant to the Spending Clause." "In a Spending Clause case," the majority adds, "the key is not what a majority of the Members of both Houses intend but what the States are clearly told regarding the conditions that go along with the acceptance of those funds." . . .

I agree that the statute on its face does not *clearly* tell the States that they must pay expert fees to prevailing parents. But I do not agree that the majority has posed the right question. For one thing, we have repeatedly examined the nature and extent of the financial burdens that the IDEA imposes without reference to the Spending Clause or any "clear-statement rule." [Citations.] Those cases did not ask whether the statute "furnishes clear notice" to the affirmative obligation or liability at issue.

For another thing, neither *Pennhurst* nor any other case suggests that *every spending detail* of a Spending Clause statute must be spelled out with unusual clarity. To the contrary, we have held that *Pennhurst's* requirement that Congress "unambiguously" set out "a condition on the grant of federal money" does *not* necessarily apply to legislation setting forth "*the remedies available against a noncomplying State.*" [Citation.] We have added that *Pennhurst* does not require Congress "specifically" to "identify" and "proscribe *each* condition in [Spending Clause] legislation." [Citations.] And we have denied any implication that "suits under Spending Clause legislation are suits in contract, or that contract-law principles apply to *all* issues that they raise." [Citation.]

. . . [T]he basic objective of *Pennhurst's* clear-statement requirement does not demand textual clarity in respect to every detail. That is because ambiguity about the precise nature of a statutory program's details— particularly where they are of a kind that States might have anticipated—is rarely relevant to the basic question: Would the States have accepted the Federal Government's funds *had they only known* the nature of the accompanying conditions? Often, the later filling-in of details through judicial interpretation will not lead one to wonder whether funding recipients would have agreed to enter the basic program at all. Given the nature of such details, it is clear that the States would have entered the program regardless. At the same time, to view each statutory detail of a highly complex federal/state program (involving, say, transportation, schools, the environment) simply through the lens of linguistic clarity, rather than to assess its meanings in terms of basic legislative purpose, is to risk a set of judicial interpretations that can prevent the program, overall, from achieving its basic objectives or that might well reduce a program in its details to incoherence.

This case is about just such a detail. . . .

B

If the Court believes that the statute's language is unambiguous, I must disagree. The provision at issue says that a court "may award reasonable attorneys' fees as part of the costs" to parents who prevail in an action brought under the Act. 20 U.S.C. § 1415(i)(3)(B). The statute neither defines the word "costs" nor points to any other source of law for a definition. And the word "costs," alone, says nothing at all about which costs fall within its scope.

Neither does the statutory phrase—"as part of the costs to the parents of a child with a disability who is the prevailing party"—taken in its entirety unambiguously foreclose an award of expert fees. I agree that, read literally, that provision does not clearly grant authority to award any costs at all. And one might read it, as the Court does, as referencing another federal statute, 28 U.S.C. § 1920, which provides that authority. [Citations.] But such a reading is not inevitable. The provision (indeed, the entire Act) says nothing about that other statute. And one can, consistent with the language, read the provision as both embodying a general authority to award costs while also specifying the inclusion of "reasonable attorneys' fees" as part of those costs (as saying, for example, that a court "may award reasonable attorneys' fees as part of [a] costs [award]").

This latter reading, while linguistically the less natural, is legislatively the more likely. The majority's alternative reading, by cross-referencing only the federal general cost-awarding statute (which applies solely *in federal courts*), would produce a jumble of different cost definitions applicable to similar IDEA administrative and state-court proceedings in different States. [Citation.] This result is particularly odd, as all IDEA actions must begin in state due process hearings, where the federal cost statute clearly does not apply, and the overwhelming majority of these actions are never appealed to *any* court. . . . [Citation.] And when parents do appeal, they can file their actions in either state or federal courts. [Citation.]

Would Congress "obviously" have wanted the content of the word "costs" to vary from State to State, proceeding to proceeding? Why? At most, the majority's reading of the text is plausible; it is not the only possible reading.

C

The majority's most persuasive argument does not focus on either the Spending Clause or lack of statutory ambiguity. Rather, the majority says that "costs" is a term of art. In light of the law's long practice of excluding expert fees from the scope of the word "costs," along with this Court's cases interpreting the word similarly in other statutes, the "legislative history is simply not enough."

I am perfectly willing to assume that the majority is correct about the traditional scope of the word "costs." . . . Regardless, here the statute itself indicates that Congress did not intend to use the word "costs" as a term of art. . . . If Congress intended the word "costs" in § 2 to authorize an award of only those costs listed in the federal cost statute, why did it use the word "expenses" in § 4(b)(3)(A) as part of the "amount . . . awarded to the prevailing party"? When used as a term of art, after all, "costs" does not cover expenses. Nor does the federal costs statute cover any expenses, at least not any that Congress could have wanted the GAO to study. [Citation.]

Further, why did Congress, when asking the GAO (in the statute itself) to study the "number of hours spent by personnel," include among those personnel both attorneys "*and consultants*"? Who but experts could those consultants be? Why would Congress want the GAO to study the hours that those experts "spent," unless it thought that it would help keep track of the "costs" that the statute imposed?

. . . We *know* what Congress intended the GAO study to cover. It *told* the GAO in its Conference Report that the word "costs" included the costs of experts. And, not surprisingly, the GAO made clear that it understood precisely what Congress asked it to do. In its final report, the GAO wrote: "Parents can receive reimbursement from state or local education agencies for some or all of their attorney fees *and related expenses* if they are the prevailing party in part or all of administrative hearings or court proceedings. *Expert witness fees, cost of tests or evaluations found to be necessary during the case, and court costs for services rendered during administrative and court proceedings are examples of reimbursable expenses.*" GAO, Briefing Report to Congressional Requesters, Special Education: The Attorney Fees Provision of Public Law 99–372 (GAO/HRD–90–22BR), p. 13 (Nov.1989) (emphasis added), online at http://archive.gao.gov/d26t7/140084.pdf. At the very least, this amounts to *some* indication that Congress intended the word "costs," not as a term of art, not as it was used in the statutes at issue in *Casey* and *Crawford Fitting,* but rather as including certain additional "expenses." If that is so, the claims of tradition, of the interpretation this Court has given other statutes, cannot be so strong as to prevent us from examining the legislative history. And that history could not be more clear about the matter: Congress intended the statutory phrase "attorneys' fees as part of the costs" to include the costs of experts.

III

For the reasons I have set forth, I cannot agree with the majority's conclusion. Even less can I agree with its failure to consider fully the statute's legislative history. That history makes Congress' purpose clear. And our ultimate judicial goal is to interpret language in light of the statute's purpose. Only by seeking that purpose can we avoid the substitution of judicial for legislative will. Only by reading language in its light can we maintain the democratic link between voters, legislators, statutes, and ultimate implementation, upon which the legitimacy of our constitutional system rests. . . .

For these reasons, I respectfully dissent.

NOTES AND QUESTIONS

1.   The majority invoked the "clear notice rule" because Congress enacted the IDEA under its Spending Clause authority. On this basis, the majority concluded that the statute must be viewed "from the perspective of a state official who is engaged in the process of deciding whether the State should accept IDEA funds and the obligations that go with those funds. We must ask whether such a state official would clearly understand that one of the obligations of the Act is the obligation to compensate prevailing parents for expert fees." Is there reason to think that such officials may interpret the statutory provision differently than, say, members of Congress, parents of disabled children, the federal Department of Education, and/or federal judges? From which perspective does the dissent seem inclined to view the statutory phrase in question? What about the concurrence?

2.   If the majority is right to interpret the statutory text differently in light of a prioritized audience, what obligation, if any, do judges have to appreciate how that audience is likely to understand a statute's meaning? In the case of the IDEA provision in question, the majority likely underestimated the knowledge and sophistication of the most plausible audience, which is state-level education officials who engage directly with the Department of Education in understanding the IDEA's requirements and deciding whether to accept conditioned federal funds. Local educators are not the state officials directly involved in the states' decision to consent to IDEA requirements; rather, since at least 1970, the IDEA has mandated that states establish advisory councils that advise both local officials and state education agencies as to requirements under the IDEA. What kind of empirical examination, if any, should judges engage in to decide how a statute gives notice to that

audience? Does it matter if their empirical claim about the audience's likely understanding may be unsupported by evidence? Should it matter if notice is provided by extratextual means, such as legislative history or agency guidance?

3.   Expecting or requiring that a term or phrase have a consistent meaning across all federal statutes seems implausible as a descriptive account of how Congress drafts statutes. Indeed, as Professors Abbe Gluck and Lisa Bressman have found in surveying legislative drafters, congressional staffers generally have no such expectations:

> . . . Although more than 93% of our respondents affirmed that the "goal" is for statutory terms to have consistent meanings throughout, our respondents emphasized time and again the significant organizational barriers that the committee system, bundled legislative deals, and lengthy, multidrafter statutes pose to the realistic operation of those rules.
>
> Our respondents told us that congressional committees are "islands" that limit communication between committees drafting different parts of the same statutes and that, because of the increasing tendency to legislate through omnibus or otherwise "unorthodox" legislative vehicles, most major statutes are now conglomerations of multiple committees' separate work. . . .
>
> For the same reasons, our respondents also vigorously disputed that the first cousin of the whole act rule—the "whole code rule," under which courts construe terms across different statutes consistently—reflects how Congress drafts or even how it tries to draft. Specifically, only 9% of respondents told us that drafters often or always intend for terms to apply consistently across statutes that are unrelated by subject matter.
>
> This presumption of consistent usage, we would note, is widely accepted in the federal courts. Indeed, leading commentators have called it one of the most important and consistently applied textual default rules, and it has been employed by textualists and purposivists alike. In the October 2011 Term of the Supreme Court alone, the whole act rule was used in at least three cases, and the leading case for the principle has been cited in at least 118 federal cases since 1995. To our knowledge, however, courts have never considered the role that committee jurisdiction plays when applying the rule, and courts have rarely focused on the type of statutory vehicle.
>
> We also note that, given the institutional factors that our respondents identified, application of the consistent-usage presumption is unlikely to exert any positive influence on the drafting process. This suggestion runs contrary to popular arguments that a strict textual approach may incentivize Congress to draft more carefully. Justice Scalia's new book offers a typical example of such an argument in support of the consistent-usage rule:

The canons ... promote better drafting. When it is widely understood in the legal community that, for example, a word used repeatedly in a document will be taken to have the same meaning throughout ... you can expect those who prepare legal documents competently to draft accordingly.

Such arguments, however, depend on the absence of other barriers to such "better" drafting. Almost all of our respondents told us that consistent term usage was the "goal" or what "should be," but they still told us that the rule was unlikely to hold because of the way that Congress is organized.

Abbe R. Gluck & Lisa Schultz Bressman, *Statutory Interpretation from the Inside: An Empirical Study of Congressional Drafting, Delegation, and the Canons: Part I*, 65 Stan. L. Rev. 901 (2013).

4. If consistent usage presumptions are difficult to justify in terms of the drafters' *intended* meaning, can they be justified on other grounds? For example, should law-literate reasonable readers like judges and lawyers be able to *expect* that a legal term of art means the same thing throughout the federal code? (Maybe not: see *Yates v. United States*, *supra*: "In law as in life, ... the same words, placed in different contexts, sometimes mean different things.") Should it matter whether other non-legal audiences might also be expected to engage with federal statutes from time to time? Or is it sufficient to answer that a client's legal counsel should be expected to do the interpreting? If so, does such an answer assume the widespread availability of affordable legal services?

E. TEMPORAL ISSUES IN STATUTORY INTERPRETATION

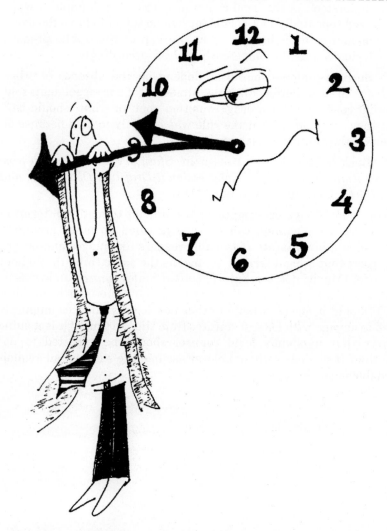

1. APPLYING OLD STATUTES TO CHANGING CIRCUMSTANCES

Whether or not legislative drafters have in mind "an evil to be remedied" when enacting a statute, the resulting statute nevertheless will likely apply to circumstances beyond those considered at the time of its enactment. Consider, for example, Justice Scalia's statement in *Oncale v. Sundowner Offshore Services, Inc.*, 523 U.S. 75, 79–80 (1998). In *Oncale*, the Court addressed whether workplace harassment against an employee of the same sex as the harasser can violate Title VII's prohibition against "discriminat[ion] ... because of ... sex," 42 U.S.C. § 2000e–2(a)(1). Justice Scalia, writing for the Court, concluded that:

> We see no justification in the statutory language or our precedents for a categorical rule excluding same-sex

harassment claims from the coverage of Title VII. As some courts have observed, male-on-male sexual harassment in the workplace was assuredly not the principal evil Congress was concerned with when it enacted Title VII. But statutory prohibitions often go beyond the principal evil to cover reasonably comparable evils, and it is ultimately the provisions of our laws rather than the principal concerns of our legislators by which we are governed. Title VII prohibits "discriminat[ion] . . . because of . . . sex" in the "terms" or "conditions" of employment. Our holding that this includes sexual harassment must extend to sexual harassment of any kind that meets the statutory requirements.

The cases in this section raise considerations about the interpretation and application of statutes in changing circumstances and over time.

Commonwealth v. Maxwell

Supreme Court of Pennsylvania, 1921.
271 Pa. 378, 114 A. 825.

■ Opinion by MR. JUSTICE SCHAFFER. In this case, the court below quashed an indictment, charging the defendants with murder, because a woman served on the grand jury which found the bill. The Commonwealth has appealed; and this brings before us the important question whether women are eligible as jurors in Pennsylvania.

It is conceded that, under the 19th Amendment to the Constitution of the United States, women are given the right to vote, and are therefore electors; but the oyer and terminer held that the provision of our Constitution (article I, section 6),—"Trial by jury shall be as heretofore and the right thereof remain inviolate,"—preserves in this State trial by jury as it existed at common law, and that neither the federal amendment nor its effect upon the Act of April 10, 1867, P.L. 62, providing for the selection of jurors, alters the ancient rule that men only may serve.

Let it be noted that what we are called upon to determine is the composition of juries, so far as the qualifications of jurors are concerned, not the conduct of trials before such a body nor the kinds of cases which under the Constitution must be decided by that character of tribunal.

At the time the provision we are considering was placed in Pennsylvania's first Constitution, in 1776, justice had been administered in the Commonwealth according to English forms for about a century. Does the word "heretofore" refer to jury trials as conducted in England or in Pennsylvania? We find the method of selecting juries and the qualifications of jurors, at the time of the promulgation of this Constitution, September 28, 1776, was regulated in Pennsylvania and in England by legislation and not by the common law, in the latter country by the Act of 3 George II, c. 25; 3 Blackstone 361. . . .

Under the Act of April 10, 1867, P.L. 62, section 2, (2 Purdon 2062, placitum 2), which expressly applies to each of the counties in the Commonwealth, except Philadelphia, the jury commissioners are required to select "from the *whole qualified electors* of the respective county, at large, a number," such as shall be designated by the court of common pleas, "of sober, intelligent and judicious persons, to serve as jurors in the several courts of such county during that year." The seventh section of this act exempts Philadelphia from its provisions. The statutory enactment which covers Philadelphia is section 2 of the Act of April 20, 1858, P.L. 354 (2 Purdon 2077, placitum 94); it sets forth: "That prior to the first day of December in each and every year, the receiver of public taxes of the said city shall lodge with the said sheriff, for the use of the said board [of judges], a duly certified list of *all taxable inhabitants of the said city,* setting out their names, places of residence and occupation; and, prior to the tenth day of December in each and every year, it shall be the duty of the said board, or a quorum thereof, to assemble together and select from the said list of taxables a sufficient number of sober, healthy and discreet citizens, to constitute the several panels of jurors, grand and petit, that may be required for service in the several courts for the next ensuing year, in due proportion from the several wards of the said city and the principal avocations."

It will thus be seen that since 1805, when the Constitution of 1790 was in force, the persons charged with the duty of jury service have been fixed, from time to time, by the legislature and have been "taxable citizens," "white male taxable citizens," "male taxable citizens," "taxable inhabitants" and "qualified electors." . . .

Without feeling called upon to determine what other matters the word "heretofore" in the Constitution of 1873 refers to, we do say that when that instrument was adopted the uniform method of selecting jurors and determining their qualification was by legislation, both here and in England. This was known to the framers of the first and all succeeding Constitutions, in the first being specifically recognized, and, in guaranteeing the right of trial by jury, it and all the others did not in any way limit the legislature from determining from time to time how juries should be composed.

We have then the Act of 1867, constitutionally providing that the jury commissioners are required to select "from the *whole qualified electors* of the respective county . . . persons to serve as jurors in the several courts of such county," and the 19th Amendment to the federal Constitution putting women in the body of electors. "The term 'elector' is a technical, generic term, descriptive of a citizen having constitutional and statutory qualifications that enable him to vote, and including not only those who vote, but also those who are qualified yet fail to exercise the right of franchise": 20 Corpus Juris 58. If the Act of 1867 is prospective in operation, and takes in new classes of electors as they come to the voting privilege from time to time, then necessarily women being electors are eligible to jury service. That the Act of 1867 does cover those who at any time shall come within the designation of electors there can be no question. "Statutes framed in general terms apply to new cases that arise, and to new subjects that are created from time to time, and which come within their general scope and policy. It is a rule of statutory construction that legislative enactments in general and comprehensive terms, prospective in operation, apply alike to all persons, subjects and business within their general purview and scope coming into existence subsequent to their passage": 25 Ruling Case Law 778.

Summing up, we conclude, (1) there was no absolute and fixed qualification of jurors at common law, and from very ancient times their qualifications were fixed by act of parliament; (2) the qualification of jurors was not the thing spoken of by the section of the Constitution under consideration; (3) the words "as heretofore" in that section refer to the kinds of cases triable before juries and the trial, not the qualifications of the jurors; (4) the designation "qualified elector" embraces all electors at the time jurors are selected from the body of electors; (5) the term "electors" embraces those who may be added to the electorate from time to time. . . .

The pending case calls for the immediate decision only of the right of women to serve as jurors in those counties which are covered by the Act of 1867. We entertain no doubt, however, that women are eligible to serve as jurors in all the Commonwealth's courts.

The order quashing the indictment is reversed, and the indictment is reinstated with direction to the court below to proceed with the trial of the defendants in due course.

Commonwealth v. Welosky

Supreme Court of Massachusetts, 1931.
276 Mass. 398, 177 N.E. 656.

Complaint, received and sworn to in the District Court of Chelsea on July 9, 1930, charging the defendant with keeping and exposing intoxicating liquor with intent unlawfully to sell the same.

Upon appeal to the Superior Court, the complaint was tried before *Hayes,* J., a judge of a district court sitting in the Superior Court under statutory provisions. The defendant's challenge to the array is described in the opinion. The judge sustained a replication by the Commonwealth thereto. The defendant was found guilty and alleged exceptions.

■ RUGG, C.J.[, joined by CROSBY, CARROLL, WAIT, and FIELD, JJ.] As the jurors were about to be empaneled for the trial of this complaint, the defendant filed a challenge to the array. Issue of law was joined thereon. [Citation.] The ground on which that challenge rests is that there were no women on the lists from which the jurors were drawn.

1.   The first question to be decided is whether the statutes of this Commonwealth require that the names of women otherwise qualified be placed upon jury lists so that they may be drawn for service as jurors.

It is plain that women could not rightly serve as jurors, save in the rare instances where a jury of matrons was called, under the Constitution and laws of this Commonwealth prior to the adoption of the Nineteenth Amendment to the Constitution of the United States. The terms of the statute, in the light of the Constitution, express decisions, universal understanding, and unbroken practice, forbid any other view. The trial by jury of the common law and that contemplated by both the Constitution of this Commonwealth and that of the United States were by a jury of twelve composed exclusively of men. [Citation.]

The statute to be interpreted is G.L. c. 234, § 1. Its relevant language is: "A person qualified to vote for representatives to the general court shall be liable to serve as a juror," with exceptions not here material.

The words of a statute are the main source for the ascertainment of a legislative purpose. They are to be construed according to their natural import in common and approved usage. The imperfections of language to express intent often render necessary further inquiry. Statutes are to be interpreted, not alone according to their simple, literal or strict verbal meaning, but in connection with their development, their progression through the legislative body, the history of the times, prior legislation, contemporary customs and conditions and the system of positive law of which they are part, and in the light of the Constitution and of the common law, to the end that they be held to cover the subjects presumably within the vision of the Legislature and, on the one hand, be not unduly constricted so as to exclude matters fairly within their scope, and, on the other hand, be not stretched by enlargement of signification to comprehend matters not within the principle and purview on which they were founded when originally framed and their words chosen. General expressions may be restrained by relevant circumstances showing a legislative intent that they be narrowed and used in a particular sense. [Citation.]

It is clear beyond peradventure that the words of G.L. c. 234, § 1, when originally enacted could not by any possibility have included or been intended by the General Court to include women among those liable to jury duty. The Constitution forbade the words, "A person qualified to vote for representatives to the general court," to comprehend women. Women have been qualified to vote in this Commonwealth only since the adoption of the Nineteenth Amendment to the Constitution of the United States. It is not argued in behalf of the defendant that the terms of the statutes preceding G.L. c. 234, § 1, that is to say of R.L. c. 176, § 1, and its predecessors in substantially the same words since a time before the adoption of the Constitution, could possibly have imposed jury duty upon women. The argument on this point is twofold: (A) that the phrase of the statute is general and therefore was intended automatically to include women if their constitutional inhibitions were ever removed; and (B) that, since the General Laws were enacted in December, 1920, after the ratification of the Nineteenth Amendment, the statute was intended to include women. These arguments will be considered in turn.

A. The Nineteenth Amendment was, on August 26, 1920, proclaimed to have been duly ratified. That amendment declared that "The right of citizens of the United States to vote shall not be denied or abridged by the United States or by any state on account of sex." It became forthwith binding upon the people and the several departments of this Commonwealth. By its own self-executing force it struck from the Constitution of this Commonwealth the word "male" wherever it occurred as a limitation upon the right to vote. . . .

Statutes framed in general terms commonly look to the future and may include conditions as they arise from time to time not even known at the time of enactment, provided they are fairly within the sweep and the meaning of the words and falling within their obvious scope and purpose. But statutes do not govern situations not within the reason of their enactment and giving rise to radically diverse circumstances presumably not within the dominating purpose of those who framed and enacted them. [Citation.]

As matter of strict and abstract verbal interpretation, apart from context, circumstances, and contemporary and antecedent history, the language of G.L. c. 234, § 1, is broad enough to comprise women. The word "person" when used in an unrestricted sense includes a woman. It has been said that "The word 'persons,' in its natural and usual signification, includes women as well as men." *Opinion of the Justices,* 136 Mass. 578, 580. Binney v. Globe National Bank, 150 Mass. 574. "The natural and obvious meaning of the word 'person' is a living human being." Sawyer v. Mackie, 149 Mass. 269, 270. Madden v. Election Commissioners of Boston, 251 Mass. 95, 98. The word "person," like many other words, has no fixed and rigid signification, but has different meanings dependent upon contemporary conditions, the connection in which it is used, and the result intended to be accomplished. It has been said to be "an ambiguous word" and may refer to those of either or both sexes. Nairn v. University of St. Andrews, [1909] A.C. 147, 162. . . . Yet it was held not to include corporations upon the facts in Commonwealth v. Phoenix Bank, 11 Met. 129, 149. Notwithstanding Pub.Sts. c. 3, § 3, Sixteenth, (G.L. c. 4, § 7, Twenty-third) to the effect that the word "person" in construing statutes shall include corporations, it was held not thus inclusive in Steel Edge Stamping & Retinning Co. v. Manchester Savings Bank, 163 Mass. 252. It has also been held not to include a woman. Mashburn v. State, 65 Fla. 470, 474. Several cases have arisen where the question was whether the word "person," when used respecting the right to hold office or to exercise the franchise, included women. In Nairn v. University of St. Andrews, [1909] A.C. 147, it appeared that, by Acts of Parliament of 1868 and 1881, the university franchise was conferred upon "every person" whose name was on the register and on whom degrees had been conferred. At that time women were not admitted to graduation and could not receive degrees. In 1889, a further act was passed for the appointment of commissioners with extensive regulatory powers over universities. These commissioners adopted an ordinance enabling the universities to confer degrees on women for satisfactory academic accomplishments. The appellants, having received degrees upon graduation, contended that they had the right to vote. In rejecting that contention, it was said by Lord Loreburn, at page 161: "It proceeds upon the supposition that the word 'person' in the Act of 1868 did include women, though not then giving them the vote, so that at some later date an Act purporting to deal only with education might enable commissioners to admit them to the degree, and thereby also indirectly confer upon them the franchise. It would require a convincing demonstration to satisfy me that Parliament intended to effect a constitutional change so momentous and far-reaching by so furtive a process. It is a dangerous assumption to suppose that the Legislature foresees every possible result that may ensue from the unguarded use of a single word, or that the language used in statutes is so precisely accurate that you can pick out from various Acts this and that expression and, skillfully piecing them together, lay a safe foundation for some remote inference." It was held that the statutory word "person" did not in these circumstances include women. It was held in *Viscountess Rhondda's Claim,* [1922] 2 A.C. 339, that an Act of Parliament passed in 1919, providing that "A person shall not be disqualified by sex or marriage from the exercise of any public function," did not entitle a peeress of the United Kingdom in her own right to receive the writ of summons to Parliament. Doubtless, as an abstract conception, it is a public function to sit in the House of Lords and to exercise the prerogatives of a member. But it was held by ten out of twelve law lords sitting in the case, among whom were the most eminent judges of the day, that the word "person" as used in the act could not rightly be interpreted to include women in those entitled to sit in the House of Lords. It was said by Lord Birkenhead in the course of an exhaustive statement reviewing many decisions, at page 369: ". . . a long stream of cases has established that general words are to be construed so as, in an old phrase, 'to pursue the intent of the makers of statutes' . . . and so as to import all those implied exceptions which arise from a close consideration of the mischiefs sought to be remedied and of the state of the law at the moment, when the statute was passed." At pages 372–373, the words of Lord Loreburn in Nairn v. University of St. Andrews, [1909] A.C. 147, at pages 160, 161, to which reference has already been made, were quoted with high commendation.

This brief review of authorities demonstrates that "person" by itself is an equivocal word. Its meaning in a statute requires interpretation. The statute here under examination (G.L. c. 234, § 1) is a reenactment of a long line of statutes of the Commonwealth running back to a time shortly after the adoption of the Constitution as well as through all intermediate revisions dealing with qualifications for jury service. Laws of the Colony and of the Province are in effect the same. In the earlier and later statutes, the same essential and almost the identical words have been employed. The word "person" occurs in them all. The selection of jurors has constantly been required to be from those qualified to vote. Qualifications for voting have been continuously established by the Constitution. By the words of that instrument and its amendments (apart from the effect of the Nineteenth Amendment to the Federal Constitution) the right to vote was confined to male inhabitants, male persons, and finally to male citizens, until the word "male" was stricken out in 1924 by Amendment 68. See c. 1, § 2, art. 2; c. 1, § 3, art. 4; arts. 3 and 32 of the Amendments. Manifestly, therefore, the intent of the Legislature must have been, in using the word "person" in statutes concerning jurors and jury lists, to confine its meaning to men. . . .

Possession of property of specified value and payment of taxes, as qualifications for voters, were required in earlier days and from time to time, but these were gradually eliminated by amendments to the Constitution until the last of such limitations disappeared with the approval of Amendment 32 in 1891. When the suffrage has been thus widened among male citizens, there has followed, without further legislation and without change in the phrase of the statute, a like extension of citizens liable to service as jurors. These concurring enlargements of those liable to jury service were simply an extension to larger numbers of the same classification of persons. Since the word "person" in the statutes respecting jurors meant men, when there was an extension of the right to vote to other men previously disqualified, the jury statutes by specific definition included them. No amendment to the statute can be conceived which could have made that meaning more clear. . . .

Changes in suffrage and in liability for jury service in the past differ in kind from the change here urged.

The Nineteenth Amendment to the Federal Constitution conferred the suffrage upon an entirely new class of human beings. It did not extend the right to vote to members of an existing classification theretofore disqualified, but created a new class. It added to qualified voters those who did not fall within the meaning of the word "person" in the jury statutes. No member of the class thus added to the body of voters had ever theretofore in this Commonwealth had the right to vote for candidates for offices created by the Constitution. The change in the legal status of women wrought by the Nineteenth Amendment was radical, drastic and unprecedented. While it is to be given full effect in its field, it is not to be extended by implication. It is unthinkable that those who first framed and selected the words for the statute now embodied in G.L. c. 234, § 1, had any design that it should ever include women within its scope. It is equally inconceivable that those who from time to time have reenacted that statute had any such design. When they used the word "person" in connection with those qualified to vote for members of the more numerous branch of the General Court, to describe those liable to jury service, no one contemplated the possibility of women becoming so qualified. The same is true in general of those who from time to time reenacted the statute in substantially the same words. No intention to include women can be deduced from the omission of the word male. That word was imbedded in the Constitution of the Commonwealth as a limitation upon those citizens who might become voters and thereby members of a class from which jurors might be drawn. It would have been superfluous also to insert that word in the statute. The words of Chief Justice Gray in *Robinson's Case,* 131 Mass. 376, at pages 380, 381, are equally pertinent to the case at bar: "Whenever the Legislature has intended to make a change in the legal rights or capacities of women, it has used words clearly manifesting its intent and the extent of the change intended. . . . In making innovations upon the long-established system of law on this subject, the Legislature appears to have proceeded with great caution, one step at a time; and the whole course of legislation precludes the inference that any change in the legal rights or capacities of women is to be implied, which has not been clearly expressed."

The conclusion is irresistible that, according to sound principles of statutory construction, it cannot rightly be held that the scope of R.L. c. 176, § 1, the statute in force on August 26, 1920, now G.L. c. 234, § 1, was extended by the ratification of the Nineteenth Amendment so as to render women liable to jury duty. To reach that result would be directly contrary to every purpose and intent of the General Court in enacting that law. . . .

NOTES AND QUESTIONS

1.   The statutory text construed in *Maxwell* directed that jurors were to be drawn "from the whole qualified electors . . . " In *Welosky,* the statute designated "persons qualified to vote . . . " Does the different statutory language explain the different outcomes in the two cases?

2.   *Maxwell's* approach to statutory interpretation seems consistent with the "plain meaning rule," while *Welosky's* interpretive techniques recall a variety of other devices to ascertain legislative intent. Do those devices seem more problematic here than, for example, in *Johnson v. Southern Pacific Co., supra*?

3.   Is it relevant that the different outcomes on the composition of juries permitted the convictions in both cases to be sustained?

4.   Once women obtained the right to vote, many hoped the Nineteenth Amendment would guarantee equal citizenship in all aspects of civic life. Because many states' jury duty statutes, like those in *Maxwell* and *Welosky,* linked jury duty with the franchise, lawsuits in many states tested the scope of women's legal equality by urging that women voters were as subject to jury service as male voters. Most of these challenges failed; the majority of

state courts ruled that the Nineteenth Amendment had no effect beyond the specific domain of voting. See Gretchen Ritter, *Jury Service and Women's Citizenship before and after the Nineteenth Amendment*, 20 LAW & HISTORY REVIEW 479, 507–09 (2002).

New Prime Inc. v. Oliveira

Supreme Court of the United States, 2019.
139 S.Ct. 532, 202 L.Ed.2d 536.

■ JUSTICE GORSUCH delivered the opinion of the Court[, in which all other Members joined, except JUSTICE KAVANAUGH, who took no part in the consideration or decision of the case.].

The Federal Arbitration Act requires courts to enforce private arbitration agreements. But like most laws, this one bears its qualifications. Among other things, § 1 says that "nothing herein" may be used to compel arbitration in disputes involving the "contracts of employment" of certain transportation workers. 9 U.S.C. § 1. And that qualification has sparked these questions: When a contract delegates questions of arbitrability to an arbitrator, must a court leave disputes over the application of § 1's exception for the arbitrator to resolve? And does the term "contracts of employment" refer only to contracts between employers and employees, or does it also reach contracts with independent contractors? . . .

New Prime is an interstate trucking company and Dominic Oliveira works as one of its drivers. But, at least on paper, Mr. Oliveira isn't an employee; the parties' contracts label him an independent contractor. Those agreements also instruct that any disputes arising out of the parties' relationship should be resolved by an arbitrator—even disputes over the scope of the arbitrator's authority.

Eventually, of course, a dispute did arise. In a class action lawsuit in federal court, Mr. Oliveira argued that New Prime denies its drivers lawful wages. The company may call its drivers independent contractors. But, Mr. Oliveira alleged, in reality New Prime treats them as employees and fails to pay the statutorily due minimum wage. In response to Mr. Oliveira's complaint, New Prime asked the court to invoke its statutory authority under the Act and compel arbitration according to the terms found in the parties' agreements.

That request led to more than a little litigation of its own. Even when the parties' contracts mandate arbitration, Mr. Oliveira observed, the Act doesn't *always* authorize a court to enter an order compelling it. In particular, § 1 carves out from the Act's coverage "contracts of employment of . . . workers engaged in foreign or interstate commerce." And at least for purposes of this collateral dispute, Mr. Oliveira submitted, it doesn't matter whether you view him as an employee or independent contractor. Either way, his agreement to drive trucks for New Prime qualifies as a "contract[ ] of employment of . . . [a] worker[ ] engaged in . . . interstate commerce." Accordingly, Mr. Oliveira argued, the Act supplied the district court with no authority to compel arbitration in this case.

Naturally, New Prime disagreed. Given the extraordinary breadth of the parties' arbitration agreement, the company insisted that any question about § 1's application belonged for the arbitrator alone to resolve. Alternatively and assuming a court could address the question, New Prime contended that the term "contracts of employment" refers only to contracts that establish an employer-employee relationship. And because Mr. Oliveira is, in fact as well as form, an independent contractor, the company argued, § 1's exception doesn't apply; the rest of the statute does; and the district court was (once again) required to order arbitration.

Ultimately, the district court and the First Circuit sided with Mr. Oliveira. [Citation] . . . . [T]he court of appeals held . . . that . . . § 1' s exclusion of certain "contracts of employment" removes from the Act's coverage not only employer-employee contracts but also contracts involving independent contractors. So under any account of the parties' agreement in this case, the court held, it lacked authority under the Act to order arbitration. . . .

Did the First Circuit correctly resolve the merits of the § 1 challenge in this case? . . . What does the term "contracts of employment" mean? If it refers only to contracts that reflect an employer-employee relationship, then § 1's exception is irrelevant and a court is free to order arbitration, just as New Prime urges. But if the term *also* encompasses contracts that require an independent contractor to perform work, then the exception takes hold and a court lacks authority under the Act to order arbitration, exactly as Mr. Oliveira argues. . . .

In taking up this question, we bear an important caution in mind. "[I]t's a 'fundamental canon of statutory construction' that words generally should be 'interpreted as taking their ordinary . . . meaning . . . at the time Congress enacted the statute.'" [Citation.] After all, if judges could freely invest old statutory terms with new meanings, we would risk amending legislation outside the "single, finely wrought and exhaustively considered, procedure" the Constitution commands. [Citation.] We would risk, too, upsetting reliance interests in the settled meaning of a statute. [Citation.] Of course, statutes may sometimes refer to an external source of law and fairly warn readers that they must abide that external source of law, later amendments and modifications included. [Citation.] But nothing like that exists here. Nor has anyone suggested any other appropriate reason that might allow us to depart from the original meaning of the statute at hand.

That, we think, holds the key to the case. To many lawyerly ears today, the term "contracts of employment" might call to mind only agreements between employers and employees (or what the common law sometimes called masters and servants). Suggestively, at least one recently published law dictionary defines the word "employment" to mean "the relationship between master and servant." Black's Law Dictionary 641 (10th ed. 2014). But this modern intuition isn't easily squared with evidence of the term's meaning at the time of the Act's adoption in 1925. At that time, a "contract of employment" usually meant nothing more than an agreement to perform work. As a result, most people then would have understood § 1 to exclude not only agreements between employers and employees but also agreements that require independent contractors to perform work.

What's the evidence to support this conclusion? It turns out that in 1925 the term "contract of employment" wasn't defined in any of the (many) popular or legal dictionaries the parties cite to us. And surely that's a first hint the phrase wasn't then a term of art bearing some specialized meaning. It turns out, too, that the dictionaries of the era consistently afforded the word "employment" a broad construction, broader than may be often found in dictionaries today. Back then, dictionaries tended to treat "employment" more or less as a synonym for "work." Nor did they distinguish between different kinds of work or workers: All work was treated as employment, whether or not the common law criteria for a master-servant relationship happened to be satisfied.[1]

What the dictionaries suggest, legal authorities confirm. This Court's early 20th-century cases used the phrase "contract of employment" to describe work agreements involving independent contractors. Many state court cases did the same.[3] So did a variety of federal statutes. And state statutes too. We see here no evidence that a "contract of employment" necessarily signaled a formal employer-employee or master-servant relationship.

More confirmation yet comes from a neighboring term in the statutory text. Recall that the Act excludes from its coverage "contracts

---

[1] *See, e.g.,* 3 J. Murray, A New English Dictionary on Historical Principles 130 (1891) (defining "employment" as, among other things, "[t]he action or process of employing; the state of being employed. The service (of a person). That on which (one) is employed; business; occupation; a special errand or commission. A person's regular occupation or business; a trade or profession"); 3 The Century Dictionary and Cyclopedia 1904 (1914) (defining "employment" as "[w]ork or business of any kind"); W. Harris, Webster's New International Dictionary 718 (1st ed. 1909) (listing "work" as a synonym for "employment"); Webster's Collegiate Dictionary 329 (3d ed. 1916) (same); Black's Law Dictionary 422 (2d ed. 1910) ("an engagement or rendering services" for oneself or another); 3 Oxford English Dictionary 130 (1933) ("[t]hat on which (one) is employed; business; occupation; a special errand or commission").

[3] See, *e.g., Lindsay v. McCaslin (Two Cases),* 123 Me. 197, 200, 122 A. 412, 413 (1923) ("When the contract of employment has been reduced to writing, the question whether the person employed was an independent contractor or merely a servant is determined by the court as a matter of law"); *Tankersley v. Webster,* 116 Okla. 208, 210, 243 P. 745, 747 (1925) ("[T]he contract of employment between Tankersley and Casey was admitted in evidence without objections, and we think conclusively shows that Casey was an independent contractor"); *Waldron v. Garland Pocahontas Coal Co.,* 89 W.Va. 426, 427, 109 S.E. 729 (1921) (syllabus) ("Whether a person performing work for another is an independent contractor depends upon a consideration of the contract of employment, the nature of the business, the circumstances under which the contract was made and the work was done"); see also App. to Brief for Respondent 1a–12a (citing additional examples).

of employment of . . . any . . . class of *workers* engaged in foreign or interstate commerce." 9 U.S.C. § 1 (emphasis added). Notice Congress didn't use the word "employees" or "servants," the natural choices if the term "contracts of employment" addressed them alone. Instead, Congress spoke of "workers," a term that everyone agrees easily embraces independent contractors. That word choice may not mean everything, but it does supply further evidence still that Congress used the term "contracts of employment" in a broad sense to capture any contract for the performance of *work* by *workers*. . . .

What does New Prime have to say about the case building against it? Mainly, it seeks to shift the debate from the term "contracts of employment" to the word "employee." Today, the company emphasizes, the law often distinguishes between employees and independent contractors. Employees are generally understood as those who work "in the service of another person (the employer) under an express or implied contract of hire, under which the employer has the right to control the details of work performance." Black's Law Dictionary, at 639. Meanwhile, independent contractors are sometimes described as those "entrusted to undertake a specific project but who [are] left free to do the assigned work and to choose the method for accomplishing it." *Id.*, at 888. New Prime argues that, by 1925, the words "employee" and "independent contractor" had already assumed these distinct meanings.[6] And given that, the company contends, the phrase "contracts of *employment*" should be understood to refer only to relationships between *employers and employees*.

Unsurprisingly, Mr. Oliveira disagrees. He replies that, while the term "employment" dates back many centuries, the word "employee" only made its first appearance in English in the 1800s. See Oxford English Dictionary (3d ed., Mar. 2014), www.oed.com/view/Entry/61374 (all Internet materials as last visited Jan. 9, 2019). At that time, the word from which it derived, "employ," simply meant to "apply (a thing) to some definite purpose." 3 J. Murray, A New English Dictionary on Historical Principles 129 (1891). And even in 1910, Black's Law Dictionary reported that the term "employee" had only "become somewhat naturalized in our language." Black's Law Dictionary 421 (2d ed. 1910).

Still, the parties do share some common ground. They agree that the word "employee" eventually came into wide circulation and came to denote those who work for a wage at the direction of another. They agree, too, that all this came to pass in part because the word "employee" didn't suffer from the same "historical baggage" of the older common law term "servant," and because it proved useful when drafting legislation to regulate burgeoning industries and their labor forces in the early 20th century. The parties even agree that the development of the term "employee" may have come to influence and narrow our understanding of the word "employment" in comparatively recent years and may be why today it might signify to some a "relationship between master and servant."

But if the parties' extended etymological debate persuades us of anything, it is that care is called for. The words "employee" and "employment" may share a common root and an intertwined history. But they also developed at different times and in at least some different ways. The only question in this case concerns the meaning of the term "contracts of *employment* " in 1925. And, whatever the word "employee" may have meant at that time, and however it may have later influenced the meaning of "employment," the evidence before us remains that, as dominantly understood in 1925, a contract of *employment* did not necessarily imply the existence of an employer-employee or master-servant relationship.

When New Prime finally turns its attention to the term in dispute, it directs us to *Coppage v. Kansas,* 236 U.S. 1, 13, 35 S.Ct. 240, 59 L.Ed. 441 (1915). There and in other cases like it, New Prime notes, courts sometimes used the phrase "contracts of employment" to describe what today we'd recognize as agreements between employers and employees. But this proves little. No one doubts that employer-employee agreements to perform work qualified as "contracts of employment" in 1925—and documenting that fact does nothing to negate the possibility that "contracts of employment" *also* embraced agreements by independent contractors to perform work. Coming a bit closer to the mark, New Prime eventually cites a handful of early 20th-century legal materials that seem to use the term "contracts of employment" to refer *exclusively* to employer-employee agreements. But from the record amassed before us, these authorities appear to represent at most the vanguard, not the main body, of contemporaneous usage.

New Prime's effort to explain away the statute's suggestive use of the term "worker" proves no more compelling. The company reminds us that the statute excludes "contracts of employment" for "seamen" and "railroad employees" as well as other transportation workers. And because "seamen" and "railroad employees" included *only* employees in 1925, the company reasons, we should understand "any other class of workers engaged in . . . interstate commerce" to bear a similar construction. But this argument rests on a precarious premise. At the time of the Act's passage, shipboard surgeons who tended injured sailors were considered "seamen" though they likely served in an independent contractor capacity. Even the term "railroad employees" may have swept more broadly at the time of the Act's passage than might seem obvious today. In 1922, for example, the Railroad Labor Board interpreted the word "employee" in the Transportation Act of 1920 to refer to anyone "engaged in the customary work directly contributory to the operation of the railroads." And the Erdman Act, a statute enacted to address disruptive railroad strikes at the end of the 19th century, seems to evince an equally broad understanding of "railroad employees." . . .

When Congress enacted the Arbitration Act in 1925, the term "contracts of employment" referred to agreements to perform work. No less than those who came before him, Mr. Oliveira is entitled to the benefit of that same understanding today. Accordingly, his agreement with New Prime falls within § 1's exception, the court of appeals was correct that it lacked authority under the Act to order arbitration, and the judgment is

Affirmed.

■ JUSTICE GINSBURG, concurring.

"[W]ords generally should be 'interpreted as taking their ordinary . . . meaning . . . at the time Congress enacted the statute.'" The Court so reaffirms, and I agree. Looking to the period of enactment to gauge statutory meaning ordinarily fosters fidelity to the "regime . . . Congress established." MCI Telecommunications Corp. v. American Telephone & Telegraph Co., 512 U.S. 218, 234 (1994).

Congress, however, may design legislation to govern changing times and circumstances. See, e.g., Kimble v. Marvel Entertainment, LLC, 135 S.Ct. 2401, 2412 (2015) ("Congress . . . intended [the Sherman Antitrust Act's] reference to 'restraint of trade' to have 'changing content,' and authorized courts to oversee the term's 'dynamic potential.'" (quoting Business Electronics Corp. v. Sharp Electronics Corp., 485 U.S. 717, 731–732 (1988))); SEC v. Zandford, 535 U.S. 813, 819 (2002) (In enacting the Securities Exchange Act, "Congress sought to substitute a philosophy of full disclosure for the philosophy of caveat emptor . . . . Consequently, . . . the statute should be construed not technically and restrictively, but flexibly to effectuate its remedial purposes." (internal quotation marks and paragraph break omitted)); H.J. Inc. v. Northwestern Bell Telephone Co., 492 U.S. 229, 243 (1989) ("The limits of the relationship and continuity concepts that combine to define a [Racketeer Influenced and Corrupt Organizations] pattern . . . cannot be fixed in advance with such clarity that it will always be apparent whether in a particular case a 'pattern of racketeering activity' exists. The development of these concepts must await future cases. . . ."). As these illustrations suggest, sometimes, "[w]ords in statutes can enlarge or contract their scope as other changes, in law or in the world, require their application to new instances or make old applications anachronistic." West v. Gibson, 527 U.S. 212, 218 (1999).

NOTE: "ORIGINAL" STATUTORY MEANING

The majority's approach in *Oliveira* has an intuitive appeal. Nevertheless, its temporally-oriented inquiry may result in potential uncertainties if applied more broadly to statutory interpretation questions of first impression.

First, this approach presents a seeming paradox concerning the legitimacy of seeking the original ordinary meaning of a statutory term. In

Oliveira, the majority gave the term "contracts of employment" its "original" meaning "at the time Congress enacted the statute," and suggested that even if the *ordinary* meaning of a term "drifts" over time, the statute's *legal* meaning should not change. Does this approach raise rule-of-law issues if the "ordinary meaning" of a statutory term as commonly used and understood *today* is not what it *legally* means according to courts? Can you imagine circumstances where this approach could undermine the capacity for the statute to give notice to those it regulates?

Second, recall the typology of interpretive methods in subsection III.A.2.a, *supra*. Broadly speaking, courts employ interpretive methods to determine one of three (potentially overlapping) meanings of a statutory term or phrase:

(1) the drafters' intended meaning;

(2) the meaning as understood by the reasonable reader of the statute; and/or

(3) the meaning that, for rule of law reasons, is the best *legal* meaning to be attributed to that statutory term or phrase.

Most textualists resist attributing to a statutory term its meaning *as intended by the statute's drafters*. (Contrast this approach with Chief Justice Rugg's conviction in *Welosky*, *supra*, that the Massachusetts legislators who enacted the statute governing jury duty could not possibly have intended that women serve as jurors.) Some textualists argue that any evidence of the drafters' intentions in the legislative history may be inherently unreliable as a source of statutory meaning. Others skeptical of "legislative intent"-based interpretive methods have noted that "Congress, is a they, not an it," and so a legislative body cannot be said to have a single coherent intention as to any given term's "intended" meaning. Textualists thus generally rule out the drafters' intended meaning as a basis for deciding on the meaning of ambiguous statutory text.

Instead, textualists generally seek to attribute to a statutory term or phrase its *"ordinary"* meaning, the meaning as understood by the reasonable reader. But recall that the "reasonable reader's understanding" may refer either to (a) the *original* reasonable reader's understanding at the time of the statute's enactment; or (b) the *contemporary* reasonable reader's understanding at the time the interpretive problem arises. Per the majority in *Oliveira*, where they might conflict, the original reasonable reader's understanding should trump the contemporary reader's. What is the basis for limiting a statute's meaning to the meaning understood by the reasonable reader *at the time of enactment*? The majority in *Oliveira* references the possibility of reliance issues. However, in any case of first impression, the term or phrase's meaning may be *inherently* unsettled, so absent authoritative guidance from relevant agency officials or courts, *either* party could make a claim of legal reliance based on *their* understanding of what the statute meant. And if the term or phrase's legal meaning has not remained fixed over time, why should the historical reader's understanding prevail over the contemporary reasonable reader's? Arguably, the enacting-era reasonable reader would understand better than today's readers what the statute meant at the time it was enacted. But whose intended meaning was that? The legislative drafters'! Unless the term was indisputably clear at the time of enactment, is there reason to think that a (potentially haphazard) collection of historical sources of ordinary usage will furnish more reliable indicia of intended meaning than the legislative history of the statute?

Importantly, the same temporality quandary may arise with respect to divining the drafters' intentions about whether they expected the statute's meaning and potential applications to evolve over time. On some occasions, evidence suggests the legislative drafters intended the meaning of the statutory provision to stay fixed at the time of its enactment (as the *Welosky* court claimed). Alternatively, legislators sometimes select an open-ended term precisely so that the statutory provision can be interpreted dynamically over time, as social problems and practices evolve (as the *Maxwell* court determined). In the latter circumstances, would a judge be an "unfaithful" agent of the legislature if she imposes a temporally-fixed meaning on a statutory term that the legislature intended to evolve over time? What clues in the statutory text might indicate that a particular term or provision should be given a dynamic rather than static meaning? For example, should common-law terms of art presumptively be given more dynamic meanings than other statutory terms that do not have common-law origins? (*Cf.* State Oil Co. v. Khan, 522 U.S. 3, 21 (1997) ("[T]he term 'restraint of trade', as used in § 1 [of the Sherman Act], also invokes the common law itself, and not merely the static content that the common law had assigned to the term in 1890." (internal quotation marks omitted)).

Third, the majority's approach also raises potential epistemological problems, because the "original reasonable reader's understanding" is a hypothetical construct developed by contemporary judges, not an actual historical person's stated understanding. But actual persons often disagree about meaning, even at the time of enactment. Recall the legal question in *King v. Burwell* in subsection III.C.2, *supra*: whether the phrase "an Exchange established by the State" as used in the Affordable Care Act included an Exchange established by the federal government (on behalf of a State). That question arose in the years immediately after the ACA's enactment, and it was heavily contested by both opponents and supporters of the law. Prior to the Supreme Court's decision in *King*, would it have made sense to say that a settled "ordinary" meaning of that statutory phrase existed? If a term or phrase's meaning was heavily contested even at the time of the statute's enactment, would it be reasonable to conclude that any future court's quest for an original ordinary meaning will necessarily be an exercise in frustration, or at least in subjectivity?

Finally, consider how, methodologically, a court is supposed to derive the original ordinary meaning of a statutory term or phrase. In *Oliveira*, the majority notes that the term "contract of employment" had no settled *legal* meaning, but that courts during the relevant period tended to include among "contract[s] of employment" any contracts that involved independent contractors. If there was no settled legal meaning, but *some* interpreters in exclusively *legal* settings attributed a particular meaning to the term, is that adequate evidence to establish a statutory term's *ordinary* meaning at that time? Note also that the contemporary interpreter must often weigh competing evidence of historical usage and meaning to decide which of two or more hypothetical historical readings is more reasonable. How much evidence of agreement about original ordinary meaning at the time of enactment must be found to conclude there *was* an established ordinary meaning? Are judges and lawyers—as opposed to historians or linguists— well suited to engage in such inquiries?

2.　APPLYING NEW STATUTES TO ONGOING CIRCUMSTANCES

Martin v. Hadix

Supreme Court of the United States, 1999.
527 U.S. 343, 119 S.Ct. 1998, 144 L.Ed.2d 347.

■ JUSTICE O'CONNOR delivered the opinion of the Court.

Section 803(d)(3) of the Prison Litigation Reform Act of 1995 (PLRA or Act), 110 Stat. 1321–66, 42 U.S.C. § 1997e(d)(3) (1994 ed., Supp. II), places limits on the fees that may be awarded to attorneys who litigate prisoner lawsuits. We are asked to decide how this section applies to cases that were pending when the PLRA became effective on April 26, 1996. We conclude that § 803(d)(3) limits attorney's fees with respect to postjudgment monitoring services performed after the PLRA's effective date but it does not so limit fees for postjudgment monitoring performed before the effective date.

I

The fee disputes before us arose out of two class action lawsuits challenging the conditions of confinement in the Michigan prison system. The first case, which we will call *Glover*, began in 1977 when a now-certified class of female prisoners filed suit under Rev. Stat. § 1979, 42 U.S.C. § 1983 (1994 ed., Supp. II), in the United States District Court for the Eastern District of Michigan. The Glover plaintiffs alleged that the defendant prison officials had violated their rights under the Equal Protection Clause of the Fourteenth Amendment by denying them access to vocational and educational opportunities that were available to male prisoners. . . . The second case at issue here, *Hadix*, began in 1980. At that time, male prisoners at the State Prison of Southern Michigan, Central Complex (SPSM-CC), filed suit under 42 U.S.C. § 1983 in the United States District Court for the Eastern District of Michigan claiming that the conditions of their confinement at SPSM-CC violated the First, Eighth, and Fourteenth Amendments to the Constitution. . . .

In 1985, the parties agreed to, and the District Court entered, an order providing that the plaintiffs were entitled to attorney's fees for postjudgment monitoring of the defendants' compliance with the court's remedial decrees. [Citation.] This order also established the system for awarding monitoring fees that was in place when the present dispute arose. Under this system, the plaintiffs submit their fee requests on a semiannual basis, and the defendants then have 28 days to submit any objections to the requested award. The District Court resolves any disputes. In an appeal from a subsequent dispute over the meaning of this order, the Court of Appeals for the Sixth Circuit affirmed that the plaintiffs were entitled to attorney's fees, at the prevailing market rate, for postjudgment monitoring. The prevailing market rate has been adjusted over the years, but it is currently set at $150 per hour. [Citation]. . . .

The fee landscape changed with the passage of the PLRA on April 26, 1996. The PLRA, as its name suggests, contains numerous provisions governing the course of prison litigation in the federal courts. It provides, for example, limits on the availability of certain types of relief in such suits, see 18 U.S.C. § 3626(a)(2) (1994 ed., Supp. III), and for the termination of prospective relief orders after a limited time, § 3626(b). The section of the PLRA at issue here, § 803(d)(3), places a cap on the size of attorney's fees that may be awarded in prison litigation suits:

"(d) Attorney's fees

"(1) In any action brought by a prisoner who is confined to any jail, prison, or other correctional facility, in which attorney's fees are authorized under [42 U.S.C. § 1988], such fees shall not be awarded, except to the extent [authorized here]. . . .

"(3) No award of attorney's fees in an action described in paragraph (1) shall be based on an hourly rate greater than 150 percent of the hourly rate established under [18 U.S.C. § 3006A (1994 ed. and Supp. III)], for payment of court-appointed counsel." § 803(d), 42 U.S.C. § 1997e(d) (1994 ed., Supp. II).

Court-appointed attorneys in the Eastern District of Michigan are compensated at a maximum rate of $75 per hour, and thus, under § 803(d)(3), the PLRA fee cap for attorneys working on prison litigation suits translates into a maximum hourly rate of $112.50.

Questions involving the PLRA first arose in both *Glover* and *Hadix* with respect to fee requests for postjudgment monitoring performed before the PLRA was enacted. In both cases, in early 1996, the plaintiffs submitted fee requests for work performed during the last half of 1995. These requests were still pending when the PLRA became effective on April 26, 1996. In both cases, the District Court concluded that the PLRA fee cap did not limit attorney's fees for services performed in these cases prior to the effective date of the Act. [Citation.] . . . Fee requests next were filed in both *Glover* and *Hadix* for services performed between January 1, 1996, and June 30, 1996, a time period encompassing work performed both before and after the effective date of the PLRA. As relevant to this case, the defendant state prison officials argued that these fee requests were subject to the fee cap found in § 803(d)(3) of the PLRA, and the District Court accepted this argument in part. In nearly identical orders issued in the two cases, the court reiterated its earlier conclusion that the PLRA does not limit fees for work performed before April 26, 1996, but concluded that the PLRA fee cap does limit fees for services performed after the effective date. . . .

In this Court, the *Hadix* and *Glover* plaintiffs are respondents, and the defendant prison officials from both cases are petitioners.

II

Petitioners contend that the PLRA applies to *Glover* and *Hadix,* cases that were pending when the PLRA was enacted. This fact pattern presents a recurring question in the law: When should a new federal statute be applied to pending cases? [Citation.] To answer this question, we ask first "whether Congress has expressly prescribed the statute's proper reach." Landgraf v. USI Film Products, 511 U.S. 244, 280 (1994). If there is no congressional directive on the temporal reach of a statute, we determine whether the application of the statute to the conduct at issue would result in a retroactive effect. Ibid. If so, then in keeping with our "traditional presumption" against retroactivity, we presume that the statute does not apply to that conduct. Ibid.

A

1

Congress has not expressly mandated the temporal reach of § 803(d)(3). Section 803(d)(1) provides that "in any action brought by a prisoner who is confined [to a correctional facility] . . . attorney's fees . . . shall not be awarded, except" as authorized by the statute. Section 803(d)(3) further provides that "no award of attorney's fees . . . shall be based on an hourly rate greater than 150 percent of the hourly rate established under [18 U.S.C. § 3006A], for payment of court-appointed counsel." Petitioners contend that this language—particularly the phrase "in *any* action *brought* by a prisoner who *is* confined," § 803(d)(1) (emphasis added)—clearly expresses a congressional intent that § 803(d) apply to pending cases. They argue that "any" is a broad, encompassing word, and that its use with "brought," a past-tense verb, demonstrates congressional intent to apply the fees limitations to all fee awards entered after the PLRA became effective, even when those awards were for services performed before the PLRA was enacted. They also contend that § 803(d)(3), by its own terms, applies to all "awards"—understood as the actual court order directing the payment of fees—entered after the effective date of the PLRA, regardless of when the work was performed.

The fundamental problem with all of petitioners' statutory arguments is that they stretch the language of § 803(d) to find congressional intent on the temporal scope of that section when we believe that § 803(d) is better read as setting substantive limits on the award of attorney's fees. Section 803(d)(1), for example, prohibits fee awards unless those fees were "directly and reasonably incurred" in the suit, and unless those fees are "proportionately related" to or "directly and reasonably incurred in enforcing" the relief ordered. 42 U.S.C. § 1997e(d)(1). Similarly, § 803(d)(3) sets substantive limits by prohibiting the award of fees based on hourly rates greater than a specified rate. In other words, these sections define the substantive availability of attorney's fees; they do not purport to define the temporal reach of these substantive limitations. This language falls short of demonstrating a "clear congressional intent" favoring retroactive application of these fees limitations. *Landgraf*, 511 U.S. at 280. It falls short, in other words, of the "unambiguous directive" or "express command" that the statute is to be applied retroactively. *Id.*, at 263, 280.

In any event, we note that "brought," as used in this section, is not a past-tense verb; rather, it is the participle in a participial phrase modifying the noun "action." And although the word "any" is broad, it stretches the imagination to suggest that Congress intended, through the use of this one word, to make the fee limitations applicable to all fee awards. Finally, we do not believe that the phrase "no award" in § 803(d)(3) demonstrates congressional intent to apply that section to all fee awards (i.e., fee payment orders) entered after the PLRA's effective date. Had Congress intended § 803(d)(3) to apply to all fee orders entered after the effective date, even when those awards compensate for work performed before the effective date, it could have used language more obviously targeted to addressing the temporal reach of that section. It could have stated, for example, that "No award entered after the effective date of this Act shall be based on an hourly rate greater than the ceiling rate."

The conclusion that § 803(d) does not clearly express congressional intent that it apply retroactively is strengthened by comparing § 803(d) to the language that we suggested in *Landgraf* might qualify as a clear statement that a statute was to apply retroactively: "The new provisions shall apply to all proceedings pending on or commenced after the date of enactment." *Id.*, at 260 (internal quotation marks omitted). This provision, unlike the language of the PLRA, unambiguously addresses the temporal reach of the statute. With no such analogous language making explicit reference to the statute's temporal reach, it cannot be said that Congress has "expressly prescribed" § 803(d)'s temporal reach. *Id.*, at 280. . . .

According to respondents, a comparison of §§ 802 and 803 of the PLRA leads to the conclusion that § 803(d) should only apply to cases filed after its enactment. The attorney's fees provisions are found in § 803 of the PLRA, and, as described above, this section contains no explicit directive that it should apply to pending cases. By contrast, § 802— addressing "appropriate remedies" in prison litigation—explicitly provides that it applies to pending cases: "[This section] shall apply with respect to all prospective relief whether such relief was originally granted or approved before, on, or after the date of the enactment of this title." § 802(b)(1), note following 18 U.S.C. § 3626 (1994 ed., Supp. III). . . .

Because §§ 802 and 803 address wholly distinct subject matters, [a] negative inference does not arise from the silence of § 803. Section 802 addresses "appropriate remedies" in prison litigation, prohibiting, for example, prospective relief unless it is "narrowly drawn" and is "the least intrusive means necessary to correct the violation." § 802(a),18 U.S.C. § 3626(a)(1)(A) (1994 ed., Supp. III). That section also creates new standards designed to encourage the prompt termination of prospective relief orders, providing, for example, for the "immediate termination of any prospective relief if the relief was approved or granted in the absence of a finding by the court that the relief is narrowly drawn, extends no further than necessary to correct the violation of the Federal right, and is the least intrusive means necessary to correct the violation of the Federal right." § 802(a), 18 U.S.C. § 3626(b)(2). Section 803(d), by contrast, does not address the propriety of various forms of relief and does not provide for the immediate termination of ongoing relief orders. Rather, it governs the award of attorney's fees. Thus, there is no reason to conclude that if Congress was concerned that § 802 apply to pending cases, it would "have been just as concerned" that § 803 apply to pending cases.

Finally, we note that respondents' reliance on the legislative history overstates the inferences that can be drawn from an ambiguous act of legislative drafting. Even if respondents are correct about the legislative history, the inference that respondents draw from this history is speculative. It rests on the assumption that the reason the fees provisions were moved was to move them away from the language applying § 802 to pending cases, when they may have been moved for a variety of other reasons. This weak inference provides a thin reed on which to rest the argument that the fees provisions, by negative implication, were intended to apply prospectively.

B

Because we conclude that Congress has not "expressly prescribed" the proper reach of § 803(d)(3), *Landgraf*, 511 U.S. at 280, we must determine whether application of this section in this case would have retroactive effects inconsistent with the usual rule that legislation is deemed to be prospective. The inquiry into whether a statute operates retroactively demands a common sense, functional judgment about "whether the new provision attaches new legal consequences to events completed before its enactment." *Id.* at 270. This judgment should be informed and guided by "familiar considerations of fair notice, reasonable reliance, and settled expectations." Ibid.

1

For postjudgment monitoring performed before the effective date of the PLRA, the PLRA's attorney's fees provisions, as construed by the respondents, would have a retroactive effect contrary to the usual assumption that congressional statutes are prospective in operation. . . . The PLRA, as applied to work performed before its effective date, would alter the fee arrangement post hoc by reducing the rate of compensation. To give effect to the PLRA's fees limitations, after the fact, would "attach new legal consequences" to completed conduct. *Landgraf*, supra, at 270.

. . . While it may be possible to generalize about types of rules that ordinarily will not raise retroactivity concerns, see, e.g., *id.* at 273–275, these generalizations do not end the inquiry. For example, in *Landgraf*, we acknowledged that procedural rules may often be applied to pending suits with no retroactivity problems, *id.* at 275, but we also cautioned that "the mere fact that a new rule is procedural does not mean that it applies to every pending case," *id.* at 275, n. 29. We took pains to dispel the "suggestion that concerns about retroactivity have no application to procedural rules." Ibid. [Citation.] When determining whether a new statute operates retroactively, it is not enough to attach a label (e.g., "procedural," "collateral") to the statute; we must ask whether the statute operates retroactively.

Moreover, petitioners' reliance on our decision in Bradley v. School Bd. of Richmond, 416 U.S. 696, 40 L. Ed. 2d 476, 94 S.Ct. 2006 (1974), to support their argument that attorney's fees provisions can be applied retroactively is misplaced. In *Bradley*, the District Court had awarded attorney's fees, based on general equitable principles, to a group of parents who had prevailed in their suit seeking the desegregation of the Richmond schools. While the case was pending on appeal, Congress passed a statute specifically authorizing the award of attorney's fees for prevailing parties in school desegregation cases. The Court of Appeals held that the new statute could not authorize fee awards for work performed before the effective date of the new law, but we reversed, holding that the fee award in that case was proper. Because attorney's fees were available, albeit under different principles, before passage of the statute, and because the District Court had in fact already awarded fees invoking these different principles, there was no manifest injustice in allowing the fee statute to apply in that case. *Id.*, at 720–721. We held that the award of statutory attorney's fees did not upset any reasonable expectations of the parties. [Citation.] In this case, by contrast, from the beginning of these suits, the parties have proceeded on the assumption that 42 U.S.C. § 1988 would govern. The PLRA was not passed until well after respondents had been declared prevailing parties and thus entitled to attorney's fees. To impose the new standards now, for work performed before the PLRA became effective, would upset the reasonable expectations of the parties.

2

With respect to postjudgment monitoring performed after the effective date of the PLRA, by contrast, there is no retroactivity problem. On April 26, 1996, through the PLRA, the plaintiffs' attorneys were on notice that their hourly rate had been adjusted. From that point forward, they would be paid at a rate consistent with the dictates of the law. After April 26, 1996, any expectation of compensation at the pre-PLRA rates was unreasonable. There is no manifest injustice in telling an attorney performing postjudgment monitoring services that, going forward, she will earn a lower hourly rate than she had earned in the past. If the attorney does not wish to perform services at this new, lower, pay rate, she can choose not to work. In other words, as applied to work performed after the effective date of the PLRA, the PLRA has future effect on future work; this does not raise retroactivity concerns.

Respondents contend that the PLRA has retroactive effect in this context because it attaches new legal consequences (a lower pay rate) to conduct completed before enactment. The pre-enactment conduct that respondents contend is affected is the attorney's initial decision to file suit on behalf of the prisoner clients. . . . [R]espondents' argument assumes that once an attorney files suit, she must continue working on that case until the decree is terminated. Respondents provide no support for this assumption, however. They allude to ethical constraints on an attorney's ability to withdraw from a case midstream, see Brief for Respondents 29 ("And finally, it is at that time that plaintiffs' counsel commit themselves ethically to continued representation of their clients to ensure that the Constitution is honored, a course of conduct that cannot lightly be altered"), but they do not seriously contend that the attorneys here were prohibited from withdrawing from the case during the postjudgment monitoring stage. It cannot be said that the PLRA changes the legal consequences of the attorneys' pre-PLRA decision to file the case.

C

In sum, we conclude that the PLRA contains no express command about its temporal scope. Because we find that the PLRA, if applied to postjudgment monitoring services performed before the effective date of the Act, would have a retroactive effect inconsistent with our assumption that statutes are prospective, in the absence of an express command by Congress to apply the Act retroactively, we decline to do so. *Landgraf*, 511 U.S. at 280. With respect to postjudgment monitoring performed after the effective date, by contrast, there is no retroactive effect, and the PLRA fees cap applies to such work. Accordingly, the judgment of the Court of Appeals for the Sixth Circuit is affirmed in part and reversed in part.

It is so ordered.

■ JUSTICE SCALIA, concurring in part and concurring in the judgment. . . .

I agree with the Court that the [PLRA's] intended temporal application is not set forth in the text of the statute, and that the outcome must therefore be governed by our interpretive principle that, in absence of contrary indication, a statute will not be construed to have retroactive application, see *Landgraf*. But that leaves open the key question: retroactive in reference to what? The various options in the present case include (1) the alleged violation upon which the fee-imposing suit is based (applying the new fee rule to any case involving an alleged violation that occurred before the PLRA became effective would be giving it "retroactive application"); (2) the lawyer's undertaking to prosecute the suit for which attorney's fees were provided (applying the new fee rule to any case in which the lawyer was retained before the PLRA became effective would be giving it "retroactive application"); (3) the filing of the suit in which the fees are imposed (applying the new fee rule to any suit brought before the PLRA became effective would be giving it "retroactive application"); (4) the doing of the legal work for which the fees are payable (applying the new fee rule to any work done before the PLRA became effective would be giving it "retroactive application"); and (5) the actual award of fees in a prisoner case (applying the new fee rule to an award rendered before the PLRA became effective would be giving it "retroactive application").

My disagreement with the Court's approach is that, in deciding which of the above five reference points for the retroactivity determination ought to be selected, it seems to me not much help to ask which of them would frustrate expectations. In varying degrees, they all would. As I explained in my concurrence in *Landgraf,* 511 U.S. at 286 (opinion concurring in judgments), I think the decision of which reference point (which "retroactivity event") to select should turn upon which activity the statute was intended to regulate. If it was intended to affect primary conduct, No. 1 should govern; if it was intended to induce lawyers to undertake representation, No. 2—and so forth.

In my view, the most precisely defined purpose of the provision at issue here was to reduce the previously established incentive for lawyers to work on prisoners' civil rights cases. If the PLRA is viewed in isolation, of course, its purpose could be regarded as being simply to prevent a judicial award of fees in excess of the referenced amount—in which case the relevant retroactivity event would be the award. In reality, however, the PLRA simply revises the fees provided for by § 1988, and it seems to me that the underlying purpose of that provision must govern its amendment as well—which purpose was to provide an appropriate incentive for lawyers to work on (among other civil rights cases) prisoner suits. That being so, the relevant retroactivity event is the doing of the work for which the incentive was offered. All work rendered in reliance upon the fee assurance contained in the former § 1988 will be reimbursed at those rates; all work rendered after the revised fee assurance of the PLRA became effective will be limited to the new rates. The District Court's announcement that it would permit future work to be billed at a higher rate operated in futuro; it sought to regulate future conduct rather than adjudicate past. It was therefore no less subject to revision by statute than is an injunction. Pennsylvania v. Wheeling & Belmont Bridge Co., 59 U.S. 421, 18 How. 421, 436 (1856).

For these reasons, I concur in the judgment of the Court and join all but Part II-B of its opinion.

■ JUSTICE GINSBURG, with whom JUSTICE STEVENS joins, concurring in part and dissenting in part.

I agree with the Court's determination that § 803(d) of the Prison Litigation Reform Act of 1995, (PLRA or Act), does not "limit fees for postjudgment monitoring performed before the [Act's] effective date," and with much of the reasoning set out in Parts I, II-A-1, and II-B-1 of the Court's opinion. I disagree, however, with the holding that § 803(d) "limits attorney's fees with respect to postjudgment monitoring services performed after . . . the effective date." Ibid. I do not find in the PLRA's text or history a satisfactory basis for concluding that Congress meant to order a midstream change, placing cases commenced before the PLRA became law under the new regime. I would therefore affirm in full the judgment of the Court of Appeals for the Sixth Circuit, which held § 803(d) inapplicable to cases brought to court prior to the enactment of the PLRA. . . .

II

. . . As the Court recognizes . . . § 803(d)'s "any action brought" language refers to the provision's substantive scope, not its temporal reach; "any" appears in the text only in proximity to provisions identifying the law's substantive dimensions. Had Congress intended that § 803(d) apply retroactively, it might easily have specified, as the Court suggests, that all post-enactment awards shall be subject to the limitation, or prescribed that the provision "shall apply in all proceedings pending on or commenced after the date of enactment of this Act." Congress instead left unaddressed § 803(d)'s temporal reach.

Comparison of § 803(d)'s text with that of a neighboring provision, § 802(b)(1) of the PLRA, is instructive for the retroactivity question we face. Section 802(b)(1), which governs "appropriate remedies" in prison litigation, applies expressly to "all prospective relief whether such relief was originally granted or approved before, on, or after the date of the enactment of this title." 110 Stat. 1321–70, note following 18 U.S.C. § 3626. "Congress [thus] saw fit to tell us which part of the Act was to be retroactively applied," i.e., § 802. Jensen v. Clarke, 94 F.3d 1191, 1203 (C.A.8 1996). While I agree with the Court that the negative implication created by these two provisions is not dispositive, Congress' silence nevertheless suggests that § 803(d) has no carryback thrust.

Absent an express statutory command respecting retroactivity, *Landgraf* teaches, the attorney's fees provision should not be applied to pending cases if doing so would "have retroactive effect." 511 U.S. at 280. As the Court recognizes, application of § 803(d) to work performed before the PLRA's effective date would be impermissibly retroactive. Instead of the court-approved market-based fee that attorneys anticipated for work performed under the old regime, counsel would be limited to the new statutory rate. We long ago recognized the injustice of interpreting a statute to reduce the level of compensation for work already performed. [Citation.]

III

In my view, § 803(d) is most soundly read to cover all and only representations undertaken after the PLRA's effective date. Application of § 803(d) to representations commenced before the PLRA became law would "attach new legal consequences to [an] event completed before [the statute's] enactment"; hence the application would be retroactive under *Landgraf*, 511 U.S. at 270. The critical event effected before the PLRA's effective date is the lawyer's undertaking to prosecute the client's civil rights claim. Applying § 803(d) to pending matters significantly alters the consequences of the representation on which the lawyer has embarked. Notably, attorneys engaged before passage of the PLRA have little leeway to alter their conduct in response to the new legal regime; an attorney who initiated a prisoner's rights suit before April 26, 1996 remains subject to a professional obligation to see the litigation through to final disposition. See American Bar Association Model Rules of Professional Conduct, Rule 1.3, and Comment [3] (1999) ("[A] lawyer should carry through to conclusion all matters undertaken for a client."). Counsel's actions before and after that date are thus "inextricably part of a course of conduct initiated prior to the law." Inmates of D. C. Jail v. Jackson, 332 U.S. App. D.C. 451, 158 F.3d 1357, 1362 (C.A.D.C.1998) (Wald, J., dissenting).

While the injustice in applying the fee limitations to pending actions may be more readily apparent regarding work performed before the PLRA's effective date, application of the statute to work performed thereafter in pending cases also frustrates reasonable reliance on prior law and court-approved market rates. Consider, for example, two attorneys who filed similar prison reform lawsuits at the same time, pre-PLRA. Both attorneys initiated their lawsuits in the expectation that, if they prevailed, they would earn the market rate anticipated by pre-PLRA law. In one case, the lawsuit progressed swiftly, and labor-intensive pretrial discovery was completed before April 26, 1996. In the other, the suit lagged through no fault of plaintiff's counsel, pending the court's disposition of threshold motions, and the attorney was unable to pursue discovery until after April 26, 1996. Both attorneys have prosecuted their claims with due diligence; both were obliged, having accepted the representations, to perform the work for which they seek compensation. There is scarcely greater injustice in denying pre-PLRA compensation for pretrial discovery in the one case than the other. Nor is there any reason to think that Congress intended these similarly situated attorneys to be treated differently.

The Court avoids a conclusion of retroactivity by dismissing as an unsupported assumption the attorneys' assertion of an obligation to continue their representations through to final disposition. It seems to me, however, that the assertion has secure support.

Like the ABA's Model Rules, the Michigan Rules of Professional Conduct, which apply to counsel in both *Hadix* and *Glover*, see Rule

83.20(j) (1999), provide that absent good cause for terminating a representation, "a lawyer should carry through to conclusion all matters undertaken for a client." Mich. Rules of Prof. Conduct, Rule 1.3 Comment (1999) It is true that withdrawal may be permitted where "the representation will result in an unreasonable financial burden on the lawyer," Rule 1.16(b)(5), but explanatory comments suggest that this exception is designed for situations in which "the client refuses to abide by the terms of an agreement relating to the representation, such as an agreement concerning fees," Rule 1.16 Comment Consistent with the Michigan Rules, counsel for petitioners affirmed at oral argument their ethical obligation to continue these representations to a natural conclusion. See Tr. of Oral Arg. 43 ("[Continuing the representation] does involve ethical concerns certainly, especially in these circumstances."). There is no reason to think counsel ethically could have abandoned these representations in response to the PLRA fee limitation, nor any basis to believe the trial court would have permitted counsel to withdraw. See Rule 1.16(c) ("When ordered to do so by a tribunal, a lawyer shall continue representation."). As I see it, the attorneys' pre-PLRA pursuit of the civil rights claims thus created an obligation, enduring post-PLRA, to continue to provide effective representation.

Accordingly, I conclude that the Sixth Circuit soundly resisted the "sophisticated construction," 143 F.3d at 252, that would split apart, for fee award purposes, a constant course of representation. "The triggering event for retroactivity purposes," I am persuaded, "is when the lawyer undertakes to litigate the civil rights action on behalf of the client." *Inmates of D. C. Jail*, 158 F.3d at 1362 (Wald, J. dissenting).

Landgraf's lesson is that Congress must speak clearly when it wants new rules to govern pending cases. Because § 803(d) contains no clear statement on its temporal reach, and because the provision would operate retroactively as applied to lawsuits pending on the Act's effective date, I would hold that the fee limitation applies only to cases commenced after April 26, 1996.

NOTE & QUESTION

1.   In *Landgraf v. USI Film Prods.*, 511 U.S. 244 (1994), referenced in all opinions in *Martin v. Hadix*, the Supreme Court clarified its caselaw on the retroactivity of statutes. *Landgraf* required the Court to determine whether the 1991 amendments to Title VII of the 1964 Civil Rights Act, which instituted a damages remedy for prohibited workplace discrimination (in that case, sexual harassment), applied to claims arising before the amendment took effect. When Ms. Landgraf suffered the alleged harassment, she would have had no monetary remedy; her claim was still pending when Congress changed the law. The Court announced a presumption against application of a new law to past conduct if a "genuinely 'retroactive'" effect would result, "i.e. whether [the new statute] would impair rights a party possessed when he acted, increase a party's liability for

past conduct, or impose new duties with respect to transactions already completed." *Martin v. Hadix* illustrates a subsequent endeavor to apply the Court's criteria to a case pending when Congress changed the law (in that instance, to restrict rather than to expand a civil rights law).

2. In *Martin v. Hadix*, the history of the case and of the legislation suggests several "retroactivity events." What are they, and at what point could the legislation, if effective as of that event, be said to have "genuinely retroactive" effect? What activity is the statute endeavoring to address and change? Which event implicates fairness concerns (such as reliance)?

Vartelas v. Holder

Supreme Court of the United States, 2012.
566 U.S. 257, 132 S.Ct. 1479, 182 L.Ed.2d 473.

■ JUSTICE GINSBURG delivered the opinion of the Court.

Panagis Vartelas, a native of Greece, became a lawful permanent resident of the United States in 1989. He pleaded guilty to a felony (conspiring to make a counterfeit security) in 1994, and served a prison sentence of four months for that offense. Vartelas traveled to Greece in 2003 to visit his parents. On his return to the United States a week later, he was treated as an inadmissible alien and placed in removal proceedings. Under the law governing at the time of Vartelas' plea, an alien in his situation could travel abroad for brief periods without jeopardizing his resident alien status. See 8 U.S.C. § 1101(a)(13) (1988 ed.), as construed in *Rosenberg* v. *Fleuti*, 374 U.S. 449 (1963).

In 1996, Congress enacted the Illegal Immigration Reform and Immigrant Responsibility Act (IIRIRA), 110 Stat. 3009–546. That Act effectively precluded foreign travel by lawful permanent residents who had a conviction like Vartelas'. Under IIRIRA, such aliens, on return from a sojourn abroad, however brief, may be permanently removed from the United States. See 8 U.S.C. §§ 1101(a)(13)(C)(v); § 1182(a)(2).

This case presents a question of retroactivity not addressed by Congress: As to a lawful permanent resident convicted of a crime before the effective date of IIRIRA, which regime governs, the one in force at the time of the conviction, or IIRIRA? If the former, Vartelas' brief trip abroad would not disturb his lawful permanent resident status. If the latter, he may be denied reentry. We conclude that the relevant provision of IIRIRA, § 1101(a)(13)(C)(v), attached a new disability (denial of reentry) in respect to past events (Vartelas' pre-IIRIRA offense, plea, and conviction). Guided by the deeply rooted presumption against retroactive legislation, we hold that § 1101(a)(13)(C)(v) does not apply to Vartelas' conviction. The impact of Vartelas' brief travel abroad on his permanent resident status is therefore determined not by IIRIRA, but by the legal regime in force at the time of his conviction.

I

A

Before IIRIRA's passage, United States immigration law established "two types of proceedings in which aliens can be denied the hospitality of the United States: deportation hearings and exclusion hearings." *Landon* v. *Plasencia*, 459 U.S. 21, 25, 103 S.Ct. 321, 74 L. Ed. 2d 21 (1982). Exclusion hearings were held for certain aliens seeking entry to the United States, and deportation hearings were held for certain aliens who had already entered this country. See *ibid.*

Under this regime, "entry" into the United States was defined as "any coming of an alien into the United States, from a foreign port or place." 8 U.S.C. § 1101(a)(13) (1988 ed.). The statute, however, provided an exception for lawful permanent residents; aliens lawfully residing here were not regarded as making an "entry" if their "departure to a foreign port or place . . . was not intended or reasonably to be expected by [them] or [their] presence in a foreign port or place . . . was not voluntary." *Ibid.* Interpreting this cryptic provision, we held in *Fleuti*, 374 U.S., at 461–462, that Congress did not intend to exclude aliens long resident in the United States upon their return from "innocent, casual, and brief excursion[s] . . . outside this country's borders." Instead, the Court determined, Congress meant to rank a once-permanent resident as a new entrant only when the foreign excursion "meaningfully interrupt[ed] . . . the alien's [U.S.] residence." *Id.*, at 462. Absent such "disrupti[on]" of the alien's residency, the alien would not be "subject . . . to the consequences of an 'entry' into the country on his return." *Ibid.*

In IIRIRA, Congress abolished the distinction between exclusion and deportation procedures and created a uniform proceeding known as "removal." See 8 U.S.C. §§ 1229, 1229a; *Judulang* v. *Holder*, 565 U.S. ___, ___, 132 S.Ct. 476 (2011). Congress made "admission" the key word, and defined admission to mean "the lawful entry of the alien into the United States after inspection and authorization by an immigration officer." § 1101(a)(13)(A). This alteration, the Board of Immigration Appeals (BIA) determined, superseded *Fleuti*. See *In re Collado-Munoz*, 21 I. & N. Dec. 1061, 1065–1066 (1998) (en banc). Thus, lawful permanent residents returning post-IIRIRA, like Vartelas, may be required to " 'see[k] an admission' into the United States, without regard to whether the alien's departure from the United States might previously have been ranked as 'brief, casual, and innocent' under the Fleuti doctrine." *Id.*, at 1066.

An alien seeking "admission" to the United States is subject to various requirements, see, *e.g.*, § 1181(a), and cannot gain entry if she is deemed "inadmissible" on any of the numerous grounds set out in the immigration statutes, see § 1182. Under IIRIRA, lawful permanent residents are regarded as seeking admission into the United States if they fall into any of six enumerated categories. § 1101(a)(13)(C). Relevant here, the fifth of these categories covers aliens who "ha[ve] committed an offense identified in section 1182(a)(2) of this title." § 1101(a)(13)(C)(v). Offenses in this category include "a crime involving moral turpitude (other than a purely political offense) or an attempt or conspiracy to commit such a crime." § 1182(a)(2)(A)(i).

In sum, before IIRIRA, lawful permanent residents who had committed a crime of moral turpitude could, under the *Fleuti* doctrine, return from brief trips abroad without applying for admission to the United States. Under IIRIRA, such residents are subject to admission procedures, and, potentially, to removal from the United States on grounds of inadmissibility.

B

Panagis Vartelas, born and raised in Greece, has resided in the United States for over 30 years. Originally admitted on a student visa issued in 1979, Vartelas became a lawful permanent resident in 1989. He currently lives in the New York area and works as a sales manager for a roofing company.

In 1992, Vartelas opened an auto body shop in Queens, New York. One of his business partners used the shop's photocopier to make counterfeit travelers' checks. Vartelas helped his partner perforate the sheets into individual checks, but Vartelas did not sell the checks or receive any money from the venture. In 1994, he pleaded guilty to conspiracy to make or possess counterfeit securities, in violation of 18 U.S.C. § 371. He was sentenced to four months' incarceration, followed by two years' supervised release.

Vartelas regularly traveled to Greece to visit his aging parents in the years after his 1994 conviction; even after the passage of IIRIRA in 1996, his return to the United States from these visits remained uneventful. In January 2003, however, when Vartelas returned from a week-long trip to Greece, an immigration officer classified him as an alien seeking "admission." The officer based this classification on Vartelas' 1994 conviction. See *United States ex rel. Volpe* v. *Smith*, 289 U.S. 422, 423, 53 S.Ct. 665, 77 L. Ed. 1298 (1933) (counterfeiting ranks as a crime of moral turpitude).

At Vartelas' removal proceedings, his initial attorney conceded removability, and requested discretionary relief from removal under the former § 212(c) of the Immigration and Nationality Act (INA). See 8 U.S.C. § 1182(c) (1994 ed.) (repealed 1996). This attorney twice failed to appear for hearings and once failed to submit a requested brief. Vartelas engaged a new attorney, who continued to concede removability and to request discretionary relief. The Immigration Judge denied the request for relief, and ordered Vartelas removed to Greece. The BIA affirmed the Immigration Judge's decision.

In July 2008, Vartelas filed with the BIA a timely motion to reopen the removal proceedings, alleging that his previous attorneys were ineffective for, among other lapses, conceding his removability. He sought to withdraw the concession of removability on the ground that IIRIRA's new "admission" provision, codified at § 1101(a)(13), did not reach back to deprive him of lawful resident status based on his pre-IIRIRA conviction. The BIA denied the motion, declaring that Vartelas had not been prejudiced by his lawyers' performance, for no legal authority prevented the application of IIRIRA to Vartelas' pre-IIRIRA conduct.

The U.S. Court of Appeals for the Second Circuit affirmed the BIA's decision, agreeing that Vartelas had failed to show he was prejudiced by his attorneys' allegedly ineffective performance. Rejecting Vartelas' argument that IIRIRA operated prospectively and therefore did not govern his case, the Second Circuit reasoned that he had not relied on the prior legal regime at the time he committed the disqualifying crime. See 620 F.3d 108, 118–120 (2010).

In so ruling, the Second Circuit created a split with two other Circuits. The Fourth and Ninth Circuits have held that the new § 1101(a)(13) may not be applied to lawful permanent residents who committed crimes listed in § 1182 (among them, crimes of moral turpitude) prior to IIRIRA's enactment. [Citation.] We granted certiorari to resolve the conflict among the Circuits.

II

As earlier explained, pre-IIRIRA, a resident alien who once committed a crime of moral turpitude could travel abroad for short durations without jeopardizing his status as a lawful permanent resident. Under IIRIRA, on return from foreign travel, such an alien is treated as a new arrival to our shores, and may be removed from the United States. Vartelas does not question Congress' authority to restrict reentry in this manner. Nor does he contend that Congress could not do so retroactively. Instead, he invokes the principle against retroactive legislation, under which courts read laws as prospective in application unless Congress has unambiguously instructed retroactivity. See *Landgraf* v. *USI Film Products*, 511 U.S. 244 (1994).

The presumption against retroactive legislation, the Court recalled in *Landgraf*, "embodies a legal doctrine centuries older than our Republic." *Id.*, at 265. Several provisions of the Constitution, the Court noted, embrace the doctrine, among them, the *Ex Post Facto* Clause, the Contract Clause, and the Fifth Amendment's Due Process Clause. *Id.*, at 266. Numerous decisions of this Court repeat the classic formulation Justice Story penned for determining when retrospective application of a law would collide with the doctrine. It would do so, Story stated, when such application would "tak[e] away or impai[r] vested rights acquired under existing laws, or creat[e] a new obligation, impos[e] a new duty, or attac[h] a new disability, in respect to transactions or considerations already past." [Citation.]

Vartelas urges that applying IIRIRA to him, rather than the law that existed at the time of his conviction, would attach a "new disability," effectively a ban on travel outside the United States, "in respect to [events] . . . already past," *i.e.*, his offense, guilty plea, conviction, and punishment, all occurring prior to the passage of IIRIRA. In evaluating Vartelas' argument, we note first a matter not disputed by the Government: Congress did not expressly prescribe the temporal reach of the IIRIRA provision in question, 8 U.S.C. § 1101(a)(13). . . .

Vartelas presents a firm case for application of the antiretroactivity principle. Neither his sentence, nor the immigration law in effect when he was convicted and sentenced, blocked him from occasional visits to his parents in Greece. Current § 1101(a)(13)(C)(v), if applied to him, would thus attach "a new disability" to conduct over and done well before the provision's enactment.

Beyond genuine doubt, we note, the restraint § 1101(a)(13)(C)(v) places on lawful permanent residents like Vartelas ranks as a "new disability." Once able to journey abroad to fulfill religious obligations, attend funerals and weddings of family members, tend to vital financial interests, or respond to family emergencies, permanent residents situated as Vartelas is now face potential banishment. We have several times recognized the severity of that sanction. [Citation.]

It is no answer to say, as the Government suggests, that Vartelas could have avoided any adverse consequences if he simply stayed at home in the United States, his residence for 24 years prior to his 2003 visit to his parents in Greece. . . . Loss of the ability to travel abroad is itself a harsh penalty, made all the more devastating if it means enduring separation from close family members living abroad. See Brief for Asian American Justice Center et al. as *Amici Curiae* 16–23 (describing illustrative cases). We have rejected arguments for retroactivity in similar cases, and in cases in which the loss at stake was less momentous.

In *Chew Heong* v. *United States*, 112 U.S. 536 (1884), a pathmarking decision, the Court confronted the "Chinese Restriction Act," which barred Chinese laborers from reentering the United States without a certificate issued on their departure. The Court held the reentry bar inapplicable to aliens who had left the country prior to the Act's passage and tried to return afterward without a certificate. The Act's text, the Court observed, was not "so clear and positive as to leave no room to doubt [retroactive application] was the intention of the legislature." *Id.*, at 559.

In *Landgraf*, the question was whether an amendment to Title VII's ban on employment discrimination authorizing compensatory and punitive damages applied to pre-enactment conduct. The Court held it did not. No doubt the complaint against the employer charged discrimination that violated the Act at the time it occurred. But compensatory and punitive damages were not then available remedies. The later provision for such damages, the Court determined, operated prospectively only, and did not apply to employers whose discriminatory conduct occurred prior to the amendment. See 511 U.S., at 280–286. And in *Hughes Aircraft* [v. *United States ex rel. Schumer*, 520 U.S. 939 (1997)], the Court held that a provision removing an affirmative defense to *qui tam* suits* did not apply to pre-enactment fraud. As in *Landgraf*, the provision attached "a new disability" to past wrongful conduct and therefore could not apply retrospectively unless Congress clearly manifested such an intention. *Hughes Aircraft*, 520 U.S., at 946–950.

Most recently, in [*INS* v.] *St. Cyr*, the Court took up the case of an alien who had entered a plea to a deportable offense. At the time of the plea, the alien was eligible for discretionary relief from deportation. IIRIRA, enacted after entry of the plea, removed that eligibility. The Court held that the IIRIRA provision in point could not be applied to the alien, for it attached a "new disability" to the guilty plea and Congress had not instructed such a result. 533 U.S. 289, 321–23 (2001).

III

The Government, echoed in part by the dissent, argues that no retroactive effect is involved in this case, for the Legislature has not attached any disability to past conduct. Rather, it has made the relevant event the alien's post-IIRIRA act of returning to the United States. We find this argument disingenuous. Vartelas' return to the United States occasioned his treatment as a new entrant, but the reason for the "new disability" imposed on him was not his lawful foreign travel. It was, indeed, his conviction, pre-IIRIRA, of an offense qualifying as one of moral turpitude. That past misconduct, in other words, not present travel, is the wrongful activity Congress targeted in § 1101(a)(13)(C)(v).

The Government observes that lower courts have upheld Racketeer Influenced and Corrupt Organizations Act prosecutions that encompassed pre-enactment conduct. [Citation.] But those prosecutions depended on criminal activity, *i.e.*, an act of racketeering occurring *after* the provision's effective date. Section 1101(a)(13)(C)(v), in contrast, does not require any showing of criminal conduct postdating IIRIRA's enactment.

Fernandez-Vargas v. *Gonzales*, 548 U.S. 30 (2006), featured by the Government and the dissent, is similarly inapposite. That case involved 8 U.S.C. § 1231(a)(5), an IIRIRA addition, which provides that an alien who reenters the United States after having been removed can be removed again under the same removal order. We held that the provision could be applied to an alien who reentered illegally before IIRIRA's enactment. Explaining the Court's decision, we said: "[T]he conduct of remaining in the country . . . is the predicate action; the statute applies to stop *an indefinitely continuing violation*. . . . It is therefore the alien's choice *to continue his illegal presence* . . . *after* the effective date of the new la[w] that subjects him to the new . . . legal regime, not a past act

---

* Editors' Note: a *qui tam* action is a statutorily-authorized civil suit brought by a private citizen (often a "whistleblower") seeking a penalty to be shared with the government against a person or entity who has violated a government regulation or contract.

that he is helpless to undo." 548 U.S., at 44 (emphasis added). Vartelas, we have several times stressed, engaged in no criminal activity after IIRIRA's passage. He simply took a brief trip to Greece, anticipating a return without incident as in past visits to his parents. No "indefinitely continuing" crime occurred; instead, Vartelas was apprehended because of a pre-IIRIRA crime he was "helpless to undo." *Ibid.*

The Government further refers to lower court decisions in cases involving 18 U.S.C. § 922(g), which prohibits the possession of firearms by convicted felons. [Citation.] "[L]ongstanding prohibitions on the possession of firearms by felons," *District of Columbia* v. *Heller*, 554 U.S. 570 (2008), however, target a present danger, *i.e.*, the danger posed by felons who bear arms. See, *e.g.*, *United States* v. *Pfeifer*, 371 F. 3d, 430, at 436 (CA8 2004) (hazardous conduct that statute targets "occurred after enactment of the statute"); Omnibus Crime Control and Safe Streets Act of 1968, § 1201, 82 Stat. 236 (noting hazards involved when felons possess firearms).[7]

Nor do recidivism sentencing enhancements support the Government's position. Enhanced punishment imposed for the later offense " 'is not to be viewed as . . . [an] additional penalty for the earlier crimes,' but instead, as a 'stiffened penalty for the latest crime, which is considered to be an aggravated offense because [it is] a repetitive one.' " *Witte* v. *United States*, 515 U.S. 389, 400 (1995) (quoting *Gryger* v. *Burke*, 334 U.S. 728, 732 (1948)). In Vartelas' case, however, there is no "aggravated . . . repetitive" offense. There is, in contrast, no post-IIRIRA criminal offense at all. Vartelas' travel abroad and return are "innocent" acts, see *Fleuti*, 374 U.S., at 462, burdened only because of his pre-IIRIRA offense.

In sum, Vartelas' brief trip abroad post-IIRIRA involved no criminal infraction. IIRIRA disabled him from leaving the United States and returning as a lawful permanent resident. That new disability rested not on any continuing criminal activity, but on a single crime committed years before IIRIRA's enactment. The antiretroactivity principle

---

[7] The dissent, notes two statutes of the same genre: laws prohibiting persons convicted of a sex crime against a victim under 16 years of age from working in jobs involving frequent contact with minors, and laws prohibiting a person "who has been adjudicated as a mental defective or who has been committed to a mental institution" from possessing guns, 18 U.S.C. § 922(g)(4). The dissent is correct that these statutes do not operate retroactively. Rather, they address dangers that arise postenactment: sex offenders with a history of child molestation working in close proximity to children, and mentally unstable persons purchasing guns. The act of flying to Greece, in contrast, does not render a lawful permanent resident like Vartelas hazardous. Nor is it plausible that Congress' solution to the problem of dangerous lawful permanent residents would be to pass a law that would deter such persons from ever leaving the United States.

As for student loans, it is unlikely that the provision noted by the dissent, 20 U.S.C. § 1091(r), would raise retroactivity questions in the first place. The statute has a prospective thrust. It concerns "[s]uspension of eligibility" when a student receiving a college loan commits a drug crime. The suspension runs "from the date of th[e] conviction" for specified periods, *e.g.*, two years for a second offense of possession. Moreover, eligibility may be restored before the period of ineligibility ends if the student establishes, under prescribed criteria, his rehabilitation.

instructs against application of the new proscription to render Vartelas a first-time arrival at the country's gateway.

IV

The Second Circuit homed in on the words "committed an offense" in § 1101(a)(13)(C)(v) in determining that the change IIRIRA wrought had no retroactive effect. 620 F. 3d, at 119–121. It matters not that Vartelas may have relied on the prospect of continuing visits to Greece in deciding to plead guilty, the court reasoned. "[I]t would border on the absurd," the court observed, "to suggest that Vartelas committed his counterfeiting crime in reliance on the immigration laws." *Id.*, at 120. This reasoning is doubly flawed.

As the Government acknowledges, "th[is] Court has not required a party challenging the application of a statute to show [he relied on prior law] in structuring his conduct." In *Landgraf*, for example, the issue was the retroactivity of compensatory and punitive damages as remedies for employment discrimination. "[C]oncerns of . . . upsetting expectations are attenuated in the case of intentional employment discrimination," the Court noted, for such discrimination "has been unlawful for more than a generation." 511 U.S., at 282, n. 35. But "[e]ven when the conduct in question is morally reprehensible or illegal," the Court added, "a degree of unfairness is inherent whenever the law imposes additional burdens based on conduct that occurred in the past." *Id.*, at 283, n. 35. . . .

The operative presumption, after all, is that Congress intends its laws to govern prospectively only. "It is a strange 'presumption," the Third Circuit commented, "that arises only on . . . a showing [of] actual reliance." *Ponnapula* v. *Ashcroft*, 373 F.3d 480, 491 (2004). The essential inquiry, as stated in *Landgraf*, 511 U.S., at 269–270, is "whether the new provision attaches new legal consequences to events completed before its enactment." That is just what occurred here.

In any event, Vartelas likely relied on then-existing immigration law. While the presumption against retroactive application of statutes does not require a showing of detrimental reliance, see *Olatunji*, 387 F. 3d, at 389–395, reasonable reliance has been noted among the "familiar considerations" animating the presumption, see *Landgraf*, 511 U.S., at 270 (presumption reflects "familiar considerations of fair notice, reasonable reliance, and settled expectations"). Although not a necessary predicate for invoking the antiretroactivity principle, the likelihood of reliance on prior law strengthens the case for reading a newly enacted law prospectively. See *Olatunji*, 387 F. 3d, at 393 (discussing *St. Cyr*).

St. Cyr is illustrative. That case involved a lawful permanent resident who pleaded guilty to a criminal charge that made him deportable. Under the immigration law in effect when he was convicted, he would have been eligible to apply for a waiver of deportation. But his removal proceeding was commenced after Congress, in IIRIRA, withdrew that dispensation. Disallowance of discretionary waivers, the Court recognized, "attache[d] a new disability, in respect to transactions or considerations already past." 533 U.S., at 321 (internal quotation marks omitted). Aliens like St. Cyr, the Court observed, "almost certainly relied upon th[e] likelihood [of receiving discretionary relief] in deciding [to plead guilty, thereby] forgo[ing] their right to a trial." *Id.*, at 325.[9] Hence, applying the IIRIRA withdrawal to St. Cyr would have an "obvious and severe retroactive effect." *Ibid.* Because Congress made no such intention plain, *ibid.*, n. 55, we held that the prior law, permitting relief from deportation, governed St. Cyr's case.

As to retroactivity, one might think Vartelas' case even easier than St. Cyr's. St. Cyr could seek the Attorney General's *discretionary* dispensation. Vartelas, under *Fleuti*, was free, without seeking an official's permission, to make trips of short duration to see and assist his parents in Greece.[10] The Second Circuit thought otherwise, compounding its initial misperception (treating reliance as essential to application of the antiretroactivity principle). . . .

Satisfied that Vartelas' case is at least as clear as St. Cyr's for declining to apply a new law retroactively, we hold that *Fleuti* continues to govern Vartelas' short-term travel.

For the reasons stated, the judgment of the Court of Appeals for the Second Circuit is reversed, and the case is remanded for further proceedings consistent with this opinion.

It is so ordered.

■ JUSTICE SCALIA, with whom JUSTICE THOMAS and JUSTICE ALITO join, dissenting.

As part of the Illegal Immigration Reform and Immigrant Responsibility Act of 1996 (IIRIRA), Congress required that lawful permanent residents who have committed certain crimes seek formal "admission" when they return to the United States from abroad. 8 U.S.C. § 1101(a)(13)(C)(v). This case presents a straightforward question of statutory interpretation: Does that statute apply to lawful permanent residents who, like Vartelas, committed one of the specified offenses before 1996, but traveled abroad after 1996? Under the proper approach to determining a statute's temporal application, the answer is yes.

---

[9] "There can be little doubt," the Court noted in *St. Cyr*, "that, as a general matter, alien defendants considering whether to enter into a plea agreement are acutely aware of the immigration consequences of their convictions." 533 U.S., at 322. Indeed, "[p]reserving [their] right to remain in the United States may be more important to [them] than any potential jail sentence." *Ibid.* (internal quotation marks omitted). See *Padilla* v. *Kentucky*, 130 S.Ct. 1473, 1478–80 (2010) (holding that counsel has a duty under the Sixth Amendment to inform a noncitizen defendant that his plea would make him eligible for deportation).

[10] Armed with knowledge that a guilty plea would preclude travel abroad, aliens like Vartelas might endeavor to negotiate a plea to a nonexcludable offense—in Vartelas' case, *e.g.*, possession of counterfeit securities—or exercise a right to trial.

I

The text of § 1101(a)(13)(C)(v) does not contain a clear statement answering the question presented here. So the Court is correct that this case is governed by our longstanding interpretive principle that, in the absence of a contrary indication, a statute will not be construed to have retroactive application. See, *e.g.*, *Landgraf* v. *USI Film Products*, 511 U.S. 244, 280 (1994). The operative provision of this text—the provision that specifies the act that it prohibits or prescribes—says that lawful permanent residents convicted of offenses similar to Vartelas's must seek formal "admission" before they return to the United States from abroad. Since Vartelas returned to the United States after the statute's effective date, the application of that text to his reentry does not give the statute a retroactive effect.

In determining whether a statute applies retroactively, we should concern ourselves with the statute's actual operation on regulated parties, not with retroactivity as an abstract concept or as a substitute for fairness concerns. It is impossible to decide whether a statute's application is retrospective or prospective without first identifying a reference point—a moment in time to which the statute's effective date is either subsequent or antecedent. (Otherwise, the obvious question— retroactive in reference to what?—remains unanswered.) In my view, the identity of that reference point turns on the activity a statute is intended to regulate. For any given regulated party, the reference point (or "retroactivity event") is the moment at which the party does what the statute forbids or fails to do what it requires. See *Martin* v. *Hadix*, 527 U.S. 343, 362–363 (1999) (SCALIA, J., concurring in part and concurring in judgment); *Landgraf, supra*, at 291 (SCALIA, J., concurring in judgments). With an identified reference point, the retroactivity analysis is simple. If a person has engaged in the primary regulated activity *before* the statute's effective date, then the statute's application *would* be retroactive. But if a person engages in the primary regulated activity *after* the statute's effective date, then the statute's application is prospective only. In the latter case, the interpretive presumption against retroactivity does not bar the statute's application.

Under that commonsense approach, this is a relatively easy case. Although the *class* of aliens affected by § 1101(a)(13)(C)(v) is defined with respect to past crimes, the *regulated activity* is reentry into the United States. By its terms, the statute is all about controlling admission at the border. It specifies six criteria to identify lawful permanent residents who are subject to formal "admission" procedures, most of which relate to the circumstances of departure, the trip itself, or reentry. The titles of the statutory sections containing § 1101(a)(13)(C)(v) confirm its focus on admission, rather than crime: The provision is located within Title III of IIRIRA ("Inspection, Apprehension, Detention, Adjudication, and Removal of Inadmissible and Deportable Aliens"), under Subtitle A ("Revision of Procedures for Removal of Aliens"), and § 301 ("Treating

Persons Present in the United States Without Authorization as Not Admitted"). 110 Stat. 3009–575. And the specific subsection of IIRIRA at issue (§ 301(a), entitled " 'Admission' Defined") is an amendment to the definition of "entry" in the general "Definitions" section of the Immigration and Nationality Act (INA). The original provision told border officials how to regulate admission—not how to punish crime— and the amendment does as well.

Section 1101(a)(13)(C)(v) thus has no retroactive effect on Vartelas because the reference point here—Vartelas's readmission to the United States after a trip abroad occurred years after the statute's effective date. Although Vartelas cannot change the fact of his prior conviction, he could have avoided *entirely* the consequences of § 1101(a)(13)(C)(v) by simply remaining in the United States or, having left, remaining in Greece. That § 1101(a)(13)(C)(v) had no effect on Vartelas until he performed a post-enactment activity is a clear indication that the statute's application is purely prospective. See *Fernandez-Vargas* v. *Gonzales*, 548 U.S. 30, 45, n. 11, 46 (2006) (no retroactive effect where the statute in question did "not operate on a completed preenactment act" and instead turned on "a failure to take timely action that would have avoided application of the new law altogether").

II

The Court avoids this conclusion by insisting that "[p]ast misconduct, . . . not present travel, is the wrongful activity Congress targeted" in § 1101(a)(13)(C)(v). That assertion does not, however, have any basis in the statute's text or structure, and the Court does not pretend otherwise. Instead, the Court simply asserts that Vartelas's "lawful foreign travel" surely could not be the "reason for the 'new disability' imposed on him." *Ibid.* (emphasis added). But the *reason* for a prohibition has nothing to do with whether the prohibition is being applied to a past rather than a future act. It may be relevant to other legal inquiries—for example, to whether a legislative act violates one of the *Ex Post Facto* Clauses in Article I, [citation,] or one of the Due Process Clauses in the Fifth and Fourteenth Amendments, see, *e.g.*, *Williamson* v. *Lee Optical of Okla., Inc.*, [citation,] or the Takings Clause in the Fifth Amendment, [citation,] or the Obligation of Contracts Clause in Article I [citation omitted]. But it has no direct bearing upon whether the statute is retroactive.

The Court's failure to differentiate between the statutory-interpretation question (whether giving certain effect to a provision would make it retroactive and hence presumptively unintended) and the validity question (whether giving certain effect to a provision is unlawful) is on full display in its attempts to distinguish § 1101(a)(13)(C)(v) from similar statutes. Take, for example, the Court's discussion of the Racketeer Influenced and Corrupt Organizations Act (RICO). That Act, which targets "patterns of racketeering," *expressly* defines those "patterns" to include some pre-enactment conduct. See 18 U.S.C.

§ 1961(5). Courts interpreting RICO therefore need not consider the presumption against retroactivity; instead, the cases cited by the majority consider whether RICO violates the *Ex Post Facto* Clause. [Citation.] The Government recognized this distinction and cited RICO to make a point about the *Ex Post Facto* Clause rather than the presumption against retroactivity; the Court evidently does not.

The Court's confident assertion that Congress surely would not have meant this statute to apply to Vartelas, whose foreign travel and subsequent return to the United States were innocent events, simply begs the question presented in this case. Ignorance, of course, is no excuse (*ignorantia legis neminem excusat*); and his return was entirely lawful only if the statute before us did not render it unlawful. Since IIRIRA's effective date in 1996, lawful permanent residents who have committed crimes of moral turpitude are forbidden to leave the United States and return without formally seeking "admission." See § 1101(a)(13)(C)(v). As a result, Vartelas's numerous trips abroad and "uneventful" reentries into the United States after the passage of IIRIRA were lawful only *if* § 1101(a)(13)(C)(v) does not apply to him—which is, of course, precisely the matter in dispute here.

The Court's circular reasoning betrays its underlying concern: Because the Court believes that reentry after a brief trip abroad *should* be lawful, it will decline to apply a statute that clearly provides otherwise for certain criminal aliens. . . . The Court's test for retroactivity—asking whether the statute creates a "new disability" in "respect to past events"—invites this focus on fairness. Understandably so, since it is derived from a Justice Story opinion interpreting a provision of the New Hampshire Constitution that *forbade* retroactive laws—a provision comparable to the Federal Constitution's *ex post facto* prohibition and bearing no relation to the presumption against retroactivity. What is unfair or irrational (and hence should be forbidden) has nothing to do with whether applying a statute to a particular act is prospective (and thus presumptively intended) or retroactive (and thus presumptively unintended). On the latter question, the "new disability in respect to past events" test provides no meaningful guidance.

I can imagine countless laws that, like § 1101(a)(13) (C)(v), impose "new disabilities" related to "past events" and yet do not operate retroactively. For example, a statute making persons convicted of drug crimes ineligible for student loans. See, *e.g.*, 20 U.S.C. § 1091(r)(1). Or laws prohibiting those convicted of sex crimes from working in certain jobs that involve repeated contact with minors. See, *e.g.*, Cal. Penal Code Ann. § 290.95(c) (West Supp. 2012). Or laws prohibiting those previously committed for mental instability from purchasing guns. See, *e.g.*, 18 U.S.C. § 922(g)(4). The Court concedes that it would not consider the last two laws inapplicable to pre-enactment convictions or commitments. The Court does not deny that these statutes impose a "new disability in respect to past events," but it distinguishes them based on the *reason* for their enactment: These statutes "address dangers that arise postenactment." So much for the new-disability-in-respect-to-past-events test; it has now become a new-disability-not-designed-to-guard-against-future-danger test. But why is guarding against future danger the *only* reason Congress may wish to regulate future action in light of past events? It obviously is not. So the Court must invent yet another doctrine to address my first example, the law making persons convicted of drug crimes ineligible for student loans. According to the Court, that statute differs from § 1101(a)(13)(C)(v) because it "has a prospective thrust." I cannot imagine what that means, other than that the statute regulates post-enactment conduct. But, of course, so does § 1101(a)(13)(C)(v). Rather than reconciling any of these distinctions with Justice Story's formulation of retroactivity, the Court leaves to lower courts the unenviable task of identifying new-disabilities-not-designed-to-guard-against-future-danger-and-also-lacking-a-prospective-thrust.

And anyway, is there any doubt that § 1101(a)(13)(C)(v) is intended to guard against the "dangers that arise postenactment" from having aliens in our midst who have shown themselves to have proclivity for crime? Must that be rejected as its purpose simply because Congress has not sought to achieve it by all possible means—by ferreting out such dangerous aliens and going through the expensive and lengthy process of deporting them? At least some of the post-enactment danger can readily be eliminated by forcing lawful permanent residents who have committed certain crimes to undergo formal "admission" procedures at our borders. Indeed, by limiting criminal aliens' opportunities to travel and then return to the United States, § 1101(a)(13)(C)(v) may encourage self-deportation. But all this is irrelevant. The positing of legislative "purpose" is always a slippery enterprise compared to the simple determination of whether a statute regulates a future event—and it is that, rather than the Court's pronouncement of some forward-looking *reason*, which governs whether a statute has retroactive effect. . . .

This case raises a plain-vanilla question of statutory interpretation, not broader questions about frustrated expectations or fairness. Our approach to answering that question should be similarly straightforward: We should determine what relevant activity the statute regulates (here, reentry); absent a clear statement otherwise, only such relevant activity which occurs after the statute's effective date should be covered (here, post-1996 re-entries). If, as so construed, the statute is unfair or irrational enough to violate the Constitution, that is another matter entirely, and one not presented here. Our interpretive presumption against retroactivity, however, is just that—a tool to ascertain what the statute means, not a license to rewrite the statute in a way the Court considers more desirable.

I respectfully dissent.

QUESTIONS

1.   In *Vartelas*, which "retroactivity event"—the past guilty plea or re-entry into the United States—makes more sense in analyzing the effect of the amended statute? If the statute is effective as of that event, could the statute be said to have "genuinely retroactive" effect? What activity is the statute endeavoring to address and change?

2.   What are the concerns underlying the antiretroactivity principle? Which approach in *Vartelas*, the majority's or dissent's, better addresses those concerns?

3.   What do you make of the dissent's statement in *Vartelas* that "[if] the statute is unfair or irrational enough to violate the Constitution, that is another matter entirely, and one not presented here." Does this statement suggest that fairness concerns are to be addressed only by means of a constitutional challenge? What, then, of the doctrine of "constitutional avoidance," which enables a court to reject a proposed statutory interpretation on the ground that, so read, the statute would be unconstitutional? Is not the anti-retroactivity principle an attempt to address fairness concerns without engaging in constitutional interpretation?

F. AGENCY INTERPRETATIONS OF STATUTES

[Reread Section I.C. Administrative Law.]

Many statutes task administrative agencies with implementing complex regulatory schemes on the basis of relatively bare statutory instructions. While legislative delegations to administrative agencies may provoke constitutional questions about the separation of powers, they also raise important and unique interpretive issues for courts. For most regulatory statutes, the relevant agencies do the bulk of the interpretive work in the course of administering statutes, and policy considerations often inform these interpretations. Under what circumstances should courts defer to agency interpretations, especially when policy considerations for which agencies—not courts—possess the relevant expertise inform those interpretations? Should these factors influence the legal methods courts employ when interpreting statutes directed primarily at agencies? This subsection explores these tensions.

Chevron, U.S.A., Inc. v. Natural Resources Defense Council, Inc.

Supreme Court of the United States, 1984.
467 U.S. 837, 104 S.Ct. 2778, 81 L.Ed.2d 694.

■ JUSTICE STEVENS delivered the opinion of the Court[, in which CHIEF JUSTICE BURGER, JUSTICE BRENNAN, JUSTICE WHITE, JUSTICE BLACKMUN, and JUSTICE POWELL joined].

In the Clean Air Act Amendments of 1977, Pub.L. 95–95, 91 Stat. 685, Congress enacted certain requirements applicable to States that had not achieved the national air quality standards established by the Environmental Protection Agency (EPA) pursuant to earlier legislation. The amended Clean Air Act required these "nonattainment" States to establish a permit program regulating "new or modified major stationary sources" of air pollution. Generally, a permit may not be issued for a new or modified major stationary source unless several stringent conditions are met. The EPA regulation promulgated to implement this permit requirement allows a State to adopt a plantwide definition of the term "stationary source." Under this definition, an existing plant that contains several pollution-emitting devices may install or modify one piece of equipment without meeting the permit conditions if the alteration will not increase the total emissions from the plant. The question presented by these cases is whether EPA's decision to allow States to treat all of the pollution-emitting devices within the same industrial grouping as though they were encased within a single "bubble" is based on a reasonable construction of the statutory term "stationary source."

I

The EPA regulations containing the plantwide definition of the term stationary source were promulgated on October 14, 1981. 46 Fed.Reg. 50766. Respondents filed a timely petition for review in the United States Court of Appeals for the District of Columbia Circuit pursuant to 42 U.S.C. § 7607(b)(1). The Court of Appeals set aside the regulations.

Natural Resources Defense Council, Inc. v. Gorsuch, 685 F.2d 718 (D.C.Cir.1982).

The court observed that the relevant part of the amended Clean Air Act "does not explicitly define what Congress envisioned as a 'stationary source,' to which the permit program . . . should apply," and further stated that the precise issue was not "squarely addressed in the legislative history." *Id.*, at 273, 685 F.2d, at 723. In light of its conclusion that the legislative history bearing on the question was "at best contradictory," it reasoned that "the purposes of the nonattainment program should guide our decision here." *Id.*, at 276, n. 39, 685 F.2d, at 726, n. 39.[5] Based on two of its precedents concerning the applicability of the bubble concept to certain Clean Air Act programs, the court stated that the bubble concept was "mandatory" in programs designed merely to maintain existing air quality, but held that it was "inappropriate" in programs enacted to improve air quality. *Id.*, at 276, 685 F.2d, at 726. Since the purpose of the permit program—its "raison d'être," in the court's view—was to improve air quality, the court held that the bubble concept was inapplicable in these cases under its prior precedents. Ibid. It therefore set aside the regulations embodying the bubble concept as contrary to law. We . . . now reverse.

The basic legal error of the Court of Appeals was to adopt a static judicial definition of the term "stationary source" when it had decided that Congress itself had not commanded that definition. . . .

II

When a court reviews an agency's construction of the statute which it administers, it is confronted with two questions. First, always, is the question whether Congress has directly spoken to the precise question at issue. If the intent of Congress is clear, that is the end of the matter; for the court, as well as the agency, must give effect to the unambiguously expressed intent of Congress.[9] If, however, the court determines Congress has not directly addressed the precise question at issue, the court does not simply impose its own construction on the statute, as would be necessary in the absence of an administrative interpretation. Rather, if the statute is silent or ambiguous with respect to the specific issue, the question for the court is whether the agency's answer is based on a permissible construction of the statute.

---

[5] The court remarked in this regard:

"We regret, of course, that Congress did not advert specifically to the bubble concept's application to various Clean Air Act programs, and note that a further clarifying statutory directive would facilitate the work of the agency and of the court in their endeavors to serve the legislators' will." 685 F.2d at 726 n.39.

[9] The judiciary is the final authority on issues of statutory construction and must reject administrative constructions which are contrary to clear congressional intent. See, e.g., FEC v. Democratic Senatorial Campaign Committee, 454 U.S. 27, 32 (1981) [further citations omitted]. If a court, employing traditional tools of statutory construction, ascertains that Congress had an intention on the precise question at issue, that intention is the law and must be given effect.

The power of an administrative agency to administer a congressionally created . . . program necessarily requires the formulation of policy and the making of rules to fill any gap left, implicitly or explicitly, by Congress. Morton v. Ruiz, 415 U.S. 199, 231 (1974). If Congress has explicitly left a gap for the agency to fill, there is an express delegation of authority to the agency to elucidate a specific provision of the statute by regulation. Such legislative regulations are given controlling weight unless they are arbitrary, capricious, or manifestly contrary to the statute. Sometimes the legislative delegation to an agency on a particular question is implicit rather than explicit. In such a case, a court may not substitute its own construction of a statutory provision for a reasonable interpretation made by the administrator of an agency.

We have long recognized that considerable weight should be accorded to an executive department's construction of a statutory scheme it is entrusted to administer, and the principle of deference to administrative interpretations

> has been consistently followed by this Court whenever decision as to the meaning or reach of a statute has involved reconciling conflicting policies, and a full understanding of the force of the statutory policy in the given situation has depended upon more than ordinary knowledge respecting the matters subjected to agency regulations.[Citation.] . . . If this choice represents a reasonable accommodation of conflicting policies that were committed to the agency's care by the statute, we should not disturb it unless it appears from the statute or its legislative history that the accommodation is not one that Congress would have sanctioned." United States v. Shimer, 367 U.S. 374, 382, 383 (1961).

Accord Capital Cities Cable, Inc. v. Crisp, 467 U.S. 691, 699–700 (1984).

In light of these well-settled principles it is clear that the Court of Appeals misconceived the nature of its role in reviewing the regulations at issue. Once it determined, after its own examination of the legislation, that Congress did not actually have an intent regarding the applicability of the bubble concept to the permit program, the question before it was not whether in its view the concept is "inappropriate" in the general context of a program designed to improve air quality, but whether the Administrator's view that it is appropriate in the context of this particular program is a reasonable one. Based on the examination of the legislation and its history which follows, we agree with the Court of Appeals that Congress did not have a specific intention on the applicability of the bubble concept in these cases, and conclude that the EPA's use of that concept here is a reasonable policy choice for the agency to make.

III

[The Court then reviewed the legislative history at length, remarking that the issue before it concerned "one phase" of a "small portion" of "a lengthy, detailed, technical, complex, and comprehensive response to a major social issue," the Clean Air Act Amendments of 1977, that in turn was only part of a much larger statutory scheme under EPA's administration. "The legislative history of the portion of the 1977 Amendments dealing with nonattainment areas," it remarked, "does not contain any specific comment on the 'bubble concept' or the question whether a plantwide definition of a stationary source is permissible under the permit program. It does, however, plainly disclose that in the permit program Congress sought to accommodate the conflict between the economic interest in permitting capital improvements to continue and the environmental interest in improving air quality."

Turning to the administrative history of implementation, the Court noted that EPA had at first proposed interpretations like that under challenge.] . . .

VI

. . . In August 1980, however, the EPA adopted a regulation that, in essence, applied the basic reasoning of the Court of Appeals in these cases. The EPA took particular note of the two then-recent Court of Appeals decisions, which had created the bright-line rule that the "bubble concept" should be employed in a program designed to maintain air quality but not in one designed to enhance air quality. Relying heavily on those cases, EPA adopted a dual definition of "source" for nonattainment areas that required a permit whenever a change in either the entire plant, or one of its components, would result in a significant increase in emissions even if the increase was completely offset by reductions elsewhere in the plant. . . .

In 1981 a new administration took office and initiated a "Government-wide reexamination of regulatory burdens and complexities." 46 Fed.Reg. 16281. In the context of that review, the EPA reevaluated the various arguments that had been advanced in connection with the proper definition of the term "source" and concluded that the term should be given the same definition in both nonattainment areas and PSD areas.

In explaining its conclusion, the EPA first noted that the definitional issue was not squarely addressed in either the statute or its legislative history and therefore that the issue involved an agency "judgment as how to best carry out the Act." Ibid. It then set forth several reasons for concluding that the plantwide definition was more appropriate. . . .

VII

. . . Based on our examination of the legislative history, we agree with the Court of Appeals that it is unilluminating. The general remarks pointed to by respondents "were obviously not made with this narrow issue in mind and they cannot be said to demonstrate a Congressional desire. . . . " Jewell Ridge Coal Corp. v. Mine Workers, 325 U.S. 161, 168–169 (1945). . . . We find that the legislative history as a whole is silent on the precise issue before us. It is, however, consistent with the view that the EPA should have broad discretion in implementing the policies of the 1977 Amendments.

More importantly, that history plainly identifies the policy concerns that motivated the enactment; the plantwide definition is fully consistent with one of those concerns—the allowance of reasonable economic growth—and, whether or not we believe it most effectively implements the other, we must recognize that the EPA has advanced a reasonable explanation for its conclusion that the regulations serve the environmental objectives as well. Indeed, its reasoning is supported by the public record developed in the rulemaking process, as well as by certain private studies.[37]

Our review of the EPA's varying interpretations of the word "source"—both before and after the 1977 Amendments—convinces us that the agency primarily responsible for administering this important legislation has consistently interpreted it flexibly—not in a sterile textual vacuum, but in the context of implementing policy decisions in a technical and complex arena. The fact that the agency has from time to time changed its interpretation of the term "source" does not, as respondents argue, lead us to conclude that no deference should be accorded the agency's interpretation of the statute. An initial agency interpretation is not instantly carved in stone. On the contrary, the agency, to engage in informed rulemaking, must consider varying interpretations and the wisdom of its policy on a continuing basis. Moreover, the fact that the agency has adopted different definitions in different contexts adds force to the argument that the definition itself is flexible, particularly since Congress has never indicated any disapproval of a flexible reading of the statute.

Significantly, it was not the agency in 1980, but rather the Court of Appeals that read the statute inflexibly to command a plantwide definition for programs designed to maintain clean air and to forbid such a definition for programs designed to improve air quality. The distinction the court drew may well be a sensible one, but our labored review of the problem has surely disclosed that it is not a distinction that Congress ever articulated itself, or one that the EPA found in the statute before the courts began to review the legislative work product. We conclude that it was the Court of Appeals, rather than Congress or any of the

---

[37] "Economists have proposed that economic incentives be substituted for the cumbersome administrative-legal framework. The objective is to make the profit and cost incentives that work so well in the marketplace work for pollution control. . . . [The 'bubble' or 'netting' concept] is a first attempt in this direction. By giving a plant manager flexibility to find the places and processes within a plant that control emissions most cheaply, pollution control can be achieved more quickly and cheaply." L. Lave & G. Omenn, Cleaning Air: Reforming the Clean Air Act 28 (1981) (footnote omitted).

decisionmakers who are authorized by Congress to administer this legislation, that was primarily responsible for the 1980 position taken by the agency.

. . . In these cases, the Administrator's interpretation represents a reasonable accommodation of manifestly competing interests and is entitled to deference: the regulatory scheme is technical and complex, the agency considered the matter in a detailed and reasoned fashion, and the decision involves reconciling conflicting policies. Congress intended to accommodate both interests, but did not do so itself on the level of specificity presented by these cases. Perhaps that body consciously desired the Administrator to strike the balance at this level, thinking that those with great expertise and charged with responsibility for administering the provision would be in a better position to do so; perhaps it simply did not consider the question at this level; and perhaps Congress was unable to forge a coalition on either side of the question, and those on each side decided to take their chances with the scheme devised by the agency. For judicial purposes, it matters not which of these things occurred.

Judges are not experts in the field, and are not part of either political branch of the Government. Courts must, in some cases, reconcile competing political interests, but not on the basis of the judges' personal policy preferences. In contrast, an agency to which Congress has delegated policy-making responsibilities may, within the limits of that delegation, properly rely upon the incumbent administration's views of wise policy to inform its judgments. While agencies are not directly accountable to the people, the Chief Executive is, and it is entirely appropriate for this political branch of the Government to make such policy choices—resolving the competing interests which Congress itself either inadvertently did not resolve, or intentionally left to be resolved by the agency charged with the administration of the statute in light of everyday realities.

When a challenge to an agency construction of a statutory provision, fairly conceptualized, really centers on the wisdom of the agency's policy, rather than whether it is a reasonable choice within a gap left open by Congress, the challenge must fail. In such a case, federal judges—who have no constituency—have a duty to respect legitimate policy choices made by those who do. The responsibilities for assessing the wisdom of such policy choices and resolving the struggle between competing views of the public interest are not judicial ones: "Our Constitution vests such responsibilities in the political branches." TVA v. Hill, 437 U.S. 153, 195 (1978).

. . . [R]eversed.

It is so ordered.

■ JUSTICE MARSHALL and JUSTICE REHNQUIST took no part in the consideration or decision of these cases.

■ JUSTICE O'CONNOR took no part in the decision of these cases.

NOTE: CHEVRON AND ITS AFTERMATH

Chevron is among the Court's most-cited statutory interpretation decisions of the past four decades. As Professor Richard Pierce has noted, the proper application of *Chevron* requires deciding first whether the question at issue is one of law or policy:

> In determining whether an agency's interpretation of a statute involves an issue of law or policy, it is useful to analyze and characterize the issue prior to Congress' enactment of the statute in question. For example, in *Chevron* most would agree that, prior to the enactment of the Clean Air Act, the question of whether to limit emissions at the plant level or the level of each piece of combustion equipment is a pure question of policy. This question is but one of hundreds of policy issues that some institution of government must resolve in order to implement any regulatory program to reduce air pollution. In the process of enacting the Clean Air Act, or any other regulatory statute, Congress invariably resolves some policy issues but leaves to some other institution of government the task of resolving many other policy issues.

> As the Court recognized in *Chevron,* Congress declines to resolve policy issues for many different reasons: Congress simply may have neglected to consider the issue; Congress may have believed that the agency was in a better position to resolve the issue; or finally, Congress may not have been able to forge a coalition or simply may have lacked the political courage necessary to resolve the issue, given that a resolution either way might damage the political future of many members of Congress. The general proposition that Congress cannot and does not resolve all the policy issues raised by its creation of a regulatory scheme probably is not at all controversial.

> A more controversial point, however, may be that Congress resolves very few issues when it enacts a statute empowering an agency to regulate. Rather, Congress typically leaves the vast majority of policy issues, including many of the most important issues, for resolution by some other institution of government. Congress accomplishes this through several different statutory drafting techniques, including the use of empty standards, lists of unranked decisional goals, and contradictory standards. Thus, Congress declines to resolve many policy issues by using statutory language that is incapable of meaningful definition and application.

> Once a court realizes that it is reviewing an agency's resolution of a policy issue, rather than an issue of law, comparative institutional analysis demonstrates that the agency is a more appropriate institution than a court to resolve the controversy. Because agencies are more accountable to the electorate than

courts, agencies should have the dominant role in policy making when the choice is between agencies and courts. A court's function in reviewing a policy decision made by an agency should be the same whether the agency policy decision is made by interpreting an ambiguous statutory provision or by any other means of agency policy making. The court should affirm the agency's policy decision, and hence its statutory interpretation, if the policy is "reasonable." The court should reverse the agency's policy decision if the policy is arbitrary and capricious. Of course, in deciding whether the agency's policy decision is "reasonable," the court should review the agency's decision making process by which the agency determined that its choice of policy was consistent with statutory goals and the contextual facts of the controversy in question.

Richard J. Pierce, Chevron *and Its Aftermath: Judicial Review of Agency Interpretations of Statutory Provisions*, 41 Vand. L. Rev. 301 (1988).

Chevron introduced a two-stage analysis: (1) has Congress expressed its intent clearly in the statute, or is the statute ambiguous as to the relevant provision?; (2) if the statute is ambiguous, is the agency's interpretation a reasonably *permissible* construction of the provision? If Congress has spoken clearly as to the provision's meaning, there is no place for a "stage two" inquiry, and the agency must carry out the clearly expressed intent of Congress. The Court has subsequently endorsed what scholars have described as *Chevron* "step zero" analysis: whether Congress has delegated to the agency lawmaking authority to bind regulated parties with the force of law, as opposed to other kinds of non-binding agency actions, such as enforcement guidelines, policy manuals, opinion letters, and no-action letters. Thus, *Chevron* deference applies only in circumstances in which the agency's interpretation will have the force of law, such as in rulemaking and in many administrative adjudications. As you read *FDA v. Brown & Williamson Tobacco Corp.*, next, consider whether the majority and dissenting opinions are debating whether the agency's interpretation was unreasonable, or whether Congress foreclosed any agency discretion with respect to the disputed issue.

FDA v. Brown & Williamson Tobacco Corp.

Supreme Court of the United States, 2000.
529 U.S. 120, 120 S.Ct. 1291, 146 L.Ed.2d 121.

■ JUSTICE O'CONNOR delivered the opinion of the Court[, joined by CHIEF JUSTICE REHNQUIST, JUSTICE SCALIA, JUSTICE KENNEDY, and JUSTICE THOMAS].

This case involves one of the most troubling public health problems facing our Nation today: the thousands of premature deaths that occur each year because of tobacco use. In 1996, the Food and Drug

Administration (FDA), after having expressly disavowed any such authority since its inception, asserted jurisdiction to regulate tobacco products. [Citation.] The FDA concluded that nicotine is a drug within the meaning of the Food, Drug, and Cosmetic Act (FDCA or Act), 52 Stat. 1040, as amended, 21 U.S.C. § 301 et seq., and that cigarettes and smokeless tobacco are combination products that deliver nicotine to the body. 61 Fed.Reg. 44397 (1996). Pursuant to this authority, it promulgated regulations intended to reduce tobacco consumption among children and adolescents. Id., at 44615–44618. The agency believed that, because most tobacco consumers begin their use before reaching the age of 18, curbing tobacco use by minors could substantially reduce the prevalence of addiction in future generations and thus the incidence of tobacco-related death and disease. Id., at 44398–44399.

Regardless of how serious the problem an administrative agency seeks to address, however, it may not exercise its authority in a manner that is inconsistent with the administrative structure that Congress enacted into law. [Citation.] And although agencies are generally entitled to deference in the interpretation of statutes that they administer, a reviewing court, as well as the agency, must give effect to the unambiguously expressed intent of Congress. Chevron U.S.A. Inc. v. Natural Resources Defense Council, Inc., 467 U.S. 837, 842–843 (1984). In this case, we believe that Congress has clearly precluded the FDA from asserting jurisdiction to regulate tobacco products. Such authority is inconsistent with the intent that Congress has expressed in the FDCA's overall regulatory scheme and in the tobacco-specific legislation that it has enacted subsequent to the FDCA. In light of this clear intent, the FDA's assertion of jurisdiction is impermissible.

I

The FDCA grants the FDA, as the designee of the Secretary of Health and Human Services, the authority to regulate, among other items, "drugs" and "devices." See 21 U.S.C. §§ 321(g)–(h), 393 (1994 ed. and Supp. III). The Act defines "drug" to include "articles (other than food) intended to affect the structure or any function of the body." 21 U.S.C. § 321(g)(1)(C). It defines "device," in part, as "an instrument, apparatus, implement, machine, contrivance, . . . or other similar or related article, including any component, part, or accessory, which is . . . intended to affect the structure or any function of the body." § 321(h). The Act also grants the FDA the authority to regulate so-called "combination products," which "constitute a combination of a drug, device, or biological product." § 353(g)(1). The FDA has construed this provision as giving it the discretion to regulate combination products as drugs, as devices, or as both. See 61 Fed.Reg. 44400 (1996). . . .

Based on [its] findings [regarding the dangerousness of tobacco], the FDA promulgated regulations concerning tobacco products' promotion, labeling, and accessibility to children and adolescents. See id., at 44615–44618. . . .

The FDA promulgated these regulations pursuant to its authority to regulate "restricted devices." See 21 U.S.C. § 360j(e). The FDA construed § 353(g)(1) as giving it the discretion to regulate "combination products" using the Act's drug authorities, device authorities, or both, depending on "how the public health goals of the act can be best accomplished." 61 Fed.Reg. 44403 (1996). Given the greater flexibility in the FDCA for the regulation of devices, the FDA determined that "the device authorities provide the most appropriate basis for regulating cigarettes and smokeless tobacco." *Id.*, at 44404. Under 21 U.S.C. § 360j(e), the agency may "require that a device be restricted to sale, distribution, or use . . . upon such other conditions as [the FDA] may prescribe in such regulation, if, because of its potentiality for harmful effect or the collateral measures necessary to its use, [the FDA] determines that there cannot otherwise be reasonable assurance of its safety and effectiveness." The FDA reasoned that its regulations fell within the authority granted by § 360j(e) because they related to the sale or distribution of tobacco products and were necessary for providing a reasonable assurance of safety. 61 Fed.Reg. 44405–44407 (1996).

Respondents, a group of tobacco manufacturers, retailers, and advertisers, filed suit in [federal district court. Citation.] They moved for summary judgment on the grounds that the FDA lacked jurisdiction to regulate tobacco products as customarily marketed, the regulations exceeded the FDA's authority under 21 U.S.C. § 360j(e). . . . The District Court granted respondents' motion in part and denied it in part. [Citation.] The court held that the FDCA authorizes the FDA to regulate tobacco products as customarily marketed and that the FDA's access and labeling regulations are permissible, but it also found that the agency's advertising and promotion restrictions exceed its authority under § 360j(e). [Citation.]

The Court of Appeals for the Fourth Circuit reversed, holding that Congress has not granted the FDA jurisdiction to regulate tobacco products[Citation.] . . .

We granted the [Government's] petition for certiorari, [citation], to determine whether the FDA has authority under the FDCA to regulate tobacco products as customarily marketed.

II

The FDA's assertion of jurisdiction to regulate tobacco products is founded on its conclusions that nicotine is a "drug" and that cigarettes and smokeless tobacco are "drug delivery devices." . . .

A threshold issue is the appropriate framework for analyzing the FDA's assertion of authority to regulate tobacco products. Because this case involves an administrative agency's construction of a statute that it administers, our analysis is governed by Chevron U.S.A. Inc. v. Natural Resources Defense Council, Inc., 467 U.S. 837 (1984). Under *Chevron*, a reviewing court must first ask "whether Congress has directly spoken to the precise question at issue." *Id.*, at 842. If Congress has done so, the inquiry is at an end; the court "must give effect to the unambiguously expressed intent of Congress." *Id.*, at 843 [other citations omitted]. But if Congress has not specifically addressed the question, a reviewing court must respect the agency's construction of the statute so long as it is permissible. [Citation]. Such deference is justified because [t]he responsibilities for assessing the wisdom of such policy choices and resolving the struggle between competing views of the public interest are not judicial ones, *Chevron*, [citation,] and because of the agency's greater familiarity with the ever-changing facts and circumstances surrounding the subjects regulated[, citation].

In determining whether Congress has specifically addressed the question at issue, a reviewing court should not confine itself to examining a particular statutory provision in isolation. The meaning—or ambiguity—of certain words or phrases may only become evident when placed in context. See Brown v. Gardner, 513 U.S. 115, 118 (1994) ("Ambiguity is a creature not of definitional possibilities but of statutory context"). It is a "fundamental canon of statutory construction that the words of a statute must be read in their context and with a view to their place in the overall statutory scheme." Davis v. Michigan Dept. of Treasury, 489 U.S. 803, 809 (1989). A court must therefore interpret the statute as a symmetrical and coherent regulatory scheme, Gustafson v. Alloyd Co., 513 U.S. 561, 569 (1995), and "fit, if possible, all parts into an harmonious whole," FTC v. Mandel Brothers, Inc., 359 U.S. 385, 389 (1959). Similarly, the meaning of one statute may be affected by other Acts, particularly where Congress has spoken subsequently and more specifically to the topic at hand. [Citation.] In addition, we must be guided to a degree by common sense as to the manner in which Congress is likely to delegate a policy decision of such economic and political magnitude to an administrative agency. [Citation.]

With these principles in mind, we find that Congress has directly spoken to the issue here and precluded the FDA's jurisdiction to regulate tobacco products.

A

Viewing the FDCA as a whole, it is evident that one of the Act's core objectives is to ensure that any product regulated by the FDA is safe and "effective" for its intended use. See 21 U.S.C. § 393(b)(2) (1994 ed., Supp. III) (defining the FDA's mission). . . . This essential purpose pervades the FDCA. For instance, 21 U.S.C. § 393(b)(2) (1994 ed., Supp. III) defines the FDA's "mission" to include "protect [ing] the public health by ensuring that . . . drugs are safe and effective and that there is reasonable assurance of the safety and effectiveness of devices intended for human use." The FDCA requires premarket approval of any new drug, with some limited exceptions, and states that the FDA "shall issue an order refusing to approve the application" of a new drug if it is not safe and effective for its intended purpose. §§ 355(d)(1)–(2), (4)–(5). If the

FDA discovers after approval that a drug is unsafe or ineffective, it "shall, after due notice and opportunity for hearing to the applicant, withdraw approval" of the drug. 21 U.S.C. §§ 355(e)(1)–(3). The Act also requires the FDA to classify all devices into one of three categories. § 360c(b)(1). Regardless of which category the FDA chooses, there must be a "reasonable assurance of the safety and effectiveness of the device." 21 U.S.C. §§ 360c(a)(1)(A)(i), (B), (C) (1994 ed. and Supp. III); 61 Fed.Reg. 44412 (1996). Even the "restricted device" provision pursuant to which the FDA promulgated the regulations at issue here authorizes the agency to place conditions on the sale or distribution of a device specifically when "there cannot otherwise be reasonable assurance of its safety and effectiveness." 21 U.S.C. § 360j(e). Thus, the Act generally requires the FDA to prevent the marketing of any drug or device where "the potential for inflicting death or physical injury is not offset by the possibility of therapeutic benefit." United States v. Rutherford, 442 U.S. 544, 556 (1979).

In its rulemaking proceeding, the FDA quite exhaustively documented that tobacco products are unsafe, dangerous, and cause great pain and suffering from illness. 61 Fed.Reg. 44412 (1996). . . . These findings logically imply that, if tobacco products were devices under the FDCA, the FDA would be required to remove them from the market. Consider, first, the FDCA's provisions concerning the misbranding of drugs or devices. The Act prohibits "[t]he introduction or delivery for introduction into interstate commerce of any food, drug, device, or cosmetic that is adulterated or misbranded." 21 U.S.C. § 331(a). . . . Thus, were tobacco products within the FDA's jurisdiction, the Act would deem them misbranded devices that could not be introduced into interstate commerce. . . .

Congress, however, has foreclosed the removal of tobacco products from the market. A provision of the United States Code currently in force states that "[t]he marketing of tobacco constitutes one of the greatest basic industries of the United States with ramifying activities which directly affect interstate and foreign commerce at every point, and stable conditions therein are necessary to the general welfare." 7 U.S.C. § 1311(a). More importantly, Congress has directly addressed the problem of tobacco and health through legislation on six occasions since 1965. . . . Nonetheless, Congress stopped well short of ordering a ban. Instead, it has generally regulated the labeling and advertisement of tobacco products, expressly providing that it is the policy of Congress that "commerce and the national economy may be . . . protected to the maximum extent consistent with" consumers "be[ing] adequately informed about any adverse health effects." 15 U.S.C. § 1331. Congress' decisions to regulate labeling and advertising and to adopt the express policy of protecting "commerce and the national economy . . . to the maximum extent" reveal its intent that tobacco products remain on the market. Indeed, the collective premise of these statutes is that cigarettes and smokeless tobacco will continue to be sold in the United States. A ban of tobacco products by the FDA would therefore plainly contradict congressional policy. . . .

The dissent contends that our conclusion means that the FDCA requires the FDA to ban outright "dangerous" drugs or devices, and that this is a "perverse" reading of the statute. This misunderstands our holding. The FDA, consistent with the FDCA, may clearly regulate many "dangerous" products without banning them. Indeed, virtually every drug or device poses dangers under certain conditions. What the FDA may not do is conclude that a drug or device cannot be used safely for any therapeutic purpose and yet, at the same time, allow that product to remain on the market. Such regulation is incompatible with the FDCA's core objective of ensuring that every drug or device is safe and effective.

Considering the FDCA as a whole, it is clear that Congress intended to exclude tobacco products from the FDA's jurisdiction. . . . [I]f tobacco products were within the FDA's jurisdiction, the Act would require the FDA to remove them from the market entirely. But a ban would contradict Congress' clear intent as expressed in its more recent, tobacco-specific legislation. The inescapable conclusion is that there is no room for tobacco products within the FDCA's regulatory scheme. If they cannot be used safely for any therapeutic purpose, and yet they cannot be banned, they simply do not fit.

B

In determining whether Congress has spoken directly to the FDA's authority to regulate tobacco, we must also consider in greater detail the tobacco-specific legislation that Congress has enacted over the past 35 years. At the time a statute is enacted, it may have a range of plausible meanings. Over time, however, subsequent acts can shape or focus those meanings. The "classic judicial task of reconciling many laws enacted over time, and getting them to 'make sense' in combination, necessarily assumes that the implications of a statute may be altered by the implications of a later statute." United States v. Fausto, 484 U.S., at 453. This is particularly so where the scope of the earlier statute is broad but the subsequent statutes more specifically address the topic at hand. As we recognized recently in United States v. Estate of Romani, "a specific policy embodied in a later federal statute should control our construction of the [earlier] statute, even though it ha[s] not been expressly amended." 523 U.S., at 530–531.

Congress has enacted six separate pieces of legislation since 1965 addressing the problem of tobacco use and human health. See *supra*, at 1322. Those statutes, among other things, require that health warnings appear on all packaging and in all print and outdoor advertisements, see 15 U.S.C. §§ 1331, 1333, 4402; prohibit the advertisement of tobacco products through any medium of electronic communication subject to regulation by the Federal Communications Commission (FCC), see §§ 1335, 4402(f); require the Secretary of Health and Human Services

(HHS) to report every three years to Congress on research findings concerning "the addictive property of tobacco," 42 U.S.C. § 290aa–2(b)(2); and make States' receipt of certain federal block grants contingent on their making it unlawful "for any manufacturer, retailer, or distributor of tobacco products to sell or distribute any such product to any individual under the age of 18," § 300x–26(a)(1).

In adopting each statute, Congress has acted against the backdrop of the FDA's consistent and repeated statements that it lacked authority under the FDCA to regulate tobacco absent claims of therapeutic benefit by the manufacturer. In fact, on several occasions over this period, and after the health consequences of tobacco use and nicotine's pharmacological effects had become well known, Congress considered and rejected bills that would have granted the FDA such jurisdiction. Under these circumstances, it is evident that Congress' tobacco-specific statutes have effectively ratified the FDA's long-held position that it lacks jurisdiction under the FDCA to regulate tobacco products. Congress has created a distinct regulatory scheme to address the problem of tobacco and health, and that scheme, as presently constructed, precludes any role for the FDA. . . .

Taken together, these actions by Congress over the past 35 years preclude an interpretation of the FDCA that grants the FDA jurisdiction to regulate tobacco products. We do not rely on Congress' failure to act—its consideration and rejection of bills that would have given the FDA this authority—in reaching this conclusion. Indeed, this is not a case of simple inaction by Congress that purportedly represents its acquiescence in an agency's position. To the contrary, Congress has enacted several statutes addressing the particular subject of tobacco and health, creating a distinct regulatory scheme for cigarettes and smokeless tobacco. In doing so, Congress has been aware of tobacco's health hazards and its pharmacological effects. It has also enacted this legislation against the background of the FDA repeatedly and consistently asserting that it lacks jurisdiction under the FDCA to regulate tobacco products as customarily marketed. Further, Congress has persistently acted to preclude a meaningful role for any administrative agency in making policy on the subject of tobacco and health. Moreover, the substance of Congress' regulatory scheme is, in an important respect, incompatible with FDA jurisdiction. Although the supervision of product labeling to protect consumer health is a substantial component of the FDA's regulation of drugs and devices, see 21 U.S.C. § 352 (1994 ed. and Supp. III), the FCLAA and the CSTHEA explicitly prohibit any federal agency from imposing any health-related labeling requirements on cigarettes or smokeless tobacco products, see 15 U.S.C. §§ 1334(a), 4406(a).

Under these circumstances, it is clear that Congress' tobacco-specific legislation has effectively ratified the FDA's previous position that it lacks jurisdiction to regulate tobacco. . . .

"It is hardly conceivable that Congress—and in this setting, any Member of Congress—was not abundantly aware of what was going on." [Citation.] Congress has affirmatively acted to address the issue of tobacco and health, relying on the representations of the FDA that it had no authority to regulate tobacco. It has created a distinct scheme to regulate the sale of tobacco products, focused on labeling and advertising, and premised on the belief that the FDA lacks such jurisdiction under the FDCA. As a result, Congress' tobacco-specific statutes preclude the FDA from regulating tobacco products as customarily marketed. . . .

[O]ur conclusion does not rely on the fact that the FDA's assertion of jurisdiction represents a sharp break with its prior interpretation of the FDCA. Certainly, an agency's initial interpretation of a statute that it is charged with administering is not "carved in stone." Chevron, 467 U.S., at 863 [other citations omitted]. As we recognized in Motor Vehicle Mfrs. Assn. of United States, Inc. v. State Farm Mut. Automobile Ins. Co., 463 U.S. 29 (1983), agencies "must be given ample latitude to 'adapt their rules and policies to the demands of changing circumstances.' " Id., at 42. The consistency of the FDA's prior position is significant in this case for a different reason: it provides important context to Congress' enactment of its tobacco-specific legislation. When the FDA repeatedly informed Congress that the FDCA does not grant it the authority to regulate tobacco products, its statements were consistent with the agency's unwavering position since its inception, and with the position that its predecessor agency had first taken in 1914. Although not crucial, the consistency of the FDA's prior position bolsters the conclusion that when Congress created a distinct regulatory scheme addressing the subject of tobacco and health, it understood that the FDA is without jurisdiction to regulate tobacco products and ratified that position.

The dissent also argues that the proper inference to be drawn from Congress' tobacco-specific legislation is "critically ambivalent." We disagree. In that series of statutes, Congress crafted a specific legislative response to the problem of tobacco and health, and it did so with the understanding, based on repeated assertions by the FDA, that the agency has no authority under the FDCA to regulate tobacco products. Moreover, Congress expressly preempted any other regulation of the labeling of tobacco products concerning their health consequences, even though the oversight of labeling is central to the FDCA's regulatory scheme. And in addressing the subject, Congress consistently evidenced its intent to preclude any federal agency from exercising significant policymaking authority in the area. Under these circumstances, we believe the appropriate inference—that Congress intended to ratify the FDA's prior position that it lacks jurisdiction—is unmistakable.

The dissent alternatively argues that, even if Congress' subsequent tobacco-specific legislation did, in fact, ratify the FDA's position, that position was merely a contingent disavowal of jurisdiction. Specifically, the dissent contends that "the FDA's traditional view was largely premised on a perceived inability to prove the necessary statutory 'intent' requirement." A fair reading of the FDA's representations prior to 1995, however, demonstrates that the agency's position was essentially unconditional. [Citation.] To the extent the agency's position could be characterized as equivocal, it was only with respect to the well-established exception of when the manufacturer makes express claims of therapeutic benefit. [Citation.] Thus, what Congress ratified was the FDA's plain and resolute position that the FDCA gives the agency no authority to regulate tobacco products as customarily marketed. . . .

Reading the FDCA as a whole, as well as in conjunction with Congress' subsequent tobacco-specific legislation, it is plain that Congress has not given the FDA the authority that it seeks to exercise here. For these reasons, the judgment of the Court of Appeals for the Fourth Circuit is affirmed.

It is so ordered.

■ JUSTICE BREYER, with whom JUSTICE STEVENS, JUSTICE SOUTER, and JUSTICE GINSBURG join, dissenting.

The Food and Drug Administration (FDA) has the authority to regulate "articles (other than food) intended to affect the structure or any function of the body. . . ." Federal Food, Drug and Cosmetic Act (FDCA), 21 U.S.C. § 321(g)(1)(C). Unlike the majority, I believe that tobacco products fit within this statutory language.

In its own interpretation, the majority nowhere denies the following two salient points. First, tobacco products (including cigarettes) fall within the scope of this statutory definition, read literally. Cigarettes achieve their mood-stabilizing effects through the interaction of the chemical nicotine and the cells of the central nervous system. Both cigarette manufacturers and smokers alike know of, and desire, that chemically induced result. Hence, cigarettes are "intended to affect" the body's "structure" and "function," in the literal sense of these words.

Second, the statute's basic purpose—the protection of public health—supports the inclusion of cigarettes within its scope. See United States v. Article of Drug . . . Bacto-Unidisk, 394 U.S. 784, 798 (1969) (FDCA "is to be given *a liberal construction consistent with [its] overriding purpose to protect the public health*" (emphasis added)). Unregulated tobacco use causes [m]ore than 400,000 people [to] die each year from tobacco-related illnesses, such as cancer, respiratory illnesses, and heart disease. 61 Fed.Reg. 44398 (1996). Indeed, tobacco products kill more people in this country every year "than . . . AIDS, car accidents, alcohol, homicides, illegal drugs, suicides, and fires, *combined*." Ibid. (emphasis added).

Despite the FDCA's literal language and general purpose (both of which support the FDA's finding that cigarettes come within its statutory authority), the majority nonetheless reads the statute as excluding tobacco products for two basic reasons:

(1) the FDCA does not "fit" the case of tobacco because the statute requires the FDA to prohibit dangerous drugs or devices (like cigarettes) outright, and the agency concedes that simply banning the sale of cigarettes is not a proper remedy; and

(2) Congress has enacted other statutes, which, when viewed in light of the FDA's long history of denying tobacco-related jurisdiction and considered together with Congress' failure explicitly to grant the agency tobacco-specific authority, demonstrate that Congress did not intend for the FDA to exercise jurisdiction over tobacco.

In my view, neither of these propositions is valid. Rather, the FDCA does not significantly limit the FDA's remedial alternatives. And the later statutes do not tell the FDA it cannot exercise jurisdiction, but simply leave FDA jurisdictional law where Congress found it. . . .

The bulk of the opinion that follows will explain the basis for these latter conclusions. In short, I believe that the most important indicia of statutory meaning—language and purpose—along with the FDCA's legislative history (described briefly in Part I) are sufficient to establish that the FDA has authority to regulate tobacco. . . .

I

Before 1938, the federal Pure Food and Drug Act contained only two jurisdictional definitions of "drug":

"[1] medicines and preparations recognized in the United States Pharmacopoeia or National Formulary . . . and [2] any substance or mixture of substances intended to be used for the cure, mitigation, or prevention of disease." Act of June 30, 1906, ch. 3915, § 6, 34 Stat. 769.

In 1938, Congress added a third definition, relevant here:

"(3) articles (other than food) intended to affect the structure or any function of the body. . . ." Act of June 25, 1938, ch. 675, § 201(g), 52 Stat. 1041 (codified at 21 U.S.C. § 321(g)(1)(C)).

It also added a similar definition in respect to a "device." See § 201(h), 52 Stat. 1041 (codified at 21 U.S.C. § 321(h)). As I have mentioned, the literal language of the third definition and the FDCA's general purpose both strongly support a projurisdiction reading of the statute. See *supra*, at 1316.

The statute's history offers further support. The FDA drafted the new language, and it testified before Congress that the third definition would expand the FDCA's jurisdictional scope significantly. . . .

That Congress would grant the FDA such broad jurisdictional authority should surprise no one. In 1938, the President and much of Congress believed that federal administrative agencies needed broad authority and would exercise that authority wisely—a view embodied in much Second New Deal legislation. . . . Thus, at around the same time that it added the relevant language to the FDCA, Congress enacted laws granting other administrative agencies even broader powers to regulate much of the Nation's transportation and communication. [Citation.] Why would the 1938 New Deal Congress suddenly have hesitated to delegate to so well established an agency as the FDA all of the discretionary authority that a straightforward reading of the relevant statutory language implies?

Nor is it surprising that such a statutory delegation of power could lead after many years to an assertion of jurisdiction that the 1938 legislators might not have expected. Such a possibility is inherent in the very nature of a broad delegation. In 1938, it may well have seemed unlikely that the FDA would ever bring cigarette manufacturers within the FDCA's statutory language by proving that cigarettes produce chemical changes in the body and that the makers "intended" their product chemically to affect the body's "structure" or "function." Or, back then, it may have seemed unlikely that, even assuming such proof, the FDA actually would exercise its discretion to regulate so popular a product. See R. Kluger, Ashes to Ashes 105 (1997) (in the 1930's "Americans were in love with smoking . . .").

But it should not have seemed unlikely that, assuming the FDA decided to regulate and proved the particular jurisdictional prerequisites, the courts would rule such a jurisdictional assertion fully authorized. Cf. United States v. Southwestern Cable Co., 392 U.S. 157, 172 (1968) (reading Federal Communications Act as authorizing FCC jurisdiction to regulate cable systems while noting that "Congress could not in 1934 have foreseen the development of" advanced communications systems). After all, this Court has read more narrowly phrased statutes to grant what might have seemed even more unlikely assertions of agency jurisdiction. See, e.g., Permian Basin Area Rate Cases, 390 U.S. 747, 774–777 (1968) (statutory authority to regulate interstate "transportation" of natural gas includes authority to regulate "prices" charged by field producers); Phillips Petroleum Co. v. Wisconsin, 347 U.S. 672, 677–684 (1954) (independent gas producer subject to regulation despite Natural Gas Act's express exemption of gathering and production facilities).

I shall not pursue these general matters further, for neither the companies nor the majority denies that the FDCA's literal language, its general purpose, and its particular legislative history favor the FDA's present jurisdictional view. Rather, they have made several specific arguments in support of one basic contention: even if the statutory delegation is broad, it is not broad enough to include tobacco. I now turn to each of those arguments.

II

A

The tobacco companies contend that the FDCA's words cannot possibly be read to mean what they literally say. The statute defines "device," for example, as "an instrument, apparatus, implement, machine, contrivance, implant, in vitro reagent, or other similar or related article . . . intended to affect the structure or any function of the body. . . ." 21 U.S.C. § 321(h). Taken literally, this definition might include everything from room air conditioners to thermal pajamas. The companies argue that, to avoid such a result, the meaning of "drug" or "device" should be confined to medical or therapeutic products, narrowly defined. [Citation.]

The companies may well be right that the statute should not be read to cover room air conditioners and winter underwear. But I do not agree that we must accept their proposed limitation. For one thing, such a cramped reading contravenes the established purpose of the statutory language. See *Bacto-Unidisk*, 394 U.S., at 798 (third definition is "clearly, broader than any strict medical definition"); 1 Leg. Hist. 108 (definition covers products "that cannot be alleged to be treatments for diseased conditions"). For another, the companies' restriction would render the other two "drug" definitions superfluous. See 21 U.S.C. §§ 321(g)(1)(A), (g)(1)(B) (covering articles in the leading pharmacology compendia and those "intended for use in the diagnosis, cure, mitigation, treatment, or prevention of disease").

Most importantly, the statute's language itself supplies a different, more suitable, limitation: that a "drug" must be a *chemical* agent. The FDCA's "device" definition states that an article which affects the structure or function of the body is a "device" only if it "does *not* achieve its primary intended purposes through chemical action within . . . the body," and "is *not* dependent upon being metabolized for the achievement of its primary intended purposes." § 321(h) (emphasis added). One can readily infer from this language that at least an article that *does* achieve its primary purpose through chemical action within the body and that *is* dependent upon being metabolized is a "drug," provided that it otherwise falls within the scope of the "drug" definition. And one need not hypothesize about air conditioners or thermal pajamas to recognize that the chemical nicotine, an important tobacco ingredient, meets this test. . . .

B

The tobacco companies' principal definitional argument focuses upon the statutory word "intended." See 21 U.S.C. § 321(g)(1)(C). The companies say that "intended" in this context is a term of art. See Brief for Respondent Brown & Williamson Tobacco Corp. 2. They assert that the statutory word "intended" means that the product's maker has made an express claim about the effect that its product will have on the body. Ibid. Indeed, according to the companies, the FDA's inability to prove that cigarette manufacturers make such claims is precisely why that agency historically has said it lacked the statutory power to regulate tobacco. See *id.*, at 19–20.

The FDCA, however, does not use the word "claimed"; it uses the word "intended." And the FDA long ago issued regulations that say the relevant "intent" can be shown not only by a manufacturer's "expressions," but also "by the circumstances surrounding the distribution of the article." 41 Fed.Reg. 6896 (1976) (codified at 21 CFR § 801.4 (1999)); see also 41 Fed.Reg. 6896 (1976) ("objective intent" shown if "article is, with the knowledge [of its makers], offered and used" for a particular purpose). Thus, even in the absence of express claims, the FDA has regulated products that affect the body if the manufacturer wants, and knows, that consumers so use the product. See, e.g., 60 Fed.Reg. 41527–41531 (1995) (describing agency's regulation of topical hormones, sunscreens, fluoride, tanning lamps, thyroid in food supplements, novelty condoms—all marketed without express claims); see also O'Reilly, Food and Drug Administration § 13.04, at 13–15 ("Sometimes the very nature of the material makes it a drug . . .").

Courts ordinarily reverse an agency interpretation of this kind only if Congress has clearly answered the interpretive question or if the agency's interpretation is unreasonable. Chevron U.S.A. Inc. v. Natural Resources Defense Council, Inc., 467 U.S. 837, 842–843 (1984). The companies, in an effort to argue the former, point to language in the legislative history tying the word "intended" to a technical concept called "intended use." But nothing in Congress' discussion either of "intended" or "intended use" suggests that an express claim (which often shows intent) is always necessary. Indeed, the primary statement to which the companies direct our attention says only that a manufacturer can determine what kind of regulation applies—"food" or "drug"—because, through his representations in connection with its sale, [the manufacturer] can determine whether an article is to be used as a "food," as a "drug," or as "both." S.Rep. No. 361, 74th Cong., 1st Sess., 4 (1935), reprinted in 3 Leg. Hist. 696.

Nor is the FDA's "objective intent" interpretation unreasonable. It falls well within the established scope of the ordinary meaning of the word "intended." See Agnew v. United States, 165 U.S. 36, 53 (1897) (intent encompasses the known consequences of an act). And the companies acknowledge that the FDA can regulate a drug-like substance in the ordinary circumstance, i.e., where the manufacturer makes an express claim, so it is not unreasonable to conclude that the agency retains such power where a product's effects on the body are so well known (say, like those of aspirin or calamine lotion), that there is no need for express representations because the product speaks for itself.

The companies also cannot deny that the evidence of their intent is sufficient to satisfy the statutory word "intended" as the FDA long has interpreted it. . . . With such evidence, the FDA has more than sufficiently established that the companies "intend" their products to "affect" the body within the meaning of the FDCA.

C

The majority nonetheless reaches the "inescapable conclusion" that the language and structure of the FDCA as a whole "simply do not fit" the kind of public health problem that tobacco creates. That is because, in the majority's view, the FDCA requires the FDA to ban outright "dangerous" drugs or devices (such as cigarettes); yet, the FDA concedes that an immediate and total cigarette-sale ban is inappropriate. Ibid.

This argument is curious because it leads with similarly "inescapable" force to precisely the opposite conclusion, namely, that the FDA does have jurisdiction but that it must ban cigarettes. More importantly, the argument fails to take into account the fact that a statute interpreted as requiring the FDA to pick a more dangerous over a less dangerous remedy would be a perverse statute, causing, rather than preventing, unnecessary harm whenever a total ban is likely the more dangerous response. And one can at least imagine such circumstances.

Suppose, for example, that a commonly used, mildly addictive sleeping pill (or, say, a kind of popular contact lens), plainly within the FDA's jurisdiction, turned out to pose serious health risks for certain consumers. Suppose further that many of those addicted consumers would ignore an immediate total ban, turning to a potentially more dangerous black-market substitute, while a less draconian remedy (say, adequate notice) would wean them gradually away to a safer product. Would the FDCA still force the FDA to impose the more dangerous remedy? For the following reasons, I think not.

First, the statute's language does not restrict the FDA's remedial powers in this way. The FDCA permits the FDA to regulate a "combination product"—i.e., a "device" (such as a cigarette) that contains a "drug" (such as nicotine)—under its "device" provisions. 21 U.S.C. § 353(g)(1). And the FDCA's "device" provisions explicitly grant the FDA wide remedial discretion. For example, where the FDA cannot "otherwise" obtain "reasonable assurance" of a device's "safety and effectiveness," the agency may restrict by regulation a product's "sale, distribution, or use" upon "*such . . . conditions as the Secretary may prescribe.*" § 360j(e)(1) (emphasis added). And the statutory section that most clearly addresses the FDA's power to ban (entitled Banned devices) says that, where a device presents "an unreasonable and substantial risk of illness or injury," the Secretary "*may*"—not *must*—"initiate a proceeding . . . to make such device a banned device." § 360f(a) (emphasis added).

The tobacco companies point to another statutory provision which says that if a device "would cause serious, adverse health consequences or death, the Secretary *shall* issue" a cease distribution order. 21 U.S.C. § 360h(e)(1) (emphasis added). But that word "shall" in this context cannot mean that the Secretary must resort to the recall remedy *whenever* a device would have serious, adverse health effects. Rather, that language must mean that the Secretary "shall issue" a cease distribution order in compliance with the section's procedural requirements if the Secretary chooses *in her discretion* to use that particular subsection's recall remedy. Otherwise, the subsection would trump and make meaningless the same section's provision of other lesser remedies such as simple "notice" (which the Secretary similarly can impose if, but only if, she finds that the device "presents an unreasonable risk of substantial harm to the public"). § 360h(a)(1). And reading the statute to compel the FDA to "recall" every dangerous device likewise would conflict with that same subsection's statement that the recall remedy "shall be *in addition to* [the other] remedies provided" in the statute. § 360h(e)(3) (emphasis added).

The statute's language, then, permits the agency to choose remedies consistent with its basic purpose—the overall protection of public health.

The second reason the FDCA does not require the FDA to select the more dangerous remedy, is that, despite the majority's assertions to the contrary, the statute does not distinguish among the kinds of health effects that the agency may take into account when assessing safety. The Court insists that the statute only permits the agency to take into account the health risks and benefits of the "product itself" as used by individual consumers and, thus, that the FDA is prohibited from considering that a ban on smoking would lead many smokers to suffer severe withdrawal symptoms or to buy possibly stronger, more dangerous, black market cigarettes—considerations that the majority calls "the aggregate health effects of alternative administrative actions." Ibid. But the FDCA expressly permits the FDA to take account of comparative safety in precisely this manner. See, e.g., 21 U.S.C. § 360h(e)(2)(B)(i)(II) (no device recall "if risk of recal[l]" presents "a greater health risk than" no recall); § 360h(a) (notification "unless" notification "would present a greater danger" than "no such notification"). . . .

I concede that, as a matter of logic, one could consider the FDA's "safety" evaluation to be different from its choice of remedies. But to read the statute to forbid the agency from taking account of the realities of consumer behavior either in assessing safety or in choosing a remedy could increase the risks of harm—doubling the risk of death to each "individual user" in my example above. Why would Congress insist that the FDA ignore such realities, even if the consequent harm would occur only unusually, say, where the FDA evaluates a product (a sleeping pill; a cigarette; a contact lens) that is already on the market, potentially habit forming, or popular? I can find no satisfactory answer to this question. And that, I imagine, is why the statute itself says nothing about any of the distinctions that the Court has tried to draw. See 21 U.S.C. § 360c(a)(2) (instructing FDA to determine the safety and effectiveness of a "device" in part by weighing "any probable benefit to health . . . against *any* probable risk of injury or illness . . .") (emphasis added). . . .

In my view, where linguistically permissible, we should interpret the FDCA in light of Congress' overall desire to protect health. That purpose requires a flexible interpretation that both permits the FDA to take into account the realities of human behavior and allows it, in appropriate cases, to choose from its arsenal of statutory remedies. A statute so interpreted easily "fit[s]" this, and other, drug-and device-related health problems.

III

In the majority's view, laws enacted since 1965 require us to deny jurisdiction, whatever the FDCA might mean in their absence. But why? Do those laws contain language barring FDA jurisdiction? The majority must concede that they do not. Do they contain provisions that are inconsistent with the FDA's exercise of jurisdiction? With one exception, the majority points to no such provision. Do they somehow repeal the principles of law (discussed in Part II, *supra*) that otherwise would lead to the conclusion that the FDA has jurisdiction in this area? The companies themselves deny making any such claim. See Tr. of Oral Arg. 27 (denying reliance on doctrine of "partial repeal"). Perhaps the later laws "shape" and "focus" what the 1938 Congress meant a generation earlier. But this Court has warned against using the views of a later Congress to construe a statute enacted many years before. See Pension Benefit Guaranty Corporation v. LTV Corp., 496 U.S. 633, 650 (1990) (later history is "a 'hazardous basis for inferring the intent of an earlier' " Congress (quoting United States v. Price, 361 U.S. 304, 313 (1960))). And, while the majority suggests that the subsequent history "control[s] our construction" of the FDCA, this Court expressly has held that such subsequent views are not "controlling." Haynes v. United States, 390 U.S. 85, 87–88, n. 4 (1968); accord, Southwestern Cable Co., 392 U.S., at 170 (such views have "very little, if any, significance"); see also Sullivan v. Finkelstein, 496 U.S. 617, 632 (1990) (SCALIA, J., concurring) ("Arguments based on subsequent legislative history . . . should not be taken seriously, not even in a footnote.").

Regardless, the later statutes do not support the majority's conclusion. That is because, whatever individual Members of Congress after 1964 may have assumed about the FDA's jurisdiction, the laws they enacted did not embody any such "no jurisdiction" assumption. And one cannot automatically infer an antijurisdiction intent, as the majority does, for the later statutes are both (and similarly) consistent with quite a different congressional desire, namely, the intent to proceed without interfering with whatever authority the FDA otherwise may have possessed. See, e.g., Cigarette Labeling and Advertising—1965: Hearings on H.R. 2248 et al. before the House Committee on Interstate and Foreign Commerce, 89th Cong., 1st Sess., 19 (1965) (hereinafter 1965 Hearings) (statement of Rep. Fino that the proposed legislation would not "erode" agency authority). . . . [Indeed], the subsequent legislative history is critically ambivalent, for it can be read either as (a) "ratif[ying]" a no-jurisdiction assumption, or as (b) leaving the jurisdictional question just where Congress found it. And the fact that both inferences are "equally tenable," *Pension Benefit Guaranty Corp., supra,* at 650 (citation and internal quotation marks omitted); Johnson v. Transportation Agency, Santa Clara Cty., 480 U.S. 616, 672 (1987) (SCALIA, J., dissenting), prevents the majority from drawing from the later statutes the firm, antijurisdiction implication that it needs. . . .

IV

I now turn to the final historical fact that the majority views as a factor in its interpretation of the subsequent legislative history: the FDA's former denials of its tobacco-related authority.

Until the early 1990's, the FDA expressly maintained that the 1938 statute did not give it the power that it now seeks to assert. It then changed its mind. The majority agrees with me that the FDA's change of positions does not make a significant legal difference. see also *Chevron,* 467 U.S., at 863 ("An initial agency interpretation is not instantly carved in stone"); accord, Smiley v. Citibank (South Dakota), N. A., 517 U.S. 735, 742 (1996) ("[C]hange is not invalidating"). Nevertheless, it labels those denials "important context" for drawing an inference about Congress' intent. In my view, the FDA's change of policy, like the subsequent statutes themselves, does nothing to advance the majority's position.

When it denied jurisdiction to regulate cigarettes, the FDA consistently stated why that was so. In 1963, for example, FDA administrators wrote that cigarettes did not satisfy the relevant FDCA definitions—in particular, the "intent" requirement—because cigarette makers did not sell their product with accompanying "therapeutic claims." Letter to Directors of Bureaus, Divisions and Directors of Districts from FDA Bureau of Enforcement (May 24, 1963), in Public Health Cigarette Amendments of 1971: Hearings on S. 1454 before the Consumer Subcommittee of the Senate Committee on Commerce, 92d Cong., 2d Sess., 240 (1972) (hereinafter FDA Enforcement Letter). And subsequent FDA Commissioners made roughly the same assertion. . . .

[A] fair reading of the FDA's denials suggests that the overwhelming problem was one of proving the requisite manufacturer intent. See Action on Smoking and Health v. Harris, 655 F.2d 236, 238–239 (C.A.D.C.1980) (FDA "comments" reveal its "understanding" that "the crux of FDA jurisdiction over drugs lay in manufacturers' representations as revelatory of their intent").

What changed? For one thing, the FDA obtained evidence sufficient to prove the necessary "intent" despite the absence of specific "claims." This evidence, which first became available in the early 1990's, permitted the agency to demonstrate that the tobacco companies knew nicotine achieved appetite-suppressing, mood-stabilizing, and habituating effects through chemical (not psychological) means, even at a time when the companies were publicly denying such knowledge.

Moreover, scientific evidence of adverse health effects mounted, until, in the late 1980's, a consensus on the seriousness of the matter became firm. . . .

Finally, administration policy changed. Earlier administrations may have hesitated to assert jurisdiction for the reasons prior Commissioners expressed. Commissioners of the current administration simply took a different regulatory attitude.

Nothing in the law prevents the FDA from changing its policy for such reasons. . . .

The upshot is that the Court today holds that a regulatory statute aimed at unsafe drugs and devices does not authorize regulation of a drug (nicotine) and a device (a cigarette) that the Court itself finds unsafe. Far more than most, this particular drug and device risks the life-threatening harms that administrative regulation seeks to rectify. The majority's conclusion is counter intuitive. And, for the reasons set forth, I believe that the law does not require it.

Consequently, I dissent.

NOTES AND QUESTIONS

1.   The majority suggests that the FDA's current determination to regulate tobacco products is illegitimate in light of the agency's prior disavowals of authority. Is this consistent with the *Chevron* approach to agency policy changes?

2.   The majority contends that, if the FDA has jurisdiction to regulate tobacco products at all, the FDA must ban them, it may not take lesser measures. As Congress has given no indication that it wished tobacco products banned, it would follow that the FDA lacks jurisdiction over tobacco products. More typically, however, if a legislature grants authority to take "greater" actions (such as totally prohibiting), it also implicitly authorizes "lesser" responses (such as regulation). Should a "greater/lesser" argument prevail here? Why or why not?

3.   The dissent argues that the majority's conclusion requires looking to later laws as "shap[ing]" and "focus[ing]" what an earlier Congress meant, a problematic approach insofar as the Court has elsewhere "warned against using the views of a later Congress to construe a statute enacted many years before." Recall the typology of interpretive methods in subsection III.A.3.a, *supra*. If one seeks to understand what Congress either objectively or subjectively intended in enacting a statute, is it appropriate to look to materials post-dating the statute's enactment? On the other hand, could the statute itself be understood to invite an evolutionary approach to its interpretation, with its "shape" and "focus" evolving as social and technological changes require new approaches to regulation? Recall Judge Leval's distinction between "micromanager" and "delegating" statutes in Section III.B, *supra*. What textual evidence in the statute supports an interpretation of the FDCA as either a micromanager or delegating statute?

4. The proper application of *Chevron* deference and the distinction between micromanager and delegating statutes raise related questions about whether courts should employ interpretive legal methods differently for statutes that are primarily addressed to administrative agencies:

> The law often designates to regulatory agencies like the IRS an "official" interpreter status, and both state and federal laws deem certain officials to be the authoritative interpreters of relevant bodies of law that fall under their jurisdiction. . . . [and so] official interpreters abound in federal administrative law. They include agencies entitled to "*Chevron*" deference because they have been delegated law-making authority by Congress to engage in legislative rulemaking with the effect of law. Peter Strauss has called this the "*Chevron* space": the area within which Congress has statutorily empowered the agency to act in a manner that creates obligations or constraints that carry legal force derived from the statute.
>
> . . . [A]gencies interpret statutes in many kinds of actions beyond the rulemaking and binding adjudications that formally warrant *Chevron* deference: these include interpretative rules, enforcement guidelines, policy manuals, opinion letters, no-action letters, and agency guidance, among others. In theory, where Congress has not delegated lawmaking authority to the agency, less deferential "*Skidmore* weight" applies, and so agency interpretations rendered in these more informal documents are not entitled to *Chevron* deference.
>
> In practice, informal or (un)official interpretations such as agency guidance nevertheless have a significant effect on how other . . . statutory audiences act to conform their conduct to law, particularly given that such official interpretive positions may effectively govern the field for years or even decades unless and until a court is called upon to review a legal challenge to the agency's interpretation. . . .
>
> [L]egislative delegations to administrative agencies are often purposefully broad and intransitive statutory instructions to develop clear and concrete rules, rather than provide precise rules themselves. Indeed, this intransitivity is one of the primary justifications for *Chevron* deference in the first place. Within this "*Chevron* space," . . . broad authorizing statutes often do not have "a single best interpretation"; instead, interpretation typically involves agency choice within a policy space defined by the range of the statute's reasonable interpretations. . . .
>
> Congress often gives important signals to an agency through the legislative drafting process itself, and so extratextual evidence provided in the legislative history of the statute may be especially useful for the agency tasked with implementing and interpreting the law. For intransitive administrative statutes, it is much rarer for agencies to make regulatory choices on the basis of an

interpretation of the semantic meaning of the text alone. In determining Congress's ambition behind an ambiguous instruction, the agency would almost certainly begin by examining sources of contextual meaning such as the legislative history. As Peter Strauss has noted, "[l]egislative history has a centrality and importance for agency lawyers that might not readily be conceived by persons who are outside government." Congressional drafters often interface directly with agencies in the course of drafting the laws the agencies will be authorized to enforce, including the production of materials that constitute the statute's legislative history. Post-enactment, agencies are staffed with both legal and policy experts who have the time and expertise to undergo such research before acting. . . .

Thus, when courts review the interpretations of such official interpreters, it would seem especially appropriate that they draw on the same resources as the agencies themselves do and that Congress often expects. This is one rationale for *Chevron* deference, and it is also borne out in judicial practice. Bill Eskridge and Lauren Baer have identified that the Supreme Court relies on legislative history more often in Chevron cases than in non-Chevron cases, which is not surprising given the relatively greater weight agencies place on legislative history in developing their own interpretations and understandings of statutory meaning.

Nevertheless, the origin of legislative history as an interpretive method cautions against its unvarnished application for statutes directed at all audiences, for its initial development as an interpretive method was motivated by its strategic advantage for particular government audiences. Nicholas Parrillo has documented how legislative history as a method of interpretation arose in the wake of the newly expanded New Deal administrative state, which was "vested with unprecedented capability to process and analyze congressional discourse and translate it into legal argument." Given federal agencies' unequalled access and resources, Parrillo has concluded that "[l]egislative history was therefore a statist tool of interpretation, in the sense that the administrative state enjoyed privileged access to such material and was a privileged provider of it to the Court, more than was true of other interpretive sources, such as statutory text."

However, agency insiders did not long remain the sole beneficiaries of legislative history. Because of the "peculiar openness of the legislative process in America," Parrillo has noted that judicial reliance on legislative history also privileged "lawyer-lobbyists above the general population of lawyers" (let alone other audiences). These lawyers entered and exited the "revolving door" between law firms, lobbying firms, and government, and after World War II "created a new kind of law firm—the 'Washington law firm'—staffed by veterans of the administrative state and dedicated to constant lobbying of that state and of Congress."

Unsurprisingly, industry and trade associations and the Washington law firms they hire are the chief antagonists of the agencies and their frequent sparring partners in litigation. While the playing field has since become more (though not entirely) level, this history demonstrates precisely why normative questions of statutory audience and interpretive methods questions must be evaluated side by side, for some methods of interpretation may be more advantageous for some audiences at the expense of others. . . .

David S. Louk, *The Audiences of Statutes*, 105 Cornell L. Rev. 137 (2019).

Consider these questions of method as you read *Babbitt v. Sweet Home, infra.*

Babbitt v. Sweet Home Chapter of Communities for a Great Oregon

Supreme Court of the United States, 1995.
515 U.S. 687, 115 S.Ct. 2407, 132 L.Ed.2d 597.

■ JUSTICE STEVENS delivered the opinion of the Court[, in which JUSTICE KENNEDY, JUSTICE SOUTER, JUSTICE GINSBURG, and JUSTICE BREYER joined].

The Endangered Species Act of 1973 . . . makes it unlawful for any person to "take" any endangered or threatened species. The Secretary has promulgated a regulation that defines the statute's prohibition on takings to include "significant habitat modification or degradation where it actually kills or injures wildlife." This case presents the question whether the Secretary exceeded his authority under the Act by promulgating that regulation.

I

. . . Section 3(19) of the [Endangered Species] Act defines the statutory term "take":

"The term 'take' means to harass, harm, pursue, hunt, shoot, wound, kill, trap, capture, or collect, or to attempt to engage in any such conduct." 16 U.S.C. § 1532(19).

The Act does not further define the terms it uses to define "take." The Interior Department regulations that implement the statute, however, define the statutory term "harm":

"*Harm* in the definition of 'take' in the Act means an act which actually kills or injures wildlife. Such act may include significant habitat modification or degradation where it actually kills or injures wildlife by significantly impairing essential behavioral patterns, including breeding, feeding, or sheltering." 50 CFR § 17.3 (1994).

This regulation has been in place since 1975.[2]

_____

[2] The Secretary, through the Director of the Fish and Wildlife Service, originally promulgated the regulation in 1975 and amended it in 1981 to emphasize that actual death or

A limitation on the § 9 "take" prohibition appears in § 10(a)(1)(B) of the Act, which Congress added by amendment in 1982. That section authorizes the Secretary to grant a permit for any taking otherwise prohibited by § 9(a)(1)(B) "if such taking is incidental to, and not the purpose of, the carrying out of an otherwise lawful activity." 16 U.S.C. § 1539(a)(1)(B). . . .

Respondents in this action are small landowners, logging companies, and families dependent on the forest products industries in the Pacific Northwest and in the Southeast, and organizations that represent their interests. They brought this declaratory judgment action against petitioners, the Secretary of the Interior and the Director of the Fish and Wildlife Service, in the United States District Court for the District of Columbia to challenge the statutory validity of the Secretary's regulation defining "harm," particularly the inclusion of habitat modification and degradation in the definition. Respondents challenged the regulation on its face. Their complaint alleged that application of the "harm" regulation to the redcockaded woodpecker, an endangered species, and the northern spotted owl, a threatened species, had injured them economically.

. . . The District Court therefore entered summary judgment for petitioners and dismissed respondents' complaint. A divided panel of the Court of Appeals initially affirmed the judgment of the District Court. [Citation.] After granting a petition for rehearing, however, the panel reversed. . . .

II

Because this case was decided on motions for summary judgment, we may appropriately make certain factual assumptions in order to frame the legal issue. First, we assume respondents have no desire to harm either the red-cockaded woodpecker or the spotted owl; they merely wish to continue logging activities that would be entirely proper if not prohibited by the ESA. On the other hand, we must assume, *arguendo*, that those activities will have the effect, even though unintended, of detrimentally changing the natural habitat of both listed species and that, as a consequence, members of those species will be killed or injured. . . . The Secretary . . . submits that the § 9 prohibition on takings, which Congress defined to include "harm," places on respondents a duty to avoid harm that habitat alteration will cause the birds unless respondents first obtain a permit pursuant to § 10.

The text of the Act provides three reasons for concluding that the Secretary's interpretation is reasonable. First, an ordinary understanding of the word "harm" supports it. The dictionary definition of the verb form of "harm" is "to cause hurt or damage to: injure." Webster's Third New International Dictionary 1034 (1966). In the context of the ESA, that definition naturally encompasses habitat

injury of a protected animal is necessary for a violation. *See* 40 Fed. Reg. 44412, 44416 (1975); 46 Fed. Reg. 54748, 54750 (1981).

modification that results in actual injury or death to members of an endangered or threatened species.

Respondents argue that the Secretary should have limited the purview of "harm" to direct applications of force against protected species, but the dictionary definition does not include the word "directly" or suggest in any way that only direct or willful action that leads to injury constitutes "harm."[10] Moreover, unless the statutory term "harm" encompasses indirect as well as direct injuries, the word has no meaning that does not duplicate the meaning of other words that § 3 uses to define "take." A reluctance to treat statutory terms as surplusage supports the reasonableness of the Secretary's interpretation.[11] [Citation.]

Second, the broad purpose of the ESA supports the Secretary's decision to extend protection against activities that cause the precise harms Congress enacted the statute to avoid. . . . [W]e have described the Act as "the most comprehensive legislation for the preservation of endangered species ever enacted by any nation." [Citation.] Whereas predecessor statutes enacted in 1966 and 1969 had not contained any sweeping prohibition against the taking of endangered species except on federal lands, [citation,] the 1973 Act applied to all land in the United States and to the Nation's territorial seas. As stated in § 2 of the Act, among its central purposes is "to provide a means whereby the ecosystems upon which endangered species and threatened species depend may be conserved. . . ." 16 U.S.C. § 1531(b).

. . . Congress' intent to provide comprehensive protection for endangered and threatened species supports the permissibility of the Secretary's "harm" regulation.

Respondents advance strong arguments that activities that cause minimal or unforeseeable harm will not violate the Act as construed in the "harm" regulation. Respondents, however, present a facial challenge to the regulation. [Citation.] Thus, they ask us to invalidate the

---

[10] Respondents and the dissent emphasize what they portray as the "established meaning" of "take" in the sense of a "wildlife take," a meaning respondents argue extends only to "the effort to exercise dominion over some creature, and the concrete effect of [sic] that creature." . . . This limitation ill serves the statutory text, which forbids not taking "some creature" but "tak[ing] any [endangered] species"—a formidable task for even the most rapacious feudal lord. More importantly, Congress explicitly defined the operative term "take" in the ESA, no matter how much the dissent wishes otherwise . . . thereby obviating the need for us to probe its meaning as we must probe the meaning of the undefined subsidiary term "harm." Finally, Congress' definition of "take" includes several words—most obviously "harass," "pursue," and "wound," in addition to "harm" itself—that fit respondents' and the dissent's definition of "take" no better than does "significant habitat modification or degradation."

[11] In contrast, if the statutory term "harm" encompasses such indirect means of killing and injuring wildlife as habitat modification, the other terms listed in § 3—"harass," "pursue," "hunt," "shoot," "wound," "kill," "trap," "capture," and "collect"—generally retain independent meanings. Most of those terms refer to deliberate actions more frequently than does "harm," and they therefore do not duplicate the sense of indirect causation that "harm" adds to the statute. In addition, most of the other words in the definition describe either actions from which habitat modification does not usually result (e.g., "pursue," "harass") or effects to which activities that modify habitat do not usually lead (e.g., "trap," "collect"). To the extent the Secretary's definition of "harm" may have applications that overlap with other words in the definition, that overlap reflects the broad purpose of the Act.

Secretary's understanding of "harm" in every circumstance, even when an actor knows that an activity, such as draining a pond, would actually result in the extinction of a listed species by destroying its habitat. Given Congress' clear expression of the ESA's broad purpose to protect endangered and threatened wildlife, the Secretary's definition of "harm" is reasonable.

Third, the fact that Congress in 1982 authorized the Secretary to issue permits for takings that § 9(a)(1)(B) would otherwise prohibit, "if such taking is incidental to, and not the purpose of, the carrying out of an otherwise lawful activity," 16 U.S.C. § 1539(a)(1)(B), strongly suggests that Congress understood § 9(a)(1)(B) to prohibit indirect as well as deliberate takings. [Citation.] The permit process requires the applicant to prepare a "conservation plan" that specifies how he intends to "minimize and mitigate" the "impact" of his activity on endangered and threatened species, 16 U.S.C. § 1539(a)(2)(A), making clear that Congress had in mind foreseeable rather than merely accidental effects on listed species. No one could seriously request an "incidental" take permit to avert § 9 liability for direct, deliberate action against a member of an endangered or threatened species, but respondents would read "harm" so narrowly that the permit procedure would have little more than that absurd purpose. "When Congress acts to amend a statute, we presume it intends its amendment to have real and substantial effect." Stone v. INS, 514 U.S. 386, 397 (1995). Congress' addition of the § 10 permit provision supports the Secretary's conclusion that activities not intended to harm an endangered species, such as habitat modification, may constitute unlawful takings under the ESA unless the Secretary permits them.

The Court of Appeals made three errors in asserting that "harm" must refer to a direct application of force because the words around it do. First, the court's premise was flawed. Several of the words that accompany "harm" in the § 3 definition of "take," especially "harass," "pursue," "wound," and "kill," refer to actions or effects that do not require direct applications of force. Second, to the extent the court read a requirement of intent or purpose into the words used to define "take," it ignored § 11's express provision that a "knowin[g]" action is enough to violate the Act. Third, the court employed *noscitur a sociis* to give "harm" essentially the same function as other words in the definition, thereby denying it independent meaning. The canon, to the contrary, counsels that a word "gathers meaning from the words around it." [Citation.] The statutory context of "harm" suggests that Congress meant that term to serve a particular function in the ESA, consistent with, but distinct from, the functions of the other verbs used to define "take." The Secretary's interpretation of "harm" to include indirectly injuring endangered animals through habitat modification permissibly interprets "harm" to have "a character of its own not to be submerged by its association." [Citation.]

. . . We need not decide whether the statutory definition of "take" compels the Secretary's interpretation of "harm," because our conclusions that Congress did not unambiguously manifest its intent to adopt respondents' view and that the Secretary's interpretation is reasonable suffice to decide this case. *See generally* Chevron U.S.A. Inc. v. Natural Resources Defense Council, Inc., 467 U.S. 837 (1984). The latitude the ESA gives the Secretary in enforcing the statute, together with the degree of regulatory expertise necessary to its enforcement, establishes that we owe some degree of deference to the Secretary's reasonable interpretation. [Citation.]

III

Our conclusion that the Secretary's definition of "harm" rests on a permissible construction of the ESA gains further support from the legislative history of the statute. The Committee Reports accompanying the bills that became the ESA do not specifically discuss the meaning of "harm," but they make clear that Congress intended "take" to apply broadly to cover indirect as well as purposeful actions. The Senate Report stressed that " '[t]ake' is defined . . . in the broadest possible manner to include every conceivable way in which a person can 'take' or attempt to 'take' any fish or wildlife." [Citation.] The House Report stated that "the broadest possible terms" were used to define restrictions on takings. [Citation.] The House Report underscored the breadth of the "take" definition by noting that it included "harassment, *whether intentional or not.*" [Citation.] The Report explained that the definition "would allow, for example, the Secretary to regulate or prohibit the activities of bird-watchers where the effect of those activities might disturb the birds and make it difficult for them to hatch or raise their young." [Citation.] These comments, ignored in the dissent's welcome but selective foray into legislative history, support the Secretary's interpretation that the term "take" in § 9 reached far more than the deliberate actions of hunters and trappers. . . .

[A floor amendment that added "harm" to the definition, noting that this and accompanying amendments would "help to achieve the purposes of the bill."] Respondents argue that the lack of debate about the amendment that added "harm" counsels in favor of a narrow interpretation. We disagree. An obviously broad word that the Senate went out of its way to add to an important statutory definition is precisely the sort of provision that deserves a respectful reading.

The definition of "take" that originally appeared in S. 1983 differed from the definition as ultimately enacted in one other significant respect: It included "the destruction, modification, or curtailment of [the] habitat or range" of fish and wildlife. [Citation.] Respondents make much of the fact that the Commerce Committee removed this phrase from the "take" definition before S. 1983 went to the floor. [Citation.] We do not find that fact especially significant. The legislative materials contain no indication why the habitat protection provision was deleted. That provision differed greatly from the regulation at issue today. Most notably, the habitat protection provision in S. 1983 would have applied far more broadly than the regulation does because it made adverse habitat modification a categorical violation of the "take" prohibition, unbounded by the regulation's limitation to habitat modifications that actually kill or injure wildlife. The S. 1983 language also failed to qualify "modification" with the regulation's limiting adjective "significant." We do not believe the Senate's unelaborated disavowal of the provision in S. 1983 undermines the reasonableness of the more moderate habitat protection in the Secretary's "harm" regulation.

The history of the 1982 amendment that gave the Secretary authority to grant permits for "incidental" takings provides further support for his reading of the Act. The House Report expressly states that "[b]y use of the word 'incidental' the Committee intends to cover situations in which it is known that a taking will occur if the other activity is engaged in but such taking is incidental to, and not the purpose of, the activity." [Citation.] This reference to the foreseeability of incidental takings undermines respondents' argument that the 1982 amendment covered only accidental killings of endangered and threatened animals that might occur in the course of hunting or trapping other animals. Indeed, Congress had habitat modification directly in mind: both the Senate Report and the House Conference Report identified as the model for the permit process a cooperative state-federal response to a case in California where a development project threatened incidental harm to a species of endangered butterfly by modification of its habitat. [Citation.] Thus, Congress in 1982 focused squarely on the aspect of the "harm" regulation at issue in this litigation. Congress' implementation of a permit program is consistent with the Secretary's interpretation of the term "harm."

IV

When it enacted the ESA, Congress delegated broad administrative and interpretive power to the Secretary. See 16 U.S.C. §§ 1533, 1540(f). The task of defining and listing endangered and threatened species requires an expertise and attention to detail that exceeds the normal province of Congress. Fashioning appropriate standards for issuing permits under § 10 for takings that would otherwise violate § 9 necessarily requires the exercise of broad discretion. The proper interpretation of a term such as "harm" involves a complex policy choice. When Congress has entrusted the Secretary with broad discretion, we are especially reluctant to substitute our views of wise policy for his. See *Chevron,* 467 U.S., at 865–866. In this case, that reluctance accords with our conclusion, based on the text, structure, and legislative history of the ESA, that the Secretary reasonably construed the intent of Congress when he defined "harm" to include "significant habitat modification or degradation that actually kills or injures wildlife." . . .

The judgment of the Court of Appeals is reversed.

It is so ordered.

[The concurring opinion of JUSTICE O'CONNOR is omitted.]

■ JUSTICE SCALIA, with whom . . . CHIEF JUSTICE [REHNQUIST] and JUSTICE THOMAS join, dissenting.

I think it unmistakably clear that the legislation at issue here (1) forbade the hunting and killing of endangered animals, and (2) provided federal lands and federal funds *for the acquisition of private lands,* to preserve the habitat of endangered animals. The Court's holding that the hunting and killing prohibition incidentally preserves habitat on private lands imposes unfairness to the point of financial ruin—not just upon the rich, but upon the simplest farmer who finds his land conscripted to national zoological use. I respectfully dissent.

I

. . . In my view . . . the regulation must fall—even under the test of Chevron U.S.A. Inc. v. Natural Resources Defense Council, Inc., 467 U.S. 837, 843 (1984). . . . The regulation has three features which, for reasons I shall discuss at length below, do not comport with the statute.

First, it interprets the statute to prohibit habitat modification that is no more than the cause-in-fact of death or injury to wildlife. *Any* "significant habitat modification" that in fact produces that result by "impairing essential behavioral patterns" is made unlawful, regardless of whether that result is intended or even foreseeable, and no matter how long the chain of causality between modification and injury. . . . Second, the regulation does not require an "act"; the Secretary's officially stated position is that an *omission* will do. . . . The third and most important unlawful feature of the regulation is that it encompasses injury inflicted, not only upon individual animals, but upon populations of the protected species. "Injury" in the regulation includes "significantly impairing essential behavioral patterns, including *breeding,*" 50 CFR § 17.3 (1994) (emphasis added). Impairment of breeding does not "injure" living creatures; it prevents them from propagating, thus "injuring" *a population* of animals which would otherwise have maintained or increased its numbers. What the face of the regulation shows, the Secretary's official pronouncements confirm. The Final Redefinition of "Harm" accompanying publication of the regulation said that "harm" is not limited to "direct physical injury to an individual member of the wildlife species," [citation,] and refers to "injury *to a population,*" [citation] (emphasis added). . . .

None of these three features of the regulation can be found in the statutory provisions supposed to authorize it. The term "harm" in § 1532(19) has no legal force of its own. An indictment or civil complaint that charged the defendant with "harming" an animal protected under the Act would be dismissed as defective, for the only *operative* term in the statute is to "take." If "take" were not elsewhere defined in the Act, none could dispute what it means, for the term is as old as the law itself. To "take," when applied to wild animals, means to reduce those animals, by killing or capturing, to human control. See, *e.g.,* 11 Oxford English Dictionary (1933) ("Take . . . To catch, capture (a wild beast, bird, fish, etc.)"); Webster's New International Dictionary of the English Language (2d ed. 1949) (take defined as "to catch or capture by trapping, snaring, etc., or as prey"); Geer v. Connecticut, 161 U.S. 519, 523, 16 S.Ct. 600, 602, 40 L.Ed. 793 (1896) ("[A]ll the animals which can be taken upon the earth, in the sea, or in the air, that is to say, wild animals, belong to those who take them") (quoting the Digest of Justinian); 2 W. Blackstone, Commentaries 411 (1766) ("Every man . . . has an equal right of pursuing and taking to his own use all such creatures as are *ferae naturae*"). This is just the sense in which "take" is used elsewhere in federal legislation and treaty. See, *e.g.,* Migratory Bird Treaty Act, 16 U.S.C. § 703 (1988 ed., Supp. V) (no person may "pursue, hunt, take, capture, kill, [or] attempt to take, capture, or kill" any migratory bird); Agreement on the Conservation of Polar Bears, Nov. 15, 1973, Art. I, 27 U.S.T. 3918, 3921, T.I.A.S. No. 8409 (defining "taking" as "hunting, killing and capturing"). And that meaning fits neatly with the rest of § 1538(a)(1), which makes it unlawful not only to take protected species, but also to import or export them (§ 1538(a)(1)(A)); to possess, sell, deliver, carry, transport, or ship any taken species (§ 1538(a)(1)(D)); and to transport, sell, or offer to sell them in interstate or foreign commerce (§§ 1538(a)(1)(E)(F)). The taking prohibition, in other words, is only part of the regulatory plan of § 1538(a)(1), which covers all the stages of the process by which protected wildlife is reduced to man's dominion and made the object of profit. It is obvious that "take" in this sense—a term of art deeply embedded in the statutory and common law concerning wildlife—describes a class of acts (not omissions) done directly and intentionally (not indirectly and by accident) to particular animals (not populations of animals).

The Act's definition of "take" does expand the word slightly (and not unusually), so as to make clear that it includes not just a completed taking, but the process of taking, and all of the acts that are customarily identified with or accompany that process ("to harass, harm, pursue, hunt, shoot, wound, kill, trap, capture, or collect"); and so as to include attempts. § 1532(19). The tempting fallacy—which the Court commits with abandon—is to assume that *once defined,* "take" loses any significance, and it is only the definition that matters. The Court treats the statute as though Congress had directly enacted the § 1532(19) definition as a self-executing prohibition, and had not enacted § 1538(a)(1)(B) at all. But § 1538(a)(1)(B) *is* there, and if the terms contained in the definitional section are susceptible of two readings, one of which comports with the standard meaning of "take" as used in application to wildlife, and one of which does not, an agency regulation that adopts the latter reading is necessarily unreasonable, for it reads the defined term "take"—the only operative term—out of the statute altogether.[2]

That is what has occurred here. The verb "harm" has a *range* of meaning: "to cause injury" at its broadest, "to do hurt or damage" in a narrower and more direct sense. *See, e.g.,* 1 N. Webster, An American Dictionary of the English Language (1828) ("Harm, *v.t.* To hurt; to injure; to damage; *to impair soundness of body, either animal* or vegetable") (emphasis added); American College Dictionary 551 (1970) ("harm . . . *n.* injury; damage; hurt: *to do him bodily harm*"). In fact the more directed sense of "harm" is a somewhat more common and preferred usage; "*harm* has in it a little of the idea of specially focused hurt or injury, as if a personal injury has been anticipated and intended." J. Opdycke, Mark My Words: A Guide to Modern Usage and Expression 330 (1949). See also American Heritage Dictionary of the English Language (1981) ("*Injure* has the widest range. . . . *Harm* and *hurt* refer principally to what causes physical or mental distress to living things"). To define "harm" as an act or omission that, however remotely, "actually kills or injures" a population of wildlife through habitat modification, is to choose a meaning that makes nonsense of the word that "harm" defines— requiring us to accept that a farmer who tills his field and causes erosion that makes silt run into a nearby river which depletes oxygen and thereby "impairs [the] breeding" of protected fish, has "taken" or "attempted to take" the fish. It should take the strongest evidence to make us believe that Congress has defined a term in a manner repugnant to its ordinary and traditional sense.

Here the evidence shows the opposite. "Harm" is merely one of 10 prohibitory words in § 1532(19), and the other 9 fit the ordinary meaning of "take" perfectly. To "harass, pursue, hunt, shoot, wound, kill, trap, capture, or collect" are all affirmative acts (the provision itself describes them as "conduct," see § 1532(19)) which are directed immediately and intentionally against a particular animal—not acts or omissions that indirectly and accidentally cause injury to a population of animals. . . .

I am not the first to notice this fact, or to draw the conclusion that it compels. In 1981 the Solicitor of the Fish and Wildlife Service delivered a legal opinion on § 1532(19) that is in complete agreement with my reading:

"The Act's definition of 'take' contains a list of actions that illustrate the intended scope of the term. . . . With the possible exception of 'harm,' these terms all represent forms of conduct that are directed against and likely to injure or kill *individual* wildlife. Under the principle of statutory construction, *ejusdem generis,* . . . the term 'harm' should be interpreted

---

[2] The Court suggests halfheartedly that "take" cannot refer to the taking of particular animals, because § 1538(a)(1)(B) prohibits "tak[ing] any [endangered] species." The suggestion is halfhearted because that reading obviously contradicts the statutory intent. It would mean no violation in the intentional shooting of a single bald eagle—or, for that matter, the intentional shooting of 1,000 bald eagles out of the extant 1,001. The phrasing of § 1538(a)(1)(B), as the Court recognizes elsewhere, is shorthand for "take any member of [an endangered] species."

to include only those actions that are directed against, and likely to injure or kill, individual wildlife." Memorandum of April 17, 1981, reprinted in 46 Fed. Reg. 29490, 29491 (emphasis in original).

I would call it *noscitur a sociis,* but the principle is much the same: the fact that "several items in a list share an attribute counsels in favor of interpreting the other items as possessing that attribute as well," [Citation.] The Court contends that the canon cannot be applied to deprive a word of all its "independent meaning." That proposition is questionable to begin with, especially as applied to long lawyers' listings such as this. If it were true, we ought to give the word "trap" in the definition its rare meaning of "to clothe" (whence "trappings")—since otherwise it adds nothing to the word "capture." See Moskal v. United States, 498 U.S. 103, 120 (1990) (Scalia, J., dissenting). . . .

The penalty provisions of the Act counsel this interpretation as well. Any person who "knowingly" violates § 1538(a)(1)(B) is subject to criminal penalties under § 1540(b)(1) and civil penalties under § 1540(a)(1); moreover, under the latter section, any person "who otherwise violates" the taking prohibition (*i.e.,* violates it *un* knowingly) may be assessed a civil penalty of $500 for each violation, with the stricture that "[e]ach such violation shall be a separate offense." This last provision should be clear warning that the regulation is in error, for when combined with the regulation it produces a result that no legislature could reasonably be thought to have intended: A large number of routine private activities—farming, for example, farming, ranching, roadbuilding, construction and logging—are subjected to strict-liability penalties when they fortuitously injure protected wildlife, no matter how remote the chain of causation and no matter how difficult to foresee (or to disprove) the "injury" may be (*e.g.,* an "impairment" of breeding). . . .

So far I have discussed only the immediate statutory text bearing on the regulation. But the definition of "take" in § 1532(19) applies "[f]or the purposes of this chapter," that is, it governs the meaning of the word *as used everywhere in the Act.* Thus, the Secretary's interpretation of "harm" is wrong if it does not fit with the use of "take" throughout the Act. And it does not. In § 1540(e)(4)(B), for example, Congress provided for the forfeiture of "[a]ll guns, traps, nets, and other equipment . . . used to aid the taking, possessing, selling, [etc.]" of protected animals. This listing plainly relates to "taking" in the ordinary sense. If environmental modification were part (and necessarily a major part) of taking, as the Secretary maintains, one would have expected the list to include "plows, bulldozers, and backhoes." As another example, § 1539(e)(1) exempts "the taking of any endangered species" by Alaskan Indians and Eskimos "if such taking is primarily for subsistence purposes"; and provides that "[n]on-edible byproducts of species taken pursuant to this section may be sold . . . when made into authentic native articles of handicrafts and clothing." Surely these provisions apply to taking only in the ordinary sense, and are meaningless as applied to species injured by environmental modification. The Act is full of like examples. [Citation.] "[I]f the Act is to be interpreted as a symmetrical and coherent regulatory scheme, one in which the operative words have a consistent meaning throughout," [citation,] the regulation must fall.

The broader structure of the Act confirms the unreasonableness of the regulation. Section 1536 provides:

"Each Federal agency shall . . . insure that any action authorized, funded, or carried out by such agency . . . is not likely to jeopardize the continued existence of any endangered species or threatened species or *result in the destruction or adverse modification of habitat* of such species which is determined by the Secretary . . . to be critical." 16 U.S.C. § 1536(a)(2) (emphasis added). . . .

This means that the "harm" regulation also contradicts another principle of interpretation: that statutes should be read so far as possible to give independent effect to all their provisions. See Ratzlaf v. United States, 510 U.S. 135, 155. By defining "harm" in the definition of "take" in § 1538(a)(1)(B) to include significant habitat modification that injures populations of wildlife, the regulation makes the habitat-modification restriction in § 1536(a)(2) almost wholly superfluous.

II

The Court makes . . . other arguments. First, "the broad purpose of the [Act] supports the Secretary's decision to extend protection against activities that cause the precise harms Congress enacted the statute to avoid." I thought we had renounced the vice of "simplistically . . . assum[ing] that *whatever* furthers the statute's primary objective must be the law." [Citation.] Deduction from the "broad purpose" of a statute begs the question if it is used to decide by what *means* (and hence to what *length*) Congress pursued that purpose; to get the right answer to that question there is no substitute for the hard job (or, in this case, the quite simple one) of reading the whole text. "The Act must do everything necessary to achieve its broad purpose" is the slogan of the enthusiast, not the analytical tool of the arbiter. . . .

III

In response to the points made in this dissent, the Court's opinion stresses two points, neither of which is supported by the regulation, and so cannot validly be used to uphold it. First, the Court and the concurrence suggest that the regulation should be read to contain a requirement of proximate causation or foreseeability, principally *because the statute does*—and "[n]othing in the regulation purports to weaken those requirements [of the statute]." I quite agree that the statute contains such a limitation, because the verbs of purpose in § 1538(a)(1)(B) denote action directed at animals. *But the Court has rejected that reading.* The critical premise on which it has upheld the regulation is that, despite the weight of the other words in § 1538(a)(1)(B), "the statutory term 'harm' encompasses indirect as well as direct injuries," (describing "the sense of indirect causation that 'harm' adds to the statute"); (stating that the Secretary permissibly interprets " 'harm' " to include "indirectly injuring endangered animals"). Consequently, unless there is some strange category of causation that is indirect and yet also proximate, the Court has already rejected its own basis for finding a proximate-cause limitation in the regulation. In fact "proximate" causation simply *means* "direct" causation. [Citation.] . . .

The only other reason given for finding a proximate-cause limitation in the regulation is that "by use of the word 'actually,' " the regulation clearly rejects speculative or conjectural effects, and thus itself invokes principles of proximate causation. . . . "actually" defines the requisite *injury,* not the requisite *causality.*

The regulation says (it is worth repeating) that "harm" means (1) an act that (2) actually kills or injures wildlife. If that does not dispense with a proximate cause requirement, I do not know what language would. And changing the regulation by judicial invention, even to achieve compliance with the statute, is not permissible. Perhaps the agency itself would prefer to achieve compliance in some other fashion. We defer to reasonable agency interpretations of ambiguous statutes precisely in order that agencies, rather than courts, may exercise policymaking discretion in the interstices of statutes. See *Chevron,* 467 U.S., at 843–845, 104 S. Ct., at 2782. Just as courts may not exercise an agency's power to adjudicate, and so may not affirm an agency order on discretionary grounds the agency has not advanced, [citation,] so also this Court may not exercise the Secretary's power to regulate, and so may not uphold a regulation by adding to it even the most reasonable of elements it does not contain.

The second point the Court stresses in its response seems to me a belated mending of its holding. It apparently *concedes* that the statute requires injury *to particular animals* rather than merely to populations of animals (referring to killing or injuring "*members of* [listed] species" (emphasis added)). The Court then rejects my contention that the regulation ignores this requirement, since, it says, "every term in the regulation's definition of 'harm' is subservient to the phrase 'an act which actually kills or injures wildlife.' " As I have pointed out, this reading is incompatible with the regulation's specification of impairment of "breeding" as one of the *modes* of "kill[ing] or injur[ing] wildlife." . . .

But since the Court is reading the regulation and the statute incorrectly in other respects, it may as well introduce this novelty as well—law à la carte. As I understand the regulation that the Court has created and held consistent with the statute that it has also created, habitat modification can constitute a "taking," but only if it results in the killing or harming of *individual animals,* and only if that consequence is the direct result of the modification. This means that the destruction of privately owned habitat that is essential, not for the feeding or nesting, but for the *breeding,* of butterflies, would not violate the Act, since it would not harm or kill any living butterfly. I, too, think it would not violate the Act—not for the utterly unsupported reason that habitat modifications fall outside the regulation if they happen not to kill or injure a living animal, but for the textual reason that only action directed at living animals constitutes a "take." . . .

The Endangered Species Act is a carefully considered piece of legislation that forbids all persons to hunt or harm endangered animals, but places upon the public at large, rather than upon fortuitously accountable individual landowners, the cost of preserving the habitat of endangered species. There is neither textual support for, nor even evidence of congressional consideration of, the radically different disposition contained in the regulation that the Court sustains. For these reasons, I respectfully dissent.

QUESTIONS

1. The dissent emphasizes that the majority's interpretation of the harm cross-definition of "take" seems to read the underlying meaning of "take" out of the statute altogether. Is this true? Does it matter whether a cross-definition seems to reach conduct beyond what the ordinary meaning of the verb it defines usually conveys?

2. The dissent contends that "[a]n indictment or civil complaint that charged the defendant with 'harming' an animal protected under the Act would be dismissed as defective, for the only *operative* term in the statute is to 'take.'" Does it seem reasonable to cabin a criminal prohibition only to a term's ordinary meaning, even if Congress elsewhere defined that term in a more expansive way? On the other hand, how much of a departure from the ordinary meaning of the term should be tolerated—either as a result of a definitions section or a cross-reference to other portions of the statute—before the statute might be thought defective in giving fair notice to members of the general public as to the conduct the statute criminalizes?

3. Even if you find the dissent's concerns about the reach of potential criminal law applications of the "harm" regulation compelling, should that matter for the resolution of the legal question in *Sweet Home*, which concerned whether the plaintiffs were required to seek a permit to engage in incidental takings? Should courts consider every potential civil and criminal application of a statute when interpreting its meaning in a given case?

4. The majority notes that Congress's 1982 amendments to the ESA seem to endorse the agency's incidental takings definition of harm by establishing the permitting system that would allow limited incidental takings notwithstanding the regulatory prohibition. Nevertheless, as the dissent notes, such an interpretation seriously complicates the meaning of "take" and "harm" as applied elsewhere in the statute. When such intra-statutory complications arise—especially with a statute that has been amended multiple times—what is the appropriate role of courts in reviewing challenges to the amended statute's application? Should courts attend to developing the most coherent interpretation of the statute as a whole, or simply ensure the integrity of the specific statutory text at issue in the

instant case? As you will see in the next subsection, special interpretive issues can arise when courts interpret a statute that has been amended in response to prior judicial interpretations of that statute.

G. The Relationships Between Statutes, and Among Judicial Interpretations of Those Statutes

1. Interpreting a Statute in Light of Related Statutes or Provisions

Peacock v. Lubbock Compress Company

United States Court of Appeals for the Fifth Circuit, 1958.
252 F.2d 892.

■ John R. Brown, Circuit Judge[, joined by Hutcheson, Chief Judge, and Jones, Circuit Judge].

This whole case turns on one word. Does the word "and" mean *and*? Does it mean *or*? May it have been primarily used as a comma?

The question arises in connection with an FLSA [Fair Labor Standards Act] suit for overtime wages brought by three night watchmen against the Compress Company who, admittedly, was subject to the Act, and had employed them for eighty-four hours each week at a wage in excess of the minimum hourly rate (75 cents) but without payment of overtime. The dispute narrows down to Section 207(c) with emphasis on the few words italicized:

"In the case of an employer engaged in the first processing of milk, buttermilk, whey, skimmed milk, or cream into dairy products, *or in the ginning and compressing of cotton*, or in the processing of cottonseed, or in the processing of sugar beets, sugar-beet molasses, sugarcane, or maple sap, into sugar * * * the provisions of subsection (a) * * * (29 U.S.C.A. § 207(a) requiring overtime) shall not apply to his employees in any place of employment where he is so engaged * * *." 29 U.S.C.A. § 207(c), Section 7 of the Act.

The statute, of course, says "ginning *and* compressing of cotton." If it is conjunctive, the watchmen are right, the Compress is wrong, and the cause must be reversed. This is so because it is admitted that the Compress Company is engaged exclusively in compressing cotton and never has engaged in the activity of ginning cotton or a combination of ginning and compressing. Actually, it cuts much deeper since it is an acknowledged undisputed fact of the cotton industry that compressing is an operation entirely removed from ginning and that the two are never carried on together. To read it literally here is to read it out of the statute.

But the word "and" is not a word with a single meaning, for chameleonlike, it takes its color from its surroundings. Nor has the law looked upon it as such. It is ancient learning, recorded authoritatively for us nearly one hundred years ago, echoing that which had accumulated in the previous years and forecasting that which was to come,[1] that, "In the construction of statutes, it is the duty of the Court to ascertain the clear intention of the legislature. In order to do this, Courts are often compelled to construe 'or' as meaning 'and,' and again 'and' as meaning 'or.' " United States v. Fisk, 70 U.S. 445, 448 (1866), and see Heydon's Case, 3 Co. 7a (1584).

In searching then for the Congressional purpose, there appears to be no basis for concluding that the exemption was to be confined to those engaging in *both* ginning and compressing. Indeed, the contrary appears. The great concern of Congress was to exempt agriculture as such from the Act. Maneja v. Waialua Agricultural Co., 349 U.S. 254. Once it set out to shore up that basic exclusion, certain operation such as those defined in Section 207(c) were specifically removed so far as *hours* were concerned, and other operations of the kind described in 213(a)(10) within the area of production to be defined administratively were taken[2] out from the Act as to both *hours* and *wages*. The latter, Section 213(a)(10), note 2, *supra*, was to make certain that for services described in it, the small farms forced to use nearby independent contractors, or the like, would not be worse off than larger integrated farms equipped

---

[1] Hundreds of cases are conveniently collected in Vol. 3, Words and Phrases, under the title word "And," at page 569, and see especially pages 583–593 under the heading of "Civil Statutes." Whatever the particular meaning attributed to the word or words may be in each of these collected cases, the universal test may be summarized. The words "and" and "or" when used in a statute are convertible, as the sense may require. A substitution of one for the other is frequently resorted to in the interpretation of statutes, when the evident intention of the lawmaker requires it.

[2] 29 U.S.C.A. § 213(a)(10): "The provisions of sections 206 and 207 * * * (29 U.S.C.A. §§ 206, 207) shall not apply with respect to * * * (10) any individual employed within the area of production (as defined by the Administrator), engaged in handling, packing, storing, *ginning, compressing*, pasteurizing, drying, preparing in their raw or natural state, or canning of agricultural or horticultural commodities for market, or in making cheese or butter or other dairy products." (Emphasis supplied.)

with their own facilities.[3] In that Section, Congress did not even find it necessary to use the descriptive term "cotton." So long as the operation is within the area of production as promulgated, the 213(a)(10) exemption applies to ginning of cotton, the compressing of cotton, or either one or both of them.

Of course the two sections, 207(c) and 213(a)(10) are not complementary and are intended to, and do, accomplish different objectives. Maneja v. Waialua Agricultural Co., *supra*. But if either of the two activities, ginning *or* compressing, was such as to warrant exemption within the geographical-population limits of the area of production, [citation,] from the whole Act, it seems highly improbable[4] that Congress in mentioning the two again deliberately set out to prescribe a standard impossible to meet as to the hours-overtime exemption of 207(c).

If Congress did not intend the Section 207(c) exemption to apply to those same operations described in 213(a)(10) "ginning, compressing," all it had to do was to omit altogether any reference to this activity in 207(c). To accomplish any such assumed objective, it was not necessary for Congress to go at it by the roundabout method of appearing to grant it only to take it away by the prerequisite of a dual combination of "ginning and compressing" of cotton.[5]

For us to conclude that Congress meant "and" in a literal conjunctive sense is to determine that Congress meant in fact to grant no relief. To do this is to ignore realities, for Congress has long been acutely aware of the manifold problems of the production, marketing and distribution of cotton. The commodity is one of the most important in the complex pattern of farm parity and production control legislation. It is inconceivable that Congress legislated in ignorance of the distinctive nature of the physical operations of ginning of cotton as compared to the compressing of cotton, or that, with full consciousness of these practicable considerations, it meant to lay down a standard which could not be met in fact.

---

[3] Maneja v. Waialua Agricultural Co., 349 U.S. 254, 268,: "Thus, for example, the cotton farmer without a gin was placed on an equal footing with farms who ginning their own cotton, since each could have their cotton ginned by employees who were covered by neither the wage nor the hour provisions of the Act."

[4] Maneja v. Waialua Agricultural Co., 349 U.S. 254, 267: That case involved the processing of sugar cane into sugar. The Court's reference to "cotton ginning" alone and not in conjunction with compressing indicates, however, that it saw no decisive significance in the coupling word "and". To the suggested argument that the express exemption in § 207(c) from overtime liabilities was a deliberate choice by Congress to limit relief to overtime, the Court said: "But we cannot be sure of this, because § 7(c) (207(c)) includes similar exemptions for operations like cotton ginning, which also come within the agricultural exemption if performed by the farmer on his own crops. More significant is the omission of sugar milling from the exemption provided by § 13(a)(10), § 213(a)(10), from various processing operations performed within the area of production."

[5] The sparse legislative history on the point as set forth in the briefs is unilluminating. Apparently in its original form, Senate Bill 2475, 75th Congress, granted the overtime exemption for "the ginning and bailing of cotton." The "bailing" is an integral part of the "ginning" process. In Committee "compressing and storing" of cotton was added.

Literalism gives way in the face of such considerations. [Citations omitted]. Under Section 207(c), the ginning of cotton, the compressing of cotton, the performance of either or both is exempt from the overtime provisions of the Act.

Affirmed.

QUESTION

1. How does section 213(a)(10) of the Fair Labor Standards Act help illuminate the meaning of section 207(c) of the same statute? Section 207(c) concerns restrictions on hours worked, while section 213(a)(10) exempts certain agriculture-related businesses from both minimum wages and hours limitations. Is it reasonable to expect that legislative drafters, when drafting a given statutory provision, attend to how similar language appears elsewhere in the statute?

2. A literal reading of the relevant provision of the Fair Labor Standards Act would have exempted from an obligation to pay overtime only employers of workers engaged in the combined activity of both ginning and compressing cotton; it would have required payment of overtime of workers engaged separately in either of those activities. The employer's preferred construction of the statute, reading "and" as "or," thus substantially broadened the scope of the employers' exemption. Given the significantly different meanings and effects of "and" and "or," as well as the overall purpose of the FLSA to improve workers' conditions, why was it appropriate for the court to substitute "or" for "and"? Is the court's interpretation any more or less problematic than interpolating a comma in *Johnson v. Southern Pacific*, or than ignoring the repeal of the bankruptcy provisions in *Adamo*?

Alaska Steamship Co. v. United States

Supreme Court of the United States, 1933.
290 U.S. 256, 54 S.Ct. 159, 78 L.Ed. 302.

Certiorari to review the affirmance of a judgment dismissing a suit against the United States under the Tucker Act.

■ MR. JUSTICE STONE delivered the opinion of the Court.

In this suit, brought under the Tucker Act, 24 Stat. 505, in the District Court for Western Washington, petitioner sought compensation at an agreed rate for the transportation of certain destitute seamen from Ketchikan, Alaska, to Seattle, under the provisions of § 4578 R.S., as amended, 46 U.S.C.A. § 679. That section imposes on masters of United States vessels homeward bound the duty, upon request of consular officers, to receive and carry destitute seamen to the port of destination at such compensation not exceeding a specified amount as may be agreed upon by the master with a consular officer, and authorizes the consular officer to issue certificates for such transportation, "which certificates shall be assignable for collection." By § 4526 R.S., 17 Stat. 269, as amended December 21, 1898, 30 Stat. 755, 46 U.S.C.A. § 593, seamen, whose term of service is terminated by loss or wreck of their vessel, are "destitute seamen," and are required to be transported as provided in § 4578.

The demand in the present case was for compensation for the transportation of the crew of the S.S. Depere, owned by petitioner, which had been wrecked on the Alaska coast and for that reason had been unable to complete her voyage. The crew was received and carried to Seattle on petitioner's S.S. Yukon, on certificate of the deputy customs collector of Alaska that he had agreed with the master for their transportation at a specified rate. The Comptroller General refused payment upon the certificate on the sole ground that it was the duty of petitioner to transport to the United States the crew of its own wrecked vessel, and that the Congressional appropriation for the relief of American seamen was not available to compensate the owner for performing that duty. Judgment of the district court dismissing the complaint, 60 F.2d 135, was affirmed by the Court of Appeals for the Ninth Circuit, on the ground that the certificate of the deputy collector authorizing the transportation did not satisfy the requirement of the statute that the certificate should be that of a consular officer. 63 F.2d 398. This court granted certiorari.

The government, conceding that the statute by long administrative practice has been construed as authorizing payment for transportation of seamen from Alaska on the certificate of deputy customs collectors, insists that it does not authorize payment to the owner for the transportation of the crew of his own wrecked vessel and that such has been its administrative construction.

1.   If the statutory language is to be taken literally, the certificate, which by R.S. § 4578 is authority for the transportation and evidence of the right of the vessel to compensation, must be that of a consular officer. Deputy collectors of customs are not consular officers and there are no consular officers in Alaska. If the right to compensation is dependent upon certification by a consular officer the statutes providing for transportation of destitute seamen can be given no effect in Alaska. But the meaning of this provision must be ascertained by reading it with related statutes and in the light of a long and consistent administrative practice.

Since 1792 the statutes of the United States have made provision for the return of destitute seamen to this country upon suitable action taken by consular officers of the United States. And since 1803 the government has undertaken to compensate for their transportation. Beginning in 1896, Congress has made provision for the relief of American seamen shipwrecked in Alaska in annual appropriation bills for the maintenance of the diplomatic and consular service. The appropriation bill for that year, 29 Stat. 186, and every later one has extended the benefits of the appropriation for the relief of American seamen in foreign countries to "American seamen shipwrecked in Alaska." The appropriation for 1922 and 1923, c. 204, 42 Stat. 599, 603; c. 21, 42 Stat. 1068, 1072, contained the proviso, not appearing in previous acts, that no part of the appropriation should be available for payment for transportation in excess of a specified rate agreed upon by a consular officer and the master of the vessel. The proviso did not appear in subsequent appropriation acts, but by Act of January 3, 1923, 43 Stat. 1072, it was transferred to its proper place in the shipping laws, where it now appears in § 680 of Title 46 of the United States Code. The Act of 1929, 45 Stat. 1098, applicable when the seamen in the present case were transported, appropriated $70,000 "for relief, protection and burial of American seamen in foreign countries, in the Panama Canal Zone, and in the Philippine Islands, and shipwrecked American seamen in the Territory of Alaska, in the Hawaiian Islands, in Porto Rico and in the Virgin Islands." By the amendment of R.S. § 5226 of December 21, 1898, 30 Stat. 755, 46 U.S.C.A., § 593, it was provided that where the service of a seaman terminates by reason of the loss or wreck of the vessel, "he shall not be entitled to wages for any period beyond such termination of the service and shall be considered as a destitute seaman, and shall be treated and transported to port of shipment," as provided in R.S. § 4578. No exception is made in the case of transportation of seamen from Alaska or other dependencies of the United States.

Thus, from 1896 to the present time, there has been a definite obligation on the part of the government to provide transportation for shipwrecked seamen without reference to the place where shipwrecked, and funds have been annually appropriated for the purpose of carrying out that obligation in the case of seamen shipwrecked in Alaska. As appears from the findings of the trial court, not challenged here, the appropriations have been expended for the transportation of shipwrecked seamen from Alaska, in conformity to a practice established and consistently followed at least since 1900. Certificates for the transportation of shipwrecked seamen have been regularly signed and issued by the collector of customs or the deputy collector in Alaska upon forms provided by the Bureau of Navigation of the Department of Commerce. That Bureau, which has a general superintendence over merchant seamen of the United States, 46 U.S.C.A., §§ 1 and 2, has regularly supplied its customs officials and its agents in Alaska with these forms, with instructions that they were to be used in arranging transportation of shipwrecked seamen to the United States, as provided by the sections of the statute to which reference has been made. The stipulated amounts due for the transportation, as certified, have been regularly paid without objection upon presentation of the certificate to the disbursing officer of the United States.

Courts are slow to disturb the settled administrative construction of a statute long and consistently adhered to. Brown v. United States, 113 U.S. 568, 571, 5 S.Ct. 648, 28 L.Ed. 1079; United States v. Philbrick, 120 U.S. 52, 59, 7 S.Ct. 413, 30 L.Ed. 559; United States v. G. Falk & Bro.,

204 U.S. 143, 151, 27 S.Ct. 191, 51 L.Ed. 411. This is especially the case where, as here, the declared will of the legislative body could not be carried out without the construction adopted. That construction must be accepted and applied by the courts when, as in the present case, it has received Congressional approval, implicit in the annual appropriations over a period of thirty-five years, the expenditure of which was effected by resort to the administrative practice, and in amendments by Congress to the statutes relating to transportation of destitute seamen without modification of that practice. United States v. G. Falk & Bro., *supra*; compare United States v. Missouri Pacific R. Co., 278 U.S. 269, 49 S.Ct. 133, 73 L.Ed. 322.

2.	The rejection of petitioner's claim by the Comptroller General rests upon the supposed duty of the owner to transport to the home port the seamen of its own wrecked vessel. Diligent search by counsel of the ancient learning of the admiralty has failed to disclose the existence of any such duty. . . .

The rulings of the Comptroller General rest upon a proposition so plainly contrary to law and so plainly in conflict with the statute as to leave them without weight as administrative constructions of it. United States v. Missouri Pacific R. Co., *supra*.

Reversed.

QUESTION

Recall the Supreme Court's use of legislative history in *Holy Trinity Church*, in which it relied on a committee report to conclude that Congress had not intended to bring "brain toilers" within the scope of the immigration prohibition on contract labor. In the report, the committee acknowledged that the statute as written could be read to include "brain toilers," but feared that time constraints would prevent redrafting the bill with more precise language. Nevertheless, some might be troubled by the Court's reliance on statements from the committee's unenacted clarification. By contrast, in *Alaska Steamship* the Court relied on subsequent legislation to clarify the meaning of the destitute seaman statute, insofar as it applied to repatriations from Alaska. Is the Court on firmer ground when it interprets a statute in light of *subsequent* (enacted) legislation that seems to inform the prior statute's meaning, as opposed to interpreting a statute in reliance on (unenacted) statements contemporaneous with the bill's passage to clarify Congress's intent?

2. INTERPRETING A STATUTE IN LIGHT OF PRIOR JUDICIAL INTERPRETATIONS OF THAT STATUTE

CASE STUDY IN THREE LITTLE WORDS: "USES OR CARRIES A FIREARM"

The following cases interpret a related provision to the one at issue in *Muscarello, supra*. Although *Muscarello* focused only on the meaning of "carries a firearm" in 18 U.S.C. § 924(c), the statute also increased by five years the duration of a sentence if the defendant "during and in relation to any crime of violence or drug trafficking crime . . . , *uses* or carries a firearm." (emphasis added). Thus, in a related set of cases, the Court had to decide what it means to "use" a firearm. To place that provision in context, we reproduce the full section, and other pertinent sections as they appeared in the statute at the time the Court decided these cases. (As indicated in *Muscarello, supra*, Congress has subsequently amended the statute.)

18 U.S.C. § 924

. . . **(b)** Whoever, with intent to commit therewith an offense punishable by imprisonment for a term exceeding one year, or with knowledge or reasonable cause to believe that an offense punishable by imprisonment for a term exceeding one year is to be committed therewith, ships, transports, or receives a firearm or any ammunition in interstate or foreign commerce shall be fined under this title, or imprisoned not more than ten years, or both.

(c)(1) Whoever, during and in relation to any crime of violence or drug trafficking crime (including a crime of violence or drug trafficking crime which provides for an enhanced punishment if committed by the use of a deadly or dangerous weapon or device) for which he may be prosecuted in a court of the United States, uses or carries a firearm, shall, in addition to the punishment provided for such crime of violence or drug trafficking crime, be sentenced to imprisonment for five years, and if the firearm is a short-barreled rifle, short-barreled shotgun, or semiautomatic assault weapon, to imprisonment for ten years, and if the firearm is a machinegun, or a destructive device, or is equipped with a firearm silencer or firearm muffler, to imprisonment for thirty years. In the case of his second or subsequent conviction under this subsection, such person shall be sentenced to imprisonment for twenty years, and if the firearm is a machinegun, or a destructive device, or is equipped with a firearm silencer or firearm muffler, to life imprisonment without release. Notwithstanding any other provision of law, the court shall not place on probation or suspend the sentence of any person convicted of a violation of this subsection, nor shall the term of imprisonment imposed under this subsection run concurrently with any other term of imprisonment including that imposed for the crime of violence or drug trafficking crime in which the firearm was used or carried.

(d)(1) Any firearm or ammunition involved in or used in any knowing violation of [various provisions], or willful violation of any other provision of this chapter or any rule or regulation promulgated thereunder, or any violation of any other criminal law of the United States, or any firearm or ammunition intended to be used in any offense referred to in paragraph (3) of this subsection, where such intent is demonstrated by clear and convincing evidence, shall be subject to seizure and forfeiture, ...

(3) The offenses referred to in paragraphs (1) and (2)(C) of this subsection are— . . .

(D) any offense described in section 922(d) of this title [making it "unlawful for any person to sell or otherwise dispose of any firearm or ammunition to any person knowing or having reasonable cause to believe that such person" is one of specified classes of persons, including convicted felons and persons under restraining orders for domestic violence] where the firearm or ammunition is intended to be used in such offense by the transferor of such firearm or ammunition; . . .

18 U.S.C. § 922

(g) It shall be unlawful for any [specified category of] person[s]—

. . . to ship or transport in interstate or foreign commerce, or possess in or affecting commerce, any firearm or ammunition; or to receive any firearm or ammunition which has been shipped or transported in interstate or foreign commerce. . . .

(j) It shall be unlawful for any person to receive, possess, conceal, store, barter, sell, or dispose of any stolen firearm or stolen ammunition, or pledge or accept as security for a loan any stolen firearm or stolen ammunition, which is moving as, which is a part of, which constitutes, or which has been shipped or transported in, interstate or foreign commerce, either before or after it was stolen, knowing or having reasonable cause to believe that the firearm or ammunition was stolen.

Smith v. United States

Supreme Court of the United States, 1993.
508 U.S. 223, 113 S.Ct. 2050, 124 L.Ed.2d 138.

■ JUSTICE O'CONNOR delivered the opinion of the Court,[in which CHIEF JUSTICE REHNQUIST, JUSTICE WHITE, JUSTICE BLACKMUN, JUSTICE KENNEDY, and JUSTICE THOMAS joined].

We decide today whether the exchange of a gun for narcotics constitutes "use" of a firearm "during and in relation to . . . [a] drug trafficking crime" within the meaning of 18 U.S.C. § 924(c)(1). We hold that it does.

I

Petitioner John Angus Smith and his companion went from Tennessee to Florida to buy cocaine; they hoped to resell it at a profit. While in Florida, they met petitioner's acquaintance, Deborah Hoag. Hoag agreed to, and in fact did, purchase cocaine for petitioner. She then accompanied petitioner and his friend to her motel room, where they were joined by a drug dealer. While Hoag listened, petitioner and the dealer discussed petitioner's MAC-10 firearm, which had been modified to operate as an automatic. The MAC-10 apparently is a favorite among criminals. It is small and compact, lightweight, and can be equipped with a silencer. Most important of all, it can be devastating: A fully automatic MAC-10 can fire more than 1,000 rounds per minute. The dealer expressed his interest in becoming the owner of a MAC-10, and petitioner promised that he would discuss selling the gun if his arrangement with another potential buyer fell through.

Unfortunately for petitioner, Hoag had contacts not only with narcotics traffickers but also with law enforcement officials. In fact, she was a confidential informant. Consistent with her post, she informed the Broward County Sheriff's Office of petitioner's activities. The Sheriff's Office responded quickly, sending an undercover officer to Hoag's motel room. Several others were assigned to keep the motel under surveillance. Upon arriving at Hoag's motel room, the undercover officer presented himself to petitioner as a pawnshop dealer. Petitioner, in turn, presented the officer with a proposition: He had an automatic MAC-10 and silencer with which he might be willing to part. Petitioner then pulled the MAC-10 out of a black canvas bag and showed it to the officer. The officer examined the gun and asked petitioner what he wanted for it. Rather than asking for money, however, petitioner asked for drugs. He was willing to trade his MAC-10, he said, for two ounces of cocaine. The officer told petitioner that he was just a pawnshop dealer and did not distribute narcotics. Nonetheless, he indicated that he wanted the MAC-10 and would try to get the cocaine. The officer then left, promising to return within an hour.

Rather than seeking out cocaine as he had promised, the officer returned to the Sheriff's Office to arrange for petitioner's arrest. But petitioner was not content to wait. The officers who were conducting surveillance saw him leave the motel room carrying a gun bag; he then climbed into his van and drove away. The officers reported petitioner's departure and began following him. When law enforcement authorities tried to stop petitioner, he led them on a high-speed chase. Petitioner eventually was apprehended.

Petitioner, it turns out, was well armed. A search of his van revealed the MAC-10 weapon, a silencer, ammunition, and a "fast-feed" mechanism. In addition, the police found a MAC-11 machine gun, a loaded .45 caliber pistol, and a .22 caliber pistol with a scope and homemade silencer. Petitioner also had a loaded 9 millimeter handgun in his waistband.

A grand jury sitting in the District Court for the Southern District of Florida returned an indictment charging petitioner with, among other offenses, two drug trafficking crimes—conspiracy to possess cocaine with intent to distribute and attempt to possess cocaine with intent to distribute in violation of 21 U.S.C. §§ 841(a)(1), 846, and 18 U.S.C. § 2. Most important here, the indictment alleged that petitioner knowingly used the MAC-10 and its silencer during and in relation to a drug trafficking crime. Under 18 U.S.C. § 924(c)(1), a defendant who so uses a firearm must be sentenced to five years' incarceration. And where, as here, the firearm is a "machinegun" or is fitted with a silencer, the sentence is 30 years. See § 924(c)(1) ("If the firearm is a machinegun, or is equipped with a firearm silencer," the sentence is "thirty years"); § 921(a)(23), 26 U.S.C. § 5845(b) (term "machinegun" includes automatic weapons). The jury convicted petitioner on all counts.

On appeal, petitioner argued that § 924(c)(1)'s penalty for using a firearm during and in relation to a drug trafficking offense covers only situations in which the firearm is used as a weapon. According to petitioner, the provision does not extend to defendants who use a firearm solely as a medium of exchange or for barter. The Court of Appeals for the Eleventh Circuit disagreed. 957 F.2d 835 (1992). The plain language of the statute, the court explained, imposes no requirement that the firearm be used as a weapon. Instead, any use of "the weapon to facilitate *in any manner* the commission of the offense" suffices.

Shortly before the Eleventh Circuit decided this case, the Court of Appeals for the District of Columbia Circuit arrived at the same conclusion. *United States* v. *Harris*, 294 U.S. App. D.C. 300, 315–316, 959 F.2d 246, 261–262 *(per curiam)*, cert. denied, 506 U.S. 932 (1992). In

United States v. *Phelps*, 877 F.2d 28 (1989), however, the Court of Appeals for the Ninth Circuit held that trading a gun in a drug-related transaction could not constitute use of a firearm during and in relation to a drug trafficking offense within the meaning of § 924(c)(1). We granted certiorari to resolve the conflict among the Circuits. 506 U.S. 814 (1992). We now affirm.

II

Section 924(c)(1) requires the imposition of specified penalties if the defendant, "during and in relation to any crime of violence or drug trafficking crime[,] uses or carries a firearm." By its terms, the statute requires the prosecution to make two showings. First, the prosecution must demonstrate that the defendant "use[d] or carrie[d] a firearm." Second, it must prove that the use or carrying was "during and in relation to" a "crime of violence or drug trafficking crime." Petitioner argues that exchanging a firearm for drugs does not constitute "use" of the firearm within the meaning of the statute. He points out that nothing in the record indicates that he fired the MAC-10, threatened anyone with it, or employed it for self-protection. In essence, petitioner argues that he cannot be said to have "use[d]" a firearm unless he used it as a weapon, since that is how firearms most often are used. See 957 F.2d at 837 (firearm often facilitates drug offenses by protecting drugs or protecting or emboldening the defendant). Of course, § 924(c)(1) is not limited to those cases in which a gun is used; it applies with equal force whenever a gun is "carrie[d]." In this case, however, the indictment alleged only that petitioner "use[d]" the MAC-10. Accordingly, we do not consider whether the evidence might support the conclusion that petitioner carried the MAC-10 within the meaning of § 924(c)(1). Instead we confine our discussion to what the parties view as the dispositive issue in this case: whether trading a firearm for drugs can constitute "use" of the firearm within the meaning of § 924(c)(1).

When a word is not defined by statute, we normally construe it in accord with its ordinary or natural meaning. [Citation.] Surely petitioner's treatment of his MAC-10 can be described as "use" within the everyday meaning of that term. Petitioner "used" his MAC-10 in an attempt to obtain drugs by offering to trade it for cocaine. Webster's defines "to use" as "to convert to one's service" or "to employ." Webster's New International Dictionary 2806 (2d ed. 1950). Black's Law Dictionary contains a similar definition: "to make use of; to convert to one's service; to employ; to avail oneself of; to utilize; to carry out a purpose or action by means of." Black's Law Dictionary 1541 (6th ed. 1990). Indeed, over 100 years ago we gave the word "use" the same gloss, indicating that it means " 'to employ' " or " 'to derive service from.' " *Astor* v. *Merritt*, 111 U.S. 202, 213, 28 L. Ed. 401, 4 S.Ct. 413 (1884). Petitioner's handling of the MAC-10 in this case falls squarely within those definitions. By attempting to trade his MAC-10 for the drugs, he "used" or "employed" it as an item of barter to obtain cocaine; he "derived service" from it because it was going to bring him the very drugs he sought.

In petitioner's view, § 924(c)(1) should require proof not only that the defendant used the firearm, but also that he used it *as a weapon*. But the words "as a weapon" appear nowhere in the statute. Rather, § 924(c)(1)'s language sweeps broadly, punishing any "use" of a firearm, so long as the use is "during and in relation to" a drug trafficking offense. See *United States* v. *Long*, 284 U.S. App. D.C. 405, 409–410, 905 F.2d 1572, 1576–1577 (Thomas, J.) (although not without limits, the word "use" is "expansive" and extends even to situations where the gun is not actively employed), cert. denied, 498 U.S. 948, 112 L. Ed. 2d 328, 111 S.Ct. 365 (1990). Had Congress intended the narrow construction petitioner urges, it could have so indicated. It did not, and we decline to introduce that additional requirement on our own.

Language, of course, cannot be interpreted apart from context. The meaning of a word that appears ambiguous if viewed in isolation may become clear when the word is analyzed in light of the terms that surround it. Recognizing this, petitioner and the dissent argue that the word "uses" has a somewhat reduced scope in § 924(c)(1) because it appears alongside the word "firearm." Specifically, they contend that the average person on the street would not think immediately of a guns-for-drugs trade as an example of "us[ing] a firearm." Rather, that phrase normally evokes an image of the most familiar use to which a firearm is put—use as a weapon. Petitioner and the dissent therefore argue that the statute excludes uses where the weapon is not fired or otherwise employed for its destructive capacity. Indeed, relying on that argument—and without citation to authority—the dissent announces its own, restrictive definition of "use." "To use an instrumentality," the dissent argues, "ordinarily means to use it for its intended purpose."

There is a significant flaw to this argument. It is one thing to say that the ordinary meaning of "uses a firearm" *includes* using a firearm as a weapon, since that is the intended purpose of a firearm and the example of "use" that most immediately comes to mind. But it is quite another to conclude that, as a result, the phrase also *excludes* any other use. Certainly that conclusion does not follow from the phrase "uses . . . a firearm" itself. As the dictionary definitions and experience make clear, one can use a firearm in a number of ways. That one example of "use" is the first to come to mind when the phrase "uses . . . a firearm" is uttered does not preclude us from recognizing that there are other "uses" that qualify as well. In this case, it is both reasonable and normal to say that petitioner "used" his MAC-10 in his drug trafficking offense by trading it for cocaine; the dissent does not contend otherwise.

The dissent's example of how one might "use" a cane, suffers from a similar flaw. To be sure, "use" as an adornment in a hallway is not the first "use" of a cane that comes to mind. But certainly it does not follow that the *only* "use" to which a cane might be put is assisting one's grandfather in walking. Quite the opposite: The most infamous use of a cane in American history had nothing to do with walking at all, see J. McPherson, Battle Cry of Freedom 150 (1988) (describing the caning of Senator Sumner in the United States Senate in 1856); and the use of a cane as an instrument of punishment was once so common that "to cane" has become a verb meaning "to beat with a cane." Webster's New International Dictionary, *supra*, at 390. In any event, the only question in this case is whether the phrase "uses . . . a firearm" in § 924(c)(1) is most reasonably read as *excluding* the use of a firearm in a gun-for-drugs trade. The fact that the phrase clearly *includes* using a firearm to shoot someone, as the dissent contends, does not answer it. . . .

We are not persuaded that our construction of the phrase "uses . . . a firearm" will produce anomalous applications. § 924(c)(1) requires not only that the defendant "use" the firearm, but also that he use it "during and in relation to" the drug trafficking crime. As a result, the defendant who "uses" a firearm to scratch his head, or for some other innocuous purpose, would avoid punishment for that conduct altogether: Although scratching one's head with a gun might constitute "use," that action cannot support punishment under § 924(c)(1) unless it facilitates or furthers the drug crime; that the firearm served to relieve an itch is not enough. Such a defendant would escape the six-point enhancement provided in USSG § 2B3.1(b)(2)(B) as well. . . .

In any event, the "intended purpose" of a firearm is not that it be used in any offensive manner whatever, but rather that it be used in a particular fashion—by firing it. The dissent's contention therefore cannot be that the defendant must use the firearm "as a weapon," but rather that he must fire it or threaten to fire it, "as a gun." Under the dissent's approach, then, even the criminal who pistol-whips his victim has not used a firearm within the meaning of § 924(c)(1), for firearms are intended to be fired or brandished, not used as bludgeons. It appears that the dissent similarly would limit the scope of the "other use[s]" covered by USSG § 2B3.1(b) (2)(B). The universal view of the courts of appeals, however, is directly to the contrary. No court of appeals ever has held that using a gun to pistol-whip a victim is anything but the "use" of a firearm; nor has any court ever held that trading a firearm for drugs falls short of being the "use" thereof. [Citation.]

To the extent there is uncertainty about the scope of the phrase "uses . . . a firearm" in § 924(c)(1), we believe the remainder of § 924 appropriately sets it to rest. Just as a single word cannot be read in isolation, nor can a single provision of a statute. As we have recognized:

> "Statutory construction . . . is a holistic endeavor. A provision that may seem ambiguous in isolation is often clarified by the remainder of the statutory scheme—because the same terminology is used elsewhere in a context that makes its meaning clear, or because only one of the permissible meanings produces a substantive effect that is compatible with the rest of

the law." *United Savings Assn. of Texas* v. *Timbers of Inwood Forest Associates, Ltd.*, 484 U.S. 365, 371, 98 L. Ed. 2d 740, 108 S.Ct. 626 (1988) (citations omitted).

Here, Congress employed the words "use" and "firearm" together not only in § 924(c)(1), but also in § 924(d)(1), which deals with forfeiture of firearms. [Citation.] Under § 924(d)(1), any "firearm or ammunition intended to be used" in the various offenses listed in § 924(d)(3) is subject to seizure and forfeiture. Consistent with petitioner's interpretation, § 924(d)(3) lists offenses in which guns might be used as offensive weapons. See §§ 924(d)(3)(A), (B) (weapons used in a crime of violence or drug trafficking offense). But it also lists offenses in which the firearm is *not* used as a weapon but instead as an item of barter or commerce. For example, any gun intended to be "used" in an interstate "transfer, sale, trade, gift, transport, or delivery" of a firearm prohibited under § 922(a)(5) where there is a pattern of such activity, see § 924(d)(3)(C), or in a federal offense involving "the exportation of firearms," § 924(d)(3)(F), is subject to forfeiture. In fact, none of the offenses listed in four of the six subsections of § 924(d)(3) involves the bellicose use of a firearm; each offense involves use as an item in commerce.* Thus, it is clear from § 924(d)(3) that one who transports, exports, sells, or trades a firearm "uses" it within the meaning of § 924(d)(1)—even though those actions do not involve using the firearm as a weapon. Unless we are to hold that using a firearm has a different meaning in § 924(c)(1) than it does in § 924(d)—and clearly we should not—we must reject petitioner's narrow interpretation.

The evident care with which Congress chose the language of § 924(d)(1) reinforces our conclusion in this regard. Although § 924(d)(1) lists numerous firearm-related offenses that render guns subject to forfeiture, Congress did not lump all of those offenses together and require forfeiture solely of guns "used" in a prohibited activity. Instead, it carefully varied the statutory language in accordance with the guns' relation to the offense. For example, with respect to some crimes, the firearm is subject to forfeiture not only if it is "used," but also if it is "involved in" the offense. § 924(d)(1). Examination of the offenses to which the "involved in" language applies reveals why Congress believed it necessary to include such an expansive term. One of the listed offenses,

---

* Section 924(d)(3)(C) lists four offenses: unlicensed manufacture of or commerce in firearms, in violation of § 922(a)(1); unlicensed receipt of a weapon from outside the State, in violation of § 922(a)(3); unlicensed transfer of a firearm to a resident of a different State, in violation of § 922(a)(5); and delivery of a gun by a licensed entity to a resident of a State that is not the licensee's, in violation of § 922(b)(3). Section 924(d)(3)(D) mentions only one offense, the transfer or sale of a weapon to disqualified persons, such as fugitives from justice and felons, in violation of § 922(d). Under § 924(d)(3)(E), firearms are subject to forfeiture if they are intended to be used in any of five listed offenses: shipping stolen firearms, in violation of § 922(i); receipt of stolen firearms, in violation of § 922(j); importation of firearms, in violation of § 922(*l*); shipment of a firearm by a felon, in violation of § 922(n); and shipment or receipt of a firearm with intent to commit a felony, in violation of § 924(b). Finally, § 924(d)(3)(F) subjects to forfeiture any firearm intended to be used in any offense that may be prosecuted in federal court if it involves the exportation of firearms.

violation of § 922(a)(6), is the making of a false statement material to the lawfulness of a gun's transfer. Because making a material misstatement in order to acquire or sell a gun is not "use" of the gun even under the broadest definition of the word "use," Congress carefully expanded the statutory language. As a result, a gun with respect to which a material misstatement is made is subject to forfeiture because, even though the gun is not "used" in the offense, it is "involved in" it. Congress, however, did not so expand the language for offenses in which firearms were "intended to be used," even though the firearms in many of those offenses function as items of commerce rather than as weapons. Instead, Congress apparently was of the view that one could use a gun by trading it. In light of the common meaning of the word "use" and the structure and language of the statute, we are not in any position to disagree.

The dissent suggests that our interpretation produces a "strange dichotomy" between "using" a firearm and "carrying" one. We do not see why that is so. Just as a defendant may "use" a firearm within the meaning of § 924(c)(1) by trading it for drugs *or* using it to shoot someone, so too would a defendant "carry" the firearm by keeping it on his person whether he intends to exchange it for cocaine or fire it in self-defense. The dichotomy arises, if at all, only when one tries to extend the phrase " 'uses . . . a firearm' " to any use " 'for any purpose whatever.' " For our purposes, it is sufficient to recognize that, because § 924(d)(1) includes both using a firearm for *trade* and using a firearm as a *weapon* as "us[ing] a firearm," it is most reasonable to construe § 924(c)(1) as encompassing both of those "uses" as well. . . .

■ JUSTICE SCALIA, with whom JUSTICE STEVENS and JUSTICE SOUTER join, dissenting.

Section 924(c)(1) mandates a sentence enhancement for any defendant who "during and in relation to any crime of violence or drug trafficking crime . . . uses . . . a firearm." 18 U.S.C. § 924(c)(1). The Court begins its analysis by focusing upon the word "use" in this passage, and explaining that the dictionary definitions of that word are very broad. It is, however, a "fundamental principle of statutory construction (and, indeed, of language itself) that the meaning of a word cannot be determined in isolation, but must be drawn from the context in which it is used." That is particularly true of a word as elastic as "use," whose meanings range all the way from "to partake of" (as in "he uses tobacco") to "to be wont or accustomed" (as in "he used to smoke tobacco"). See Webster's New International Dictionary 2806 (2d ed. 1950).

In the search for statutory meaning, we give nontechnical words and phrases their ordinary meaning. [Citation.] To use an instrumentality ordinarily means to use it for its intended purpose. When someone asks, "Do you use a cane?," he is not inquiring whether you have your grandfather's silver-handled walking stick on display in the hall; he wants to know whether you *walk* with a cane. Similarly, to speak of "using a firearm" is to speak of using it for its distinctive purpose, *i.e.*, as a weapon. To be sure, "one can use a firearm in a number of ways," including as an article of exchange, just as one can "use" a cane as a hall decoration—but that is not the ordinary meaning of "using" the one or the other.[1] The Court does not appear to grasp the distinction between how a word *can be* used and how it *ordinarily is* used. It would, indeed, be "both reasonable and normal to say that petitioner 'used' his MAC-10 in his drug trafficking offense by trading it for cocaine." *Ibid.* It would also be reasonable and normal to say that he "used" it to scratch his head. When one wishes to describe the action of employing the instrument of a firearm for such unusual purposes, "use" is assuredly a verb one could select. But that says nothing about whether the *ordinary* meaning of the phrase "uses a firearm" embraces such extraordinary employments. It is unquestionably *not* reasonable and normal, I think, to say simply "do not use firearms" when one means to prohibit selling or scratching with them. . . .

The Court seeks to avoid this conclusion by referring to the next subsection of the statute, § 924(d), which does not employ the phrase "uses a firearm," but provides for the confiscation of firearms that are "used in" referenced offenses which include the crimes of transferring, selling, or transporting firearms in interstate commerce. The Court concludes from this that *whenever* the term appears in this statute, "use" of a firearm must include nonweapon use. I do not agree. We are dealing here not with a technical word or an "artfully defined" legal term, cf. *Dewsnup* v. *Timm*, 502 U.S. 410, 423, 116 L. Ed. 2d 903, 112 S.Ct. 773 (1992) (SCALIA, J., dissenting), but with common words that are, as I have suggested, inordinately sensitive to context. Just as adding the direct object "a firearm" to the verb "use" *narrows* the meaning of that verb (it can no longer mean "partake of"), so also adding the modifier "in the offense of transferring, selling, or transporting firearms" to the phrase "use a firearm" *expands* the meaning of that phrase (it then includes, as it previously would not, nonweapon use). But neither the narrowing nor the expansion should logically be thought to apply to *all* appearances of the affected word or phrase. Just as every appearance of the word "use" in the statute need not be given the narrow meaning that word acquires in the phrase "use a firearm," so also every appearance of the phrase "use a firearm" need not be given the expansive connotation that phrase acquires in the broader context "use a firearm in crimes such as unlawful sale of firearms." When, for example, the statute provides that its prohibition on certain transactions in firearms "shall not apply to the loan or rental of a firearm to any person for temporary use for

---

[1]   The Court asserts that the "significant flaw" in this argument is that "to say that the ordinary meaning of 'uses a firearm' *includes* using a firearm as a weapon" is quite different from saying that the ordinary meaning "also *excludes* any other use." The two are indeed different—but it is precisely the latter that I assert to be true: The ordinary meaning of "uses a firearm" does *not* include using it as an article of commerce. I think it perfectly obvious, for example, that the objective falsity requirement for a perjury conviction would not be satisfied if a witness answered "no" to a prosecutor's inquiry whether he had ever "used a firearm," even though he had once sold his grandfather's Enfield rifle to a collector.

lawful sporting purposes," 18 U.S.C. §§ 922(a)(5)(B), (b)(3)(B), I have no doubt that the "use" referred to is *only* use as a sporting *weapon*, and not the use of pawning the firearm to pay for a ski trip. Likewise when, in § 924(c)(1), the phrase "uses . . . a firearm" is not employed in a context that necessarily envisions the unusual "use" of a firearm as a commodity, the normally understood meaning of the phrase should prevail.

Another consideration leads to the same conclusion: § 924(c)(1) provides increased penalties not only for one who "uses" a firearm during and in relation to any crime of violence or drug trafficking crime, but also for one who "carries" a firearm in those circumstances. The interpretation I would give the language produces an eminently reasonable dichotomy between "using a firearm" (as a weapon) and "carrying a firearm" (which in the context "uses or carries a firearm" means carrying it in such manner as to be ready for use as a weapon). The Court's interpretation, by contrast, produces a strange dichotomy between "using a firearm for any purpose whatever, including barter," and "carrying a firearm."[3] . . .

QUESTIONS

1. Consider the arguments for and against implying the "as a weapon" condition on "uses." Which do you find most persuasive? Why?

2. 15 U.S.C. § 1644(a) imposes criminal liability on any person who:

    knowingly in a transaction affecting interstate or foreign commerce, uses or attempts or conspires to use any counterfeit, fictitious, altered, forged, lost, stolen, or fraudulently obtained credit card to obtain money, goods, services, or anything else of value which within any one-year period has an aggregating value of $1,000 or more.

"Credit card" is defined as "any card, plate, coupon book or other credit device existing for the purpose of obtaining money, property, labor, or services on credit." 15 U.S.C. § 1702(k). Can a person be convicted under this statute if the government can show that the defendant made use of a credit card number, but not the credit card itself? See United States v. Bice-Bey, 701 F.2d 1086 (4th Cir.1983).

---

[3] The Court responds to this argument by abandoning all pretense of giving the phrase "uses a firearm" even a *permissible* meaning, much less its ordinary one. There is no problem, the Court says, because it is not contending that "uses a firearm" means "uses for *any* purpose," only that it means "uses as a weapon or for trade." Unfortunately, that is not one of the options that our mother tongue makes available. "Uses a firearm" can be given a broad meaning ("uses for any purpose") or its more ordinary narrow meaning ("uses as a weapon"); but it can not possibly mean "uses as a weapon or for trade."

Bailey v. United States

Supreme Court of the United States, 1995.
516 U.S. 137, 116 S.Ct. 501, 133 L.Ed.2d 472.

■ JUSTICE O'CONNOR delivered the [unanimous] opinion of the Court.

These consolidated petitions each challenge a conviction under 18 U.S.C. § 924(c)(1). In relevant part, that section imposes a 5-year minimum term of imprisonment upon a person who "during and in relation to any crime of violence or drug trafficking crime . . . uses or carries a firearm." We are asked to decide whether evidence of the proximity and accessibility of a firearm to drugs or drug proceeds is alone sufficient to support a conviction for "use" of a firearm during and in relation to a drug trafficking offense under 18 U.S.C. § 924(c)(1).

I

In May 1989, petitioner Roland Bailey was stopped by police officers after they noticed that his car lacked a front license plate and an inspection sticker. When Bailey failed to produce a driver's license, the officers ordered him out of the car. As he stepped out, the officers saw Bailey push something between the seat and the front console. A search of the passenger compartment revealed one round of ammunition and 27 plastic bags containing a total of 30 grams of cocaine. After arresting Bailey, the officers searched the trunk of his car where they found, among a number of items, a large amount of cash and a bag containing a loaded 9-mm. pistol.

Bailey was charged on several counts, including using and carrying a firearm in violation of 18 U.S.C. § 924(c)(1). A prosecution expert testified at trial that drug dealers frequently carry a firearm to protect their drugs and money as well as themselves. Bailey was convicted by the jury on all charges, and his sentence included a consecutive 60-month term of imprisonment on the § 924(c)(1) conviction.

The Court of Appeals for the District of Columbia Circuit rejected Bailey's claim that the evidence was insufficient to support his conviction under § 924(c)(1). *United States v. Bailey,* 995 F.2d 1113 (C.A.D.C.1993). The court held that Bailey could be convicted for "using" a firearm during and in relation to a drug trafficking crime if the jury could reasonably infer that the gun facilitated Bailey's commission of a drug offense. *Id.,* at 1119. In Bailey's case, the court explained, the trier of fact could reasonably infer that Bailey had used the gun in the trunk to protect his drugs and drug proceeds and to facilitate sales. Judge Douglas H. Ginsburg, dissenting in part, argued that prior circuit precedent required reversal of Bailey's conviction.

In June 1991, an undercover officer made a controlled buy of crack cocaine from petitioner Candisha Robinson. The officer observed Robinson retrieve the drugs from the bedroom of her one-bedroom apartment. After a second controlled buy, the police executed a search warrant of the apartment. Inside a locked trunk in the bedroom closet, the police found, among other things, an unloaded, holstered .22-caliber Derringer, papers and a tax return belonging to Robinson, 10.88 grams of crack cocaine, and a marked $20 bill from the first controlled buy.

Robinson was indicted on a number of counts, including using or carrying a firearm in violation of § 924(c)(1). A prosecution expert testified that the Derringer was a "second gun," *i.e.*, a type of gun a drug dealer might hide on his or her person for use until reaching a "real gun." The expert also testified that drug dealers generally use guns to protect themselves from other dealers, the police, and their own employees. Robinson was convicted on all counts, including the § 924(c)(1) count, for which she received a 60-month term of imprisonment. The District Court denied Robinson's motion for a judgment of acquittal with respect to the "using or carrying" conviction and ruled that the evidence was sufficient to establish a violation of § 924(c)(1).

A divided panel of the Court of Appeals reversed Robinson's conviction on the § 924(c)(1) count. *United States v. Robinson,* 997 F.2d 884 (C.A.D.C.1993). The court determined, "[g]iven the way section 924(c)(1) is drafted, even if an individual intends to use a firearm in connection with a drug trafficking offense, the conduct of that individual is not reached by the statute unless the individual actually uses the firearm for that purpose." *Id.,* at 887. The court held that Robinson's possession of an unloaded .22-caliber Derringer in a locked trunk in a bedroom closet fell significantly short of the type of evidence the court had previously held necessary to establish actual use under § 924(c)(1). The mere proximity of the gun to the drugs was held insufficient to support the conviction. Judge Henderson dissented, arguing among other things that the firearm facilitated Robinson's distribution of drugs because it protected Robinson and the drugs during sales.

In order to resolve the apparent inconsistencies in its decisions applying § 924(c)(1), the Court of Appeals for the District of Columbia Circuit consolidated the two cases and reheard them en banc. In a divided opinion, a majority of the court held that the evidence was sufficient to establish that each defendant had used a firearm in relation to a drug trafficking offense and affirmed the § 924(c)(1) conviction in each case. 36 F.3d 106 (C.A.D.C.1994) (en banc).

The majority . . . "[held] that one uses a gun, i.e., avails oneself of a gun, and therefore violates [§ 924(c)(1)], whenever one puts or keeps the gun in a particular place from which one (or one's agent) can gain access to it if and when needed to facilitate a drug crime." *Id.,* at 115. The court applied this new standard and affirmed the convictions of both Bailey and Robinson. In both cases, the court determined that the gun was sufficiently accessible and proximate to the drugs or drug proceeds that the jury could properly infer that the defendant had placed the gun in order to further the drug offenses or to protect the possession of the drugs.

Judge Wald, [dissented]. . . . Judge Williams, joined by Judges Silberman and Buckley, also dissented. He explained his understanding that "use" under § 924(c)(1) denoted active employment of the firearm "rather than possession with a contingent intent to use." *Id.*, at 121. "[B]y articulating a 'proximity' plus 'accessibility' test, however, the court has in effect diluted 'use' to mean simply possession with a floating intent to use." *Ibid.*

As the debate within the District of Columbia Circuit illustrates, § 924(c)(1) has been the source of much perplexity in the courts. The Circuits are in conflict both in the standards they have articulated, compare *United States* v. *Torres-Rodriguez,* 930 F.2d 1375, 1385 (C.A.9 1991) (mere possession sufficient to satisfy § 924(c)) with *United States* v. *Castro-Lara,* 970 F.2d 976, 983 (C.A.1 1992), cert. denied, 508 U.S. 962 (1993) (mere possession insufficient); and in the results they have reached, compare *United States* v. *Feliz-Cordero,* 859 F.2d 250, 254 (C.A.2 1988) (presence of gun in dresser drawer in apartment with drugs, drug proceeds, and paraphernalia insufficient to meet § 924(c)(1)) with *United States* v. *McFadden,* 13 F.3d 463, 465 (C.A.1 1994) (evidence of gun hidden under mattress with money, near drugs, was sufficient to show "use") and *United States* v. *Hager,* 969 F.2d 883, 889 (C.A.10), cert. denied, 506 U.S. 964 (1992) (gun in boots in living room near drugs was "used"). We granted certiorari to clarify the meaning of "use" under § 924(c)(1). 514 U.S. 1062 (1995).

II

Section 924(c)(1) requires the imposition of specified penalties if the defendant, "during and in relation to any crime of violence or drug trafficking crime . . . uses or carries a firearm." Petitioners argue that "use" signifies active employment of a firearm. Respondent opposes that definition and defends the proximity and accessibility test adopted by the Court of Appeals. We agree with petitioners, and hold that § 924(c)(1) requires evidence sufficient to show an *active employment* of the firearm by the defendant, a use that makes the firearm an operative factor in relation to the predicate offense.

This case is not the first one in which the Court has grappled with the proper understanding of "use" in § 924(c)(1). In *Smith,* we faced the question whether the barter of a gun for drugs was a "use," and concluded that it was. Smith v. United States, 508 U.S. 223 (1993). As the debate in *Smith* illustrated, the word "use" poses some interpretational difficulties because of the different meanings attributable to it. Consider the paradoxical statement: "I *use* a gun to protect my house, but I've never had to *use* it." "Use" draws meaning from its context, and we will look not only to the word itself, but also to the statute and the sentencing scheme, to determine the meaning Congress intended.

We agree with the majority below that "use" must connote more than mere possession of a firearm by a person who commits a drug offense. [Citation.] Had Congress intended possession alone to trigger liability under § 924(c)(1), it easily could have so provided. This obvious conclusion is supported by the frequent use of the term "possess" in the gun-crime statutes to describe prohibited gun-related conduct. See, *e.g.*, §§ 922(g), 922(j), 922(k), 922(*o*)(1), 930(a), 930(b).

Where the Court of Appeals erred was not in its conclusion that "use" means more than mere possession, but in its standard for evaluating whether the involvement of a firearm amounted to something more than mere possession. Its proximity and accessibility standard provides almost no limitation on the kind of possession that would be criminalized; in practice, nearly every possession of a firearm by a person engaged in drug trafficking would satisfy the standard, "thereby eras[ing] the line that the statutes, and the courts, have tried to draw." *United States* v. *McFadden, supra,* at 469 (Breyer, C.J., dissenting). Rather than requiring actual use, the District of Columbia Circuit would criminalize "simpl[e] possession with a floating intent to use." 36 F.3d, at 121 (Williams, J., dissenting). The shortcomings of this test are succinctly explained in Judge Williams' dissent:

> "While the majority attempts to fine-tune the concept of facilitation (and thereby, use) through its twin guideposts of proximity and accessibility, the ultimate result is that possession amounts to 'use' because possession enhances the defendant's confidence. Had Congress intended that, all it need have mentioned is possession. In this regard, the majority's test is either so broad as to assure automatic affirmance of any jury conviction or, if not so broad, is unlikely to produce a clear guideline." *Id.,* at 124–125 (citations omitted).

An evidentiary standard for finding "use" that is satisfied in almost every case by evidence of mere possession does not adhere to the obvious congressional intent to require more than possession to trigger the statute's application.

This conclusion—that a conviction for "use" of a firearm under § 924(c)(1) requires more than a showing of mere possession—requires us to answer a more difficult question. What must the Government show, beyond mere possession, to establish "use" for the purposes of the statute? We conclude that the language, context, and history of § 924(c)(1) indicate that the Government must show active employment of the firearm.

We start, as we must, with the language of the statute. See United States v. Ron Pair Enterprises, Inc., 489 U.S. 235, 241 (1989). The word "use" in the statute must be given its "ordinary or natural" meaning, a meaning variously defined as "[t]o convert to one's service," "to employ," "to avail oneself of," and "to carry out a purpose or action by means of." *Smith, supra,* at 228–229, 113 S.Ct., at 2054 (slip op., at 5) (internal quotation marks omitted) (citing Webster's New International Dictionary of English Language 2806 (2d ed. 1949) and Black's Law Dictionary 1541 (6th ed. 1990)). These various definitions of "use" imply action and implementation. See also *McFadden,* 13 F.3d, at 467 (Breyer, C.J., dissenting) ("the ordinary meanings of the words 'use and carry' . . . connote activity beyond simple possession").

We consider not only the bare meaning of the word but also its placement and purpose in the statutory scheme. " '[T]he meaning of statutory language, plain or not, depends on context.' " [Citation.] Looking past the word "use" itself, we read § 924(c)(1) with the assumption that Congress intended each of its terms to have meaning. "Judges should hesitate . . . to treat [as surplusage] statutory terms in any setting, and resistance should be heightened when the words describe an element of a criminal offense." Ratzlaf v. United States, 510 U.S. 135 (1994) (slip op., at 5–6). Here, Congress has specified two types of conduct with a firearm: "uses" or "carries."

Under the Government's reading of § 924(c)(1), "use" includes even the action of a defendant who puts a gun into place to protect drugs or to embolden himself. This reading is of such breadth that no role remains for "carry." The Government admits that the meanings of "use" and "carry" converge under its interpretation, but maintains that this overlap is a product of the particular history of § 924(c)(1). Therefore, the Government argues, the canon of construction that instructs that "a legislature is presumed to have used no superfluous words," [citation] is inapplicable. We disagree. Nothing here indicates that Congress, when it provided these two terms, intended that they be understood to be redundant.

We assume that Congress used two terms because it intended each term to have a particular, nonsuperfluous meaning. While a broad reading of "use" undermines virtually any function for "carry," a more limited, active interpretation of "use" preserves a meaningful role for "carries" as an alternative basis for a charge. Under the interpretation we enunciate today, a firearm can be used without being carried, *e.g.,* when an offender has a gun on display during a transaction, or barters with a firearm without handling it; and a firearm can be carried without being used, *e.g.,* when an offender keeps a gun hidden in his clothing throughout a drug transaction.

This reading receives further support from the context of § 924(c)(1). As we observed in *Smith,* "using a firearm" should not have a "different meaning in § 924(c)(1) than it does in § 924(d)." 508 U.S., at 235 (slip op., at 11). See also *United Savings Assn.* v. *Timbers of Inwood Forest Assocs., Ltd.,* 484 U.S. 365, 371 (1988) ("A provision that may seem ambiguous in isolation is often clarified by the remainder of the statutory scheme"). Section 924(d)(1) provides for the forfeiture of any firearm that is "used" or "intended to be used" in certain crimes. In that provision, Congress recognized a distinction between firearms "used" in commission of a crime and those "intended to be used," and provided for forfeiture of a weapon even before it had been "used." In § 924(c)(1), however, liability attaches only to cases of actual use, not intended use, as when an offender places a firearm with the intent to use it later if necessary. The difference between the two provisions demonstrates that, had Congress meant to broaden application of the statute beyond actual "use," Congress could and would have so specified, as it did in § 924(d)(1).

The amendment history of § 924(c) casts further light on Congress' intended meaning. The original version, passed in 1968, read:

> "(c) Whoever—
>
> "(1) uses a firearm to commit any felony which may be prosecuted in a court of the United States, or
>
> "(2) carries a firearm unlawfully during the commission of any felony which may be prosecuted in a court of the United States, shall be sentenced to a term of imprisonment for not less than one year nor more than 10 years." § 102, 82 Stat. 1224.

The phrase "uses ... to commit" indicates that Congress originally intended to reach the situation where the firearm was actively employed during commission of the crime. This original language would not have stretched so far as to cover a firearm that played no detectable role in the crime's commission. For example, a defendant who stored a gun in a nearby closet for retrieval in case the deal went sour would not have "use[d] a firearm to commit" a crime. This version also shows that "use" and "carry" were employed with distinctly different meanings.

Congress' 1984 amendment to § 924(c) altered the scope of predicate offenses from "any felony" to "any crime of violence," removed the "unlawfully" requirement, merged the "uses" and "carries" prongs, substituted "during and in relation to" the predicate crimes for the earlier provisions linking the firearm to the predicate crimes, and raised the minimum sentence to five years. § 1005(a), 98 Stat. 2138–2139. The Government argues that this amendment stripped "uses" and "carries" of the qualifications ("to commit" and "unlawfully during") that originally gave them distinct meanings, so that the terms should now be understood to overlap. Of course, in *Smith* we recognized that Congress' subsequent amendments to § 924(c) employed "use" expansively, to cover both use as a weapon and use as an item of barter. But there is no evidence to indicate that Congress intended to expand the meaning of "use" so far as to swallow up any significance for "carry." If Congress had intended to deprive "use" of its active connotations, it could have simply substituted a more appropriate term—"possession"—to cover the conduct it wished to reach.

The Government nonetheless argues that our observation in *Smith* that "§ 924(c)(1)'s language sweeps broadly," 508 U.S. at 229 (slip op., at 5), precludes limiting "use" to active employment. But our decision today is not inconsistent with *Smith*. Although there we declined to limit "use" to the meaning "use as a weapon," our interpretation of § 924(c)(1) nonetheless adhered to an active meaning of the term. In *Smith,* it was clear that the defendant had "used" the gun; the question was whether that particular use (bartering) came within the meaning of § 924(c)(1). *Smith* did not address the question we face today of what evidence is required to permit a jury to find that a firearm had been used at all.

To illustrate the activities that fall within the definition of "use" provided here, we briefly describe some of the activities that fall within "active employment" of a firearm, and those that do not.

The active-employment understanding of "use" certainly includes brandishing, displaying, bartering, striking with, and most obviously, firing or attempting to fire, a firearm. We note that this reading compels the conclusion that even an offender's reference to a firearm in his possession could satisfy § 924(c)(1). Thus, a reference to a firearm calculated to bring about a change in the circumstances of the predicate offense is a "use," just as the silent but obvious and forceful presence of a gun on a table can be a "use."

The example given above—"I *use* a gun to protect my house, but I've never had to *use* it"—shows that "use" takes on different meanings depending on context. In the first phrase of the example, "use" refers to an ongoing, inactive function fulfilled by a firearm. It is this sense of "use" that underlies the Government's contention that "placement for protection"—*i.e.,* placement of a firearm to provide a sense of security or to embolden—constitutes a "use." It follows, according to this argument, that a gun placed in a closet is "used," because its mere presence emboldens or protects its owner. We disagree. Under this reading, mere possession of a firearm by a drug offender, at or near the site of a drug crime or its proceeds or paraphernalia, is a "use" by the offender, because its availability for intimidation, attack, or defense would always, presumably, embolden or comfort the offender. But the inert presence of a firearm, without more, is not enough to trigger § 924(c)(1). Perhaps the nonactive nature of this asserted "use" is clearer if a synonym is used: storage. A defendant cannot be charged under § 924(c)(1) merely for storing a weapon near drugs or drug proceeds. Storage of a firearm, without its more active employment, is not reasonably distinguishable from possession.

A possibly more difficult question arises where an offender conceals a gun nearby to be at the ready for an imminent confrontation. Cf. 36 F.3d, at 119 (Wald, J., dissenting) (discussing distinction between firearm's accessibility to drugs or drug proceeds, and its accessibility to defendant). Some might argue that the offender has "actively employed" the gun by hiding it where he can grab and use it if necessary. In our view, "use" cannot extend to encompass this action. If the gun is not disclosed or mentioned by the offender, it is not actively employed, and it is not "used." To conclude otherwise would distort the language of the statute as well as create an impossible line-drawing problem. How "at the ready" was the firearm? Within arm's reach? In the room? In the house? How long before the confrontation did he place it there? Five minutes or 24 hours? Placement for later active use does not constitute "use." An alternative rationale for why "placement at the ready" is a "use"—that such placement is made with the intent to put the firearm to a future active use—also fails. As discussed above, § 924(d)(1) demonstrates that Congress knew how to draft a statute to reach a firearm that was "intended to be used." In § 924(c)(1), it chose not to include that term, but instead established the five-year mandatory minimum only for those defendants who actually "use" the firearm.

While it is undeniable that the active-employment reading of "use" restricts the scope of § 924(c)(1), the Government often has other means available to charge offenders who mix guns and drugs. The "carry" prong of § 924(c)(1), for example, brings some offenders who would not satisfy the "use" prong within the reach of the statute. And Sentencing Guidelines § 2D1.1(b)(1) provides an enhancement for a person convicted of certain drug-trafficking offenses if a firearm was possessed during the offense. United States Sentencing Commission, Guidelines Manual § 2D1.1(b)(1) (Nov. 1994). But the word "use" in § 924(c)(1) cannot support the extended applications that prosecutors have sometimes placed on it, in order to penalize drug-trafficking offenders for firearms possession.

The test set forth by the Court of Appeals renders "use" virtually synonymous with "possession" and makes any role for "carry" superfluous. The language of § 924(c)(1), supported by its history and context, compels the conclusion that Congress intended "use" in the active sense of "to avail oneself of." To sustain a conviction under the "use" prong of § 924(c)(1), the Government must show that the defendant actively employed the firearm during and in relation to the predicate crime.

III

Having determined that "use" denotes active employment, we must conclude that the evidence was insufficient to support either Bailey's or Robinson's conviction for "use" under § 924(c)(1).

The police stopped Bailey for a traffic offense and arrested him after finding cocaine in the driver's compartment of his car. The police then found a firearm inside a bag in the locked car trunk. There was no evidence that Bailey actively employed the firearm in any way. In Robinson's case, the unloaded, holstered firearm that provided the basis for her § 924(c)(1) conviction was found locked in a footlocker in a bedroom closet. No evidence showed that Robinson had actively employed the firearm. We reverse both judgments.

Bailey and Robinson were each charged under both the "use" and "carry" prongs of § 924(c)(1). Because the Court of Appeals did not consider liability under the "carry" prong of § 924(c)(1) for Bailey or Robinson, we remand for consideration of that basis for upholding the convictions.

It is so ordered.

NOTES AND QUESTIONS

1.   Do you understand why the term "use" as used in 18 U.S.C. § 924(c)(1) does not encompass all the meanings the term used to have?

2.   Are you persuaded by the court's attempt to reconcile *Bailey* with *Smith*? Should the Court simply have overruled *Smith*? See *infra*, *Watson v. United States*.

Watson v. United States

Supreme Court of the United States, 2007.
552 U.S. 74, 128 S.Ct. 579, 169 L.Ed.2d 472.

■ JUSTICE SOUTER delivered the opinion of the Court[, in which CHIEF JUSTICE ROBERTS, JUSTICE STEVENS, JUSTICE SCALIA, JUSTICE KENNEDY, JUSTICE THOMAS, JUSTICE BREYER, and JUSTICE ALITO joined].

The question is whether a person who trades his drugs for a gun "uses" a firearm "during and in relation to . . . [a] drug trafficking crime" within the meaning of 18 U.S.C. § 924(c)(1)(A). We hold that he does not.

I

A

Section 924(c)(1)(A) sets a mandatory minimum sentence, depending on the facts, for a defendant who, "during and in relation to any crime of violence or drug trafficking crime[,] . . . uses or carries a firearm."[2] The statute leaves the term "uses" undefined, though we have spoken to it twice before.

Smith v. *United States*, 508 U.S. 223, 113 S.Ct. 2050, 124 L. Ed. 2d 138 (1993) raised the converse of today's question, and held that "a criminal who trades his firearm for drugs 'uses' it during and in relation to a drug trafficking offense within the meaning of § 924(c)(1)." We rested primarily on the "ordinary or natural meaning" of the verb in context, and understood its common range as going beyond employment as a weapon: "it is both reasonable and normal to say that petitioner 'used' his MAC-10 in his drug trafficking offense by trading it for cocaine."

Two years later, the issue in *Bailey* v. *United States*, 516 U.S. 137, 116 S.Ct. 501, 133 L. Ed. 2d 472 (1995) was whether possessing a firearm kept near the scene of drug trafficking is "use" under § 924(c)(1). We looked again to "ordinary or natural" meaning, and decided that mere possession does not amount to "use": "§ 924(c)(1) requires evidence sufficient to show an *active employment* of the firearm by the defendant,

---

[2]   Any violation of § 924(c)(1)(A), for example, demands a mandatory minimum sentence of 5 years. See 18 U.S.C. § 924(c)(1)(A)(i). If the firearm is brandished, the minimum goes up to 7 years, see § 924(c)(1)(A)(ii); if the firearm is discharged, the minimum jumps to 10 years, see § 924(c)(1)(A)(iii).

a use that makes the firearm an operative factor in relation to the predicate offense."[3]

B

This third case on the reach of § 924(c)(1)(A) began to take shape when petitioner, Michael A. Watson, told a Government informant that he wanted to acquire a gun. On the matter of price, the informant quoted no dollar figure but suggested that Watson could pay in narcotics. Next, Watson met with the informant and an undercover law enforcement agent posing as a firearms dealer, to whom he gave 24 doses of oxycodone hydrocholoride (commonly, OxyContin) for a .50 caliber semiautomatic pistol. When law enforcement officers arrested Watson, they found the pistol in his car, and a later search of his house turned up a cache of prescription medicines, guns, and ammunition. Watson said he got the pistol "to protect his other firearms and drugs."

A federal grand jury indicted him for distributing a Schedule II controlled substance and for "using" the pistol during and in relation to that crime, in violation of § 924(c)(1)(A). Watson pleaded guilty across the board, reserving the right to challenge the factual basis for a § 924(c)(1)(A) conviction and the added consecutive sentence of 60 months for using the gun. The Court of Appeals affirmed, [citation,] on Circuit precedent foreclosing any argument that Watson had not "used" a firearm. [Citation.]

We granted certiorari to resolve a conflict among the Circuits on whether a person "uses" a firearm within the meaning of 18 U.S.C. § 924(c)(1)(A) when he trades narcotics to obtain a gun. We now reverse.

II

A

The Government's position that Watson "used" the pistol under § 924(c)(1)(A) by receiving it for narcotics lacks authority in either precedent or regular English. To begin with, neither *Smith* nor *Bailey* implicitly decides this case. While *Smith* held that firearms may be "used" in a barter transaction, even with no violent employment, the case addressed only the trader who swaps his gun for drugs, not the trading partner who ends up with the gun. *Bailey*, too, is unhelpful, with its rule that a gun must be made use of actively to satisfy § 924(c)(1)(A), as "an operative factor in relation to the predicate offense." The question here is whether it makes sense to say that Watson employed the gun at all; *Bailey* does not answer it.

With no statutory definition or definitive clue, the meaning of the verb "uses" has to turn on the language as we normally speak it; there is no other source of a reasonable inference about what Congress

---

[3] In 1998, Congress responded to *Bailey* by amending § 924(c)(1). The amendment broadened the provision to cover a defendant who "in furtherance of any [crime of violence or drug trafficking] crime, possesses a firearm." 18 U.S.C. § 924(c)(1)(A). The amendment did not touch the "use" prong of § 924(c)(1).

understood when writing or what its words will bring to the mind of a careful reader. So, in *Smith* we looked for "everyday meaning," revealed in phraseology that strikes the ear as "both reasonable and normal." [Citation.] See also *Bailey, supra*. This appeal to the ordinary leaves the Government without much of a case.

The Government may say that a person "uses" a firearm simply by receiving it in a barter transaction, but no one else would. A boy who trades an apple to get a granola bar is sensibly said to use the apple, but one would never guess which way this commerce actually flowed from hearing that the boy used the granola. Cf. *United States* v. *Stewart*, 345 U.S. App. D.C. 384, 246 F.3d 728, 731 (CADC 2001) ("When a person pays a cashier a dollar for a cup of coffee in the courthouse cafeteria, the customer has not used the coffee. He has only used the dollar bill"). So, when Watson handed over the drugs for the pistol, the informant or the agent "used" the pistol to get the drugs, just as *Smith* held, but regular speech would not say that Watson himself used the pistol in the trade. "A seller does not 'use' a buyer's consideration," *United States* v. *Westmoreland*, 122 F.3d 431, 436 (CA7 1997), and the Government's contrary position recalls another case; [we previously] rejected the Government's interpretation of 18 U.S.C. § 924(c)(2) because "we do not normally speak or write the Government's way."[7]

B

The Government would trump ordinary English with two arguments. First, it relies on *Smith* for the pertinence of a neighboring provision, 18 U.S.C. § 924(d)(1), which authorizes seizure and forfeiture of firearms "intended to be used in" certain criminal offenses listed in § 924(d)(3). Some of those offenses involve receipt of a firearm,[8] from which the Government infers that "use" under § 924(d) necessarily includes receipt of a gun even in a barter transaction. *Smith* is cited for the proposition that the term must be given the same meaning in both subsections, and the Government urges us to import "use" as "receipt in barter" into § 924(c)(1)(A).

We agree with the Government that § 924(d) calls for attention; the reference to intended use in a receipt crime carries some suggestion that receipt can be "use" (more of a hint, say, than speaking of intended "use" in a crime defined as exchange). But the suggestion is a tepid one and

---

[7] Dictionaries confirm the conclusion. "Use" is concededly "elastic," *Smith* v. *United States*, 508 U.S. 223, 241, 113 S.Ct. 2050, 124 L. Ed. 2d 138 (1993) (SCALIA, J., dissenting), but none of its standard definitions stretch far enough to reach Watson's conduct, see, *e.g.,* Webster's New International Dictionary of the English Language 2806 (2d ed. 1939) ("to employ"); The Random House Dictionary of the English Language 2097 (2d ed. 1987) (to "apply to one's own purposes"; "put into service; make use of"); Black's Law Dictionary 1541 (6th ed. 1990) ("to avail oneself of; . . . to utilize"); see also *Smith, supra,* at 228–229, 241, 113 S.Ct. 2050, 124 L. Ed. 2d 138 (listing various dictionary definitions).

[8] See, *e.g.,* 18 U.S.C. § 922(j) (prohibiting, *inter alia,* the receipt of a stolen firearm in interstate commerce); § 924(b) (prohibiting, *inter alia,* the receipt of a firearm in interstate commerce with the intent to commit a felony).

falls short of supporting what is really an attempt to draw a conclusion too specific from a premise too general.

The *Smith* majority rested principally on ordinary speech in reasoning that § 924(c)(1) extends beyond use as a weapon and includes use as an item of barter, [citation,] and the *Smith* opinion looks to § 924(d) only for its light on that conclusion. It notes that the "intended to be used" clause of § 924(d)(1) refers to offenses where "the firearm is *not* used as a weapon but instead as an item of barter or commerce," [citation,] with the implication that Congress intended "use" to reach commercial transactions, not just gun violence, in § 924(d) generally. It was this breadth of treatment that led the *Smith* majority to say that, "unless we are to hold that using a firearm has a different meaning in § 924(c)(1) than it does in § 924(d)—and clearly we should not—we must reject petitioner's narrow interpretation"; [citation] see also *Bailey, supra* ("Using a firearm should not have a different meaning in § 924(c)(1) than it does in § 924(d)" (internal quotation marks omitted)).

The Government overreads *Smith*. While the neighboring provision indicates that a firearm is "used" nonoffensively, and supports the conclusion that a gun can be "used" in barter, beyond that point its illumination fails. This is so because the utility of § 924(d)(1) is limited by its generality and its passive voice; it tells us a gun can be "used" in a receipt crime, but not whether both parties to a transfer use the gun, or only one, or which one. The nearby subsection (c)(1)(A), however, requires just such a specific identification. It provides that a person who uses a gun in the circumstances described commits a crime, whose perpetrator must be clearly identifiable in advance.

The agnosticism on the part of § 924(d)(1) about who does the using is entirely consistent with common speech's understanding that the first possessor is the one who "uses" the gun in the trade, and there is thus no cause to admonish us to adhere to the paradigm of a statute "as a symmetrical and coherent regulatory scheme, . . . in which the operative words have a consistent meaning throughout," *Gustafson* v. *Alloyd Co.*, 513 U.S. 561, 569, 115 S.Ct. 1061, 131 L. Ed. 2d 1 (1995), or to invoke the "standard principle of statutory construction . . . that identical words and phrases within the same statute should normally be given the same meaning," *Powerex Corp.* v. *Reliant Energy Servs.*, 551 U.S. 224, 127 S.Ct. 2411, 168 L. Ed. 2d 112 (2007) Subsections (d)(1) and (c)(1)(A) as we read them are not at odds over the verb "use"; the point is merely that in the two subsections the common verb speaks to different issues in different voices and at different levels of specificity. The provisions do distinct jobs, but we do not make them guilty of employing the common verb inconsistently.[9]

---

[9] For that matter, the Government's argument that "use" must always have an identical meaning in §§ 924(c)(1)(A) and 924(d)(1) would upend *Bailey* v. *United States*, 516 U.S. 137, 116 S.Ct. 501, 133 L. Ed. 2d 472 (1995). One of the relevant predicate offenses referred to by § 924(d)(1) is possession of "any stolen firearm . . . [in] interstate or foreign commerce." 18 U.S.C.

C

The second effort to trump regular English is the claim that failing to treat receipt in trade as "use" would create unacceptable asymmetry with *Smith*. At bottom, this atextual policy critique says it would be strange to penalize one side of a gun-for-drugs exchange but not the other: "the danger to society is created not only by the person who brings the firearm to the drug transaction, but also by the drug dealer who takes the weapon in exchange for his drugs during the transaction," Brief for United States 23.

The position assumes that *Smith* must be respected, and we join the Government at least on this starting point. A difference of opinion within the Court (as in *Smith*) does not keep the door open for another try at statutory construction, where *stare decisis* has "special force [since] the legislative power is implicated, and Congress remains free to alter what we have done." What is more, in 14 years Congress has taken no step to modify *Smith*'s holding, and this long congressional acquiescence "has enhanced even the usual precedential force" we accord to our interpretations of statutes,

The problem, then, is not with the sturdiness of *Smith* but with the limited malleability of the language *Smith* construed, and policy-driven symmetry cannot turn "receipt-in-trade" into "use." Whatever the tension between the prior result and the outcome here, law depends on respect for language and would be served better by statutory amendment (if Congress sees asymmetry) than by racking statutory language to cover a policy it fails to reach.

The argument is a peculiar one, in fact, given the Government's take on the current state of § 924(c)(1)(A). It was amended after *Bailey* and now prohibits not only using a firearm during and in relation to a drug trafficking crime, but also possessing one "in furtherance of" such a crime. 18 U.S.C. § 924(c)(1)(A); see n. 3, *supra*. The Government is confident that "a drug dealer who takes a firearm in exchange for his drugs generally will be subject to prosecution" under this new possession prong. Brief for United States 27; see Tr. of Oral Arg. 41 (Watson's case "could have been charged as possession"); cf. *United States* v. *Cox*, 324 F.3d 77, 83, n. 2 (CA2 2003) ("For defendants charged under § 924(c) after [the post-*Bailey*] amendment, trading drugs for a gun will probably result in . . . possession [in furtherance of a drug trafficking crime]"). This view may or may not prevail, and we do not speak to it today, but it does leave the appeal to symmetry underwhelming in a contest with the English language, on the Government's very terms.

---

§ 922(j). If we were to hold that all criminal conduct covered by the "intended to be used" clause in § 924(d)(1) is "use" for purposes of § 924(c)(1)(A), it would follow that mere possession is use. But that would squarely conflict with our considered and unanimous decision in *Bailey* that " 'use' must connote more than mere possession of a firearm." 516 U.S., at 143, 116 S.Ct. 501, 133 L. Ed. 2d 472.

Given ordinary meaning and the conventions of English, we hold that a person does not "use" a firearm under § 924(c)(1)(A) when he receives it in trade for drugs. The judgment of the Court of Appeals is reversed, and the case is remanded for further proceedings consistent with this opinion.

■ JUSTICE GINSBURG, concurring in the judgment.

It is better to receive than to give, the Court holds today, at least when the subject is guns. Distinguishing, as the Court does, between trading a gun for drugs and trading drugs for a gun, for purposes of the 18 U.S.C. § 924(c)(1) enhancement, makes scant sense to me. I join the Court's judgment, however, because I am persuaded that the Court took a wrong turn in *Smith* v. *United States*, 508 U.S. 223, 113 S.Ct. 2050, 124 L. Ed. 2d 138 (1993), when it held that trading a gun for drugs fits within § 924(c)(1)'s compass as "use" of a firearm "during and in relation to any . . . drug trafficking crime." For reasons well stated by JUSTICE SCALIA in his dissenting opinion in *Smith,* 508 U.S., at 241, 113 S.Ct. 2050, 124 L. Ed. 2d 138, I would read the word "use" in § 924(c)(1) to mean use as a weapon, not use in a bartering transaction. Accordingly, I would overrule *Smith,* and thereby render our precedent both coherent and consistent with normal usage. Cf. *Henslee* v. *Union Planters Nat. Bank & Trust Co.*, 335 U.S. 595, 600, 69 S.Ct. 290, 93 L. Ed. 259, 1949–1 C.B. 223 (1949) (Frankfurter, J., dissenting) ("Wisdom too often never comes, and so one ought not to reject it merely because it comes late.").

QUESTIONS

1. Is *Smith* still good law after *Watson*? Under what circumstances might employment of a firearm for any purpose other than as a weapon still warrant application of the § 924(c) sentence enhancer?

2. How should the court's interpretation of "uses" to mean "actively employs" affect the understanding of "or carries" in the same statutory section? Is there a risk that a broad interpretation of "uses" could swallow any independent meaning to the term "or carries?" See *Muscarello v. United States, supra.*

3. INTERPRETING LEGISLATIVE RESPONSES TO PRIOR JUDICIAL INTERPRETATIONS

a. WHEN THE LEGISLATURE DECLINES, OR FAILS, TO RESPOND

Girouard v. United States
Supreme Court of the United States, 1946.
328 U.S. 61, 66 S.Ct. 826, 90 L.Ed. 1084.

Certiorari to the United States Circuit Court of Appeals for the First Circuit.

■ MR. JUSTICE DOUGLAS delivered the opinion of the Court[, in which JUSTICE BLACK, JUSTICE MURPHY, JUSTICE RUTLEDGE, and JUSTICE BURTON joined].

In 1943 petitioner, a native of Canada, filed his petition for naturalization in the District Court of Massachusetts. He stated in his application that he understood the principles of the government of the United States, believed in its form of government, and was willing to take the oath of allegiance (54 Stat. 1157, 8 U.S.C.A. § 735(b)), which reads as follows:

"I hereby declare, on oath, that I absolutely and entirely renounce and abjure all allegiance and fidelity to any foreign prince, potentate, state, or sovereignty of whom or which I have heretofore been a subject or citizen; that I will support and defend the Constitution and laws of the United States of America against all enemies, foreign and domestic; that I will bear true faith and allegiance to the same; and that I take this obligation freely without any mental reservation or purpose of evasion: So help me God."

To the question in the application "If necessary, are you willing to take up arms in defense of this country?" he replied, "No (Noncombatant) Seventh Day Adventist." He explained that answer before the examiner by saying "it is a purely religious matter with me, I have no political or personal reasons other than that." He did not claim before his Selective Service board exemption from all military service, but only from combatant military duty. At the hearing in the District Court petitioner testified that he was a member of the Seventh Day Adventist denomination, of whom approximately 10,000 were then serving in the armed forces of the United States as non-combatants, especially in the medical corps; and that he was willing to serve in the army but would not bear arms. The District Court admitted him to citizenship. The Circuit Court of Appeals reversed, one judge dissenting. 1 Cir., 149 F.2d 760. It took that action on the authority of United States v. Schwimmer, 279 U.S. 644, 49 S.Ct. 448, 73 L.Ed. 889; United States v. Macintosh, 283 U.S. 605, 51 S.Ct. 570, 75 L.Ed. 1302, and United States v. Bland, 283 U.S. 636, 51 S.Ct. 569, 75 L.Ed. 1319, saying that the facts of the present case brought it squarely within the principles of those cases. The case is here on a petition for a writ of certiorari which we granted so that those authorities might be re-examined.

The *Schwimmer, Macintosh* and *Bland* cases involved, as does the present one, a question of statutory construction. At the time of those cases, Congress required an alien, before admission to citizenship, to declare on oath in open court that "he will support and defend the Constitution and laws of the United States against all enemies, foreign and domestic, and bear true faith and allegiance to the same." It also required the court to be satisfied that the alien had during the five year period immediately preceding the date of his application "behaved as a man of good moral character, attached to the principles of the Constitution of the United States, and well disposed to the good order and happiness of the same." Those provisions were reenacted into the present law in substantially the same form.

While there are some factual distinctions between this case and the *Schwimmer* and *Macintosh* cases, the *Bland* case on its facts is indistinguishable. But the principle emerging from the three cases obliterates any factual distinction among them. As we recognized in In re Summers, 325 U.S. 561, 572, 577, 65 S.Ct. 1307, 1313, 1316, they stand for the same general rule—that an alien who refuses to bear arms will not be admitted to citizenship. As an original proposition, we could not agree with that rule. The fallacies underlying it were, we think, demonstrated in the dissents of Mr. Justice Holmes in the *Schwimmer* case and of Mr. Chief Justice Hughes in the *Macintosh* case.

The oath required of aliens does not in terms require that they promise to bear arms. Nor has Congress expressly made any such finding a prerequisite to citizenship. To hold that it is required is to read it into the Act by implication. But we could not assume that Congress intended to make such an abrupt and radical departure from our traditions unless it spoke in unequivocal terms.

The bearing of arms, important as it is, is not the only way in which our institutions may be supported and defended, even in times of great peril. Total war in its modern form dramatizes as never before the great cooperative effort necessary for victory. The nuclear physicists who developed the atomic bomb, the worker at his lathe, the seaman on cargo vessels, construction battalions, nurses, engineers, litter bearers, doctors, chaplains—these, too, made essential contributions. And many of them made the supreme sacrifice. Mr. Justice Holmes stated in the *Schwimmer* case, 279 U.S. at page 655, 49 S.Ct. at page 451, 73 L.Ed. 889, that "the Quakers have done their share to make the country what it is." And the annals of the recent war show that many whose religious scruples prevented them from bearing arms, nevertheless were unselfish participants in the war effort. Refusal to bear arms is not necessarily a sign of disloyalty or a lack of attachment to our institutions. One may serve his country faithfully and devotedly though his religious scruples make it impossible for him to shoulder a rifle. Devotion to one's country can be as real and as enduring among non-combatants as among combatants. One may adhere to what he deems to be his obligation to God and yet assume all military risks to secure victory. The effort of war is indivisible; and those whose religious scruples prevent them from killing are no less patriots than those whose special traits or handicaps result in their assignment to duties far behind the fighting front. Each is making the utmost contribution according to his capacity. The fact that his role may be limited by religious convictions rather than by physical characteristics has no necessary bearing on his attachment to his country or on his willingness to support and defend it to his utmost.

Petitioner's religious scruples would not disqualify him from becoming a member of Congress or holding other public offices. While Article VI, Clause 3 of the Constitution provides that such officials, both of the United States and the several States, "shall be bound by Oath or Affirmation, to support this Constitution," it significantly adds that "no religious Test shall ever be required as a Qualification to any Office or public Trust under the United States." The oath required is in no material respect different from that prescribed for aliens under the Naturalization Act. It has long contained the provision "that I will support and defend the Constitution of the United States against all enemies, foreign and domestic; that I will bear true faith and allegiance to the same; that I take this obligation freely, without any mental reservation or purpose of evasion." R.S. § 1757, 5 U.S.C.A. § 16. As Mr. Chief Justice Hughes stated in his dissent in the *Macintosh* case, 283 U.S. at page 631, 51 S.Ct. at page 577, 75 L.Ed. 1302, "the history of the struggle for religious liberty, the large number of citizens of our country from the very beginning who have been unwilling to sacrifice their religious convictions, and in particular, those who have been conscientiously opposed to war and who would not yield what they sincerely believed to be their allegiance to the will of God"—these considerations make it impossible to conclude "that such persons are to be deemed disqualified for public office in this country because of the requirement of the oath which must be taken before they enter upon their duties."

There is not the slightest suggestion that Congress set a stricter standard for aliens seeking admission to citizenship than it did for officials who make and enforce the laws of the nation and administer its affairs. It is hard to believe that one need forsake his religious scruples to become a citizen but not to sit in the high councils of state.

As Mr. Chief Justice Hughes pointed out (United States v. Macintosh, *supra*, 283 U.S. at page 633, 51 S.Ct. at page 578, 75 L.Ed. 1302), religious scruples against bearing arms have been recognized by Congress in the various draft laws. This is true of the Selective Training and Service Act of 1940, 54 Stat. 889, 50 U.S.C.A. Appendix, § 305(g), as it was of earlier acts. He who is inducted into the armed services takes an oath which includes the provision "that I will bear true faith and allegiance to the United States of America; that I will serve them honestly and faithfully against all their enemies whomsoever." 41 Stat. 809, 10 U.S.C.A. § 1581. Congress has thus recognized that one may adequately discharge his obligations as a citizen by rendering non-combatant as well as combatant services. This respect by Congress over the years for the conscience of those having religious scruples against bearing arms is cogent evidence of the meaning of the oath. It is recognition by Congress that even in time of war one may truly support and defend our institutions though he stops short of using weapons of war.

That construction of the naturalization oath received new support in 1942. In the Second War Powers Act, 56 Stat. 176, 182, 8 U.S.C.A. § 1001, Congress relaxed certain of the requirements for aliens who served honorably in the armed forces of the United States during World War II and provided machinery to expedite their naturalization. Residence requirements were relaxed, educational tests were eliminated, and no fees were required. But no change in the oath was made; nor was any change made in the requirement that the alien be attached to the principles of the Constitution. Yet it is clear that these new provisions cover non-combatants as well as combatants. If petitioner had served as a non-combatant (as he was willing to do), he could have been admitted to citizenship by taking the identical oath which he is willing to take. Can it be that the oath means one thing to one who has served to the extent permitted by his religious scruples and another thing to one equally willing to serve but who has not had the opportunity? It is not enough to say that petitioner is not entitled to the benefits of the new Act since he did not serve in the armed forces. He is not seeking the benefits of the expedited procedure and the relaxed requirements. The oath which he must take is identical with the oath which both non-combatants and combatants must take. It would, indeed, be a strange construction to say that "support and defend the Constitution and laws of the United States of America against all enemies, foreign and domestic" demands something more from some than it does from others. That oath can hardly be adequate for one who is unwilling to bear arms because of religious scruples and yet exact from another a promise to bear arms despite religious scruples.

Mr. Justice Holmes stated in the *Schwimmer* case, 279 U.S. at pages 654, 655, 49 S.Ct. at page 451, 73 L.Ed. 889: "if there is any principle of the Constitution that more imperatively calls for attachment than any other it is the principle of free thought—not free thought for those who agree with us but freedom for the thought that we hate. I think that we should adhere to that principle with regard to admission into, as well as to life within this country." The struggle for religious liberty has through the centuries been an effort to accommodate the demands of the State to the conscience of the individual. The victory for freedom of thought recorded in our Bill of Rights recognizes that in the domain of conscience there is a moral power higher than the State. Throughout the ages men have suffered death rather than subordinate their allegiance to God to the authority of the State. Freedom of religion guaranteed by the First Amendment is the product of that struggle. As we recently stated in United States v. Ballard, 322 U.S. 78, 86, 64 S.Ct. 882, 886, 88 L.Ed. 1148, "Freedom of thought, which includes freedom of religious belief, is basic in a society of free men. West Virginia State Board of Education v. Barnette, 319 U.S. 624, 63 S.Ct. 1178, 87 L.Ed. 1628, 147 A.L.R. 674." The test oath is abhorrent to our tradition. Over the years Congress has meticulously respected that tradition and even in time of war has sought to accommodate the military requirements to the religious scruples of the individual. We do not believe that Congress intended to reverse that policy when it came to draft the naturalization oath. Such an abrupt and radical departure from our traditions should not be implied. See Schneiderman v. United States, 320 U.S. 118, 132, 63 S.Ct. 1333, 1340, 87 L.Ed. 1796. Cogent evidence would be necessary to convince us that Congress took that course.

We conclude that the *Schwimmer, Macintosh* and *Bland* cases do not state the correct rule of law.

We are met, however, with the argument that even though those cases were wrongly decided, Congress has adopted the rule which they announced. The argument runs as follows: Many efforts were made to amend the law so as to change the rule announced by those cases; but in every instance the bill died in committee. Moreover, in 1940 when the new Naturalization Act was passed, Congress reenacted the oath in its pre-existing form, though at the same time it made extensive changes in the requirements and procedure for naturalization. From this it is argued that Congress adopted and reenacted the rule of the *Schwimmer, Macintosh*, and *Bland* cases. Cf. Apex Hosiery Co. v. Leader, 310 U.S. 469, 488, 489, 60 S.Ct. 982, 989, 990, 84 L.Ed. 1311, 128 A.L.R. 1044.

We stated in Helvering v. Hallock, 309 U.S. 106, 119, 60 S.Ct. 444, 451, 84 L.Ed. 604, 125 A.L.R. 1368, that "It would require very persuasive circumstances enveloping Congressional silence to debar this Court from re-examining its own doctrines." It is at best treacherous to find in Congressional silence alone the adoption of a controlling rule of law. We do not think under the circumstances of this legislative history that we can properly place on the shoulders of Congress the burden of the Court's own error. The history of the 1940 Act is at most equivocal. It contains no affirmative recognition of the rule of the *Schwimmer, Macintosh* and *Bland* cases. The silence of Congress and its inaction are as consistent with a desire to leave the problem fluid as they are with an adoption by silence of the rule of those cases. But for us, it is enough to say that since the date of those cases Congress never acted affirmatively on this question but once and that was in 1942. At that time, as we have noted, Congress specifically granted naturalization privileges to noncombatants who like petitioner were prevented from bearing arms by their religious scruples. That was affirmative recognition that one could be attached to the principles of our government and could support and defend it even though his religious convictions prevented him from bearing arms. And, as we have said, we cannot believe that the oath was designed to exact something more from one person than from another. Thus the affirmative action taken by Congress in 1942 negatives any inference that otherwise might be drawn from its silence when it re-enacted the oath in 1940.

Reversed.

■ MR. JUSTICE JACKSON took no part in the consideration or decision of this case.

■ MR. CHIEF JUSTICE STONE dissenting.

I think the judgment should be affirmed, for the reason that the court below, in applying the controlling provisions of the naturalization statutes, correctly applied them as earlier construed by this Court, whose construction Congress has adopted and confirmed.

In three cases decided more than fifteen years ago, this Court denied citizenship to applicants for naturalization who had announced that they proposed to take the prescribed oath of allegiance with the reservation or qualification that they would not, as naturalized citizens, assist in the defense of this country by force of arms or give their moral support to the government in any war which they did not believe to be morally justified or in the best interests of the country. See United States v. Schwimmer, 279 U.S. 644, 49 S.Ct. 448, 73 L.Ed. 889; United States v. Macintosh, 283 U.S. 605, 51 S.Ct. 570, 75 L.Ed. 1302; United States v. Bland, 283 U.S. 636, 51 S.Ct. 569, 75 L.Ed. 1319.

In each of these cases this Court held that the applicant had failed to meet the conditions which Congress had made prerequisite to naturalization by § 4 of the Naturalization Act of June 29, 1906, c. 3592, 34 Stat. 596, the provisions of which, here relevant, were enacted in the Nationality Act of October 14, 1940. See c. 876, 54 Stat. 1137, as amended by the Act of March 27, 1942, c. 199, 56 Stat. 176, 182, 183, and by the Act of December 7, 1942, c. 690, 56 Stat. 1041, 8 U.S.C.A. §§ 707, 723a, 735, 1001 et seq. Section 4 of the Naturalization Act of 1906, paragraph "Third", provided that before the admission to citizenship the applicant should declare on oath in open court that "he will support and defend the Constitution and laws of the United States against all enemies, foreign and domestic, and bear true faith and allegiance to the same." And paragraph "Fourth" required that before admission it be made to appear "to the satisfaction of the court admitting any alien to citizenship" that at least for a period of five years immediately preceding his application the applicant "has behaved as a man of good moral character, attached to the principles of the Constitution of the United States, and well disposed to the good order and happiness of the same." In applying these provisions in the cases mentioned, this Court held only that an applicant who is unable to take the oath of allegiance without the reservations or qualifications insisted upon by the applicants in those cases manifests his want of attachment to the principles of the Constitution and his unwillingness to meet the requirements of the oath, that he will support and defend the Constitution of the United States and bear true faith and allegiance to the same, and so does not comply with the statutory conditions of his naturalization. No question of the constitutional power of Congress to withhold citizenship on these grounds was involved. That power was not doubted. See Selective Draft Law Cases [(Arver v. United States)], 245 U.S. 366[, 38 S.Ct. 159, 62 L.Ed. 349, L.R.A.1918C, 361, Ann.Cas.1918B, 856]; Hamilton v. Regents, 293 U.S. 245[, 55 S.Ct. 197, 79 L.Ed. 343]. The only question was of construction of the statute which Congress at all times has been free to amend if dissatisfied with the construction adopted by the Court.

With three other Justices of the Court I dissented in the *Macintosh* and *Bland* cases, for reasons which the Court now adopts as ground for overruling them. Since this Court in three considered earlier opinions has rejected the construction of the statute for which the dissenting Justices contended, the question, which for me is decisive of the present case, is whether Congress has likewise rejected that construction by its subsequent legislative action, and has adopted and confirmed the Court's earlier construction of the statutes in question. A study of Congressional action taken with respect to proposals for amendment of the naturalization laws since the decision in the *Schwimmer* case, leads me to conclude that Congress has adopted and confirmed this Court's earlier construction of the naturalization laws. For that reason alone I think that the judgment should be affirmed.

The construction of the naturalization statutes, adopted by this Court in the three cases mentioned, immediately became the target of an active, publicized legislative attack in Congress which persisted for a period of eleven years, until the adoption of the Nationality Act in 1940. Two days after the *Schwimmer* case was decided, a bill was introduced in the House, H.R. 3547, 71st Cong., 1st Sess., to give the Naturalization Act a construction contrary to that which had been given to it by this Court and which, if adopted, would have made the applicants rejected by this Court in the *Schwimmer, Macintosh* and *Bland* cases eligible for citizenship. This effort to establish by Congressional action that the construction which this Court had placed on the Naturalization Act was not one which Congress had adopted or intended, was renewed without success after the decision in the Macintosh and Bland cases, and was continued for a period of about ten years. All of these measures were of substantially the same pattern as H.R. 297, 72d Cong., 1st Sess., introduced December 8, 1931, at the first session of Congress, after the decision in the Macintosh case. It provided that no person otherwise qualified "shall be debarred from citizenship by reason of his or her religious views or philosophical opinions with respect to the lawfulness of war as a means of settling international disputes, but every alien admitted to citizenship shall be subject to the same obligation as the native-born citizen." H.R. 3547, 71st Cong., 1st Sess., introduced immediately after the decision in the *Schwimmer* case, had contained a like provision, but with the omission of the last clause beginning "but every alien." Hearings were had before the House Committee on Immigration and Naturalization on both bills at which their proponents had stated clearly their purpose to set aside the interpretation placed on the oath of allegiance by the *Schwimmer* and *Macintosh* cases. There was opposition on each occasion. Bills identical with H.R. 297 were introduced in three later Congresses. None of these bills were reported out of Committee. The other proposals, all of which failed of passage . . . , had the same purpose and differed only in phraseology.

Thus, for six successive Congresses, over a period of more than a decade, there were continuously pending before Congress in one form or another proposals to overturn the rulings in the three Supreme Court decisions in question. Congress declined to adopt these proposals after full hearings and after speeches on the floor advocating the change. 72 Cong.Rec. 6966–7; 75th Cong.Rec. 15354–7. In the meantime the decisions of this Court had been followed in Clarke's Case, 301 Pa. 321, 152 A. 92; Beale v. United States, 8 Cir., 71 F.2d 737; In re Warkentin, 7 Cir., 93 F.2d 42. In Beale v. United States, *supra*, [71 F.2d 737] the court pointed out that the proposed amendments affecting the provisions of the statutes relating to admission to citizenship had failed saying: "We must conclude, therefore, that these statutory requirements as construed by the Supreme Court have Congressional sanction and approval."

Any doubts that such were the purpose and will of Congress would seem to have been dissipated by the reenactment by Congress in 1940 of Paragraphs "Third" and "Fourth" of § 4 of the Naturalization Act of 1906, and by the incorporation in the Act of 1940 of the very form of oath which had been administratively prescribed for the applicants in the *Schwimmer, Macintosh* and *Bland* cases. See Rule 8(c), Naturalization Regulations of July 1, 1929.

The Nationality Act of 1940 was a comprehensive, slowly matured and carefully considered revision of the naturalization laws. The preparation of this measure was not only delegated to a Congressional Committee, but was considered by a committee of Cabinet members, one of whom was the Attorney General. Both were aware of our decisions in the *Schwimmer* and related cases and that no other question pertinent to the naturalization laws had been as persistently and continuously before Congress in the ten years following the decision in the *Schwimmer* case. The modifications in the provisions of Paragraphs "Third" and "Fourth" of § 4 of the 1906 Act show conclusively the careful attention which was given to them.

In the face of this legislative history the "failure of Congress to alter the Act after it had been judicially construed, and the enactment by

Congress of legislation which implicitly recognizes the judicial construction as effective, is persuasive of legislative recognition that the judicial construction is the correct one. This is the more so where, as here, the application of the statute . . . has brought forth sharply conflicting views both on the Court and in Congress, and where after the matter has been fully brought to the attention of the public and the Congress, the latter has not seen fit to change the statute." Apex Hosiery Co. v. Leader, 310 U.S. 469, 488, 489, 60 S.Ct. 982, 989, 84 L.Ed. 1311, 128 A.L.R. 1044. And see to like effect United States v. Ryan, 284 U.S. 167–175, 52 S.Ct. 65–68, 76 L.Ed. 224; United States v. Elgin, J. & E.R. Co., 298 U.S. 492, 500, 56 S.Ct. 841, 843, 80 L.Ed. 1300; State of Missouri v. Ross, 299 U.S. 72, 75, 57 S.Ct. 60, 62, 81 L.Ed. 46; cf. Helvering v. Winmill, 305 U.S. 79, 82, 83, 59 S.Ct. 45, 46, 47, 83 L.Ed. 52. It is the responsibility of Congress, in reenacting a statute, to make known its purpose in a controversial matter of interpretation of its former language, at least when the matter has, for over a decade, been persistently brought to its attention. In the light of this legislative history, it is abundantly clear that Congress has performed that duty. In any case it is not lightly to be implied that Congress has failed to perform it and has delegated to this Court the responsibility of giving new content to language deliberately readopted after this Court has construed it. For us to make such an assumption is to discourage, if not to deny, legislative responsibility. By thus adopting and confirming this Court's construction of what Congress had enacted in the Naturalization Act of 1906 Congress gave that construction the same legal significance as though it had written the very words into the Act of 1940.

The only remaining question is whether Congress repealed this construction by enactment of the 1942 amendments of the Nationality Act. That Act extended special privileges to applicants for naturalization who were aliens and who have served in the armed forces of the United States in time of war, by dispensing with or modifying existing requirements, relating to declarations of intention, period of residence, education, and fees. It left unchanged the requirements that the applicant's behavior show his attachment to the principles of the Constitution and that he take the oath of allegiance. In adopting the 1942 amendments Congress did not have before it any question of the oath of allegiance with which it had been concerned when it adopted the 1940 Act. In 1942 it was concerned with the grant of special favors to those seeking naturalization who had worn the uniform and rendered military service in time of war and who could satisfy such naturalization requirements as had not been dispensed with by the amendments. In the case of those entitled to avail themselves of these privileges, Congress left it to the naturalization authorities, as in other cases, to determine whether, by their applications and their conduct in the military service they satisfy the requirements for naturalization which had not been waived.

It is pointed out that one of the 1942 amendments, 8 U.S.C.A. § 1004, provided that the provisions of the amendment should not apply to "any conscientious objector who performed no military duty whatever or refused to wear the uniform." It is said that the implication of this provision is that conscientious objectors who rendered noncombatant service and wore the uniform were, under the 1942 amendments, to be admitted to citizenship. From this it is argued that since the 1942 amendments apply to those who have been in noncombatant, as well as combatant, military service, the amendment must be taken to include some who have rendered noncombatant service who are also conscientious objectors and who would be admitted to citizenship under the 1942 amendments, even though they made the same reservations as to the oath of allegiance as did the applicants in the *Schwimmer, Macintosh* and *Bland* cases. And it is said that although the 1942 amendments are not applicable to petitioner, who has not been in military service, the oath cannot mean one thing as to him and another as to those who have been in the noncombatant service.

To these suggestions there are two answers. One is that if the 1942 amendment be construed as including noncombatants who are also conscientious objectors, who are unwilling to take the oath without the reservations made by the applicants in the *Schwimmer, Macintosh* and *Bland* cases, the only effect would be to exempt noncombatant conscientious objectors from the requirements of the oath, which had clearly been made applicable to all objectors, including petitioner, by the Nationality Act of 1940, and from which petitioner was not exempted by the 1942 amendments. If such is the construction of the 1942 Act, there is no constitutional or statutory obstacle to Congress' taking such action. Congress if it saw fit could have admitted to citizenship those who had rendered noncombatant service, with a modified oath or without any oath at all. Petitioner has not been so exempted.

Since petitioner was never in the military or naval forces of the United States, we need not decide whether the 1942 amendments authorized any different oath for those who had been in noncombatant service than for others. The amendments have been construed as requiring the same oath, without reservations, from conscientious objectors, as from others. In re Nielsen, D.C., 60 F.Supp. 240. Not all of those who rendered noncombatant service were conscientious objectors. Few were. There were others in the noncombatant service who had announced their conscientious objections to combatant service, who may have waived or abandoned their objections. Such was the experience in the First World War. See "Statement Concerning the Treatment of Conscientious Objectors in the Army", prepared and published by direction of the Secretary of War, June 18, 1919. All such could have taken the oath without the reservations made by the applicants in the *Schwimmer, Macintosh* and *Bland* cases and would have been entitled to the benefits of the 1942 amendments provided they had performed military duty and had not refused to wear the uniform. The fact that Congress recognized by indirection, in 8 U.S.C.A. § 1004, that those who had appeared in the role of conscientious objectors, might become citizens by taking the oath of allegiance and establishing their attachment to the principles of the Constitution, does not show that Congress dispensed with the requirements of the oath as construed by this Court and plainly confirmed by Congress in the Nationality Act of 1940. There is no necessary inconsistency in this respect between the 1940 Act and the 1942 amendments. Without it repeal by implication is not favored. United States v. Borden Co., 308 U.S. 188, 198, 199, 203–206, 60 S.Ct. 182, 188, 189, 190–192, 84 L.Ed. 181; State of Georgia v. Pennsylvania R. Co., 324 U.S. 439, 457, 65 S.Ct. 716, 726; United States Alkali Export Ass'n v. United States, 325 U.S. 196, 209, 65 S.Ct. 1120, 1128. The amendments and their legislative history give no hint of any purpose of Congress to relax, at least for persons who had rendered no military service, the requirements of the oath of allegiance and proof of attachment to the Constitution as this Court had interpreted them and as the Nationality Act of 1940 plainly required them to be interpreted. It is not the function of this Court to disregard the will of Congress in the exercise of its constitutional power.

■ MR. JUSTICE REED and MR. JUSTICE FRANKFURTER join in this opinion.

QUESTION

How pointed must Congress' non-response to a controversial statutory interpretation be before Congress should be deemed to have "ratified" that interpretation? Would it matter if no bills to amend the statute to "overrule" the judicial interpretation were ever proposed? If bills were repeatedly submitted, but no action taken? Submitted and hearings held? Submitted and committee reports issued? Voted on but failed to pass? Is this kind of inquiry helpful at all?

b. WHEN CONGRESS DOES RESPOND

Newport News Shipbuilding and Dry Dock Co. v. EEOC

Supreme Court of the United States, 1983.
462 U.S. 669, 103 S.Ct. 2622, 77 L.Ed.2d 89.

■ JUSTICE STEVENS delivered the opinion of the Court[, in which CHIEF JUSTICE BURGER, JUSTICE BRENNAN, JUSTICE WHITE, JUSTICE MARSHALL, JUSTICE BLACKMUN, and JUSTICE O'CONNOR joined].

In 1978 Congress decided to overrule our decision in General Electric Co. v. Gilbert, 429 U.S. 125 (1976), by amending Title VII of the Civil Rights Act of 1964 "to prohibit sex discrimination on the basis of pregnancy."[1] On the effective date of the Act, petitioner amended its health insurance plan to provide its female employees with hospitalization benefits for pregnancy-related conditions to the same extent as for other medical conditions.[2] The plan continued, however, to provide less favorable pregnancy benefits for spouses of male employees. The question presented is whether the amended plan complies with the amended statute.

Petitioner's plan provides hospitalization and medical-surgical coverage for a defined category of employees and a defined category of dependents. Dependents covered by the plan include employees' spouses .... Prior to April 29, 1979, the scope of the plan's coverage for eligible dependents was identical to its coverage for employees. All covered males, whether employees or dependents, were treated alike for purposes of hospitalization coverage. All covered females, whether employees or dependents, also were treated alike. Moreover, with one relevant exception, the coverage for males and females was identical. The exception was a limitation on hospital coverage for pregnancy that did not apply to any other hospital confinement.

After the plan was amended in 1979, it provided the same hospitalization coverage for male and female employees themselves for all medical conditions, but it differentiated between female employees and spouses of male employees in its provision of pregnancy-related benefits. ...

On September 20, 1979, one of petitioner's male employees filed a charge with the EEOC alleging that petitioner had unlawfully refused to provide full insurance coverage for his wife's hospitalization caused by pregnancy; a month later the United Steelworkers filed a similar charge on behalf of other individuals. App. 15–18. Petitioner then commenced an action in the United States District Court for the Eastern District of Virginia, challenging the Commission's guidelines and seeking both declaratory and injunctive relief. ... Concluding that the benefits of the new Act extended only to female employees, and not to spouses of male employees, the District Court held that petitioner's plan was lawful and enjoined enforcement of the EEOC guidelines relating to pregnancy benefits for employees' spouses. 510 F.Supp. 66 (1981). It also dismissed

---

[1] Pub.L. 95–555, 92 Stat. 2076 (quoting title of 1978 Act). The new statute (the Pregnancy Discrimination Act) amended the "Definitions" section of Title VII, 42 U.S.C. § 2000e, to add a new subsection (k) reading in pertinent part as follows:

"The terms 'because of sex' or 'on the basis of sex' include, but are not limited to, because of or on the basis of pregnancy, childbirth, or related medical conditions; and women affected by pregnancy, childbirth, or related medical conditions shall be treated the same for all employment-related purposes, including receipt of benefits under fringe benefit programs, as other persons not so affected but similar in their ability or inability to work, and nothing in section 2000e–2(h) of this title shall be interpreted to permit otherwise. ... " § 2000e(k) (1976 ed., Supp. V).

[2] The amendment to Title VII became effective on the date of its enactment, October 31, 1978, but its requirements did not apply to any then-existing fringe benefit program until 180 days after enactment—April 29, 1979. 92 Stat. 2076. The amendment to petitioner's plan became effective on April 29, 1979.

the EEOC's complaint. App. to Pet. for Cert. 21a. The two cases were consolidated on appeal.

A divided panel of the United States Court of Appeals for the Fourth Circuit reversed, reasoning that since "the company's health insurance plan contains a distinction based on pregnancy that results in less complete medical coverage for male employees with spouses than for female employees with spouses, it is impermissible under the statute." 667 F.2d, at 451. After rehearing the case en banc, the court reaffirmed the conclusion of the panel over the dissent of three judges who believed the statute was intended to protect female employees "in their ability or inability to work," and not to protect spouses of male employees. 682 F.2d 113 (1982). Because the important question presented by the case had been decided differently by the United States Court of Appeals for the Ninth Circuit, EEOC v. Lockheed Missiles & Space Co., 680 F.2d 1243 (1982), we granted certiorari 459 U.S. 1069 (1982).

Ultimately the question we must decide is whether petitioner has discriminated against its male employees with respect to their compensation, terms, conditions, or privileges of employment because of their sex within the meaning of § 703(a)(1) of Title VII.[11] Although the Pregnancy Discrimination Act has clarified the meaning of certain terms in this section, neither that Act nor the underlying statute contains a definition of the word "discriminate." In order to decide whether petitioner's plan discriminates against male employees because of *their* sex, we must therefore go beyond the bare statutory language. Accordingly, we shall consider whether Congress, by enacting the Pregnancy Discrimination Act, not only overturned the specific holding in General Electric Co. v. Gilbert, 429 U.S. 125 (1976), but also rejected the test of discrimination employed by the Court in that case. We believe it did. Under the proper test petitioner's plan is unlawful, because the protection it affords to married male employees is less comprehensive than the protection it affords to married female employees.

I

At issue in *General Electric Co. v. Gilbert* was the legality of a disability plan that provided the company's employees with weekly compensation during periods of disability resulting from nonoccupational causes. Because the plan excluded disabilities arising from pregnancy, the District Court and the Court of Appeals concluded that it

---

[11]   Section 703(a), 42 U.S.C. § 2000e–2(a), provides in pertinent part:

"It shall be an unlawful employment practice for an employer—

"(1) to fail or refuse to hire or discharge any individual, or otherwise to discriminate against any individual with respect to his compensation, terms, conditions, or privileges of employment, because of such individual's race, color, religion, sex, or national origin. . . . "

Although the 1978 Act makes clear that this language should be construed to prohibit discrimination against a female employee on the basis of her own pregnancy, it did not remove or limit Title VII's prohibition of discrimination on the basis of the sex of the employee—male or female—which was already present in the Act. As we explain *infra,* at 682–685, petitioner's plan discriminates against male employees on the basis of their sex.

discriminated against female employees because of their sex. This Court
reversed.

After noting that Title VII does not define the term "discrimination,"
the Court applied an analysis derived from cases construing the Equal
Protection Clause of the Fourteenth Amendment to the Constitution. *Id.,*
at 133. The *Gilbert* opinion quoted at length from a footnote in Geduldig
v. Aiello, 417 U.S. 484 (1974), a case which had upheld the
constitutionality of excluding pregnancy coverage under California's
disability insurance plan.[12] "Since it is a finding of sex-based
discrimination that must trigger, in a case such as this, the finding of an
unlawful employment practice under § 703(a)(1)," the Court added,
"*Geduldig* is precisely in point in its holding that an exclusion of
pregnancy from a disability-benefits plan providing general coverage is
not a gender-based discrimination at all." 429 U.S., at 136.

The dissenters in *Gilbert* took issue with the majority's assumption
"that the Fourteenth Amendment standard of discrimination is
coterminous with that applicable to Title VII." *Id.,* at 154, n. 6 (Brennan,
J., dissenting); *id.,* at 160–161 (Stevens, J., dissenting). As a matter of
statutory interpretation, the dissenters rejected the Court's holding that
the plan's exclusion of disabilities caused by pregnancy did not constitute
discrimination based on sex. As Justice Brennan explained, it was
facially discriminatory for the company to devise "a policy that, but for
pregnancy, offers protection for all risks, even those that are 'unique to'
men or heavily male dominated." *Id.,* at 160. It was inaccurate to describe
the program as dividing potential recipients into two groups, pregnant
women and nonpregnant persons, because insurance programs "deal
with future *risks* rather than historic facts." Rather, the appropriate
classification was "between persons who face a risk of pregnancy and
those who do not." *Id.,* at 161–162, n. 5 (Stevens, J., dissenting). The
company's plan, which was intended to provide employees with
protection against the risk of uncompensated unemployment caused by
physical disability, discriminated on the basis of sex by giving men
protection for all categories of risk but giving women only partial
protection. Thus, the dissenters asserted that the statute had been

---

[12] " 'While it is true that only women can become pregnant, it does not follow that every
legislative classification concerning pregnancy is a sex-based classification like those considered
in *Reed* [*v. Reed,* 404 U.S. 71 (1971)], and *Frontiero* [*v. Richardson,* 411 U.S. 677 (1973)]. Normal
pregnancy is an objectively identifiable physical condition with unique characteristics. Absent
a showing that distinctions involving pregnancy are mere pretexts designed to effect an
invidious discrimination against the members of one sex or the other, lawmakers are
constitutionally free to include or exclude pregnancy from the coverage of legislation such as
this on any reasonable basis, just as with respect to any other physical condition.

" 'The lack of identity between the excluded disability and gender as such under this
insurance program becomes clear upon the most cursory analysis. The program divides
potential recipients into two groups—pregnant women and nonpregnant persons. While the first
group is exclusively female, the second includes members of both sexes.' [417 U.S.], at 496–497,
n. 20." 429 U.S., at 134–135.

The principal emphasis in the text of the *Geduldig* opinion, unlike the quoted footnote, was
on the reasonableness of the State's cost justifications for the classification in its insurance
program.

violated because conditions of employment for females were less favorable than for similarly situated males.

When Congress amended Title VII in 1978, it unambiguously expressed its disapproval of both the holding and the reasoning of the Court in the *Gilbert* decision. It incorporated a new subsection in the "definitions" applicable "[f]or the purposes of this subchapter." 42 U.S.C. § 2000e (1976 ed., Supp. V). The first clause of the Act states, quite simply: "The terms 'because of sex' or 'on the basis of sex' include, but are not limited to, because of or on the basis of pregnancy, childbirth, or related medical conditions." § 2000e(k).[14] The House Report stated: "It is the Committee's view that the dissenting Justices correctly interpreted the Act."[15] Similarly, the Senate Report quoted passages from the two dissenting opinions, stating that they "correctly express both the principle and the meaning of title VII."[16] Proponents of the bill repeatedly emphasized that the Supreme Court had erroneously interpreted congressional intent and that amending legislation was necessary to reestablish the principles of Title VII law as they had been understood prior to the *Gilbert* decision. Many of them expressly agreed with the views of the dissenting Justices.[17]

As petitioner argues, congressional discussion focused on the needs of female members of the work force rather than spouses of male employees. This does not create a "negative inference" limiting the scope of the Act to the specific problem that motivated its enactment. See

---

[14] The meaning of the first clause is not limited by the specific language in the second clause, which explains the application of the general principle to women employees.

[15] H.R.Rep. No. 95–948, p. 2 (1978), Legislative History of the Pregnancy Discrimination Act of 1978 (Committee Print prepared for the Senate Committee on Labor and Human Resources), p. 148 (1979) (hereinafter Leg. Hist.).

[16] S.Rep. No. 95–331, pp. 2–3 (1977), Leg. Hist., at 39–40.

[17] *Id.,* at 7–8 ("the bill is merely reestablishing the law as it was understood prior to *Gilbert* by the EEOC and by the lower courts"); H.R.Rep. No. 95–948, *supra,* at 8 (same); 123 Cong.Rec. 10581 (1977) (remarks of Rep. Hawkins) ("H.R. 5055 does not really add anything to title VII as I and, I believe, most of my colleagues in Congress when title VII was enacted in 1964 and amended in 1972, understood the prohibition against sex discrimination in employment. For, it seems only commonsense, that since only women can become pregnant, discrimination against pregnant people is necessarily discrimination against women, and that forbidding discrimination based on sex therefore clearly forbids discrimination based on pregnancy"); *id.,* at 29387 (remarks of Sen. Javits) ("this bill is simply corrective legislation, designed to restore the law with respect to pregnant women employees to the point where it was last year, before the Supreme Court's decision in *Gilbert . . .* "); *id.,* at 29647; *id.,* at 29655 (remarks of Sen. Javits) ("What we are doing is leaving the situation the way it was before the Supreme Court decided the Gilbert case last year"); 124 Cong.Rec. 21436 (1978) (remarks of Rep. Sarasin) ("This bill would restore the interpretation of title VII prior to that decision").

For statements expressly approving the views of the dissenting Justices that pregnancy discrimination is discrimination on the basis of sex, see Leg.Hist., at 18 (remarks of Sen. Bayh, Mar. 18, 1977, 123 Cong.Rec. 8144); 24 (remarks of Rep. Hawkins, Apr. 5, 1977, 123 Cong.Rec. 10582); 67 (remarks of Sen. Javits, Sept. 15, 1977, 123 Cong.Rec. 29387); 73 (remarks of Sen. Bayh, Sept. 16, 1977, 123 Cong.Rec. 29641); 134 (remarks of Sen. Mathias, Sept. 16, 1977, 123 Cong.Rec. 29663–29664); 168 (remarks of Rep. Sarasin, July 18, 1978, 124 Cong.Rec. 21436). See also Discrimination on the Basis of Pregnancy, 1977, Hearings on S. 995 before the Subcommittee on Labor of the Senate Committee on Human Resources, 95th Cong., 1st Sess., 13 (1977) (statement of Sen. Bayh); *id.,* at 37, 51 (statement of Assistant Attorney General for Civil Rights Drew S. Days).

United States v. Turkette, 452 U.S. 576, 591 (1981). Cf. McDonald v. Santa Fe Trail Transp. Co., 427 U.S. 273, 285–296 (1976).[18] Congress apparently assumed that existing plans that included benefits for dependents typically provided no less pregnancy-related coverage for the wives of male employees than they did for female employees. . . .[19] Proponents of the legislation stressed throughout the debates that Congress had always intended to protect *all* individuals from sex discrimination in employment—including but not limited to pregnant women workers.[21] Against this background we review the terms of the amended statute to decide whether petitioner has unlawfully discriminated against its male employees.

II

Section 703(a) makes it an unlawful employment practice for an employer to "discriminate against any individual with respect to his compensation, terms, conditions, or privileges of employment, because of such individual's race, color, religion, sex, or national origin. . . ." 42 U.S.C. § 2000e–2(a)(1). Health insurance and other fringe benefits are "compensation, terms, conditions, or privileges of employment." Male as well as female employees are protected against discrimination. Thus, if a private employer were to provide complete health insurance coverage for the dependents of its female employees, and no coverage at all for the dependents of its male employees, it would violate Title VII. Such a practice would not pass the simple test of Title VII discrimination that we enunciated in Los Angeles Dept. of Water & Power v. Manhart, 435 U.S. 702, 711 (1978), for it would treat a male employee with dependents " 'in a manner which but for that person's sex would be different.' " The same result would be reached even if the magnitude of the discrimination

---

[18] In *McDonald,* the Court held that 42 U.S.C. § 1981, which gives "[a]ll persons within the jurisdiction of the United States . . . the same right in every State and Territory to make and enforce contracts . . . as is enjoyed by white citizens," protects whites against discrimination on the basis of race even though the "immediate impetus for the bill was the necessity for further relief of the constitutionally emancipated former Negro slaves." 427 U.S., at 289.

[19] This, of course, was true of petitioner's plan prior to the enactment of the statute. See *supra,* at 672. See S.Rep. No. 95–331, *supra* n. 16, at 6, Leg.Hist., at 43 ("Presumably because plans which provide comprehensive medical coverage for spouses of women employees but not spouses of male employees are rare, we are not aware of any Title VII litigation concerning such plans. It is certainly not this committee's desire to encourage the institution of such plans"); 123 Cong.Rec. 29663 (1977) (remarks of Sen. Cranston); Brief for Respondent 31–33, n. 31.

[21] See, *e.g.,* 123 Cong.Rec. 7539 (1977) (remarks of Sen. Williams) ("the Court has ignored the congressional intent in enacting title VII of the Civil Rights Act—that intent was to protect all individuals from unjust employment discrimination, including pregnant workers"); *id.,* at 29385, 29652. In light of statements such as these, it would be anomalous to hold that Congress provided that an employee's pregnancy is sex-based, while a spouse's pregnancy is gender-neutral.

During the course of the Senate debate on the Pregnancy Discrimination Act, Senator Bayh and Senator Cranston both expressed the belief that the new Act would prohibit the exclusion of pregnancy coverage for spouses if spouses were otherwise fully covered by an insurance plan. See *id.,* at 29642, 29663. Because our holding relies on the 1978 legislation only to the extent that it unequivocally rejected the *Gilbert* decision, and ultimately we rely on our understanding of general Title VII principles, we attach no more significance to these two statements than to the many other comments by both Senators and Congressmen disapproving the Court's reasoning and conclusion in *Gilbert.* See n. 17, *supra.*

were smaller. For example, a plan that provided complete hospitalization coverage for the spouses of female employees but did not cover spouses of male employees when they had broken bones would violate Title VII by discriminating against male employees.

Petitioner's practice is just as unlawful. Its plan provides limited pregnancy-related benefits for employees' wives, and affords more extensive coverage for employees' spouses for all other medical conditions requiring hospitalization. Thus the husbands of female employees receive a specified level of hospitalization coverage for all conditions; the wives of male employees receive such coverage except for pregnancy-related conditions. Although *Gilbert* concluded that an otherwise inclusive plan that singled out pregnancy-related benefits for exclusion was nondiscriminatory on its face, because only women can become pregnant, Congress has unequivocally rejected that reasoning. The 1978 Act makes clear that it is discriminatory to treat pregnancy-related conditions less favorably than other medical conditions. Thus petitioner's plan unlawfully gives married male employees a benefit package for their dependents that is less inclusive than the dependency coverage provided to married female employees.

There is no merit to petitioner's argument that the prohibitions of Title VII do not extend to discrimination against pregnant spouses because the statute applies only to discrimination in employment. A two-step analysis demonstrates the fallacy in this contention. The Pregnancy Discrimination Act has now made clear that, for all Title VII purposes, discrimination based on a woman's pregnancy is, on its face, discrimination because of her sex. And since the sex of the spouse is always the opposite of the sex of the employee, it follows inexorably that discrimination against female spouses in the provision of fringe benefits is also discrimination against male employees. Cf. Wengler v. Druggists Mutual Ins. Co., 446 U.S. 142, 147 (1980). By making clear that an employer could not discriminate on the basis of an employee's pregnancy, Congress did not erase the original prohibition against discrimination on the basis of an employee's sex.

In short, Congress' rejection of the premises of *General Electric Co. v. Gilbert* forecloses any claim that an insurance program excluding pregnancy coverage for female beneficiaries and providing complete coverage to similarly situated male beneficiaries does not discriminate on the basis of sex. Petitioner's plan is the mirror image of the plan at issue in *Gilbert*. The pregnancy limitation in this case violates Title VII by discriminating against male employees.

The judgment of the Court of Appeals is

Affirmed.

■ JUSTICE REHNQUIST, with whom JUSTICE POWELL joins, dissenting.

In *General Electric Co. v. Gilbert,* 429 U.S. 125 (1976), we held that an exclusion of pregnancy from a disability-benefits plan is not discrimination "because of [an] individual's ... sex" within the meaning of Title VII of the Civil Rights Act of 1964, § 703(a)(1), 78 Stat. 255, 42 U.S.C. § 2000e–2(a)(1). ... Under our decision in *Gilbert,* petitioner's otherwise inclusive benefits plan that excludes pregnancy benefits for a male employee's spouse clearly would not violate Title VII. For a different result to obtain, *Gilbert* would have to be judicially overruled by this Court or Congress would have to legislatively overrule our decision in its entirety by amending Title VII.

Today, the Court purports to find the latter by relying on the Pregnancy Discrimination Act of 1978, Pub.L. 95–555, 92 Stat. 2076, 42 U.S.C. § 2000e(k) (1976 ed., Supp. V), a statute that plainly speaks only of female employees affected by pregnancy and says nothing about spouses of male employees. Congress, of course, was free to legislatively overrule *Gilbert* in whole or in part, and there is no question but that the Pregnancy Discrimination Act manifests congressional dissatisfaction with the result we reached in *Gilbert.* But I think the Court reads far more into the Pregnancy Discrimination Act than Congress put there, and that therefore it is the Court, and not Congress, which is now overruling *Gilbert.*

In a case presenting a relatively simple question of statutory construction, the Court pays virtually no attention to the language of the Pregnancy Discrimination Act or the legislative history pertaining to that language. The Act provides in relevant part:

"The terms 'because of sex' or 'on the basis of sex' include, but are not limited to, because of or on the basis of pregnancy, childbirth, or related medical conditions; and women affected by pregnancy, childbirth, or related medical conditions shall be treated the same for all employment-related purposes, including receipt of benefits under fringe benefit programs, as other persons not so affected but similar in their ability or inability to work. ... " 42 U.S.C. § 2000e(k) (1976 ed., Supp. V).

The Court recognizes that this provision is merely definitional and that "[u]ltimately the question we must decide is whether petitioner has discriminated against its male employees ... because of their sex within the meaning of § 703(a)(1)" of Title VII. Section 703(a)(1) provides in part:

"It shall be an unlawful employment practice for an employer ... to fail or refuse to hire or to discharge any individual, or otherwise to discriminate against any individual with respect to his compensation, terms, conditions, or privileges of employment, because of such individual's race, color, religion, sex, or national origin. ... " 42 U.S.C. § 2000e–2(a)(1).

It is undisputed that in § 703(a)(1) the word "individual" refers to an employee or applicant for employment. As modified by the first clause of the definitional provision of the Pregnancy Discrimination Act, the proscription in § 703(a)(1) is for discrimination "against any individual ... because of such individual's ... pregnancy, childbirth, or related medical conditions." This can only be read as referring to the pregnancy of an employee.

That this result was not inadvertent on the part of Congress is made very evident by the second clause of the Act, language that the Court essentially ignores in its opinion. When Congress in this clause further explained the proscription it was creating by saying that "women affected by pregnancy . . . shall be treated the same . . . as other persons not so affected but *similar in their ability or inability to work*" it could only have been referring to *female employees*. The Court of Appeals below stands alone in thinking otherwise. . . .

The plain language of the Pregnancy Discrimination Act leaves little room for the Court's conclusion that the Act was intended to extend beyond female employees. The Court concedes that "congressional discussion focused on the needs of female members of the work force rather than spouses of male employees." In fact, the singular focus of discussion on the problems of the *pregnant worker* is striking.

When introducing the Senate Report on the bill that later became the Pregnancy Discrimination Act, its principal sponsor, Senator Williams, explained:

> "Because of the Supreme Court's decision in the *Gilbert* case, this legislation is necessary to provide fundamental protection against sex discrimination for our Nation's 42 million *working women*." . . .

. . . [T]he Congressional Record is overflowing with similar statements by individual Members of Congress expressing their intention to ensure with the Pregnancy Discrimination Act that working women are not treated differently because of pregnancy. Consistent with these views, all three Committee Reports on the bills that led to the Pregnancy Discrimination Act expressly state that the Act would require employers to treat pregnant employees the same as "other employees."

The Court tr[ie]s to avoid the impact of this legislative history by saying that it "does not create a 'negative inference' limiting the scope of the Act to the specific problem that motivated its enactment." This reasoning might have some force if the legislative history was silent on an arguably related issue. But the legislative history is not silent. . . .

Under our decision in *General Electric Co. v. Gilbert,* petitioner's exclusion of pregnancy benefits for male employees' spouses would not violate Title VII. Since nothing in the Pregnancy Discrimination Act even arguably reaches beyond female employees affected by pregnancy, *Gilbert* requires that we reverse the Court of Appeals. Because the Court concludes otherwise, I dissent.

QUESTIONS

1.   The *Newport News* majority held that Congress, in enacting the 1978 pregnancy discrimination amendments, rejected the rationale of the *Gilbert*

decision. There, Justice Rehnquist identified two classes of individuals, pregnant persons, and non-pregnant persons. This was not sex discrimination, according to the majority, because the second class consisted of both women and men. While the pregnancy discrimination amendments prohibited classifications based on pregnancy, by subsuming them under sex discrimination, do those amendments discredit other classification exercises of the *Gilbert* variety?

2.   Consider how the Pregnancy Discrimination Act (PDA) would function in a different context (see footnote 1 in *Newport News* for an excerpt of the PDA). Suppose that a company provides health care benefits to its employees. The plan includes coverage of routine physical exams and other preventative measures such as immunization shots, but it excludes both male and female contraceptive methods, prescription and non-prescription, when used for the sole purpose of contraception. A female employee of child-bearing age brings a suit against the company claiming that the company discriminates against its female employees under the PDA by not providing coverage of contraception.

Is contraception "related" to pregnancy under the PDA? Does it make a difference that both male and female contraception is excluded under the health plan? Does it make a difference that prescription contraception is currently only available for women?

The PDA was enacted to amend Title VII of the Civil Rights Act, which states generally that "[i]t shall be an unlawful employment practice for an employer . . . to discriminate against any individual with respect to his compensation, terms, conditions, or privileges of employment, because of such individual's . . . sex." Suppose that the health plan discussed above covers prescription drugs, devices, and services that are used to prevent the occurrence of medical conditions that occur only in men, such as prostate cancer and male-pattern baldness. How does this affect the female employee's claim?

Suppose that female contraception is a lot more expensive than male contraception. Therefore, women have greater out-of-pocket expenses than men on the same plan. How would a claim based on this fact fare under Title VII? See In re Union Pacific Railroad Employment Practices Litigation, 479 F.3d 936 (8th Cir. 2007).

3.   The majority took as a given that "since the sex of the spouse is always the opposite of the sex of the employee, it follows inexorably that discrimination against female spouses in the provision of fringe benefits is also discrimination against male employees." In 2015, in Obergefell v. Hodges, 135 S.Ct. 2584 (2015), the Supreme Court ruled that couples of the same-sex may not be deprived of the right to marry. By that time, several dozen state legislatures had already enacted laws permitting same-sex marriage. In the wake of these developments, does the *Newport News* majority's assumption still hold? If it does not, can an employee benefits policy of the kind at issue in *Newport News* still be said to discriminate on the basis of sex?

c.   WHEN LEGISLATIVE RESPONSES TO JUDICIAL INTERPRETATIONS
     TAKE EFFECT

Where, as in the 1978 Pregnancy Discrimination Act, Congress concludes that the Supreme Court has wrongly interpreted prior legislation, Congress may amend the statute to correct and clarify its meaning. But to what conduct does the new legislation apply? Only to events occurring after enactment, or to prior events (at least within the statute of limitations) as well? The latter prospect, potentially entailing the retroactive application of a new law, raises fairness (or due process) concerns, if the new law would change the legal consequences of prior conduct to the detriment of the prior actor. But as we have seen, not every statutory correction of, or change to, a past legal standard is "genuinely retroactive" in this sense. As the ensuing cases illustrate, in order to assess whether a statute has retroactive effect, it is necessary to identify what conduct Congress sought to impact.

Congress may in any event specify the temporal application of a new statute, including one that corrects past judicial errors. Interpretive problems arise when Congress fails to make clear its intention (if any, and if so, to what extent) to confer retrospective effect on new legislation. Courts must then search the text and related sources for clues. In the absence or insufficiency of indicia of Congressional intent, courts will generally construe a new or a corrective enactment only prospectively. (Contrast this rule of construction with the general rule you saw in Part II that judge-made rules apply not only forward but also backward in time.) The Supreme Court considered the temporal effect of the Pregnancy Discrimination Act in *AT&T Corp. v. Noreen Hulteen et al.*

AT&T Corp. v. Noreen Hulteen et al.

Supreme Court of the United States, 2009.
556 U.S. 701, 129 S.Ct. 1962, 173 L.Ed. 2d 898.

■ JUSTICE SOUTER delivered the opinion of the Court[, in which CHIEF JUSTICE ROBERTS, JUSTICE STEVENS, JUSTICE SCALIA, Justice KENNEDY, JUSTICE THOMAS, and JUSTICE ALITO joined].

The question is whether an employer necessarily violates the Pregnancy Discrimination Act (PDA), 42 U.S.C. § 2000e(k), when it pays pension benefits calculated in part under an accrual rule, applied only prior to the PDA, that gave less retirement credit for pregnancy leave than for medical leave generally. We hold there is no necessary violation; and the benefit calculation rule in this case is part of a bona fide seniority system under § 703(h) of Title VII of the Civil Rights Act of 1964, 42 U.S.C. § 2000e–2(h), which insulates it from challenge.

I

Since 1914, AT&T Corporation (then American Telephone & Telegraph Company) and its Bell System Operating Companies, including Pacific Telephone and Telegraph Company (hereinafter, collectively, AT&T), have provided pensions and other benefits based on a seniority system that relies upon an employee's term of employment, understood as the period of service at the company minus uncredited leave time.

In the 1960s and early to mid-1970s, AT&T employees on "disability" leave got full service credit for the entire periods of absence, but those who took "personal" leaves of absence received maximum service credit of 30 days. Leave for pregnancy was treated as personal, not disability. AT&T altered this practice in 1977 by adopting its Maternity Payment Plan (MPP), entitling pregnant employees to disability benefits and service credit for up to six weeks of leave. If the absence went beyond six weeks, however, it was treated as personal leave, with no further benefits or credit, whereas employees out on disability unrelated to pregnancy continued to receive full service credit for the duration of absence. This differential treatment of pregnancy leave, under both the pre-1977 plan and the MPP, was lawful: in *General Elec. Co.* v. *Gilbert*, 429 U.S. 125, 97 S.Ct. 401, 50 L. Ed. 2d 343 (1976), this Court concluded that a disability benefit plan excluding disabilities related to pregnancy was not sex-based discrimination within the meaning of Title VII of the Civil Rights Act of 1964, 78 Stat. 253, as amended, 42 U.S.C. § 2000e *et seq.*

In 1978, Congress amended Title VII by passing the PDA, 92 Stat. 2076, 42 U.S.C. § 2000e(k), which superseded *Gilbert* so as to make it "clear that it is discriminatory to treat pregnancy-related conditions less favorably than other medical conditions." *Newport News Shipbuilding & Dry Dock Co.* v. *EEOC*, 462 U.S. 669, 684, 103 S.Ct. 2622, 77 L. Ed. 2d 89 (1983). On April 29, 1979, the effective date of the PDA, AT&T adopted its Anticipated Disability Plan which replaced the MPP and provided service credit for pregnancy leave on the same basis as leave taken for other temporary disabilities. AT&T did not, however, make any retroactive adjustments to the service credit calculations of women who had been subject to the pre-PDA personnel policies.

Four of those women are named respondents in this case. Each of them received less service credit for pregnancy leave than she would have accrued on the same leave for disability: seven months less for Noreen Hulteen; about six months for Eleanora Collet; and about two for Elizabeth Snyder and Linda Porter. Respondents Hulteen, Collet, and Snyder have retired from AT&T respondent Porter has yet to. If her total term of employment had not been decreased due to her pregnancy leave, each would be entitled to a greater pension benefit.

Eventually, each of the individual respondents and respondent Communications Workers of America (CWA), the collective-bargaining representative for the majority of AT&T's nonmanagement employees, filed charges of discrimination with the Equal Employment Opportunity Commission (EEOC), alleging discrimination on the basis of sex and pregnancy in violation of Title VII. In 1998, the EEOC issued a Letter of

Determination finding reasonable cause to believe that AT&T had discriminated against respondent Hulteen and "a class of other similarly-situated female employees whose adjusted [commencement of service] date has been used to determine eligibility for a service or disability pension, the amount of pension benefits, and eligibility for certain other benefits and programs, including early retirement offerings." The EEOC issued a notice of right to sue to each named respondent and the CWA (collectively, Hulteen), and Hulteen filed suit in the United States District Court for the Northern District of California.

On dueling motions for summary judgment, the District Court held itself bound by a prior Ninth Circuit decision, *Pallas* v. *Pacific Bell*, 940 F.2d 1324 (1991), which found a Title VII violation where post-PDA retirement eligibility calculations incorporated pre-PDA accrual rules that differentiated on the basis of pregnancy. [Citation.] The Circuit, en banc, affirmed and held that *Pallas*'s conclusion that "calculation of service credit excluding time spent on pregnancy leave violates Title VII was, and is, correct." 498 F.3d 1001, 1003 (2007).

The Ninth Circuit's decision directly conflicts with the holdings of the Sixth and Seventh Circuits that reliance on a pre-PDA differential accrual rule to determine pension benefits does not constitute a current violation of Title VII. See *Ameritech Benefit Plan Comm.* v. *Communication Workers of Am.*, 220 F.3d 814 (CA7 2000) (finding no actionable Title VII violation given the existence of a bona fide seniority system); *Leffman* v. *Sprint Corp.*, 481 F.3d 428 (CA6 2007) (characterizing claim as challenging the continuing effects of past discrimination rather than alleging a current Title VII violation). We granted certiorari in order to resolve this split, 554 U.S. __, 128 S.Ct. 2957, 171 L. Ed. 2d 883 (2008), and now reverse the judgment of the Ninth Circuit.

II

Title VII makes it an "unlawful employment practice" for an employer "to discriminate against any individual with respect to his compensation, terms, conditions, or privileges of employment, because of such individual's . . . sex." 42 U.S.C. § 2000e–2(a)(1). Generally, a claim under Title VII must be filed "within one hundred and eighty days after the alleged unlawful employment practice occurred," § 2000e–5(e)(1). In this case, Hulteen has identified the challenged practice as applying the terms of AT&T's seniority system to calculate and pay pension benefits to women who took pregnancy leaves before April 29, 1979. She says the claim is timely because the old service credit differential for pregnancy leave was carried forward through the system's calculations so as to produce an effect in the amount of the benefit when payments began.

There is no question that the payment of pension benefits in this case is a function of a seniority system, given the fact that calculating benefits under the pension plan depends in part on an employee's term of employment. As we have said, "[a] 'seniority system' is a scheme that, alone or in tandem with non-'seniority' criteria, allots to employees ever improving employment rights and benefits as their relative lengths of pertinent employment increase." *California Brewers Assn.* v. *Bryant*, 444 U.S. 598, 605–606, 100 S.Ct. 814, 63 L. Ed. 2d 55 (1980) (footnote omitted). Hulteen is also undoubtedly correct that AT&T's personnel policies affecting the calculation of any employee's start date should be considered "ancillary rules" and elements of the system, necessary for it to operate at all, being rules that "define which passages of time will 'count' towards the accrual of seniority and which will not." *Id.*, at 607, 100 S.Ct. 814, 63 L. Ed. 2d 55.

But contrary to Hulteen's position, establishing the continuity of a seniority system whose results depend in part on obsolete rules entailing disadvantage to once-pregnant employees does not resolve this case. Although adopting a service credit rule unfavorable to those out on pregnancy leave would violate Title VII today, a seniority system does not necessarily violate the statute when it gives current effect to such rules that operated before the PDA. "[S]eniority systems are afforded special treatment under Title VII," *Trans World Airlines, Inc.* v. *Hardison*, 432 U.S. 63, 81, 97 S.Ct. 2264, 53 L. Ed. 2d 113 (1977), reflecting Congress's understanding that their stability is valuable in its own right. Hence, § 703(h):

> "Notwithstanding any other provision of this subchapter, it shall not be an unlawful employment practice for an employer to apply different standards of compensation, or different terms, conditions, or privileges of employment pursuant to a bona fide seniority . . . system . . . provided that such differences are not the result of an intention to discriminate because of race, color, religion, sex, or national origin . . . ." 42 U.S.C. § 2000e–2(h).

Benefit differentials produced by a bona fide seniority-based pension plan are permitted unless they are "the result of an intention to discriminate." *Ibid.*

In *Teamsters* v. *United States*, 431 U.S. 324, 97 S.Ct. 1843, 52 L. Ed. 2d 396 (1977), advantages of a seniority system flowed disproportionately to white, as against minority, employees, because of an employer's prior discrimination in job assignments. We recognized that this "disproportionate distribution of advantages does in a very real sense operate to freeze the status quo of prior discriminatory employment practices[,] [b]ut both the literal terms of § 703(h) and the legislative history of Title VII demonstrate that Congress considered this very effect of many seniority systems and extended a measure of immunity to them." *Id.*, at 350, 97 S.Ct. 1843, 52 L. Ed. 2d 396 (internal quotation marks omitted). "[T]he unmistakable purpose of § 703(h) was to make clear that the routine application of a bona fide seniority system would not be unlawful under Title VII." *Id.*, at 352, 97 S.Ct. 1843, 52 L. Ed. 2d 396. The seniority system in *Teamsters* exemplified a bona fide system without any discriminatory terms (the discrimination having occurred in executive action hiring employees and assigning jobs), so that the Court could conclude that the system "did not have its genesis in . . . discrimination, and . . . has been maintained free from any illegal purpose." *Id.*, at 356, 97 S.Ct. 1843, 52 L. Ed. 2d 396.

AT&T's system must also be viewed as bona fide, that is, as a system that has no discriminatory terms, with the consequence that subsection (h) controls the result here, just as in *Teamsters*. It is true that in this case the pre-April 29, 1979 rule of differential treatment was an element of the seniority system itself; but it did not taint the system under the terms of subsection (h), because this Court held in *Gilbert* that an accrual rule limiting the seniority credit for time taken for pregnancy leave did not unlawfully discriminate on the basis of sex. As a matter of law, at that time, "an exclusion of pregnancy from a disability-benefits plan providing general coverage [was] not a gender-based discrimination at all." 429 U.S., at 136, 97 S.Ct. 401, 50 L. Ed. 2d 343. Although the PDA would have made it discriminatory to continue the accrual policies of the old rule, AT&T amended that rule as of the effective date of the Act, April 29, 1979; the new one, treating pregnancy and other temporary disabilities the same way, remains a part of AT&T's seniority system today. . . .

The only way to conclude here that the subsection would not support the application of AT&T's system would be to read the PDA as applying retroactively to recharacterize the acts as having been illegal when done, contra *Gilbert*. But this is not a serious possibility. As we have said,

> "Because it accords with widely held intuitions about how statutes ordinarily operate, a presumption against retroactivity will generally coincide with legislative and public expectations. Requiring clear intent assures that Congress itself has affirmatively considered the potential unfairness of retroactive application and determined that it is an acceptable price to pay for the countervailing benefits." *Landgraf* v. *USI Film Products*, 511 U.S. 244, 272–273, 114 S.Ct. 1483, 128 L. Ed. 2d 229 (1994).

There is no such clear intent here, indeed, no indication at all that Congress had retroactive application in mind; the evidence points the other way. Congress provided for the PDA to take effect on the date of enactment, except in its application to certain benefit programs, as to which effectiveness was held back 180 days. Act of Oct. 31, 1978, § 2(b), 92 Stat. 2076, note following 42 U.S.C. § 2000e(k) (1976 ed. Supp. III). The House Report adverted to these benefit schemes:

> "As the *Gilbert* decision permits employers to exclude pregnancy-related coverage from employee benefit plans, [the bill] provides for [a] transition period of 180 days to allow employees *[sic]* to comply with the explicit provisions of this amendment. It is the committee's intention to provide for an orderly and equitable transition, with the least disruption for employers and employees, consistent with the purposes of the

bill." H. R. Rep. No. 95–948, p. 8 (1978), U.S. Code Cong. & Admin. News 1978, pp. 4749, 4756.

This is the language of prospective intent, not retrospective revision.

Hulteen argues that she nonetheless has a challenge to AT&T's current payment of pension benefits under § 706(e)(2) of Title VII, believing (again mistakenly) that this subsection affects the validity of any arrangement predating the PDA that would be facially discriminatory if instituted today. Brief for Respondents 27–29. Section 706(e)(2) provides that

> "an unlawful employment practice occurs, with respect to a seniority system that has been adopted for an intentionally discriminatory purpose in violation of this subchapter (whether or not that discriminatory purpose is apparent on the face of the seniority provision), when the seniority system is adopted, when an individual becomes subject to the seniority system, or when a person aggrieved is injured by the application of the seniority system or provision of the system." 42 U.S.C. § 2000e–5(e)(2).

But, as the text makes clear, this subsection determines the moments at which a seniority system violates Title VII only if it is a system "adopted for an intentionally discriminatory purpose in violation of this subchapter." As discussed above, the Court has unquestionably held that the feature of AT&T's seniority system at issue was not discriminatory when adopted, let alone intentionally so in violation of this subchapter. That leaves § 706(e)(2) without any application here. . . .

III

We have accepted supplemental briefing after the argument on the possible effect on this case of the recent amendment to § 706(e) of Title VII, adopted in response to *Ledbetter* v. *Goodyear Tire & Rubber Co.*, 550 U.S. 618, 127 S.Ct. 2162,167 L. Ed. 2d 982 (2007), and dealing specifically with discrimination in compensation:

> "For purposes of this section, an unlawful employment practice occurs, with respect to discrimination in compensation in violation of this title, when a discriminatory compensation decision or other practice is adopted, when an individual becomes subject to a discriminatory compensation decision or other practice, or when an individual is affected by application of a discriminatory compensation decision or other practice, including each time wages, benefits, or other compensation is paid, resulting in whole or in part from such a decision or other practice." Lilly Ledbetter Fair Pay Act of 2009, Pub. L. 111–2, § 3(A), 123 Stat. 5–6.

Hulteen argues that payment of the pension benefits at issue in this case marks the moment at which she "is affected by application of a discriminatory compensation decision or other practice," and she reads the statute as providing that such a "decision or other practice" may not be applied to her disadvantage.

But the answer to this claim is essentially the same as the answer to Hulteen's argument that § 706(e)(2) helps her. For the reasons already discussed, AT&T's pre-PDA decision not to award Hulteen service credit for pregnancy leave was not discriminatory, with the consequence that Hulteen has not been "affected by application of a discriminatory compensation decision or other practice." § 3(A), 123 Stat. 6.

IV

Bona fide seniority systems allow, among other things, for predictable financial consequences, both for the employer who pays the bill and for the employee who gets the benefit. [Citation.] As § 703(h) demonstrates, Congress recognized the salience of these reliance interests and, where not based upon or resulting from an intention to discriminate, gave them protection. Because the seniority system run by AT&T is bona fide, the judgment of the Court of Appeals for the Ninth Circuit is reversed.

It is so ordered.

■ JUSTICE STEVENS, concurring.

Today my appraisal of the Court's decision in *General Elec. Co.* v. *Gilbert*, 429 U.S. 125, 97 S.Ct. 401, 50 L. Ed. 2d 343 (1976), is the same as that expressed more than 30 years ago in my dissent. I therefore agree with much of what Justice GINSBURG has to say in this case. Nevertheless, I must accept *Gilbert*'s interpretation of Title VII as having been the governing law until Congress enacted the Pregnancy Discrimination Act. Because this case involves rules that were in force only prior to that Act, I join the Court's opinion.

■ JUSTICE GINSBURG, with whom JUSTICE BREYER joins, dissenting.

In *General Elec. Co.* v. *Gilbert*, 429 U.S. 125, 97 S.Ct. 401, 50 L. Ed. 2d 343 (1976), this Court held that a classification harmful to women based on pregnancy did not qualify as discrimination "because of . . . sex" prohibited by Title VII of the Civil Rights Act of 1964. 42 U.S.C. § 2000e–2(a)(1). Exclusion of pregnancy from an employer's disability benefits plan, the Court ruled, "is not a gender-based discrimination at all." 429 U.S., at 136, 97 S.Ct. 401, 50 L. Ed. 2d 343. See also *id.*, at 138, 97 S.Ct. 401, 50 L. Ed. 2d 343 (describing G. E.'s plan as "facially nondiscriminatory" and without "any gender-based discriminatory effect"). In dissent, JUSTICE STEVENS wondered how the Court could come to that conclusion, for "it is the capacity to become pregnant which primarily differentiates the female from the male." *Id.*, at 162, 97 S.Ct. 401, 50 L. Ed. 2d 343.

Prior to *Gilbert*, all Federal Courts of Appeals presented with the question had determined that pregnancy discrimination violated Title VII. Guidelines issued in 1972 by the Equal Employment Opportunity

Commission (EEOC or Commission) declared that disadvantageous classifications of employees based on pregnancy-related conditions are "in prima facie violation of Title VII." 37 Fed. Reg. 6837 (1972). In terms closely resembling the EEOC's current Guideline, see 29 CFR § 1604.10 (2008), the Commission counseled:

> "Written and unwritten employment policies and practices involving . . . the accrual of seniority and other benefits and privileges . . . shall be applied to disability due to pregnancy or childbirth on the same terms and conditions as they are applied to other temporary disabilities." 37 Fed. Reg. 6837.

The history of women in the paid labor force underpinned and corroborated the views of the lower courts and the EEOC. In generations preceding—and lingering long after—the passage of Title VII, that history demonstrates, societal attitudes about pregnancy and motherhood severely impeded women's employment opportunities. [Citation.]

Congress swiftly reacted to the *Gilbert* decision. Less than two years after the Court's ruling, Congress passed the Pregnancy Discrimination Act of 1978 (PDA or Act) to overturn *Gilbert* and make plain the legislators' clear understanding that discrimination based on pregnancy *is* discrimination against women. The Act amended Title VII to require that women affected by pregnancy "be treated the same for all employment-related purposes, including receipt of benefits under fringe benefit programs, as other persons not so affected but similar in their ability or inability to work." 42 U.S.C. § 2000e(k).

The PDA does not require redress for past discrimination. It does not oblige employers to make women whole for the compensation denied them when, prior to the Act, they were placed on pregnancy leave, often while still ready, willing, and able to work, and with no secure right to return to their jobs after childbirth.[4] But the PDA does protect women, from and after April 1979, when the Act became fully effective, against repetition or continuation of pregnancy-based disadvantageous treatment.

Congress interred *Gilbert* more than 30 years ago, but the Court today allows that wrong decision still to hold sway. The plaintiffs (now respondents) in this action will receive, for the rest of their lives, lower pension benefits than colleagues who worked for AT&T no longer than

---

[4] For examples of once prevalent restrictions, see *Turner* v. *Utah Dept. of Employment Security*, 423 U.S. 44, 96 S.Ct. 249, 46 L. Ed. 2d 181 (1975) *(per curiam)* (state statute made pregnant women ineligible for unemployment benefits for a period extending from 12 weeks before the expected date of childbirth until six weeks after childbirth); *Cleveland Bd. of Ed.* v. *LaFleur*, 414 U.S. 632, 634–635, 94 S.Ct. 791, 39 L. Ed. 2d 52 (1974) (school board rule forced pregnant public school teachers to take unpaid maternity leave five months before the expected date of childbirth, with no guarantee of re-employment). Cf. *Nev. Dep't of Human Res.* v. *Hibbs*, 538 U.S. 721, 736–737, 123 S.Ct. 1972, 155 L. Ed. 2d 953 (2003) (sex discrimination, Congress recognized, is rooted, primarily, in stereotypes about "women when they are mothers or mothers-to-be" (internal quotation marks omitted)).

they did. They will experience this discrimination not simply because of the adverse action to which they were subjected pre-PDA. Rather, they are harmed today because AT&T has refused fully to heed the PDA's core command: Hereafter, for "*all* employment-related purposes," disadvantageous treatment "on the basis of pregnancy, childbirth, or related medical conditions" must cease. 42 U.S.C. § 2000e(k) (emphasis added). I would hold that AT&T committed a current violation of Title VII when, post-PDA, it did not totally discontinue reliance upon a pension calculation premised on the notion that pregnancy-based classifications display no gender bias.

I

Enacted as an addition to the section defining terms used in Title VII, the PDA provides:

> "The terms 'because of sex' or 'on the basis of sex' include, but are not limited to, because of or on the basis of pregnancy, childbirth, or related medical conditions; and women affected by pregnancy, childbirth, or related medical conditions shall be treated the same for all employment-related purposes, including receipt of benefits under fringe benefit programs, as other persons not so affected but similar in their ability or inability to work. . . ." 42 U.S.C. § 2000e(k).

The text of the Act, this Court has acknowledged, "unambiguously expressed [Congress'] disapproval of both the holding and the reasoning of the Court in the *Gilbert* decision." *Newport News Shipbuilding & Dry Dock Co.* v. *EEOC*, 462 U.S. 669, 678, 103 S.Ct. 2622, 77 L. Ed. 2d 89 (1983). "Proponents of the [PDA]," the Court observed, "repeatedly emphasized that the Supreme Court had erroneously interpreted congressional intent and that amending legislation was necessary to reestablish the principles of Title VII law as they had been understood prior to the *Gilbert* decision." *Id.,* at 679, 103 S.Ct. 2622, 77 L. Ed. 2d 89. See also *California Federal Sav. & Loan Ass'n* v. *Guerra,* 479 U.S. 272, 284–285, 107 S.Ct. 683, 93 L. Ed. 2d 613 (1987) (explaining that "the first clause of the PDA reflects Congress' disapproval of the reasoning in *Gilbert*," while "the second clause . . . illustrate[s] how discrimination against pregnancy is to be remedied"). Cf. *Newport News,* 462 U.S., at 694, 103 S.Ct. 2622, 77 L. Ed. 2d 89 (Rehnquist, J., dissenting) (criticizing the Court for concluding that the PDA "renders all of *Gilbert* obsolete").

Today's case presents a question of time. As the Court comprehends the PDA, even after the effective date of the Act, lower pension benefits perpetually can be paid to women whose pregnancy leaves predated the PDA. As to those women, the Court reasons, the disadvantageous treatment remains as *Gilbert* declared it to be: "facially nondiscriminatory," and without "any gender-based discriminatory effect," 429 U.S., at 138, 97 S.Ct. 401, 50 L. Ed. 2d 343.

There is another way to read the PDA, one better attuned to Congress' "unambiguou[s] . . . disapproval of both the holding and the reasoning" in *Gilbert*. *Newport News*, 462 U.S., at 678, 103 S.Ct. 2622, 77 L. Ed. 2d 89. On this reading, the Act calls for an immediate end to any pretense that classification on the basis of pregnancy can be "facially nondiscriminatory." While the PDA does not reach back to redress discrimination women encountered before Congress overruled *Gilbert*, the Act instructs employers forthwith to cease and desist: From and after the PDA's effective date, classifications treating pregnancy disadvantageously must be recognized, "for all employment-related purposes," including pension payments, as discriminatory both on their face and in their impact. So comprehended, the PDA requires AT&T to pay Noreen Hulteen and others similarly situated pension benefits untainted by pregnancy-based discrimination.

II

The Court's rejection of plaintiffs' claims to pension benefits undiminished by discrimination "because of [their] sex," 42 U.S.C. § 2000e–2(h), centers on § 703(h) of Title VII, as construed by this Court in *Teamsters* v. *United States*, 431 U.S. 324, 97 S.Ct. 1843, 52 L. Ed. 2d 396 (1977). Section 703(h) permits employers "to apply different standards of compensation . . . pursuant to a bona fide seniority . . . system." 42 U.S.C. § 2000e–2(h). Congress enacted § 703(h), *Teamsters* explained, to "exten[d] a measure of immunity" to seniority systems even when they "operate to 'freeze' the status quo of prior discriminatory employment practices." 431 U.S., at 350, 97 S.Ct. 1843, 52 L. Ed. 2d 396 (quoting *Griggs* v. *Duke Power Co.*, 401 U.S. 424, 430, 91 S.Ct. 849, 28 L. Ed. 2d 158 (1971)).

Teamsters involved a seniority system attacked under Title VII as perpetuating race-based discrimination. Minority group members ranked low on the seniority list because, pre-Title VII, they were locked out of the job category in question. But the seniority system itself, the Court reasoned, "did not have its genesis in . . . discrimination," contained no discriminatory terms, and applied "equally to all races and ethnic groups," 431 U.S., at 355–356, 97 S.Ct. 1843, 52 L. Ed. 2d 396. Therefore, the Court concluded, § 703(h) sheltered the system despite its adverse impact on minority group members only recently hired for, or allowed to transfer into, more desirable jobs. See *id.*, at 356, 97 S.Ct. 1843, 52 L. Ed. 2d 396.

This case differs from *Teamsters* because AT&T's seniority system itself was infected by an overt differential. ("[R]ule of differential treatment was an element of the seniority system itself . . . ."). One could scarcely maintain that AT&T's scheme was "neutral on [its] face and in intent," discriminating against women only "in effect." Cf. *Teamsters*, 431 U.S., at 349, 97 S.Ct. 1843, 52 L. Ed. 2d 396. Surely not a term fairly described as "equally [applicable] to all," *id.*, at 355, 97 S.Ct. 1843, 52 L. Ed. 2d 396, AT&T's prescription regarding pregnancy leave would gain no immunity under § 703(h) but for this Court's astonishing declaration in *Gilbert:* "[E]xclusion of pregnancy from a disability-benefits plan providing general coverage," the Court decreed, "[was] not a gender-based discrimination at all." 429 U.S., at 136, 97 S.Ct. 401, 50 L. Ed. 2d 343. See *ante,* (because of *Gilbert,* AT&T's disadvantageous treatment of pregnancy leave "did not taint the system under the terms of [§ 703(h)]").

Were the PDA an ordinary instance of legislative revision by Congress in response to this Court's construction of a statutory text, I would not dissent from today's decision. But Congress made plain its view that *Gilbert* was not simply wrong about the character of a classification that treats leave necessitated by pregnancy and childbirth disadvantageously. In disregarding the opinions of other courts, of the agency that superintends enforcement of Title VII[5] and, most fundamentally, the root cause of discrimination against women in the paid labor force, this Court erred egregiously. Congress did not provide a remedy for pregnancy-based discrimination already experienced before the PDA became effective. I am persuaded by the Act's text and legislative history, however, that Congress intended no continuing reduction of women's compensation, pension benefits included, attributable to their placement on pregnancy leave.

III

A few further considerations influence my dissenting view. Seeking equal treatment only from and after the PDA's effective date, plaintiffs present modest claims. As the Court observes, they seek service credit, for pension benefit purposes, for the periods of their pregnancy leaves. For the named plaintiffs, whose claims are typical, the uncounted leave days are these: "seven months . . . for Noreen Hulteen; about six months for Eleanora Collet; and about two for Elizabeth Snyder and Linda Porter." [Citation.] Their demands can be met without disturbing settled expectations of other workers, the core concern underlying the shelter § 703(h) provides for seniority systems. See *Franks* v. *Bowman Transp. Co.,* 424 U.S. 747, 766, 773, and n. 33, 96 S.Ct. 1251, 47 L. Ed. 2d 444 (1976) (" 'benefit' seniority," unlike " 'competitive status' seniority," does not conflict with economic interests of other employees).

Furthermore, as Judge Rymer explained in her opinion dissenting from the Ninth Circuit's initial panel opinion, 441 F.3d 653, 665–666 (2006), the relief plaintiffs request is not retroactive in character. Plaintiffs request no backpay or other compensation for past injury. They seek pension benefits, now and in the future, equal to the benefits received by others employed for the same length of time. The actionable conduct of which they complain is AT&T's denial of equal benefits to plaintiffs "in the post-PDA world." *Id.,* at 667.

Nor does it appear that equal benefits for plaintiffs during their retirement years would expose AT&T to an excessive or unmanageable cost. The plaintiffs' class is not large; it comprises only women whose pregnancy leaves predated April 29, 1979 and whose employment continued long enough for their pensions to vest. The periods of service involved are short—several weeks or some months, not years. And the cost of equal treatment would be spread out over many years, as eligible women retire.

IV

Certain attitudes about pregnancy and childbirth, throughout human history, have sustained pervasive, often law-sanctioned, restrictions on a woman's place among paid workers and active citizens. This Court so recognized in *Nev. Dep't of Human Res.* v. *Hibbs*, 538 U.S. 721, 123 S.Ct. 1972, 155 L. Ed. 2d 953 (2003). *Hibbs* rejected challenges, under the Eleventh and Fourteenth Amendments, to the Family and Medical Leave Act of 1993, 107 Stat. 6, 29 U.S.C. § 2601 *et seq.*, as applied to state employees. The Court's opinion featured Congress' recognition that,

> "[h]istorically, denial or curtailment of women's employment opportunities has been traceable directly to the pervasive presumption that women are mothers first, and workers second. This prevailing ideology about women's roles has in turn justified discrimination against women when they are mothers or mothers-to-be." Joint Hearing before the Subcommittee on Labor-Management Relations and the Subcommittee on Labor Standards of the House Committee on Education and Labor, 99th Cong., 2d Sess., 100 (1986) (quoted in *Hibbs*, 538 U.S., at 736, 123 S.Ct. 1972, 155 L. Ed. 2d 953).

Several of our own decisions, the opinion in *Hibbs* acknowledged, 538 U.S., at 729, 123 S.Ct. 1972, 155 L. Ed. 2d 953, exemplified the once "prevailing ideology." [Citation.] The *Hibbs* opinion contrasted [those decisions] with more recent opinions: Commencing in 1971, the Court had shown increasing awareness that traditional sex-based classifications confined or depressed women's opportunities. 538 U.S., at 728–730, 123 S.Ct. 1972, 155 L. Ed. 2d 953. . . .

Gilbert is aberrational not simply because it placed outside Title VII disadvantageous treatment of pregnancy rooted in "stereotype-based beliefs about the allocation of family duties," *Hibbs*, 538 U.S., at 730, 123 S.Ct. 1972, 155 L. Ed. 2d 953; *Gilbert* also advanced the strange notion that a benefits classification excluding some women ("pregnant women") is not sex-based because other women are among the favored class ("nonpregnant persons"). . . .

Grasping the connection *Gilbert* failed to make, a District Court opinion pre-*Gilbert*, *Wetzel v. Liberty Mut. Ins. Co.*, 372 F. Supp. 1146 (WD Pa. 1974), published this deft observation. In response to an employer's argument that its disadvantageous maternity leave and pregnancy disability income protection policies were not based on sex, the court commented: "[I]t might appear to the lay mind that we are treading on the brink of a precipice of absurdity. Perhaps the admonition of Professor Thomas Reed Powell to his law students is apt; 'If you can think of something which is inextricably related to some other thing and not think of the other thing, you have a legal mind.' " *Id.*, at 1157.

Congress put the Court back on track in 1978 when it amended Title VII to repudiate *Gilbert*'s holding and reasoning. See *Newport News*, 462 U.S., at 678, 103 S.Ct. 2622, 77 L. Ed. 2d 89; *California Fed.*, 479 U.S., at 284–285, 107 S.Ct. 683, 93 L. Ed. 2d 613; *supra*, at 4–5. Congress' swift and strong repudiation of *Gilbert*, the Court today holds, does not warrant any redress for the plaintiffs in this case. They must continue to experience the impact of their employer's discriminatory—but, for a short time, *Gilbert*-blessed—plan. That outcome is far from inevitable. It is at least reasonable to read the PDA to say, from and after the effective date of the Act, no woman's pension payments are to be diminished by the pretense that pregnancy-based discrimination displays no gender bias.

I would construe the Act to embrace plaintiffs' complaint, and would explicitly overrule *Gilbert* so that the decision can generate no more mischief. . . .

For the reasons stated, I would affirm the Ninth Circuit's judgment.

QUESTIONS

1. How does AT&T's pension system perpetuate pregnancy discrimination?

2. Is Hulteen demanding back pay to cover the period of her uncompensated maternity leave?

3. Imagine a timeline from the date of the *Gilbert* decision, the dates of Hulteen's maternity leave, the PDA's effective date, and the date Ms. Hulteen began collecting her pension. If retroactivity changes the consequences of past conduct, what is the conduct the PDA changes, and when did it occur?

PART IV

REVIEW PROBLEMS

A. COMMON LAW LEGAL METHODS REVIEW PROBLEMS

PROBLEM 1

Harris Enterprises is a real festate company that owns several office buildings in Ryanville. Harris rents office space to commercial tenants. On June 1, 2007, at the height of the real estate market, Harris granted the law firm of Bell & Young a ten-year lease on twelve floors in its most prestigious building, Pegasus Place, at $100,000 per month.

In September 2012, in the depths of the real estate market, Bell & Young obtained more favorable rental terms in an office building in the nearby city of Saperstown. Bell & Young therefore vacated Pegasus Place, and stopped paying rent to Harris Ents. Harris Ents. nonetheless continued to send monthly invoices. By the time Bell & Young left Pegasus Place, comparable office space in Ryanville was being leased at $50,000 per month. Bell & Young's departure dismayed Harris not only because of the loss of rental income, but because of the security problems posed by the vacant space. A recent article in the Ryanville Record described several incidents in which visitors and tenants of office buildings similar to Pegasus Place had been accosted, forced into the vacant space, and then robbed. In response to this danger, in December Harris changed the locks to all the doors of the offices it had leased to Bell & Young.

Harris found a new tenant for the Bell & Young space beginning March 1, 2013, and continuing through the end of Bell & Young's lease term (May 31, 2017), at $50,000 per month. Taking into account the six months during which the office space remained vacant, the difference between the rent Harris is now receiving and the rent Harris would have received had Bell & Young remained is $365,000. Can Harris recover this sum from Bell & Young? Your research has revealed the following two decisions from the Supreme Court of New Hazard (the State in which Ryanville and Saperstown are located).

Metro-TV v. Dayal Realty Co.
Supreme Court of New Hazard, 1990.

■ ZLOTCHEW, CHIEF JUSTICE,

Appellee Dayal Realty brought this action against appellant Metro-TV, an electronics retailer, for outstanding rent on a five-year commercial lease entered into on July 1, 1984. The trial and appellate courts held Metro liable for the 37 months of unpaid rent, from June 1, 1986 through June 30, 1989. We reverse.

The undisputed facts are as follows. On June 1, 1986, Metro failed to make its monthly rent payment, and has made no rent payments since. Over the Fourth of July weekend, while Metro's store was closed for the holiday, Ashima Dayal, President of Dayal Realty, changed the locks on the store, and sent a registered letter to Metro's president, stating "You are still obligated to pay me under our lease agreement, and until you make back payments I will not give you a key to the new lock." Metro did not pay, and the store remained unoccupied through June 30, 1989.

Metro claims that Dayal's changing the locks released Metro from its obligation to pay rent. We agree, holding that when Dayal Realty changed the locks, that act constituted an eviction. An eviction terminates a tenant's duty to pay rent for the remainder of the lease term. Thus, we find Metro liable for only the one month's rent corresponding to the period after which Metro had stopped paying but during which it was still occupying the store.

University of New Hazard v. Giannou
Supreme Court of New Hazard, 2002.

■ KIM, JUSTICE.

Appellant, the University of New Hazard, brought this action against appellee, a residential tenant, for one years' outstanding rent on a three-year lease. The trial and appellate courts held that appellant's changing of the lock on appellee's apartment discharged his duty to pay rent. We reverse.

The University owns several residential apartment buildings near its main campus in Ryanville. It rents these apartments to students and staff members. In this case, the University granted a three-year lease to appellee, Nicholas Giannou, then-Chairman of the Department of Greek and Classical Philosophy. After two years, Giannou went out of state on sabbatical leave to the Agora Academy. He left his university apartment empty, and left his key in the lock.

Following complaints from neighbors that squatters were living in Giannou's apartment, the university changed the locks, and sent Giannou a letter informing him of the lock change, and instructing him to contact the University real estate office to obtain a new key.

Giannou did not request a new key. Instead, at the conclusion of his sabbatical year, he resigned from the University of New Hazard, in order to remain at Agora Academy. He has refused to respond to the University's demands for back rent.

We hold that, under these circumstances, the landlord's changing of the lock did not constitute an eviction. The University is entitled to one year's back rent.

PROBLEM 2

You are a law clerk to Judge Celia Taylor of the United States Court of Appeals for the Fourteenth Circuit. Judge Taylor has been assigned to the panel that will hear defendants' appeal in *United States v. Walker and Powell*. Below are the pertinent facts regarding the trial and the district court's determination.

In 2012, Florenz Walker and Tanya Powell were indicted and tried for a variety of federal drug-related offenses, including the illicit importation of heroin. A number of government witnesses agreed to testify only if they could remain overseas. As a result, the government deposed these witnesses on video, and offered the videotapes as evidence. Walker and Powell objected to major portions of the tapes, and the Court ruled that much of the tapes had to be edited as a result. Written transcripts of the videotapes were prepared, in which the deleted taped portions were highlighted. During the trial, the jury viewed the edited tapes, but the written transcripts were not entered as an exhibit.

Nonetheless, the transcripts were inadvertently included with the exhibits that the jurors asked to review during their deliberations. As a result, the jurors discovered the transcripts, highlighting and all. The jury, unaware of the mistake, asked District Judge Lorne Sossin if they could make use of the highlighted portions of the transcripts, to which they had not been exposed during the trial. Up to this point, the jurors had not carefully read the transcripts, but had skimmed their contents, including the highlighted portions. Walker and Powell immediately moved for a mistrial on the basis of juror bias due to the inadvertent disclosure of the transcripts.

The district judge conducted a hearing at which he questioned each of the jurors. Defense counsel and the prosecution were present at this hearing, and also questioned the jurors on their state of mind. Based on this investigation, the district judge ruled that there was "a good probability that none of the jurors had actually read the highlighted portions," but rather, "had only read far enough to recognize it as forbidden fruit." The district judge therefore denied the motion for a mistrial, instead instructing the jury to disregard the transcripts and to rely only on what they had seen and heard during the trial.

The jury convicted both defendants. Both have appealed to this court. They contend that the government should have borne the burden of disproving that juror bias resulted from the disclosure of the transcripts. Judge Taylor informs you that the sole relevant authority consists of four decisions (following): the United States Supreme Court's decisions in *Remmer v. United States* and *Smith v. Phillips,* and two decisions from the Ninth and Sixth Circuits, respectively, *United States v. Littlefield,* and *United States v. Pennell.* No court in the 14th Circuit (apart from the district court here) has yet addressed this issue.

Judge Taylor asks, first, that you articulate all the methods of allocating the burdens that the opinions of these courts suggest. Second, she asks that you determine which of these methods of allocation this Circuit should apply here in light of the facts of this case. Please be sure to explain fully the analysis leading to your conclusion.

Remmer v. United States

Supreme Court of the United States, 1954.
347 U.S. 227, 74 S.Ct. 450, 98 L.Ed. 654.

■ MR. JUSTICE MINTON delivered the opinion of the Court.

The petitioner was convicted by a jury on several counts charging willful evasion of the payment of federal income taxes. A matter admitted by the Government to have been handled by the trial court in a manner that may have been prejudicial to the petitioner, and therefore confessed as error, is presented at the threshold and must be disposed of first.

After the jury had returned its verdict, the petitioner learned for the first time that during the trial a person unnamed had communicated with a certain juror, who afterwards became the jury foreman, and remarked to him that he could profit by bringing in a verdict favorable to the petitioner. The juror reported the incident to the judge, who informed the prosecuting attorneys and advised with them. As a result, the Federal Bureau of Investigation was requested to make an investigation and report, which was accordingly done. The F.B.I. report was considered by the judge and prosecutors alone, and they apparently concluded that the statement to the juror was made in jest, and nothing further was done or said about the matter. Neither the judge nor the prosecutors informed the petitioner of the incident, and he and his counsel first learned of the matter by reading of it in the newspapers after the verdict.

The above-stated facts were alleged in a motion for a new trial, together with an allegation that the petitioner was substantially prejudiced, thereby depriving him of a fair trial, and a request for a hearing to determine the circumstances surrounding the incident and its effect on the jury. A supporting affidavit of the petitioner's attorneys recited the alleged occurrences and stated that if they had known of the incident they would have moved for a mistrial and requested that the juror in question be replaced by an alternate juror. Two newspaper articles reporting the incident were attached to the affidavit. The Government did not file answering affidavits. The District Court, without holding the requested hearing, denied the motion for a new trial. The Court of Appeals held that the District Court had not abused its discretion, since the petitioner had shown no prejudice to him. 205 F.2d 277, 291. The case is here on writ of certiorari. 346 U.S. 884.

In a criminal case, any private communication, contact, or tampering directly or indirectly, with a juror during a trial about the matter pending before the jury is, for obvious reasons, deemed presumptively prejudicial, if not made in pursuance of known rules of the court and the instructions and directions of the court made during the trial, with full knowledge of the parties. The presumption is not conclusive, but the burden rests heavily upon the Government to establish, after notice to and hearing of the defendant, that such contact with the juror was harmless to the defendant. Mattox v. United States, 146 U.S. 140, 148–150; Wheaton v. United States, 133 F.2d 522, 527.

We do not know from this record, nor does the petitioner know, what actually transpired, or whether the incidents that may have occurred were harmful or harmless. The sending of an F.B.I. agent in the midst of a trial to investigate a juror as to his conduct is bound to impress the juror and is very apt to do so unduly. A juror must feel free to exercise his functions without the F.B.I. or anyone else looking over his shoulder. The integrity of jury proceedings must not be jeopardized by unauthorized invasions. The trial court should not decide and take final action ex parte on information such as was received in this case, but should determine the circumstances, the impact thereof upon the juror, and whether or not it was prejudicial, in a hearing with all interested parties permitted to participate.

We therefore vacate the judgment of the Court of Appeals and remand the case to the District Court with directions to hold a hearing to determine whether the incident complained of was harmful to the petitioner, and if after hearing it is found to have been harmful, to grant a new trial.

Judgment vacated.

Smith v. Phillips

Supreme Court of the United States, 1982.
455 U.S. 209, 102 S.Ct. 940, 71 L.Ed.2d 78.

■ JUSTICE REHNQUIST delivered the opinion of the Court.

Respondent was convicted in November 1974 by a New York state-court jury on two counts of murder and one count of attempted murder. After trial, respondent moved to vacate his conviction, and a hearing on his motion was held. The hearing was held before the justice who presided at respondent's trial, and the motion to vacate was denied by him in an opinion concluding that the events giving rise to the motion did not influence the verdict. People v. Phillips, 87 Misc.2d 613, 614, 630 (1975). The Appellate Division of the Supreme Court, First Judicial Department, affirmed the conviction without opinion. 52 App.Div.2d 758 (1976). The New York Court of Appeals denied leave to appeal. 39 N.Y.2d 949 (1976).

Respondent subsequently sought relief in the United States District Court for the Southern District of New York on the same ground which had been asserted in the state post-trial hearing. The District Court granted the writ, 485 F.Supp. 1365 (1980), and the United States Court of Appeals for the Second Circuit affirmed on a somewhat different ground. 632 F.2d 1019 (1980). We granted certiorari and now reverse.

I

A

Respondent's original motion to vacate his conviction was based on the fact that a juror in respondent's case, one John Dana Smith, submitted during the trial an application for employment as a major felony investigator in the District Attorney's Office.[3] Smith had learned of the position from a friend who had contacts within the office and who had inquired on Smith's behalf without mentioning Smith's name or the fact that he was a juror in respondent's trial. When Smith's application was received by the office, his name was placed on a list of applicants but he was not then contacted and was not known by the office to be a juror in respondent's trial.

During later inquiry about the status of Smith's application, the friend mentioned that Smith was a juror in respondent's case. The attorney to whom the friend disclosed this fact promptly informed his superior, and his superior in turn informed the Assistant District Attorney in charge of hiring investigators. The following day, more than one week before the end of respondent's trial, the assistant informed the

---

[3] Smith's letter of application was addressed to the District Attorney and stated:
"I understand that a federally funded investigative unit is being formed in your office to investigate major felonies. I wish to apply for a position as an investigator."
The letter did not mention that Smith was a juror in respondent's trial. Appended to the letter was a resume containing biographical information about Smith. People v. Phillips, 87 Misc.2d 613, 616 (1975).

two attorneys actually prosecuting respondent that one of the jurors had applied to the office for employment as an investigator.

The two prosecuting attorneys conferred about the application but concluded that, in view of Smith's statements during *voir dire* [the jury selection process],[4] there was no need to inform the trial court or defense counsel of the application. They did instruct attorneys in the office not to contact Smith until after the trial had ended, and took steps to insure that they would learn no information about Smith that had not been revealed during the jury selection process. When the jury retired to deliberate on November 20th, three alternate jurors were available to substitute for Smith, and neither the trial court nor the defense counsel knew of his application. The jury returned its verdict on November 21st.

The District Attorney first learned of Smith's application on December 4th. Five days later, after an investigation to verify the information, he informed the trial court and defense counsel of the application and the fact that its existence was known to attorneys in his office at some time before the conclusion of the trial. Respondent's attorney then moved to set aside the verdict.

At the hearing before the trial judge, Justice Harold Birns, the prosecuting attorneys explained their decision not to disclose the application and Smith explained that he had seen nothing improper in submitting the application during the trial. Justice Birns, from all the evidence adduced at the hearing, found that Smith's letter was indeed an indiscretion but that it in no way reflected a premature conclusion as to the respondent's guilt, or prejudice against the respondent, or an inability to consider the guilt or innocence of the respondent solely on the evidence. Id., at 627. With respect to the conduct of the prosecuting attorneys, Justice Birns found "no evidence" suggesting "a sinister or dishonest motive with respect to Mr. Smith's letter of application." Id., at 618–619.

B

In his application for federal relief, respondent contended that he had been denied due process of law under the Fourteenth Amendment to the United States Constitution by Smith's conduct. The District Court found insufficient evidence to demonstrate that Smith was actually biased. 485 F.Supp., at 1371. Nonetheless, the court imputed bias to Smith because "the average man in Smith's position would believe that

---

[4] The trial judge described the jury selection process in respondent's case as "ten days of meticulous examination." Id., at 614. During his jury selection, Smith stated that he intended to pursue a career in law enforcement and that he had applied for employment with a federal drug enforcement agency. He also disclosed that his wife was interested in law enforcement, an interest which arose out of an incident in which she was assaulted and seriously injured. Smith stated that he had previously worked as a store detective for Bloomingdale's Department Store, and, in that capacity, had made several arrests which led to contact with the District Attorney's Office. In response to close inquiry by defense counsel, Smith declared his belief that he could be a fair and impartial juror in the case. This assurance apparently satisfied defense counsel, for Smith was permitted to take his seat among the jurors even though the defense could have removed him.

the verdict of the jury would directly affect the evaluation of his job application." Id., at 1371–1372. Accordingly, the court ordered respondent released unless the State granted him a new trial within 90 days.

The United States Court of Appeals for the Second Circuit affirmed by a divided vote. The court noted that "it is at best difficult and perhaps impossible to learn from a juror's own testimony after the verdict whether he was in fact 'impartial,'" but the court did not consider whether Smith was actually or impliedly biased. 632 F.2d, at 1022. Rather, the Court of Appeals affirmed respondent's release simply because "the failure of the prosecutors to disclose their knowledge denied [respondent] due process." Ibid. The court explained: "To condone the withholding by the prosecutor of information casting substantial doubt as to the impartiality of a juror, such as the fact that he has applied to the prosecutor for employment, would not be fair to a defendant and would ill serve to maintain public confidence in the judicial process." Id., at 1023.

II

This Court has long held that the remedy for allegations of juror partiality is a hearing in which the defendant has the opportunity to prove actual bias. For example, in Remmer v. United States, 347 U.S. 227 (1954), a juror in a federal criminal trial was approached by someone offering money in exchange for a favorable verdict. An FBI agent was assigned to investigate the attempted bribe, and the agent's report was reviewed by the trial judge and the prosecutor without disclosure to defense counsel. When they learned of the incident after trial, the defense attorneys moved that the verdict be vacated, alleging that "they would have moved for a mistrial and requested that the juror in question be replaced by an alternate juror" had the incident been disclosed to them during trial. Id., at 229.

This Court recognized the seriousness not only of the attempted bribe, which it characterized as "presumptively prejudicial," but also of the undisclosed investigation, which was "bound to impress the juror and [was] very apt to do so unduly." Ibid. Despite this recognition, and a conviction that "[the] integrity of jury proceedings must not be jeopardized by unauthorized invasions," ibid., the Court did not require a new trial like that ordered in this case. Rather, the Court instructed the trial judge to "determine the circumstances, the impact thereof upon the juror, and whether or not [they were] prejudicial, in a hearing with all interested parties permitted to participate." Id., at 230. In other words, the Court ordered precisely the remedy which was accorded by Justice Birns in this case.

This case demonstrates that due process does not require a new trial every time a juror has been placed in a potentially compromising situation. Were that the rule, few trials would be constitutionally acceptable. The safeguards of juror impartiality are not infallible; it is virtually impossible to shield jurors from every contact or influence that might theoretically affect their vote. Due process means a jury capable and willing to decide the case solely on the evidence before it, and a trial judge ever watchful to prevent prejudicial occurrences and to determine the effect of such occurrences when they happen. Such determinations may properly be made at a hearing like that ordered in Remmer and held in this case.

Therefore, the prosecutors' failure to disclose Smith's job application, although requiring a post-trial hearing on juror bias, did not deprive respondent of the fair trial guaranteed by the Due Process Clause. Accordingly, the judgment of the Court of Appeals is reversed.

■ JUSTICE MARSHALL, with whom JUSTICE BRENNAN and JUSTICE STEVENS join, dissenting.

Juror John Smith vigorously pursued employment with the office of the prosecutor throughout the course of his jury service in respondent's state criminal trial. The prosecutors learned of Smith's efforts during the trial, but improperly failed to disclose this information until after the jury had returned a verdict of guilty against respondent. The state court conducted a post-trial evidentiary hearing and determined that the juror was not actually biased. Thus, it ruled that respondent was not prejudiced, and refused to set aside the conviction. Respondent subsequently filed for relief in the United States District Court for the Southern District of New York, claiming that he was denied his constitutional right to an impartial jury. The District Court ruled that the conviction should be set aside, and the United States Court of Appeals for the Second Circuit affirmed. A majority of this Court now reverses, holding that the post-trial evidentiary hearing provided sufficient protection to respondent's right to an impartial jury. Because I find the majority's analysis completely unpersuasive, I dissent.

The majority concedes the importance of the right to a trial by an impartial jury. It claims, however, that respondent's right was adequately protected here, because the state trial judge conducted a postverdict evidentiary hearing and concluded that Smith was not actually biased. According to the majority, the Constitution requires only that the defendant be given an opportunity to prove actual bias. Indeed, it would apparently insist on proof of actual bias, not only when a juror had applied for employment with the prosecutor's office, but also when the juror was already employed in the prosecutor's office, or when he served as a prosecuting attorney. The majority relies on the premise that an evidentiary hearing provides adequate assurance that prejudice does not exist. This premise, however, ignores basic human psychology. In cases like this one, an evidentiary hearing can never adequately protect the right to an impartial jury.

Despite the majority's suggestions to the contrary, juror Smith was not a passive, indifferent job applicant.[5] He began pursuing employment as an investigator in the Office of the District Attorney on September 23, 1974, the same day he was sworn in. He asked a friend, Criminal Court Officer Rudolph Fontaine, to determine the proper method of applying for employment. Once he had completed his application, he gave it to Fontaine for hand delivery to the District Attorney's Office, apparently because he assumed that the court officer had a personal contact in the office. In addition, after the application had been filed, he met regularly with Fontaine and Jury Warden Mario Piazza in order to determine the progress of his application. On November 21, 1974, the jury returned a verdict of guilt and the trial ended. The very next day, Smith phoned the District Attorney's Office to check on the status of his application. When he was unable to get in touch with anyone who knew about his application, he asked his former supervisor to make inquiries in his behalf.

When a juror vigorously and actively pursues employment in the prosecutor's office throughout the course of a trial, the probability of bias is substantial. This bias may be conscious, part of a calculated effort to obtain a job. The juror may believe that his application will be viewed favorably if the defendant is found guilty. Thus, he may decide to vote for a verdict of guilty regardless of the evidence, and he may attempt to persuade the other jurors that acquittal is not justified. There is also a very serious danger of unconscious bias. Only individuals of extraordinary character would not be affected in some way by their interest in future employment. Subconsciously, the juror may tend to favor the prosecutor simply because he feels some affinity with his potential employer. Indeed, the juror may make a sincere effort to remain impartial, and yet be unable to do so.

Not only is the probability of bias high, it is also unlikely that a post-trial evidentiary hearing would reveal this bias. As the Court of Appeals stated, given the human propensity for self-justification, it is very difficult "to learn from a juror's own testimony after the verdict whether he was in fact 'impartial.' " 632 F.2d 1019, 1022 (CA2 1980). Certainly, a juror is unlikely to admit that he had consciously plotted against the defendant during the course of the trial. Such an admission would have subjected juror Smith to criminal sanctions. It would also have damaged his prospects for a career in law enforcement. A law enforcement agency is unlikely to hire an investigator whose credibility could always be impeached by an admission that he had disregarded his juror's oath in a criminal trial.

---

[5]   The majority notes that during jury selection, the defense chose not to challenge Smith, even though he had stated that he had a strong interest in a law enforcement career. However, since the defendant was himself a law enforcement officer, such an interest would not necessarily have been unfavorable to the defense. I think it clear that a general career interest in law enforcement is very different from an application for a job with the prosecutor in a particular case.

Even when the bias was not part of an affirmative course of misconduct, however, but was unconscious, a juror is unlikely to admit that he had been unable to weigh the evidence fairly. If he honestly believes that he remained impartial throughout the trial, no amount of questioning will lead to an admission. Rather the juror will vehemently deny any accusation of bias.[7]

In the past, the Court has recognized that the question whether a juror is prejudiced poses substantial problems of proof.

> "Bias or prejudice is such an elusive condition of the mind that it is most difficult, if not impossible, to always recognize its existence, and it might exist in the mind of one (on account of his relations with one of the parties) who was quite positive that he had no bias, and said that he was perfectly able to decide the question wholly uninfluenced by anything but the evidence." Crawford v. United States, 212 U.S. 183, 196 (1909).

I believe that in cases like this one, where the probability of bias is very high, and where the evidence adduced at a hearing can offer little assurance that prejudice does not exist, the juror should be deemed biased as a matter of law. Specifically, where a juror pursues employment with the office of the prosecutor, under circumstances highly suggestive of misconduct or conflict of interest, bias should be "implied," and he should be automatically disqualified, despite the absence of proof of actual bias. If the juror's efforts to secure employment are not revealed until after the trial, the conviction must be set aside. The right to a trial by an impartial jury is too important, and the threat to that right too great, to justify rigid insistence on actual proof of bias. Such a requirement blinks reality.

The majority adopts a completely unrealistic view of the efficacy of a post-trial hearing, and thus fails to accord any meaningful protection to the right to an impartial jury, one of the most valuable rights possessed by criminal defendants. I would affirm the judgment of the Court of Appeals on the ground that a juror who applies for employment with the office of the prosecutor and vigorously pursues that employment throughout the course of the trial is impliedly biased.

---

[7]   The petitioner emphasizes that during the hearing, the trial judge had an opportunity to observe the juror's demeanor. Thus, argues the petitioner, even where the juror denies that he was biased, the trial judge will be able to measure the juror's integrity, and decide whether to credit his claim that he fairly weighed the evidence. It may be true that the opportunity to observe the juror will be of assistance in some cases. However, it will be of little value where the juror honestly but falsely believes that he was impartial.

United States v. Littlefield

United States Court of Appeals for the Ninth Circuit, 1985.
752 F.2d 1429.

■ GOODWIN, CIRCUIT JUDGE:

Littlefield, Nicoladze, and Solomon appeal their convictions for conspiracy to violate the tax laws and for various tax-related criminal offenses arising from tax shelter activities. We remand for a new trial because a Time magazine article on similarly fraudulent tax shelters was carried by one of the jurors into the jury room during deliberations and was read and discussed by one or more of the other jurors.

The district judge determined that it could be concluded that the extrinsic evidence did not influence the verdict. We reverse because this finding fails to satisfy the standard of proof required to show lack of jury bias.

The government argues that defendants rather than the government bear the burden of proving jury partiality in a hearing on the matter. We believe that this argument misinterprets the meaning of Smith v. Phillips, 455 U.S. 209 (1982).

In Remmer v. United States, 347 U.S. 227 (1954), the Supreme Court placed the burden of proof on the government to overcome a presumption of prejudice where there is "any private communication, contact or tampering directly or indirectly with a juror during a trial about the matter pending before the jury." 347 U.S. at 229. In a hearing to determine whether contact with a juror was harmless, "the burden rests heavily upon the Government to establish . . . that such contact with the juror was harmless to the defendant." Id. The government maintains that *Phillips* overruled *Remmer* by holding that the remedy for allegations of juror partiality is a hearing "in which the defendant has the opportunity to prove actual bias." 455 U.S. at 215. Quite simply, the government misread the *Phillips* "opportunity to prove actual bias" as a shifting of the burden of proof to the defendant.

The *Phillips* case did not confront the issue of burden or proof but rather concerned the necessity for a hearing on the issue of jury partiality. It was on that issue that the Court discussed the relevance of *Remmer*; its conclusion that the state hearing was constitutionally adequate did not even address the burden of proof issue. *Phillips*, 455 U.S. at 215–18.

In light of *Phillips*, therefore, we reject the government's assertion that Remmer is no longer good law. The government had an obligation here to prove beyond a reasonable doubt that the juror's reading of the Time magazine article was harmless.

Vacated and remanded.

■ WALLACE, CIRCUIT JUDGE, dissenting:

The district judge held a hearing to determine whether the Time magazine article influenced the jury's verdict.

The Court has stated "that due process does not require a new trial every time a juror has been placed in a potentially compromising situation. Were that the rule, few trials would be constitutionally acceptable." Smith v. Phillips, 455 U.S. 209, 217 (1982). The Court suggested that the government meets its burden of proof in a partiality hearing if it shows that the "jury [was] capable and willing to decide the case solely on the evidence before it, and [the] trial judge [was] ever watchful to prevent prejudicial occurrences and to determine the effect of such occurrences when they happen." Id.

I believe the majority fails to follow this sound advice. In this case at least, I would defer to the district judge's conclusion that the magazine did not influence the jury's verdict.

United States v. Pennell

United States Court of Appeals for the Sixth Circuit, 1984.
737 F.2d 521.

■ CONTIE, CIRCUIT JUDGE:

Gordon Pennell, the defendant, appeals from jury convictions for one count of conspiracy to possess with intent to distribute cocaine, and one count of attempt to possess with intent to distribute cocaine. For the reasons set forth below, we affirm.

Pennell contends that the district court should have declared a mistrial after five jurors were contacted at their homes by an anonymous telephone caller. Jury deliberations began on Friday, January 28, 1983. Between 1:00 A.M. and 1:30 A.M. on Sunday, January 30, five jurors received anonymous telephone calls. Juror Larson was told, "Urness Larson, you had better find him guilty." Juror Page's daughter answered her father's telephone and was told, "tell Charles [Page] he better vote guilty." Juror Burgess was told, "Mrs. Burgess, find him guilty or you will wish you had." The caller told Juror Saveski, "is this Janet? You had better find him guilty." Finally, the caller instructed Juror Wilcox, "Ms. Wilcox, find him guilty." In all five instances, the caller urged the juror to convict and then quickly hung up.[9]

On the morning of Monday, January 31, the five jurors informed their counterparts of what had happened and then notified the court. The court proceeded individually to question the five who had received calls out of the presence of the other jurors. Juror Wilcox stated that her impartiality had not been compromised and that she did not feel

---

[9]   Although the government contends that the caller's statements should not be regarded as threats, similar statements were so regarded in United States v. Brown, 571 F.2d 980, 987 (6th Cir.1978).

intimidated. She indicated that the call could have been a prank by a young person attending the school at which she taught. Juror Burgess also assured the court that her impartiality had not been affected, but indicated that Juror Saveski had exhibited apprehension and nervousness about the telephone call. Burgess also stated that Saveski had not said "one way or the other whether the (telephone call) would have anything to do with her decision."

When asked if the telephone call would impair his ability to render a fair verdict, Juror Page responded, "I don't believe it is impaired in the least." Page did indicate, however, that Juror Saveski was "disturbed" about the matter and was "unsure" of herself. The court next questioned Saveski. During the ensuing discussion, Saveski stated four times in response to different questions that the telephone call had not affected her impartiality or her ability to decide the case on the basis of the testimony and exhibits. Finally, Juror Larson assured the court three times that she would exclude the telephone calls from consideration during deliberations.

With the concurrence of counsel for both parties, the court then summoned the entire jury and asked a series of questions designed to elicit whether any juror's impartiality had been compromised and whether any juror would find it difficult to render a verdict based upon the evidence and the court's instructions. When no juror responded, the court ordered the jury to resume deliberations. Defense counsel then moved for a mistrial.

After the jury resumed deliberations, the forewoman sent a note to the court which read in its entirety:

> Attention Honorable John Cook. We do have a juror Linda Lorenz, that does feel that the phone calls will influence her judgment in this case. Forewoman Darlene Patterson.

The court immediately summoned Juror Lorenz, who had not received a telephone call, back to the courtroom. In response to questions, Lorenz stated that listening to the other jurors had made her nervous and that she did not wish to receive a telephone call. Nevertheless, she twice indicated that the calls received by the others would not affect her verdict.

After Juror Lorenz returned to the jury room, the court denied the motion for mistrial. As to Juror Lorenz, the court found:

> After examining Ms. Lorenz in the presence of counsel and on the record, this Court believes that Ms. Lorenz, while nervous and apprehensive about potential harm to herself, that she is nevertheless able and willing to continue as a juror and, moreover, that I am satisfied that Ms. Lorenz, being aware of her responsibilities as a juror, will confine her assessment of the facts in this case to the testimony of the witnesses, the exhibits that have been received into evidence and the instructions that

were presented to the Jury by the Court. Moreover, the last juror, Linda Lorenz, advised the Court that she could confine her evaluations to those three categories that I have just mentioned.

Regarding the jury as a whole, the court found:

> It is my personal opinion, in speaking with the jurors prior to the—to this session and during the session that they were resolute in their belief that their opinion would not be swayed one way or the other by the telephone call. More specifically, I am satisfied that the jurors, in responding to my questions, were desirous of continuing in their roles as jurors and that the telephone calls would not play any part in their decision. Thus, I am satisfied that a verdict from the Jury, whether it is guilty or not guilty, will not be tainted or affected in any way by the telephone calls that were received by them on Sunday morning, between the hours of 1:00 and 1:30.

The court did offer the jury the opportunity to be sequestered. The jury declined this offer and deliberated for three more days without incident before rendering its verdict.

Remmer v. United States, 347 U.S. 227 (1954), has generally been regarded as the leading case on the issue of how a district court should treat unauthorized communications with jurors. The Supreme Court in Remmer fashioned the following rule:

> In a criminal case, any private communication, contact, or tampering, directly or indirectly, with a juror during a trial about the matter pending before the jury is, for obvious reasons, *deemed presumptively prejudicial,* if not made in pursuance of known rules of the court and the instructions and directions of the court made during the trial, with full knowledge of the parties. *The presumption is not conclusive, but the burden rests heavily upon the Government to establish, after notice to and hearing of the defendant, that such contact with the juror was harmless to the defendant.* [Emphasis supplied.]

Id. at 229.

The Supreme Court, has more recently filed an opinion that is relevant to the case at hand. Smith v. Phillips, 455 U.S. 209 (1982). Thus, the question is whether *Phillips* has so changed the rules relating to unauthorized communications with jurors that the presumptive prejudice standard no longer governs. We conclude that *Phillips* has indeed altered the law concerning unauthorized communications with jurors.

Although *Phillips* involved bias resulting from a juror's potential employment relationship with a law enforcement agency, the principles set forth in the opinion apply to allegations of jury partiality generally. In essence, *Phillips* reinterpreted *Remmer.* Although the Court in

Phillips referred to the *Remmer* presumptive prejudice standard, the Court nevertheless stated:

> This court has long held that the remedy for allegations of juror partiality is a *hearing* in which the defendant has the opportunity to prove actual bias. [Emphasis supplied.]

455 U.S. at 215. Thus, the Court held that *Remmer* does not govern the question of the burden of proof where potential jury partiality is alleged. Instead, *Remmer* only controls the question of how the district court should proceed where such allegations are made, i.e., a hearing must be held during which the defendant is entitled to be heard. 455 U.S. at 216. In light of *Phillips*, the burden of proof rests upon a defendant to demonstrate that unauthorized communications with jurors resulted in actual juror partiality. Prejudice is not to be presumed.[10]

Moreover, the Court in *Phillips* implied that deference should be accorded a district court's findings made after a properly conducted hearing. Accordingly, we hold that if a district court views juror assurances of continued impartiality to be credible, the court may rely upon such assurances in deciding whether a defendant has satisfied the burden of proving actual prejudice.

The judgment of the district court is Affirmed.

■ CELEBREZZE, SENIOR CIRCUIT JUDGE, dissenting.

The majority holds that a presumption of prejudice should not be applied in a hearing to determine juror bias when five jurors receive late night threatening phone calls, the entire jury discussed the phone calls during deliberations, and one juror expresses privately doubts as to whether she can render an objective decision based solely on the evidence. Respectfully, I dissent.

Generally, the remedy for allegations of juror bias is a hearing to determine whether actual bias exists. E.g., Smith v. Phillips, 455 U.S. 209 (1982).

In *Phillips*, the issue was whether a conclusive presumption of prejudice should apply. The issue of a conclusive presumption, more often termed the doctrine of "implied bias," involves a different line of cases than those which address a presumption of prejudice.[1] *Phillips* is merely another case which rejects the use of a conclusive presumption of prejudice under circumstances which are not extreme. In less extreme cases, such as those in *Phillips* and the case at bar, a post-conviction

---

[10] We read *Remmer* as requiring the government to do more than come forward with evidence that unauthorized communications with jurors were harmless. As the quotation cited supra, indicates, *Remmer* placed a heavy burden of proof upon the government. Accordingly, *Phillips* worked a substantive change in the law.

[1] In extreme cases, such as when a juror is involved in serious misconduct, bias is to be presumed conclusively. Under less serious circumstances, such as when a jury might be affected by the misconduct of a third party, a *Remmer* type hearing safeguards adequately a defendant's right to an impartial jury.

hearing, where the defendant is aided by the presumption of prejudice, will suffice to determine whether juror bias exists.

There is no precedent in support of the majority's conclusion that the Supreme Court has abandoned the application of the presumption of prejudice when unauthorized contacts are made with jurors.

There is no evidence in the record to suggest that the trial court applied the presumption of prejudice at the hearing to determine whether the improper jury contact was prejudicial. Because the court did not apply a presumption required by the law, the hearing was defective. In my view, the conviction should be reversed and the case remanded for a new trial.

B. STATUTORY INTERPRETATION LEGAL METHODS REVIEW PROBLEMS

PROBLEM 1

Brutus Forte is a musician who, under the pseudonym Brute Force, is an extremely popular entertainer, performing in the "heavy metal" genre of rock music. Brute Force has a distinctive vocal style, consisting in part of grunts and squawks that evoke a variety of barnyard fauna, principally pigs and turkeys. Perhaps not surprisingly, the song with which Brute Force opens and closes his live performances is his own, rather violent and idiosyncratic, version of "Old MacDonald Had A Farm." Brute Force often appears on stage, in music videos, and on album covers dressed in a turkey suit.

Brute Force has become a pop culture icon, and advertisers have sought to take advantage of his popularity by soliciting his participation in a variety of commercials. However, seeking to maintain his artistic purity, Brute Force has refused to perform in or to authorize any commercials incorporating sounds or images from his live or recorded performances.

Tina's Turkeys is a successful poultry producer in the State of New Hazard. Tina's has just aired a commercial on a local New Hazard television station that depicts a person in a turkey suit, striking an aggressive attitude. The turkey suit completely encloses its wearer. Next to the individual in the turkey suit is a roast turkey attractively arranged on a serving platter. The sound track plays "Old Mac Donald's Farm" in a traditional arrangement, but accompanied by sounds of squawking turkeys and grunting pigs. These sounds were taken from a sound effects recording. A voice-over declares "As tough as this turkey is (close up of the person in the turkey suit), that's how tender ours is (close up of the roast turkey). You don't have to be a brute to enjoy a good turkey . . . Tina's Turkeys."

Mr. Forte asks you, his lawyer, whether he has a valid claim against Tina's Turkeys. In the State of New Hazard, there is a potentially applicable statute, reproduced below. Assume that there is no legislative history to this statute.

Were Mr. Forte to bring a claim under the statute, it would present a case of first instance for the New Hazard courts. Nor is there any common law case law on point. Basing your analysis solely on the text of the statute, advise Mr. Forte whether he has a claim under the statute; what arguments he should expect to encounter from Tina's Turkeys in opposition to his claim; how he should respond to these arguments; and how you think the court would resolve the issue. Mr. Forte is highly argumentative, and likes to have things clearly spelled out, so make sure you state your points clearly, and supply well elaborated rationales for your conclusions.

New Hazard Collected Statutes, section 1995

a.   Any person who uses for advertising purposes, or for purposes of trade, the name, picture or likeness of any person, without first having obtained the written consent of such person, shall be liable in a civil action to such person.

b.   Any person who, in connection with any goods or services, uses any word, term, name, symbol or device, or any combination thereof, which is likely to cause confusion, or to cause mistake, or to deceive as to the affiliation, connection, or association of such person with another person, or as to the origin, sponsorship, or approval of his or her goods, services, or commercial activities by another person, shall be liable in a civil action by any person who believes that he or she is or is likely to be damaged by such act.

PROBLEM 2

In July of 2013, lured by end of season specials, Judy Church journeyed to a used car dealership outside of the city of Cacophony, serving the tri-state area of New Hazard (the state in which Cacophony is located), Harmony and North Bedlam. There she found the Trans Am of her dreams—black with tinted windows. The man with the loud tie informed her that with her purchase she was entitled to a pair of fuzzy dice, a set of beer mugs and a free car alarm.

Church bought the car, hung up the dice, put the mugs in the trunk and glanced briefly at the sticker on the back of the alarm. The alarm was capable of being operated by remote or activated on contact. According to the sticker, at least two pounds of direct pressure is necessary to activate the alarm, and there is a one-minute lag time between the activating of the alarm and its sounding "to allow the owner to de-activate the alarm before causing an inconvenience to others should the alarm be accidentally activated." Once the alarm sounds, it does so continuously for three minutes before ceasing. It then remains silent for three minutes, and if it is not deactivated, it resets and begins again.

Church was told she could trade in the alarm for a set of second-hand mag tires, which was tempting, but Church had fallen in love with her Trans Am and knew it would be the envy of the whole neighborhood— she decided she would feel more secure having the alarm. Church left the car at the dealer for a few days to have the alarm installed. This was done off the premises.

Church picked up the car and drove it for a month or two without incident. Then one day during a storm she parked it on the street in front of a friend's apartment building in Cacophony. She went inside and listened to the new Megadeath CD a few times while chatting with her friend. Later, she glanced out the window and spied a police cruiser alongside her cherished black Trans Am. When she arrived at the scene, the police officer said, "the alarm on your car has been going off every few minutes for over an hour. Four residents of the building called to complain. One of them saw a branch from the tree fall onto your car during the storm, which apparently set it off, though it did not begin to sound until after a short delay." The officer gave Church a $100.00 ticket, explaining that she was in violation of a statute dealing with motor vehicle alarms. The statute is set forth below.

Church asks you, her lawyer, whether she may successfully contest the ticket. Assume that there is no legislative history and that this is a case of first impression. Your discussion must therefore be based solely on the text of the statute.

NEW HAZARD STATUTES

GENERAL BUSINESS LAW

ARTICLE 26. MISCELLANEOUS

§ 369   **Motor Vehicle Alarms**

1.   On and after the effective date of this section, all devices offered for sale or installed in the state as alarms for motor vehicles shall be so equipped and shall function so that the audible portion of the alarm resets and ceases to sound not more than three minutes after it is activated and commences sounding. No audible burglar alarm in a motor vehicle shall be capable of being activated except by:

a)   direct physical contact with that motor vehicle; or

b)   through the use of an individual remote activation that is designed to be used with the motor vehicle alarm so long as the alarm activated by such device ceases to sound within not more than three minutes

2.   This Act shall take effect immediately.

3.   A violation of the provisions of this section shall constitute an offense punishable by a fine of not more than one hundred dollars for the

first offense and not more than two hundred fifty dollars for a second and subsequent offense.

Approved July 21, 2020.

C. COMPREHENSIVE LEGAL METHODS REVIEW PROBLEMS

The following problems require the reader to work her way through a statute and apply it while also synthesizing cases interpreting the statute in sometimes apparently inconsistent ways.

PROBLEM 1

The Plaintiff, Henry Hurtz, worked as one of five waiters in the Caffe Violenti in the state of New Hazard. The Defendant, Bobbie Basher, also worked at the restaurant. On the evening of August 21, 2013, after closing, Hurtz was washing trays when Basher pointed a loaded handgun in the direction of Hurtz's feet and fired. Basher intended merely to frighten Hurtz, for she believed the gun was filled with blank cartridges. Needless to say, the cartridges were not blank and Hurtz suffered serious and permanent injuries when a bullet struck him in the left foot. After several other restaurants in the vicinity had been robbed, Basher began carrying the weapon to protect herself and the employer's money when making night bank deposits of the day's proceeds.

Having received workers compensation from his employer, Mr. Hurtz has filed a common law action in tort against Basher in the New Hazard trial court, alleging that the accident was proximately caused by Basher's wrongful conduct. Basher has moved to dismiss the action on the ground that the plaintiff's exclusive remedy is under the New Hazard Workers Compensation Act.

You are the law clerk to the judge who must decide the motion. She has asked you to prepare a draft opinion for her on the question of whether the case should be dismissed. Draft the analysis of the court's opinion (i.e. it is not necessary to repeat the facts in a "Facts" section) in the case of Hurtz v. Basher, taking into account the statute and other relevant authority.

The State of New Hazard enacted a Workers Compensation Act in 2010 which is set out in relevant part below. No New Hazard courts have yet ruled on the Workers Compensation Act.

The New Hazard Workers Compensation Act is identical to the workers compensation acts of South Tranquility, enacted in 1999, and New Bedlam, enacted in 1996. Decisions from the Supreme Courts in these jurisdictions follow.

NEW HAZARD WORKERS COMPENSATION ACT, 2010

Section 1.   Definitions

When used in this Act:

(a) The term "employment" includes employment by the state and all political subdivisions thereof and all public and quasi-public corporations therein and all private employments in which three or more employees are employed in the same business or establishment.

(b) The term "employee" means every person engaged in an employment under appointment or contract of hire or apprenticeship, express or implied, oral or written.

(c) The term "employer" means the state and all political subdivisions thereof, and every person, firm or corporation carrying on any employment, or the legal representative of a deceased person or the receiver or trustees of any person.

(d) The term "injury" means personal injury or death arising out of and in the course of employment and such diseases or infections as naturally or unavoidably result from such injury.

Section 2.   Coverage—Liability for Compensation

(a) Compensation shall be payable under this Act in respect of disability or death of an employee if the disability or death results from an injury.

(b) Every employer, as defined in this Act, shall be liable for and shall secure the payment to his employees of the compensation payable under this Act.

(c) Compensation shall be payable irrespective of fault as a cause for the injury.

Section 3.   Exclusiveness of Liability

The liability of an employer prescribed in section 2 shall be exclusive and in place of all other liability of such employer to the employee, his or her legal representative, husband or wife, parents, dependents, next of kin, or anyone otherwise entitled to recover damages from such employer on account of injury to the employee.

Section 4.   Compensation for Injuries Where Third Persons Are Liable

If an employee is injured or killed in the course of his or her employment by the negligence or wrongful act of any person other than the employer, such injured employee, or in the case of his or her death his or her dependents, may accept compensation benefits under the provision of this law and, in addition, may pursue his or her remedy by action at law or otherwise against such third party tort-feasor.

Majors v. Moneymaker

Supreme Court of New Bedlam, 2004.

■ DRUMBLE, C. J.

The plaintiff, Elsie N. Majors, sued the defendant, Elizabeth Moneymaker, in the Circuit Court of Knox County for damages arising out of an automobile accident. Mrs. Majors was riding as an invited guest when the car, which was being operated by the defendant, came in violent collision with another automobile.

The defendant, Elizabeth Moneymaker, filed a motion to dismiss and averred therein that she and the plaintiff were fellow workers and employees of the American National Insurance Company, working out of the Knoxville office of said company; were acting in concert within the scope and course of their employment; that the Insurance Company and the parties had agreed to be bound by the terms of the Workers Compensation Law of New Bedlam, and that both the plaintiff and defendant were bound by the provisions of said statute. It is further alleged in the plea that both the plaintiff and the defendant were paid compensation by the Indemnity Insurance Company of North America for injuries resulting from the said accident; that the "defendant is not such other or third party or person within the meaning of the Workers Compensation Law of New Bedlam as would permit her to be sued for negligence at common law, the plaintiff's rights against her employer and/or its workers compensation insurance company being the only right and exclusive remedy of the plaintiff against either this defendant or her employer."

The plaintiff demurred to the motion to dismiss, as follows: "Defendant's motion to dismiss is not sufficient in law because: the injuries sustained by plaintiff for which she claims damages in a tort action were caused by the act or acts of the defendant under circumstances creating a legal liability against the defendant to pay damages, the defendant not being plaintiff's employer or such other person legally liable to pay workers compensation to her."

The trial judge sustained the motion to dismiss and dismissed the plaintiff's suit. The sole question made in the assignment of error is that it was error by the trial judge to sustain the motion to dismiss because the plaintiff's remedy is not exclusive as provided in the Statute; her right was to prosecute her common law action against the defendant, she being "any person other than the employer" as provided in Section 4.

Now in the case at bar the demurrer admits as true the averment in the motion to dismiss that the employer, American National Insurance Company, and both the plaintiff and the defendant are within the compensation system, i.e. all were subject to the provisions of the New Bedlam Workers' Compensation Act. Both Mrs. Majors and Mrs. Moneymaker were paid workers' compensation benefits by their employer's insurance carrier, Indemnity Insurance Company of North America.

In the case at bar it is clear that the alleged negligence of the defendant is chargeable to her principal, American National Insurance Company, who is also the common employer of both the plaintiff and the defendant. The negligence of the defendant, Elizabeth Moneymaker, created a legal liability against her employer. But, as forcibly and clearly argued by defendant's counsel, the language used in the quoted Statute specifically limits the action to circumstances creating a legal liability against "any person other than the employer".

If we should adopt the construction of the Act according to the plaintiff's contention it would create an unfair result.

One purpose of the Workers Compensation Act was to sweep within its provisions all claims for compensation flowing from personal injuries arising out of and in the course of employment by a common employer insured under the act, and not to preserve for the benefit of the insurer or of the insurer and those injured liabilities between those engaged in the common employment which but for the act would exist at common law.

The defendant, Moneymaker, being a co-employee of the plaintiff, is exempt from liability by the Workers' Compensation Law. As an employee acting within the scope of her employment, and not "on a frolic of her own," she was the agent of the employer. Her acts and conduct became the acts and conduct of the employer, and the exemption from damages at law extended to the employer by the Workers Compensation Law is also by that act extended to co-employees through whom the employer acts. Thus, the co-employee becomes merged in the employer and is not a third person, within the meaning of the compensation law, against whom a damage action may be maintained.

Another purpose of the workers compensation scheme is to place the cost of work related injuries on the employer. Suits against fellow employees shift the burden to the employees and circumvent the theory of workers compensation. The insurance company, who paid workers compensation benefits to both the plaintiff and the defendant, would in the case at bar recover, by means of subrogation, from the defendant all sums of money which it had paid the plaintiff, Elsie N. Majors. And while the defendant, Elizabeth Moneymaker, could recover only a limited amount under the Workers Compensation Act, the plaintiff, Mrs. Majors, and the insurance carrier could recover from the defendant unlimited damages under the common law. The foregoing is in substance the argument of the defendant's counsel in support of the latter's construction of the statute. We think it is logical and give it our unqualified approval.

We furthermore take notice of the fact that in many cases arising under the Workers Compensation Act the injury results from the negligence of some fellow employee. If the insurance carrier is subrogated to the rights of an employee against his fellow servant, the result would be a flood of litigation over claims that were never contemplated by the statute. The statute was never designed to permit the employer and his insurance carrier to sue employees for damages for negligent injuries arising out of and in the course of the employment. In all such cases the injured defendant employee sometimes suffering either death or total and permanent injuries would, by force of the statute, be required to surrender all his compensation benefits to the insurance carrier, and in many cases a sizable amount in addition thereto by way of damages. This is certainly contrary to the spirit, if not the letter of the statute, in that the right of every employee to compensation is made to depend upon whether or not he is free from some proximate negligent act committed during his employment.

The judgment of the trial court is affirmed.

Victor Hockett v. J.E. Chapman

Supreme Court of South Tranquility, 2011.

■ HANIGSBERG, C. J.

This is a personal injury action. The appeal results from the dismissal of appellant's complaint on the ground that appellant, having received workers compensation benefits, may not recover for the negligence of a coemployee where the damages sought are based on injuries received in an accident arising out of and in the course of employment and where such injuries were caused by the negligence of a coemployee.

Appellant and appellees were fellow employees. Appellant was injured as the result of a collision between a truck driven by appellee Chapman, in which he was a passenger, and a truck driven by appellee Bachus. The accident arose out of and in the course of their employment. Appellant received workers compensation benefits and thereafter brought a negligence action against the appellees. The employer's insurance carrier intervened as a plaintiff and appellant.

The sole question presented by this appeal is whether, under the South Tranquility Workers Compensation Act, a coemployee is a "person other than the employer" against whom a negligence action may be maintained, or whether a coemployee comes within the immunity from such an action which is granted to the employer.

The Workers Compensation Act provides that an employee, or someone claiming through him or on his behalf, is not denied his common-law right to recover damages caused by the negligence of a third person because he has received workers' compensation benefits for the same injury. The pertinent provision of the Act reads as follows:

Section 4.   Compensation for Injuries Where Third Persons Are Liable

If an employee is injured or killed in the course of his or her employment by the negligence or wrongful act of any person other than the employer, such injured employee, or in the case of his or her death his or her dependents, may accept compensation benefits under the provision of this law and, in addition, may pursue his or her remedy by action at law or otherwise against such third party tort-feasor.

It is clear, therefore, that our Workers Compensation Act was not intended to relieve one other than the employer, his insurer, guarantor or surety from liability imposed by statute or by common law, while providing against a double recovery by an employee.

Appellees urge upon this court that since they were employees of the same employer, and were admittedly within the scope of their employment, they were the agents or servants of the employer, and that as such their liability is limited, the same as that of an employer. We are unable to agree with appellees' analysis of the statute. Section 3 deals with the exclusiveness of the remedy between an employer and employee. We see nothing in this section of the Act which could be said to mean that a fellow employee shall be the same as the employer for the purpose of limiting his liability thereunder.

The appellees, Chapman and Bachus, have cited authorities supporting their position that an employee is immune from a negligence action by a coemployee. In these jurisdictions, the courts have held that a coemployee is not a "person other than the employer," either on the theory of agency, making the conduct of an employee the conduct of the employer, or on the broad ground that the Workers Compensation Act intended to cover by its terms all liability arising out of and in the course of employment by a common employer insured under the Act.

Despite appellees' arguments, in the states having workers' compensation laws similar to those of South Tranquility, in that they provide the Act shall not affect any cause of action an employee may have against "a person other than his employer," or against a third party, or a "third party tortfeasor", most, albeit not all, courts have held that a coemployee is a third person, or a person other than the employer, and that such an action may be maintained. The basic reasoning behind these holdings is that the workers compensation laws have predicated an employer's liability to his employee on the employer-employee relationship and not in tort; that consequently the right of an employee to receive benefits under workers compensation is not based on fault or negligence, but is contractual in nature; that a negligent employee is not liable for compensation and is, therefore, a stranger to the Act, being a person other than the employee entitled to receive compensation and the employer liable to pay it. Further, that coemployees are in no way subject to the provisions of the compensation act in their relationship with each other. Some of these courts have said that to hold otherwise would be to unjustly confer upon a worker freedom to neglect his duty towards a fellow employee and immunize him against all liability for damages proximately caused by his negligence.

Where it was the intention in other states, in enacting workers compensation laws, to include fellow employees within the limited liability of the employer, the acts have expressly restricted actions by an employee by providing that action may be maintained by an employee "provided such third person be not a fellow servant" or against "third persons who are not in the same employ," or they have provided that actions may not be so maintained against an employer "or any worker," or "his employees" or "persons in the same employ," or "those conducting his (the employer's) business." The judicial decisions in these jurisdictions have, therefore, by virtue of the express legislative intent, excluded suits against a coemployee.

In the absence of express language in the South Tranquility Workers Compensation Act denying an employee the right to maintain a negligence action against a coemployee, and in view of the sound reasoning upon which we consider the weight of authority to be based, we must conclude that a coemployee is "a person other than the employer" against whom such an action for damages may be maintained and that the court below erred in dismissing appellant's complaint.

This reasoning is consistent with the generally recognized rule that a co-employee who causes injury while acting outside the course of his employment is not protected from liability in common law actions arising out of the injury. Likewise, when an employee is injured by a coemployee who intentionally inflicts injuries upon him, the employee-victim may maintain a common law action against his co-employee. In accepting employment, a worker does not render himself vulnerable to every type of wrong, with the workers compensation laws being his sole remedy.

The judgment is reversed with directions to the trial court to proceed in a manner not inconsistent with the views expressed herein.

It is so ordered.

PROBLEM 2

Marci Messy works for the New Hazard Garbage Collection Service ("GCS") as a garbage collector in the City of Blissville, a state government competitive service position, and she is also President of the Blissville Chapter of the Sanitation Workers Union ("SWU"). Marci's job involves driving door-to-door across Blissville collecting garbage in a GCS garbage truck. As Marci has strongly held political beliefs, she often scrolls through her "Twizzler" social messaging feed when the freeway is jammed on the way to and from her garbage pickup route, and sometimes when stuck in traffic while on her collection route. This fall is an election year, and so during these traffic jams Marci has taken to "retweezing" messages from her preferred candidates running for office in the New

Hazard House and Senate. Some of these "tweezes" are links to contribute funds to the candidates' campaigns, while others address particular issues, such as the science behind climate change, the outsourcing of jobs from New Hazard factories, and—most important to her—caustic partisan attacks and calls to vote out New Hazard Representatives and Senators who support cuts to the pay and benefits of garbage collectors like herself. Although Marci rarely directly tweezes herself, when she does, it is usually about the insufficient pay and benefits of her job or calls to donate to candidates who support garbage collectors. In one memorably angry "tweeze-storm," Marci threatened to stop picking up the garbage from houses with yard signs for candidates promising to cut garbage collector pay and benefits, and she posted tweezes with pictures of several such houses to shame their inhabitants.

Not contented with tweezing, Marci decides to get involved with the local branch of the Muckraking Party, one of New Hazard's main political parties and the party most opposed to cutting pay and benefits for garbage collectors. There is an upcoming election for mayor of Blissville, which is a non-partisan office for which candidates do not identify as a member of a particular party. Among the mayor's responsibilities are important decisions about the number of garbage collectors, garbage collection routes, and garbage collector pay scale. Although never formally enacted, the Muckraking Party's practice has been that whoever wins the Party's internal election for Party President will be the only Party member who will run for mayor of Blissville, and the Party will throw its support entirely behind that candidate in the mayoral election. To support her campaign for Muckraking Party President, Marci solicits donations from several of the trainee garbage collectors she supervises at work.

Marci wins the internal Muckraking Party election and then declares her candidacy for mayor via the following tweeze: "Marci Messy, President of the Blissville Muckraking Party, is running to be your Mayor this fall! Vote Marci for Mayor!" Many self-identified members of the Muckraking Party are active on Twizzler, and Marci sometimes retweezes their messages that every party member should support her campaign. To make time for her mayoral campaign, Marci resigns from her position as the Blissville SWU President.

Shortly before the Blissville mayoral election, the polling suggests the election between Marci and her opponent, local lawyer Roger Rulefollower, will be very close, in part due to expected record low turnout. To drum up votes, the SWU, puts up old posters and newspaper articles of Marci from her time as Union President around the employee break rooms of GCS branches, just to remind GCS employees of the upcoming election. Union members also hand out "Marci for Mayor!" campaign buttons and hats before they clock in and after they clock out of their shifts, and fellow garbage collectors sometimes ask for, and receive, the campaign gear during work hours when they are chatting in the break room. The weekend before the election, the new SWU President sends out several tweezes calling for contributions to the Union's political action fund, which helps to support candidates for office who favor stronger pay and benefits for sanitation workers, including Marci.

The day before the election, Marci's car breaks down at a campaign event and she is late to a radio interview. Marci's husband Mark, a New Hazard Marshal, is having a very slow work day, so he picks her up in his patrol car and takes her to the radio station. On the way, Mark advises Marci about what to say in her latest campaign fundraising tweeze, and helps her decide on the order of speakers at that evening's fundraising event. While Mark waits for Marci to conduct her radio interview, he chats with the radio station's security personnel—all undecided voters—about how wonderful she is as a partner, and how those same traits are so important for the town's mayor. Afterward, he takes her to a campaign rally, where Marci has Mark pose by her side while she gives a speech about the importance of supporting law enforcement. Mark briefly addresses the crowd, extolling Marci's leadership skills in their home and at their church, and aided by Mark's winning smile, Marci raises several thousand dollars at the event.

On election night, Marci prevails by only 7 votes, and Roger Rulefollower, after hearing about her campaign activities, files a complaint before the New Hazard Electoral Integrity Board ("EIB") asking the Board to investigate possible violations of the New Hazard Anti-Partisanship in Government Act ("APGA").

* * *

You are a law clerk to a Commissioner on the EIB, and you have been asked to write a memo identifying whether the EIB should bring charges against any of the public employees discussed above for possible violations of APGA. In your memo, identify all possible actions taken by the public employees that may constitute a violation of APGA. For each activity, provide your assessment as to whether the EIB should bring a charge, as well as any potential counter-arguments to your position.

For some of activities, you will need to interpret only APGA, while other activities will also require application of the two New Hazard decisions included below. Another law clerk is examining whether there are any other constitutional or legal issues, so you should focus only on possible violations of APGA. If you believe you would need more information to make an informed decision, identify what information would be relevant and how it would affect your decision.

New Hazard Anti-Partisanship in Government Act ("APGA") § 7322. Definitions

For the purpose of this subchapter—

(1) "employee" means any individual, other than the New Hazard Governor and the Lieutenant Governor, employed or holding office in—

(A) an Executive agency other than the New Hazard Accountability Office;

(B) a government competitive service position; or

(C) an agency identified in § 7323(b)(1)(B)(i) of this subchapter.

(2) "partisan political office" means any office for which any candidate is nominated or elected as representing a registered political party, but shall exclude any office or position within a political party or affiliated organization; and

(3) "political contribution"—

(A) means any gift, subscription, loan, advance, or deposit of money or anything of value, made for any political purpose;

(B) includes any contract, promise, or agreement, express or implied, whether or not legally enforceable, to make a contribution for any political purpose;

(C) includes any payment by any person, other than a candidate or a political party or affiliated organization, of compensation for the personal services of another person which are rendered to any candidate or political party or affiliated organization without charge for any political purpose; and

(D) includes the provision of personal services for any political purpose.

APGA § 7323. Political activity authorized and prohibited

(a) Subject to the provisions of subsection (b), an employee may take an active part in political management or in political campaigns, except an employee may not—

(1) use his official authority or influence for the purpose of interfering with or affecting the result of an election; or

(2) knowingly solicit, accept, or receive a political contribution from any person, unless such person is—

(A) a member of the same organized labor organization; and

(B) not a subordinate employee; or

(3) run for the nomination or as a candidate for election to a partisan political office.

(b)(1)(A) No employee described under subparagraph (B) may take an active part in political management or political campaigns.

(B) The provisions of subparagraph (A) shall apply to—

(i) an employee of—

(I) the New Hazard Electoral Integrity Board; (II) the New Hazard Marshals Agency; (III) the New Hazard Anti-Terrorism Agency; (IV) the New Hazard Secret Service Agency.

(c) An employee retains the right to vote as he chooses and to express his opinion on political subjects and candidates.

APGA § 7324. Political activities on duty

(a) An employee may not engage in political activity—

(1) while the employee is on duty;

(2) in any room or building occupied in the discharge of official duties by an individual employed or holding office in the Government of the New Hazard or any agency or instrumentality thereof;

(3) while wearing a uniform or official insignia identifying the office or position of the employee; or

(4) using any vehicle owned or leased by the Government of New Hazard or any agency or instrumentality thereof.

In re 2000 Election

Supreme Court of New Hazard, 2005.
404 N.Hz.3d 1320.

■ DILLON, C.J.

I. BACKGROUND

This case concerns charges brought by the New Hazard Electoral Integrity Board ("EIB") in connection with alleged violations of the Anti-Partisanship in Government Act during the 2000 election: two charges brought against Mike McEntee, a mayoral candidate, and one charge brought against the Police Benevolent Association of Blissville ("PBAB").

A. McEntee

In August 1999, Mike McEntee declared himself a candidate for Mayor of Blissville, New Hazard. According to city ordinances, the mayoral race is intended to be nonpartisan and the names of the candidates are listed on the ballot without party or other designation. At the time he became a candidate, McEntee was a state employee.

The McEntee campaign distributed leaflets stating "Mike McEntee—the ONLY CONSERVATIVE REPUBLICAN in the race for Mayor." The same leaflet included the statement "[f]inally, Republicans have a chance to elect a Conservative to lead our city" and the following quote from "Former Republican State Representative Frank Bird:"

For years Republicans have been forced to hold their nose and accept the policies that city government forced on them by Jim Baca, Marty Chavez and the rest of the liberal Democrats. Now, for the first time in years we have a chance to elect one of us, a conservative Republican to clean up the mess in City Hall.

The campaign also distributed a "Dear Friend" letter from Jack Stahl, "Former Republican Lieutenant Governor," which included the following statements:

In two months, we can FINALLY elect a REPUBLICAN MAYOR to lead this city!

The letter further listed McEntee's opponents, all identified as "Democrat."

The McEntee campaign solicited campaign contributions in a variety of ways. The "Dear Friend" letter from "Former Republican Lieutenant Governor" Jack Stahl included the statements "I'VE JUST SENT MY CHECK TO MIKE MCENTEE. WON'T YOU PLEASE SEND YOUR CHECK TODAY? . . . You [sic] contribution of $25, $50, $100 or even $1000 is vital. Please let us know in the next 10 days if you can help elect the only conservative candidate." At least two fundraising events were held in support of the McEntee campaign, one on June 21, 2000, and another on September 14, 2000, where Jack Stahl spoke at length about McEntee's conservative credentials.

B. PBAB

The PBAB represents approximately 350 City of Blissville police officers.

In September and October, 2000, PBAB leadership developed and distributed a poster comparing the campaign positions and voting records of the Republican and Democratic party candidates for the New Hazard House and Senate on issues of concern to the PBAB and its membership. While the poster purported to present only factual information, the PBAB does not seriously dispute that it was intended to generate support for Democratic candidates. However, the evidence is that the poster was not produced in cooperation or coordination with the Democratic Party or New Hazard Democratic Congressional Campaign Committee.

II. PROCEDURAL HISTORY

After the 2000 election, the New Hazard EIB cited both Candidate McEntee and the PBAB for violations of the New Hazard Anti-Partisanship in Government Act ("APGA"). The court of appeals affirmed as to the citations of McEntee, but vacated the citation of the PBAB, holding that the PBAB was entitled to advocate the election of candidates through display of posters and like materials on designated union bulletin boards in non-public areas of police departments, so long as the display is not coordinated with or in concert with a political party or candidate. McEntee and the Board appealed the respective decisions.

III. McENTEE

The EIB found that McEntee had engaged in two forms of conduct prohibited by APGA: 1) running as a candidate for election to a partisan political office in violation of § 7323(a)(3); and 2) knowingly soliciting and receiving a political contribution in violation of § 7323(a)(2). The court of appeals grounded its findings for both violations in its determination that the McEntee campaign introduced partisan politics to the 2000 City of

Blissville mayoral election, effectively rebutting the presumption that the race was not an election for partisan political office.

McEntee asserts that elections designated as nonpartisan under state or local law cannot meet the statutory requirements to be considered a "partisan political office." To reach this conclusion, McEntee reads the language of § 7322(2) as requiring that a candidate be elected or nominated to represent a major political party. Under this theory, because elections designated as nonpartisan do not provide a mechanism for parties to choose or identify their representative candidates, participation in such elections cannot constitute running for a "partisan political office."

We reject McEntee's reading of § 7322(2) on the ground that it is contrary to the plain meaning of the statutory language. Here, McEntee presumes that the term "nominated or elected" modifies the phrase "as representing a party" thereby creating a requirement that the candidates represent a party by nomination or election. A careful reading of the statute, however, reveals that the phrase "as representing a party" actually modifies the term "nominated or elected" and the entire clause "any candidate is nominated or elected as representing a party" identifies the office sought. Accordingly, the definition of a "partisan political office" expressly encompasses offices for which candidates are either nominated as representing a party or elected as representing a party.

While the term "nominated . . . as representing" a party suggests a formal party endorsement or selection process, the term "elected as representing a party" is broader and imposes no such implication. In order to give meaning to all the words of the statute, as we must, we do not read the term "elected as representing a party" to require formal endorsement or selection by a major political party. Thus, the terms of § 7322(2) do not preclude an election designated as nonpartisan under state law from constituting an election for a "partisan political office."

In a prior case, *Campbell v. Electoral Integrity Bd.*, 27 N.Hz.3d 1560 (N.Hz. S. Ct. 1995), we refused to limit the definition of an "independent candidate" to the strictures of state law, primarily out of concern that "reducing the factual inquiry into 'independence' to an examination of a person's registration card and ballot billing would exalt form over substance and permit circumvention of the substantive congressional policy of keeping partisan politics out of the routine administration of the laws and the running of the bureaucracy." Accordingly, we resolved *Campbell* by considering the facts presented to determine whether the employee's conduct in associating himself with the Democratic Party comported with the common meaning of the word "independent." *Id.* at 1568–69.

McEntee's invitation to define the regulatory term "nonpartisan election" by reference solely to local election laws presents the identical risk of exalting form over substance that we identified and avoided in *Campbell*. Accordingly, we affirm the lower court's finding that

McEntee's participation in a presumptively nonpartisan election constituted a violation of APGA.

Although we do not attempt to establish the minimum level of partisan politics necessary to rebut the presumption that an election designated as nonpartisan under state and local law is, in fact, a prohibited political race, there is no question that the record here amply supports the conclusion that the presumption of nonpartisanship afforded the 2000 City of Blissville mayoral race was so rebutted. Here, McEntee openly solicited members of the Republican Party for campaign contributions and made it clear that he was requesting donations on the basis of party affiliation in order to further the party's agenda. He trumpeted his endorsement by the Executive Committee of the Tranquility County Republican Party and individual Republican Party figures and appeared at press conferences with his endorsers. Furthermore, leaders of the local and state Republican Party actively supported McEntee by publicly associating themselves with his campaign, advocating his election, and helping to raise funds in support of his candidacy. While we leave open the possibility that less blatant invocation of party status may not justify rebutting the presumption of nonpartisanship, there can be no doubt that the combination of McEntee's conduct as a candidate and the Republican Party's acquiescence in that conduct constitutes representing a major political party such that the race in which he participated constituted an election for partisan political office. The Board had substantial evidence to support its findings.

IV. PBAB

As to the PBAB, the EIB found that the PBAB violated APGA § 7324 by participating in political activities on duty. Whereas § 7323's provisions are not limited by time or place, the § 7324 concerns on-the-job activities and is the dispositive provision regarding the issues in this case. The PBAB argues—and the court of appeals agreed—that the display of the posters does not constitute "political activity" within the meaning of APGA because § 7324's term "political activity," like § 7323's term "active part in political management or in political campaigns," has been interpreted to refer only to activity "coordinated with or in concert with a political party or candidate." *Burrus v. Vegliante*, 547 N.Hz.App. 3d 372, 375 (N.Hz. Ct. App. 2002). However, the term "political activity" is broader than the quoted language in § 7323 and does not imply that the particular conduct be in concert with a candidate's campaign or party. The language of the statute is plain.

Moreover, the pertinent regulations define political activity in a way that clearly includes the PBAB poster. The definition covers any and all activity "directed toward the success or failure of a political party, candidate for partisan political office, or partisan political group," 5 C.N.Hz.R. § 734.101, and clearly reaches the poster. Indeed, one of the illustrative examples provided in the regulation includes an employee's "display [of] partisan political . . . signs . . . at his or her place of work," 5 C.N.Hz.R. § 734.306 (Example 16).

The view that § 7324 places broad prohibitions on on-the-job and at-the-workplace conduct is entirely consistent with the legislative history of the enactment of § 7324. The New Hazard Senate Report characterizes APGA as follows:

[APGA] would retain and strengthen current law prohibitions against political activity "on-the-clock"—on Government time and in Government premises. It would broaden the current law to also provide State civilian and sanitation employees the opportunity to participate voluntarily in political activities as private citizens "off-the-clock."

When signing the amendments into law, Governor Krainer echoed this understanding: "While employees will now be entitled to volunteer on their own time for the candidate of their choice, all political activity in the New Hazard state workplace will be prohibited, including the wearing of campaign buttons." Statement of Governor Krainer (Oct. 6, 1990); *see also* 139 N.Hz. Leg. Rec. 15,366 (July 13, 1990) (statement of Sen. Bernhardt) ("[N]o political activity on the job, zero.").

The court of appeals also suggested that, even if displaying the posters constituted "political activity" for purposes of § 7324, it would still fall outside that Section's prohibitions because it did not involve "interference with official 'duty,' " or "appropriation of a 'room or building occupied in the discharge of official duties.' " However, the prohibitions of § 7324 do not turn on a showing of "interference" with duty or "appropriation" of workplace rooms or buildings. The Section requires only that an employee be "on duty," § 7324(a)(1), or be "in any room or building occupied in the discharge of official duties by [a government employee]," § 7324(a)(2).

Therefore, we also disagree with the court appeals' further implication that § 7324(a)(1) and (2) prohibits political activity by an employee only while "on duty" or "in the discharge of official duties." Rather, the statutory text prohibits political activity while either on duty or in a room or building occupied in the discharge of official duties by any government employee. *See* APGA § 7324(a).

Finally, the court of appeals stated that § 7323(c), which provides that an employee "retains the right to . . . express his opinion on political subjects and candidates," exempts the display of the posters from attack under § 7324. We disagree. § 7323(c) qualifies only the off-the-job active participation prohibitions contained in § 7323(b) and the prohibitions on official coercion in § 7323(a).

Section 7323(c) defines permitted passive and noncoercive conduct under § 7323. As noted, § 7324 is a more particularized provision, dealing not with overall conduct, but with conduct on the job or at the workplace. Indeed, if § 7323(c) gives employees the right to express opinions on political subjects under all circumstances, then § 7324 has little effect.

Where possible we avoid construing a statute so as to render a provision mere surplusage.

V. CONCLUSION

For the foregoing reasons, we affirm the judgment of the court of appeals as to McEntee, but reverse the judgment of the court of appeals as to the PBAB.

Bill & Sombretto v. Electoral Integrity Board

New Hazard Court of Appeals, 1995.
357 N.Hz.App. 3d 600.

■ LOUK, J.

BACKGROUND

Morris Biller and Vincent R. Sombrotto are the presidents of, respectively, the Blissville Teachers Union and the Blissville Association of Educators. Both unions are organizations that represent public school teacher bargaining units in the State of New Hazard Public School System. Like all public school teachers in the State of New Hazard, Biller and Sombrotto's positions are government competitive service positions.

Both unions circulate official monthly magazines. As presidents of their Unions, petitioners contribute regular columns to these magazines. The unions also publish newsletters and other periodicals which frequently report statements by petitioners. In their regular magazine columns and in other statements made in 1991 and 1992 and quoted in the union periodicals, the subject of petitioners' discussion was the upcoming gubernatorial election. Their statements generally expressed support for Democratic gubernatorial candidate Malter Wondale and opposition to incumbent Governor Donald Deagan and sometimes criticized the Deagan Administration on issues of interest to public school teachers. Petitioners' articles encouraged union members to vote for Wondale and to contribute to the unions' political action funds, which are funds segregated from the unions' own finances.

The theme of most of Biller's articles in the "Blissville Educator Magazine" was to urge the teachers union to help the defeat of Governor Deagan: "[w]e must raise a half-million dollars as our contribution to changing the tenant in the Governor's Mansion"; "[w]e have got to get a Governor who will be sensitive to the needs of organized labor"; "[i]n addition to seeking a new tenant in the Governor's Mansion, it is imperative that we play a role to help elect Congressmen and Senators who are sensitive to our needs. . . ." A typical example of Sombrotto's writing in "Blissville Class Notes" follows: "[t]o recapture New Hazard and save our jobs and benefits, teachers unions must join with other working men and women to support the Democratic nomination, the candidate of the New Hazard labor movement—Malter Wondale."

DISCUSSION

We think a line may be discerned that solves the definitional problem of sorting out what activity is permitted from that which is prohibited. APGA carefully distinguishes between partisan political activities and mere expressions of views. The very purposes of APGA and the evils it sought to eliminate demonstrate, in fact, that it is engaging in organized political activity by New Hazard employees that threatens government integrity and efficiency. The dangers of politicized administration of the laws, of "machine politics" in the state bureaucracy, of coercion of public employees and of reducing public confidence in governmental activities are present especially when employees participate or are directly affiliated with a political party. Put another way, the concern is that New Hazard state employees—through coercion or machine politics—will act in concert and produce an inordinate influence on the way government executes the laws and provides services. Thus, finding "partisan activity" implicitly requires a nexus between the government employee and the effort to promote the political party or elect its candidate. It is not enough that the state employee and the candidate pursue the same political goals independently; the two must work in tandem or be linked together for there to be a violation of the APGA.

It is undisputed that neither Biller nor Sombrotto acted in concert with a political party or campaign organization. In fact, neither of the petitioners had any connection with a political party. The Board itself conceded that there was no nexus between petitioners and the Wondale campaign or the Democratic Party. The nexus required to establish their activities as partisan under the Act is therefore lacking. Thus, petitioners' actions were the individual expression of permitted personal opinion on political subjects and candidates. Consequently, petitioners were erroneously held by the respondent Board to have violated the Act on the first charge.

The second charge, that Biller and Sombrotto violated APGA by urging union members to contribute to the unions' political action funds, presents a closer question. The instant charges were based on statements in petitioner's articles that exhorted union members to contribute to their respective unions' political action funds. Thus, the question is whether petitioners solicited the funds in concert with a partisan political campaign or organization. As with the first charge, we think the answer in this case is "no."

Although the plain purpose of the challenged writings was to raise funds, it cannot be demonstrated that the funds were solicited for use by a partisan political campaign or organization. To the contrary, the funds were "not designated for any political campaign, party, committee or candidate at the time they were made." Finally, there is no proof in the record that suggests either that petitioners were acting in concert with a partisan political campaign or that the funds were actually distributed or spent for that purpose. On that subject, the record is silent.

Moreover, the Board's findings make clear that none of the evils of solicitation sought to be rooted out by the statute or its implementing regulations are present in this case. The Board found that petitioners had no connection with the money the unions' political action funds received—that is, they did not personally collect or administer contributions. Nor did petitioners have any supervisory authority over any union employees from whom contributions were sought—the readers of the magazines. Petitioners' columns obviously did not "strong-arm" employees into contributing. Again, the Act's concern with the creation of a bureaucratic political machine and with coercion of public employees is not adequately implicated to constitute a violation of the Act. As a result, we conclude that the second charge against petitioners alleging violations of APGA fails for lack of proof.

For the reasons stated, the order finding petitioners Biller and Sombrotto guilty of violating APGA is reversed and vacated.

PROBLEM 3

Melody Harmony rents a nice home with a large lot which backs onto a public park in a residential area of Blissville in the state of New Hazard. Melody operates a catering business from her kitchen and sells baked products out of her garage. Business had been slow of late, and she canvassed friends and relatives about how to market her pies more aggressively. As a result of these consultations, she decided on the following scheme.

Melody parked her pick-up truck alongside her front yard. She mounted a cannon, which she leases from a circus, on the bed of the truck. The cannon operates using a small generator, which every forty-five minutes, must be recharged using the battery of the truck. At the back of her yard, just before the boundary of the public park, she placed a trampoline, building a concrete foundation around it to ensure its stability. Experimenting with her own durable two children, she discovered that a child shot out of the cannon would land exactly (more or less) in the center of the trampoline, bounce five to ten feet in the air, and then descend to earth gently on a mattress placed beside the trampoline. Her children confirmed it was a thrill to be remembered.

The kids spread word of this unique entertainment experience throughout the neighborhood. Melody advertised in the local paper. The use of the cannon was free to all those children whose parents bought either two cherry pies or a cheesecake. To Melody's delight, many Blissville parents showed up at her house to see their children propelled out of a cannon. She could barely keep up with the demand for her pies and cakes.

While no children were injured in flight or landing, the trampoline itself posed a hazard to people utilizing the park. It was positioned just outside the area used as the outfield to the baseball diamond in the park, and as no fence separated Melody's yard from the park, a number of wayward little-leaguers had crashed into it chasing fly balls. One such child had to be hospitalized.

Unfortunately for Melody, the parents of that child live in the same neighborhood and are alarmed at the traffic and carnival atmosphere that now characterizes their once serene residential street. They would like the town to initiate legal action against Melody. You are the Town Attorney, charged with enforcing compliance with the Blissville Town Code. Based on your analysis of the pertinent sections of the Town Code (below) and of the case law construing the Code (also below), explain whether and why (or why not), Melody has violated the Town Code.*

BLISSVILLE TOWN CODE

1. (a) Amusement. An amusement is any form of entertainment open to the public and generally conducted in the outdoors with the presence of tents, booths or temporary structures erected for such purpose or any combination of the foregoing, including but not limited to the following forms of entertainment commonly known as carnivals, circuses, fairs, bazaars, menageries, or sideshows. Such forms of entertainment are deemed to be generally characterized by the presence of any of the following activities or any combination of activities thereof: mechanical rides, exhibitions of skill, animal exhibitions, games of skill or games of chance where otherwise permitted by local regulation.

(b) Amusement Device. An amusement device is any device whereby, upon the deposit therein of a coin or token, any apparatus is released or set in motion or put in a position where it may be set in motion for the purpose of playing any game including but not exclusively such devices as are commonly known as juke boxes, bowling games, pinball and video machines or pool tables.

2. Site Plan Review and Approval. A site plan review and approval is required in all zoning districts for all new buildings and structures or land use and/or for all alterations or changes in use thereto. The Town Board shall have the authority to impose such reasonable conditions and restrictions as are directly related and incidental to a proposed site plan.

3. (a) Special Use Permit. A special use permit is required for all amusements or amusement devices, where admission is charged, which occur on property zoned as a business district, or where a licensed restaurant, bar or eatery places on its property amusements or amusement devices for the enjoyment of customers.

---

* The parents of the child have also initiated a tort action against Melody but that claim is of no concern to you.

(b)   Certification. No amusement or amusement device may be used for purposes of amusement unless it possesses certification from the Blissville Amusement Devices Safety Board (BADSB) as to its safety, and is operated under the supervision of a qualified operator.

(c)   Restrictions. Any amusement or amusement device operating within 200 yards of a public school which students 13 years old or younger attend, may only be used between the hours of 4:00 p.m. to 9:00 p.m. on weekdays.

4.   Public Safety or Welfare. Owners of property may not allow their premises to be used for purposes detrimental to public safety or welfare.

5.   Stationary Motor Vehicles. No motor vehicle may operate for a period longer than three minutes in any hour while the vehicle is stationary, while the vehicle is parked on a public right-of-way, and while the vehicle is within 150 feet of a residential area, for reasons other than traffic congestion or emergency work.

The Town of Blissville in the State of New Hazard v. Donald Sossin

Supreme Court of New Hazard, 2009.

■ RADIN, J.

The defendant is the owner of a bar/restaurant known as Avenues Night Club located in the town of Blissville, County of Pleasant, New Hazard. On June 26, 2008 the defendant was charged with four violations of the Blissville Town Code (hereinafter BTC). The alleged violations are all related to the activity of bungee jumping. The Superior Court found that Sossin had violated the BTC. The Court of Appeals affirmed.

The defendant had a crane brought onto the outdoor area of the property on which the night club was situated. Attached to the crane lift was a partially enclosed platform. A participant paid a fee to the operator, was secured to the platform by a bungee-type cord, then was lifted to a designated height from which a jump was made above a designated area. The defendant was charged with violating the BTC after several patrons had performed bungee jumps. The court shall now consider each of the charges.

Count one alleges that the defendant failed to obtain a site plan review and approval for the bungee jumping as mandated by BTC § 2. Said ordinance provides in pertinent part: "Site plan review and approval is required in all zoning districts for all new buildings and structures or land use and/or for all alterations or changes in use thereto." In the court's opinion the Town failed to prove that the mobile crane from which the bungee jumps were made is either a building, structure or land use as set out in BTC § 2, hence, a site plan review and approval was not necessary therefor.

Count two charges violations under BTC § 3(a) which sets out the requirements for obtaining a Special Use Permit for the operation of amusements. Section 3(a) prohibits the use of designated property as a place of amusement without a special permit. An amusement is defined in BTC § 1. In the court's opinion the instant activity of bungee jumping does not fall within the definition of an amusement. An amusement is generally characterized by the presence of multiple activities with more than one booth, tent or structure. Conversely, bungee jumping, as described herein, entails a singular activity. Therefore, the defendant was not mandated to obtain the Special Use Permit under BTC § 3(a) for which he is charged.

Count three alleges a violation of BTC § 4 in that the defendant allowed the premises to be used for purposes detrimental to public safety or welfare. It is the court's opinion that the Town failed to prove that the activity of bungee jumping, as described herein and conducted on defendant's property, was detrimental to the safety of the public. The Court's analysis might have been different had the Town shown that injuries resulted from the bungee jumps.

Finally, count four alleges a violation of BTC § 5 in that the defendant allowed a motor vehicle to operate for a period of longer than three minutes in any hour while the vehicle was stationary. The ordinance prohibits such operation of a vehicle on a public right-of-way, in a public space, and within 150 feet of a residential area for reasons other than traffic congestion or emergency work. The Town does not allege and did not prove that the crane as used for the bungee jumps was operated on a public right-of-way or public space within 150 feet of a residential area. Such are necessary elements of the offense charged.

Accordingly, the court reverses the decision below.

The Town of Blissville in the State of New Hazard v. Barney's Pizzeria

Supreme Court of New Hazard, 2011.

■ ELLIS, J.

This case comes before us on appeal from a judgment entered in the Superior Court, affirmed by the Court of Appeals, enjoining the defendant, Barney's Pizzeria, from operating an amusement device on its property. Defendant is charged with four separate violations of the Blissville Town Code ("the Code") sections 3(a), (b), and (c) and 4.

Barney's Pizzeria is located in Blissville across the street from Serenity Junior High. In order to attract students from the school, the restaurant installed a "Bronco Barney" machine on the back patio. The machine was in the form of a giant purple dinosaur wearing a saddle. The owner of Barney's purchased the amusement device from Melron Amusements Corp. Customers who satisfied the minimum height drequirement (4 feet) paid an additional dollar on top of the price of a slice of pizza to use the machine. The machine worked by jerking in all directions while the customer attempted to stay on. Mattresses were placed near the machine to soften the fall of those customers who were unsuccessful. Melron Amusements recommended the use of mattresses or similar cushioning devices but did not supply them to the restaurant. One of the waiters at the Pizzeria, recruited from the neighboring Blissville Community College, supervised the machine after receiving one day of training by Melron personnel.

It is alleged that Barney's Pizzeria violated § 3(a) of the Code, which provides that "[a] special use permit is required for all amusements or amusement devices, where admission is charged, which occur on property zoned as a business district, or where a licensed restaurant, bar or eatery places on its property, amusements or amusement devices for the enjoyment of customers." We find, as Barney's Pizzeria clearly falls within the category of an "eatery," a special use permit was required for the operation of the amusement device.

Section 3(b) of the Blissville Town Code stipulates that, "[n]o amusement or amusement device may be used for purposes of amusement unless it possesses certification from the Blissville Amusement Devices Safety Board (BADSB) as to its safety, and is operated under the supervision of a qualified operator." On these facts, Barney's Pizzeria adduced no evidence of certification of any kind. Further, one day of training by the manufacturer is not sufficient to qualify the employee as a "qualified operator."

Additionally, it is clear that the defendant has violated § 3(c) of the Code by allowing the Bronco Barney machine to be operated during the hours 12:00 p.m. to 1:00 p.m. contrary to the clear language of this section.

Finally, § 4 of the Code provides that, "Owners of property may not allow their premises to be used for purposes detrimental to public safety or welfare." The evidence in the record establishes that the Town Board was concerned that the availability of these amusement devices to school-age children during school hours would encourage truancy and related problems. In addition, because children will tend to congregate where these devices are clustered, the Town Board was also concerned about traffic congestion and the possibility of accident. These legislative determinations are made in furtherance of the protection of the public health, safety, and general welfare. However, in view of the foregoing violations, it is not necessary to determine in addition whether the operation of the Bronco Barney machine was detrimental to the public safety or welfare.

We affirm the determination that the defendant has violated the Blissville Town Code and the "Bronco Barney" device shall be shut down until such time as the defendant is in full compliance with the provisions of the Code.

PROBLEM 4

You are a member of the Bar of the State of New Hazard, where, as a solo practitioner, you specialize in Legal Ethics. Your client, Clara Grubsnig, a fellow member of the Bar who is a partner in the leading Metropolis firm of Grubsnig & Areps, is concerned about her possible exposure to disciplinary action under the New Hazard Rules of Professional Conduct, and consults you regarding the following problem.

Grubsnig's client, Mega Industries Conglomerated, has asked her to draft a contract between Mega and Kiddie Kable TV, to place advertisements for its Choco-Cruncho Cereal during Kiddie's Saturday morning cartoon programs. Choco-Cruncho Cereal features the cuddly Cruncho character on its boxes and in the shape of the cereal morsels. Cruncho is a loveable, if toothy, reptilian figure, somewhat reminiscent of the wildly popular children's television purple dinosaur, Barney. The Choco-Cruncho advertisements would include animated versions of the Cruncho character. Grubsnig has just learned from Mega that Mega's TV ads contain subliminal messages promoting another Mega Product, WayCool Cigarettes. The ads depict Cruncho smoking WayCools with great pleasure. Kiddie Kable is unaware of the subliminal messages hidden in the ads.

Grubsnig has attempted to dissuade her client, Mega, from placing the advertisements, but Mega persists in its intent to air the ads containing the subliminal messages.

Based on the following New Hazard authorities (disregard any possibly relevant federal authorities), what would you advise Grubsnig to do?

NEW HAZARD COMPILED STATUTES, COURT RULES NEW HAZARD SUPREME COURT RULES ARTICLE VIII. NEW HAZARD RULES OF PROFESSIONAL CONDUCT

PREAMBLE

The practice of law is a public trust. Lawyers are the trustees of the system by which citizens resolve disputes among themselves, punish and deter crime, and determine their relative rights and responsibilities toward each other and their government. Lawyers therefore are responsible for the character, competence and integrity of the persons whom they assist in joining their profession; for assuring access to that system through the availability of competent legal counsel; for maintaining public confidence in the system of justice by acting competently and with loyalty to the best interests of their clients; by working to improve that system to meet the challenges of a rapidly changing society; and by defending the integrity of the judicial system against those who would corrupt, abuse or defraud it.

To achieve these ends the practice of law is regulated by the following rules. Violation of these rules is grounds for discipline. No set of prohibitions, however, can adequately articulate the positive values or goals sought to be advanced by those prohibitions. Lawyers seeking to conform their conduct to the requirements of these rules should look to the values described in this preamble for guidance in interpreting the difficult issues which may arise under the rules.

The policies which underlie the various rules may, under certain circumstances, be in some tension with each other. Wherever feasible, the rules themselves seek to resolve such conflicts with clear statements of duty. For example, a lawyer must disclose, even in breach of a client confidence, a client's intent to commit a crime involving a serious risk of bodily harm. In other cases, lawyers must carefully weigh conflicting values, and make decisions, at the peril of violating one or more of the following rules. Lawyers are trained to make just such decisions, however, and should not shrink from the task. To reach correct ethical decisions, lawyers must be sensitive to the duties imposed by these rules and, whenever practical, should discuss particularly difficult issues with their peers.

Lawyers also must assist in the policing of lawyer misconduct. The vigilance of the bar in preventing and, where required, reporting misconduct can be a formidable deterrent to such misconduct, and a key to maintaining public confidence in the integrity of the profession as a whole in the face of the egregious misconduct of a few.

Legal services are not a commodity. Rather, they are the result of the efforts, training, judgment and experience of the members of a learned profession. These rules reflect the sensitive task of striking a balance between making available useful information regarding the availability and merits of lawyers and the need to protect the public against deceptive or overreaching practices. All communications with clients and potential clients should be consistent with these values.

The lawyer-client relationship is one of trust and confidence. Such confidence only can be maintained if the lawyer acts competently and zealously pursues the client's interests within the bounds of the law. "Zealously" does not mean mindlessly or unfairly or oppressively. Rather, it is the duty of all lawyers to seek resolution of disputes at the least cost in time, expense and trauma to all parties and to the courts. . . .

Rule 1.6.   Confidentiality of Information

(a)   Except when required under Rule 1.6(b) or permitted under Rule 1.6(c), a lawyer shall not, during or after termination of the professional relationship with the client, use or reveal a confidence or secret of the client known to the lawyer unless the client consents after disclosure.

(b)   A lawyer shall reveal information about a client to the extent it appears necessary to prevent the client from committing an act that would result in death or serious bodily harm.

(c)   A lawyer may use or reveal:

(1) confidences or secrets when required by law or court order;

(2) the intention of a client to commit a crime in circumstances other than those enumerated in Rule 1.6(b); or

(3) confidences or secrets necessary to establish or collect the lawyer's fee or to defend the lawyer or the lawyer's employees or associates against an accusation of wrongful conduct.

Rule 1.7.   Declining or Terminating Representation

(a) A lawyer representing a client before a tribunal shall withdraw from employment (with permission of the tribunal if such permission is required) if:

(1) the lawyer knows or reasonably should know that the client is bringing the legal action, conducting the defense, or asserting a position in the litigation, or is otherwise having steps taken, merely for the purpose of harassing or maliciously injuring any person;

(2) the lawyer knows or reasonably should know that such continued employment will result in violation of the law;

(b) Except as required in Rule 1.7(a), a lawyer shall not request permission to withdraw in matters pending before a tribunal, unless such request or such withdrawal is because:

(1) the client:

(A) insists upon presenting a claim or defense that is not warranted under existing law and cannot be supported by a reasonable argument for an extension, modification, or reversal of existing law;

(B) seeks to pursue an illegal course of conduct;

(C) insists that the lawyer pursue a course of conduct that is illegal or that is prohibited by these Rules;

(2) the lawyer's inability to work with co-counsel indicates that the best interests of the client likely will be served by withdrawal;

(3) the client consents to termination of the lawyer's employment after disclosure; or

(4) the lawyer reasonably believes that a tribunal will, in a proceeding pending before the tribunal, find the existence of other good cause for withdrawal.

(c) A lawyer shall not withdraw from representing a client in a matter not pending before a tribunal, unless such withdrawal is because the client:

(1) insists that the lawyer pursue a course of conduct that is illegal; or

(2) insists that the lawyer engage in conduct that is contrary to the judgment and advice of the lawyer although not prohibited by these Rules.

NEW HAZARD COMPILED STATUTES THE PUBLIC HEALTH CIGARETTE SALES ACT, 2002

WHEREAS the New Hazard State Legislature finds that cigarettes are potentially dangerous, lethal and addictive;

The New Hazard State Legislature enacts the Public Health Cigarette Sales Act of 2002, which provides:

§ 1234. Sale of tobacco products to minors

The sale of tobacco products to minors shall be considered unlawful and shall subject the seller, and all those acting in concert with him or her, to civil liability.

Balla v. Gambro, Inc.

Supreme Court of New Hazard, 2009.

■ BELL, J.,

The issue in this case is whether in-house counsel should be allowed the remedy of an action for retaliatory discharge.

Appellee, Roger Balla, formerly in-house counsel for Gambro, Inc. (Gambro), filed a retaliatory discharge action against Gambro. Appellee alleged that he was fired in contravention of New Hazard public policy and sought damages for the discharge. The trial court dismissed the action on appellants' motion for summary judgment. The appellate court reversed. We granted appellant's petition for leave to appeal.

Gambro is a distributor of kidney dialysis equipment manufactured by Gambro (Germany). The manufacture and sale of dialyzers is regulated by the federal government, including the United States Food and Drug Administration (FDA).

Appellee, Roger J. Balla, is and was at all times throughout this controversy an attorney licensed to practice law in the State of New Hazard. Appellee held the title of director of administration at Gambro. As director of administration, appellee's specific responsibilities included coordinating and overseeing corporate activities to assure compliance with applicable laws and regulations.

In July 2005, Gambro learned that certain dialyzers its affiliated company (Gambro Germany) had manufactured were about to be shipped to Gambro and that they did not comply with federal regulations. Appellee told the president of Gambro about the violations and told the president to reject the shipment. The president notified Gambro Germany of its decision to reject the shipment on July 12, 2005.

However, one week later the president informed Gambro Germany that Gambro would accept the dialyzers. Appellee contends that he was not informed by the president of the decision to accept the dialyzers but became aware of it through other Gambro employees. Appellee maintains that he spoke with the president in August regarding the company's decision to accept the dialyzers and told the president that he would do whatever necessary to stop the sale of the dialyzers.

On September 4, 2005, appellee was discharged from Gambro's employment by its president. The following day, appellee reported the shipment of the dialyzers to the FDA. The FDA seized the shipment.

On March 19, 2006, appellee filed a four-count complaint in tort for retaliatory discharge seeking $22 million in damages.

On July 28, 2007, Gambro filed a motion for summary judgment. Gambro argued that appellee, as an attorney, was precluded from filing a retaliatory discharge.

On November 30, 2008, the trial court granted appellants' motion for summary judgment. The trial court concluded that the duties appellee was performing which led to his discharge were conduct clearly within the attorney-client relationship and that Gambro had the absolute right to discharge its attorney. On appeal, the court below held that an attorney is not barred as a matter of law from bringing an action for retaliatory discharge.

We agree with the trial court that appellee does not have a cause of action against Gambro for retaliatory discharge under the facts of the case at bar. Generally, this court adheres to the proposition that an employer may discharge an employee-at-will for any reason or for no reason at all. However, this court has recognized the limited and narrow tort of retaliatory discharge. This court stressed that if employers could fire employees for filing workers' compensation claims, the public policy behind the enactment of the Workers' Compensation Act would be frustrated.

In this case it appears that Gambro discharged appellee, an employee of Gambro, in retaliation for his activities, and this discharge was in contravention of a clearly mandated public policy. Appellee allegedly told the president of Gambro that he would do whatever was necessary to stop the sale of the "misbranded and/or adulterated" dialyzers. In appellee's eyes, the use of these dialyzers could cause death or serious bodily harm to patients. There is no public policy more important or more fundamental than the one favoring the effective protection of the lives and property of citizens. However, in this case, appellee was not just an employee of Gambro, but also general counsel for Gambro.

In-house counsel do not have a claim under the tort of retaliatory discharge. We base our decision as much on the nature and purpose of the tort of retaliatory discharge, as on the effect on the attorney-client relationship that extending the tort would have. We caution that our holding is confined by the fact that appellee is and was at all times throughout this controversy an attorney licensed to practice law in the State of New Hazard. Appellee is and was subject to the New Hazard Code of Professional Responsibility adopted by this court.

In this case, the public policy to be protected, that of protecting the lives and property of citizens, is adequately safeguarded without extending the tort of retaliatory discharge to in-house counsel. Appellee was required under the Rules of Professional Conduct to report Gambro's intention to sell the "misbranded and/or adulterated" dialyzers. Rule 1.6(b) of the Rules of Professional Conduct reads: "A lawyer shall reveal information about a client to the extent it appears necessary to prevent the client from committing an act that would result in death or serious bodily injury." (N. Haz. Prof. Resp. R. 1.6(b).)

Appellee alleges, and the FDA's seizure of the dialyzers indicates, that the use of the dialyzers would cause death or serious bodily injury. Thus, under the above-cited rule, appellee was under the mandate of this court to report the sale of these dialyzers.

In his brief to this court, appellee argues that not extending the tort of retaliatory discharge to in-house counsel would present attorneys with a "Hobson's choice." According to appellee, in-house counsel would face two alternatives: either comply with the client/employer's wishes and risk both the loss of a professional license and exposure to criminal sanctions, or decline to comply with client/employer's wishes and risk the loss of a full-time job and the attendant benefits.

We disagree. In-house counsel do not have a choice of whether to follow their ethical obligations as attorneys licensed to practice law, or follow the illegal and unethical demands of their clients. In-house counsel must abide by the Rules of Professional Conduct. Appellee had no choice but to report to the FDA Gambro's intention to sell or distribute these dialyzers.

We recognize that under the New Hazard Rules of Professional Conduct, attorneys shall reveal client confidences or secrets in certain situations (see N. Haz. Prof. Resp. R. 1.6(a), (b), (c)), and thus one might expect employers/clients to be naturally hesitant to rely on in-house counsel for advice regarding this potentially questionable conduct. However, the danger exists that if in-house counsel are granted a right to sue their employers in tort for retaliatory discharge, employers might further limit their communication with their in-house counsel. The attorney-client privilege is supposed to encourage full and frank communication between attorneys and their clients and thereby promote broader public interests in the observance of law and administration of justice. The privilege recognizes that sound legal advice or advocacy serves public ends and that such advice or advocacy depends upon the lawyer being fully informed by the client. If extending the tort of retaliatory discharge might have a chilling effect on the communications between the employer/client and the in-house counsel, we believe that it is more wise to refrain from doing so.

However difficult economically and perhaps emotionally it is for in-house counsel to discontinue representing an employer/client, we refuse to allow in-house counsel to sue their employer/client for damages because they obeyed their ethical obligations. In this case, appellee, in addition to being an employee at Gambro, is first and foremost an attorney bound by the Rules of Professional Conduct. These Rules of Professional Conduct hope to articulate in a concrete fashion certain values and goals such as defending the integrity of the judicial system, promoting the administration of justice and protecting the integrity of the legal profession. (N. Haz. Prof. Resp. R., Preamble.) An attorney's obligation to follow these Rules of Professional Conduct should not be the foundation for a claim of retaliatory discharge.

For the foregoing reasons, the decision of the appellate court is reversed, and the decision of the trial court is affirmed.

Spaulding v. Zimmerman

Supreme Court of New Hazard, 1998.

■ HITTSON, J.

Appeal from an order of the trial vacating and setting aside a prior order of such court dated May 8, 1995, approving a settlement made on behalf of David Spaulding on March 5, 1995, at which time he was a minor of the age of 20 years.

The prior action was brought against defendants by Theodore Spaulding, as father and natural guardian of David Spaulding, for injuries sustained by David in an automobile accident, arising out of a collision which occurred August 24, 1994, between an automobile driven by John Zimmerman, in which David was a passenger, and one owned by John Ledermann and driven by Florian Ledermann.

After the accident, David's injuries were diagnosed by his family physician, Dr. James H. Cain, as a severe crushing injury of the chest with multiple rib fractures; a severe cerebral concussion, probably with petechial hemorrhages of the brain; and bilateral fractures of the clavicles. At Dr. Cain's suggestion, on January 3, 1995, David was examined by Dr. John F. Pohl, an orthopedic specialist, who made X-ray studies of his chest and found that his heart and aorta were normal.

In the meantime, on February 22, 1995, at defendants' request, David was examined by Dr. Hewitt Hannah, a neurologist. On February 26, 1995, the latter reported to Messrs. Field, Arveson, & Donoho, attorneys for defendant John Zimmerman, as follows:

> The one feature of the case which bothers me more than any other part of the case is the fact that this boy of 20 years of age has an aneurysm, which means a dilatation of the aorta and the arch of the aorta. Whether this came out of this accident I cannot say with any degree of certainty and I have discussed it with the Roentgenologist and a couple of Internists.... Of course an aneurysm or dilatation of the aorta in a boy of this age is a serious matter as far as his life. This aneurysm may dilate

further and it might rupture with further dilatation and this would cause his death.

Prior to the negotiations for settlement, the contents of the above report were made known to counsel for defendants Florian and John Ledermann, but not to counsel for plaintiff.

The case was called for trial on March 4, 1995, at which time the respective parties and their counsel possessed such information as to David's physical condition as was revealed to them by their respective medical examiners as above described. It is thus apparent that neither David nor his father, the nominal plaintiff in the prior action, was then aware that David was suffering the aorta aneurysm but on the contrary believed that he was recovering from the injuries sustained in the accident.

On the following day an agreement for settlement was reached wherein, in consideration of the payment of $6,500, David and his father agreed to settle in full for all claims arising out of the accident.

Richard S. Roberts, counsel for David, thereafter presented to the court a petition for approval of the settlement, wherein David's injuries were described as: " * * * severe crushing of the chest, with multiple rib fractures, severe cerebral concussion, with petechial hemorrhages of the brain, bilateral fractures of the clavicles." At no time was there information disclosed to the court that David was then suffering from an aorta aneurysm which may have been the result of the accident. The court on May 8, 1995, made its order approving the settlement.

Early in 1997, David was required by the army reserve, of which he was a member, to have a physical checkup. For this, he again engaged the services of Dr. Cain. In this checkup, the latter discovered the aorta aneurysm. He then reexamined the X rays which had been taken shortly after the accident and at this time discovered that they disclosed the beginning of the process which produced the aneurysm. He promptly sent David to Dr. Jerome Grismer for an examination and opinion. The latter confirmed the finding of the aorta aneurysm and recommended immediate surgery therefor. This was performed by him at Mount Sinai Hospital in Metropolis on March 10, 1997.

Shortly thereafter, David, having attained his majority, instituted the present action for additional damages due to the more serious injuries including the aorta aneurysm which he alleges proximately resulted from the accident. As indicated above, the prior order for settlement was vacated. The trial court noted that, by reason of the failure of plaintiff's counsel to use available rules of discovery, plaintiff's doctor and all of plaintiff's representatives did not learn the seriousness of his plaintiff's injuries.

That defendants' counsel concealed the knowledge they had is not disputed. There is no doubt, however, of the good faith of both defendants' counsel. During the course of the negotiations, when the parties were in an adversary relationship, no rule required or duty rested upon defendants or their representatives to disclose this knowledge. Under Rule 1.6 of the New Hazard Rules of Professional Responsibility, a lawyer is required to disclose information about an act that would lead to death or serious bodily harm. The application of this rule often requires a delicate balance of competing interests. On the one hand, a lawyer must uphold the sanctity of the attorney-client relationship by strictly maintaining client confidences. At the same time, however, a lawyer has an obligation to society and to the physical well-being of the very people our system of justice is designed to protect. In considering these countervailing interests and the express language of Rule 1.6, we conclude that defense counsel's conduct in this case did not violate the New Hazard Rules of Professional Responsibility.

Despite the lack of any ethical obligation to disclose the life threatening condition, the concealment was of such character as to result in an unconscionable advantage over plaintiff's ignorance or mistake during settlement discussions. The court may vacate such a settlement for mistake.

From the foregoing it is clear that in the instant case the court did not abuse its discretion in setting aside the settlement which it had approved on plaintiff's behalf while he was still a minor. It is undisputed that neither he nor his counsel nor his medical attendants were aware that at the time settlement was made he was suffering from an aorta aneurysm which may have resulted from the accident. The seriousness of this disability is indicated by Dr. Hannah's report indicating the imminent danger of death therefrom. This was known by counsel for both defendants but was not disclosed to the court at the time it was petitioned to approve the settlement. While no canon of ethics or legal obligation may have required them to inform plaintiff or his counsel with respect thereto, or to advise the court therein, it did become obvious to them at the time, that the settlement then made did not contemplate or take into consideration the disability described. This fact opened the way for the court to later exercise its discretion in vacating the settlement.

Affirmed.

PROBLEM 5

Morning Site Security, Inc. ("MSS"), a private corporation in the State of New Hazard, was established in 1910 to provide security personnel for private businesses. Its original services included, for example, the provision of trained security guards for private office buildings and factories. In 1914, at the suggestion of a new wealthy investor, MSS expanded its operations by entering into a series of contracts with the State of New Hazard's Department of Corrections, pursuant to which MSS would construct and operate private prison facilities to house New Hazard state prisoners. Under these contracts, which have been renewed every year from 1916 to the present, MSS has agreed to keep state prisoners incarcerated in private facilities that are comparable (in terms of, *e.g.*, security, safety, sanitation and comfort) to prison facilities owned and operated by the state. In return, the Department of Corrections provides a fee to MSS, adjusted yearly to account for both inflation and the number of state prisoners housed that year in MSS facilities.

MSS's first private prison (which was also, incidentally, the first private prison in the state) was completed in late 1916, and in its first full year of operation housed about 3% of all state prisoners then incarcerated in the State of New Hazard. MSS's private-prison business grew rapidly, however, and by 1950, over half of state prisoners in New Hazard were housed in MSS's private facilities. The numbers continued to climb steadily as the decades passed. By early 2010, 72% of New Hazard prisoners were housed in private MSS facilities.

There are no other private corporations operating prisons in the state; thus, all state prisoners are housed in either MSS prisons or in prisons operated by the state's Department of Corrections.

MSS's business of providing security personnel to other private corporations—now called its "CorProtection" branch—has also grown rapidly over the years. In recent decades, CorProtection has accounted for roughly half of MSS's business activities and revenues. Since 1990, for example, MSS's prison-operating business has accounted for 51 to 53 percent of its activities and revenue every year, with its CorProtection branch accounting for the remaining 47 to 49 percent. The only exception was 2002, when there was a temporary spike in demand for private security services; that year, CorProtection's services and sales accounted for approximately 56% of MSS's total business activities and revenue, with the prison-operating business accounting for the remaining 44%.

As the number of prisoners in MSS's facilities has risen over the years, state legislators have attempted (with varying degrees of success) to ensure that state laws governing prisons apply to both public *and* private prison facilities. The Prison Security Act of 1997, for example, provides that "any prisoner in any prison facility, whether public or private, who commits any Class A security violation under this Act, shall be subject to appropriate penalties at the discretion of the prison's director, in addition to any criminal charges brought by the state." The Act defines "Class A security violation" to include, among other things, "the possession or use, on prison property, of any weapon or other material capable of causing serious bodily harm."

Janet Jones, convicted of multiple nonviolent felonies in 1998, is serving a sentence of 35 years in one of MSS's private prisons in New Hazard. In early 2010, after converting to Wicca—a Neopagan religion— she began to wear a large pentagram around her neck (about 5.5 inches in diameter). She had received the pentagram from a friend who came during visiting hours; guards at the time had not noticed the gift. Jones initially wore the pentagram under her prison uniform, as she did not want to draw attention to herself, and she suspected that jewelry might be prohibited under prison regulations. The five points of the pentagram's star, however, were unusually sharp, and they jutted out slightly beyond the edge of the pentagram's circle. If Jones made abrupt movements or sat in certain positions, the sharp points would poke into her skin, causing her mild pain and discomfort. After several days, she decided to fix that problem by wearing the pentagram on the outside of her uniform instead.

Moments after Jones pulled the pentagram out from under her uniform, however, a prison guard spotted it and confiscated it. Alarmed by the pentagram's five sharp points, the guard brought it immediately to the prison's director, Deidre Doe, who determined that, for purposes of the 1997 Prison Security Act, the pentagram qualified as a "weapon or other material capable of causing serious bodily harm," and that Jones had therefore committed a Class A security violation. Relying on the Prison Security Act clause regarding the imposition by prison directors of appropriate penalties for Class A security violations, Doe ordered that Jones be prohibited from any contact with outside visitors for a period of one year. Doe also refused to return the pentagram to Jones.

Within six weeks, Jones filed a lawsuit against Doe, alleging that Doe's implementation and enforcement of the 1997 Prison Security Act violated Jones's rights under the State of New Hazard's 2009 Freedom of Religious Exercise and Expression Act ("FREE Act"). In her complaint, Jones requests that the court invalidate the one-year ban on visitor contact and that the Court order Doe to return the pentagram.

ASSIGNMENT

You are a law clerk to the Honorable Y'not Ekruoro, the New Hazard trial judge assigned to Ms. Jones's case. Judge Ekruoro has asked you to write a memorandum analyzing two threshold issues that will help determine whether Jones has stated a valid claim.

Your memorandum must be limited to the following two questions only:

(1) Does Doe fall within the definition of "government" under the FREE Act?

(2) Assuming, for the sake of argument, that your answer to the first question is "no," can Jones nevertheless sue Doe under the FREE Act, or does Doe's status as a non-government actor preclude Jones from doing so? In other words, can the FREE Act's protections be invoked even if the defendant here is not an official or entity of the "government" (as defined by the Act), or does the Act only apply where a "government" (as defined by the Act) is a party to the case?

Though you might answer "yes" to the first question, you must still address the second question, as Judge Ekruoro wants to understand both issues fully. For each question, please address the strongest arguments available to each side, using the statute and cases provided below, and the facts set forth above. (In writing your memorandum, you should assume the truth of the facts on pages two and three of this exam.) Advise Judge Ekruoro on how he should rule on these issues.

Because your memorandum is limited to the threshold issues identified above, you should not address a variety of other legal issues that the case might involve. For example, you should not address whether Director Doe properly interpreted the 1997 Prison Security Act. Nor should you address the FREE Act claim on the merits. That is, you should not address whether Wicca qualifies as a "religion" under the Act or whether Doe's actions imposed a "substantial burden" on religion; nor should you address whether Doe's actions were the "least restrictive means" to further a "compelling state interest." FREE Act § 3, *infra*. You also should not address any constitutional issues that you believe the case may present. Your co-clerk is writing a separate memorandum to address all of these separate issues.

No court in New Hazard has yet applied or interpreted the FREE Act, but the highest courts of two neighboring states, North Bedlam and South Tranquility, have issued decisions interpreting identical statutes enacted in those states.* A trial court in North Bedlam also issued a decision last week that might be relevant to Jones's case. These court decisions, along with the full text of New Hazard's FREE Act, are provided below.

The State of New Hazard's 2009 Freedom of Religious Exercise and Expression Act:

Section 1. Purpose and applicability.

(A) Purpose. The legislature enacts this Freedom of Religious Exercise and Expression Act ("FREE Act" or "Act") to expand legal protections for religious conduct and religious expression for all of the state's residents, by providing a claim or defense to persons whose religious exercise is substantially burdened by the government. Recent reports indicate that some public officials have not shown appropriate respect for religious conduct and expression in a variety of contexts. New Hazard residents representing a range of religious faiths have reported discrimination in their interactions with, for example, property zoning authorities, state prosecutors, police and public employers. Current legal protections are insufficient to remedy the problem.

---

* The North Bedlam and South Tranquility FREE Acts are identical to New Hazard's FREE Act, except that where the New Hazard FREE Act refers specifically to "New Hazard," the North Bedlam FREE Act refers to "North Bedlam," and the South Tranquility FREE Act refers to "South Tranquility."

(B) Application. The FREE Act applies to all New Hazard state law, and the implementation and enforcement of that law, whether statutory or otherwise, and whether adopted before or after the enactment of the FREE Act. The Act goes into effect on July 9, 2009.

Section 2. Definitions.

For purposes of the FREE Act, the following definitions apply:

(A) The term "**government**" includes the following New Hazard state authorities: (i) all branches, departments, commissions and divisions of state and municipal governments, and subdivisions thereof; (ii) law enforcement authorities, including both state and local police authorities; and (iii) quasi-public entities as defined in Subsection B of this Section. "Government" also includes officials and employees of the aforementioned entities.

(B) "**Quasi public entity**" means any private corporation or other private entity that: (i) exists principally to assist the State of New Hazard in carrying out traditionally public functions and (ii) carries out those traditionally public functions pursuant to a contract with any entity covered by Subsections (i) or (ii) of Section 2(A) of this Act.

(C) The term "**demonstrates**" means "meets the burdens of going forward with the evidence and of persuasion" in a proceeding under this Act.

(D) The term "**person**" includes a natural person as well as a corporation, a non-profit organization and any other association.

Section 3. Prohibition and exception.

(A) Government shall not substantially burden a person's exercise of religion, even if the burden results from a neutral rule of general applicability, except as provided in Subsection (B).

(B) Government may substantially burden a person's exercise of religion only where the government demonstrates that application of the burden to the person (i) is in furtherance of a compelling state interest and (ii) is the least restrictive means of furthering that compelling state interest.

Section 4. Remedies.

A person whose religious exercise or expression has been burdened in violation of this Act may assert that violation as a claim or defense in a judicial proceeding and obtain appropriate relief against a government.

Amsterdam Christian Community House v. Amsterdam Christian Community Home

Supreme Court of the State of South Tranquility, 2010.

■ QUINLAN, J., writing for the Court:

This case presents an issue of first impression in this State: Whether the South Tranquility Freedom of Religious Exercise and Expression Act ("FREE Act") can be raised as a defense in a lawsuit alleging unfair competitive practices by a private religious organization. The district court answered in the negative, holding that the Act did not apply to suits between private parties. We vacate the court's judgment and remand for additional proceedings consistent with this opinion.

A.

The Amsterdam Christian Community House (the "Community House"), a charitable religious organization in the South Tranquility Town of Amsterdam, has provided various services to low-income individuals and families for over 25 years. It distributes warm meals to the homeless, offers tuition assistance to low-income residents enrolled in various education programs, provides free space to prayer and support groups, and engages in other charitable activities. To provide these services, it relies entirely on private donations from individuals and corporations.

Nevae H. Kalling, the former assistant director of the Community House, was dismissed from the organization in the summer of 2008. While the parties dispute the reason for the dismissal, they agree that Ms. Kalling's relationship with the Community House had terminated by July 2008. They also agree that by early September 2008, Ms. Kalling had—with the help of three philanthropists who had previously donated to the Community House—formed a new charitable religious organization three blocks from the Community House. Based on what she has called a "divine revelation" that came to her in a dream, Ms. Kalling named her new organization the Amsterdam Christian Community Home (the "Community Home").

Community House leaders, fearing that the similarity between "Amsterdam Christian Community House" and "Amsterdam Christian Community Home" would confuse current and potential donors and thereby lead to a loss of donations to the Community House, demanded that Ms. Kalling choose a different name for her organization. Community House leaders also suspected that Ms. Kalling, acting out of spite stemming from her 2008 dismissal, would purposefully exploit the confusion among donors to build her new organization and to undermine her former employer.

Ms. Kalling denied any illicit motive and, citing her divine revelation, refused to change the name of the Community Home. After several additional, unsuccessful attempts to negotiate an amicable solution, the Community House filed a lawsuit, alleging violations of South

Tranquility's Unfair Competitive Practices Act ("UCPA"). The lawsuit seeks damages and various other forms of relief, including an injunction requiring the Community Home to change its name.

The Community Home filed a motion for judgment as a matter of law, arguing that because its name was inspired by a divine revelation, any court order requiring the organization to change its name would constitute a substantial and unjustified burden on religious exercise in violation of the FREE Act. In short, the Community Home argued that regardless of the merits of the Community House's UCPA claim, the FREE Act protected the Community Home from any court-mandated name change. The Community House opposed the motion, arguing the FREE Act only applies to suits in which the government is a party. The trial court agreed with the Community House and denied the Community Home's motion. The Community Home, relying on South Tranquility Rule of Appellate Procedure 1.16, filed an interlocutory appeal of the denial of its FREE Act motion, and urges this Court to vacate the trial court's ruling.

B.

Case law involving our state's FREE Act has until now involved only disputes in which a government entity or official is a party to the case. *See, e.g., Foyad v. Dep't of Motor Vehicles*, 45 S.T. 98 (2009) (holding that a public employer's failure to recognize an employee's religious holiday constituted a "substantial[ ] burden" on religion under the FREE Act, and remanding to the trial court to consider the employer's "compelling interest" argument). There is thus no case law in this state addressing whether the FREE Act applies where, as here, a private party seeks to invoke the Act's protections to defend itself against a suit brought by another private party. The Act's language, however, surely seems broad enough to encompass this case. Section 1 of the Act states that it applies to "*all* South Tranquility state law, and the implementation and enforcement of that law," FREE Act § 1(B) (emphasis added), and Section 4 provides that a defendant arguing that a law substantially burdens the exercise of religion "may assert [a] violation" of the FREE Act as a "defense in a judicial proceeding." *Id.* § 4. This language easily covers the present action, in which a plaintiff seeks to implement and enforce a state law through a statutorily authorized civil action. The only conceivably narrowing language is the phrase immediately following: "and obtain appropriate relief against a government." *Id.* Contrary to what the Community House argues, however, this language would seem most reasonably read as broadening, rather than narrowing, the rights of a party asserting a FREE Act defense. The legislature most likely included Section 4's government-specific language to ensure that courts would not block relief against the government by invoking common-law principles of sovereign immunity, under which governments may not be sued absent their consent. As there is no analogous principle disfavoring suits against private parties, there was no need to expressly specify that the

FREE Act afforded relief against such parties. In light of these background principles, as well as the FREE Act's broad purposes and scope, *see* § 1(A)–(B), we find it unreasonable to interpret language that ensures the availability of relief against the government as a prohibition on relief in all other cases. If the legislature meant to categorically bar relief in lawsuits between private parties, it would have included language to say so; it would not have expected courts to somehow infer that the rights-*granting* language in Section 4 is actually a drastic *restriction* on the FREE Act's protections.

The Community House makes much of the fact that, where a substantial burden on religion exists, the FREE Act requires the *"government* [to] demonstrate[ ]" that the burden is the least restrictive means of furthering a compelling state interest. FREE Act § 3(B) (emphasis added). In the Community House's view, this indicates that the FREE Act can only be applied to suits where the government is a party to the case. We are required, however, to read the statute as a coherent whole, keeping in mind its broad purposes and taking care not to construe any particular clause in a way that would undermine the Act's core provisions or create unnecessary inconsistencies in their application. In our view, the Community House's narrow and mechanical reading of the "government demonstrates" clause fails to accord appropriate weight to, among other things, the sweeping language of the Act's central prohibition, which bars substantial governmental burdens on religious exercise without any reference to whether the burden is imposed through a private lawsuit or direct government enforcement. *Id.* § 3(A). The Community House's argument also fails to account for the statute's broadly stated purposes, which include protecting "all" state residents, *see id.* § 1(A), and the legislature's express intention that the Act apply to *all* state law, *see id.* § 1(B).

We find it significant, moreover, that UCPA—like many laws potentially implicating the FREE Act—authorizes enforcement not only through private lawsuits, but also through administrative actions initiated independently by the State Commission on Fair Business Practices. In cases initiated by the State Commission, there can be no dispute that the FREE Act applies, given that the Commission is a government entity. *See* FREE Act § 2(A). It would be absurd, however, to hold that the substance of the UCPA's prohibitions and the availability of the FREE Act's protections depend entirely on whether UCPA is enforced in a given case by the Commission or, as here, by an aggrieved private party.

Accordingly, we read the "government demonstrates" language from Subsection 3(B) as creating, at most, a procedural ambiguity as to how courts should go about applying the law in cases where the government is not a party. We can resolve that ambiguity by requiring, in cases such as this, that the trial court assess both the existence of compelling state interests and the availability of less restrictive forms of government regulation based on the parties' submissions and the court's independent judgment.

In sum, we hold that the Community Home may invoke the FREE Act as a defense to the UCPA claim in this case, notwithstanding the fact that no government entity is a party to the suit. We express no opinion, however, on whether the Community Home's FREE Act defense should prevail on its merits. We leave it to the trial court, in other words, to determine in the first instance whether there is actually a "substantial[ ] burden" on religious exercise in this case, and/or whether application of the UCPA is nevertheless justified as the least restrictive means of furthering a compelling state interest.

The trial court's judgment denying the Community Home's FREE Act motion is vacated, and the case is remanded for further proceedings consistent with this opinion.

It is so ordered.

Yevak v. New Yooth Church

Supreme Court of the State of North Bedlam, 2010.

■ TEW, C.J., writing for the Court:

This case requires us to determine whether the state's 2004 Freedom of Religious Exercise and Expression Act ("FREE Act") applies to suits between private parties. We hold that it does not.

A.

The facts are undisputed. Plaintiff Ekim Yevak was ordained as a clergy member of the Defendant New Yooth Church (the "Church") in 1992, and served from 1993 to 2008 as a minister at a local New Yooth Church congregation in the North Bedlam Town of Greene Hall. In early 2008, shortly after Yevak turned 70 years old, the Church's governing officials directed him to retire from his position as minister of the Greene Hall congregation pursuant to the Church's mandatory retirement policy, which bars any member of its clergy older than 69 from serving as the minister of a congregation. The Church offered Yevak a "desk job" at the Church's central offices, which Yevak rejected. Yevak instead attempted to negotiate a five-year exception to the retirement policy, and presented Church officials with a letter, signed by 96% of the adult members of Yevak's congregation, urging the Church to reconsider. The Church, however, refused to reconsider or grant an exception, and Yevak left his position as minister in July 2008.

In November 2008, Yevak filed a lawsuit in North Bedlam trial court, alleging that the New Yooth Church's mandatory retirement policy violated the North Bedlam's Age Discrimination in Employment Act ("ADEA"), which prohibits employment discrimination based on age against workers above the age of 40. The Church moved to dismiss, arguing that enforcement of the ADEA against the Church would substantially burden its religious freedom in violation of North Bedlam's Freedom of Religious Exercise and Expression Act ("FREE Act"), which prohibits government entities from substantially burdening religious exercise except where the government can demonstrate that the burden is the least restrictive means of furthering a compelling state interest. FREE Act § 3(A)–(B). The trial court denied the Church's motion, holding that the FREE Act applied only to suits where the government (as defined in the Act) is a party. The Church, the court held, could not rely on the FREE Act as a defense to a lawsuit brought by a non-government party. The Church field an interlocutory appeal, and a sharply divided panel of the North Bedlam Intermediate Appellate Court affirmed the trial court's judgment. The Church appealed to this Court. We affirm as well.

B.

In response to reports of religious discrimination by government officials in a variety of contexts, several states—including our own—have enacted statutes to provide enhanced protections to religious exercise. The statutes—known as "FREE Acts"—allow parties to file suit against a government entity that substantially burdens the exercise of their religion. *See* FREE Act § 4. If a court agrees that the government has substantially burdened religion, the government must remove the burden (and possibly provide other "appropriate relief") unless it can justify its actions under certain standards set forth in the statute. *Id.* §§ 3–4. In one case, for example, a Muslim inmate in a North Bedlam state prison sued the state Department of Corrections under the FREE Act because the Department refused to provide halal meals to state prisoners. Finding that this constituted a substantial burden on the plaintiff's religion, a North Bedlam trial court directed the Department of Corrections either to provide the halal meals to plaintiff or to demonstrate that its refusal to do so was the least restrictive means of furthering a compelling state interest. *See Teid v. Pub. Univ. Hosp.*, 100 N.B. 101, 102 (2006). The Department agreed to provide the meals, and the parties stipulated to a dismissal of the case.

Parties may also invoke the FREE Act's protections as a *defense* where the government initiates a proceeding against them. *See* FREE Act § 4. In *People v. Evitan*, for example, two members of a Native American tribe were convicted under the North Bedlam Narcotics Law for illegal possession of peyote. *See* 59 N.B.2d 46 (2007). The defendants appealed their convictions to this Court, arguing that they ingested the peyote for purely spiritual purposes in accordance with the tenants of their faith, and that the government's application of the Narcotics Law to their religious use of peyote constituted a substantial burden on their religion, in violation of the FREE Act. We agreed that the FREE Act provided a potential defense to the criminal charges, and that the Narcotics Law, as applied to the two defendants, substantially burdened their religion. We remanded to the trial court for consideration of the government's "compelling interest" argument. *Evitan*, 59 N.B.2d at 51.

C.

The present dispute involves only private parties—a Church and a member of its clergy—and thus differs fundamentally from *Teid, Evitan* and the cases like them. We agree with the courts below that North Bedlam's FREE Act does not apply in these circumstances.

The Church argues that application of the ADEA substantially burdens the Church's free exercise of religion by interfering with its ability to choose its spiritual leaders. The Church further maintains that it makes no difference for purposes of the FREE Act that this ADEA dispute involves only private parties, because the FREE Act applies to "all" state law as well as any "implementation and enforcement of that law." FREE Act § 1(B).

The Church is correct that the enforcement of the ADEA would necessarily involve government action (*e.g.*, court-ordered compliance with the ADEA's terms), even where the underlying lawsuit is a civil action between two private parties. And it is possible that the enforcement of the ADEA could, in some circumstances, substantially burden religious exercise. The problem with the Church's argument, however, is that the legislature has not chosen to make the FREE Act's special protections available in *every* action implicating religious freedoms. In enacting the FREE Act, the legislature only provided a claim or defense in actions where a *government* (as defined in the Act) is a party to the suit. This Court has no authority to expand the FREE Act's remedies to provide a defense to the Church in this action.

Two provisions of the FREE Act make clear that the Act applies only to disputes to which the government is a party. Section 4 of the FREE Act provides that "[a] person whose religious exercise has been burdened in violation of this Act may assert that violation as a claim or defense in a judicial proceeding and obtain appropriate relief against a government." The phrase "*against a government*" (emphasis added) would serve no purpose if Section 4 were read to authorize relief *regardless* of whether that relief is sought against the government or a private party.* Section 3(B) of the Act, moreover, provides that where a law imposes a substantial burden on religion, the "*government*" must "demonstrate[ ] that application of the burden . . . is the least restrictive means of furthering [a] compelling state interest" (emphasis added). The Act defines "demonstrates" as "meet[ing] the burdens of going forward with the evidence and of persuasion." *Id.* § 2(C). Where, as here, the government is not a party, it cannot "go[ ] forward" with any evidence.

---

*   We find it implausible that the legislature included this language merely to overcome background presumptions regarding the government's immunity from suit, particularly because language elsewhere in Section 4 as well as other sections of the Act already make abundantly clear that the Act authorizes suits against the government. *See, e.g.*, FREE Act §§ 1(A), 3(A), (B). If the legislature had intended to authorize relief against private parties *as well as* the government, it could have easily so specified. Instead, the legislature chose language referring only to "relief against a government." *Id.* § 4.

This demonstrates that the legislature did not contemplate or intend to authorize FREE Act suits between purely private parties.

We recognize that according to the FREE Act's "[a]pplicability" section, the statute applies to "all" North Bedlam state law. FREE Act § 1(B). This provision, however, is not inconsistent with our holding that the statute does not apply to suits between private parties. Read in conjunction with the rest of the statute, the provision simply requires courts to apply the FREE Act "to all North Bedlam state law" in any lawsuit to which a government is a party.

The Church observes that in some cases, the ADEA is enforced not through private litigation, but through actions brought by a state entity—specifically, the North Bedlam Equal Employment Opportunities Commission ("EEOC"). In such cases, the FREE Act could certainly apply, since the EEOC is a "government." FREE Act § 2(A). Emphasizing this possibility of EEOC enforcement, the Church argues that the ADEA's prohibitions and the availability of a FREE Act remedy should not and "cannot" change depending on whether the ADEA is enforced by the EEOC or a private litigant. Church Brief at 7. The Church does not explain, however, why this is so. If the FREE Act effectively amends all North Bedlam statutes as they apply to suits in which the government is a party, then the substance of the ADEA's prohibitions and the availability of the FREE Act's protections most certainly *can* change depending on who initiates a suit. Although the Church apparently finds this unwise or unreasonable from a policy perspective, there is no acceptable reading of the statute that would yield the kind of consistency the Church desires. This Court's duty is to apply the statute's plain language, not to re-write or "improve" the statute to conform to the parties' or the Court's preferred policies.

Accordingly, we hold that New Yooth Church cannot invoke the FREE Act as a defense in this case. We affirm the denial of the Church's motion to dismiss based on the FREE Act, and remand the case to the trial court for consideration of the Church's alternative defenses, including its First Amendment defense.

It is so ordered.

Jewish Community Center v. Historic Landmark Institute

Trial Court, 116th Judicial District, State of North Bedlam, 2010.

■ ROCHER, DISTRICT JUDGE:

The Jewish Community Center (the "JCC") is a religious organization in the North Bedlam Village of Little Warren. The JCC has sought unsuccessfully for over three years to find an appropriate site in Little Warren for the construction of a new temple.

The Historic Landmark Institute ("HLI"), is a private organization authorized under contracts with the state to make certain property zoning decisions. Specifically, the contracts authorize HLI to designate buildings and lots within the state as "property of significant historical interest." Such a designation by HLI triggers a state statute that prohibits new construction on the land. Those affected by the designation can contest it before a state regulatory body called the State Zoning Board, but the appeals are notoriously slow and costly.

In Little Warren, HLI's influence is unusually broad, because the Village, which is over two hundred and fifty years old, retains many of its original buildings. Since mid-2007, HLI has effectively thwarted the JCC's efforts to build a new temple by repeatedly designating JCC's preferred construction sites as "property of significant historical interest." Rather than contest the designations before the State Zoning Board, the JCC has sued HLI, alleging that HLI's zoning designations have substantially burdened the JCC's religious exercise in violation of the state's Freedom of Religious Exercise and Expression Act ("FREE Act"). HLI has moved to dismiss the FREE Act claim, arguing that as a private organization, it is not a "government" under the Act.

This Court agrees with HLI. The only possible basis for holding that HLI is a "government" under the FREE Act lies in Subsections 2(A)(iii) and 2(B), which define "government" to include "quasi-public entities," and which further define "quasi-public entity" to include any private entity that "(i) exists principally to assist" the state "in carrying out traditionally public functions" and that "(ii) carries out these traditionally public functions pursuant to a contract with [a state] entity." Applying these definitions, the Court concludes that HLI is not a "government." HLI is a large, multi-state organization engaged in a wide array of educational activities and related community services; as the JCC's complaint concedes, HLI spends only a tiny fraction of its resources assisting the state with its zoning decisions. HLI was founded, moreover, over sixty years before it entered into its first state contract regarding zoning designations. In view of these uncontested facts, it borders on frivolous to claim that HLI *"exists principally* to assist" the state in carrying out traditionally public functions. FREE Act § 2(B) (emphasis added). Thus, HLI is not a "government" for purposes of the FREE Act, and JCC's claim against it must be dismissed. *See also Yevak v. New Yooth Church*, 100 N.B. 101 (N. Bedlam S.Ct. 2010) (holding that the FREE Act does not apply to suits between private parties).

HLI's motion to dismiss the FREE Act claim is granted. JCC may contest HLI's zoning designations on other grounds through the normal appeals process before the State Zoning Board.*

It is so ordered.

---

*   Given the increasing frequency with which North Bedlam municipalities have authorized private organizations to make historic-landmark designations over the last 25 years,

PROBLEM 6

FACTS

The Gates University Law School is a leading law school in the State of New Hazard. For the 2013–14 academic year, it admitted just over two hundred students, amounting to less than three per cent of the total applications received. The law school prides itself on its innovative and influential faculty, many of whom are recognized leaders in their scholarly fields. Several of the school's professors have received the New Hazard Academy of Arts and Sciences's prestigious Blackstone Award for outstanding contributions to the study of law.

The first week of law school classes was due to begin on Monday, September 9, 2013. That morning, when they arrived at their offices at the law school, professors who looked at their office telephones saw that the phone's notification light was blinking, indicating a pending voicemail message. Those who dialed in to check their voicemail were informed by the system that a voice message had been left by an unknown caller at 3:03 AM that morning. The system then played back the following message, recorded in a sinister, raspy voice:

> Dearest Professors of the Gates University Law School: You do not know me. You never had any reason to care about who I am . . . until now. Who am I? I am one of the 97 per cent! One of the many to whom your law school denied admission this year. You assumed you could reject me without any consequences. Well I have news for you. There will be serious consequences! I'm sure you would love to know what they are. . . . You will find out in good time. If you are interested I suggest you wait patiently by your phone. I assure you, you won't want to miss my next message!

Word of this message spread quickly amongst the faculty. It turned out that every professor had received the same voicemail. The professors also found that their office phones would no longer work properly—the only thing they would do was play the sinister caller's message. No other calls could be made or received. Any other voicemails that had previously been stored were now deleted.

While some of the professors laughed off the message and proceeded to teach their classes as scheduled, others were traumatized. Indeed, a few professors were so distressed that they could not bring themselves to leave their offices, or even to speak to anyone, for several hours after they heard the message. Two adjunct professors, who jointly taught a class on securities law and practice and were registered broker-dealers with the New Hazard Securities and Exchange Commission, had been planning to make certain trades from their law school office phones by a 9:00 AM

---

it is also unclear whether such designations are still a "traditionally public function." *See* FREE Act § 2(B). Resolution of that issue, however, is unnecessary in this case.

deadline, but were unable to do so solely due to the impaired phone system. (They did not have cell phones, and their only other phones registered with the Commission for compliance purposes were at their trading desks on the other side of town.)

The Law School I.T. department attempted to diagnose what had happened to the office telephone system. The system is a state of the art "Phonesoft 3.4" hardware and software system designed specifically for the Law School in 2010. For instance, it stores voicemail for a week after initial deletion, in case a user inadvertently deleted a message and in fact wants to keep it. The system also provides several voicemail options, such as out-of-office messages. It is run from electronic servers located in a locked room in the Law School I.T. department. The system operated via an intranet, but could only be accessed over the internet using an online portal that required users to enter a unique security code. It appeared that the sinister caller had gained access to the server by running a sophisticated code-breaking program that guessed millions of codes a second until it hit upon the correct one. The I.T. department located the source of the code-breaking attack to be a computer at an internet café a few miles from the Law School.

It proved to be very difficult to repair the telephone system. The Law School I.T. department had to bring in outside consultants, and completely refresh the software that was running on the telephone servers. All told, the repair took two weeks and cost the law school just over $20,000.

Meanwhile, the police had identified a suspect. Security camera footage from the internet café showed a very tall, red-headed man using the relevant computer at the time of the attack. Working through the law school's list of rejected applicants, the police eventually found the man who appeared on the camera, a Mr. Chuck Babbage. Mr. Babbage immediately confessed that he had hacked into the Law School phone system and left the voicemail message, in order to "get back" at the school for rejecting his application. Mr. Babbage admitted that he was aware that his actions would render the phones inoperable for any purpose other than listening to the message.

The Law School decided to bring a civil action against Mr. Babbage under the New Hazard Computer Fraud and Abuse Act of 1986. It filed a complaint in the District of New Hazard, alleging the above facts. The Law School sought compensation from Mr. Babbage for the cost of the repairs it had to carry out to fix its phone system. Several of the traumatized professors joined the law school's action, seeking a cumulative $500,000 in damages for the emotional distress inflicted by Babbage's acts. Furthermore, the two adjunct professors sought damages of $4,000 each for losses suffered because they were unable to execute their trades. Mr. Babbage filed a motion to dismiss the complaint.

ASSIGNMENT

You are a law clerk to the Honorable Emily Gerry of the District Court for the District of New Hazard. Judge Gerry has asked you to write a memorandum analyzing whether defendant's motion to dismiss should be granted. For purposes of this analysis, the New Hazard Rules of Civil Procedure provide that a plaintiff's allegations are assumed to be true.

Confine your answer to responding to this question only. Please address the strongest arguments available to each side, using the statute and cases provided below, and the facts set forth above.

The New Hazard Computer Fraud and Abuse Act, 18 N.H.C. § 1030 (1986)

Purpose and application

(1) (a) Purpose. The legislature enacts this Computer Fraud and Abuse Act ("CFAA" or "Act") in order to ensure the integrity of the computer-based systems that are increasingly important both to government and to commercial enterprise.

(b) Application. The Act goes into effect on January 1, 1987.

Offenses

An offense under this Act is committed by any person who—

(2) intentionally accesses a computer without authorization or exceeds authorized access, and thereby obtains—

(a) information contained in a financial record of a financial institution, or of a credit card issuer, or contained in a file of a consumer credit reporting agency on a consumer;

(b) information from any department or agency of the State; or

(c) information from any protected computer;

(3) knowingly and with intent to defraud, accesses a protected computer without authorization, or exceeds authorized access, and by means of such conduct furthers the intended fraud and obtains anything of value, unless the object of the fraud and the thing obtained consists only of the use of the computer and the value of such use is not more than $5,000 in any 1-year period; or

(4) (a) knowingly causes the transmission of a program, information, code, or command, and as a result of such conduct, intentionally causes damage without authorization, to a protected computer;

(b) intentionally accesses a protected computer without authorization, and as a result of such conduct, recklessly causes damage; or

(c) intentionally accesses a protected computer without authorization, and as a result of such conduct, causes damage and loss;

Liability

(5) The punishment for an offense under sections 2, 3, or 4 of this Act is a fine, imprisonment for not more than ten years, or both, if the offense caused (or, in the case of an attempted offense, would, if completed, have caused)—

(a) loss to one or more persons during any 1-year period aggregating at least $5,000 in value;

(b) the modification or impairment, or potential modification or impairment, of the medical examination, diagnosis, treatment, or care of 1 or more individuals;

(c) physical injury to any person;

(d) a threat to public health or safety;

(e) damage affecting a computer used by or for an entity of the New Hazard Government in furtherance of the administration of justice, national defense, or national security; or

(f) damage affecting 10 or more protected computers during any 1-year period

(6) Any person who suffers damage or loss by reason of an offense under sections 2, 3, or 4 of this Act may maintain a civil action against the violator to obtain compensatory damages and injunctive relief or other equitable relief. A civil action for an offense under sections 2, 3, or 4 of this Act may be brought only if the conduct involves one of the factors set forth in subsections (a), (b), (c), (d), or (e) of section 5. Damages for a violation involving only conduct described in subsection (a) of section 5 are limited to economic damages.

(7) No action may be brought under this Act unless such action is begun within 2 years of the date of the act complained of or the date of the discovery of the damage. No action may be brought under this Act for the negligent design or manufacture of computer hardware, computer software, or firmware.

Definitions

(8) As used in this Act—

(a) the term "computer" means an electronic, magnetic, optical, electrochemical, or other data processing device performing storage functions, and includes any data storage facility or communications facility directly related to or operating in conjunction with such device, but such term does not include an automated typewriter or typesetter, a portable hand held calculator, or other similar device;

(b) the term "protected computer" means a computer exclusively for the use of a financial institution or the New Hazard Government, or, in the case of a computer not exclusively for such use, used by or for a financial institution or the New Hazard

Government and the conduct constituting the offense affects that use by or for the financial institution or the Government.

(c) the term "financial institution" means—

(1) an institution, with deposits insured by the New Hazard Deposit Insurance Corporation;

(2) the New Hazard Reserve or a member of the New Hazard Reserve including any New Hazard Reserve Bank;

(3) a credit union with accounts insured by the New Hazard Credit Union Administration;

(4) a member of the New Hazard home loan bank system and any home loan bank;

(5) any institution of the New Hazard Farm Credit System; or

(6) a broker-dealer registered with the New Hazard Securities and Exchange Commission.

(d) the term "financial record" means information derived from any record held by a financial institution pertaining to a customer's relationship with the financial institution;

(e) the term "exceeds authorized access" means to access a computer with authorization and to use such access to obtain or alter information in the computer that the accesser is not entitled so to obtain or alter;

(f) the term "damage" means any impairment to the integrity or availability of data, a program, a system, or information.

New Hazard v. Amitra
Supreme Court of New Hazard, 2013.
413 N.H. 1.

■ SAGE, C.J.

New Hazard City uses a radio system for police, fire, ambulance, and other emergency communications. The Smartnet 1.2, made by Motorola, automatically assigns voice traffic to one of 20 radio channels. One of the channels is designated the "control" channel. To initiate a call a user calls the control channel by pressing a "call" button on a Smartnet-compliant mobile radio unit. Other users who have heard the call on the control channel can press a "join" button on their radio. Computer hardware and software located at the City's emergency call center then assign all of the users who wish to join the conversation to one of the radio channels that is not being used. If the control channel is interfered with, however, the mobile radio units will show a message stating "no system" and communication will be impossible.

Between January and August 2010 mobile units encountered occasional puzzling "no signal" conditions. On Halloween of that year the "no signal" condition spread citywide; a powerful signal had blanketed all of the City's communications towers and prevented the computer from receiving, on the control channel, data essential to parcel traffic among the other 19 channels. The City was hosting between 50,000 and 100,000 visitors that day. When disturbances erupted, public safety departments were unable to coordinate their activities because the radio system was down.

By then the City had used radio direction finders to pin down the source of the intruding signals. Police arrested Rajib Amitra, a student in the University of New Hazard's graduate business school. They found the radio hardware and computer gear that he had used to monitor communications over the Smartnet system, analyze how it operated, and send the signals that took control of the system. Amitra, who in 2007 had received a B.S. in computer science from the University, possessed two other credentials for this kind of work: two criminal convictions for hacking into computers in order to perform malicious mischief. A jury convicted Amitra of two counts of interference with computer-related systems under 18 N.H.C. § 1030. He has been sentenced to 96 months imprisonment. On appeal he says that his conduct does not violate § 1030.

The prosecutor's theory is that Smartnet 1.2 is a "computer" because it contains a chip that performs processing in response to signals received on the control channel, and as a whole is a "communications facility directly related to or operating in conjunction" with that computer chip.

Amitra submits that the New Hazard state legislature could not have intended the statute to work this way. Amitra did not invade a bank's system to steal financial information, or erase data on an ex-employer's system, see *Old Hazard v. Lloyd*, 269 O.H. 228 (2001), or plaster a corporation's web site with obscenities that drove away customers, or unleash a worm that slowed and crashed computers across the world, see *Old Hazard v. Morris*, 259 O.H. 504 (1991), or break into military computers to scramble a flight of interceptors to meet a nonexistent threat, or plant covert programs in computers so that they would send spam without the owners' knowledge. All he did was gum up a radio system. Surely that cannot be a New Hazard crime, Amitra insists. Under the prosecutor's theory, every cell phone and cell tower is a "computer" under this statute's definition; so is every iPod, and many another gadgets. Reading § 1030 to cover all of these, and police radio too, would give the statute very wide coverage, which according to Amitra means that the New Hazard legislature cannot have contemplated such breadth.

Of course the New Hazard legislature did not contemplate or intend this particular application of the statute. The New Hazard legislature is a "they" and not an "it"; a committee lacks a brain (or, rather, has so many brains with so many different objectives that it is almost facetious to impute a joint goal or purpose to the collectivity). See Kenneth A.

Shepsle, The New Hazard Legislature is a "They," Not an "It": Legislative Intent as Oxymoron, 12 Int'l Rev. L. & Econ. 239 (1992). Legislation is an objective text approved in constitutionally prescribed ways; its scope is not limited by the cerebrations of those who voted for or signed it into law.

Electronics and communications change rapidly, while each legislator's imagination is limited. The Smartnet system was invented after the first version of § 1030 was enacted, and none of the many amendments to this statute directly addresses them. But although legislators may not know about this particular communications system, they do know that complexity is endemic in the modern world and that each passing year sees new developments. That's why they write general statutes rather than enacting a list of particular forbidden acts. And it is the statutes they enacted—not the thoughts they did or didn't have—that courts must apply. What the New Hazard legislature would have done about various radio systems, had they been present to the mind of any Senator or Representative, is neither here nor there. As more devices come to have built-in intelligence, the effective scope of the statute grows. This might prompt the New Hazard legislature to amend the statute but does not authorize the judiciary to give the existing version less coverage than its language portends.

Nevertheless, we agree with Amitra that the Smartnet system is not a "computer" within the meaning of § 1030. The prosecutor is correct that the system performs electronic processing. However, the system does not perform any real storage function. Each time a user initiates a call, the system checks which radio channels are free, and randomly assigns the relevant users to that channel. After this is done, the system's activity is complete.

Notably, the definition of "computer" carves out exceptions for automatic typewriters, typesetters, handheld calculators, and other similar devices. The Smartnet system is analogous to typewriters and calculators in that those devices are not generally used to store information provided by users for any significant amount of time.

We therefore reverse the district court.

New Hazard v. Kramer

New Hazard Supreme Court, Appellate Division, 2011.
411 N.H. Supp. 1.

■ SARADHI, J.

Weve Stozniak, co-founder of Pear Computer, recently mused: "Everything has a computer in it nowadays."* But is an ordinary cellular phone—used only to place calls and send text messages—a computer?

---

  *   See Ark Ilian, Pear's Weve Stozniak: 'We've lost a lot of control', NCC (Dec. 8, 2010, 12:16 PM).

The district court, relying on the definition of "computer" found in the Computer Fraud and Abuse Act ("CAFA"), concluded that Neil Kramer's was, and imposed an enhanced prison sentence for its use in committing an offense. We affirm.

I.

Neil Kramer pleaded guilty to transporting a minor in interstate commerce with the intent to engage in criminal sexual activity with her. He also acknowledged that he used his cellular telephone to make voice calls and send text messages to the victim for a six-month period leading up to the offense.

The district court increased Kramer's sentence for this offense by applying a provision in the Sentencing Guidelines Manual, § 2G1.3(b)(3), which allows for a sentence enhancement where a "computer" is used to facilitate the offense. The Sentencing Guidelines provide that "computer" has the meaning given that term in the Computer Fraud and Abuse Act, 18 N.H.C. § 1030.

The district court sentenced Kramer to 168 months' imprisonment. The court acknowledged that without the enhancement it would have sentenced Kramer to only 140 months' imprisonment.

Kramer argues that application of the enhancement was procedural error because a cellular telephone, when used only to make voice calls and send text messages, cannot be a "computer" as defined in 18 N.H.C. § 1030.

II.

The Sentencing Guidelines Manual § 2G1.3(b)(3) provides a two-level enhancement for "the use of a computer . . . to . . . persuade, induce, entice, coerce, or facilitate the travel of, the minor to engage in prohibited sexual conduct. . . ." " 'Computer' has the meaning given that term in 18 N.H.C. § 1030," that is, it "means an electronic, magnetic, optical, electrochemical, or other data processing device performing storage functions, and includes any data storage facility or communications facility directly related to or operating in conjunction with such device." It does not, however, "include an automated typewriter or typesetter, a portable hand held calculator, or other similar device."

Kramer argues that the district court incorrectly interpreted the term "computer" to include a "basic cell phone" being used only to call and text message the victim. In his view, the sentencing enhancement should apply only when a device is used to access the Internet. We disagree.

The definition of "computer" is very broad. If a device is "an electronic . . . or other data processing device performing storage functions," it is a computer. This definition captures any device that makes use of an electronic data processor, examples of which are legion. Accord Rin Err, Vagueness Challenges to the Computer Fraud and Abuse

Act, 94 Minn. L. Rev. 1561, 1577 (2010) ("Just think of the common household items that include microchips and electronic storage devices, and thus will satisfy the statutory definition of 'computer.' That category can include coffeemakers, microwave ovens, watches, telephones, children's toys, MP3 players, refrigerators, heating and air-conditioning units, radios, alarm clocks, televisions, and DVD players, in addition to more traditional computers like laptops or desktop computers." (footnote omitted)).

Furthermore, there is nothing in the statutory definition that purports to exclude devices because they lack a connection to the Internet. To be sure, the term computer "does not include an automated typewriter or typesetter, a portable hand held calculator, or other similar device." But this hardly excludes all non-Internet-enabled devices from the definition of "computer"—indeed, this phrasing would be an odd way to do it. Whatever makes an automated typewriter "similar" to a hand held calculator—the statute provides no further illumination—we find few similarities between those items and a modern cellular phone containing an electronic processor. Therefore we conclude that cellular phones are not excluded by this language.[*]

Of course, the enhancement does not apply to every offender who happens to use a computer-controlled microwave or coffeemaker. Application note 4 to § 2G1.3(b)(3) limits application of the enhancement to those offenders who use a computer "to communicate directly with a minor or with a person who exercises custody, care, or supervisory control of the minor." Sentencing Guidelines Manual § 2G1.3(b)(3) cmt. n.4 (2009). Therefore, the note continues, the enhancement "would not apply to the use of a computer or an interactive computer service to obtain airline tickets for the minor from an airline's Internet site." *Id.* This is a meaningful limitation on the applicability of the enhancement, but it is no help to Kramer.

We acknowledge that a "basic" cellular phone might not easily fit within the colloquial definition of "computer." We are bound, however, not by the common understanding of that word, but by the specific—if broad—definition set forth in § 1030. Now it may be that neither the Sentencing Commission nor the New Hazard legislature anticipated that

---

[*] Kramer's reliance on *Old Hazard v. Lay*, 277 O.H. 436 (2009) (Tew, J.), is misplaced. To be sure, Old Hazard has a Computer Fraud and Abuse Act and Sentencing Guidelines that are identical in all relevant parts to our statutes. But in *Lay*, the Old Hazard Court of Appeals affirmed a sentencing enhancement on the ground that the defendant used a computer to develop a relationship with the victim, even though future communications were exclusively by mobile phone and other "offline" modes. The court said that "[t]o allow a predator to use a computer to develop relationships with minor victims, so long as the ultimate consummation is first proposed through offline communication, would not serve the purpose of the enhancement." 277 O.H. at 447. As Kramer sees it, *Lay* "implicitly distinguishes use of a cellular telephone from use of a traditional computer when applying the enhancement." Appellant's Br. at 16. That may be so. But in that case the government never argued that the mobile phone itself was a computer, nor did the court ever consider or decide that issue. Whether the court in *Lay* would have expressly adopted this implicit distinction we do not know, because the issue was never squarely presented to it. *Lay*, therefore, does not help us decide this case.

a cellular phone would be included in that definition.* As technology continues to develop, § 1030 may come to capture still additional devices that few industry experts, much less the Commission or the New Hazard legislature, could foresee.** But to the extent that such a sweeping definition was unintended or is now inappropriate, it is a matter for the Commission or the New Hazard legislature to correct. We cannot provide relief from plain statutory text.

For these reasons, we affirm Kramer's sentence.

---

*   Indeed the Commission, explaining its reasons for "expand[ing] the enhancement" found in guidelines § 2G2.2(b)(5) to include the use of an "interactive computer service," expressed its view that "the term 'computer' did not capture all types of Internet devices." Sentencing Guidelines Manual supp. to app. C, amend. 664, at 59 (2009). Therefore, it continued, "the amendment expands the definition of 'computer' to include other devices that involve interactive computer services (e.g., Web-Tv)." *Id.*

**   In a now-famous understatement, Popular Mechanics once predicted: "Where a calculator like the ENIAC today is equipped with 18,000 vacuum tubes and weighs 30 tons, computers in the future may have only 1000 vacuum tubes and perhaps weigh only 1.5 tons." Drew Amilton, Brains that Click, Unpopular Mechanics, Mar. 1949, at 162, 258.

INDEX

References are to Pages